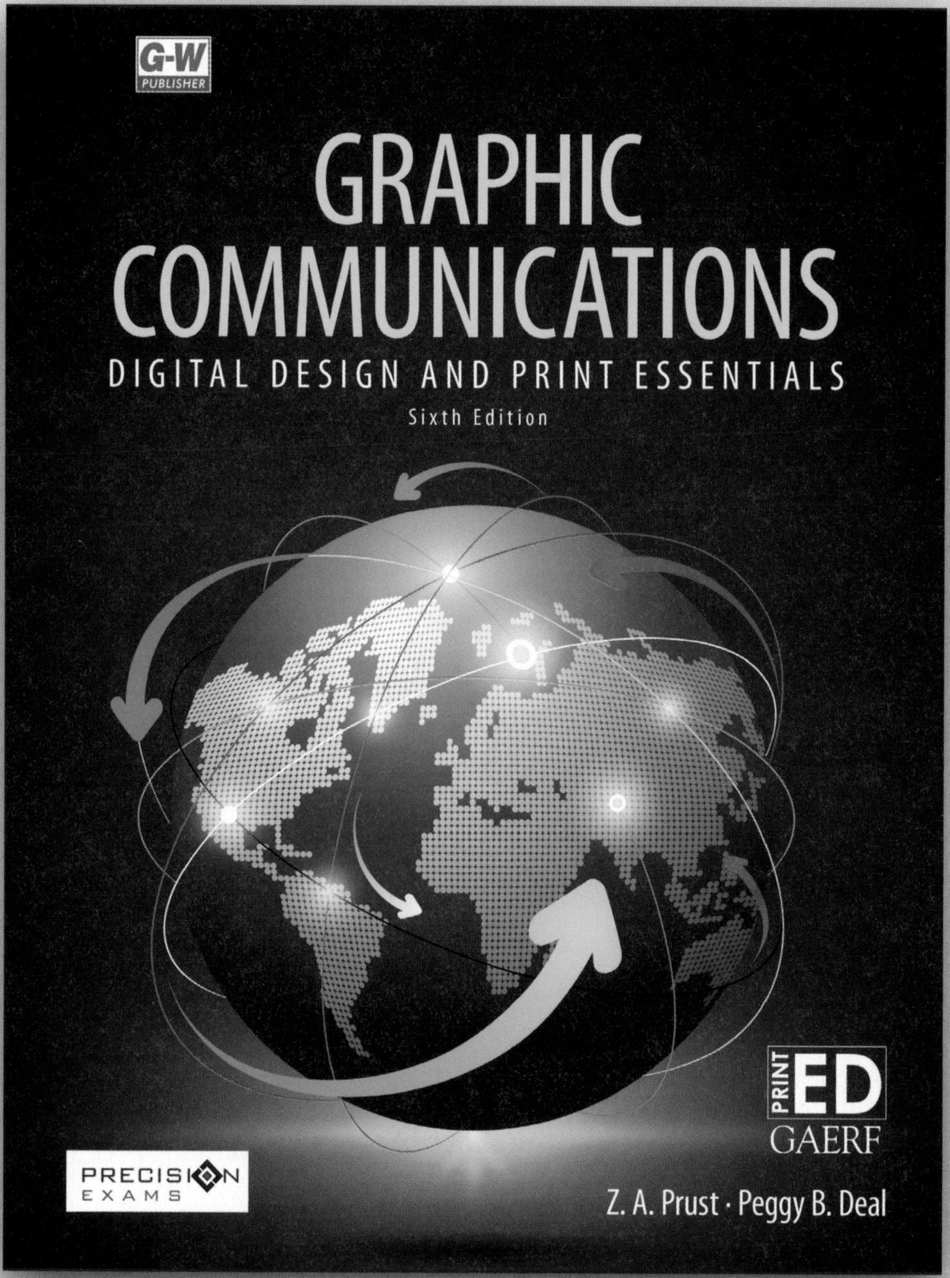

The introductory theory and applications of digital design and delivery for today's student and today's world!

Guided Tour

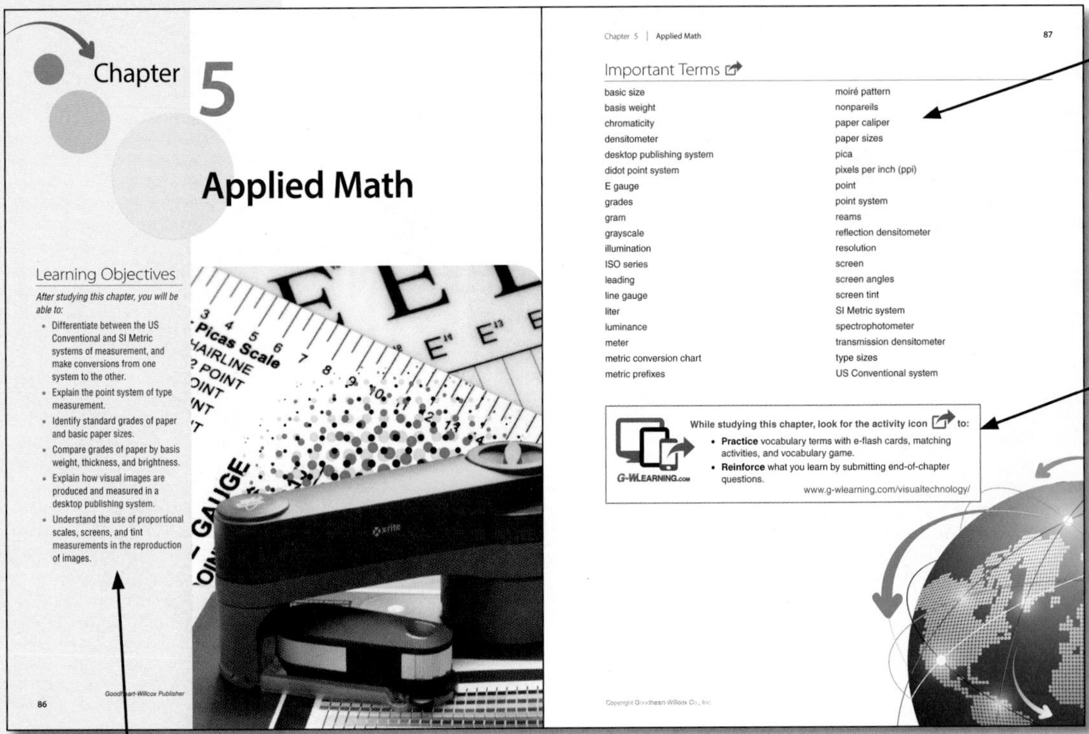
Chapter 5

Applied Math

Learning Objectives

After studying this chapter, you will be able to:

- Differentiate between the US Conventional and SI Metric systems of measurement, and make conversions from one system to the other.
- Explain the point system of type measurement.
- Identify standard grades of paper and basic paper sizes.
- Compare grades of paper by basis weight, thickness, and brightness.
- Explain how visual images are produced and measured in a desktop publishing system.
- Understand the use of proportional scales, screens, and tint measurements in the reproduction of images.

86 Goodheart-Willcox Publisher

Chapter 5 | Applied Math 87

Important Terms

basic size	moiré pattern
basis weight	nonpareils
chromaticity	paper caliper
densitometer	paper sizes
desktop publishing system	pica
didot point system	pixels per inch (ppi)
E gauge	point
grades	point system
gram	reams
grayscale	reflection densitometer
illumination	resolution
ISO series	screen
leading	screen angles
line gauge	screen tint
liter	SI Metric system
luminance	spectrophotometer
meter	transmission densitometer
metric conversion chart	type sizes
metric prefixes	US Conventional system

While studying this chapter, look for the activity icon to:

- **Practice** vocabulary terms with e-flash cards, matching activities, and vocabulary game.
- **Reinforce** what you learn by submitting end-of-chapter questions.

www.g-wlearning.com/visualtechnology/

Copyright Goodheart-Willcox Co., Inc.

Important Terms list the key terms to be learned in the chapter.

G-W Learning Companion Website Activity Icon identifies related content available on the G-W Learning companion website.

Learning Objectives clearly identify the knowledge and skills to be obtained when the chapter is completed.

Illustrations have been designed to clearly and simply communicate the specific topic. Photographic images have been updated to show the latest equipment.

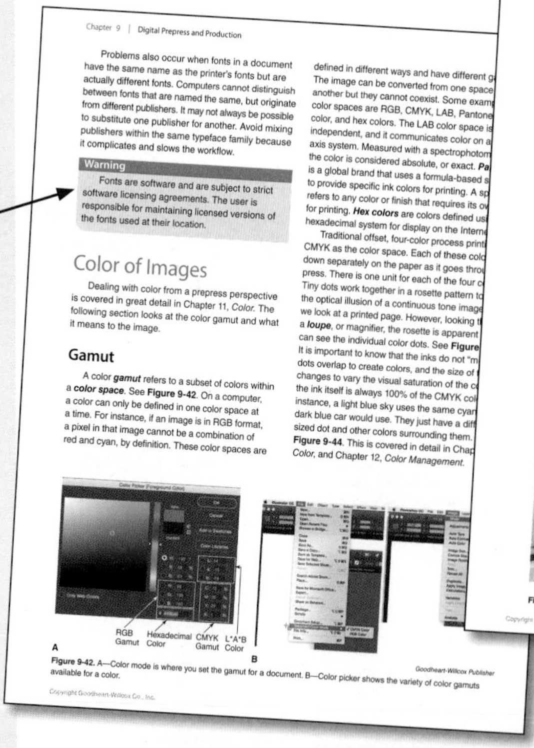
Chapter 9 | Digital Prepress and Production

Problems also occur when fonts in a document have the same name as the printer's fonts but are actually different fonts. Computers cannot distinguish between fonts that are named the same, but originate from different publishers. It may not always be possible to substitute one publisher for another. Avoid mixing publishers within the same typeface family because it complicates and slows the workflow.

Warning

Fonts are software and are subject to strict software licensing agreements. The user is responsible for maintaining licensed versions of the fonts used at their location.

Color of Images

Dealing with color from a prepress perspective is covered in great detail in Chapter 11, *Color.* The following section looks at the color gamut and what it means to the image.

Gamut

A color **gamut** refers to a subset of colors within a **color space**. See **Figure 9-42**. On a computer, a color can only be defined in one color space at a time. For instance, if an image is in RGB format, a pixel in that image cannot be a combination of red and cyan, by definition. These color spaces are

Figure 9-42. A—Color mode is where you set the gamut for a document. B—Color picker shows the variety of color gamuts available for a color. Goodheart-Willcox Publisher

Copyright Goodheart-Willcox Co., Inc.

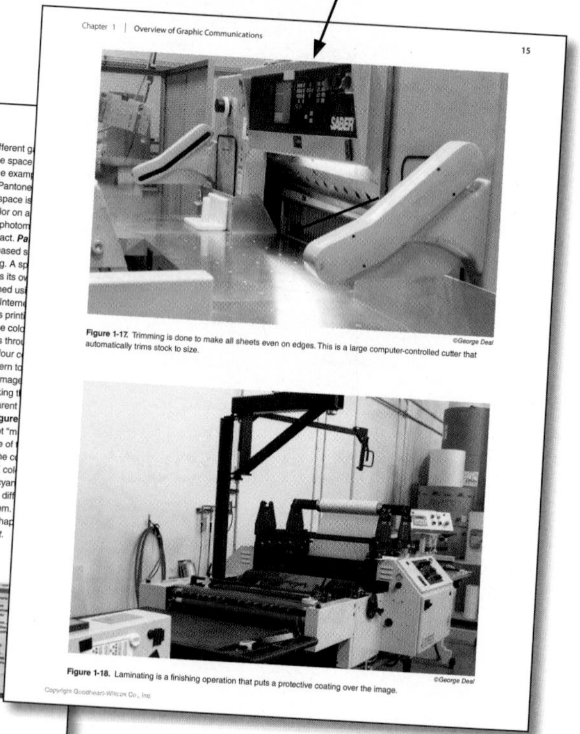
Chapter 1 | Overview of Graphic Communications 15

Figure 1-17. Trimming is done to make all sheets even on edges. This is a large computer-controlled cutter that automatically trims stock to size. ©George Deal

Figure 1-18. Laminating is a finishing operation that puts a protective coating over the image. ©George Deal

Copyright Goodheart-Willcox Co., Inc.

Warning notes alert you to potentially dangerous materials and practices.

Academic Link uses questions and activities to relate chapter content to math, science, and history.

Career Links highlight career opportunities in the graphic communications industry. Helpful quotes from industry experts are included in each link.

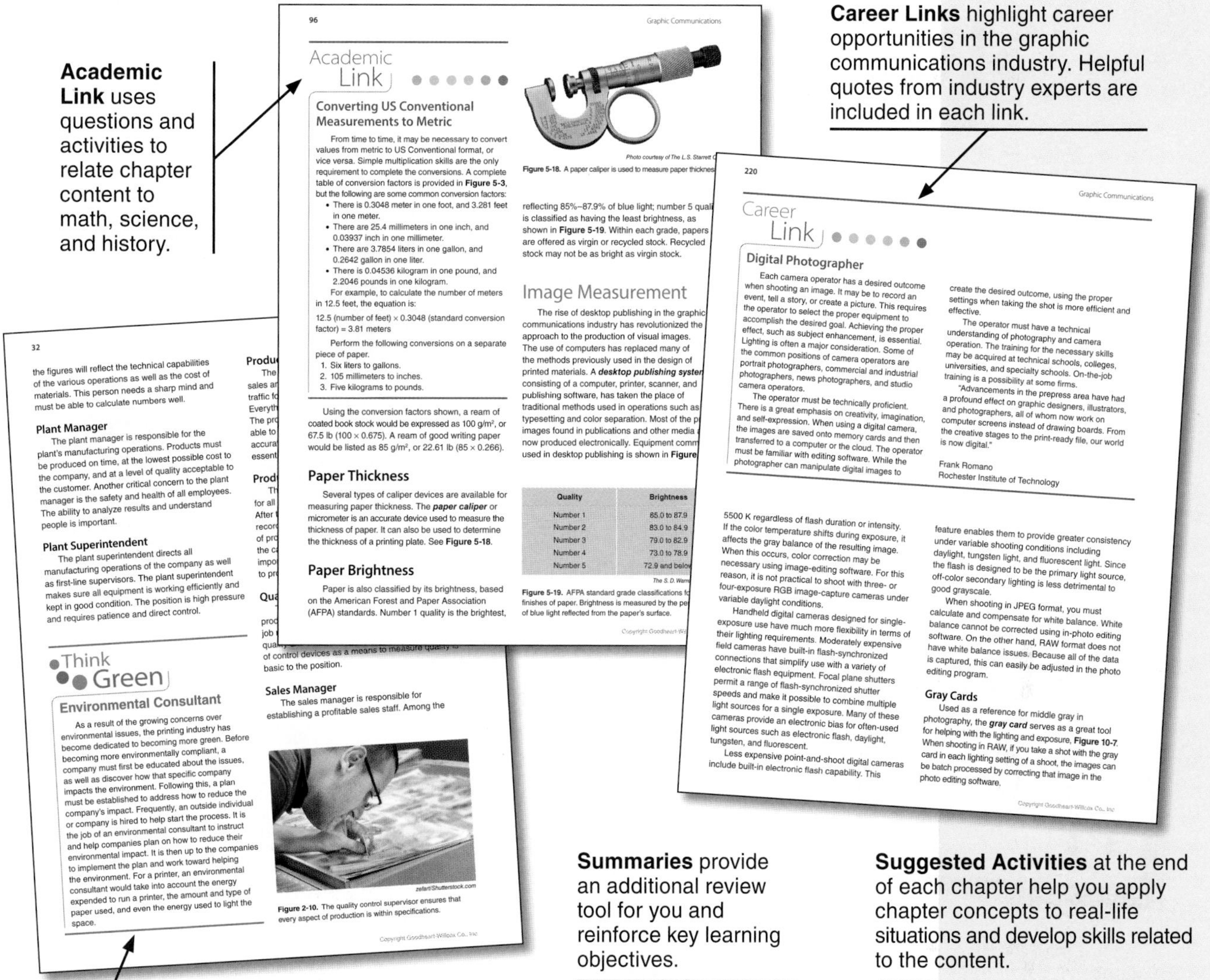

Think Green features touch on chapter-related topics and give an example of how the industry is working toward making products and processes safer for the environment.

Summaries provide an additional review tool for you and reinforce key learning objectives.

Suggested Activities at the end of each chapter help you apply chapter concepts to real-life situations and develop skills related to the content.

Review Questions allow you to demonstrate knowledge, identification, and comprehension of chapter material.

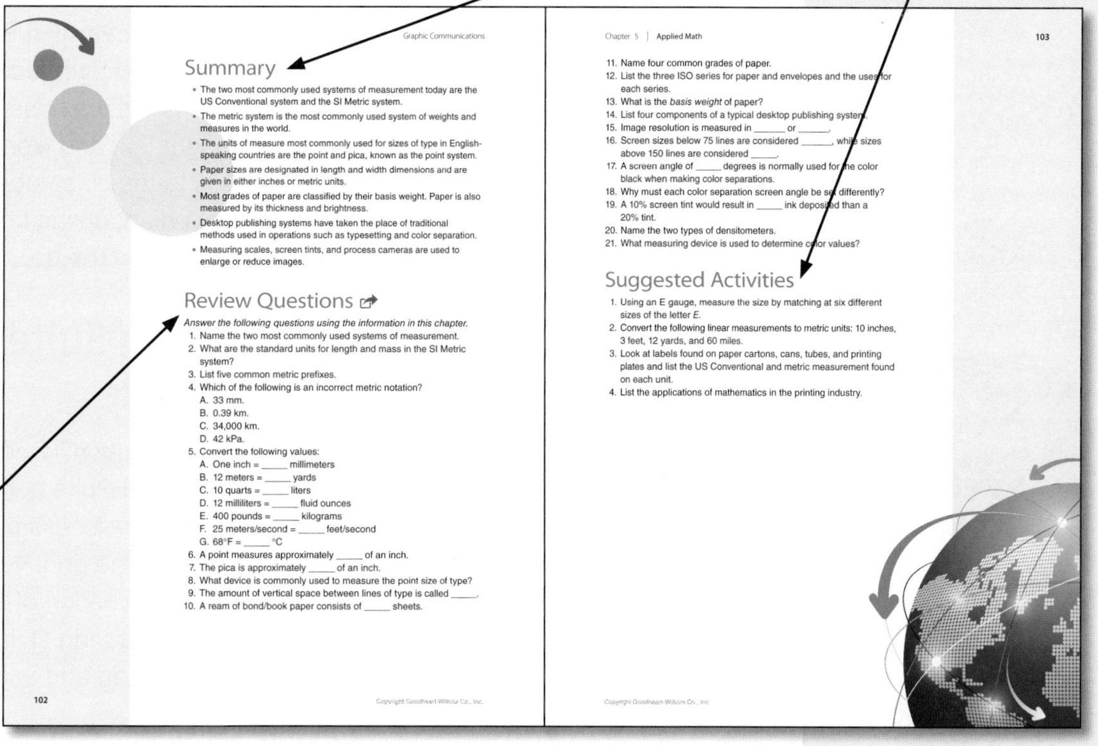

Student Resources

Textbook

The ***Graphic Communications*** textbook provides an exciting, full-color, and highly illustrated learning resource. The textbook is available in print or online versions.

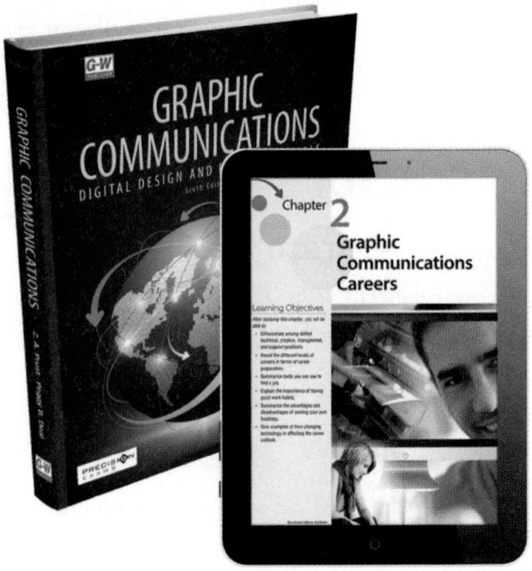

G-W Learning Companion Website

The G-W Learning companion website is a study reference that contains review questions, vocabulary exercises, and more! Accessible from any digital device, the G-W Learning companion website complements the textbook and is available to the student at no charge.

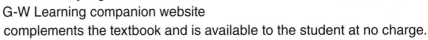

Workbook

The student workbook provides minds-on practice with questions and activities. Each chapter corresponds to the text and reinforces key concepts and applied knowledge.

Online Learning Suite

Available as a classroom subscription, the Online Learning Suite provides the foundation of instruction and learning for digital and blended classrooms. An easy-to-manage shared classroom subscription makes it a hassle-free solution for both students and instructors. An online student text and workbook, along with rich supplemental content, brings digital learning to the classroom. All instructional materials are found on a convenient online bookshelf and are accessible at home, at school, or on the go.

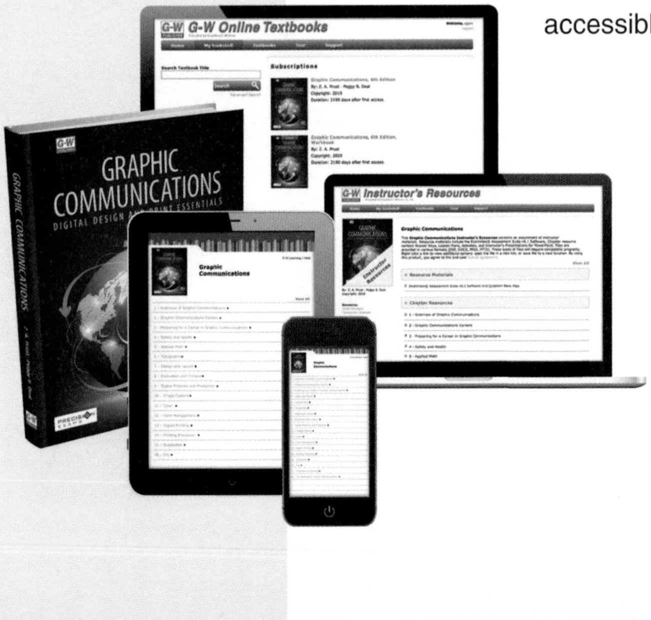

Online Learning Suite/Student Textbook Bundle

Looking for a blended solution? Goodheart-Willcox offers the Online Learning Suite bundled with the printed text in one easy-to-access package. Students have the flexibility to use the print version, the Online Learning Suite, or a combination of both components to meet their individual learning style. The convenient packaging makes managing and accessing content easy and efficient.

Instructor Resources

Instructor resources provide information and tools to support teaching, grading, and planning; class presentations; and assessment.

Instructor's Presentations for PowerPoint® CD

Help teach and visually reinforce key concepts with prepared lectures. These presentations are designed to allow for customization to meet daily teaching needs. They include objectives, outlines, and images from the textbook.

ExamView® Assessment Suite CD

Quickly and easily prepare, print, and administer tests with the ExamView® Assessment Suite. With hundreds of questions in the test bank corresponding to each chapter, you can choose which questions to include in each test, create multiple versions of a single test, and automatically generate answer keys. Existing questions may be modified and new questions may be added. You can prepare pretests, formative assessments, and summative assessments easily with the ExamView® Assessment Suite.

Instructor's Resource CD

One resource provides instructors with time-saving preparation tools such as answer keys; lesson plans; correlation charts to standards; and other teaching aids.

Online Instructor Resources

Online Instructor Resources provide all the support needed to make preparation and classroom instruction easier than ever. Available in one accessible location, support materials include Answer Keys, Lesson Plans, Instructor Presentations for PowerPoint®, ExamView® Assessment Suite, and more! Online Instructor Resources are available as a subscription and can be accessed at school or at home.

G-W Integrated Learning Solution

Together, We Build Careers

At Goodheart-Willcox, we take our mission seriously. Since 1921, G-W has been serving the career and technical education (CTE) community. Our employee-owners are driven to deliver exceptional learning solutions to CTE students to help prepare them for careers. Our authors and subject matter experts have years of experience in the classroom and industry. We combine their wisdom with our expertise to create content and tools to help students achieve success. Our products start with theory and applied content based upon a strong foundation of accepted standards and curriculum. To that base, we add student-focused learning features and tools designed to help students make connections between knowledge and skills. G-W recognizes the crucial role instructors play in preparing students for careers. We support educators' efforts by providing time-saving tools that help them plan, present, assess, and engage students with traditional and digital activities and assets. We provide an entire program of learning in a variety of print, digital, and online formats, including economic bundles, allowing educators to select the right mix for their classroom.

Student-Focused Curated Content

Goodheart-Willcox believes that student-focused content should be built from standards and/or accepted curriculum coverage. Standards from Precision Exams were used as a foundation in this text. PrintED's "Introduction to Graphic Communications" Graphic Communications Skills Competencies (GCSC) were also used to build this text. ***Graphic Communications*** uses an easy-to-understand approach to teach the processes, methods, and equipment used in the field, with a focus on careers. We call on industry experts and teachers from across the country to review and comment on our content, presentation, and pedagogy. Finally, in our refinement of curated content, our editors are immersed in content checking, securing and sometimes creating figures that convey key information, and revising language and pedagogy.

Precision Exams Certification

Goodheart-Willcox is pleased to partner with Precision Exams by correlating ***Graphic Communications*** to their Graphic Communications—Intro Standards. Precision Exams Standards and Career Skills Exams™ were created in concert with industry and subject matter experts to match real-world job skills and marketplace demands. Students who pass the exam and performance portion of the exam can earn a Career Skills Certification™.

Visit www.g-w.com/graphic-communications-2019 and click on the Correlations tab. For more information on Precision Exams, including a complete listing of their 150+ Career Skills Exams™ and Certificates, please visit www.precisionexams.com.

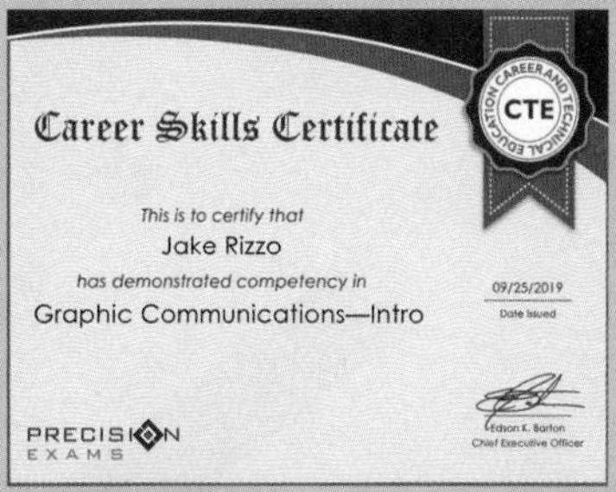

PrintED Accreditation and Certification

Since 1983, The Graphic Arts Education and Research Foundation (GAERF) has served to advance knowledge and education in graphic communications by supporting programs that prepare a skilled workforce for the industry. The PrintED accreditation program ensures instructional content that is current, relevant, consistent across the nation, and aligned with industry standards. ***Graphic Communications*** has been thoroughly reviewed by GAERF and is correlated to PrintED's "Introduction to Graphic Communications" Graphic Communications Skills Competencies (GCSC). All PrintED accredited programs must teach at least 85% of the competencies and meet the PrintED standards in this area.

Students who pass any of the PrintED/SkillsUSA Career Essentials: Assessments receive a PrintED/SkillsUSA Student Certification. These certifications provide students a way to validate their mastery of academic and workplace competencies and serve as a first step toward a career path in the graphic communications industry. For more information on GAERF and PrintED, please visit www.gaerf.org.

PRINT ED
GAERF

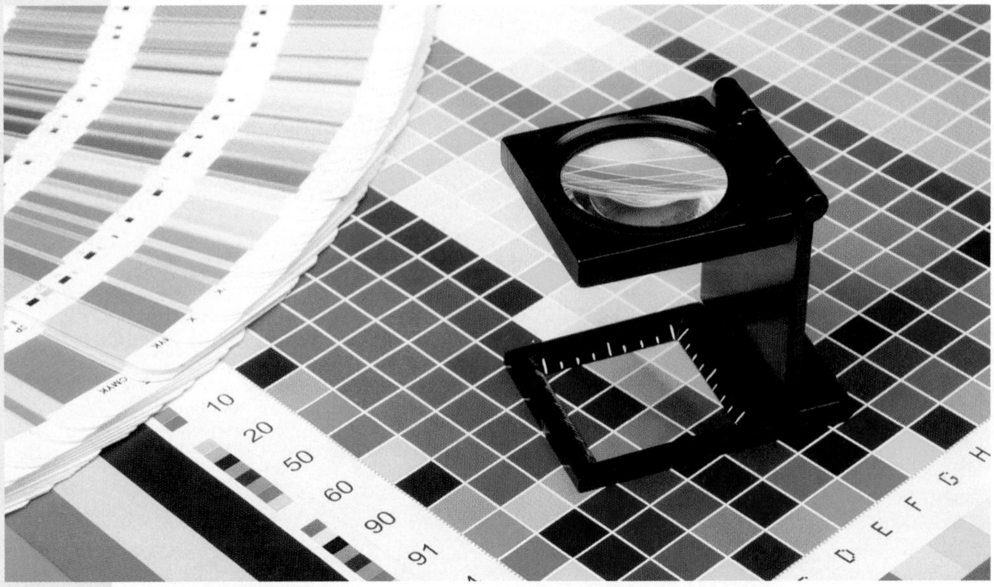
CMYK
10
20
50
60
90
91
D E F G H

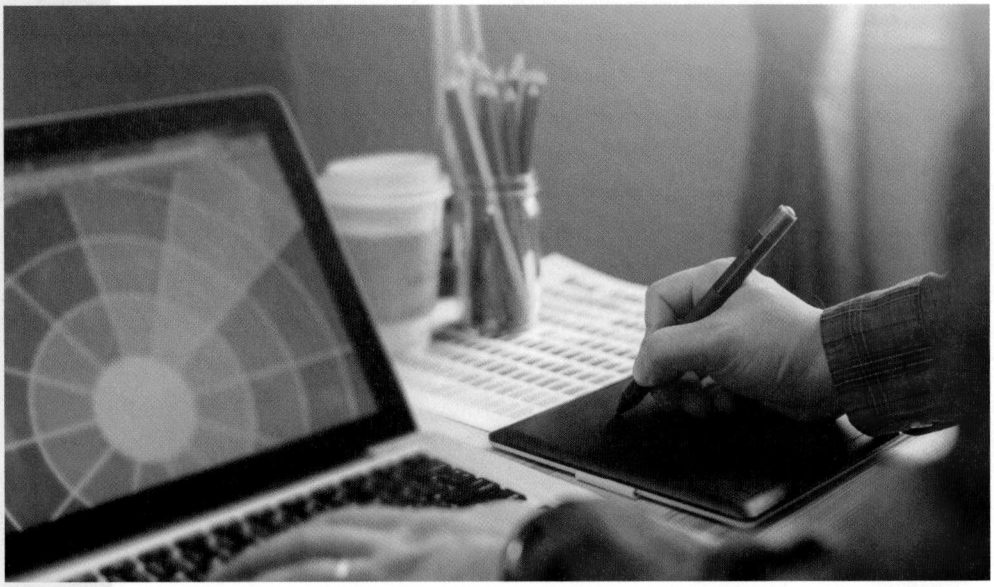

GRAPHIC COMMUNICATIONS

DIGITAL DESIGN AND PRINT ESSENTIALS

Sixth Edition

Z.A. Prust · Peggy B. Deal

Publisher
The Goodheart-Willcox Company, Inc.
Tinley Park, IL
www.g-w.com

Manufactured in the United States of America.

ISBN 978-1-63126-876-2

1 2 3 4 5 6 7 8 9 – 19 – 22 21 20 19 18 17

Cover image: Sanrunyu_foto/Shutterstock.com
Back cover image: pumpuija/Shutterstock.com

Preface

The graphic communications field (sometimes called *graphic arts* or simply *printing*) has undergone sweeping changes with the introduction of computers and digital technology in virtually every aspect of the industry. Digital image capture and manipulation, electronic prepress operations, computer-based systems for managing most aspects of a business, computer-to-plate technology, electronic control systems on presses and bindery equipment, and many other advances have changed the fundamental ways that most printing and related operations are performed. These technological changes have altered workflows and transferred responsibility and accountability from the very beginning of the creation process to the end of the project. In this deadline-driven industry, it is imperative that a full understanding of the process be analyzed. It is probably safe to say that the industry has seen more extensive changes in the last 25 years than have taken place in the five centuries since Johannes Gutenberg began printing from movable type in the mid-1400s.

Graphic Communications reflects these changes in the industry, with chapters devoted to in-depth coverage of color science, electronic prepress and digital printing, digital image capture, and color management. Other chapters provide important information on design and layout, text composition, page composition, prepress and imposition, the business aspects of printing, and careers in graphic communications. Strong emphasis has been placed on safety and workplace health matters and on environmental consideration.

Information on new methods and equipment has been incorporated throughout the book, while information on processes that have become obsolete has been condensed and treated in a historical context. The aim is to better prepare today's graphic communications student for a career in this rapidly evolving field.

Since "a picture is worth a thousand words," ***Graphic Communications*** is highly illustrated. To clarify the complex processes of the industry, literally hundreds of full-color illustrations are used. Color is also used to enhance the educational value of many of the line art illustrations.

Graphic Communications is a valuable source of information for anyone entering any area of the printing industry today. This text will help you become well-versed in most aspects of printing technology.

Z.A. Prust
Peggy B. Deal

About the Authors

Z.A. Prust retired after having taught for over 40 years. He received a bachelor's degree from the University of Wisconsin-Stout, a master's degree from the University of Minnesota, and a doctoral degree from the University of Northern Colorado. He co-owned Rock Ledge Printing Service in Sheboygan Falls, Wisconsin. His teaching career included teaching Graphic Communications at the junior high school, high school, and university levels. He spent 27 years at Arizona State University, and he retired as the Associate Director of the Division of Technology and Coordinator of the Graphic Communications program within the College of Engineering and Applied Science. After retiring from ASU, he incorporated and was the Executive Director of the Printing Industries Association, Inc., of Arizona. His awards include the Ben Franklin Society of the Printing Industries of America, the Fred J. Hartman Award, the Elmer G. Voigt Award, the Award of Excellence from the Graphic Arts Technical Foundation, the Distinguished Achievement Award, the Award of Recognition from Arizona State University, and the French Legion of Honor Medal. He served as chair and member of many local, regional, and national professional and social groups. In addition to ***Graphic Communications***, Dr. Prust authored several textbooks as well as articles in professional publications. Two awards have been given in his name since he retired: the Z.A. (Zeke) Prust Award of Recognition at Arizona State University and the Z.A. Prust Industry Achievement Award, Printing Industries Association, Inc., of Arizona.

Peggy B. Deal has been a graphic designer for more than 40 years, is a graduate of Indiana University with a BA in fine arts and graphic design, and is the owner of Deal in Design. She transitioned from traditional typesetting and printing technology to embrace the current digital revolution. In addition to her graphic design firm, she is the Graphic Design program director for the Fredrick D. Kagy Education Award of Excellence–winning program at Scottsdale Community College in Scottsdale, Arizona, where she teaches Typography, Digital Prepress, Graphic Design Self Promotion, Graphic Design I, II, and III, and Creative Brand Strategy. Peggy has received several industry awards including the Z.A. Prust Industry Achievement Award, the Maricopa Community Colleges Adjunct of the Year award, and the Excellence in Service Award from the Printing Industries of Arizona/New Mexico. She is the Chairman of the Graphic Communications Education Foundation, a 501(c)(3) that works with high school teachers and students, providing support, awareness, and financial endowments to encourage the advancement of instruction in the graphic communications industry. She coauthored the graphic design standards for the Arizona Career and Technical Education program. Peggy also sits on several advisory boards for high school and community college programs throughout the state and chairs the SkillsUSA regional and state competitions. She is the Operations Director for the Arizona chapter of the Adobe InDesign User Group and the advisor for the CreativeConnect SCC, a networking club designed to unite all creatives on the Scottsdale Community College campus. While graphic design is her chosen profession, teaching is her passion.

Reviewers

The authors and publisher wish to thank the following industry and teaching professionals for their valuable input into the development of ***Graphic Communications***.

Janet Bass
Crowley ISD
Crowley, TX

Ronald Berenato
Bartlett High School
Bartlett, TN

Brad Bond
Hononegah Community High School
Rockton, IL

Cathleen Carlson
Graham-Kapowsin High School
Graham, WA

Mike E. Crumley, M. Ed.
Science Hill High School
Johnson City, TN

Joseph Fantozzi
Davies Career and Technical High School
Lincoln, RI

Kathi Farmer
Andrew P. Hill High School
San Jose, CA

Nancy Hallsworth
Dalton High School
Dalton, GA

Frank Kanonik
Intellective Solutions, LLC
Pittsburgh, PA

Matt Kriftcher
Springfield Technical Community College
Springfield, MA

Judith Showell Loeber
Sussex Central High School
Georgetown, DE

Laura Roberts
Mattoon High School
Mattoon, IL

Michael Stinnett
Royal Oak High School
Royal Oak, MI

Acknowledgments

The author and publisher would like to thank the following companies, organizations, and individuals for their contribution of resource material, images, or other support in the development of ***Graphic Communications***. The publisher and author would like to acknowledge Margie Garr for her diligent contributions. A very special thanks goes to Prisma Graphic for allowing us to use their expansive facility for our photo shoots.

3M Company
A.B. Dick Company
Accurate Steel Rule Die Mfg., Inc.
Amanda Hall
American Roller Company
ATF
Baker Perkins Limited
basysPrint Corporation
Bernie Fritts
Bob Anderson
Bowling Green State University, Visual Communication Technology Program
Brookfield Engineering Laboratories, Inc.
Canvas Magazine, May 2015
Carpenter-Offutt Paper Co.
Caryn Butler
Center for Metric Education, Western Michigan University
Dana Thelander
Domino Printing Sciences plc
Duplo USA
Earmark, Inc.
Fuji Hunt Photographic Chemicals, Inc.
General Binding Corp.
George Deal
GIT, Arizona State University
Graphic Arts Education and Research Foundation (GAERF)
Graphic Arts Technical Foundation
GretagMacbeth, New Windsor, NY
GSMA
Hagen Systems, Inc.
Heidelberg Harris
Heidelberg, Inc.
Illinois Environmental Protection Agency of Pollution Prevention
Inter-City Paper Co.
International Sign Association/CSG Creative (Design Agency)
Interthor, Inc.
Jeremy Hamman
Justrite Manufacturing Company
Kevin Runbeck
Konica Minolta
Lab Safety Supply, Inc., Janesville, WI
Linotype-Hell
Mark Marerro
Martin Marietta Corp.
Mead Publishing Paper Division
Mee Industries Inc.
Nathan Deal
National Association of Quick Printers, Inc.
National Soy Ink Information Center
NPES The Association for Suppliers of Printing, Publishing and Converting Technologies
NuArc
PIA
Presstek, Inc.
Randy Burnett
Rollem
Safety-Kleen
Screen Printing Association International
Sonoco Products Co.
Southern Forest Products Assn.
Strachan Henshaw Machinery, Inc.
Tetko, Inc.
The L.S. Starrett Co.
The S. D. Warren Company
Thomas Detrie
US Sublimation
Van Son Holland Ink
Variquick
Westvaco Corporation
www.PrintingTips.com, owned by Austec Data Inc. dba Tecstra Systems
Xanté Corporation
X-Rite

Brief Contents

Contents

Features

Think Green

Career Link

Academic Link

Chapter 1

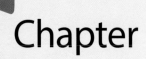

Overview of Graphic Communications

Learning Objectives

After studying this chapter, you will be able to:

- Explain the important role of graphic communications in our technological society.
- Identify the major processes commonly associated with the graphic communications industry.
- Summarize the four printing processes.
- Recall the segments of the printing industry.
- Describe the various aspects of electronic delivery.

Goodheart-Willcox Publisher

Important Terms

animation
artwork
binding
book printing
commercial printing
computer-to-plate (CTP)
content management systems (CMS)
continuous tone copy
copy
editing
e-pubs
electrostatic printing
financial printing
finishing
flexography
forms printing
graphic communications
image assembly
image carrier
impactless printing
in-plant printing
line art
newspaper printing
package printing
page composition
periodical printing
printing
printing press
process colors
quick printing
responsive design
substrate
wysiwyg

G-WLEARNING.com

While studying this chapter, look for the activity icon to:

- **Practice** vocabulary terms with e-flash cards, matching activities, and vocabulary game.
- **Reinforce** what you learn by submitting end-of-chapter questions.

www.g-wlearning.com/visualtechnology/

The term *graphic* relates to the visual, or things we can see. The term *communication* refers to the exchange of information in any form. Therefore, ***graphic communications*** is the exchange of information in a visual form, such as words, drawings, photographs, or a combination of these.

For years, the term *graphic arts* was used as the common name for the study of the processes used in the printing industry. Graphic communications is now a more accurate term because the printing industry creates products that visually convey messages. You will find the terms *multimedia* and *cross media* used in conjunction with graphic communications applications.

This is an extremely challenging time for anyone involved in graphic communications. Advances in electronics and the application of these advances to graphic communications processes have made it vital to keep up-to-date with changes in equipment capabilities and operating procedures.

One fact is crystal clear: if you fail to keep up with new technology, you could fall behind and not be aware of more efficient types of equipment and processes. This could cause your company to lose any competitive edge. The result could be antiquated techniques and inferior products, or higher costs. Either could cause you to lose customers and profits.

The purpose of this chapter is to present a brief history of printing, explain the role of graphic communications in a technological society, and identify the basic processes in this fast-changing industry. It will help prepare you to more fully comprehend the many aspects of graphic communications that are presented in detail in later chapters.

The Printing Press

It has been said that printing is truly the art of all arts since it is capable of duplicating and preserving images. The printing press, invented in 1440, made possible the printing of books, magazines, and newspapers in large quantities. This made reading material available to more people than ever before, which helped promote literacy to mankind. See **Figure 1-1**. Many modifications to the printing press have taken place over the centuries, but the processing principles are essentially the same.

15,000 BCE	Prehistoric man first painted art on the walls of his caves in what is now northern France and southern Spain.
5,000 BCE	The earliest Babylonian writings appeared.
3,500 BCE	Papyrus came into use as a writing surface.
750 BCE	Greek inscriptions were carved into stone slabs with a hammer and chisel.
200 BCE	A method of refining parchment from sheepskin was discovered—supposedly by the King of Pergamum.
105 CE	Ts'ai Lun, a Chinese monk, announced the invention of paper to Emperor Chien Ch'u. The first paper was made from mulberry and other barks, fish nets, hemp, and rags.
400 CE	True ink was invented from lampblack and used in China for brush writing and later for woodblock printing.
868 CE	*The Diamond Sutra*, the first printed book, was printed. It is a roll sixteen feet in length.
1035 CE	Waste paper was first repulped and used as a material for papermaking. The birth of recycling.
1298 CE	Marco Polo reported that during his trip to China, he witnessed the printing of paper money.
1423 CE	The earliest dated European woodblock print. It shows St. Christopher bearing the infant Christ.
1450 CE	The earliest and first dated document printed from movable type in Europe, attributed to Gutenberg.
1455 CE	The Gutenberg Bible was the first major effort in Europe using movable type. Gutenberg started the printing, but it was finished by Fust and Schoeffer.

(Continued)

Goodheart-Willcox Publisher

Figure 1-1. This is a chronological time line depicting the history of printing.

1469 CE	The first use of Roman type in printing by Nicolas Jenson, considered one of the greatest typeface designers of all time.
1477 CE	William Caxton brought the art of printing to England.
1530 CE	First type foundry opened by Claude Garamond to develop and sell fonts to printers.
1655 CE	The oldest existing and first true English language newspaper, *The London Gazette*, was published.
1724 CE	Benjamin Franklin arrived in London and obtained employment as a printer's apprentice in the shop of Samuel Palmer.
1769 CE	The first printing press made by an American craftsman was the work of Isaac Doolittle, a clockmaker and watchmaker.
1794 CE	Aloys Senefelder invented the planographic method of printing known as lithography.
1824 CE	William Pickering introduced his *Diamond Classics*, the first books to be bound in bookcloth. Prior to this, you took your folded signatures from the printer to your favorite bookbinder.
1833 CE	The first mass produced newspaper in America, *The New York Sun*, was issued. The publication was sold for one penny, and thus the name, "the penny press."
1880 CE	Stephen Horgan printed the famous *Shantytown* in the *New York Daily Graphic*. This was the first halftone photograph printed.
1886 CE	Ottmar Mergenthaler set up the first successful automatic typesetting machine in the offices of *The New York Tribune*.
1902 CE	Albert Munsell developed a color system based on three color dimensions: hue, value, and chroma.
1931 CE	The CIE 1931 RGB and CIE 1931 XYZ color spaces were defined mathematically by the International Commission on Illumination (CIE).
1952 CE	With the printing of *The Wonderful World of Insects*, electronics had at last come to the printing plant. It was the first book that used the phototype process to commercially set type.
1961 CE	The introduction of the first Xerox® machine.
1972 CE	First "laptop" called the Dynabook described in paper by Alan Kay at Xerox® PARC.
1976 CE	First Apple® computer—the Apple 1.
1980 CE	Modern Internet was introduced with the Internet protocol suite, after being started in the 1950s by the US Government.
1982 CE	John Warnock and Chuck Geschke founded Adobe® Systems and introduced PostScript, a page description language.
1984 CE	The Apple Macintosh makes its debut.
1985 CE	Aldus Pagemaker introduced the first Desktop Publishing page layout application. Apple produces the LaserWriter, the first desktop printer to contain PostScript.
1990 CE	Version 1 of Adobe Photoshop® was released.
1993 CE	The Indigo, the first digital color printing press was introduced.
1996 CE	Microsoft®and Adobe® partnered to develop OpenType fonts.
2003 CE	First version of Adobe Creative Suite® introduced.
2014 CE	Adobe launches Creative Cloud® 2014.

Goodheart-Willcox Publisher

Figure 1-1. *(Continued)*

Why Is Communication Important?

People are constantly communicating. We take part in the communication process when we talk, surf the Web, watch television, send text messages, blog, or obey a one-way street sign.

The method or medium of communication used will vary based on the specific needs of the individuals involved. For example, speech, or verbal communication, is satisfactory in certain situations, but has its limitations. With verbal communication, there is no record of the exchange of ideas or thoughts. People can misunderstand or even totally forget the message. This is one of many reasons graphic or visual images are and continue to be extremely important. The ability to exchange complex data in so many different ways sets humans apart from other living organisms. Without the ability to communicate, the human race would live in a far different world.

Graphic communications is the lifeblood of our technological society, influencing the population of the world wherever and whenever a product is printed. It affects education to a very high degree: how individuals think, see things, and draw conclusions result from what they have read and seen.

People often have a need for practical knowledge, such as directions on how to build a shed or repair a computer. For such knowledge, they often turn to manuals and textbooks (or more recently, online videos). Textbooks are a form of organized knowledge that can be consulted for immediate use or stored for future reference. Without books and other printed materials, as well as websites and online videos, people seeking knowledge would be greatly deprived. Much of our heritage and knowledge would be lost.

Textbooks, magazines, and journals, in both print and digital form, all advance the information needs of our society. Advertising is another form of information. The printed advertisement, whether in a local newspaper or a national magazine, is a widely used means of conveying selling messages to potential buyers. With the advent of the Internet, companies had to adjust their advertising budgets and resources to include online advertising aimed at personal computer and handheld device users. The variety of printed and digital products seems to be endless. Books, newspapers, greeting cards, packages, stamps, fabrics, labels, order forms, advertisements, manuals, and maps are only a few examples of products available in both hard and soft form.

Producing Visual Images

In the past, the term *printing* was used to cover all facets of the graphic communications industry. However, with present technology, printing is too limited a term to include the advanced technology found in a typical facility. Many electronic systems, such as digital printing, have been added to the production of graphic images. Today, traditional printing (electronic delivery is discussed later in this chapter) is just one part or aspect of the rapidly growing graphic communications industry.

Printing is now understood to imply using ink to place an image on a ***substrate***. The many operations necessary to reach that point, as well as the steps completed to prepare a printed product for final use, are detailed in this book. See **Figure 1-2**.

©George Deal

Figure 1-2. This web of printed images is leaving the press to start the binding process. This machine folds, perforates, and chops web sheets into signatures.

Before any job can be printed, the product must be thought out from beginning to end. It must be properly designed. Specifications or measurements for all variables must be given, and a quote, or an estimate of costs, must be calculated.

Design ensures the printed image conveys the intended message. The graphic designer takes an idea and puts it in an appropriate visual presentation. The selection of the type style and pictorial material, which includes art forms and photographs, can make the final product either acceptable or unacceptable.

Specifications are guidelines used to determine the format and cost of the final product. The development of specifications varies considerably from one facility to another, but typically includes such items as paper weight or thickness, color use, type of binding, and finishing methods.

A quote or quotation lists the prices and quantities for production of printed goods and services. The cost estimate is based on the job specifications and represents the final cost to manufacture the printed product. If the quote is accepted, which means there is agreement between two parties, work can begin. See **Figure 1-3**.

Copy and Art Preparation

Most printed products have a combination of written material, called ***copy***, and pictures, called ***artwork***. Although one or the other may be more important in some situations, they are usually equally important in communicating information, **Figure 1-4**.

Goodheart-Willcox Publisher

Figure 1-4. A printed product usually includes both copy and artwork.

bikeriderlondon/Shutterstock.com

Figure 1-3. The quote is given to the customer after evaluation of issues, including the cost of materials, size of run, and use of color.

The amount of copy, also termed the *manuscript* or *text,* will vary with each type of job. For instance, a magazine article and an advertisement will differ significantly in length, style, content, and purpose.

Most writers today use a computer and word processing software to develop their manuscript. The use of the computer has become almost universal because it allows easy modification of copy and correction of spelling, sentence structure, and punctuation errors. The completed text can be output to a printer to provide a paper (hard) copy, and saved in electronic format for use in succeeding steps of the production process. See **Figure 1-5**.

Line art, also called line copy, is an object-oriented graphic drawn by a graphic artist. Traditionally, line art was produced manually, using technical ink pens to draw solid black lines on a white background. Most line art today is produced using computer software. Line art is also available in the form of electronic clip art. See **Figure 1-6**.

Another form of artwork is the photograph, or ***continuous tone copy***. Unlike line copy, which has only solid black and white tones, continuous tone copy has gradations of tones or shades from light to dark. Continuous tone copy must be converted to a halftone image, or tiny dots, for printing. Various mechanical or electronic devices are used to create the gradated dots. The press plate or ***image carrier*** needs distinct solid and nonsolid areas (provided by the dots and surrounding spaces) to place inked images on the substrate. **Figure 1-7** shows a greatly magnified view of the dots in a halftone image.

Editing

Editing is the final preparation of the author's or writer's manuscript for publication. It involves checking the text, line art, and photographs. The two classifications of editing are content editing and copy editing.

In content editing, an editor checks the material to make sure it is up-to-date, technically accurate, organized in a logical sequence, and covers all important ideas.

Copy editing is usually done after content editing. Copy editing is done to correct spelling and punctuation, to mark for style, and to ensure proper grammar. Consistency within the designated format or style is critical during copy editing.

As with writing, editing is usually done on a computer. The writer's manuscript will typically be submitted in electronic form. The edited electronic file, in effect, becomes the typeset text. In many operations, the file will be imported to a page composition program and combined with graphic elements to create a finished page or other product, such as a brochure or multipage catalog.

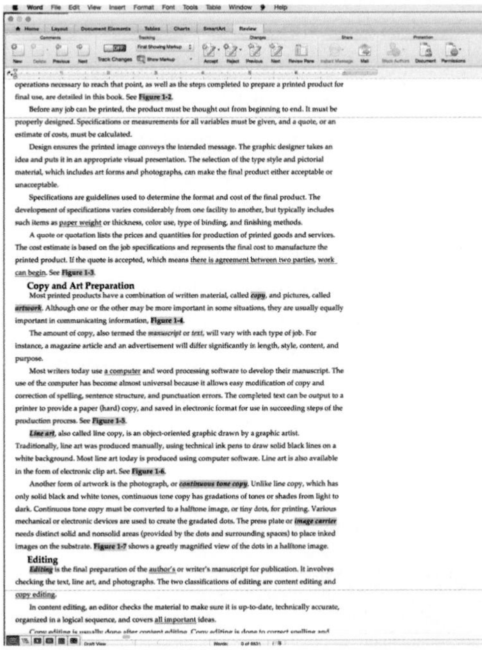

operations necessary to reach that point, as well as the steps completed to prepare a printed product for final use, are detailed in this book. See **Figure 1-2**.

Before any job can be printed, the product must be thought out from beginning to end. It must be properly designed. Specifications or measurements for all variables must be given, and a quote, or an estimate of costs, must be calculated.

Design ensures the printed image conveys the intended message. The graphic designer takes an idea and puts it in an appropriate visual presentation. The selection of the type style and pictorial material, which includes art forms and photographs, can make the final product either acceptable or unacceptable.

Specifications are guidelines used to determine the format and cost of the final product. The development of specifications varies considerably from one facility to another, but typically includes such items as paper weight or thickness, color use, type of binding, and finishing methods.

A quote or quotation lists the prices and quantities for production of printed goods and services. The cost estimate is based on the job specifications and represents the final cost to manufacture the printed product. If the quote is accepted, which means there is agreement between two parties, work can begin. See **Figure 1-3**.

Copy and Art Preparation

Most printed products have a combination of written material, called ***copy***, and pictures, called ***artwork***. Although one or the other may be more important in some situations, they are usually equally important in communicating information, **Figure 1-4**.

The amount of copy, also termed the *manuscript* or *text*, will vary with each type of job. For instance, a magazine article and an advertisement will differ significantly in length, style, content, and purpose.

Most writers today use a computer and word processing software to develop their manuscript. The use of the computer has become almost universal because it allows easy modification of copy and correction of spelling, sentence structure, and punctuation errors. The completed text can be output to a printer to provide a paper (hard) copy, and saved in electronic format for use in succeeding steps of the production process. See **Figure 1-5**.

Line art, also called line copy, is an object-oriented graphic drawn by a graphic artist. Traditionally, line art was produced manually, using technical ink pens to draw solid black lines on a white background. Most line art today is produced using computer software. Line art is also available in the form of electronic clip art. See **Figure 1-6**.

Another form of artwork is the photograph, or ***continuous tone copy***. Unlike line copy, which has only solid black and white tones, continuous tone copy has gradations of tones or shades from light to dark. Continuous tone copy must be converted to a halftone image, or tiny dots, for printing. Various mechanical or electronic devices are used to create the gradated dots. The press plate or ***image carrier*** needs distinct solid and nonsolid areas (provided by the dots and surrounding spaces) to place inked images on the substrate. **Figure 1-7** shows a greatly magnified view of the dots in a halftone image.

Editing

Editing is the final preparation of the author's or writer's manuscript for publication. It involves checking the text, line art, and photographs. The two classifications of editing are content editing and copy editing.

In content editing, an editor checks the material to make sure it is up-to-date, technically accurate, organized in a logical sequence, and covers all important ideas.

Goodheart-Willcox Publisher

Figure 1-5. The computer has become an important part of every phase of graphic communications. Writers and editors commonly use computers or word processors because they allow for easy revision and formatting of text.

Goodheart-Willcox Publisher

Figure 1-6. Electronic clip art is a readily available source of illustrations for printed materials. With suitable software, clip art images can be combined or altered to meet specific situations.

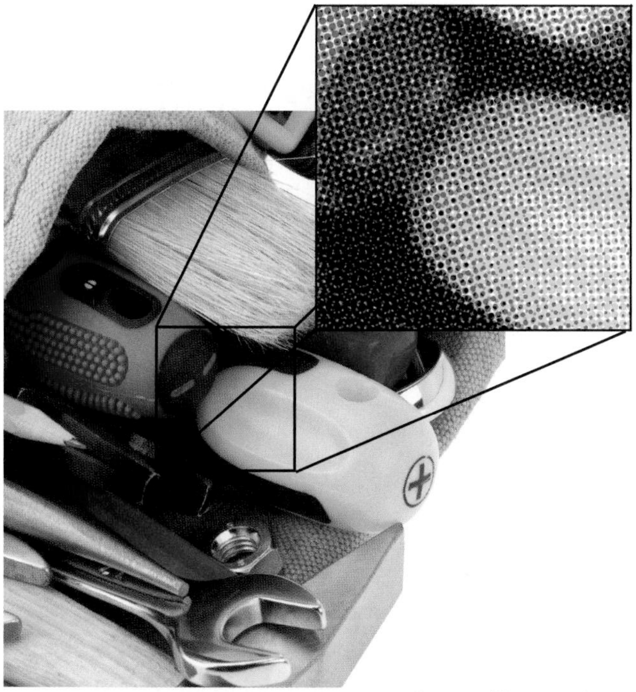

Seregam/Shutterstock.com

Figure 1-7. An original photo is a continuous tone that has different shades or gradations of color or light and darkness. A halftone, or screened photo, is made up of tiny dots that look like a continuous tone when printed. The screen can be seen easily in the enlarged section at right.

Page Composition

It is essential that printed material be attractive in design, hold attention, and transmit the desired message to the reader. To make this possible, text and graphic elements must be arranged on a page or pages. The process begins with design, progresses to layout, and is finally completed as ***page composition***.

The initial design, or idea in basic form, is worked out by making a series of thumbnail sketches. Next, a rough layout is prepared. This is an actual-size visual of the page that accurately shows the space for type and position of different illustrations. Finally, a comprehensive layout is done. This detailed sketch clearly shows style, size, and format to be used in the final printed piece.

The assembly of all the necessary components or elements on the page (matching the layout) is typically done electronically. The text, line art, and photographs, which are all in digital form, can be arranged and manipulated to assemble the design. See **Figure 1-8**. The completed pages are then output to a printer or image carrier.

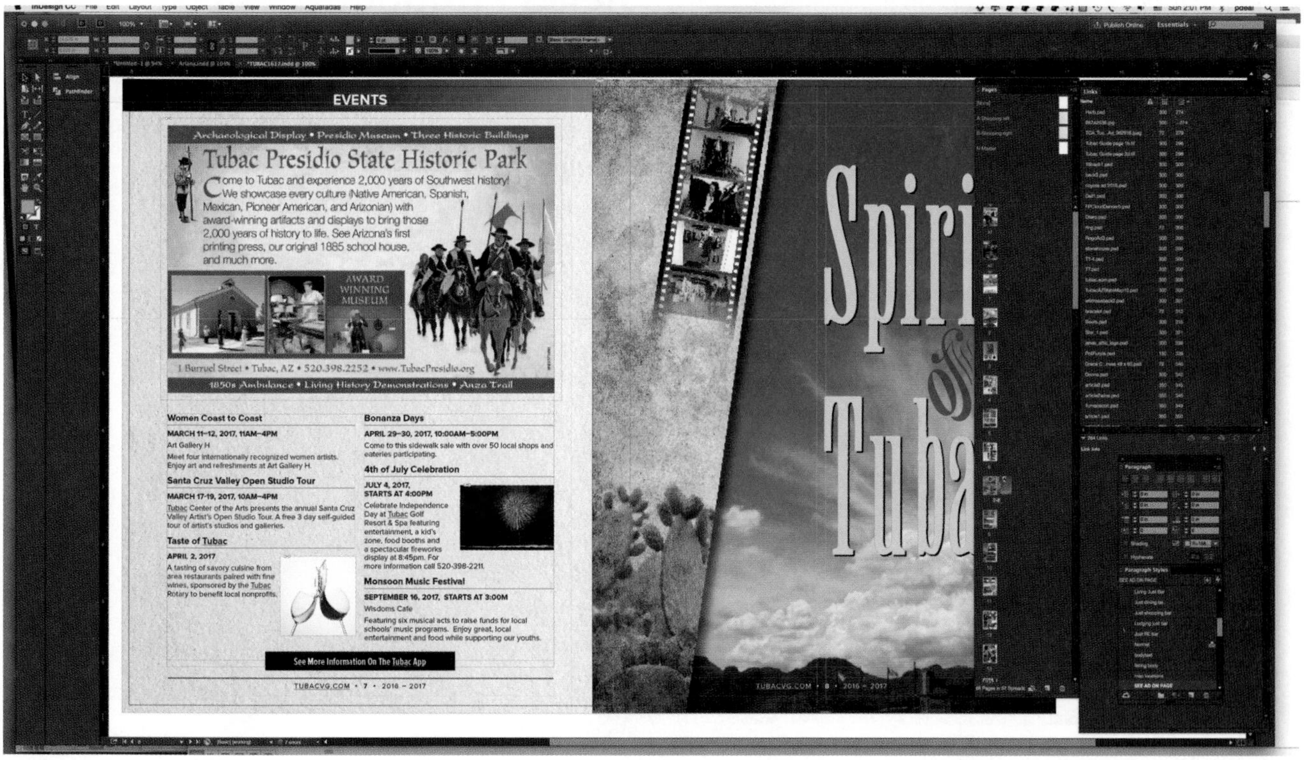

Goodheart-Willcox Publisher; Mark Marerro

Figure 1-8. Electronic page composition has replaced manual paste-up in most operations. Page composition software allows the operator to position elements on the page and make all needed alterations.

Separations

When color photographs must be reproduced in a printed piece, separations are needed. Each separation is a halftone positive or negative representing one of the ***process colors*** used for printing: cyan, magenta, yellow, and black. Each separation is used to make the image carrier for that color. When run on the press, each color is printed in register, or alignment, with the others to produce a full-color illustration. See **Figure 1-9**.

Image Assembly

The process of assembling line and halftone negatives or positives into pages has traditionally been called stripping. Today, the process of putting together pages is done electronicly and is referred to as ***image assembly***.

A number of pages may be assembled as a unit called a form. Location of the pages on the form is in a particular order, or imposition, so the pages will be in proper order when printed and folded.

Image assembly is done electronically, with all the page elements in the proper size and place. Electronic imposition software has allowed the computer to take over these tasks as well.

Platemaking

The process of placing an image on a plate is called *platemaking*. The plates are the means by which many copies can be made as duplicates of the original through the printing process. Printing plates transfer identical images onto a substrate.

The method used to make a plate varies with each printing process. Plates can be produced mechanically, electronically, or photographically. The most commonly prepared type of plate is used for offset lithography. The ***computer-to-plate (CTP)***, or direct-to-plate system, is prepared directly from the electronic file.

Printing Processes

Printing can be considered as a process involving the use of a ***printing press*** to transfer an image from an image carrier to a substrate, usually paper. Most often, printing involves making duplicates of the printed product in large quantities.

The graphic communications industry generally recognizes four major printing processes: relief, offset lithography, intaglio, and porous. A fifth category, impactless printing, has come into general use in recent years. See **Figure 1-10**.

Relief Printing

The relief process is the oldest method of printing, and requires a raised image. Ink is spread on the raised image areas, and transferred to paper by direct pressure. See **Figure 1-11**. Two types of relief printing are letterpress and

Westvaco Corporation

Figure 1-9. To print a full-color image, color separations have to be made of a full-color photo. Each separation represents one of the three primary colors (cyan, magenta, and yellow). A fourth separation is made for black. Then, the four colors of ink are deposited on top of each other as the paper runs through the press.

Academic Link

Printing Press

The invention of the printing press was one of the most influential events in our history. Johannes Gutenberg's creation caused a radical change in the way many people viewed the world and the universe. It has been said that the printing press ushered in the "period of Modernity" because of its impact on the masses.

The two basic types of presses are *sheet-fed* and *web-fed*. The sheet-fed press prints on single or individual sheets of paper. A web-fed press uses a long, single sheet or ribbon of paper. Web-fed presses are used for longer runs than sheet-fed presses. A *run* is a press operation for complete job. See **A**.

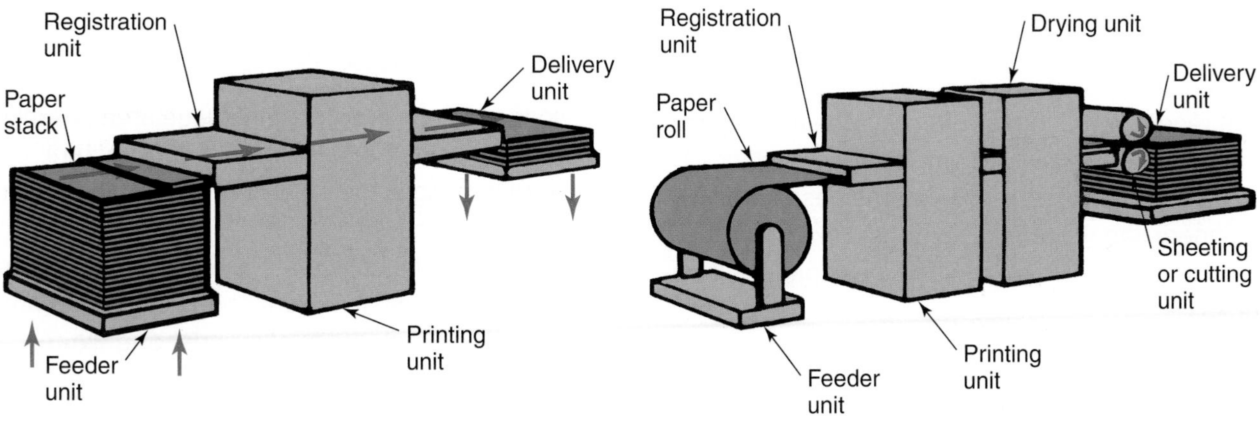

Figure A. The two basic types of printing presses. A—The sheet-fed press moves single sheets of paper through the impression system. B—The web-fed press prints on a long ribbon of paper. It is used for longer press runs.

Process	How It Works
Relief	Ink is spread on raised image areas and transferred to paper by direct pressure.
Planography	A flat printing plate accepts ink and repels water. The image is transferred from the plate to a cylinder, then onto the paper.
Intaglio	The image area is etched into the plate and then inked. The cylinders then transfer the images onto the paper.
Porous	A plate is attached to a screen and ink is forced through the screen mesh.
Impactless	Ink or toner is used to produce images from a computer.

Goodheart-Willcox Publisher

Figure 1-10. The five major types of printing processes.

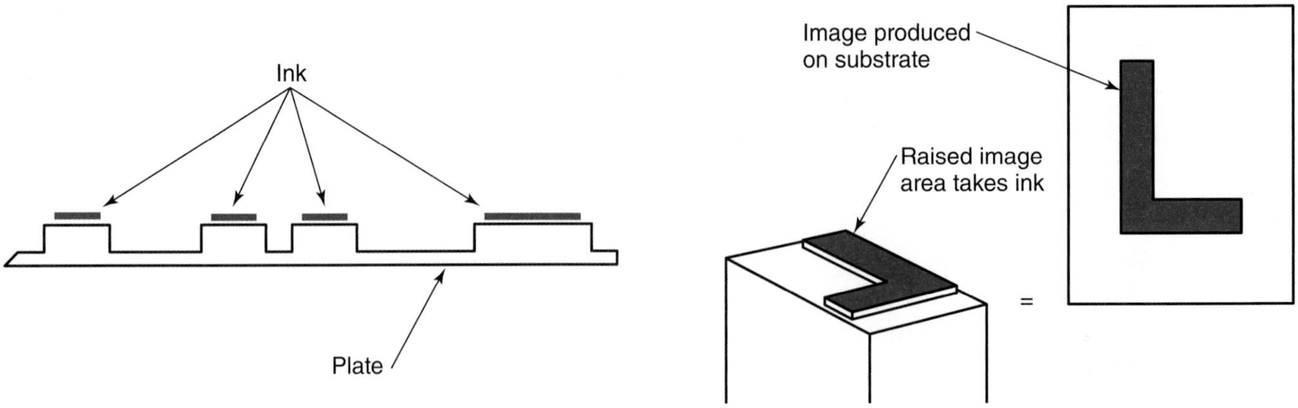

Goodheart-Willcox Publisher

Figure 1-11. Letterpress printing transfers ink from a raised image area to a substrate.

flexography. The letterpress process prints from metal plates; this process is seldom used today. Until recent years, however, it was the most widely used printing process. Examples of products once printed by letterpress are business cards, stationery, labels, business forms, tickets, cartons, magazines, reports, wrappings, newspapers, and books.

Although letterpress use has declined, another relief printing process has been growing in popularity. The process of ***flexography*** uses a flexible plastic or synthetic plate with a relief image to print on a substrate. Plastic bags, labels, and other packaging materials are commonly printed by this process. Some of today's newspapers and books are printed by flexography.

Offset Lithography

Offset lithography is the process of printing from a flat (nonraised) surface, and is based on the concept that water and oil do not readily mix. Water keeps ink from sticking, so nonimage areas are made to accept water. In this process, the image areas of the printing plate accept ink and repel water; nonimage areas accept water, which keeps ink from sticking. See **Figure 1-12**.

In this form of printing, the inked image is first transferred, or offset, from the printing plate to a rubber cylinder or roller, then from the roller to a substrate. Both sheet-fed and web-fed presses are used in offset lithography. Lithography is used for all forms of commercial printing and publishing.

Intaglio Process

In the intaglio process, the image area is sunken into the image carrier, as shown in **Figure 1-13**. Gravure printing is the most commonly used type of the intaglio process.

Two characteristics are common to the gravure process. First, both line work and photographs are screened. In effect, the total cylinder or gravure plate is a halftone. Once the images are etched in the plate, it is very difficult to alter them. Second, the gravure cylinder, which carries the image and nonimage area, is dipped into a tray of ink. The nonimage area must have the ink removed before the image is printed. The doctor blade is important because it removes the ink from the nonimage area. The blade is a steel strip that is fitted into a clip, and

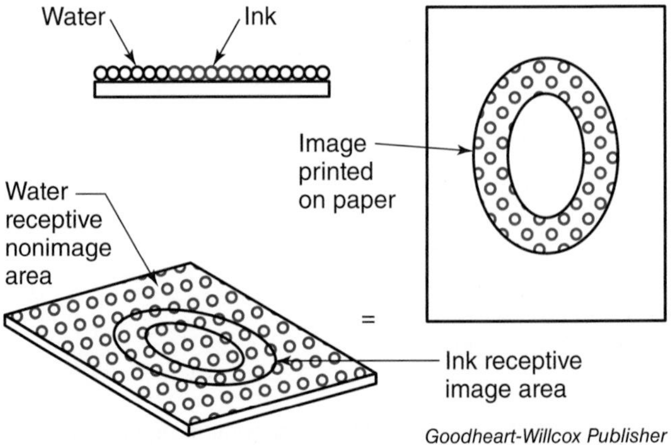

Goodheart-Willcox Publisher

Figure 1-12. Offset lithography has the image area and nonimage areas on a flat surface. The image area is receptive to ink, and the nonimage area is receptive to water.

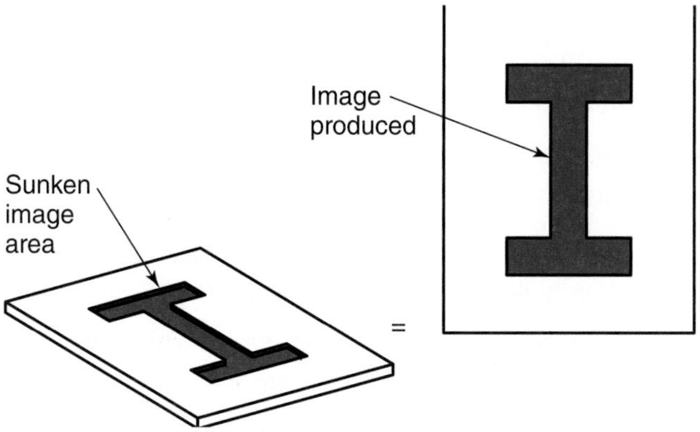

Goodheart-Willcox Publisher

Figure 1-13. Gravure or intaglio printing has an image area that is sunken below the plate surface to hold ink.

it is in contact with the cylinder. This leaves ink only in the sunken areas of the cylinder.

The gravure process is considered to be an excellent, high-speed, long-run means of producing a superior product. Some of the typical materials printed by this method are magazines, catalogs, newspaper supplements, package printing, metal surfaces, and vinyl surfaces.

Porous Printing

Porous printing is basically a stencil process, in which an image carrier is attached to a screen and ink is forced through the open mesh areas. Screen printing is the most used of the porous printing methods. See **Figure 1-14**.

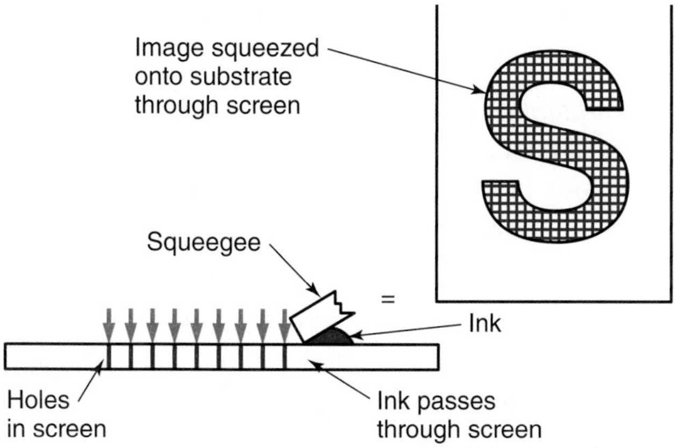

Goodheart-Willcox Publisher

Figure 1-14. Screen printing is a form of porous printing. Small holes in the image permit ink to pass through and deposit on substrate.

Screen printing is a versatile method of printing on many types of surfaces. It is capable of doing line and halftone work. Some of the screen printing work in the electronics field is very precise and the equipment highly sophisticated. Special inks are required for screen printing.

The artwork is assembled much like that for lithographic work. Laying out to size, with all of the elements in position, will generally be acceptable. Overlays are necessary for additional color work. The techniques vary slightly when using photographic or hand-cut stencils. The presses for the screen process can be manual or highly automated.

A wide variety of applications exists, including packaging, clothing and other fabric items, and printing on nonabsorbent surfaces, such as glass. Many tiny electronic circuits are produced with a type of screen printing. Another unusual application is printing the conductive materials on automobile rear windows for defrosting circuits.

Impactless Printing

Impactless printing, also called pressureless printing, does not require direct contact between an image carrier and the substrate. These terms are not as familiar as the system terms. Digital printing is a typical system and ink-jet printing is an example of the impactless processes. Ink droplets are formed and forced through very small nozzles onto the substrate. Most of the units use a computer to control the image generation. The computer controls where, and how much, ink is forced onto the substrate. See **Figure 1-15**.

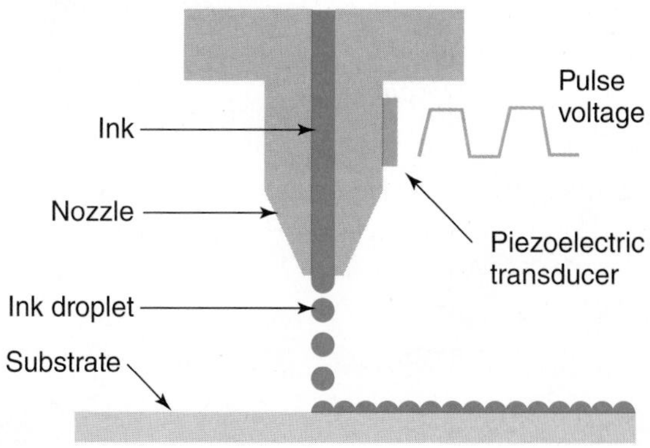

Goodheart-Willcox Publisher

Figure 1-15. This diagram illustrates the basic principle of ink-jet printing.

Electrostatic printing systems and laser printers are also being used to produce high-quality images. The electrostatic method uses the forces of electric current and static electricity. It is commonly found in office copying machines. Machines capable of producing copies in multiple colors are prevalent in the industry.

Binding and Finishing

Once an image has been printed onto a substrate, some form of binding and finishing is usually required. These are the final steps to completing the printing job.

Binding

Binding is the process of joining together multiple pages of a printed product by various means including sewing, stapling, spiral wire, and adhesives. Binding requires complex equipment, as shown in **Figure 1-16**.

The binding process for most printed products requires one or more of the following steps: scoring, folding, gathering, collating, stitching, and trimming.

- *Scoring* is the creasing of a heavier sheet of paper or paperboard to assist in the folding of the material.
- *Folding* is required when a large sheet contains two or more pages of a product. Sheets containing 8, 16, or 32 pages are common in the production of books and periodicals. The folded groups of pages are called *signatures*.
- *Gathering* is the process of bringing several signatures together in the proper order.
- *Collating* is the process of placing pages (usually single sheets) in the correct sequence.
- *Stitching* is a stapling process by which pages of a signature are held together.
- *Trimming* is the cutting of material after printing to produce even edges. **Figure 1-17** shows an example of a semiautomatic operation for cutting stock.

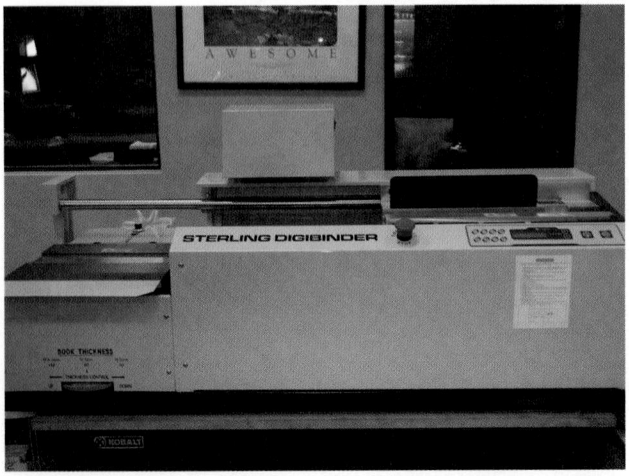

Goodheart-Willcox Publisher

Figure 1-16. A binding machine is used to hold multiple sheets together to form one product, such as a book.

Finishing

Finishing includes various processes that enhance the final printed product. Some of the more common finishing operations include embossing, die-cutting, stamping, punching, drilling, round cornering, and padding. Laminating and coating are also considered finishing processes.

- *Embossing* produces a raised design on paper or other material. This process uses pressure and heat to mold the paper fibers.
- *Die-cutting* uses rules or blades to cut paper or other sheet materials into designs.
- *Perforating* is a similar operation that cuts a series of holes or slits in the stock to allow part of it to be torn off easily. It is used extensively for tickets and coupons, often in conjunction with the process of numbering.
- *Numbering* is the process of printing numbers in sequence on each piece.
- *Stamping* refers to the application of a metal foil to almost any type of material, such as leather, paper, or cloth. A combination of embossing and foil stamping can also be done in one operation.
- *Lamination* is the process of bonding plastic film, by heat and pressure, to a sheet of paper to protect its surface and improve appearance. See **Figure 1-18**.
- *Coating* is done for the same purpose, and may be done as a finishing operation, or as part of the printing process, depending on the application. For example, a spot coating of gloss

©George Deal

Figure 1-17. Trimming is done to make all sheets even on edges. This is a large computer-controlled cutter that automatically trims stock to size.

©George Deal

Figure 1-18. Laminating is a finishing operation that puts a protective coating over the image.

Academic Link

History of Print

The invention of printing is directly correlated to the development of a substrate on which an image could be printed. The earliest examples of recorded information are generally considered to be art forms, not printing.

The earliest form of a book was created by the Sumerians on clay tablets around 3300 BCE. A stylus was used to press characters into wet clay. Ancient Egyptian writings on papyrus have been discovered that date to approximately 2600 BCE. Papyrus was made from the stalks of papyrus plants, which were abundant along the Nile River. The papyrus stalks were cut into thin strips, layered, and pressed or pounded together to form a smooth sheet.

The beginning of paper as we know it today is attributed to Ts'ai Lun in China, about 105 CE. He used bark, cotton, and fishnets to make pulp and strained the fibers using a large, framed screen. When the strained pulp dried, the sheets of paper that remained were thin, flexible, and smooth.

Over the next 1000 years, papermaking spread to India, the Middle East, Spain, Italy, and Europe. As each region implemented this method, small changes were made that affected the appearance, durability, and cost of the paper. For example, Arabians used linen fibers instead of wood in the pulp. Also, Italian papermakers began using watermarks in the late 1200s as a way of identifying their products.

or dull varnish to part of a page is often applied during printing. The varnish is a design element to draw attention to the area of the page where it is applied.

Segments of the Industry

The graphic communications industry can be divided into segments or classifications, **Figure 1-19**. A few of the major segments are described briefly in the following paragraphs.

Commercial Printing

The ***commercial printing*** segment of the industry encompasses all sizes and types of printing operations. These range from small local shops with one or two employees to large companies with several plant locations and hundreds or thousands of employees. Products produced in the commercial printing segment are as varied as the company sizes, from simple one-color envelopes and letterheads, to full-color product brochures and sales displays, to complex and sophisticated annual reports for giant corporations. See **Figure 1-20**.

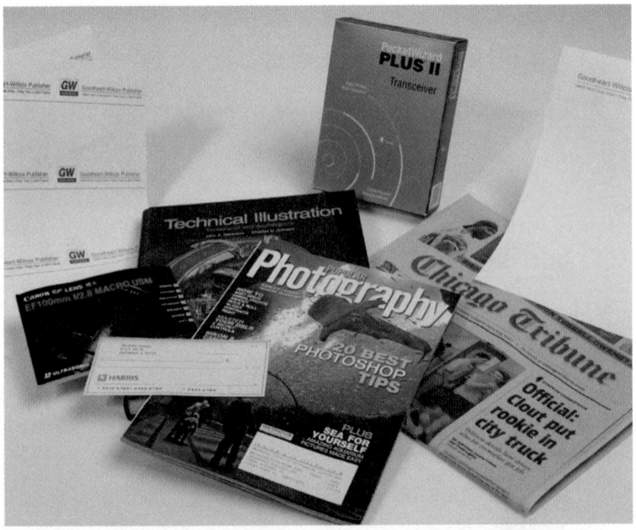

Goodheart-Willcox Publisher

Figure 1-19. Products from each segment of the printing industry.

©George Deal

Figure 1-20. This is a large sheet-fed offset lithographic press, one of the types widely used in commercial printing. Paper sheets are picked up on the right. They are then pulled to the left for printing.

Quick printing consists of shops specializing in rapid turnaround short-run printing and copying services. Both independently owned and franchised quick printing operations are designed to serve the needs of business customers. Equipment in such shops often includes digital equipment with varying capabilities, including color.

Periodical Printing

The ***periodical printing*** segment of the industry consists of plants that are designed primarily to print magazines. Web-fed offset lithography and gravure printing commonly produce periodical publications.

Newspaper Printing

Although ***newspaper printing*** was done for many years on web-fed presses using the letterpress process, most operations have switched to offset lithography. Because of the widespread use of computer technology and satellite transmission, national newspapers are published through a network of regional printing sites. This greatly simplifies distribution of the product. See **Figure 1-21**.

©George Deal

Figure 1-21. A magazine is being printed on a web press where the paper is fed from a large roll and threads through the press.

Think Green

Overview

The graphic communications industry affects the environment in several ways. It uses large amounts of paper, water, chemicals, and energy. The process of printing introduces vast amounts of carbon dioxide into the air. For the past several decades, companies have been working toward “going green,” or becoming environmentally friendly, in an effort to conserve resources without adversely affecting the environment.

Book Printing

Book printing includes the production of trade books, such as general interest nonfiction and fiction, sold in bookstores and other retail locations and textbooks providing instruction on a great variety of subjects. At one time, many book publishers operated their own printing facilities. Today, however, most contract with large specialized printing operations. Web-fed offset lithography and flexography are the two processes usually used in book production.

In-Plant Printing

The ***in-plant printing*** segment of the industry covers printing facilities operated by companies whose business is not the production of printed materials. A typical use of in-plant printing is the production of owner’s manuals, repair manuals, and parts lists for such products as power tools, material-handling equipment, or vehicles of various types. These manuals are usually available for printing directly from the companies’ websites.

Forms Printing

The ***forms printing*** segment of the industry designs and prints special paper forms used in many businesses. The types of forms vary from simple sales receipts or message pads, to multipart carbonless order forms, to continuous perforated forms for use in special impact printers. Label printing is also done by some forms printers, as well as by companies specializing in labels. Most label printing is done on papers with a pressure-sensitive adhesive backing, using specially designed small web-offset lithographic presses. Labels can also be printed directly from one’s own computer by inserting blank labels into the printer’s paper tray and using the software program to enter the label information. Business forms printing is declining because the public is choosing to use digital equipment to print forms.

Financial Printing

Financial printing involves a variety of printed materials. Typical products include checks, bonds, currency, lottery tickets, legal documents, various certificates, registration material, and loan materials. This printing classification is highly specialized and generally controlled by the federal government. Maintaining security of many of these documents is imperative.

Package Printing

Package printing has become one of the largest segments of the industry. Look at all the packages you see in the grocery store. Would you buy cereal if you did not see what it looked like? The images are printed on many different types of materials. Plastic, paper, cardboard, corrugated board, and foil are a sampling of the many types of materials used for packaging.

Electronic Delivery

Success in today’s graphic communications industry requires looking beyond ink on paper. The way consumers get their information and communication materials has evolved to encompass more complex and integrated methods of delivery. Providing only a printed method is no longer acceptable in this electronic age.

Regardless of the delivery, it is more critical than ever for the designer to present a consistent visual experience to the viewer throughout all forms of media.

Web Design

Designing for the web has a totally different perspective from designing for print. While graphic design principles still apply, the way the viewer interacts with the visual is entirely different. Printed materials are the original form of interactive media. You form a tactile relationship with a printed material while holding it. The connection is through touch as much as through the eyes. Viewing a web page is entirely different.

Web design is all about the "front end" of the site, focusing on the looks and interaction. Usability should be the main focus. The visual appeal is secondary to functionality and, yes, even predictability. Web pages must load quickly. The average person will wait about two seconds for a web response. It took you longer to read that sentence. The viewer wants easy access to information, and they want it now! If it is not available to them in a timely manner, they will just move on to something else.

Web Development

A web developer works on the "back end" of the website. Development is about how the site works and functions. It also encompasses long-term maintenance to ensure continued success. A good web developer knows the current programming codes and markup languages and how to choose the right one for a project.

Common ***content management systems (CMS)*** make it easy to wear both the design *and* development hats for websites that are not complex. See **Figure 1-22**. Some systems allow people who do not have an advanced knowledge of coding and markup languages to create web pages. These programs

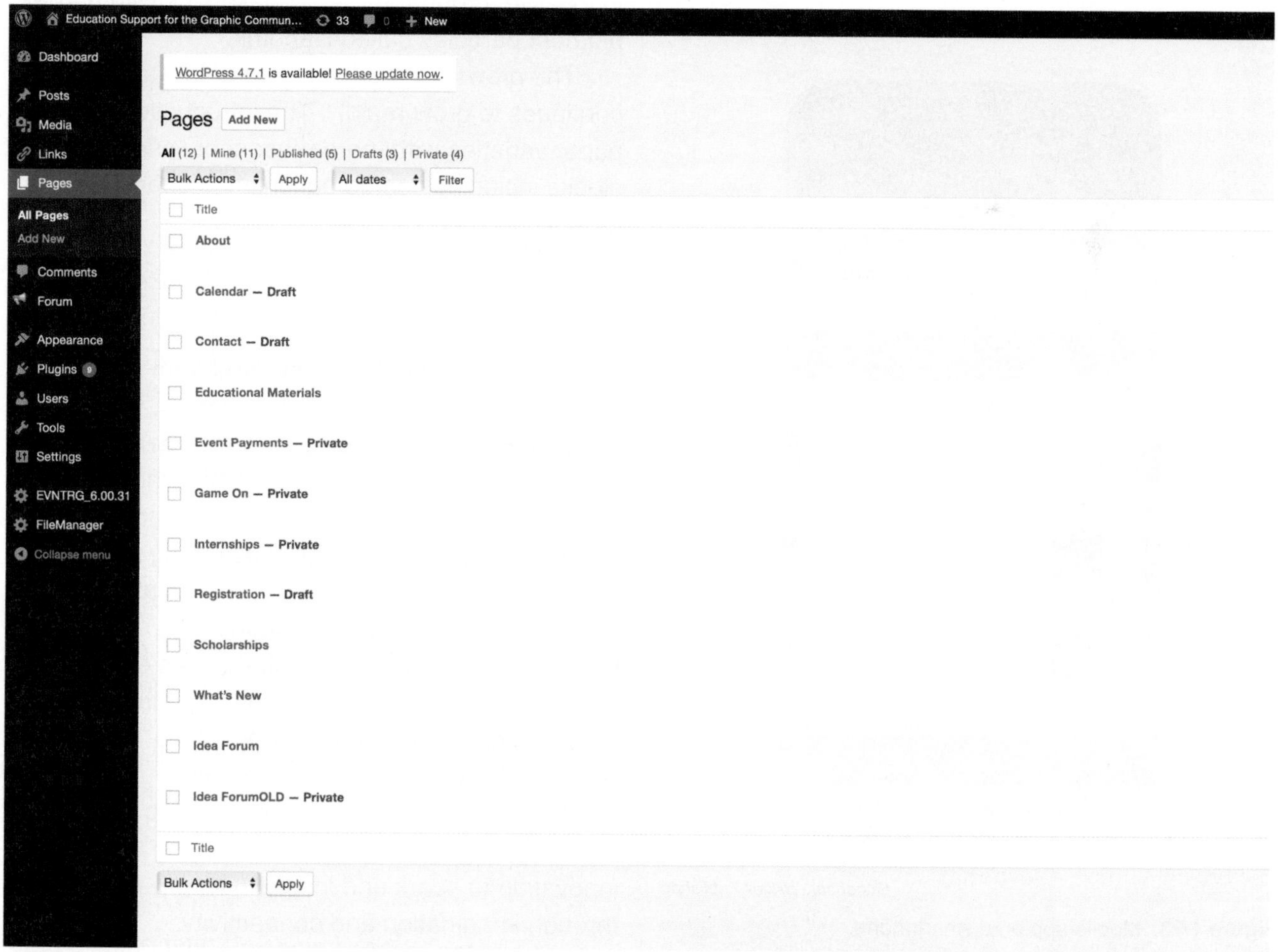

Goodheart-Willcox Publisher

Figure 1-22. A content management system allows novice web developers to create professional-looking websites.

look and function similarly to our traditional page layout software and contain familiar ***WYSIWYG*** (what you see is what you get) interfaces.

Mobile Media

Smartphones and tablets are no longer the exception but the rule. Never before have we had a single device that allows us constant connectivity and global accessibility in real time. These devices allow us to communicate, play games, watch movies, read books, shop, work, bank, schedule, store personal information, take and store photos, monitor our heart rates, go to school, and so much more. And we carry them around in our pockets.

Web design is conforming to ***responsive design***, which enables a smooth transition from the size of a computer screen to the size of the mobile device. Mobile media is an essential part of our day-to-day lives. Marketers and designers must embrace it to be effective in this digital economy. See **Figure 1-23**.

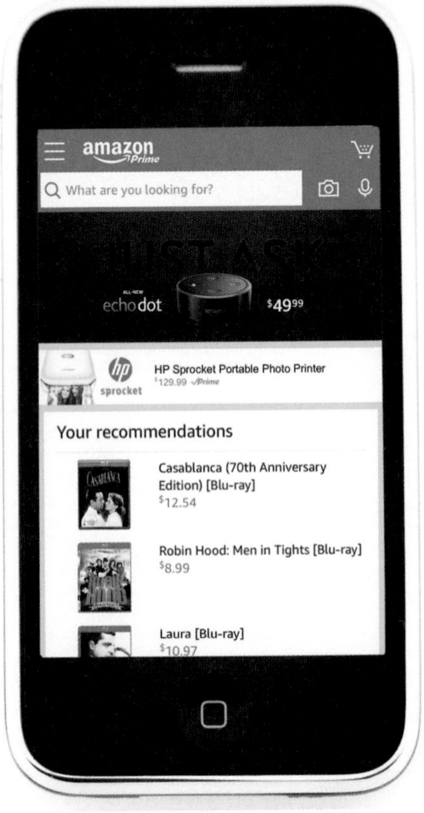

Goodheart-Willcox Publisher

Figure 1-23. Mobile app on a smartphone.

Digital Publishing

The electronic publishing revolution is becoming incredibly significant due to the technological advancements that transition almost daily. With the popularity of tablets and smartphones, and the growing compatibility of software applications to devices, distributing published materials electronically as apps, portable document format (PDF) files, or ***e-pubs*** (digital publications), to name a few, has become a standard method of delivery.

This method of publishing still goes through many of the same preliminary steps as its printed counterpart, but the production itself is very different. Benefits of digital publishing include more cost-effective updates and revisions, as well as easier and instant delivery options.

A new category of digital printing has been developed. Nanography was designed to join the versatility of digital printing with the quality and performance of offset printing by using an innovative, proprietary water-based ink with nano-pigment particles called NanoInk.

The growth of production color ink-jet printers continues to grow rapidly. The introduction of new paper varieties with more reasonably priced treated stocks including coated options has opened doors for new revenue streams.

Gaming

The gaming world has evolved from arcades, to personal computers, to game consoles, to mobile devices. Rather than being a narrow market niche for nerdy computer users, the gaming industry has spilled over into mainstream life. Encompassing programming, game design, illustrators, and animators, today's games are sophisticated and detailed. The gaming software industry drives the hardware and software industries in an endless circle of "if you can dream it, you can make it happen" mindset, producing games that are ever faster and containing realistic, detailed graphics.

The interactive nature of the gaming industry has progressed to a new level, allowing design innovation to spark and inspire user creativity through imagination and connectivity.

Animation

By definition, ***animation*** is taking individual still images with slight variations and running them together to create the illusion of motion. From sophisticated movie productions with 3D reality to simple cartoons, animation intersects with many other channels of delivery. Often incorporated into digital publishing, gaming, mobile media, and online resources, animation covers the gamut in the science and mathematics of technology and the imaginative side of creativity.

3D Printing

The additive process of laying down layers of a specific material over and over to create an object is called 3D printing. 3D modeling software is used to create a virtual design. The files for the design are sent to the printer to create a three-dimensional product that can be cut apart and cross-sectioned. There are many different processes, hardware, and final materials available to produce these amazing objects. This technology is already changing many aspects of manufacturing and new product development.

Future

It is difficult to predict where the technology will take us in five years, three years, even in six months. New and exciting technology advancements keep this industry constantly evolving to meet the needs of the consumer.

Far from being "old" and "stuffy," the world of graphic communications is revolutionary, creative, and visionary. Embracing keywords such as connectivity, transition, and accessibility, the science from the collective history of graphic communications has provided a solid foundation for transformation beyond our wildest imaginations.

Summary

- *Graphic communications* is an umbrella term to identify printing processes that place an image on a variety of surfaces we call substrates. It has a rich history that has preserved the art of communication. It is a dynamic, challenging industry.
- Graphic communications is the lifeblood of our technological society, influencing the population of the world wherever and whenever a product is printed.
- Individuals working in the industry have skills that vary greatly. The creative person, the writer, the manager, the operator, the technician, and the engineer have typical skills needed by employees of a printing facility.
- These facilities use various processes to create a product that records and preserves thoughts and ideas of individuals.
- The printing process for graphic communications includes relief printing, planography, intaglio process, porous printing, and impactless printing.
- The eight printing classifications are commercial, periodical, newspaper, book, in-plant, forms, financial, and package.
- The products produced by various segments of the industry reflect the capabilities of each process.
- Electronic delivery media includes websites, mobile devices, digital publishing, and gaming.

Review Questions

Answer the following questions using the information in this chapter.

1. Why are graphic images considered important compared to verbal communication?
2. Any material on which printing can be done is called a(n) _____.
3. A quote lists the _____ and _____ for production of printed goods and services.
4. Which of the following is the most common way of generating copy for printing?
   A. Computer.
   B. Hot type.
   C. Scanning.
   D. Photocomposing.
5. *True or False?* Line art is a type of drawing consisting of continuous tones.
6. Explain the term *halftone*.

7. Which of the following is *not* a process color used in printing a full-color photograph?
   A. Magenta.
   B. Yellow.
   C. Green.
   D. Cyan.
8. Describe the following types of printing: flexography, gravure, screen printing, impactless printing.
9. _____ printing does not require direct contact between an image carrier and the substrate.
10. What type of printing is laser printing?
11. Name at least three steps that are considered part of the binding process.
12. What subdivision of commercial printing specializes in rapidly completing short-run printing and photocopying work?
13. What processes are usually used in book production?
14. Web design is about the _____ end and web development is about the _____ end of a website.
15. The ability of a website to adjust properly for multiple devices is called _____.

Suggested Activities

1. After getting permission to visit a printing plant, identify the variety of products the plant produces. What is the printing process used to produce these printed products?
2. Select an individual or a discovery that has contributed to the advancement of the industry. Present your findings to the class.
3. Explain the basic differences among the following printing processes: relief printing, planography, intaglio process, porous printing, and impactless printing.

Chapter 2

Graphic Communications Careers

Learning Objectives

After studying this chapter, you will be able to:

- Differentiate among skilled technical, creative, management, and support positions.
- Recall the different levels of careers in terms of career preparation.
- Summarize tools you can use to find a job.
- Explain the importance of having good work habits.
- Summarize the advantages and disadvantages of owning your own business.
- Give examples of how changing technology is affecting the career outlook.

Goodheart-Willcox Publisher

Important Terms

apprenticeship
careers
craft-centered jobs
electronic information transfer
entrepreneur
journeyman
lifelong learning
managers
outsourcing
robotics
turnaround
work ethic

G-WLEARNING.com

While studying this chapter, look for the activity icon to:

- **Practice** vocabulary terms with e-flash cards, matching activities, and vocabulary game.
- **Reinforce** what you learn by submitting end-of-chapter questions.

www.g-wlearning.com/visualtechnology/

The graphic communications industry encompasses a multitude of challenging ***careers*** for skilled technical, creative, management, and support personnel. Educators, engineers, and scientists can also find positions in the graphic communications industry. Entrepreneurship is yet another avenue open to someone who wants to own and operate a company. This chapter will summarize and help you more fully understand these positions.

Careers in the Graphic Communications Industry

The graphic communications industry needs people with many different interests, talents, and abilities. The workforce can be organized into seven general categories:

- Skilled technical positions include those who can operate sophisticated machinery and carry out tasks that directly involve machines, materials, and products.
- Creative positions include those who have skills in writing, art, and design.
- Management positions include those who like to work with people and can supervise the work of others.
- Support positions include people who are the link between products and customers.
- Engineers and scientists are people whose jobs focus on research.
- Educators are people who teach students to prepare for careers in the graphic communications industry.
- Service operation positions are available to those who want to work for a company that provides a specific service to other printing companies.

Skilled Technical Positions

Skilled technical workers are involved in the prepress and press stages of production. Changes in technology have brought about changes in these career positions. Many formerly ***craft-centered jobs*** that were traditionally performed by artisans or others with manual skills now require specialized technical skills.

Prepress Imaging Specialist

Technological changes have and continue to change in the prepress area. Most of the prepress work is accomplished by using electronic devices and software. Preflighting of customer materials is one of the first activities commonly preformed in the prepress area. Image manipulation is accomplished to produce the desired results. Some of the tasks performed by personnel in the department include scanning images into digital format, creating digital artwork, and checking and fitting files. Working closely with customers is also imperative.

Pressroom Personnel

No matter what printing process is involved, pressroom workers are responsible for the quality of the final printed product, **Figure 2-1**. The efforts of many individuals are needed to transfer the image from an image carrier to a substrate. The number of people involved depends on the type and size

O'Neil Printing

Figure 2-1. Press operators are checking a run of a printed product.

of the press. Some presses are small and simple to operate, but many are complex and require extensive technical knowledge.

Controlling ink, solutions, and substrates are basic activities of pressroom workers. Quality control is imperative. Knowledge of paper, ink, and press operations is essential. Mechanical aptitude is a desirable quality.

Activities performed by lithographic press operators include positioning plates, filling the ink fountain, loading stock; controlling ink flow, fountain solution, and press speed; and inspecting finished sheets, **Figure 2-2**.

The web lithographic press operator must set up a press using huge rolls of paper, rather than sheets of stock, **Figure 2-3**. Press size and complexity varies. Newspaper and other large presses print on both sides of the stock, fold, and deliver a finished product with great speed. Press assistants working under experienced press operators are common on many of the large presses.

The letterpress operator runs a smaller press. Common job-shop printing includes letterheads, forms, cards, and envelopes. Today, these presses are used primarily for finishing operations, such as die cutting and numbering.

The gravure press operator runs a press at very high speeds and usually has a crew assigned to specific responsibilities. See **Figure 2-4**.

Screen presses have a configuration uncommon to the other processes. The screen press operator must set up the press to print on a

Strachan Henshaw Machinery, Inc.

Figure 2-3. The operator of this web offset book printing press is responsible for maintaining quality on very long runs.

©George Deal

Figure 2-2. Press operators must set up, run, and maintain complex printing presses. Mechanical aptitude and knowledge of ink, paper, and solutions are important.

variety of materials. Knowledge of inks, screens, and image carriers is essential.

Digital presses and large format ink jet printers rip files to produce products from static and variable data files. Color calibration set-up manipulation is required to meet expectations.

Bindery and Finishing Personnel

Accuracy and mechanical aptitude are required of bindery and finishing personnel. Physical strength is sometimes necessary. Workers use sophisticated equipment to cut stock to size for the press or once it has been printed, **Figure 2-5**. Machine operators must have knowledge of cutting, gathering, collating, trimming, slitting, perforating, and folding techniques. Gathering and collating operations require machine operators and setup personnel who can do accurate work. Skills in die cutting, embossing, foil stamping, and printing are also utilized.

Linotype-Hell

Figure 2-4. This technician is operating a gravure cylinder engraving machine. The finished cylinders will be transported to the pressroom.

Creative Positions

Creative people are needed in many roles within the graphic communications industry. Talented designers, editors, illustrators, writers, and photographers conceptualize and create products that go to print.

Writer

As the name implies, the writer generates any copy to be printed. Creative writing talent and thorough knowledge of the language is imperative. A willingness to write on a wide variety of topics is usually needed. Many times the writer is not employed by the printer, but by an agency or other business firm.

Graphic Designers

Graphic designers are artists who are responsible for planning printed pieces. Creative talent is imperative. Expressing an idea visually is the primary role of a graphic designer. An

©Dana Thelander

Figure 2-5. Bindery and finishing personnel must operate and maintain various types of complex equipment, including this cutter.

appreciation for beauty and an eye for composition and color are essential traits. These skills may be natural in an individual or developed through training and experience, **Figure 2-6**.

The computer has replaced the traditional cut-and-paste method of production. Familiarity with design programs is a standard job requirement, with small variations in software proficiency. Working knowledge of several of the common drawing, image editing, and page layout programs is expected. See **Figure 2-7**.

Despite the advances in computer technology, traditional artistic composition and design skills remain important. Some graphic designers design exclusively on the computer, while others may use both the computer and hand drawing or painting. The future trend in hiring will focus on creative talent.

ESB Professional/Shutterstock.com

Figure 2-6. Artists must understand color theory and be able to visualize a concept.

Editor

The editor prepares the written material and illustrations for publication by revising and rewriting copy and checking it for accuracy. Copyediting entails sequencing content, marking the copy for style, and ensuring consistency throughout the manuscript. A command of the language is essential. Sometimes technical expertise is also needed.

Publishers of books, magazines, and newspapers employ editors. Freelance editorial work is also possible for those who prefer self-employment.

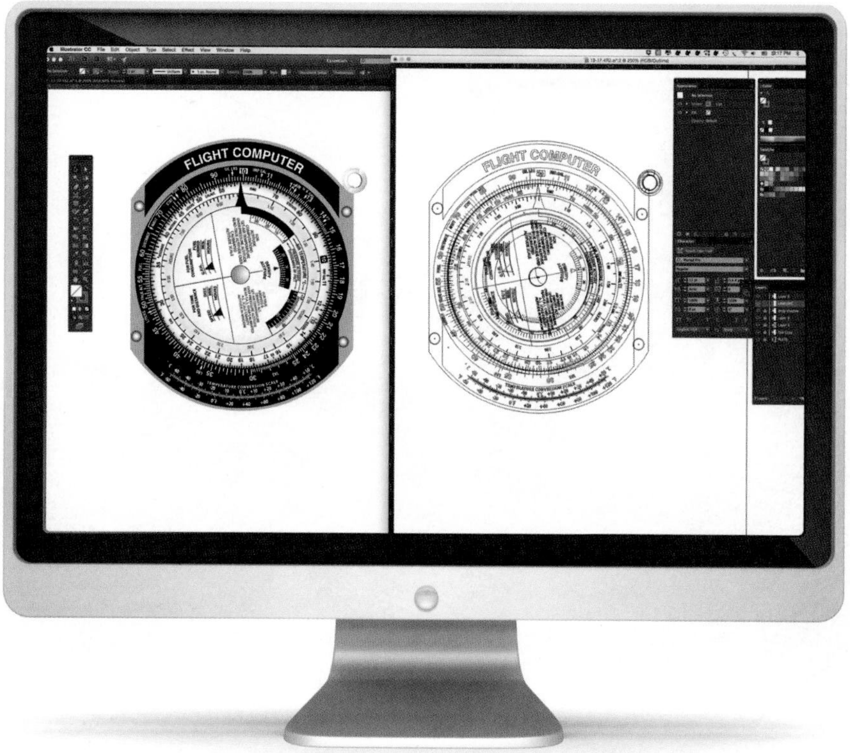

Goodheart-Willcox Publisher

Figure 2-7. Graphic artists use computers to design and lay out text and images for print.

Photographer

A photographer may be called on to take high-quality photographic images for a publication. The photographer must create the image based on the customer's stated objective and parameters. A working knowledge of traditional and digital camera equipment and photographic techniques is expected.

Many photographers work independently, while others are employed by newspaper and magazine publishers. Advertising and public relations agencies also employ photographers.

Page-Layout Artist

The page-layout artist completes the designer's layout by using a computer to assemble the components. The artist must follow directions as the job requires precision, neatness, and accuracy. Because of publishing programs, the page-layout artist may also perform the tasks of a graphic designer and illustrator.

Management Positions

Managers direct a team of workers who affect the entire organization. Part of being a good manager is being able to get work done through other people. It also requires excellent organizational abilities. See **Figure 2-8**.

Management must work in a team with other employees to accomplish the objectives of the company. Communication, cooperation, and understanding between departments are the ingredients for a productive, innovative workforce. Managers are responsible for ensuring a job gets done right and on time.

Management-level employees in a graphic communications facility typically include executive officers, plant managers, plant superintendents, managing editors, production managers and schedulers, controllers, sales managers, supervisors, estimators, and planners.

Rawpixel.com/Shutterstock.com

Figure 2-8. Managers are part of a team. They must be able to plan, organize, and direct activities.

Characteristics important to being an effective member of the management team include being able to:

- Make logical decisions.
- Get work done through others.
- Communicate well with others.
- Motivate personnel.
- Apply factual information and not opinions.
- Act maturely and fairly.

The management team must be concerned with the following aspects of the business:

- Increased specialization of production equipment.
- High investment requirements for new equipment.
- Rising costs of materials and energy.
- Shortages or lead times for critical materials.
- Rapid introduction of new technology.
- High interest rates for capital equipment purchases and short-term borrowing.
- Excess production capacity.
- Slow real business growth in market areas.
- Threat of increased international competition.
- Government regulations affecting manpower, fiscal and manufacturing operations, and environmental compliance.

Typically, management personnel have several responsibilities in different areas. At times, the executive officer can be the chief financial officer and also have responsibilities for sales. Such a mix of duties is common to the graphic communications industry.

Chief Executive Officer

The president or chief executive officer (CEO) of a company is the top administrator. He or she is the policymaker and overseer of the total operation. The president is interested in employing skilled and reliable personnel to contribute to the effective and efficient operation of the company.

Controller

The controller is responsible for the financial operation of a company. He or she ensures the company operates by sound methods and practices. Contact with financial institutions, as well as preparing budgets, forecasts, analyses, reports, and statements are functions of this position. An aptitude for mathematics and a thorough knowledge of accounting practices are essential. The controller or accounts manager monitors the client's print or digital media jobs through the production process. See **Figure 2-9**.

EDP Supervisor

The EDP supervisor is in charge of all the electronic data processing (EDP) functions in the plant. Knowledge of computer programming and applications is essential.

Cost Estimator

The estimator calculates the costs used to bid or price a job. Understanding all plant operations is essential. Accurate calculations are required, since

Goodheart-Willcox Publisher

Figure 2-9. Controllers are responsible for all financial aspects of a company. They must have an aptitude for mathematics and a knowledge of accounting practices.

the figures will reflect the technical capabilities of the various operations as well as the cost of materials. This person needs a sharp mind and must be able to calculate numbers well.

Plant Manager

The plant manager is responsible for the plant's manufacturing operations. Products must be produced on time, at the lowest possible cost to the company, and at a level of quality acceptable to the customer. Another critical concern to the plant manager is the safety and health of all employees. The ability to analyze results and understand people is important.

Plant Superintendent

The plant superintendent directs all manufacturing operations of the company as well as first-line supervisors. The plant superintendent makes sure all equipment is working efficiently and kept in good condition. The position is high pressure and requires patience and direct control.

Think Green

Environmental Consultant

As a result of the growing concerns over environmental issues, the printing industry has become dedicated to becoming more green. Before becoming more environmentally compliant, a company must first be educated about the issues, as well as discover how that specific company impacts the environment. Following this, a plan must be established to address how to reduce the company's impact. Frequently, an outside individual or company is hired to help start the process. It is the job of an environmental consultant to instruct and help companies plan on how to reduce their environmental impact. It is then up to the companies to implement the plan and work toward helping the environment. For a printer, an environmental consultant would take into account the energy expended to run a printer, the amount and type of paper used, and even the energy used to light the space.

Production Manager

The production manager is a liaison between sales and production personnel. This person directs traffic for all manufacturing tasks through the plant. Everything must be in place at the designated time. The production manager must be well organized, be able to plan ahead, and foresee problems. Keeping accurate records and getting along with others is essential.

Production Scheduler

The production scheduler sets up timetables for all jobs in an efficient and effective manner. After the job is in production, each phase must be recorded so the product can be traced at any phase of production. Being able to plan and understand the capabilities of equipment and personnel is important. The application of computer technology to production scheduling must be understood.

Quality Control Supervisor

The quality control supervisor sets standards for production and finished products, **Figure 2-10**. The job requires constant sampling to ensure consistent quality and to reduce waste or spoilage. Knowledge of control devices as a means to measure quality is basic to the position.

Sales Manager

The sales manager is responsible for establishing a profitable sales staff. Among the

zefart/Shutterstock.com

Figure 2-10. The quality control supervisor ensures that every aspect of production is within specifications.

manager's responsibilities are supervising sales activities, customer relations, and budgeting; setting sales quotas and profit margins; and overseeing sales service. The sales manager must have a good aptitude for business and leave a favorable impression on people.

Support Personnel

Support personnel reinforce the work of the technical, creative, and managerial departments through two main channels: customer service, and sales and marketing. These employees are the important link between products and customers.

Customer Service Representative

A customer service representative is the liaison between customers, management, and the sales force. Knowledge of job schedules and job progress is essential. Understanding the operation of the firm is also imperative. Good interpersonal skills, whether in person, on the telephone, via email, or through website instant messaging, are necessary to the position.

Sales Representative

A sales representative position requires basic sales techniques, but it also requires a knowledge of printing processes. In a way, a sales representative is a trusted advisor to the customer. The representative must be able to provide the greatest product or service for the customer's investment. Meeting and being accepted by people is a prime requisite for the position. Being ambitious, highly organized, and able to project a professional image are contributors to success. See **Figure 2-11**.

Heidelberg, Inc.

Figure 2-11. Sales representatives must understand processes and be able to work with customers.

Marketing Coordinator

The fundamental objective of any company is to market its products or services profitably. Personnel with positions in marketing, advertising, and public relations are responsible for promotional activities, including identifying potential customers. In a small firm, a single marketing coordinator may handle all these activities. The marketing and sales departments often work together closely. Both managerial- and support-level positions are available in marketing.

Preflight Technician

The preflight technician is a person who works with computers and software applications. This person is a troubleshooter. When a computer file arrives, the preflight technician goes over the file and identifies problems within the file that could prevent the job from printing successfully.

Color Specialist

The color specialist works closely with the printer and the customer. If, for example, the customer indicates that "the green is not green enough," the color specialist checks the copy and informs the printer what changes need to be made to produce a job acceptable to the customer. A thorough knowledge of color theory as it relates to printing processes is essential.

Premedia Technician

Premedia technicians perform a host of duties on powerful computers. Their job functions in electronic prepress include preflighting, scanning images, electronic file repair, trapping, imposition, and outputting film, proofs, and plates.

Web-to-Print E-commerce Manager

The web-to-print e-commerce manager oversees the company's online sales and presence on the web. This person is responsible for creating and updating all online information, and ensuring the information is accurate. The web-to-print e-commerce manager also oversees the work of the web designer and is responsible for the creation of marketing materials.

Cross-media/Multimedia Developer

These developers generate and manipulate images, both video and audio, into multimedia applications. These applications include interactive training, data presentation, and entertainment and educational products. The developer prepares a variety of images and manages the development and implementation of the products.

Engineers and Scientists

Engineers and scientists are able to find positions in research and development in the graphic communications industry. Engineers are needed to improve industrial processes, **Figure 2-12**. Positions are often product-oriented and exist to provide quality control.

Scientists, particularly those with a strong background in chemistry, are also hired as researchers. They may experiment with and test equipment, inks, and printing paper. The paper and pulp industry, in particular, conducts much of its own research.

With the ever-increasing focus on environmental issues, environmental engineers and scientists are being hired by industry to ensure compliance standards are met, **Figure 2-13**.

Positions for engineering and science technicians are also available. Often, four or five

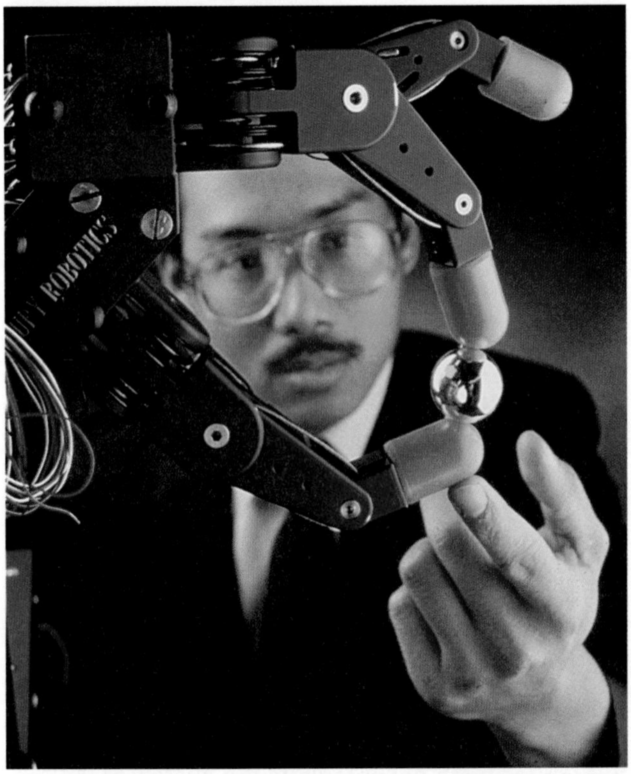

Martin Marietta Corp.

Figure 2-12. Engineers in industrial settings work to improve processes and products.

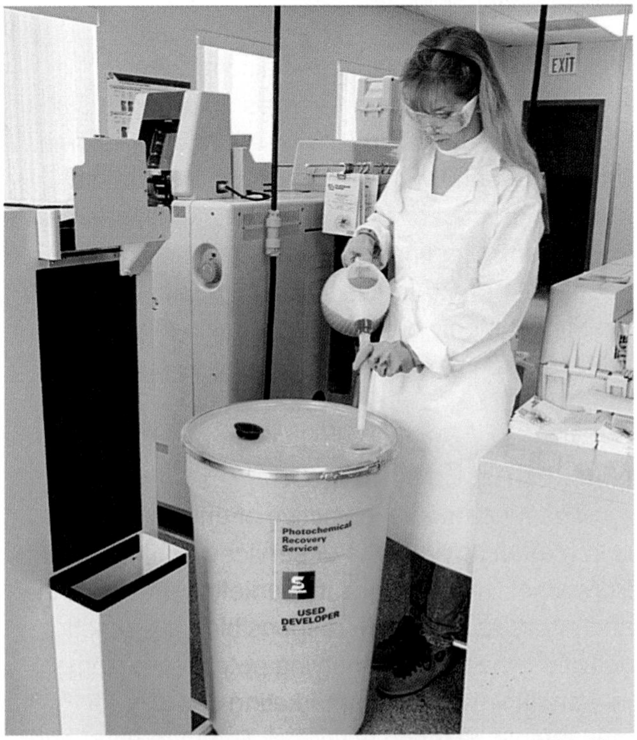

Safety-Kleen

Figure 2-13. Stringent federal, state, and local waste-reclamation standards have created a need for waste management professionals with a background in science.

technicians are hired to support the activities of a single scientist or engineer.

Educator

Educators have the responsibility of preparing capable people for careers in the graphic communications industry. An effective educator must have an in-depth knowledge of the industry, have a strong desire to work with young people, and be a strong communicator.

Positions with Service Operations

Printing is a cooperative enterprise; one component depends on another. Since most firms do not have an integrated facility, ***outsourcing*** to service companies is essential for the completion of a product. Positions supporting the printing process are available in all service operations.

Agency or Studio

An agency or studio is a type of service operation. It helps a larger company with advertising, packaging, and producing printed or media-oriented materials. Many graphic communications positions are available in agencies.

Bindery and Finishing Services

Specialized bindery and finishing operations are often beyond the capability of a printing facility. The operations are subcontracted to a company that has equipment capable of rapidly folding, trimming, and packaging printed products.

Typographic Service

Typographic service facilities design, lay out, compose, assemble, and output on a variety of materials using electronic means. Computer-oriented imaging operations have become very sophisticated as a result of the technological advances in the industry.

Vendors

The graphic communications industry depends on many types of machines and materials. Suppliers provide opportunities for the plant owner to buy equipment, but from time to time the equipment needs to be serviced. Someone must also supply inks, solutions, and paper.

Jobs exist for people to sell and service products used by the graphic communications industry, **Figure 2-14**. Ink manufacturers, for example, supply a great service to the industry. Chemists have the important job of formulating ink so it is compatible with the press, substrate, and various other requirements of the process.

basysPrint Corporation

Figure 2-14. Manufacturing provides the materials and machinery that equip graphic communications plants.

Quick Printing and Copy Services

The role of quick printing and copy services is to provide printing services quickly, with different levels of quality. The level of technical knowledge and skills needed depends on the job. Some operators have more manual skills, while others are highly skilled technicians operating sophisticated systems.

Positions in quick printing require employees to be versatile. They may be responsible for managing others, selling services, estimating job costs, or operating equipment. Job requirements vary with the owner or franchise, and should be made clear to prospective employees. See **Figure 2-15**.

Screen Process Service

Screen printing drives the need for specialty-type printing facilities and workers with a wide variety of skills. Typical screen applications include sign printing, fabric imaging, printing on vinyl, and the manufacture of printed electronic circuit boards and components. See **Figure 2-16**.

Specialty Printing Service

Specialty printing shops do not have a wide market but provide a service for specialized products. These shops do engraving, label-making, and similar types of printing. Engraving, for example, is needed for producing high-quality business cards, stationery, and invitations.

Entrepreneur

Many entrepreneurs have started small businesses. The hours of an entrepreneur may be long, and business opportunities often require taking part in networking events. The feeling of freedom often drives the entrepreneur.

Preparing for a Career in the Graphic Communications Industry

Choosing a career is one of the most important decisions you will ever make. It can affect many aspects of your life, including level of education, income potential, working conditions, and types of coworkers. A career choice can also affect your family. It determines your geographic location, the number of hours spent on the job, possibilities for advancement, and many other considerations. Above all, your career choice can affect your satisfaction with life in general.

Job satisfaction is important. You need to feel good about your work and your future. Choosing the right career requires you to look ahead. What kind of work do you expect to be doing five years from now? Ten years from now? Which occupation

KOKTARO/Shutterstock.com

Figure 2-15. Service companies include advertising agencies, quick printing shops, specialty printers, and composing services. These smaller companies do work for larger companies or individuals.

aodaodaodaod/Shutterstock.com

Figure 2-16. Screen process services fill a niche for such specialty products as T-shirts with images.

will offer advancement and bring satisfaction? What areas are in demand?

Begin your search for a career by listing your aptitudes and goals. Then, try to match those to a career. The Interest Survey given on the States' Career Clusters website may help you better define your interests by listing the knowledge and skills needed for a particular career. You will then need to learn the requirements of different jobs in a particular field.

What are the entry-level jobs within the graphic communications industry? Most of the skill areas require at least a high school education, general equivalency diploma (GED), or vocational/technical training. See **Figure 2-17**. Students who apply for part-time work during high school can get a head start toward full-time employment after graduation.

GIT, Arizona State University

Figure 2-17. These young people are in training for positions as skilled technicians.

The ***apprenticeship*** educational plan is another entry method. In union shops, it is the only means of becoming a ***journeyman***, or experienced worker. Under this plan, the employee is a registered apprentice for a designated period of time (usually four to six years). An agreement is signed that the apprentice will receive classroom and on-the-job training in specific skill areas.

Formal training is available in private or public postsecondary institutions. These schools provide technical education, where specific skills are being developed for jobs within an industry. Because many jobs now require higher-level skills, community colleges are offering technical skills training programs. A four-year program in graphic communications is another career path, **Figure 2-18**.

Phovoir/Shutterstock.com

Figure 2-18. Many students prepare for careers in graphics and printing at a four-year educational institution.

Teaching or educational administration opportunities in the field of graphic communications require a college degree from an accredited institution. Positions including technologists, scientists, researchers, and engineers also require a degree. Constantly changing technology will make necessary ongoing retraining and upgrading of skills and knowledge, a trend in education and business commonly called ***lifelong learning***, or continuing education.

Try to obtain a broad knowledge of products and processes. Courses in basic electronics and computer science should be taken during high school and college. Graphic design, quality assurance, cost analysis, inventory, prepress, production scheduling and planning, and web development are just a few of the careers that require the use of electronic equipment. Computer literacy is a necessity.

Finding a Job

Several resources are available to help you search for a job. The Internet has many sites dedicated to finding employment. Another tool is the *Occupational Outlook Handbook* published by the United States Department of Labor and Bureau of Statistics. Another is the States' Career Clusters Initiative, which provides detailed pathways for different careers.

Once you have chosen a job you want, you must apply and possibly interview for it. You will likely have to fill out a job application, and you must submit your résumé. Contact a company's human resources department for more information on how to apply. Your résumé should include your personal information, objective, educational background, previous work experience, any special skills, organizations and activities, and personal references. See **Figure 2-19**.

After filling out the application and creating your résumé, you must prepare for a job interview. Before the interview, research the company. Prepare to ask questions about the position and company if necessary. Be prompt when arriving at the interview. During the interview, be sure to answer all the employer's questions concisely and honestly.

Jane Doe

1234 W. Main St.
Anytown, AZ 85213
(480) 123-4567

As a strong and experienced professional leader, I am able to actively schedule and supervise multiple employees while being in a fast-paced customer centric work environment. Being a creative and analytical problem solver, I have developed and instituted detailed instructional and visual documents to assist in the training and growth of new employees. I am exceptionally organized, detailed-oriented, and have remarkable self-motivation to coordinate and prioritize effectively and meet specified deadlines.

Skills

• Adobe Creative Suite	• Microsoft Office	• Web Design	• Adaptive
• Analytical	• Communication	• Conflict Resolution	• Creative
• Detail Oriented	• Digital Prepress	• Leadership	• Loyal
• Multi-task	• Organized	• Self Motivated	• Time Management

Accomplishments

- Developed & Implemented a new creative instructional program to foster technical and creative skills
- Designed training manual & instructional tools for several employment positions
- Launched and redesigned website for an independent business
- Received Scholarship from the Paradise Valley Art Department
- Entered into WSPA Premier Print Awards

Education

AAS in Graphic Design: Visual Communication Scottsdale Community College May 2016

Experience

Graphic Design Freelance Graphic Design Work December 2014 – Present

Goodheart-Willcox Publisher

Figure 2-19. Example of a résumé, highlighting the main points that should be included.

Work Habits

Good work habits are important for keeping a job. Having a good ***work ethic*** means being dependable. You must be honest, cooperative, and respectful with your coworkers. It is also important to develop your communication skills. These traits will translate into skills for becoming a good team member. They will also help you progress into a position of leadership.

Solving problems often requires you to work with other people as a member of a team. A team usually consists of team members and one or more team leaders. Teamwork can help get a job done more quickly than doing it alone, and it allows for more possible solutions to be considered. Problems are successfully solved using teamwork when all the members provide their ideas and abilities. See **Figure 2-20**. Working in teams takes organization and cooperation among the team members, and the exercise of leadership skills by the team's leaders.

The team's leaders are in command of the rest of the team. The quality of their leadership determines whether the team will be a success or a failure. Some people are natural leaders, others require training. Either way, there are important characteristics of leadership. Good leaders:

- Have a vision of what must be done and look for ways to reach the team's goals.
- Are skilled communicators who are able to encourage the team members to assist each other and cooperate. They work to ensure all the team members contribute to the team's success.
- Are willing to work as long as it takes to achieve success. They can organize and direct the team's activities.
- Are fair and honest. They take responsibility for their own actions and give credit to others when it is due.
- Know how to delegate authority. They may even assign leadership roles to other team members to get the job done as efficiently as possible.

©Dana Thelander

Figure 2-20. Teamwork is an important aspect of a career. Working in teams helps get jobs done more quickly and can produce different perspectives on solutions.

Entrepreneurship

An ***entrepreneur*** is someone who starts his or her own business. In the graphic communications field, it might be a small print shop, silk screen facility, color specialist house, or similar endeavor.

Thousands of new businesses are started every year. Small businesses provide over 50% of all jobs in the United States.

A good entrepreneur must be a self-starter, in good health, and self-confident. He or she should be able to differentiate a calculated risk from a foolish chance. An entrepreneur must be responsible, dependable, hardworking, and able to motivate the workers and utilize their talents. He or she will set specific goals and work until these goals are achieved. See **Figure 2-21**.

Advantages and Disadvantages of Entrepreneurship

Before deciding to start your own business, consider the advantages and disadvantages of entrepreneurship. Some advantages are:

- More control over income if the business is successful and grows.
- More control over job responsibilities.
- Meaningful professional relationships with talented people.
- Recognition as a leader.

Some disadvantages are:

Monkey Business Images/Shutterstock.com

Figure 2-21. An owner of a facility has responsibilities similar to an executive officer or president of a company. Overseeing operations and accomplishing work through others is vital.

- Working long hours to keep the business profitable.
- Work worries go home with you.
- Success or failure is on your shoulders.
- Loss of money, possibly even life savings, if the business fails.
- Repaying business loans for many years.
- Inconsistent or unpredictable income.
- Large amount of paperwork for recordkeeping.
- Need to discipline workers for unsatisfactory performance.

Starting the Business

You can either buy an existing business or start a new one. When buying an existing business, you have the advantage of being able to check financial records to determine if it has been profitable in the past. Also, you will already have customers that know about and patronize the business. Equipment costs, facility planning, and other concerns are taken care of.

If you decide to start a new business, much more work is involved. You must find a suitable location, rent or build a facility, order equipment and supplies, and more. Until customers start patronizing the facility, it can be difficult to meet financial obligations. Financial backing can also be more difficult to obtain with a new business because of the high risk of failure.

To obtain information on buying or starting a business, you can contact the Small Business Administration or small business assistance centers at community colleges.

Do not expect instant fame and fortune when starting a business. Instead, look realistically at the inherent advantages and disadvantages. It is easy to get excited about starting a business and overlook how much work and money is involved. You may not realize the consequences of failure. Keep in mind that there may be less stress and more money working for someone else.

Technological Growth

Changes in technology have brought about changes in traditional careers in printing. For example, the manual aspects of prepress, in most cases, have been replaced by a fast-paced, all-digital workflow.

Technological advancements in computer speed and power have made for faster work patterns, with clients expecting fast ***turnaround***, the time needed to complete a project. Also, the Internet has changed how work gets done by improving the ability to function and communicate, **Figure 2-22.**

Telecommunications and ***electronic information transfer*** over the Internet permits almost instant transmission of digitized (computer-coded) images and proofs around the globe. Subsequently, information management positions are being created to handle job ticketing, tracking, processing, and billing.

Beyond prepress considerations are the capabilities for multimedia. Printing customers want to tap into the mass-marketing capability of the Internet, creating positions for web designers, computer graphics designers, and people in sales and marketing. Web-to-print, mentioned earlier, is a factor of the future the industry cannot overlook.

Robotics, the use of machines to do repetitive tasks, is utilized in various manufacturing venues. Robots are ideal in the bindery area of a printing plant where highly repetitive tasks are done. While many traditionally labor-intensive activities are being eliminated by robots, positions requiring higher technical skills are opening in other areas.

Our technological age has revolutionized the way we communicate and work. The field of graphic communications is in the forefront of this revolution. Diverse employment opportunities will continue to emerge in such a dynamic, global industry.

violetkaipa/Shutterstock.com

Figure 2-22. The computer terminals in an office are electronically linked to each other. Internet services link computers and mobile devices around the world.

Summary

- Many positions are available in the graphic communications industry. The skills range from very creative to very technical.
- Leadership and science-oriented positions are also found in the industrial environment.
- The level of educational requirements varies. It is imperative that you match your interests, aptitudes, and goals in life.
- Finding a job includes searching for open positions, creating a résumé, applying for the job, and interviewing with the prospective employer.
- Having a good work ethic is important for getting and maintaining a job.
- Entrepreneurs must understand the risks as well as the benefits of starting their own businesses.
- A successful career in printing means keeping up with the latest technologies.

Review Questions

Answer the following questions using the information in this chapter.

1. What are the seven general employment categories in graphic communications?
2. How have changes in technology brought about changes in careers in prepress and press work?
3. Who is responsible for the quality of the final printed product?
4. List six characteristics important to the management team.
5. Name three methods for entering a career in graphic communications.
6. What is *lifelong learning*?
7. What courses should someone preparing for a career in graphic communications take in high school and college?
8. List at least three types of information to be included on your résumé.
9. What is a *work ethic*?
10. Name three advantages and three disadvantages of entrepreneurship.
11. Name three things that must be done when starting a new business.
12. In what area of a printing plant is the use of robots ideal?

Suggested Activities

1. What types of jobs are found in the printing plants in your area?
2. Write the job description for a specific job that has the greatest interest to you. Be sure to include responsibilities of that job and the potential career growth.
3. Contact one of your local printing organizations and find out what opportunities are available in the local area of the country. Research the salaries and benefits packages available for several local companies. Discuss the importance of the benefits package when ecaluating a job offer.
4. Explain the qualifications and duties of a position within the prepress area of the plant.
5. Working with a partner, conduct a mock job interview. Take turns being the interviewer and the interviewee. Create a list of questons to ask when you are the interviewer. What questions would the interviewee ask to learn more about the company and the position.

Chapter

3

Preparing for a Career in Graphic Communications

Learning Objectives

After studying this chapter, you will be able to:

- Create an effective résumé.
- Explain the advantages of different types of portfolios.
- Research different kinds of networking opportunities.
- Describe basic copyright laws.
- List what is necessary to start an independent graphic design business.

Goodheart-Willcox Publisher

Important Terms

competitive advantage
copyright
Creative Commons
definition statement
elevator pitch
entrepreneurship
fair use
flush mount
intellectual property
interactive PDF
job boards
lay-flat
networking
nondisclosure
public domain
random access memory (RAM)
résumé
storage
word-of-mouth marketing (WOMM)
work for hire

G-WLEARNING.COM

While studying this chapter, look for the activity icon to:

- **Practice** vocabulary terms with e-flash cards, matching activities, and vocabulary game.
- **Reinforce** what you learn by submitting end-of-chapter questions.

www.g-wlearning.com/visualtechnology/

Today's graphic communications industry is a blend of different skill sets. Many jobs encompass high-tech, creative, and innovative skills. Others are machine based, administrative, or customer service. As this industry evolves and expands, the jobs become more complex. Strong verbal and written communication skills support critical thinking and problem solving.

Education

As in other industries, graphics communications usually requires a strong educational background to enhance career advancement. Although it is not required, a four-year college degree is seen as favorable by many industry employers. An associate degree, while requiring only two years of study, offers advantages over those with no formal education.

Specialty fields are more specifically focused on certain skills, and can be more limiting if the skill set is too narrow. Even after securing a job, it is important to periodically continue your education to keep up with the latest technological advancements.

Four-Year Degree

Selecting an accredited school that will meet the needs for a particular job is an important first step. According to the US Bureau of Labor Statistics, most jobs in the graphic communications industry list as a requirement a bachelor's degree in a related field. The National Association of Schools of Art and Design lists more than 300 postsecondary colleges, universities, and independent institutes that offer degrees in art and design. More and more online schools are offering streamlined degrees to fit virtually every area.

There are two kinds of undergraduate degrees for graphic communications studies: liberal arts and professional. A liberal arts degree has a major focus on a specific area within a broader program of general studies. A professional degree will focus mainly on the specific area and be supported by the general studies program. See **Figure 3-1**. Schools have academic counselors to help students decide which program is best suited for them.

Goodheart-Willcox Publisher

Figure 3-1. Academic counselors will help students decide on a type of two- or four-year program before graduation.

Associate Degree

Many two-year programs are vocational or occupational. These degrees, known as associate degrees, will focus mainly on a specific area of study. These programs *can* articulate to four-year programs, but often do not convert smoothly. It is important to know which classes, if any, transfer over to four-year programs. If classes taken in the associate program are not recognized by the four-year school, then the student will have to retake those classes, incurring further time and tuition costs. All details should be thoroughly evaluated before making continuing education decisions.

Often, an associate degree will qualify for an entry level position that will allow advancement as experience is gained.

Specialty

Selecting a general area of specialty is a good idea, but a focus that is too narrow can limit job options. For example, being great with Photoshop® is not the same as being adept with Adobe® Creative Cloud® and the processes of graphic communications. Limiting your skill set could hinder your chance for advancement.

Continuing Education

Above all, the key to successful entry into the graphic communications industry is to stay current with the frequently updated technological advancements in hardware, software, and processes. Many professional organizations and networking groups offer courses and training to keep your skills polished.

With the continuous development of technology and electronics, graphic communications is rapidly evolving. To be viable in the profession, it is ideal to have a breadth of skills that include both traditional printing and newer digital techniques. Having experience in business management and organization, including pricing, accounting, marketing, sales, and communications, is a plus.

Résumé

Having a current ***résumé*** is critical to the process of applying for a job. Historically, résumés have been used to outline experience and capabilities. Developing a résumé to enter the graphic communications industry would suggest you make it very creative and unique to stand out from the others. Unfortunately, a single résumé in the Internet age is not enough. Today, a résumé is not designed to *get* a job; it is most often used to *eliminate* the applicant from consideration. With large companies or agencies, the first "reader" of a résumé is often electronic, and it is looking for specific keywords for the position. Having a creative and clever format can, in fact, make it more difficult to find and register the necessary keywords.

The solution is to create two résumés. One should be a standard format that is easily adaptable to specific job postings, and contains search terms that résumé web crawlers are programmed to spot. The other can be more creative and fun. This can be presented personally at an interview, where the person who sees it can appreciate the skills and talent it took to create, **Figure 3-2**.

Alexis Hale

Figure 3-2. This is a sample of a creative résumé for a graphic design student.

What a Résumé Should Include

Your résumé should include your personal contact information: your name, address, home telephone and/or cell phone, and e-mail address. Your e-mail address should be professional. (Having an e-mail of partyon@server.com is not going to get the response you are looking for because it does not conjure an image of a serious worker.) Make sure your voicemail is professional and clear. Check your messages and e-mail often for responses.

Résumés should contain as much descriptive information about the candidate as possible, **Figure 3-3.** Here are a few items that help convey the message of what you, the candidate, have to offer an employer.

- **Definition statement.** The opening for a résumé should be a clear ***definition statement*** that is tailored to that specific job opportunity. Create the statement by outlining strengths and skills. First, make a list of personal accomplishments that shows an achieved goal. Next, list life skills developed through school, home, or outside activities. Include creative skills as they apply to graphic communications. Spend some time considering the list and have others offer opinions; there are probably more than you think. Combine the items from these lists, using the best and most relevant to create a definition statement. This statement should clearly define who you are and what you can offer.
- **Job history.** A chronology of a job history is not as important as the skills listed as a result of those jobs. Be clear as to what benefits will be brought to the company. Include any quantifiable examples of past successes.
- **Skills.** List your core competencies here. This can be a simple column of bulleted points, such as team leadership and schedule management, taken from the life skills list. Even jobs not in the projected field require basic skills that can be highlighted. Use strong and descriptive words, such as "meticulous organization."
- **Education.** Include education and degrees or, if they are not too far into the future, projected dates of degree completion. Make sure to include any specialized training or attended seminars that are relevant.
- **Other.** This category can boost credentials if you have awards, internships, or activities that highlight a specific benefit.

Including social media information shows another level of competency. It is important to not include anything a potential employer could find offensive.

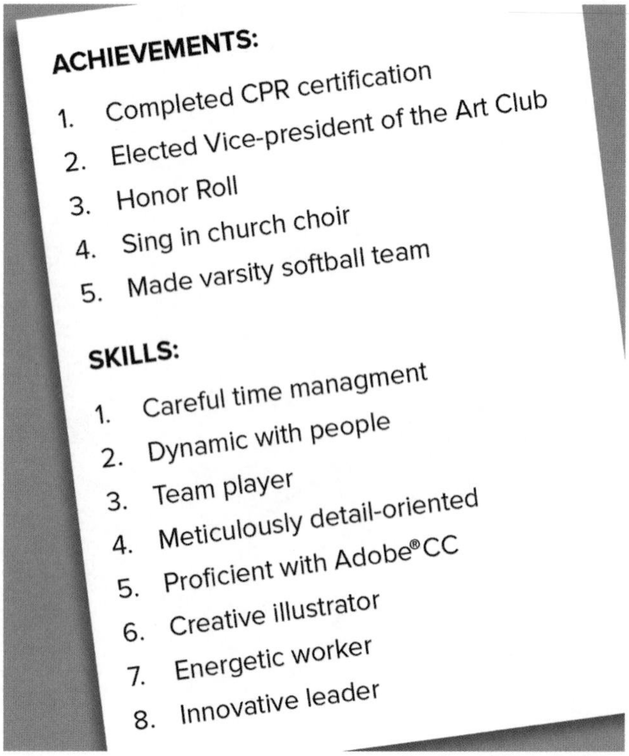
ACHIEVEMENTS:
1. Completed CPR certification
2. Elected Vice-president of the Art Club
3. Honor Roll
4. Sing in church choir
5. Made varsity softball team

SKILLS:
1. Careful time managment
2. Dynamic with people
3. Team player
4. Meticulously detail-oriented
5. Proficient with Adobe® CC
6. Creative illustrator
7. Energetic worker
8. Innovative leader

Goodheart-Willcox Publisher

Figure 3-3. A résumé should include a list that shows achievements and skills.

Important Tips

There are some important tips to creating an effective résumé:

- Proofread yourself. Then have someone else proofread.
- Do not lie, exaggerate, or embellish. It could come back to haunt you.
- Be clear and keep it simple.
- Use action verbs when possible. For example, "Spearheaded a campaign ..." as opposed to "was part of a campaign ..."
- Use professional layout software to create; do not use a word processor or templates.
- Choose the right fonts with a professional and clear voice. For more on voice, see Chapter 6.

Portfolio

Long gone are the days you carry a large portfolio bag with student projects mounted on black paper. The market is too digital and too competitive for this to be an effective option. A portfolio needs to have many faces and the flexibility to fit many requirements. Include work you are the most proud of and that highlights your strengths as a designer.

Printed Book

Your portfolio is a visual calling card. Having a printed portfolio to present at an interview is a major ***competitive advantage***. Discussing and interacting with the interviewer presents the opportunity to explain details regarding the processes as they apply to that person specifically. Printed picture books or online books are economical and they can make student work look polished and professional. Choosing a ***lay-flat*** or ***flush mount*** option makes it easier to present and view. Customize the book to highlight specific skills. Show only your best work. Do *not* include mediocre projects just to fill space. Organize them in a way that flows well and makes sense. Attention to detail is very important. Proofread and make sure the layout is as professional as the project. **Figure 3-4** and **Figure 3-5** show examples of effective portfolios.

Practice, practice, and practice your presentation of the book. Practice out loud to your friends and family. Let them ask questions, and practice giving clear answers. Know the processes used to create it and how the solution is effective.

Goodheart-Willcox Publisher

Figure 3-4. A lay-flat binding example shows specific skills.

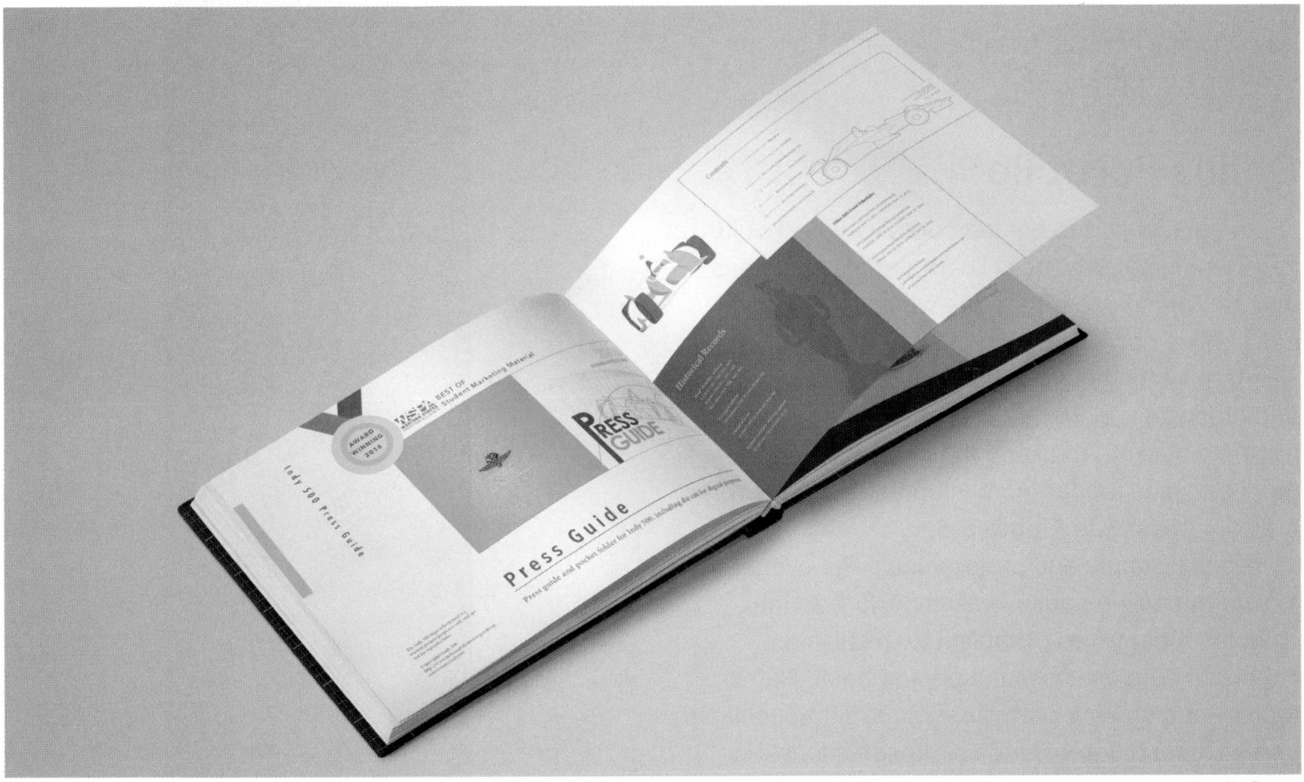

Yoo-Jin Seong

Figure 3-5. A lay-flat portfolio looks polished and professional.

Think Green

Carbon Footprint

A carbon footprint is a measurement of how much the everyday behaviors of an individual, company, or nation can impact the environment. It includes the average amount of carbon dioxide put into the air by energy and gas used at home and in travel, as well as other more detailed aspects. The graphic communications industry as a whole has a large carbon footprint. The processes used in printing plants, such as in producing inks and paper, greatly impact the environment. The electricity that goes into producing these products causes the emission of great quantities of carbon dioxide. Recently, companies have begun to determine their carbon footprints. Simply learning the details of a carbon footprint has become motivation enough for a company to work toward reducing it. However, not all companies have taken this first step. It is up to each company to determine if it wants to reduce its carbon dioxide emissions, and by how much.

Be confident and comfortable with what you are showing and saying.

Online Portfolio

In addition to the printed portfolio, you should have an online presence. There are many options that are free to use. There are websites that allow easy online portfolio setup and maintenance. As with the printed book, select only the best work and organize it thoughtfully. Make sure to include a variety of skills and keep the focus clear. A few great samples are far more impressive than several ordinary ones. See **Figure 3-6**.

Keep it simple and professional. The overall look of the online pages is as important as the samples themselves. Attention to detail is as important here as it is in the printed book. Rather than mixing up your portfolio's focus, set up multiple portfolios for different kinds of presentations. For instance, if photography and graphic design are both strengths, create a site for each individually.

Jeremy Hamman

Figure 3-6. A creative designer's online portfolio.

PDF

Sometimes a job posting will ask for samples of your work. Including a link to an online portfolio is an option, but that is sometimes more than they want to see. Creating a smaller, customizable portfolio that can be sent via e-mail eliminates any concerns about browser issues or coding problems. ***Interactive PDF*** (portable document format) documents can be done in standard page layout software and do not require the Internet to view. Create a template that includes contact information, then customize the examples to show the best skill set for each job posting. This file can also highlight layout and design skills.

Finding a Job

How do you go about finding the job that is right for you? Develop career goals based on interests, aptitudes, and research. Knowing what kind of jobs are available and what kind of company you would like to work for are important parts of setting your goals. The definition statement from the résumé will help identify what kind of job to focus on.

Research the local area and see what companies offer those kinds of positions. Most of that information can be found by doing detailed online searches. If there is a specific company of interest, find out who the decision-maker is and send a cover letter (which introduces you and your qualifications) and résumé, inviting him or her to view your online portfolio. Follow up with a phone call in 7–10 days and request an interview. Sometimes you just have to "get a foot in the door," meaning that all you need is one chance to showcase your skills to win over the employer.

Many schools offer placement offices or career centers. They often have valuable leads. School libraries, online resources, and trade magazines also provide good resources for contacts.

Networking, or using your web of friends and relatives, is key to finding a job. Check out local and student organizations that are applicable to the field. Get involved in that community and get your face and name in front of the right people. Do not be pushy, but be engaged. Check with alumni from your school or teachers who have contacts. Somebody will usually know somebody who can be of help. Also, mention to your family and friends that you are in the job market. They may be able to refer you to an opening.

Job boards are good to check out, but statistically they are not the most effective use of time. Most positions are filled from referrals or within the company, and fewer than 20% are through job boards. Social media helps you stay involved and in touch. Make sure to do so in a professional manner. Recruiting agencies can be helpful, but check them out thoroughly and make sure they are a good fit. Because their interest is in receiving a finder's fee from the company, agencies are interested in finding you *any* job, not necessarily the job you want.

Work Habits

Graphic communications is primarily a deadline-driven industry. It is important to establish good work habits from the start to be effective and efficient. Graphic designers have the especially difficult task of being creative on demand. Embracing the process of graphic design helps develop successful solutions regardless of the situation.

Work Ethic

All employers want people with integrity and discipline. Dedication to your job stems from your own attitude and character. Teamwork and an enthusiastic commitment from employees to do their best at all times is an integral component of a company's success.

Copyright Laws and Ethics

The Internet has raised a number of copyright issues for creatives in the graphic communications industry. The instant a work is created in a fixed and tangible form, it is considered an ***intellectual property*** and is protected by ***copyright***. That copyright belongs to the one who created the work, the employer, or the school, depending on contract fine print. Posting that work to the Internet does not make it free for anyone to use. Even if it does not officially say it is copyrighted, someone owns the rights to the material. If it specifically states that it is copyright free, be sure and read the fine print as to acceptable usage. It is the responsibility of the user to research the information.

Public Domain

Works that were published in the United States before 1923 belong to the ***public domain***. Unpublished works remain under federal copyright for a minimum of 70 years beyond the life of the author. Published works in the United States before 1964 that have not renewed their terms of copyright also belong to the public domain.

Creative Commons

Creative Commons is a nonprofit organization that grants a type of license that allows free use under specified terms. The work is still bound by normal copyright law.

Fair Use

Fair use is a limitation on the exclusive rights of copyright holders. It allows others to use a portion of the copyrighted material with explicit permission from the owner. It is based on several factors:

- The purpose and character of use, known as transformation.
- What is the nature of the copyrighted material? Is it fact or creative?
- How much of the work did you use?
- What effect does it have on the value of the original? Is yours a replacement? Is it a different audience?
- Altering someone's work by tracing it into a software application does not automatically make it comply. Are you using the work in a new and different way? Is it for commercial or non-commercial use? Will you be making money from the use?

The kinds of use that have been determined fair use by the courts include news reporting, art, search engines, parady, criticism, commentary, and research.

Counterfeiting

While also a copyright or intellectual property infringement, counterfeiting refers to making an exact duplicate of something that has value or importance, with the intent to defraud or mislead someone into thinking that it is the original or official. Usually done for dishonest or illegal purposes, counterfeiting generally involves lower quality components or reproductions designed for financial gain.

Entrepreneurship

Starting a graphic design business appeals to some because of the low start-up costs, the ability to work from home, and making your own schedule. Self-employment may sound like an easy way to be your own boss. In reality, ***entrepreneurship*** requires strong discipline and attention to all the details.

What You Need

It is very important for a graphic designer to have a reliable, high-end computer with enough ***random access memory (RAM)*** and ***storage***. Having the newest industry software and knowing how to use it shows you are current and taking your position seriously. Other critical supplies are a fast Internet connection and good printer, **Figure 3-7**.

Self-Promotion

While finding customers and building a client base, the work can be sporadic. Promoting yourself in a consistent and reliable manner is important in establishing your brand. Have a business card, portfolios of all kinds, a professional e-mail address, and perhaps a website. Get out there and network! Interact through professional social media sites and blogs. Reach out to people you know. Once a job is complete, send a thank you and remind the client you are available for more business. Promote your successes. Customers cannot find you if you stay home and hide behind your computer. See **Figure 3-8**.

Goodheart-Willcox Publisher

Figure 3-7. A good printer, which may print, copy, scan, and fax, is necessary when starting a business.

AntartStock/Shutterstock.com

Figure 3-8. You can help promote yourself and your business by obtaining business cards.

Word of Mouth

The number one reason companies will steer away from independent designers is reliability. Make sure to thoroughly discuss goals, details, and schedule with a client before beginning the job. Be a good listener. Always return e-mails and calls promptly and, above all else, meet your deadlines. ***Word-of-mouth marketing (WOMM)*** is a powerful tool. Studies show that a dissatisfied client will tell between 8–15 people about his or her experience. On the other hand, selecting a brand or service recommended by a friend rises to more than 70% according to marketing resources. Make sure what they are saying about you is positive.

Elevator Pitch

The ***elevator pitch*** is a 30 to 90 second description of you as a professional. It is designed to be given in the length of time it takes to ride an elevator, should you happen to run into someone important or any potential employer. This speech should be persuasive and succinct. Most of all, it should excite and energize you. Practice it until it sounds natural.

Self-Discipline

Hours can be as flexible as you want them to be as long as clients' needs and deadlines are met. Working from home may be comfortable and convenient, but it can work only as long as you have rigid self-discipline. It is easy to get sidetracked and think there is plenty of time to "do it later." Maintain clear time-recorded documentation for each job. Schedule the calendar to allow for a good mix of work time and personal time. Being organized and methodical and keeping detailed records is imperative to successful self-employment.

Rates

Do not be afraid to charge what you are worth. Sources say that the range should be somewhere around 2.5 times what you would make working for someone else to cover the cost of business expenses. Work up a business plan in writing to help establish clear goals and step-by-step procedures for starting a business. Remember, you have to pay for hardware, software, continued learning, taxes, and insurance.

Contract

There are many legal issues involved working as an independent contractor. Even if you know and trust your client, use a contract. A contract is nothing more than an agreement between parties for services, fees, schedules, and responsibilities. It is designed to protect both parties and make sure everyone is in agreement on critical information. ***Work for hire*** and ***nondisclosure*** forms are common documents you might be asked to sign. Read everything thoroughly, and if you have questions, ask them. These documents are designed to establish ownership and outline ethical issues so there is no room for error or misinterpretation. A comprehensive contract can avert many disputes that may arise over the course of a project, and perhaps prevent costly litigation. See **Figure 3-9**.

Self-employment is hard work and takes commitment, effort, and patience. Building a strong customer base requires dedication and energy. Because each job is unique and has its own set of parameters, new issues and situations will come up continually. Handle each step with open communication and integrity, and always put your best foot forward.

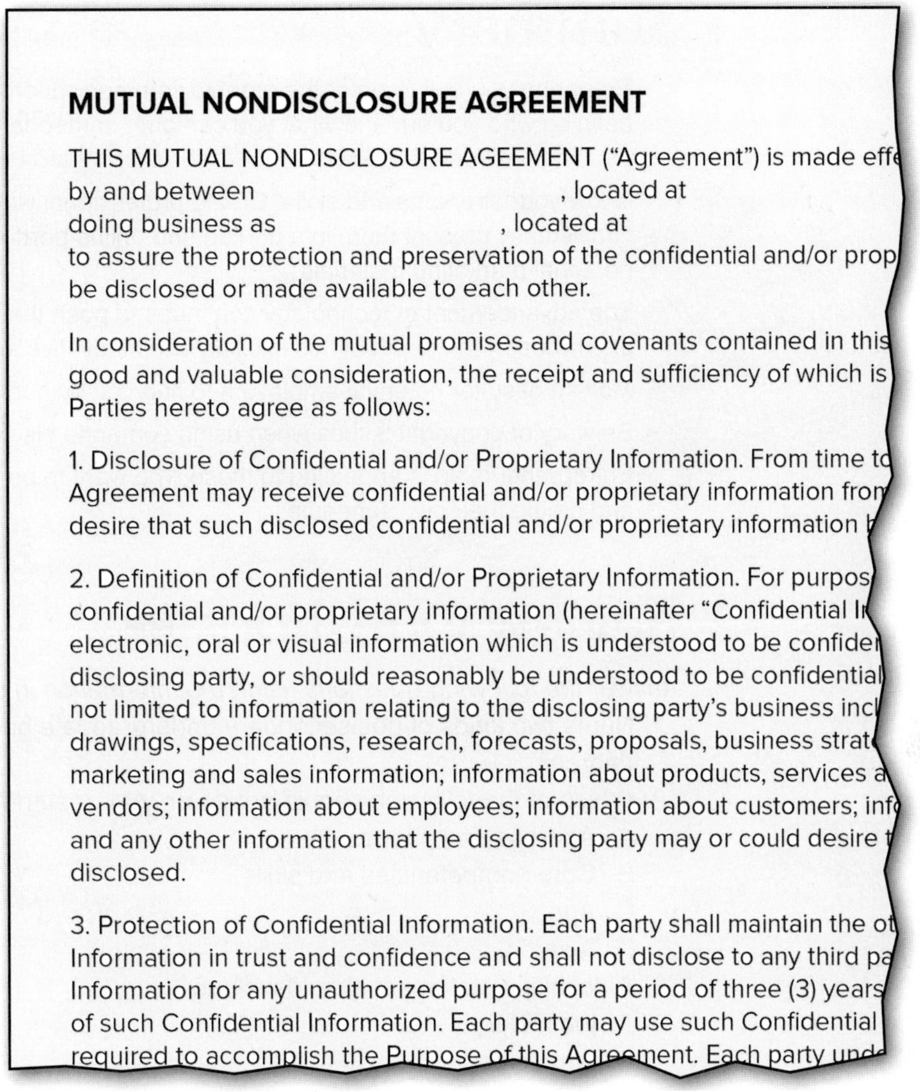

MUTUAL NONDISCLOSURE AGREEMENT

THIS MUTUAL NONDISCLOSURE AGEEMENT ("Agreement") is made eff
by and between , located at
doing business as , located at
to assure the protection and preservation of the confidential and/or prop
be disclosed or made available to each other.

In consideration of the mutual promises and covenants contained in this
good and valuable consideration, the receipt and sufficiency of which is
Parties hereto agree as follows:

1. Disclosure of Confidential and/or Proprietary Information. From time to
Agreement may receive confidential and/or proprietary information from
desire that such disclosed confidential and/or proprietary information b

2. Definition of Confidential and/or Proprietary Information. For purpos
confidential and/or proprietary information (hereinafter "Confidential In
electronic, oral or visual information which is understood to be confiden
disclosing party, or should reasonably be understood to be confidential
not limited to information relating to the disclosing party's business incl
drawings, specifications, research, forecasts, proposals, business strat
marketing and sales information; information about products, services a
vendors; information about employees; information about customers; inf
and any other information that the disclosing party may or could desire t
disclosed.

3. Protection of Confidential Information. Each party shall maintain the ot
Information in trust and confidence and shall not disclose to any third pa
Information for any unauthorized purpose for a period of three (3) years
of such Confidential Information. Each party may use such Confidential
required to accomplish the Purpose of this Agreement. Each party und

Goodheart-Willcox Publisher

Figure 3-9. Part of a nondisclosure form.

Summary

- Preparing yourself to enter the graphic communications field requires defining who you are and what you can offer someone. This is done by creating a résumé.
- Know your strengths and skills. Create professional ways to consistently present them in a printed and online portfolio, as well as personal marketing materials.
- The advancement of technology continues to push the learning curve and broaden the depth of this exciting and innovative industry.
- Make it easy for potential employers to find you by networking.
- Be wary of copyright issues when using someone else's work.
- Entrepreneurship is appealing to those who want to be their own boss and create their own schedules.

Review Questions

Answer the following questions using the information in this chapter.

1. Name two kinds of postsecondary undergraduate bachelor's degrees.
2. Which of the following should *not* go on your résumé?
   A. Address and phone.
   B. Core competencies and skills.
   C. Age.
   D. Awards.
3. A definition statement should include _____.
   A. job history
   B. education
   C. skills and strengths
   D. address
4. When printing your portfolio book, a(n) _____ or _____ option makes it easier to present.
5. *True or False?* You do not need a printed portfolio.
6. Online portfolios should include all of your work.
7. List four ways to get job leads.
8. *True or False?* Images posted on the Internet are all copyright free.
9. Works published in the United States before 1923 belong to the _____.

10. *True or False?* Creative Commons licenses are bound by normal copyright law.
11. List four considerations for fair use.
12. *True or False?* Startup costs for a graphic design business are fairly low.
13. Before beginning a job with a new client, discuss _____, _____, and _____ first.
14. A short speech that defines you as a professional is called a(n) _____.
15. What is the purpose of having a contract with a customer before work begins?

Suggested Activities

1. Make a list of three companies you would like to work for. Describe the job you want and why you think they should hire you.
2. Make a list of your core competencies as they apply to the jobs you listed in question 1.
3. Make a list of the items you want to include in your portfolio. Categorize them according to skill sets.
4. Research the copyright information for three well-known products.

Chapter

4

Safety and Health

Learning Objectives

After studying this chapter, you will be able to:

- Recall the purpose of a plant safety and health program.
- Explain the importance of machine guards and personal protection.
- Apply the safe handling of materials, tools, and equipment, as well as proper techniques for lifting.
- Identify the correct handling, storage, and disposal of chemicals and other materials.
- Explain plans for fire prevention within a plant.
- Explain proper noise control in a plant.
- Summarize an ergonomically correct computer workstation.
- Explain ways to reduce and eliminate waste for environmental compliance.

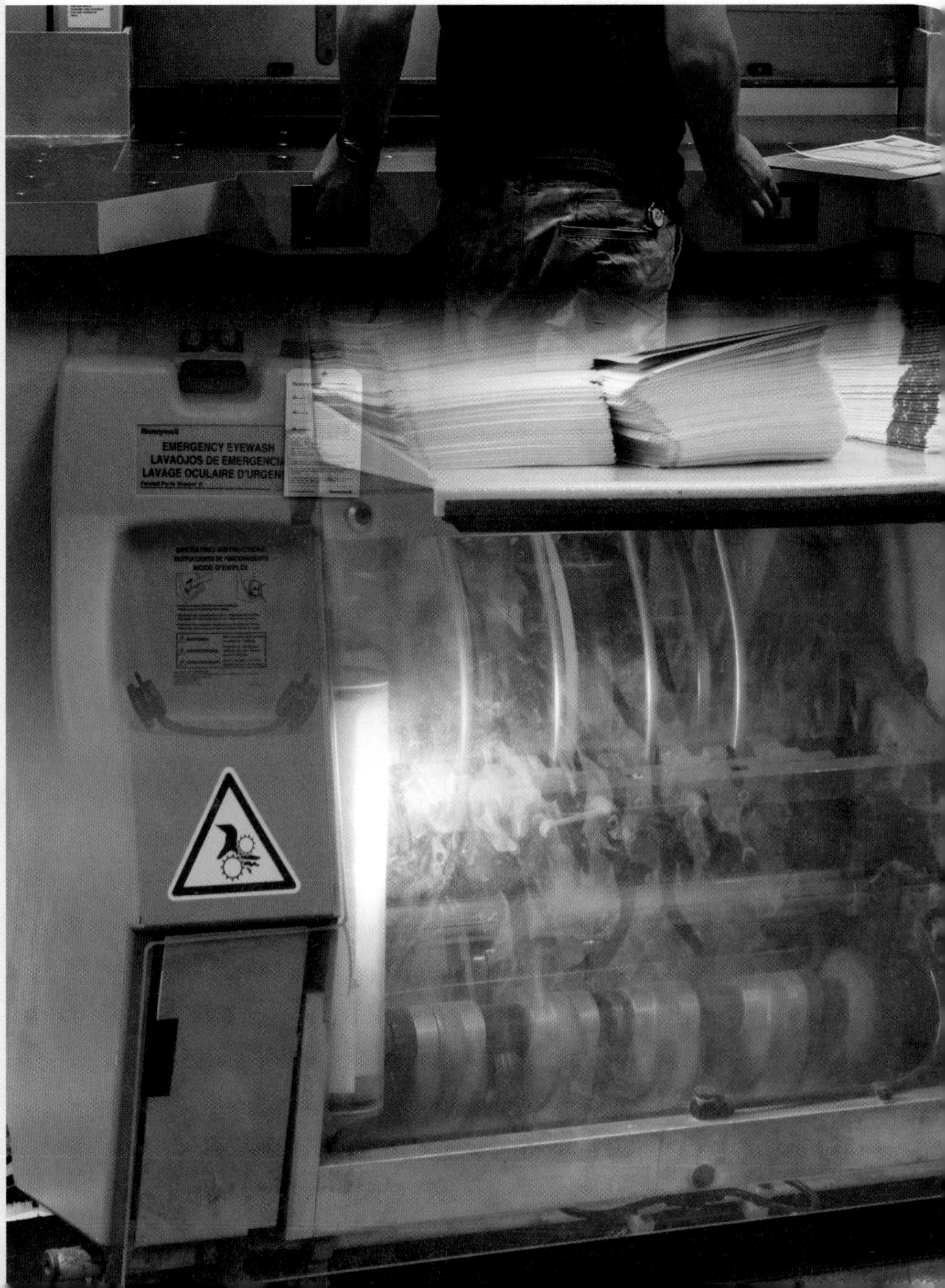

Goodheart-Willcox Publisher

Important Terms

barrier guards
decibels (dBA)
ergonomics
hazard
lockout devices
machine guards
Hazard Communication Standard (HCS)
nip points
personal protective devices
Safety Data Sheets (SDS)
spontaneous combustion
tagout device
toxic substance
volatile organic compounds (VOCs)
waste stream

G-WLEARNING.com

While studying this chapter, look for the activity icon to:

- **Practice** vocabulary terms with e-flash cards, matching activities, and vocabulary game.
- **Reinforce** what you learn by submitting end-of-chapter questions.

www.g-wlearning.com/visualtechnology/

Personnel in the graphic communications industry may be confronted with many hazards in the course of performing their duties. These include hazards of a mechanical, chemical, flammable, or electrical nature. While the industry has many safety and health problems common to other fields, this chapter will emphasize the recognition and control of those areas with the greatest potential for injury, illness, or environmental contamination. Later chapters will describe safety rules for specific processes performed in a graphic communications facility. Other sources of health and safety information available to you on the job are equipment manuals and machine labels.

It is vital for workers in a graphic communications plant to know basic safety practices. Because of the wide variety of processes performed, the potential for injury, illness, or even death always exists. It is up to you to keep the work environment safe and healthy for your coworkers and for yourself. The Ergonomics Hazards section of this chapter displays checklists that will be helpful in performing a safety inspection of a graphic communications facility.

Safety and Health Program

A safety and health program is an effective means of providing a safe working environment. The purpose of such a program is to recognize, evaluate, and control potential hazards in the workplace. See **Figure 4-1**.

Unguarded machinery, improper lifting methods, chemical contaminants, flammable and combustible materials, ungrounded wires, noise, and even poorly designed computer workstations are all potential health hazards.

OSHA has defined a ***hazard*** as anything with the potential to cause personal injury or illness. In addition to injuries to humans, a hazard has the possibility of damaging property or the environment.

These are some of the personal safety hazard risks present within the work environment:

- Crushing action of machinery.
- Cuts from a variety of sources.
- Burns from hot or chemical sources.
- Fall hazards.
- Falling from elevated places.

Variquick

Figure 4-1. A graphic communications facility can be a safe and enjoyable place to work. However, if safety rules are not followed, it can be very dangerous.

An effective safety program begins with informed employees. The Occupational Safety and Health Administration (OSHA) has issued a revised ***Hazard Communication Standard (HCS)*** to correspond with the United Nations' Globally Harmonized System of Classification and Labeling of Chemicals (GHS). This change is designed to give employees a better understanding of hazards. It generally requires employees to be afforded a safe and healthy work environment, be advised and properly trained concerning any hazardous materials to which they are routinely exposed, have access to information about chemicals used, and be advised of their rights and obligations under the act.

To ensure the success of the safety and health program, management leadership is essential. The person responsible for the safety and health program must have the authority to carry it out. Everyone in the establishment must be aware of the program. A safe operation largely depends on all plant personnel being properly informed and having an understanding of all potential hazards.

Safe conditions depend on a constant vigilance for possible hazards. That is why periodic inspections are one of the most important aspects of a successful safety and health program. **Figure 4-2** provides a safety checklist for identifying problems in a graphic communications facility so corrective action can be taken.

Safety Inspection Checklist

	Satisfactory	Unsatisfactory	Not Applicable	Dangerous	Remarks
I. Housekeeping					
A. Clean and orderly work area					
B. Proper materials available for housekeeping					
C. Floor holes (drains) covered					
D. Materials available for cleaning					
E. Maintenance schedule used					
F. Properly marked aisles					
G. Proper storage facilities					
H. Proper disposal systems					
I. Warnings and cautions posted					
J. Containers labeled					
K. Open aisles and fire lanes					
L. Proper handling devices					
M. Vacuuming used where possible					
II. Personal Protective Equipment					
A. Eye protection					
B. Foot protection					
C. Head protection					
D. Protective clothing					
E. Ear protection					
F. Respiratory equipment					
III. Administration					
A. Safety program					
1. Education-safety personnel					
2. Incentives					
B. Procedures					
1. Recordkeeping					
2. Accident and injury handling					
3. Emergency evacuation plan					
4. Posting					
C. Job hazard analysis					

(Continued)

Goodheart-Willcox Publisher

Figure 4-2. A safety inspection checklist that can be used for evaluating workplace safety conditions.

	Satisfactory	Unsatisfactory	Not Applicable	Dangerous	Remarks
IV. Equipment/Machinery					
A. Fixed guarding					
B. Movable guarding					
C. Equipment placement					
D. Maintenance					
E. Mechanical controls					
F. Proper enclosure					
V. Electrical					
A. Grounding					
B. Wiring					
C. Circuits identified					
D. Switch location					
E. Extension cords					
F. Portable electrical equipment					
VI. Chemicals					
A. Storage					
B. Ventilation					
C. Proper identification					
D. Handling devices					
E. Clean-up methods					
F. Disposal					
VII. Fire Protection					
A. Flammable materials					
1. Safe storage (cabinet)					
2. Proper labeling					
3. Proper containers					
4. Disposal of rags					
B. Fire equipment					
1. Fire extinguishers					
a. Right type for location					
b. Clearly visible					
2. Automatic sprinkler					
3. Blankets (same as fire extinguishers)					
4. Smoke detectors					
5. Flame and fume arrestors					
6. Proper waste disposal					
C. Fire drills					
1. Proper exit signs					
2. Availability of exits					
3. Dissemination of exit information					
4. Education of employees					
D. Periodic checking					
VIII. First Aid					
A. First aid facility provided					
B. Qualified first aid personnel					
1. Nurse provided					
2. First aid training available					

Goodheart-Willcox Publisher

Figure 4-2. *(Continued)*

Mechanical Hazards

Many on-the-job physical injuries are the result of mechanical hazards that can be controlled if:

- Machines are properly guarded.
- Energy-isolating devices are locked out and tagged out during maintenance.
- Workers properly use personal protective equipment.
- Workers are trained and have an understanding of how to handle materials, tools, and equipment safely.

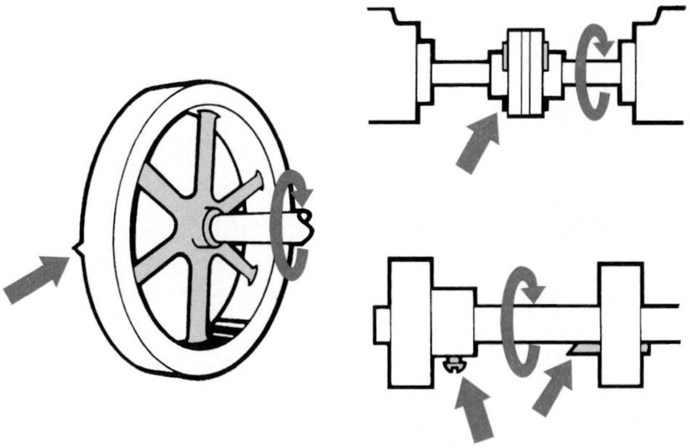

Goodheart-Willcox Publisher

Figure 4-4. Rotating objects, especially those with projecting parts, pose a constant danger on presses and other equipment. They can cause serious cuts, wrap clothing around shafts, and pull the operator into the equipment.

Machine Guarding

Hazards are posed by the reciprocating, rotating, and shearing actions of various types of machinery in the industry. See **Figure 4-3**. Therefore, properly placed guards on mechanical equipment are very important for the operator's protection.

Rotating motions create hazards in two areas: at the point of operation and at the points where power or motion is being transmitted from one part to another. Any rotating or reciprocating part is dangerous. Contact with loose clothing, hair, and even skin can cause severe injury.

Typical rotating mechanisms are spindles, flywheels, horizontal or vertical shafts, cams, and collars, **Figure 4-4**. Whenever something projects from the rotating unit, the machine becomes even more dangerous. Extreme care must be taken when working in an area with rotating units, even if they are properly guarded.

Machine guards protect parts of the human body from being electrocuted, cut, crushed, or hit by flying fragments. Guards also protect the equipment from foreign objects. Metal and plastic are two materials commonly used as guards. Most machines in the graphic communications industry require some type of guard. See **Figure 4-5**. If a guard is in place, do not remove it to perform an operation. Likewise, do not use equipment when guards are missing, broken, or out of adjustment. The risk of severe injury to yourself or to others is too great.

Machine guards are necessary wherever hazardous machine parts are within reach of the operator. Make sure guards are in place over belts, chains, flywheels, cutters, pulleys, shafting,

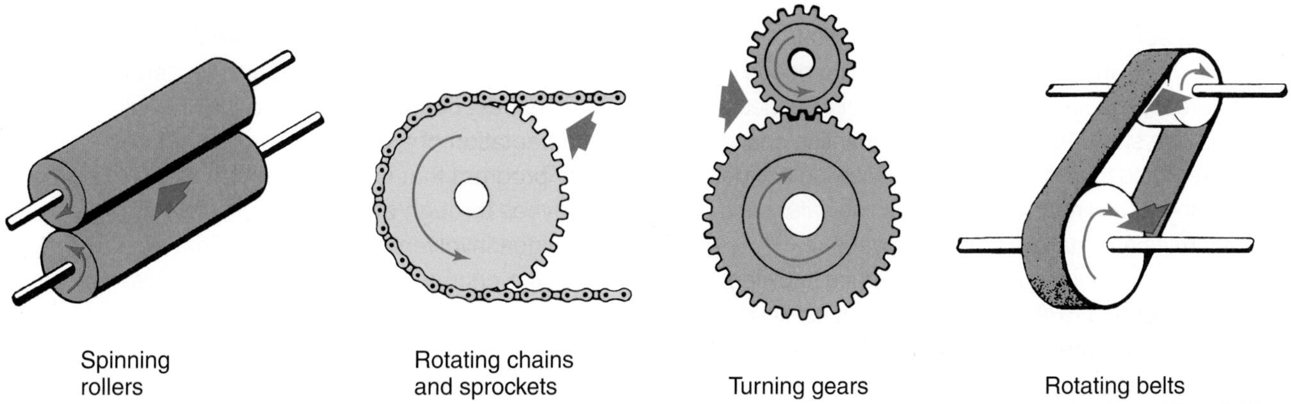

Goodheart-Willcox Publisher

Figure 4-3. These mechanisms found in a graphic communications facility can cause serious injury.

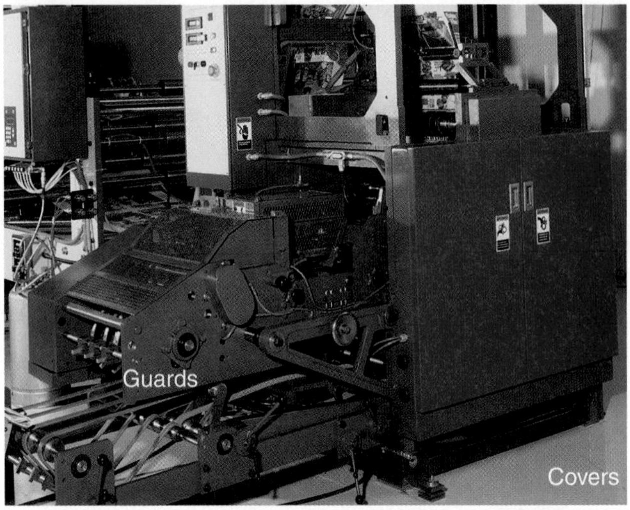

Heidelberg Harris

Figure 4-5. Always keep guards and covers in position when you operate a press or other type of equipment. Guards primarily protect people from injury, but they also keep objects from entering and damaging the press. Covers perform the same general function.

fasteners, punches, drills, clamps, gears, rollers, cylinders, shears, and all other points of operation.

Nip points exist where two cylinders meet or come close to one another. Cylinders can produce tremendous pulling and crushing force that can severely injure a person, sometimes causing permanent disability. Gears and rollers also have nip points. Many guards are pressure-sensitive and automatically stop the movement of the machine when an object becomes wedged between the guard and the cylinder. See **Figure 4-6**.

Barrier guards keep a person out of the operation area but can be hinged or moved. On newer equipment, when the guard is moved out of position, power is cut off, and the machine will not run.

Just because a machine or press looks small does not mean it is incapable of causing serious injury. Without a guard, the operator's clothing can

Career Link

Safety Specialist

Employee health and safety is an important concern in businesses of all sizes. From the operation of equipment and work environment, to the resources available to employees, federal and state regulations help companies create and maintain a safe workplace. Many larger companies hire a safety and health specialist, or safety supervisor, to oversee the implementation and maintenance of appropriate health and safety guidelines.

The duties of this specialist are listed as examples and may vary with levels of job classification. Typical duties include establishing training needs for work areas; keeping records and reporting issues; conducting safety inspections; implementing changes that are found to lack compliance; reviewing accident, injury and illness reports; and explaining safety and health rules and standards to employees.

Some of the job qualifications require knowledge of basic OSHA and EPA rules and regulations; knowledge of safety techniques and applications; knowledge of safety practices in the industry; and the ability to coordinate, organize, and supervise work activities.

The safety specialist must have a basic knowledge of mathematics, physics, and chemistry. He or she must have good communication skills. This individual should also have a basic knowledge of accounting and budgeting. Some companies may specify that they be certified as safety professionals. Most safety professionals have graduated with a bachelor's degree in safety management. The degree title may vary from one educational institution to another. Seminar courses may also be taken to prepare for certification. An exam must be taken and passed for the person to be certified.

"The best companies emphasize the full implementation of a comprehensive written safety program that is clearly communicated to all employees through effective employee training, safety idea involvement, and disciplinary action for those who choose to break the safety rules."

John Holland
Assured Compliance Solutions

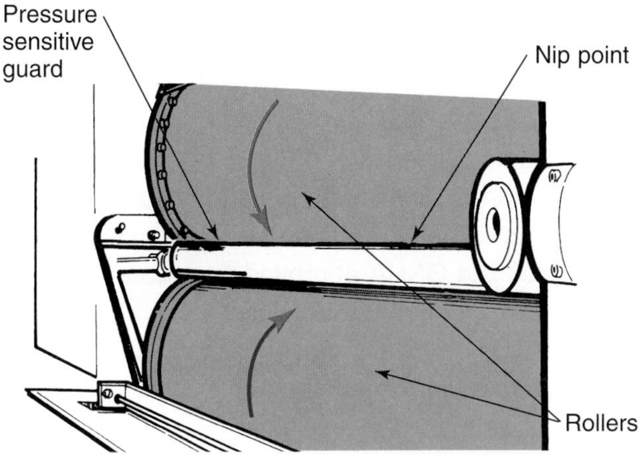

Goodheart-Willcox Publisher

Figure 4-6. A nip point occurs where two rollers come together. This press has a pressure-sensitive guard that shuts it off if anything is pulled into the nip point.

easily be caught and pulled into the nip point. Long hair can also get drawn into nip points. Always tie back long hair and wear an industrial hairnet, a cap, or headband when operating machinery. Do not wear jewelry of any kind, not even a watch, when operating equipment, **Figure 4-7**.

Some machines require specialized types of guarding. For instance, a typical safety device on a guillotine paper cutter prevents cutting until the pressure clamp is in position. A similar safety feature is one that will not permit machine operation if a light beam is blocked by some object, such as a hand. A common control device on a paper cutter requires both hands of the operator to be on the operating controls, **Figure 4-8**.

Goodheart-Willcox Publisher

Figure 4-7. Always dress properly for work. This press operator is not wearing jewelry or a watch and is wearing an apron to keep clothing out of the press.

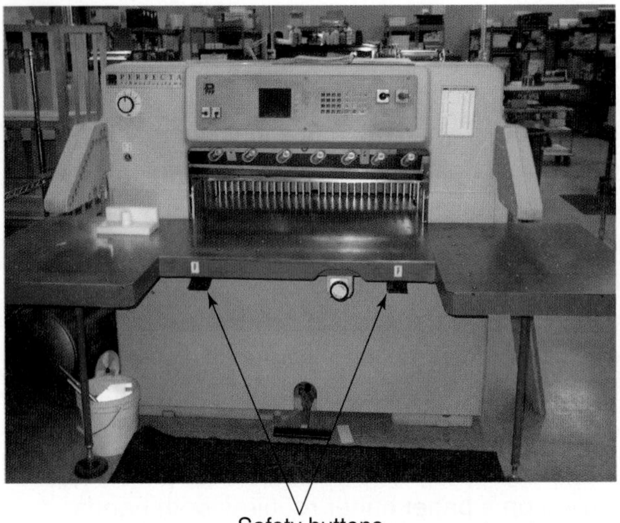

Goodheart-Willcox Publisher

Figure 4-8. Note the two control buttons on this cutter. Both safety buttons must be pressed simultaneously to operate the blade. The dual mechanism ensures the hands are out of the way when cutting.

A paper cutter blade is very sharp; all precautions should be taken to avoid injury when cutting stock or handling the blade. When operating a cutter, make it a habit to never reach for a jammed piece of paper. Follow safety procedures indicated on the machine labels or equipment manual.

Cleaning and maintaining equipment should be done when the machine is disconnected. Do not rely on a safety interlock when working on a piece of equipment. Make sure the power is *off* at the main switch!

Lockout Devices

When someone is working on a piece of equipment, the electrical power supply must be cut off. "Locking out" equipment is the only sure way to prevent injuries that could result from unexpected energizing or startup of the machine. ***Lockout devices*** utilize either a key or combination-type lock to hold an energy-isolating device, such as a manually operated electrical circuit breaker, in the safe position to prevent the machine from energizing.

A ***tagout device*** is a prominent warning, such as a tag securely fastened to an energy-isolating device. When you find a tagged power box, make no attempt to restore the power. The tag should be removed by the person who placed it. See **Figure 4-9**.

Many pieces of equipment have flip covers to prevent run/reverse or inch buttons from accidentally being pressed. The inch button on the press allows the operator to move the press a very short distance. The cover on the run/reverse button must be flipped shut during plate gumming, blanket work, or any other operation that requires a press to be inched. The OSHA-approved "inch safe service" method is very often utilized when washing the rollers on the press and when washing blankets on the press and binding equipment.

Personal Protection

Besides making sure machines are properly guarded and locked out, you can take additional steps to protect yourself and others from injury.

As cautioned earlier, never wear watches, rings, ties, bracelets, scarves, or loose clothing while working with machinery. Remember that loose, long hair is a hazard, as is a rag partially tucked in a pocket and hanging out.

Wear appropriate safety equipment, **Figure 4-10**. Eye protection should be worn when you are pouring/pumping hazardous chemicals, when you are operating a saw, a grinder, or

Goodheart-Willcox Publisher

Figure 4-9. Lockout devices and tags are used to prevent accidental operation of machinery.

any machine that can cause material to fly and strike you or other plant workers. Use earplugs or another type of hearing protection in noisy areas. Wear gloves to protect your hands when necessary. Choose gloves that suit the job while giving you the best possible protection and freedom of movement. Nitrile or butyl rubber gloves will protect your hands when handling inks, oils, solvents, and other chemicals. Wear an apron to keep clothing from being pulled into machinery. A dust mask is suitable for some airborne particles, but an approved respirator must be worn when operations produce ink mists. Certain operations, such as press, bindery, and storage, may require foot protection.

Tools, Materials, and Equipment Handling

Keep the graphic communications facility organized. Return all tools, equipment, and supplies to their proper storage areas after use.

To prevent falls, keep floors dry and clear of tools and supplies. Clean up liquid spills immediately. Nonskid mats, adhesive strips, or coating materials may be applied to the floor around work areas, **Figure 4-11**.

Do not stand skid pads or pallets on edge. They are heavy enough to cause serious foot or leg injuries if they fall on someone. Always store them flat in a designated area.

Cuts from sharp materials are common injuries. Never carry sharp objects in your pockets. They can easily puncture the skin. Some materials are banded with metal strapping. When cut, the strapping can spring and cause severe lacerations. Use extreme care if you must cut strapping, and wear proper protective equipment, such as safety glasses with side panels, a full face shield, and leather gloves.

As described earlier, keep all guards, shields, and covers in place. They perform the important function of keeping your hands and other body parts out of the equipment.

Never use or adjust any equipment unless you have been properly trained to do so. Make sure you have seen a demonstration or have supervision before using any equipment. Only properly certified employees should operate a forklift, straddle lift, or motorized pallet jack. Riders are never permitted on material handling equipment.

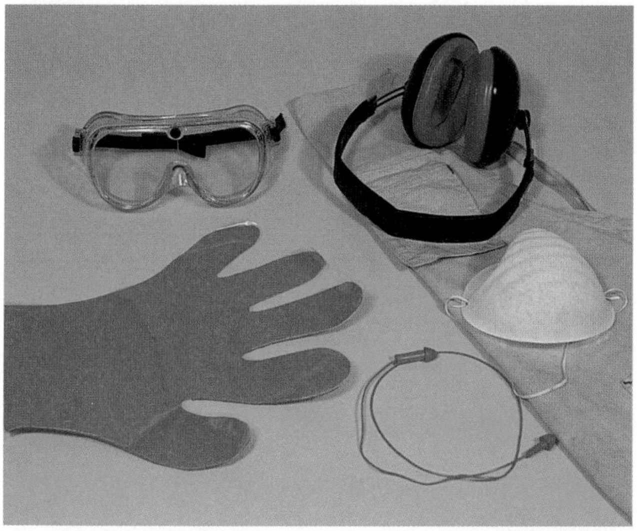

Goodheart-Willcox Publisher

Figure 4-10. Wear personal protective equipment. Shown are approved eye protection, an apron to protect clothing, plastic gloves for handling oils and solvents, earplugs, and a dust mask. For some situations, a respirator must be worn, since it provides much greater protection than a dust mask.

Courtesy of Lab Safety Supply, Inc., Janesville, WI

Figure 4-11. Nonskid mats help prevent slipping.

Always work and act as a professional when in a graphic communications facility. Horseplay endangers the safety of individuals. A joke is an accident waiting to happen. If you are not sure about a safety rule or procedure, ask your supervisor.

When operating a press, keep these factors in mind:

- Never turn on a press unless you are sure all tools have been removed from it and all mechanisms have been set correctly.
- Make sure no one is near the press before starting the equipment.
- Check to make sure all press guards are in place.
- Keep your hands clear of the press when it is running.
- Do not try to grab paper, lubricate parts, or do anything that places your hands near the rollers and nip points while the press is running.
- Have an assistant present whenever you are cleaning or running a press. If you were to get caught in the machinery, the assistant could turn off the press.

Tips for Safe Lifting

Routine on-the-job lifting and materials handling can lead to injury. Too often, a person lifts a heavy load without seeking assistance from another person or from a mechanical device. See **Figure 4-12**. When lifting an object, keep your knees bent and your back straight. Leaning over while lifting is poor practice, **Figure 4-13**. These safety instructions will lessen the risk of serious injury to the worker who is using his or her body to lift or move materials:

- **Clear a pathway.** Before you move things from one place to another, be sure you have a clear pathway.
- **Check weight.** Check the object's weight to see if you will need help lifting it.
- **Request help.** Ask for help from another person if you need it, or use mechanical lifting equipment.

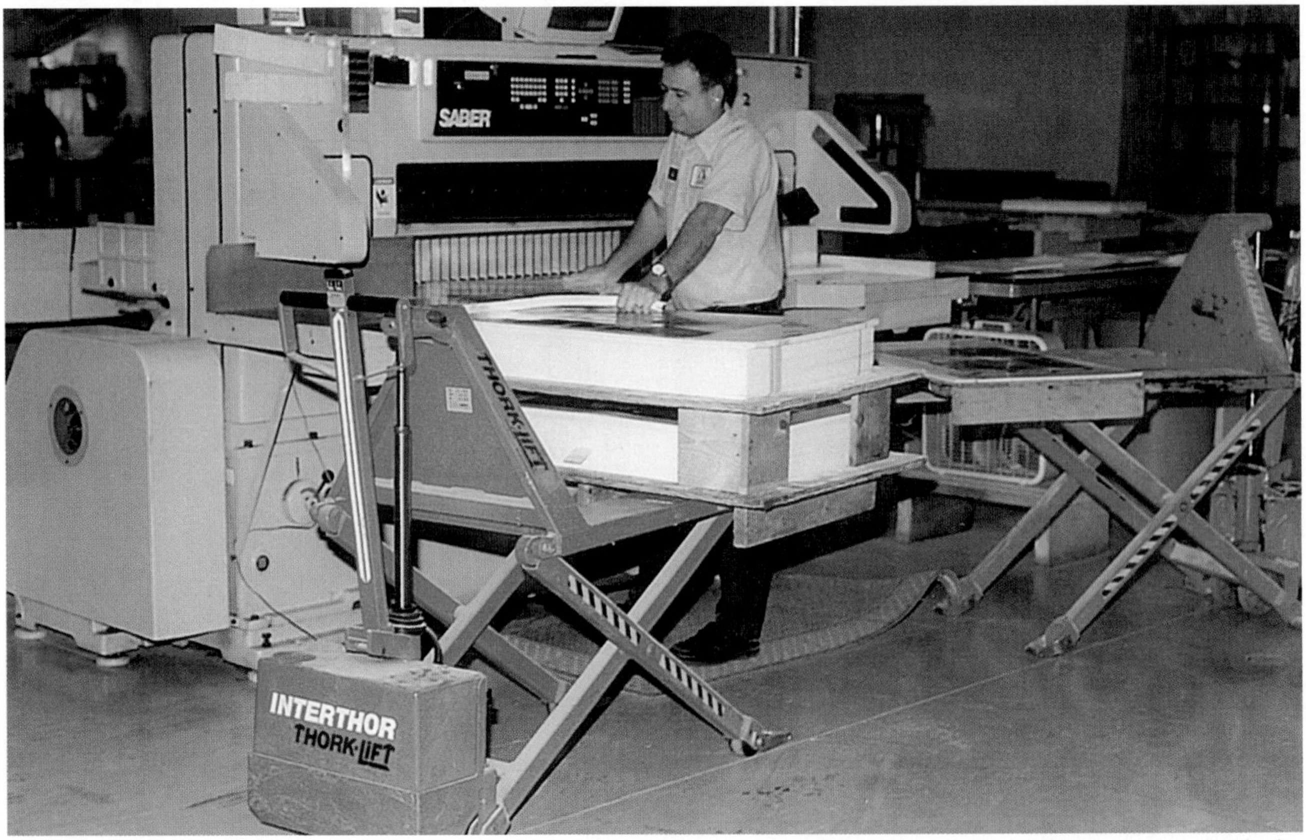

Interthor, Inc.

Figure 4-12. A combination lift table and pallet truck eliminates bending and lifting.

- **Keep your back straight.** Your back should be straight and vertical to the ground. Keeping your head up and looking straight ahead will help maintain this position.
- **Lift with your knees.** If you can, bend your knees when lifting; don't stoop over the object.
- **Keep objects close to your body.** Always bring the object as close to your body as possible. Never twist your body. Move your feet to turn and place a load next or behind your body.
- **Tighten your stomach.** Tighten your stomach muscles. This helps your back stay in balance.
- **Deliver carefully.** Use care when you put the object down. Follow the same guidelines as you would for lifting.

Compressed Air

Compressed air should *never* be used to clean off clothes or do general cleanup work. An air nozzle can force air through the skin and into the bloodstream, a condition that can cause death. Compressed air can also stir up paper dust, making breathing difficult and causing eye irritation.

When compressed air is used for an acceptable purpose, nozzle pressure should not exceed 30 psi (pounds per square inch) or 207 kPa (kilopascals). Always wear safety glasses when using an air nozzle.

Chemical Hazards

Several chemicals are used in the printing industry. You may come into contact with substances such as solvents, platemaking chemicals, ink mists, and various fumes and gases. In order to work safely, you should know how to handle these chemicals and dispose of them properly.

Chemical Handling and Disposal

Depending on their chemical structure, certain substances are more harmful than others. A poisonous substance is termed a ***toxic substance***. The amount of a toxic substance an individual is exposed to and the duration of that exposure affect the degree of harm the substance can cause. For example, oxygen is part of the air we breathe, and in normal amounts, it keeps us alive. However, a very high concentration of oxygen can be toxic.

The first line of defense against toxic substances is to know the types of chemicals you are using and the hazards involved. Chemicals should be handled with extreme care. Read the labels on chemical containers to learn specific handling procedures and potential health hazards. See **Figure 4-14**.

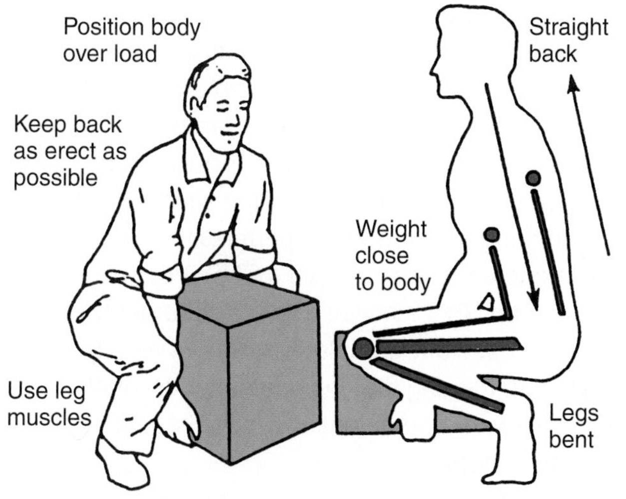

Goodheart-Willcox Publisher

Figure 4-13. Prevent painful back injuries by using the correct lifting technique. To help maintain a straight back, keep your head up and look straight ahead.

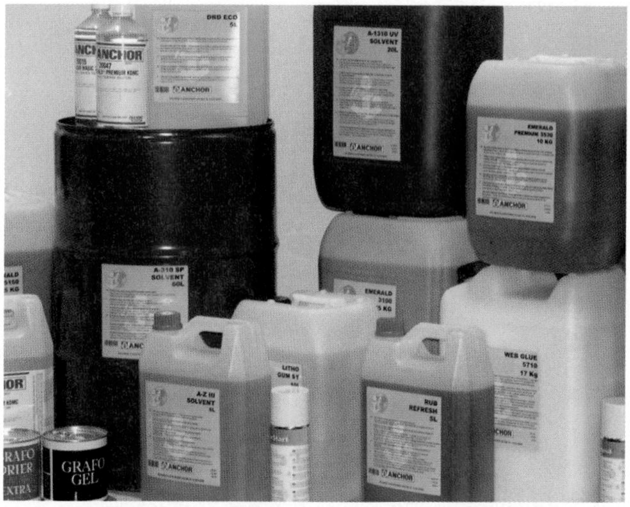

Goodheart-Willcox Publisher

Figure 4-14. All chemical containers should be labeled. Read labels carefully before using chemicals, and note safety warning and actions to take in an emergency.

Be aware of the health risks posed by toxic substances in a graphic communications facility, and take measures to avoid harm. Chemicals can enter the body through the skin, by inhalation, or by ingestion. Wear ***personal protective devices*** appropriate to the level of hazard. Protective devices for working with chemicals include safety glasses, face shields, plastic or rubber gloves, respirators, boots, and full safety suits. See **Figure 4-15**. While exposure to some chemicals may have short-term effects, exposure to others may cause long-term health problems, even cancer.

When disposing of chemicals, do not pour them down a drain or sewer. They must be discarded in an environmentally safe manner. Check the manufacturer's recommendations, as well as state and local environmental protection requirements, for proper disposal. Stiff fines are imposed for improper disposal of hazardous waste.

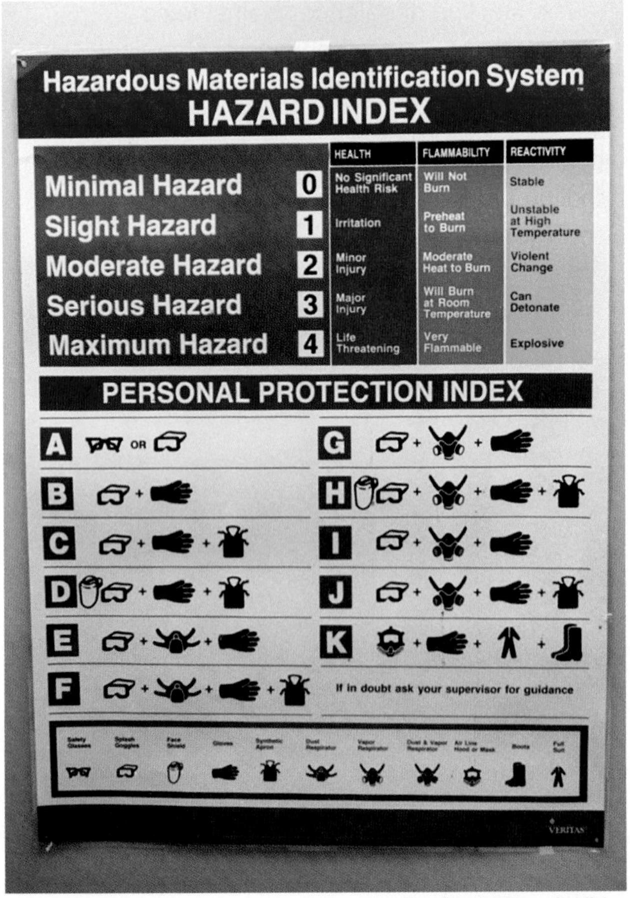

Goodheart-Willcox Publisher

Figure 4-15. A typical hazard identification chart with icons identifying personal protection required for various hazard categories.

Types of Chemicals and Agents

The chemicals and chemical agents that pose hazards to workers in the graphic communications industry are commonly classified in four categories:

- Organic solvents.
- Various chemicals.
- Ink mists.
- Gases, fumes, and dust.

Volatile Organic Solvents

Some of the most common organic solvents found in the industry are blanket and roller washes, fountain solutions, plate cleaners, glaze removers, degreasers, and film cleaners. Many blanket washes used to clean the press blankets contain ***volatile organic compounds (VOCs)***, toxic substances that help the washes work well and evaporate quickly. However, the VOCs pass into the air in the pressroom, the workers' lungs, and the outside air.

Some solvents are more harmful than others, but the following should *not* be used: benzene, carbon tetrachloride, gasoline, chloroform, and carbon disulfide.

Breathing solvent vapors can be very harmful. Do not rely on your sense of smell to warn you of vapors. Specialists need to be employed to measure airborne solvents and determine safe levels.

Vapors should be exhausted away from the operator and the area kept well ventilated. Some vapors may require the operator to wear a respirator. The proper respirator for each situation must be selected by an expert, **Figure 4-16**. Be sure to wear a respirator if the vapors in the surrounding air exceed the permissive exposure levels shown on the product's SDS. For any industry that has an SDS allowable levels statement, you must successfully complete extensive respirator protection training that includes an individual medical exam and fit testing, as well as other training factors.

Solvents can also be harmful to skin or eyes. Read the container label *before* using a chemical to determine what to do in case of contact. Typically, it is recommended that the affected area be flushed with water for at least 15 minutes and then treated by a doctor. Personal protective devices, such as goggles, face shields, gloves, and aprons, must be worn when handling chemicals and solvents.

Whenever you are working with chemicals, take these general precautions against harmful chemicals and solvent vapors:

- Do not attempt to identify a solvent by sniffing it.
- Keep lids and covers on cans and drums.
- Do not use large quantities of solvents in one area.
- Clean up spills immediately.
- Know the proper handling, cleanup, and disposal procedures for the chemical you are using.
- Place soiled rags in an approved safety can, keeping its lid closed.
- Ventilate the work area as needed.
- Wash your hands before touching anything and eating.

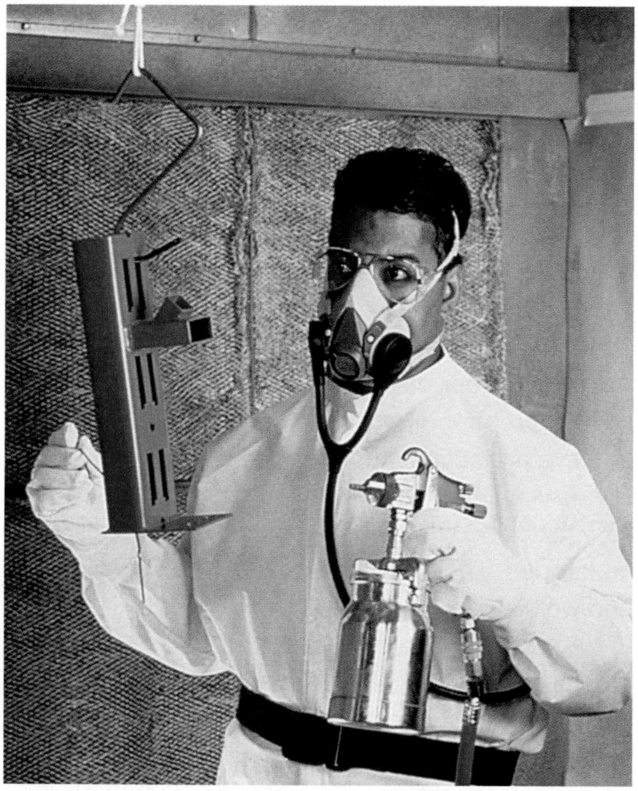

3M Company

Figure 4-16. In many industrial occupations, an approved respirator is required whenever fine airborne mists of chemicals, inks, dust, paint, or other contaminants are present.

Platemaking Chemicals

The chemicals used to prepare image carriers can irritate the skin and cause burns. Always wear rubber or plastic gloves or apply barrier creams when working with platemaking chemicals. Inspect gloves for pinholes before working. Never touch your face or eyes with gloves that have been in contact with a chemical.

Academic Link

Measuring Sound

Sound is measured in decibels, which is a value that represents the pressure of a sound. OSHA mandates that sound measurements be taken when exposure reaches 85 decibels and above. When the sound level is greater than 90 dBA over an 8-hour workday, hearing protection is necessary.

For the purpose of standardized measurement, the threshold of human hearing is 0 dBA. Prolonged exposure to any sound over 85 dBA can cause permanent hearing damage. Pain caused by sound can occur around 120 dBA. The following are some examples of common sounds and the approximate decibel level of each:

Jet engine on takeoff	140 dBA
Front row of a rock concert	120 dBA
Chain saw or pneumatic drill	100 dBA
Lawn mower	95 dBA
Vacuum cleaner or hair dryer	70 dBA
Normal conversation	60 dBA
The hum of a refrigerator	40 dBA
Quiet library	30 dBA
Rustling leaves	10 dBA
Threshold of human hearing	0 dBA

Goodheart-Willcox Publisher

Consider the sounds you are exposed to every day. Do any of the sounds reach dangerous levels? Is ear protection available in areas of prolonged exposure to high levels of sound?

Contact lenses should *not* be worn when working with chemicals. If splashed in the eyes, the chemicals can seep under the lenses and cause severe burns. Face shields and splash goggles are the best form of eye and face protection.

Wearing an appropriate apron will keep chemicals from reaching clothing and soaking through to the skin. Food and beverages should never be allowed to come into contact with chemicals. Chemicals that are corrosive, flammable, or poisonous should be properly labeled and stored in a safety cabinet, **Figure 4-17**.

Warning

Many chemicals are concentrated. When diluting an acid, always pour the acid into the water. The opposite method would produce a dangerous splattering of the acid. Never add water to concentrated acid.

Ink Mists

Rapidly rotating press rollers throw tiny droplets of ink into the air, creating an ink mist. These droplets are tiny enough to be inhaled. Ink mists often contain pigments, polymers, plasticizers, resins, and solvents that can prove harmful. Face shields and respirators should be worn for protection. Controls, such as face shields and respirators, are necessary where a relatively large amount of ink mist is produced.

Justrite Manufacturing Company

Figure 4-17. Chemicals, safety cans, and flammable containers should be stored in an approved safety cabinet.

Gases, Fumes, and Dust

Gases, fumes, and dust are chemical agents commonly found in graphic communications facilities. Proper ventilation is imperative in areas where vapors and particulate matter are generated.

Ozone (O_3) is a great concern. It is a colorless, poisonous gas in the upper atmosphere, where it occurs naturally in what is known as the ozone layer, and it shields the earth from the sun's dangerous ultraviolet rays. However, at ground-level, it is a pollutant with highly toxic effects. Ozone damages human health, the environment, crops, and a wide range of natural and artificial materials. One source of ground-level ozone is the breakdown of VOCs found in solvents. Ozone gas is also created by carbon arcs, some antistatic devices, and ultraviolet ink-curing units used in printing plants.

Another hazard is carbon monoxide (CO), an odorless and colorless gas. CO is produced by the incomplete combustion of carbon-based fuels and natural and synthetic products. After being inhaled, CO molecules enter the bloodstream, where they inhibit the delivery of oxygen throughout the body. Low concentrations can cause dizziness, headaches, and fatigue; high concentrations can be fatal.

Fumes can be produced by molten materials. Acids or corrosives also give off fumes. Corrosive-resistant rubber or plastic gloves and aprons and eye protection must be worn when handling corrosives. Many fume-producing materials are very toxic and should be considered extremely hazardous. The work area must be well-ventilated and well-lit.

A common cause of dust in graphic communications facilities is paper. Microscopic particles of dust can be inhaled and lodge in lung tissue, causing respiratory disease and lung damage. Respirators with dust filters should be worn in areas where paper dust exists. Systems for controlling dust and scrubbing the air are available for use in large industrial settings, **Figure 4-18**.

Mee Industries Inc.

Figure 4-18. Tiny fog droplets sprayed by an overhead humidification system scrub dust and chemicals from the air in this graphic communications facility.

Hazard Communication Standard

As stated earlier, the Hazard Communication Standard has been updated. Known as the employee "right to know" standard, it now puts emphasis on the right to understand. The three major changes to the standard that will take effect by June 1, 2016 are:

Hazard Classification. Specific criteria must be provided for every health and physical hazard. The chemical manufacturer and the importer are required to evaluate the hazards of the chemicals they produce or transport.

Labels for Chemical Containers. Any producer or importer of chemicals must prepare labels that inform of all hazard information relating to the specific chemicals used in the graphic communications facilities. See **Figure 4-19**.

Safety Data Sheets. The producer, distributer, and importer must prepare ***Safety Data Sheets (SDS)*** for all chemicals used in the graphic communications plant. The employees are to be trained and understand how to handle and work with the hazardous material.

The following information is required in the following format for the SDS:

Section 1: Identification

Section 2: Hazard(s) Identification

Section 3: Composition/Information on Ingredients

Section 4: First-Aid Measures

Section 5: First-Fighting Measures

Section 6: Accidental Release Measures (Emergency procedures, etc.)

Section 7: Handling and Storage

Section 8: Exposure Controls/Personal Protection

Section 9: Physical and Chemical Properties

Section 10: Stability and Reactivity

Section 11: Toxicological Information

Section 12: Ecological Information*

Section 13: Disposal Considerations*

Section 14: Transport Information*

Section 15: Regulatory Information*

Section 16: Other Information

* Since other agencies regulate this information, OSHA will not enforce this section.

The Safety Data Sheets must be readily accessible to all employees. For complete information, consult www.osha.gov.

Goodheart-Willcox Publisher

Figure 4-19. Chemicals must be labeled to inform of any hazardous materials.

Fire Prevention

Most graphic communications facilities use flammable and combustible materials. Therefore, fire prevention is a crucial part of a plant safety program.

Paper dust or anti-set-off powders may explode if concentrated where a spark could ignite the mixture. Anti-set-off powders are sprayed on printed sheets to eliminate the possibility of the fresh ink from transferring to the backside of the next printed sheet. Solvent vapors are another source of explosion danger. Avoid spillage. When pouring solvent, make sure the area is properly vented and no ignition source is present.

Ink- and solvent-soaked rags must be placed in an approved and covered metal waste can, **Figure 4-20.** The volatile vapors are then trapped inside the container. The contents of the waste can be disposed of daily to minimize the possibility of ***spontaneous***

Justrite Manufacturing Company

Figure 4-20. An approved waste container should be used to dispose of flammable rags or towels. Empty the can regularly.

combustion. Do not store oily or ink-soaked towels in a container that does not meet safety regulations.

Fire prevention should be a priority on the shop floor. Practice these safety precautions to reduce the risk of fire:

- Pick up dust using a vacuum cleaner; do *not* blow dust with an air hose.
- Report leaking solvent containers.
- Wipe up solvent and oil spills.
- Always use a spouted safety can when transferring small amounts of solvent, **Figure 4-21**. Make sure flame arrestors in safety cans are intact.
- In solvent-transfer operations, properly ground and bond equipment to prevent sparking, **Figure 4-22**.
- Properly label solvents and other flammable materials.
- Do not dump solvents into drains; store and dispose of them in compliance with state and local environmental protection standards.
- Watch for potential sources of fire, such as an overflowing safety container, dust buildup on equipment, and open chemical containers.
- Do not smoke! Inks, solutions, chemicals, paper, paper dust, and other substances all pose a serious fire hazard.

Know where fire extinguishers are located and how to use them. See **Figure 4-23**. Do not attempt to fight a fire if you are not trained or authorized by your employer, if more than a couple of ounces of chemicals are burning, or if you cannot fight the fire with your back to an exit for easy escape. Also know the fire evacuation routes. For higher visibility, many facilities outline aisles and walkways with yellow paint. Keep walkways, stairways, and exits free of obstructions. Being able to respond quickly and efficiently in a fire can mean the difference between a simple incident and a disaster.

Noise

Unwanted and excessively loud noise is found in many industrial facilities. Excessive noise can lead to permanent hearing loss. The best way to protect against ear damage is to control the noise. When those controls do not reduce the noise to an acceptable level, ear protection must be worn.

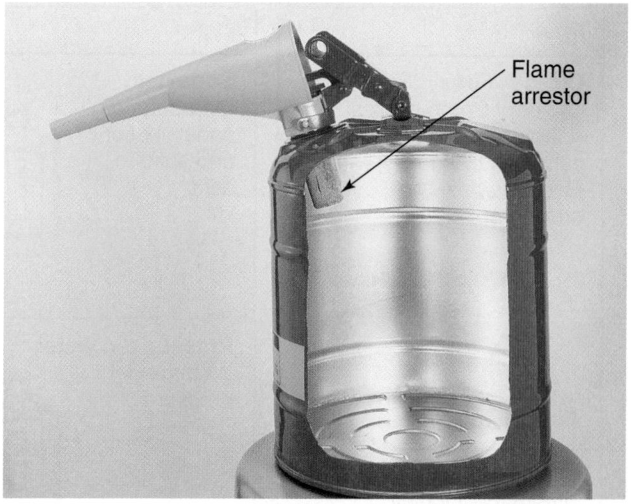

Justrite Manufacturing Company

Figure 4-21. Flame arrestors are an important feature of safety cans. Heat is dissipated and absorbed as it passes through the arrestor.

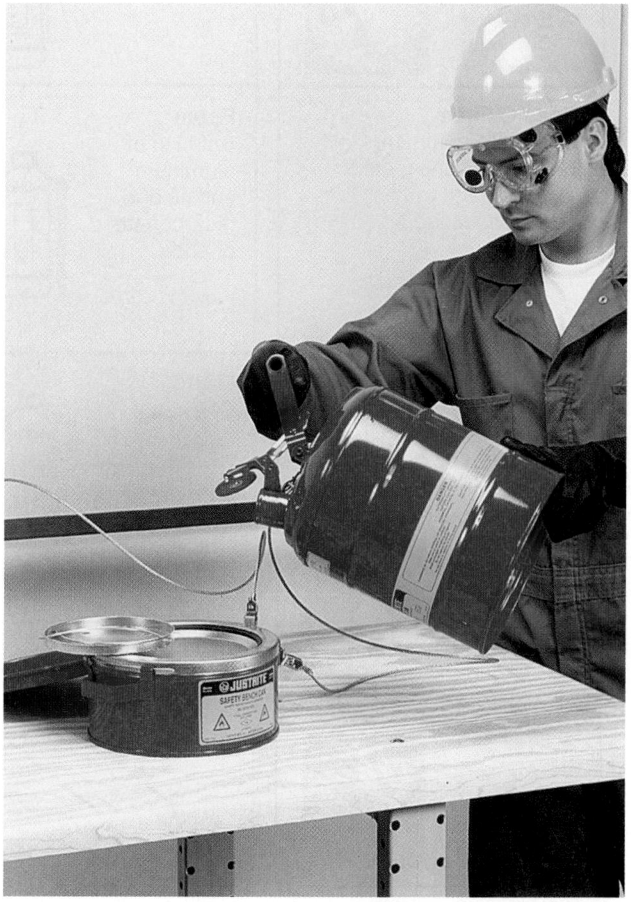

Justrite Manufacturing Company

Figure 4-22. Flowing liquids can charge cans with static electricity. Static buildup can cause fires and explosions. Bonding and grounding wires prevent sparks from jumping by allowing the electric charge to balance safely.

Fires
Class A Fires Ordinary Combustibles (Materials such as wood, paper, textiles.) *Requires... cooling-quenching* Old: A New: 
Class B Fires Flammable Liquids (Liquids such as grease, gasoline, oils, and paints.) *Requires...blanketing or smothering.* Old: B New: 
Class C Fires Electrical Equipment (Motors, switches, etc.) *Requires... a nonconducting agent.* Old: C New: 
Class D Fires Combustible Metals (Flammable metals such as magnesium and lithium.) *Requires...blanketing or smothering.* Old: D New: 

Type	Use	Operation
Soda-acid Bicarbonate of soda solution and sulfuric acid 	Okay for use on: A Not for use on: B C D	Direct stream at base of flame.
Pressurized Water Water under pressure 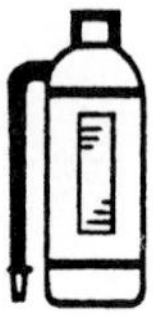	Okay for use on: A Not for use on: B C D	Direct stream at base of flame.
Carbon Dioxide (CO_2) Carbon dioxide (CO_2) gas under pressure 	Okay for use on: B C Not for use on: A D	Direct discharge as close to fire as possible, first at edge of flames and gradually forward and upward.
Foam Solution of aluminum sulfate and bicarbonate of soda 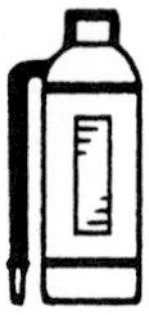	Okay for use on: A B Not for use on: C D	Direct stream into the burning material or liquid. Allow foam to fall lightly on fire.
Dry Chemical 	Multi-purpose type — Okay for: A B C; Not okay for: D Ordinary BC type — Okay for: B C; Not okay for: A D	Direct stream at base of flames. Use rapid left-to-right motion toward flames.
Dry Chemical Granular type material	Okay for use on: D Not for use on: A B C	Smother flames by scooping granular material from bucket onto burning metal.

Goodheart-Willcox Publisher

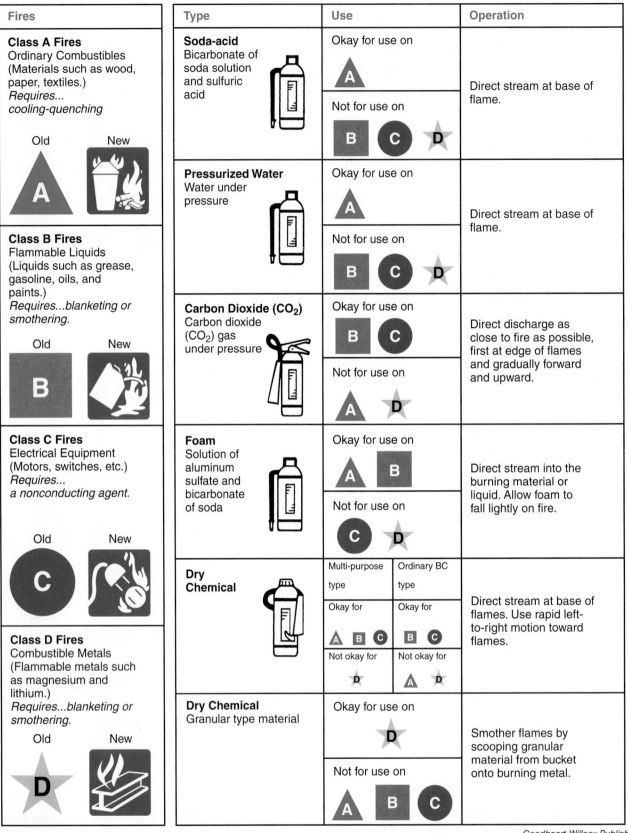

Figure 4-23. Not every fire extinguisher will put out every kind of fire. Check the label on the extinguisher. Using the wrong extinguisher may electrocute you or produce toxic fumes.

Noise levels are measured in units called ***decibels (dBA)***. **Figure 4-24** illustrates allowable exposure time to various decibels. A reading of 90 dBA is the maximum allowable limit for an eight-hour day. If the amount is greater than 90 dBA, a specific time limit is established.

If noise exceeds permissible levels, unwanted sound must be engineered out of the operation, or personal hearing protection devices must be provided and worn. Hearing protection devices include earmuffs, earplugs, moldable inserts, and noise-reducing headsets, **Figure 4-25**. Folder and web press operators usually need to wear hearing protection as their equipment typically produces noises over 90 dBA.

Light Hazards

Light sources common to graphic communications facilities can be hazardous. Ultraviolet (UV) light, for example, can damage unprotected skin and eyes. Potentially harmful sources of light include pulsed xenon and mercury vapor lamps, UV-ink curing units, and the ozone lights used on anti-set-off devices. True UV rays cannot be seen but *are* harmful; avoid contact with them. See **Figure 4-26**.

Even though most new equipment is shielded, care must be taken to protect the eyes when working in areas with platemaking equipment and drying systems. Infrared (IR) light and laser beams are also potentially

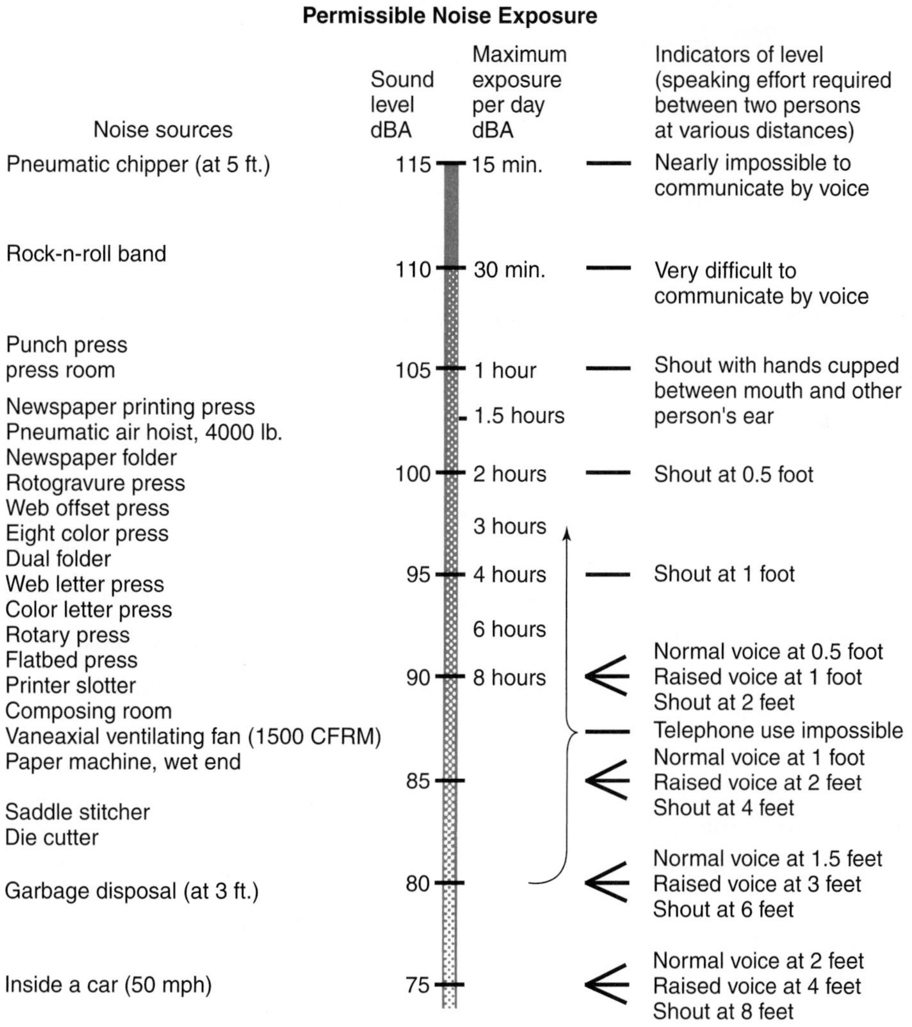

Goodheart-Willcox Publisher

Figure 4-24. Some permissible noise exposures established by OSHA. When employees are subjected to sound exceeding the levels prescribed, administrative or engineering controls must be made. If such controls fail to reduce sound levels within the permissible levels, personal protective equipment must be provided.

Earmark, Inc.

Figure 4-25. Ear protection is often needed in the pressroom or the bindery where equipment noise is loud enough to damage your hearing. This radio headset reduces noise by 23 dBA while allowing for team communication.

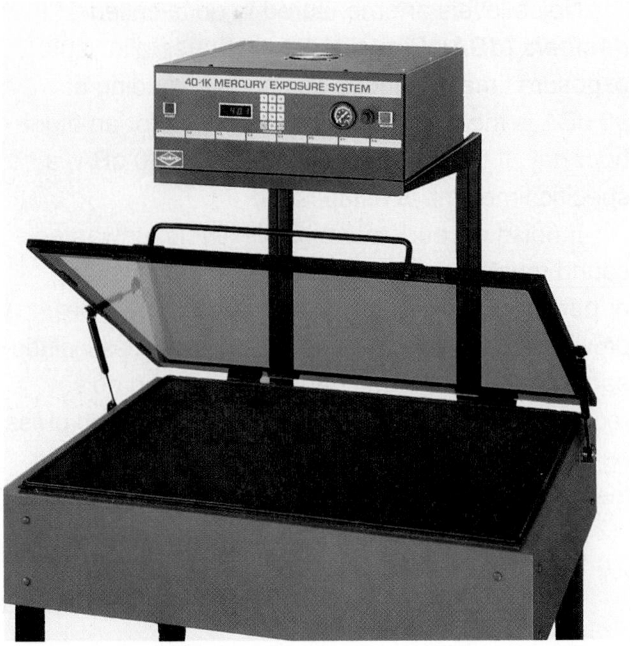

NuArc

Figure 4-26. Wear approved eye protection if you are near harmful sources of light that produce ultraviolet or infrared rays. Do not look directly at bright light when working with platemakers and cameras.

harmful. When working in areas where they are in use, take special precautions to protect your eyes.

Ergonomic Hazards

A mismatch between the physical requirements of the job and the physical capacity of the worker can cause painful conditions. ***Ergonomics*** is the science of fitting the job to the worker.

In recent years, the body of knowledge about ergonomics has expanded along with the use of computers in the workplace. In graphic communications, a task such as page layout and design, formerly performed by manually cutting and pasting text and images to boards, is now done electronically utilizing desktop publishing software. Therefore, consideration must be given to the effects of computer use on human health, **Figure 4-27**.

The following checklist can be used as an evaluation tool to determine if computer workstations are appropriate for the worker.

- When seated, the operator should maintain proper posture. Are thighs horizontal?
- Are the lower legs vertical?
- Are the feet flat on the floor or on a footrest?
- Are the wrists flat?
- Is the chair easy to adjust?
- Does the chair have a padded seat with a rounded front?
- Does the chair have an adjustable backrest?
- Does the chair provide lumbar support?
- Does the chair have casters?
- Is the keyboard detachable?
- Are the height and tilt of the work surface on which the keyboard is located adjustable?
- Do keying actions require minimal force?
- Is there an adjustable document holder?
- Are the document holder and the screen the same distance from the eyes?
- Are the document holder and the screen close together to avoid excessive head movement?
- Are armrests provided where needed?
- Are glare and reflections avoided?
- Does the monitor have brightness and contrast controls?

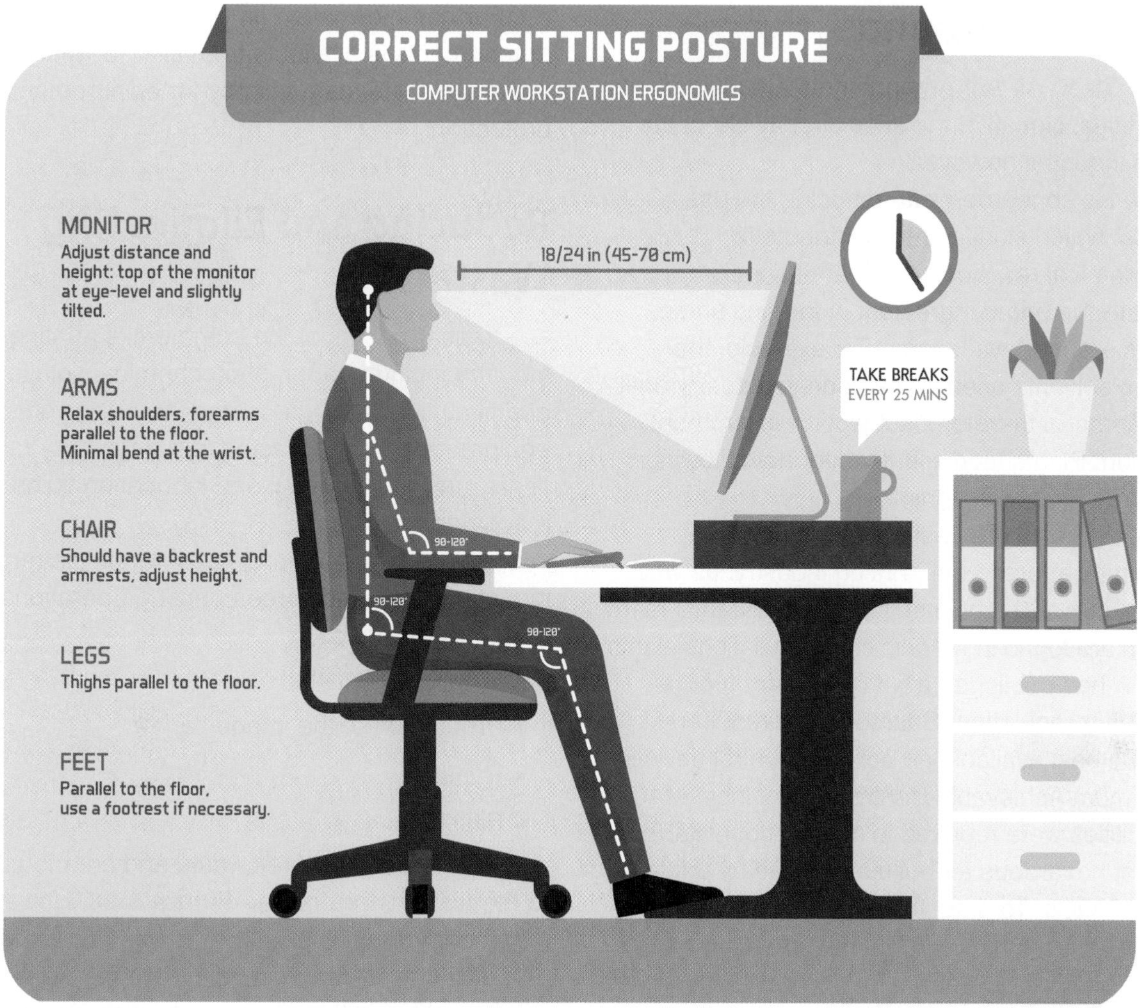
CORRECT SITTING POSTURE
COMPUTER WORKSTATION ERGONOMICS
MONITOR
Adjust distance and height: top of the monitor at eye-level and slightly tilted.
ARMS
Relax shoulders, forearms parallel to the floor. Minimal bend at the wrist.
CHAIR
Should have a backrest and armrests, adjust height.
LEGS
Thighs parallel to the floor.
FEET
Parallel to the floor, use a footrest if necessary.
18/24 in (45-70 cm)
TAKE BREAKS
EVERY 25 MINS
90-120°
90-120°
90-120°

enabsi/Shutterstock.com

Figure 4-27. Workstations that are designed for health and comfort are important when you spend hours working at a computer.

- Does the operator judge the distance between eyes and work to be satisfactory for viewing?
- Is the topmost line of display no higher than the operator's eyes?
- Is there sufficient space for knees and feet?
- Are adequate rest breaks provided for task demands?
- Have employees had training for posture at the workstation?
- Have employees been trained in proper work methods?

Ergonomic issues are presently not regulated by OSHA, but their "general duty" clause has been used to cite ergonomic hazards. California has a state ergonomics standard and several other states are moving in that direction.

Environmental Compliance

Most of the safety and health guidelines discussed in this chapter are mandated by OSHA for the protection of the individual worker. Another federal initiative, the Clean Air Act Amendments (CAAA), requires the Environmental Protection Agency (EPA) to periodically review and revise national air quality standards to ensure they fully protect human health.

The CAAA continue to significantly impact lithographic printers. An EPA standard changed the National Ambient Air Quality Standards (NAAQS) for ozone and particulate matter from 0.12 parts per million (ppm) to 0.07 ppm measured over an eight-hour period. Printers must now fully comply with the emission standard.

CAAA Background

The Clean Air Act Amendments are divided into eleven titles. Not all of the titles directly affect the printing industry, however.

Title I is concerned with reducing the use of VOCs, which significantly contribute to photochemical reactions in the atmosphere. VOCs are the prime ingredient in forming smog, which is ground-level ozone. For example, the cleaning solvents used in the printing industry emit VOCs and are, therefore, subject to government regulation. Plants face stiff fines for not following VOC emission regulations.

The Air Toxins Provisions of Title III have significantly affected the printing industry, as well. The Title lists 189 regulated toxic air pollutants, many of which are found in graphic communications plants. The EPA has published a list of industry groups targeted for regulation. Sources were required to install the best available air pollution control devices or Maximum Achievable Control Technology (MACT); new facilities were required to comply upon startup.

Most hazardous air pollutants used by printers are also VOCs. To date, the use of materials that contain low amounts of VOCs has provided a popular, alternative method for printers to meet state and federal VOC emission requirements without the costs of additional control equipment.

Under Title V, each state is required to establish rules for issuing permits for all major sources of VOCs and air toxins. The title requires facilities to obtain air permits if their emissions exceed certain limits, based on where they operate.

Clean Water Act (CWA)

The Clean Water Act (CWA) governs water pollution control, regulating discharges of pollutants to US waters. The commercial printing industry produces a number of pollutants potentially regulated by the CWA. Provisions and permit regulations are broad and administered by the US EPA. Laundry effluent (waste material) guidelines will most affect printers who send their shop rags to laundries. Hazardous oil spill regulations may apply to a printing facility if it works with oil and is located near a municipal storm sewer that discharges to or near a body of water.

Further information on these acts and amendments is available from the US EPA or the appropriate state agency for environmental protection.

Reducing and Eliminating Waste

Typical wastes of the commercial printing industry include paper, photochemical solutions and films, inks and ink-contaminated solvents, equipment cleaning wastes (solvents, dirty rags, filters, and absorbents), and lubricating fluids from machinery.

Lithographic, gravure, flexographic, letterpress, digital printing, and screen printing operations share four primary steps:

- Image processing.
- Production of the image carrier.
- Printing.
- Finishing.

Each step generates waste and contributes to the ***waste stream***. See **Figure 4-28**. However, many opportunities exist for reducing or eliminating these wastes. Described below are the wastes generated by each step in the printing operation and some pollution prevention practices that can be employed. The Safety Data Sheets are a good source of information for understanding these sources.

Image Processing

Systems are also available for onsite reclamation for plants using films and materials that contain silver. The silver is collected by a refiner for reuse, **Figure 4-29**.

Technologies, such as computer-to-plate technology, have eliminated some of the waste streams associated with films. This is also true of digital printing. See **Figure 4-30**.

Production of the Image Carrier

Some of the lithographic platemaking systems generate wastewater that may contain acids, alkalies, solvents, plate coatings, and developers. Wastewater from letterpress and flexographic plates may contain heavy metals.

Wastes Generated by Printing Operations		
Waste Stream	**Process**	**Composition**
Solid waste	Image processing	Empty containers, used film packages, outdated material
	Platemaking	Damaged plates, developed film, dated materials
	Printing	Test production, bad printings, empty ink containers
	Finishing	Damaged products, scrap
Wastewater	Image processing	Photographic chemicals, silver
	Platemaking	Acids, alkali, solvents, plate coatings (may contain dyes, photopolymers, binders, resins, pigment, organic acids), developers (may contain isopropanol, gum arabic, lacquers, caustics), and rinse water
	Printing	Spent fountain solutions (may contain chromium)
Cleanup solvents and waste ink	Printing	Lubricating oils, waste ink, cleanup solvent (halogenated and nonhalogenated), rags
Air emissions	Makeready, printing	Solvent from heat-set inks, isopropyl alcohol fountain solution, and cleaning solvents

Illinois Environmental Protection Agency of Pollution Prevention

Figure 4-28. Wastes generated by printing processes.

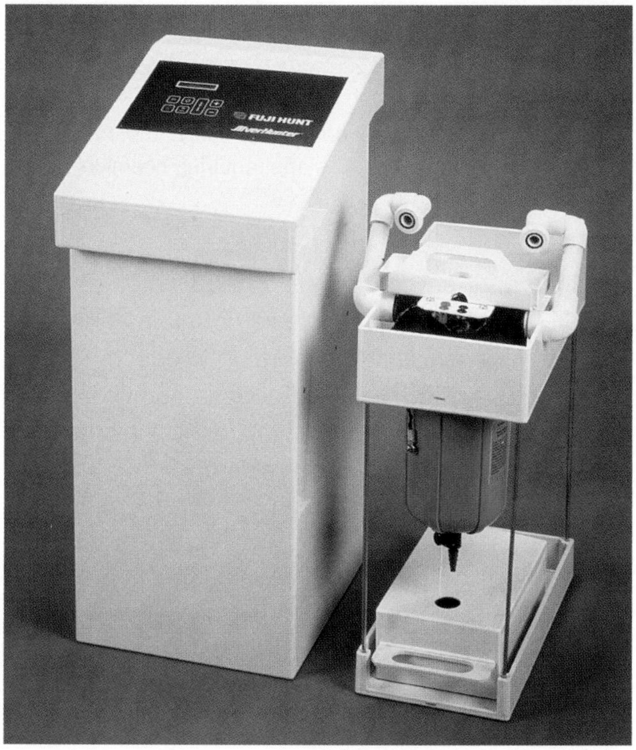

Fuji Hunt Photographic Chemicals, Inc.

Figure 4-29. An electrolytic, recirculating silver recovery unit. The unit maintains low silver levels in the fixer tank, minimizing the amount of silver carried over into the wash tank. The complete system, including secondary metal ion exchange columns, will recover 99% or more of the available silver, meeting hazardous discharge requirements of 5.0 ppm or less.

Printing

Cleaning solvents and waste ink are the primary wastes associated with the printing process. Air emissions containing VOCs from petroleum-based inks and cleaning solvents are also part of the waste stream.

If printers are manually cleaning the printing equipment, they are using a rag wetted with an organic solvent. These solvents normally contain alcohol and have low flash points that are usually less than 140°F (60°C). The rag often drips excess solvent onto the floor during cleaning. Furthermore, the solvent quickly evaporates, generating VOC emissions. Dirty rags containing solvents, waste ink, oil, dirt, and other contaminants are often sent to commercial laundries. Ink and "spent" solvents in the towels cause two major concerns for laundries and local sanitary sewer systems handling the laundry's effluent: volatility and flammability.

Several manufacturers have developed low-VOC solvents with high flash points and low toxicity. Blanket washes made from vegetable oils and their fatty acid esters, terpenes (found in essential oils and plant resins), less volatile petroleum components, or a mixture of these substances have proven suitable substitutes. Compared to standard

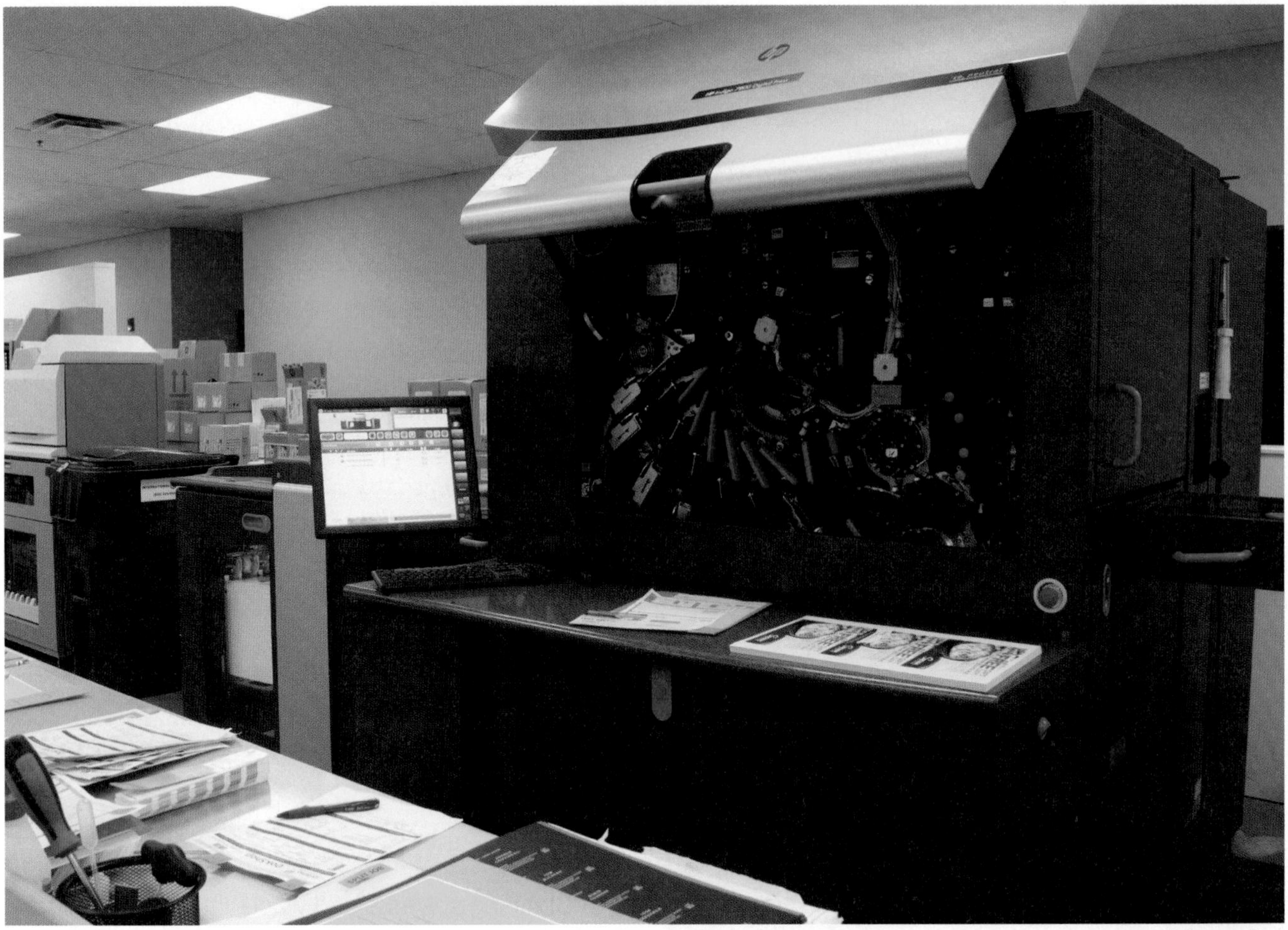

© George Deal

Figure 4-30. Digital color press. Digital printing is an increasingly popular alternative to offset printing for short- to medium-run length jobs. One of its benefits is minimizing impact on the environment by eliminating prepress steps requiring chemicals.

solvent-based washes that can contain up to 100% VOCs, the VOC content of vegetable ester washes is typically 12% to 30%. Vegetable and water mixtures drop to as low as 2%.

Some viable pollution prevention measures include using a less-volatile solvent, applying solvents conservatively using squeeze bottles or plunger cans, and wringing out excess solvent from rags using a centrifuge and reusing the recovered solvent.

Ink recovery machines make onsite reclaiming an option. Solvent recycling companies can also perform the task for printing operations that generate small quantities of ink and solvent wastes.

Substitute inks, such as UV-cured inks and water- or vegetable-based inks, are suitable for some printing applications. UV-cured inks contain no solvent and dry by exposure to ultraviolet light. They are nearly 100% solids and have a VOC content of 1% or less. UV-printed papers can be repulped and recycled as an added environmental benefit. Vegetable oils use fewer fountain additives than do mineral oils and accordingly reduce chemical use, **Figure 4-31**. Fountain additives are added to speed the drying of ink, as well as the flow characteristics and abrasion resistance.

Finishing

Most of the waste from finishing operations is scrap paper. Scrap paper from printing operations can be recycled into new paper. The market for recycled paper is good, shaped by depleted landfill space, tightening access to forest resources, changes in consumer awareness and preferences, and government restrictions. Technological improvements in recycled paper, such as stronger fiber and improved pulp, will continue to provide incentives for printers to send wastepaper to commercial paper recyclers and to buy recycled paper for printing.

National Soy Ink Information Center

Figure 4-31. Vegetable oils in inks are a sustainable resource and free of VOCs. While soybeans are the primary oil source for these inks, oils from linseed, rapeseed, and sunflower seeds are also used.

Buying recycled paper is just the beginning. States are increasingly adopting totally chlorine-free paper purchasing policies. Chlorine, a chemical compound used to bleach paper products, has been linked with ozone depletion. Legislation for state purchase of chlorine-free paper is being modeled after laws mandating state purchase of recycled products.

Process Evaluation

An excellent way to uncover new methods for reducing and eliminating waste is to evaluate the steps in the printing process. The review can be incorporated into the plant's overall safety and health program. Follow these directions for conducting a review:

- Record each step in your printing process, from purchasing raw materials to shipping the finished product.
- Diagram the process, noting every point where materials are used and wastes are created. (Include steps that are indirectly part of the process, such as waste disposal and electricity use.)
- Where wastes are generated, estimate the cost of lost raw material and costs resulting from collecting, tracking, and disposing of the wastes.
- Examine the diagram to pinpoint where the wastes are produced, and determine a plan for waste reduction. For example, you may be able to consolidate chemicals, replacing infrequently used ones with multiple-use chemicals.

Maintaining Tools, Equipment, and Machines

To operate safely and efficiently, the tools, equipment, and machines used in graphic communications facilities must be regularly maintained according to the manufacturer's requirements and recommended procedures. Failing to perform required maintenance or not following recommended procedures can cause injury to workers or damage to equipment and machines. It can also void the manufacturer's warranty and require costly repairs or replacement.

For many tools, equipment, and machines, maintenance procedures and requirements can be found in the owner's manual. More complex machines, such as printing presses, usually will have a separate maintenance manual.

Maintenance activities typically include:

- Cleaning, adjustment, and lubrication of specific areas or assemblies.
- Measuring to find whether tolerances are correct and making necessary adjustments to bring them "into spec."
- Checking alignment of parts and tightness of fasteners.
- Measuring wear on moving parts and adjusting or replacing parts as needed.
- Testing and calibrating electronic equipment to provide correct output.

To be sure maintenance is done at the recommended intervals, many companies keep a maintenance log. It lists the procedures to be done and the time when they should be performed. As each maintenance task is completed, the worker responsible signs and dates the log.

Summary

- Accidents in the workplace are very costly to the person involved and the company.
- Efforts need to be made to inform all personnel in the facility of hazardous areas and conditions.
- Coexistence of people and machines requires the establishment of a safe working environment.
- Machines must be used in the manner they were intended.
- Proper use of protective devices is a safeguard against hazardous areas and materials.
- Every plant safety program should address fire prevention.
- Noise levels are measured in units called decibels (dBA).
- Common dangers in graphic communications facilities are light hazards and ergonomic hazards.
- Production in the printing facility has an impact on the environment.
- It is imperative to handle resources responsibly.

Review Questions

Answer the following questions using the information in this chapter.

1. What is the purpose of a workplace safety and health program?
2. What four precautions can be taken to protect against injury from mechanical hazards?
3. Which dangerous condition exists where two cylinders meet or come close to each other?
   A. Shear point.
   B. Rip point.
   C. Nip point.
   D. Cut point.
4. What safety equipment can be worn to protect against injury?
5. How can you help maintain a straight back when lifting a heavy object?

6. What are inks, blanket wash, fountain solutions, and plate cleaners examples of?
   A. Inorganic solutions.
   B. Organic compounds.
   C. Tetrachlorides.
   D. Benzenes.
7. What is the purpose of the Safety Data Sheets?
8. How should you dispose of ink- and solvent-soaked rags?
9. A dBA reading of _____ is the maximum allowable limit for an 8-hour day without ear protection.
10. What is *ergonomics*?
11. Environmental compliances are meant to reduce contribution to the _____.
12. Standard solvent-based washes can contain up to 100% VOCs, while vegetable ester washes contain _____% VOCs.

Suggested Activities

1. Using the checklist in this chapter, inspect the graphic communications laboratory.
2. Select a specific piece of equipment and make a safety checklist.
3. Check the location of fire extinguishers within the school building(s).
4. What is the maximum legal weight to be lifted by a person?
5. Demonstrate the proper way to lift an object.
6. Choose a liquid that is used in the laboratory, and find the Hazard Communication Safety Data Sheet of the material on the Internet. Report on the hazards listed for your consideration.

Chapter 5

Applied Math

Learning Objectives

After studying this chapter, you will be able to:

- Differentiate between the US Conventional and SI Metric systems of measurement, and make conversions from one system to the other.
- Explain the point system of type measurement.
- Identify standard grades of paper and basic paper sizes.
- Compare grades of paper by basis weight, thickness, and brightness.
- Explain how visual images are produced and measured in a desktop publishing system.
- Understand the use of proportional scales, screens, and tint measurements in the reproduction of images.

Goodheart-Willcox Publisher

Important Terms

basic size
basis weight
chromaticity
densitometer
desktop publishing system
didot point system
E gauge
grades
gram
grayscale
illumination
ISO series
leading
line gauge
liter
luminance
meter
metric conversion chart
metric prefixes
moiré pattern
nonpareils
paper caliper
paper sizes
pica
pixels per inch (ppi)
point
point system
reams
reflection densitometer
resolution
screen
screen angles
screen tint
SI Metric system
spectrophotometer
transmission densitometer
type sizes
US Conventional system

G-WLEARNING.COM

While studying this chapter, look for the activity icon to:

- **Practice** vocabulary terms with e-flash cards, matching activities, and vocabulary game.
- **Reinforce** what you learn by submitting end-of-chapter questions.

www.g-wlearning.com/visualtechnology/

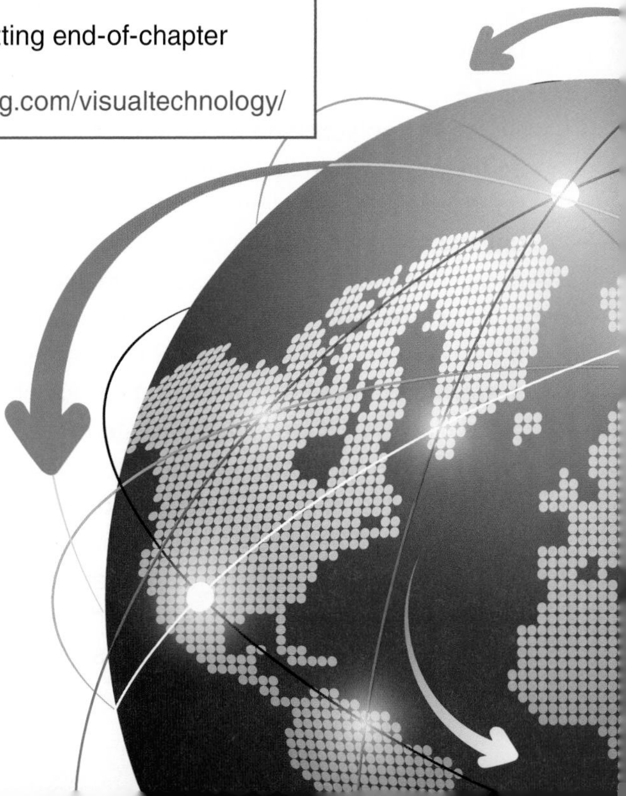

Measurement is used in almost every aspect of graphic reproduction. This chapter covers different systems and methods of measurement and demonstrates how vital they are to the graphic communications industry. The chapter begins with a discussion of the two most widely used systems of measurement: US Conventional and SI Metric. The point system of measurement, used throughout applications in graphics and design, is also discussed. The different standards used to measure paper sizes and weights are then covered. The chapter concludes with a discussion on developing technology in the production of images and the use of common measuring devices in the graphic communications industry. A thorough understanding of this chapter will prepare you for later chapters that apply different uses of measurement.

Measurement Principles

Throughout history, systems of measurement have been necessary in all parts of society. Different forms of measure have not only served as a means to describe quantities or values, but have also provided the basic functions required for communication. Some of the first measuring terms used referred to parts of the human body. For instance, the distance spanned by four fingers was known as four digits, while the hand was also a common measuring unit, representing about 4″. The length of a forearm was once called a cubit, and the length of a person's foot represented the distance of 1′.

More sophisticated measuring systems evolved as the growth of industry and trade created the need for standardization. Common agreement on units of measure developed as more accurate and consistent methods of measurement came into use.

The two most commonly used systems of measurement today are the ***US Conventional system*** and the ***SI Metric system***, or simply, metric system. The US Conventional system was derived from the English system of weights and measures, which evolved from traditional standards and was established in many parts of the world by the nineteenth century. The metric system, by contrast, was designed specifically as a standard measuring system in response to the need for standardization. It originated in France in 1790 and became recognized as a worldwide coordinated system.

The US Constitution empowered Congress to establish uniform standards for weights and measures. Today, the National Bureau of Standards ensures uniformity. The most common conventional and metric measurements are listed in **Figure 5-1**.

In 1866, the United States legalized the metric system as a standard for weights and measures. But the system has remained largely unused in US industry despite the Metric Conversion Act of 1975, which established a national policy to coordinate conversion to metric standards.

Metric System

The metric system is the most commonly used system of weights and measures in the world. While the system is not typically used in the United States, it is recognized as the international standard.

The metric system is a decimal system based on values of 10. The system was originally developed with the ***meter*** as the standard unit of length, the ***gram*** as the standard unit of mass, and the ***liter*** as the standard unit of capacity. The SI Metric system (the *Systeme International d'Unites*, or *International System of Units*) is a modernized version of the metric system established by international agreement. The SI Metric system is built on a foundation of seven base units of measure, as listed below:

- **Length** = *meter (m)*
- **Mass** = *kilogram (kg)*
- **Time** = *second (s)*
- **Electric current** = *ampere (A)*
- **Temperature** = *Kelvin (K)* or *degree Celsius (°C)*
- **Amount of substance** = *mole (mol)*
- **Luminous intensity** = *candela (cd)*

Metric Prefixes

The process of making different computations involving measure is simpler when using the metric system because metric units are structured in multiples of 10. ***Metric prefixes*** indicate multiples or divisions of these units. See **Figure 5-2**.

Approximate Equivalents			
Unit	**US Conventional**	**SI Metric**	**Uses**
Length	inch (in) feet (ft) yard (yd) mile (mi)	millimeter (mm) meter (m) meter (m) kilometer (km)	Paper, wrapping material, plates, wire rolls, scales, press calibration Covers, tapes, binders
Pressure	pounds per square inch (psi)	kilopascal (kPa)	Web press ink pressure, air pressure, vacuum
Power	horsepower (hp)	kilowatt (kw)	Electric motor rating
Torque	pound-feet (lb-ft)	newton-meter (N•m)	Bolt tightening
Volume or capacity	fluid ounce (oz) quart (qt) cubic inch (in^3)	milliliter (mL) liter (L) cubic centimeter (cc)	Ink, oil Plate chemicals Storage, shipping
Mass or weight	ounce (oz) pound (lb)	gram (g) kilogram (kg)	Postage, padding cement, chemicals, shipping, supplies
Speed	feet per second (ft/s) miles per hour (mph) revolutions per minute (rpm)	meters per second (m/s) kilometers per hour (km/h) revolutions per minute (rpm)	Web press speed
Application rates	fluid ounces per square foot (fl-oz/ft^2) ounces per square foot (oz/ft^2)	milliliters per square meter (mL/m^2) grams per square meter (g/m^2)	Applying materials, ink coverage, estimating

Goodheart-Willcox Publisher

Figure 5-1. Customary units of measure and metric equivalents. Common uses for each measurement are listed at right.

Common Metric Prefixes				
mega (M)	=	1 000 000	or	10^6
kilo (k)	=	1000	or	10^3
hecto (h)	=	100	or	10^2
centi (c)	=	0.01	or	10^{-2}
milli (m)	=	0.001	or	10^{-3}
micro (μ)	=	0.000 001	or	10^{-6}
Examples				
kilogram	=	1000	grams	
milligram	=	0.001	gram	
dekometer	=	10	meters	
centimeter	=	0.01	meter	
hectoliter	=	100	liters	
decimeter	=	0.1	meter	

Goodheart-Willcox Publisher

Figure 5-2. Prefixes are used to identify units in the metric system.

Rules of Metric Notation

Several rules are observed when expressing figures in metric notation. The following are standards used when abbreviating metric quantities:

- Unit symbols are not followed by periods (mm).
- Unit symbols are not pluralized in an abbreviation (10 g).
- A space separates the numeral from the unit symbols (2 mm).
- Spaces, not commas, are used to separate large numbers into groups of three digits (21 210 km).
- A zero precedes the decimal point if the numeral is less than one (0.11 g).

Metric Conversion

Since there is still widespread use of US Conventional measures in the graphic communications industry, it is sometimes necessary to convert to or from metric values. For instance, if a chemical quantity is given in liters and the equipment uses mixture ratios in quarts, one of the values has to be converted to the other system.

A ***metric conversion chart*** can be used to change a metric value to a conventional value or a conventional value to a metric value. See **Figure 5-3**. Values are converted from one system to another by multiplying known quantities by a specific number.

Type Measurement

Type sizes are used to distinguish different measures of printed type. The units of measure most commonly used for sizes of type in English-speaking countries are the point and pica, known as the ***point system***, or the American point system. Type sizes are measured in points, while line lengths are often given in picas and points.

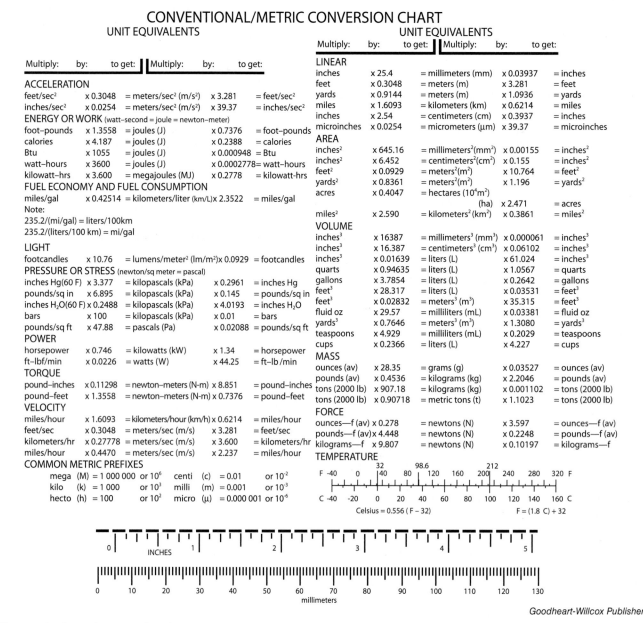

CONVENTIONAL/METRIC CONVERSION CHART

UNIT EQUIVALENTS

Multiply:	by:	to get: / Multiply:	by:	to get:
ACCELERATION				
feet/sec^2	x 0.3048	= meters/sec^2 (m/s^2)	x 3.281	= feet/sec^2
inches/sec^2	x 0.0254	= meters/sec^2 (m/s^2)	x 39.37	= inches/sec^2
ENERGY OR WORK (watt-second = joule = newton-meter)				
foot-pounds	x 1.3558	= joules (J)	x 0.7376	= foot-pounds
calories	x 4.187	= joules (J)	x 0.2388	= calories
Btu	x 1055	= joules (J)	x 0.000948	= Btu
watt-hours	x 3600	= joules (J)	x 0.0002778	= watt-hours
kilowatt-hrs	x 3.600	= megajoules (MJ)	x 0.2778	= kilowatt-hrs
FUEL ECONOMY AND FUEL CONSUMPTION				
miles/gal	x 0.42514	= kilometers/liter (km/L)	x 2.3522	= miles/gal
Note: 235.2/(mi/gal) = liters/100km; 235.2/(liters/100 km) = mi/gal				
LIGHT				
footcandles	x 10.76	= lumens/meter^2 (lm/m^2)	x 0.0929	= footcandles
PRESSURE OR STRESS (newton/sq meter = pascal)				
inches Hg(60 F)	x 3.377	= kilopascals (kPa)	x 0.2961	= inches Hg
pounds/sq in	x 6.895	= kilopascals (kPa)	x 0.145	= pounds/sq in
inches H_2O(60 F)	x 0.2488	= kilopascals (kPa)	x 4.0193	= inches H_2O
bars	x 100	= kilopascals (kPa)	x 0.01	= bars
pounds/sq ft	x 47.88	= pascals (Pa)	x 0.02088	= pounds/sq ft
POWER				
horsepower	x 0.746	= kilowatts (kW)	x 1.34	= horsepower
ft-lbf/min	x 0.0226	= watts (W)	x 44.25	= ft-lb/min
TORQUE				
pound-inches	x 0.11298	= newton-meters (N-m)	x 8.851	= pound-inches
pound-feet	x 1.3558	= newton-meters (N-m)	x 0.7376	= pound-feet
VELOCITY				
miles/hour	x 1.6093	= kilometers/hour (km/h)	x 0.6214	= miles/hour
feet/sec	x 0.3048	= meters/sec (m/s)	x 3.281	= feet/sec
kilometers/hr	x 0.27778	= meters/sec (m/s)	x 3.600	= kilometers/hr
miles/hour	x 0.4470	= meters/sec (m/s)	x 2.237	= miles/hour

COMMON METRIC PREFIXES

mega	(M)	= 1 000 000	or 10^6	centi	(c)	= 0.01	or 10^{-2}
kilo	(k)	= 1 000	or 10^3	milli	(m)	= 0.001	or 10^{-3}
hecto	(h)	= 100	or 10^2	micro	(µ)	= 0.000 001	or 10^{-6}

UNIT EQUIVALENTS

Multiply:	by:	to get: / Multiply:	by:	to get:
LINEAR				
inches	x 25.4	= millimeters (mm)	x 0.03937	= inches
feet	x 0.3048	= meters (m)	x 3.281	= feet
yards	x 0.9144	= meters (m)	x 1.0936	= yards
miles	x 1.6093	= kilometers (km)	x 0.6214	= miles
inches	x 2.54	= centimeters (cm)	x 0.3937	= inches
microinches	x 0.0254	= micrometers (µm)	x 39.37	= microinches
AREA				
inches^2	x 645.16	= millimeters^2(mm^2)	x 0.00155	= inches^2
inches^2	x 6.452	= centimeters^2(cm^2)	x 0.155	= inches^2
feet^2	x 0.0929	= meters^2(m^2)	x 10.764	= feet^2
yards^2	x 0.8361	= meters^2(m^2)	x 1.196	= yards^2
acres	x 0.4047	= hectares (10^{4}m^2) (ha)	x 2.471	= acres
miles^2	x 2.590	= kilometers^2 (km^2)	x 0.3861	= miles^2
VOLUME				
inches^3	x 16387	= millimeters^3 (mm^3)	x 0.000061	= inches^3
inches^3	x 16.387	= centimeters^3 (cm^3)	x 0.06102	= inches^3
inches^3	x 0.01639	= liters (L)	x 61.024	= inches^3
quarts	x 0.94635	= liters (L)	x 1.0567	= quarts
gallons	x 3.7854	= liters (L)	x 0.2642	= gallons
feet^3	x 28.317	= liters (L)	x 0.03531	= feet^3
feet^3	x 0.02832	= meters^3 (m^3)	x 35.315	= feet^3
fluid oz	x 29.57	= milliliters (mL)	x 0.03381	= fluid oz
yards^3	x 0.7646	= meters^3 (m^3)	x 1.3080	= yards^3
teaspoons	x 4.929	= milliliters (mL)	x 0.2029	= teaspoons
cups	x 0.2366	= liters (L)	x 4.227	= cups
MASS				
ounces (av)	x 28.35	= grams (g)	x 0.03527	= ounces (av)
pounds (av)	x 0.4536	= kilograms (kg)	x 2.2046	= pounds (av)
tons (2000 lb)	x 907.18	= kilograms (kg)	x 0.001102	= tons (2000 lb)
tons (2000 lb)	x 0.90718	= metric tons (t)	x 1.1023	= tons (2000 lb)
FORCE				
ounces—f (av)	x 0.278	= newtons (N)	x 3.597	= ounces—f (av)
pounds—f (av)	x 4.448	= newtons (N)	x 0.2248	= pounds—f (av)
kilograms—f	x 9.807	= newtons (N)	x 0.10197	= kilograms—f

TEMPERATURE

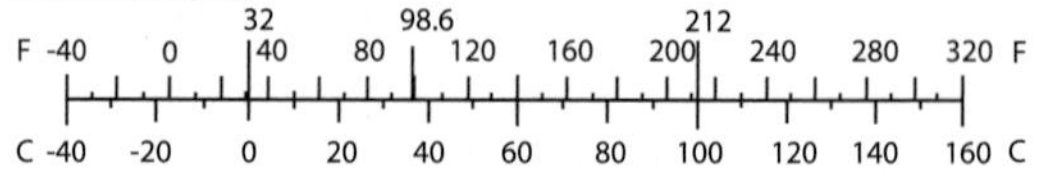

Celsius = 0.556 (F − 32) F = (1.8 C) + 32

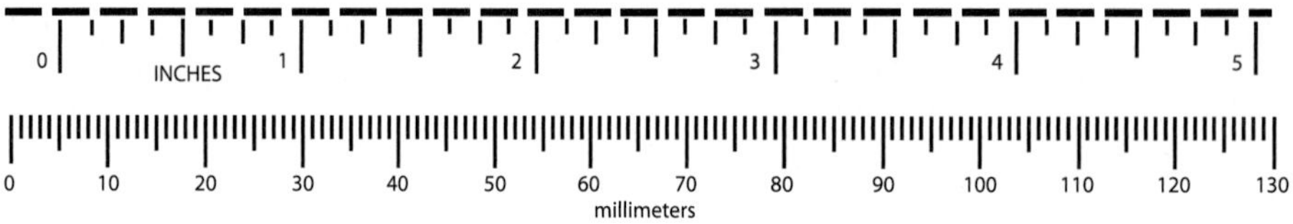

Goodheart-Willcox Publisher

Figure 5-3. A metric conversion chart can be used to change values from one measuring system to another.

The ***point*** measures approximately 0.01383″.
The ***pica*** measures approximately 0.166″.
Twelve points equal a pica, and six picas equal approximately one inch.

A ***line gauge*** is an instrument used to measure type sizes and line lengths in picas or inches. See **Figure 5-4**. Line gauges typically measure up to 72 picas (approximately 12″). One side of the gauge is marked in inches, and the other side is marked in picas and ***nonpareils***.

The latest software applications recognize all forms of measure and Adobe® products do the conversion for you. You can input any form of measure into a menu field, and the software will convert that number to whatever the default setting is for that document. For example, if your document is set up in inches, you can input the width of a box in points and picas, and it will convert on the fly.

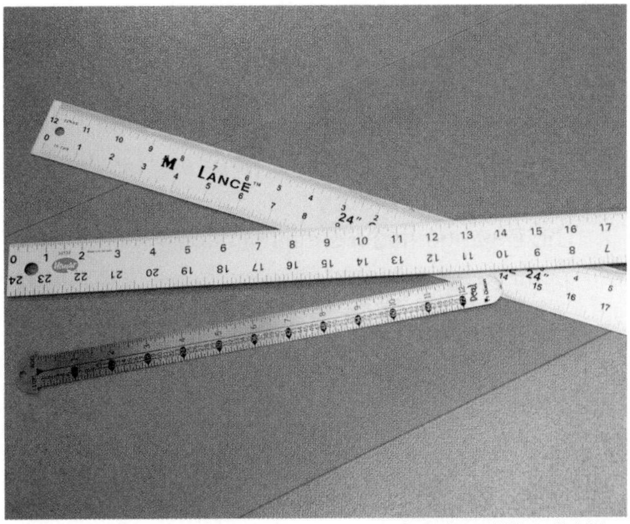

Goodheart-Willcox Publisher

Figure 5-4. A set of line gauges with scales in both picas and inches, used to measure type sizes and line lengths.

Didot Point System

The American point system was adopted for use in the United States in 1886. It was based on the Fournier point system developed in 1737 by Pierre Simon Fournier, a French typographer. The Fournier point was later modified by the Didot printing family of France. The ***didot point system***, based on the French inch, became the conventional printer's measure used in Europe and remains the standard today. The didot point is equal to 0.0148″. Twelve didot points equal the didot pica. A didot pica is equal to 0.1776″.

Metric Type Sizes

Metric units are also used to measure sizes of type. For example, millimeters can be used to give the equivalent sizes for either pica point (American point system) or didot point (European point system) sizes. One pica point equals 0.351 mm. One didot point equals 0.376 mm. Equivalent measures for the metric, pica, and didot point systems are shown in **Figure 5-5**.

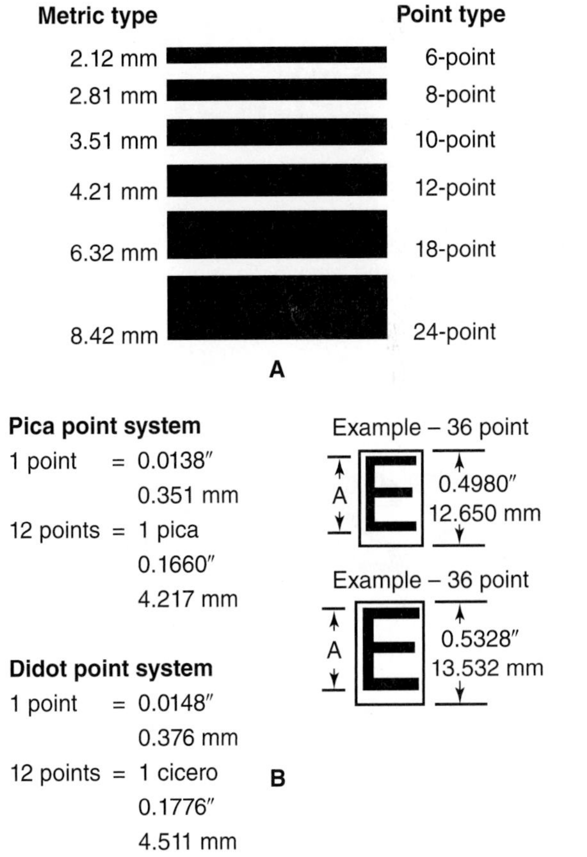

Goodheart-Willcox Publisher

Figure 5-5. Standard point and metric sizes type. A—Metric type is measured in millimeters, while type in the point system is measured in points. B—Different equivalents for type sizes in point, metric, and didot units.

Measuring Point Size

The point size or metric size of a letter is not a measurement from the top to the bottom of the letter itself. The point size also includes a small amount of white space above and below the letter for line spacing. Different styles of type have different amounts of white space above and below the letter shape. Some typographers can identify a point size on sight. Others use an ***E gauge*** or similar measuring device, **Figure 5-6**.

The E gauge has a series of capital *E* letters with point sizes indicated for each letter. The correct point size can be determined by placing the gauge flat over a line of type and matching the letter *E* closest in size to the letters in the line.

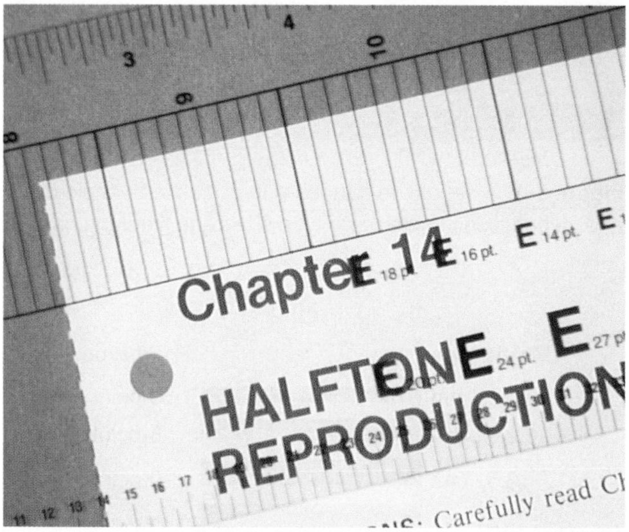

Goodheart-Willcox Publisher

Figure 5-6. An E gauge is a measuring device for different point sizes of type and leading. The uppercase "E" in the chapter title is set in 24-point type.

A comparison of two different typefaces having the same point size but different letter heights is shown in **Figure 5-7**. The typefaces are both printed in 72-point type. However, the actual size of the letters is different. Identifying the correct point size is difficult without having typographical experience or without using an E gauge to at least get you close to the correct measure.

The amount of vertical space between lines of type is also measured in points and is called ***leading***. An E gauge has a series of line spacing grids marked with point sizes that can be used to approximate leading. When the gauge is placed over several lines of type, aligning the gauge lines to the baseline of the text, the grid that most closely matches the spacing between the lines indicates the leading point size. Refer to **Figure 5-6**.

Measuring Paper Sizes

Paper sizes are designated in length and width dimensions and are given in either inches or metric units. Paper for business use is commonly packaged in ***reams***, which consist of 500 sheets.

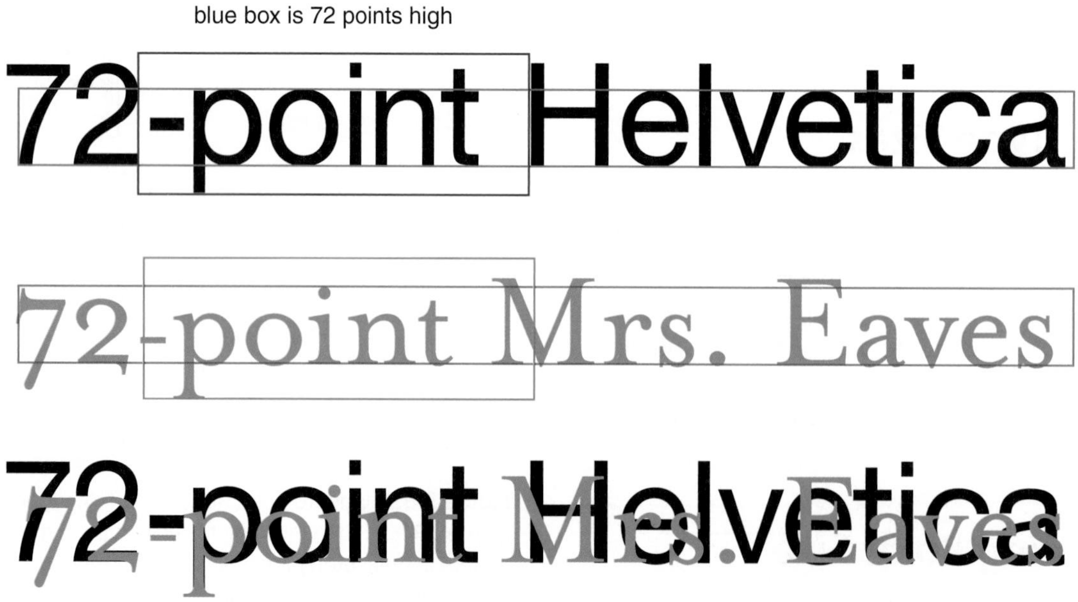

Goodheart-Willcox Publisher

Figure 5-7. Two typefaces with the same point size but different letter heights. The point size of a letter includes the measurement of white space above and below the letter.

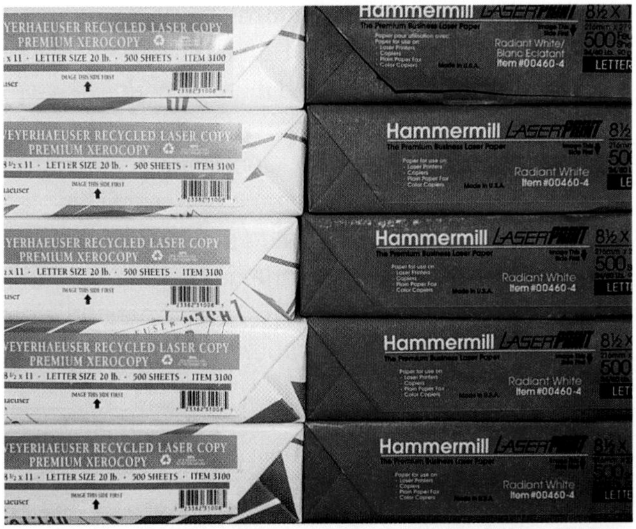

Goodheart-Willcox Publisher

Figure 5-8. Paper packaged in reams of 500 sheets. Labels identify the paper size.

See **Figure 5-8**. Different types of paper are known as ***grades*** and are classified with a ***basic size***. The classification of paper grades lacks universal agreement. End use is one way to grade paper, but some sheets may be used successfully in more than one area. Some commonly used grades of paper and their basic sizes are listed:

- **Bond** = 17″ × 22″
- **Book** = 25″ × 38″
- **Offset** = 25″ × 38″
- **Cover** = 20″ × 26″
- **Text** = 25″ × 38″

Envelopes

Envelopes are classified by size and distinguished by styles that serve a special use. Business envelope sizes are usually designated by number. The most commonly used size is a Number 10, which measures 4 1/8″ × 9 1/2″. Window envelopes are available in the same size and are generally used for invoices or statements.

Envelopes used for wedding announcements and invitations or other formal occasions commonly measure 5″ × 6″. Open-end envelopes are larger types used for mailing reports, pamphlets, magazines, and other materials. Common sizes are 9″ × 12″ and 8 3/4″ × 11 1/4″.

Postal regulations should be reviewed in order to meet current mailing standards. Envelope sizes must comply with regulations so additional charges are not assessed for mail deliveries. See **Figure 5-9**.

ISO Sizes

Standard sizes for paper and envelopes have been established by the International Organization for Standardization (ISO). The sizes, known as the ***ISO series***, are given in both SI Metric units (millimeters) and US Conventional units (inches). ISO sizes are commonly grouped into three series. A-series sizes are used for general printing requirements; B-series sizes are used for posters; C-series sizes are used for postcards, folders, and envelopes.

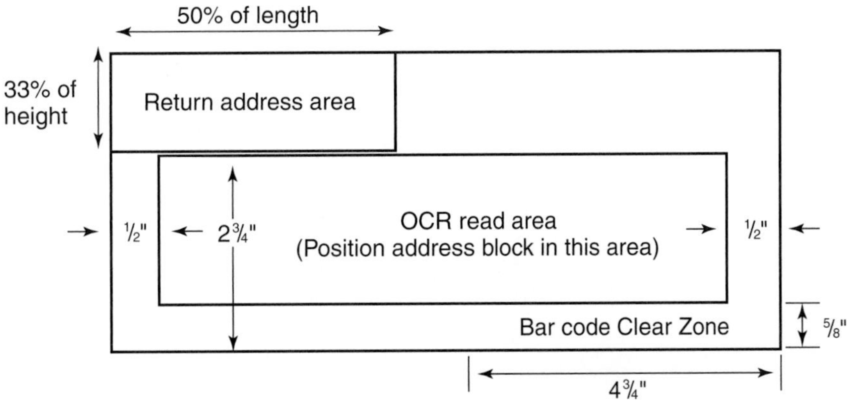

Goodheart-Willcox Publisher

Figure 5-9. A dimensional standards template used to determine if letter size is acceptable for normal handling in mail delivery.

The A-series and B-series metric paper sizes are rectangular. Their sizes are based on the ratio of the two sides having the proportion of one to the square root of two (1:1.416).

The ISO-A size of paper is based on the area of one square meter, as shown in **Figure 5-10**. Each cut reduces the size of the sheet by 50% of the previous size; for example, the size of A2 is double that of A3. Each ISO-A measurement is listed in **Figure 5-11**.

ISO-A and ISO-B metric paper sizes are considered to be trimmed sizes. However, there are other series used to classify sizes for normal trims, bleed work, and extra trims. See **Figure 5-12**. Nearly all folded and gathered printed material needs to have a normal trim, but an image that runs off a printed page must have greater trim area. Control devices on the printed sheet require more space and extra trim.

ISO-B paper sizes are listed in **Figure 5-13**. The different sizes are based on the same ratio used in measuring ISO-A sizes (1:1.416). A comparison of ISO-A, ISO-B, and ISO-C paper sizes is shown in **Figure 5-14**.

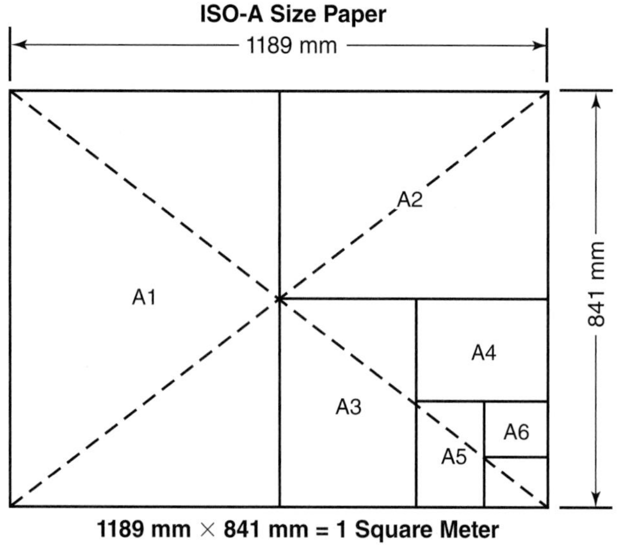

Goodheart-Willcox Publisher

Figure 5-10. ISO-A metric size paper. The dimensions are based on the area of one square meter.

ISO Sizes for Normal Trims		
ISO Size	**Metric (mm)**	**Conventional (″)**
RA0	860 × 1220	33.66 × 48.03
RA1	610 × 860	24.02 × 33.86
RA2	430 × 610	16.93 × 24.02
ISO Sizes for Bleed Work or Extra Trims		
ISO Size	**Metric (mm)**	**Conventional (″)**
SRA0	900 × 1280	35.43 × 50.39
SRA1	640 × 900	25.20 × 35.43
SRA2	450 × 640	17.72 × 25.20

Center for Metric Education, Western Michigan University

Figure 5-12. ISO trimmed paper sizes for normal trims, bleed work, and extra trims.

ISO Sizes	Metric (mm)	Conventional (″)
A0	841 × 1189	33.11 × 46.81
A1	594 × 841	23.39 × 33.11
A2	420 × 594	16.54 × 23.39
A3	297 × 420	11.69 × 16.54
A4	210 × 297	8.27 × 11.69
A5	148 × 210	5.83 × 8.27
A6	105 × 148	4.13 × 5.83
A7	74 × 105	2.91 × 4.13
A8	52 × 74	2.05 × 2.91
A9	37 × 52	1.46 × 2.05
A10	26 × 37	1.02 × 1.46

Goodheart-Willcox Publisher

Figure 5-11. ISO-A metric and conventional paper sizes.

ISO Sizes	Metric (mm)	Conventional (″)
B0	1000 × 1414	39.37 × 55.67
B1	707 × 1000	27.83 × 39.37
B2	500 × 707	19.68 × 27.83
B3	353 × 500	13.90 × 19.68
B4	250 × 353	9.84 × 13.90
B5	176 × 250	6.93 × 9.84
B6	125 × 176	4.92 × 6.93
B7	88 × 125	3.46 × 4.92
B8	62 × 88	2.44 × 3.46
B9	44 × 62	1.73 × 2.44
B10	31 × 44	1.22 × 1.73

Center for Metric Education, Western Michigan University

Figure 5-13. ISO-B metric and conventional paper sizes.

The sizes for ISO-A sheets are compatible with the sizes for ISO-C envelopes. See **Figure 5-15**. One envelope size is not derived from ISO-A, ISO-B, or ISO-C sizes. It is the German Din Lang, designated DL. DL are special envelope sizes and are not North American designations.

Paper Weight

Most grades of paper are classified by their ***basis weight***, which is a measure of the number of pounds in a ream of paper cut to its basic size. Each grade of paper is available in many different weights. See **Figure 5-16**.

The Technical Association of the Pulp and Paper Industry uses metric units to measure the weight of paper. The weight is expressed in grams per square meter (g/m^2). Factors for converting conventional weights of paper to metric units are listed in **Figure 5-17**. The conversion factors for changing from conventional weights of 500 sheets to grams per square meter are listed in column A. The conversion factors for changing weights from grams per square meter to conventional weights are listed in column B.

ISO-A, B, and C Paper Sizes

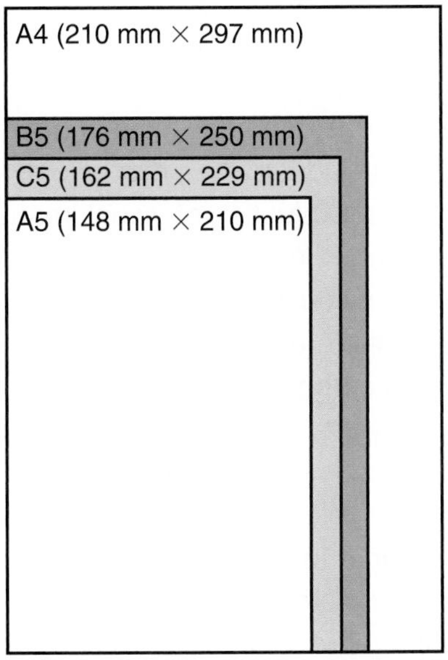

Goodheart-Willcox Publisher

Figure 5-14. Common ISO-A, B, and C paper sizes.

Common Paper Weights (1000 sheets)

Grade	Size (″)	Weight (pounds)
Bond	17 × 22	26, 32, 40, 48, 56
Book	25 × 38	60, 70, 80, 90, 100
Offset	25 × 38	50, 60, 70, 80, 100
Cover	20 × 26	100, 120, 130, 160, 180

Goodheart-Willcox Publisher

Figure 5-16. Common grades of paper are available in a number of weights.

Conversion Factors for Ream Weights

Grade of Paper	Conventional Size (″)	A Metric to Conventional	B Conventional to Metric
Writing	12 × 22	0.266	3.760
Cover	20 × 26	0.370	2.704
Cardboard	22 × 28	0.438	2.282
News	24 × 36	0.614	1.627
Book	25 × 38	0.675	1.480

Goodheart-Willcox Publisher

Figure 5-17. Multiplying factors for converting paper weights from metric or conventional units.

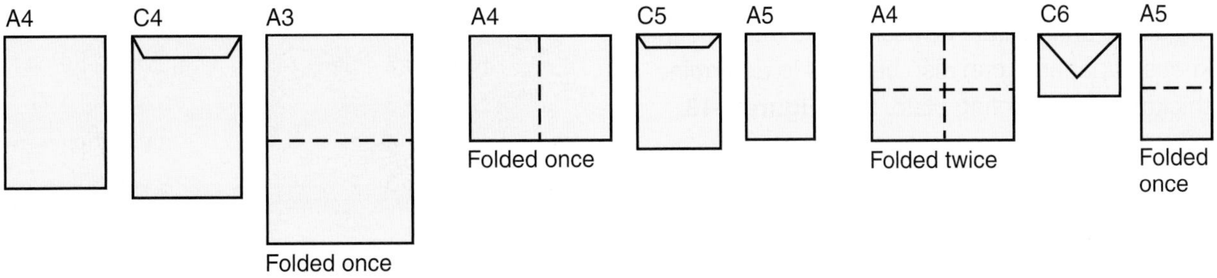

Goodheart-Willcox Publisher

Figure 5-15. ISO-A sheets of paper and ISO-C envelopes have compatible sizes.

Academic Link

Converting US Conventional Measurements to Metric

From time to time, it may be necessary to convert values from metric to US Conventional format, or vice versa. Simple multiplication skills are the only requirement to complete the conversions. A complete table of conversion factors is provided in **Figure 5-3**, but the following are some common conversion factors:

- There is 0.3048 meter in one foot, and 3.281 feet in one meter.
- There are 25.4 millimeters in one inch, and 0.03937 inch in one millimeter.
- There are 3.7854 liters in one gallon, and 0.2642 gallon in one liter.
- There is 0.04536 kilogram in one pound, and 2.2046 pounds in one kilogram.

For example, to calculate the number of meters in 12.5 feet, the equation is:

12.5 (number of feet) × 0.3048 (standard conversion factor) = 3.81 meters

Perform the following conversions on a separate piece of paper.

1. Six liters to gallons.
2. 105 millimeters to inches.
3. Five kilograms to pounds.

Using the conversion factors shown, a ream of coated book stock would be expressed as 100 g/m^2, or 67.5 lb (100 × 0.675). A ream of good writing paper would be listed as 85 g/m^2, or 22.61 lb (85 × 0.266).

Paper Thickness

Several types of caliper devices are available for measuring paper thickness. The ***paper caliper*** or micrometer is an accurate device used to measure the thickness of paper. It can also be used to determine the thickness of a printing plate. See **Figure 5-18**.

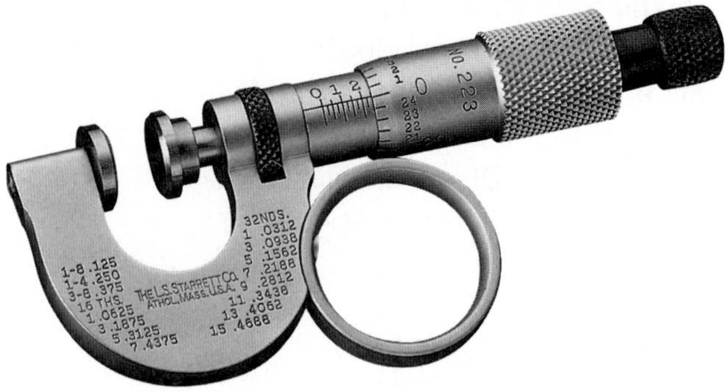

Photo courtesy of The L.S. Starrett Co.

Figure 5-18. A paper caliper is used to measure paper thickness.

Paper Brightness

Paper is also classified by its brightness, based on the American Forest and Paper Association (AFPA) standards. Number 1 quality is the brightest, reflecting 85%–87.9% of blue light; number 5 quality is classified as having the least brightness, as shown in **Figure 5-19**. Within each grade, papers are offered as virgin or recycled stock. Recycled stock may not be as bright as virgin stock.

Quality	Brightness
Number 1	85.0 to 87.9
Number 2	83.0 to 84.9
Number 3	79.0 to 82.9
Number 4	73.0 to 78.9
Number 5	72.9 and below

The S. D. Warren Company

Figure 5-19. AFPA standard grade classifications for all finishes of paper. Brightness is measured by the percentage of blue light reflected from the paper's surface.

Image Measurement

The rise of desktop publishing in the graphic communications industry has revolutionized the approach to the production of visual images. The use of computers has replaced many of the methods previously used in the design of printed materials. A ***desktop publishing system***, consisting of a computer, printer, scanner, and publishing software, has taken the place of traditional methods used in operations such as typesetting and color separation. Most of the printed images found in publications and other media are now produced electronically. Equipment commonly used in desktop publishing is shown in **Figure 5-20**.

©Dana Thelander

Figure 5-20. The components of a desktop publishing system include a computer, scanner, and publishing software. Output is typically to a laser printer.

The growth of digital technology has led to improvements in image quality and higher levels of productivity. As technology continues to expand, desktop publishing will play an even greater role in graphic communications.

Monitor Viewing Conditions

Color monitors may be used to display and view digital images. The latest version of *ISO 3664—Viewing Conditions for Graphic Technology and Photography* establishes specifications for viewing of a monitor independent of any form of hard copy. The specifications given in the ISO standard include guidelines for adjusting such controls as ***chromaticity***, or color quality; ***luminance***, or amount of light; ***illumination***, or brightness of light; and environmental conditions, such as surrounding conditions and glare.

Resolution

Resolution describes the visual quality of an image and is a measure of elements that define the image. The resolution of an image is measured in ***pixels per inch (ppi)***. A pixel is a tiny rectangle that is only visible as a dot on a computer screen. The screen display of a computer monitor is measured in horizontal rows and vertical columns of pixels. A high-resolution computer monitor rated at 2560 × 1080 pixels is able to display a resolution of 2560 pixels horizontally and 1080 pixels vertically.

Laser printers and electronic scanners used in desktop publishing are identified by a measure of dpi for image resolution. A laser printer rated at 600 dpi can produce a resolution of 600 dots for each horizontal or vertical inch. A scanner that scans images at 1200 ppi can produce a file with an image resolution of 1200 pixels per inch.

Scanning and File Sizes

The Warren Standard indicates that there is a simple way to govern how images should be scanned. Photographic material must be screened to break it down into tonal ranges. Various designated line screen figures are recommended for various types of stock. Doubling the line screen at which the image will be printed provides an approximation of the number of pixels per inch at which the image should be scanned. Scanning at different resolutions will change the file size and the amount of storage space needed. Changing the type of file will have the same effect. A bitmap file contains the smallest amount of color information, while a CMYK color file contains the largest amount. See **Figure 5-21**.

File Sizes at Various Resolutions					
		Bitmap	**Grayscale**	**RGB**	**CMYK**
4″ × 5″	120 ppi	36 KB	282 KB	844 KB	1.10 MB
	220 ppi	119 KB	946 KB	2.77 MB	3.69 MB
	300 ppi	220 KB	1.72 MB	5.15 MB	6.87 MB
	400 ppi	391 KB	3.05 MB	9.16 MB	12.2 MB
	600 ppi	879 KB	6.87 MB	20.6 MB	27.5 MB
8″ × 10″	120 ppi	141 KB	1.10 MB	3.30 MB	4.39 MB
	220 ppi	473 KB	3.69 MB	11.1 MB	14.8 MB
	300 ppi	879 KB	6.87 MB	20.6 MB	27.5 MB
	400 ppi	1.53 MB	12.2 MB	36.6 MB	48.8 MB

Goodheart-Willcox Publisher

Figure 5-21. File sizes that will result from scanning images of different sizes at various resolutions in the common formats: bitmap, grayscale, RGB color, and CMYK color.

Scaling an Image

The proper scale for an image in a design is easy to determine, as industry software allows you easily to fit the image to the appropriate box. See **Figure 5-22**. While working with digital images makes this process a few simple steps, it is important to realize that some of the "automatic" sizing options will create some unexpected and unsavory results. Selecting either of the proportional options keeps the ratio of the image the same. Selecting any of the other options will cause anamorphic scaling where the image is no longer proportional to the original. It is also important to consider what the scaling of the image does to the resolution. See Chapter 9.

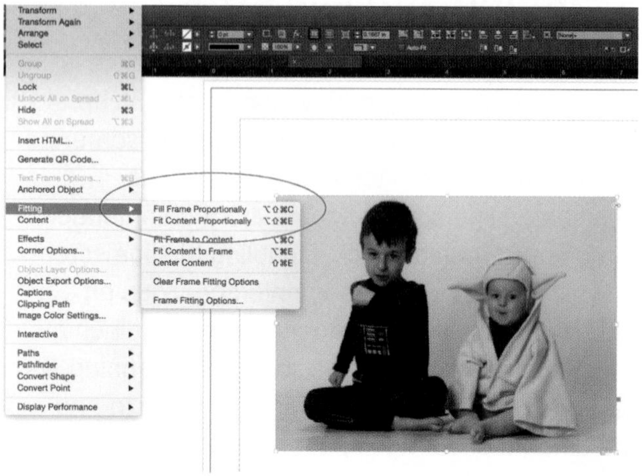

Goodheart-Willcox Publisher

Figure 5-22. Software allows you to fit an image to a picture box. Selecting one of the proportional options will keep your image from distorting.

Screens

Digital images are converted to a series of dots for printing called *halftone dots*. The size of the dots is determined by ***screens***. Screens are measured in lines per inch in conventional units and lines per centimeter in metric units. In conventional units, screen sizes below 75 lines are considered to be coarse, while sizes above 150 lines are considered fine. The greater the number of lines, the finer the screen. See **Figure 5-23**.

Conventional screen sizes can be converted to metric units by dividing the number of lines per inch by 2.54. To convert metric screen sizes to lines per inch, multiply the number of lines per centimeter by 2.54. A comparison of conventional and metric screen sizes is shown in **Figure 5-24**.

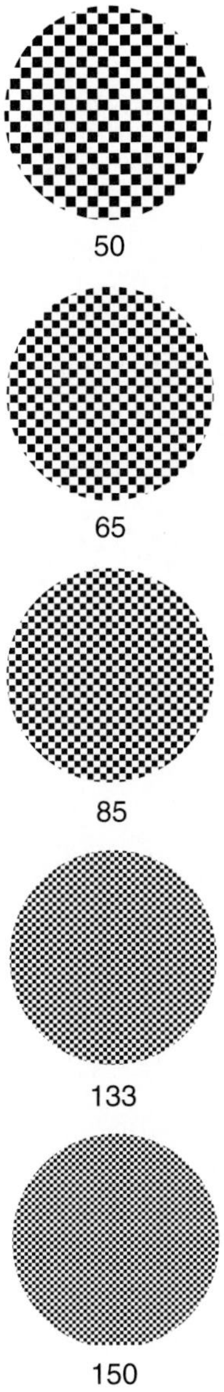

Goodheart-Willcox Publisher

Figure 5-23. Screens used to make dotted halftones. Larger screen numbers mean finer screens.

Screen Rulings per Inch	Screen Rulings per Centimeter
50	20
65	26
75	30
100	40
120	48
133	54
150	60
175	70
200	80

Goodheart-Willcox Publisher

Figure 5-24. Screen sizes compared in conventional and metric units.

Think Green

ISO 14001

The International Organization for Standardization has also created standards based on the idea of reducing the impact organizations and industry have on the environment. The ISO 14001 standard deals with several aspects of environmental management. For example, this standard covers the general stages of controlling environmental impact by listing ways to set goals within an organization. While it does not specify how to reduce waste and VOC emissions, it does list guidelines for managing an organizational plan to reduce environmental impact. This standard is not required in the United States, although several companies are working toward certification.

Screen Angle Measurement

When printing using a traditional halftone dot, different ***screen angles*** are used for each primary color for four-color printing. Screen angles are measured in degrees. A scale giving the screen angles for each color is shown in **Figure 5-25**.

To print properly, each separation must have the correct screen angle: a 45° screen angle is normally used for black, a 75° angle for magenta, a 90° angle for yellow, and a 105° angle for cyan. The line patterns on each screen have a specific angular relationship that creates a rosette and prevents a ***moiré pattern***.

Tint Percentages

A ***screen tint*** provides a smaller dot that represents a tone percentage of a solid color. See **Figure 5-26**.

A 10% tint, for example, would result in 90% less ink deposited than an image printed without a screen tint. The resulting image would be very light. A 90% tint would print with 10% less ink and would produce a dark image.

Goodheart-Willcox Publisher

Figure 5-25. Standard screen angles used in offset printing.

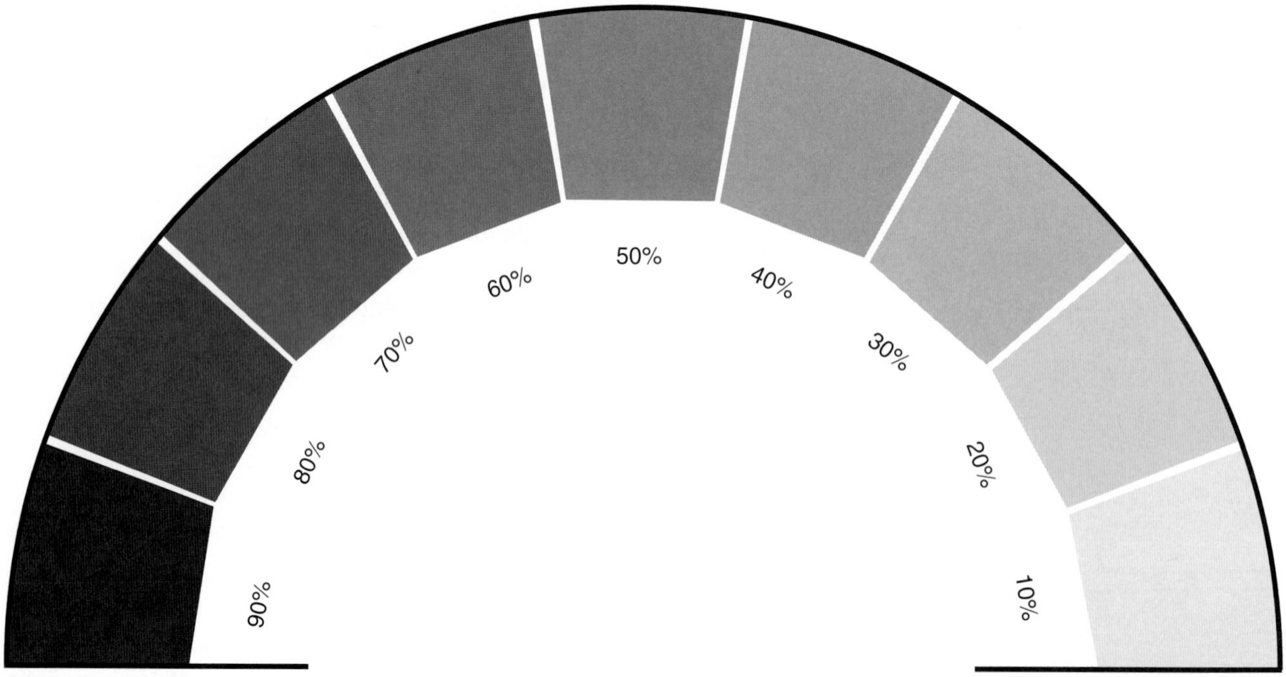

Goodheart-Willcox Publisher

Figure 5-26. Common screen tint percentages. Larger percentages produce a darker screen, while smaller percentages result in a lighter screen.

Grayscale

A ***grayscale*** is a continuous tone strip with different shades of gray ranging from light to dark. It is used for visually gauging film exposure and development during chemical processing. Numerical values along the scale indicate the density of an image. See **Figure 5-27**.

Digital Control Strip

In industry, the digital control strip is called the target and is primarily used as a control device for pre-press proofs. It is also used to monitor and control production printing presses. The target must go through all of the steps required to create and print a product. See **Figure 5-28**.

Densitometer

A ***densitometer*** is a device used to measure the density of an image. See **Figure 5-29**. There are two types of densitometers commonly used in graphic reproduction. One measures the reflection of light; the other measures the transmission of light.

A ***reflection densitometer*** is used to give a reflected light measurement that indicates the tone values of printed materials or photographic prints. A ***transmission densitometer*** is used to measure light passing through a material. Both devices measure the tone range, or contrast, of an image.

A densitometer can be used to determine the correct exposure for making a halftone screen from a photographic print. Measurements are taken to identify the lightest and darkest areas of the print or any other areas needed to calculate exposures.

Spectrophotometer

A ***spectrophotometer*** is a measuring device used to determine color values, such as chromatic value (h*; hue), brightness (L*), and saturation (C*; chroma), with which color can be clearly classified quantitatively in accordance with the color perception of the human eye. It operates on the principle that any color can be described as an additive mixture of spectral colors.

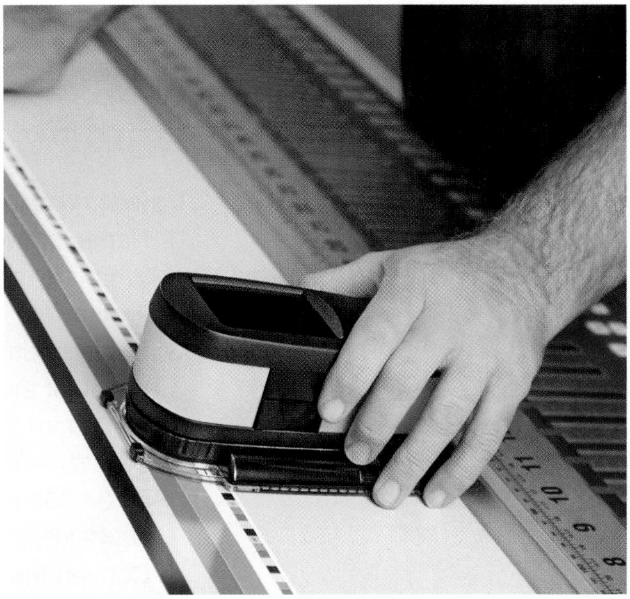

X-Rite

Figure 5-29. A densitometer measures reflected or transmitted light to read the density of an image.

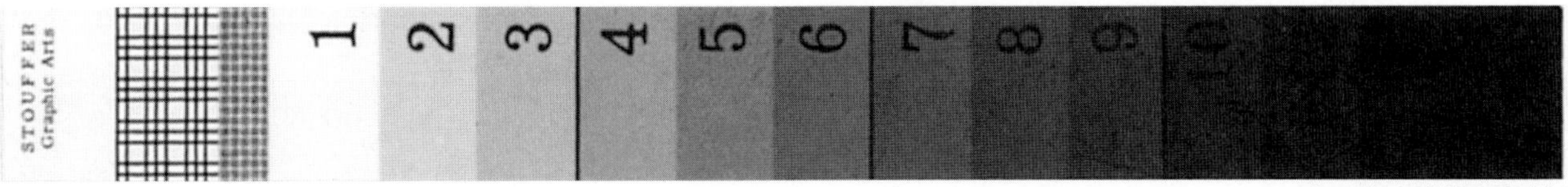

Goodheart-Willcox Publisher

Figure 5-27. A grayscale uses a series of tones to measure image density.

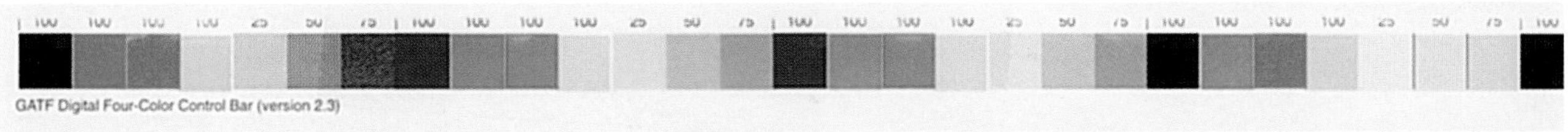

Goodheart-Willcox Publisher

Figure 5-28. A digital control strip.

Summary

- The two most commonly used systems of measurement today are the US Conventional system and the SI Metric system.
- The metric system is the most commonly used system of weights and measures in the world.
- The units of measure most commonly used for sizes of type in English-speaking countries are the point and pica, known as the point system.
- Paper sizes are designated in length and width dimensions and are given in either inches or metric units.
- Most grades of paper are classified by their basis weight. Paper is also measured by its thickness and brightness.
- Desktop publishing systems have taken the place of traditional methods used in operations such as typesetting and color separation.
- Measuring scales, screen tints, and process cameras are used to enlarge or reduce images.

Review Questions

Answer the following questions using the information in this chapter.

1. Name the two most commonly used systems of measurement.
2. What are the standard units for length and mass in the SI Metric system?
3. List five common metric prefixes.
4. Which of the following is an incorrect metric notation?
   A. 33 mm.
   B. 0.39 km.
   C. 34,000 km.
   D. 42 kPa.
5. Convert the following values:
   A. One inch = _____ millimeters
   B. 12 meters = _____ yards
   C. 10 quarts = _____ liters
   D. 12 milliliters = _____ fluid ounces
   E. 400 pounds = _____ kilograms
   F. 25 meters/second = _____ feet/second
   G. 68°F = _____ °C
6. A point measures approximately _____ of an inch.
7. The pica is approximately _____ of an inch.
8. What device is commonly used to measure the point size of type?
9. The amount of vertical space between lines of type is called _____.
10. A ream of bond/book paper consists of _____ sheets.

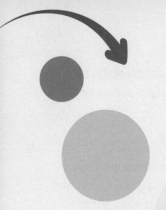

11. Name four common grades of paper.
12. List the three ISO series for paper and envelopes and the uses for each series.
13. What is the *basis weight* of paper?
14. List four components of a typical desktop publishing system.
15. Image resolution is measured in ______ or ______.
16. Screen sizes below 75 lines are considered ______, while sizes above 150 lines are considered _____.
17. A screen angle of _____ degrees is normally used for the color black when making color separations.
18. Why must each color separation screen angle be set differently?
19. A 10% screen tint would result in _____ ink deposited than a 20% tint.
20. Name the two types of densitometers.
21. What measuring device is used to determine color values?

Suggested Activities

1. Using an E gauge, measure the size by matching at six different sizes of the letter *E*.
2. Convert the following linear measurements to metric units: 10 inches, 3 feet, 12 yards, and 60 miles.
3. Look at labels found on paper cartons, cans, tubes, and printing plates and list the US Conventional and metric measurement found on each unit.
4. List the applications of mathematics in the printing industry.

Chapter 6

Typography

Learning Objectives

After studying this chapter, you will be able to:

- Identify the basic terms used to describe type.
- Summarize the development of type styles.
- Summarize seven typeface classifications.
- Explain the difference between a family, a series, and a font of type.
- Identify the common type sizes and units used in typography.
- Explain the factors that contribute to the legibility of type.
- Describe how typography has changed with the advent of web browsers.

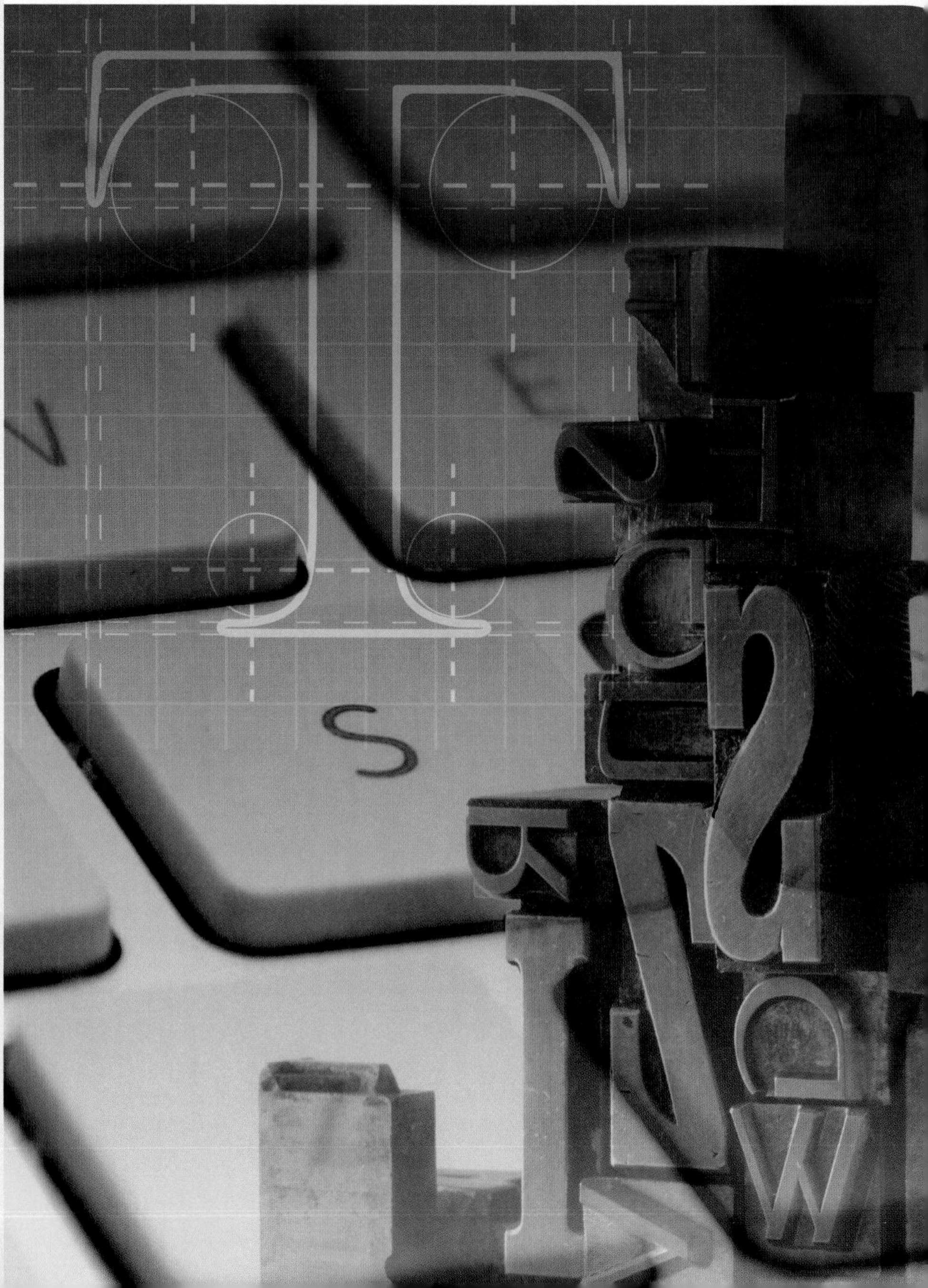

Goodheart-Willcox Publisher

Important Terms

body type
brightness
centered text
character
composition depth
concordant
conflict
contrast
cursive
decorative typeface
definition
display type
display typeface
em dash
en dash
eye span
fillet
flush left
flush right
font
font stack
foundry type
geometric sans serif
glyph
grotesque
heavy element
humanist sans serif
hyphen
ink darkness
italic type
justify
kerning
kerning pair
legibility
letterform
letterspacing
ligature
light element
line length
linespacing
manuscript
Modern Roman typefaces
monospace
neo-grotesque
oblique
Old English
oldstyle
Oldstyle Roman typeface
opacity
orphan
pi character
point size
Roman typeface
sans serif
script typeface
sentence case
serif
set size
small caps
smoothness
Subiaco face
text
title case
tracking
Transitional Roman typeface
type metal
typeface
typeface family
typeface series
typographer
typographer's quote
typography
visibility
web font
web-safe font
widow
wordspacing
x-height

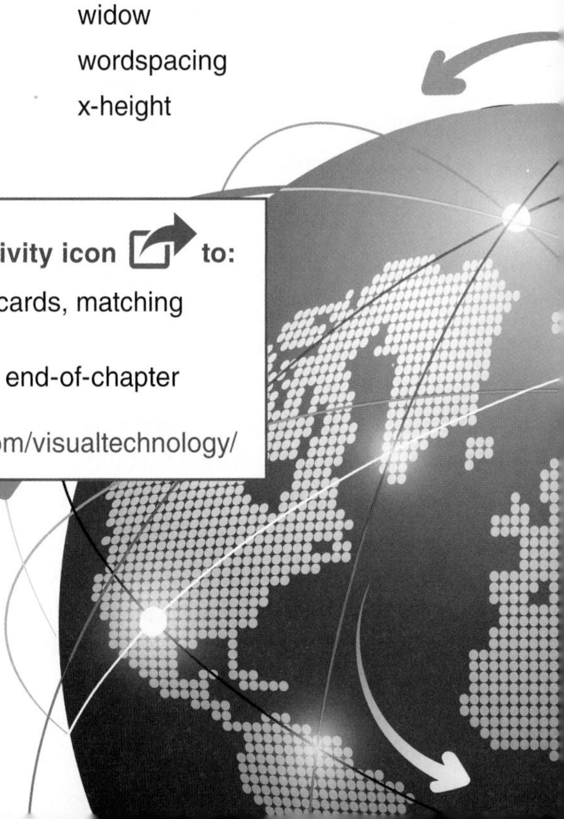

G-WLEARNING.COM

While studying this chapter, look for the activity icon to:

- **Practice** vocabulary terms with e-flash cards, matching activities, and vocabulary game.
- **Reinforce** what you learn by submitting end-of-chapter questions.

www.g-wlearning.com/visualtechnology/

This chapter introduces the role that typefaces play in producing printed images. Typefaces are important, not only to the communication of thoughts, but to the overall appearance or aesthetic characteristics of the printed image. Careful study of this chapter will help you understand the information presented in later chapters.

Typefaces

Typefaces are distinctive visual symbols that are used to compose printed pages on paper or another substrate. ***Characters*** are the individual visual symbols in a particular typeface. An assortment of characters, such as letters, numerals, punctuation marks, and special symbols, is necessary to put words into print.

Just as every person has a name, every typeface has a name. It would be very difficult to identify specific typefaces without names, just as it would be difficult to identify individual human beings if there were no names. There are over 150,000 typefaces available to the designer, and more being added every day.

Typography

Typography is the art of expressing ideas in printed form through the selection of appropriate typefaces. The ***typographer*** must determine how the manuscript should be expressed in type, as well as other details of reproduction and physical format.

For example, if the typographer is selecting a typeface to use in an advertisement for a new electronic device, he or she would *not* select an old-fashioned-appearing type style with ornate, curly letters. A modern, clean-looking type would be more appropriate and representative.

Typography has undergone some of the most radical changes of the graphic communication process. From original calligraphy through modern digital typesetting, the evolution of beautifully crafted typefaces has been dynamic. With the advent of desktop publishing and the move to electronic output, typefaces were forced through a strict review process to meet industry criteria for successful reproduction. Newer digital technology, self-publishing, and better quality desktop printers have eliminated the need for such stringent control. As a result, many of the new typefaces introduced daily are inferior in quality from a technical and aesthetic perspective.

Typeface Terminology

The alphabet used for English and most European languages consists of only 26 letters. However, since there are thousands of typefaces, the letters of that alphabet are represented in many different ways. To be able to differentiate among the various typefaces, you must understand the basic terms relating to type and know how typeface characteristics affect the printed image.

Each of these different characteristics affects the structure of the type and gives each typeface a unique look. The combination of the details will affect the final printed image.

The fundamental terms relating to a typeface and characters are shown in **Figure 6-1**. They include:

- **Ascender.** The part of a letter that extends above the x-height (defined on the next page).
- **Ascent line.** The imaginary line that extends along the top of the ascenders.
- **Baseline.** An imaginary line drawn along the base of x-height letters. Everything is measured from this line.
- **Bowl.** The fully closed part of a letter, such as in the letters *d* and *o*.
- **Cap line.** The imaginary line that extends along the top of uppercase letters. It is not always the same height as the ascent line.
- **Counter.** The open space of a closed or partially closed letter, such as in the letters *p* and *x*.
- **Descender.** The part of a letter that extends below the baseline.
- **Descent line.** The imaginary line that extends along the bottom of the descenders.
- **Eye.** The counter area of the lowercase *e*.
- **Ligature.** Two or more letters that are joined to form one glyph or character. These can sometimes be specific sounds or used for aesthetic reasons. Common examples are *tt*, *ti*, *fl*, *fi*, *ir*, and *AE*.

- **Lowercase.** Body letters; abbreviated as *lc*.
- **Point size.** A vertical measurement used to identify or specify the size of a typeface.

Loosely based on the measurement from the top of the ascender to the bottom of the descender, type size was originally determined by the em space, or square of the point size defined. For example, if the point size is 12, the em space would be 12 × 12 points. With the enormous array of typefaces available, this measurement is more arbitrary and varies with each type style.

- **Serif.** The thickened tips or short finishing-off strokes at the top and bottom of a character.
- **Set width.** The distance across a character from side to side.
- **Stem.** The vertical part of the character.
- **Stress.** The slant or tilt of a character. Also known as *axis*.
- **Stroke.** The thickness of a line forming a character element.
- **Terminal.** The end of a stroke that does not have a serif.
- **Tittle.** The dot over the lowercase *j* or *i*.
- **Uppercase.** The capital letters, usually abbreviated as *caps*.
- **x-height.** The distance from top to bottom of the lowercase *x*.

Later sections of this chapter and other chapters will discuss these terms in greater detail. You will learn how these typeface components and characteristics can be used to alter the form and function of words, sentences, and the general "look" of the printed image.

Type Style Development

Throughout history, humans have strived to perfect the art of making written or printed images. The scribes of medieval Europe produced hundreds of beautiful and masterful letter forms as they hand-lettered book pages. The scribes developed very beautiful lettering, making each character into an art form. Across Europe, the style of the letters varied from country to country, or sometimes even from region to region within a country.

When the process of mechanical printing from individual pieces of type was introduced in Europe in the fifteenth century, typographers modeled their letters on those drawn by scribes. Each letter was cut by hand from hard metal to form a punch, which then was driven into softer metal to make a mold. The mold, in turn, was used to produce many copies of the letter. Molten ***type metal*** (an alloy of lead, tin, and antimony) was poured into the mold to form an individual piece of type that could be aligned with type containing other letters to form words and sentences. **Figure 6-2** shows a piece of ***foundry type*** produced by the modern version of this method. Although it is used only in a few specialized applications today, foundry type was the major form of type used for printing from the 1400s through the mid-1900s.

Printing methods introduced in the past 60 years have given rise to photographic and electronic

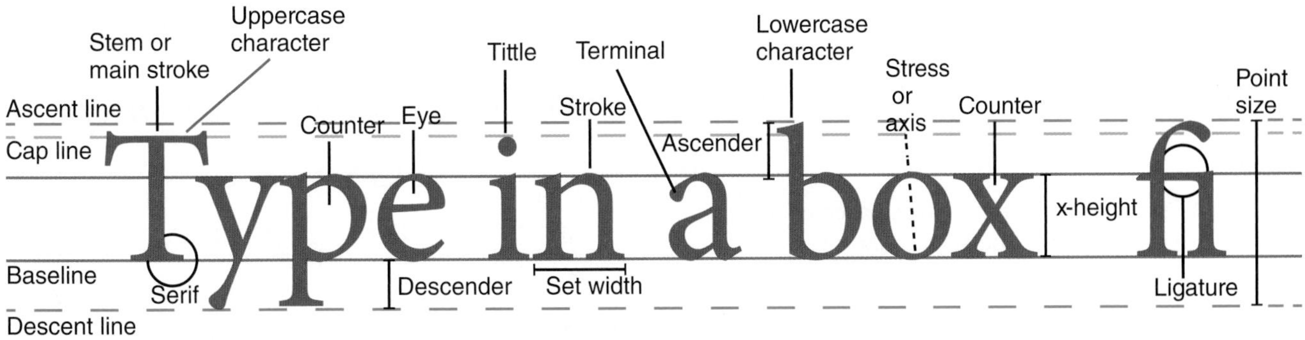

Goodheart-Willcox Publisher

Figure 6-1. Anatomy of a typeface.

Goodheart-Willcox Publisher

Figure 6-2. Foundry type, cast in metal, was the major form of type used by printers for more than 500 years. Ink was applied to the raised surface of the letter and transferred to paper to form an image.

methods of typesetting. These methods, which will be described later, also made it easier to design and produce new typefaces. Many of these new faces are radically different from those that have been widely used for many years.

Black Letter

The ***manuscript*** style of lettering used by the scribes of Germany, France, Holland, and other countries was similar to the type style known today as ***Old English***, also called *black letter* or *text*, **Figure 6-3**. This letter style was the basis for development of the earliest metal type, since the typographer or printer typically imitated the manuscript style common to a locality or geographic area.

Graphic Arts Display of Fine Printing Reveals
Skillful Arrangement of Type

ATF

Figure 6-3. Black letter is a style of type based on hand lettering done by scribes in European countries.

Development of the Roman Type Style

As the art of printing developed, changes in type styles also increased. This was especially true in Italy, where many of the German printers had migrated. The German black letter type styles gradually were replaced by a more delicate and lighter type style that became known as the *Roman typeface*. Several books were printed in an early version of the Roman face known as the ***Subiaco face***.

A major figure in the development of the Roman type style was Nicolas Jenson. Jenson was a master engraver for the French government. He learned the new craft of printing in Mainz, Germany, and later moved to Italy.

Jenson is credited with designing and cutting the Roman letter forms that first appeared in printed pieces in 1469 and 1470. His designs, **Figure 6-4**, were based on the letters cut into stone monuments by the ancient Romans. Since the letters on the monuments were all capitals, Jenson developed Roman lowercase letters that would merge readily into word forms. This was significant, since we recognize words by their shapes. The Jenson designs were the models used by type designers for hundreds of years. Nicolas Jenson is credited with printing about 150 books during his 10 years in Italy.

Jenson followed the traditions of the manuscript scribe in designing his lowercase letters. When enlarged, these letters revealed the feeling of the pen-drawn letter on a parchment surface. Each letter could be considered independently, yet they merged into the identity of the word.

ABCDEFGHIJKLMNOPQR
STUVWXYZ
abcdefghijklmnopqrstuvwxyz

Goodheart-Willcox Publisher

Figure 6-4. Nicolas Jenson modified Roman letters and developed a lowercase alphabet so that it would more readily form words. This is a modern version of his typeface.

Oldstyle, a subset of the Roman typefaces, included thick and thin stroke ***serifs*** that visually and smoothly merged into the main strokes. The letters are round and open. Many other designers produced type styles in Italy during the same period. The slanted italic type, modeled on a form of handwriting, was developed and first used by Aldus Manutius, a printer in Venice.

The black letter, Roman, and italic type styles were used universally in Europe for two centuries. For a time, black letter was dominant in Germany, and the Roman face was used primarily in Italy. Eventually, however, Roman became the principal letter style used in all countries except Germany.

Modern Typefaces and Typographers

As noted, the early type styles were adapted from hand-drawn or stone-carved letters. By the 1700s, however, the emphasis changed to producing typefaces by copying from those styles that already existed, rather than working from original sources. Aesthetics were no longer an important design factor. Types became thinner and lines became much sharper.

The decline in the quality of type design throughout Europe and England continued through much of the 1800s. The decline was reflected in the poorly printed books of the era.

In 1890, William Morris, an English architect, artist, and poet set out to demonstrate that books could again be beautiful. His interest brought about the revival of many early typefaces, such as Jenson, Garamond, Janson, and Caslon. These faces are the basis for many of the typefaces used today in book publication.

Influential Typographers

Claude Garamond, a French printer, was influenced by Nicholas Jenson's Roman typeface, but designed a more elegant and refined face that was typically French. Garamond's 1540 design was redesigned in 1919 in the United States. The redesign resulted in a light-lined, more open design that would print more clearly.

The Janson typeface of today is a recutting of the face issued in about the year 1675 by Anton Janson (not to be confused with Nicolas *Jenson*). Janson modified the manuscript letter by lightening the lines for better printing on a rough-surfaced stock.

Also designed for printing on rough stock was the typeface issued by William Caslon in England in about 1722. Caslon's typeface was an immediate success. The design by Caslon continued the trend toward lighter lines and more open design for better printing.

The English printer John Baskerville developed a typeface that is considered the beginning of the transition from Oldstyle with letters based on manuscript to modern letters designed solely for printing. Known as transitional, these serifs maintained their emphases on thickness and thinness, but were also gracefully bracketed to be suitable for printing on smooth paper. Baskerville established a paper mill, type foundry, and printing office in Birmingham, England, and conducted extensive experiments with type and paper from 1750 to 1758. Baskerville's principle of considering type, paper, ink, and presswork together was the basis of today's planning of a printed job.

Modern typefaces evolved from transitional. With much greater variation in thickness and thinness, the serifs are horizontal and the transitions more dramatic.

Around 1780, François-Ambroise Didot developed the point system of measuring type. Based on a value of 1/72 of the pre-metric inch, the point became the standard unit of measure for type.

Another widely used type style was designed by Giambattista Bodoni, an Italian printer active in the late 1700s and early 1800s. Bodoni's typeface had greater differences between the light and heavy elements than any other face at that time, and is considered to be a modern Roman typeface. Bodoni typefaces used today show extreme differences between light and heavy elements. The typeface known as *Bodoni Book* has less pronounced contrast between elements, and is closer to Bodoni's earlier designs.

Contemporary Typefaces

Contemporary typefaces are primarily the contributions of the twentieth century, and can be divided into three groups. First, there are the modern versions of the basic book faces of the early printers, as described in the preceding section. Second, there are the modifications of the basic book faces made for newspapers. Third, there are the many new display faces. The substantial increase in the number of typefaces paralleled the rapid growth of advertising and commercial printing during the first half of the twentieth century.

Today, tens of thousands of faces are in existence. While this number seems large, think of the carpenter or auto technician who keeps a large chest of tools so the right one will be available when needed. In the same way, a typographer needs many tools so he or she can choose the correct typeface for a specific job.

Sometimes, typefaces will look very much alike, yet have different names. In the United States, typefaces generally cannot be copyrighted. Fonts that qualify as computer software are protected by copyright, but it is the software, not the artistic design, that is covered. Therefore, it is possible for a designer to change a typeface slightly, give the style a new name, and not be in violation of a copyright. Remember that different countries have different copyright laws as they apply to typefaces.

Typeface Classifications

There are several different typeface classifications. Discussed below are seven typeface classifications, including Roman, slab serif, sans serif, display, script, ornamental, and italic.

Roman or Serif

The ***Roman typefaces***, or *serif typefaces*, are numerous in number and are the most widely used. The characteristics commonly associated with Roman types are the contrast between the ***heavy elements*** and ***light elements***, and the use of the serifs.

Roman typefaces are further classified into three groups: Oldstyle, Transitional, and Modern. These are shown in **Figure 6-5**.

Oldstyle or Humanist

The ***Oldstyle Roman typefaces***, or *humanist typefaces*, have a rugged appearance with relatively little contrast between heavy and light elements. Based on the handlettering of scribes, they appear to be drawn with a wedge-tipped pen. The ***fillets*** of the serifs, or where two fillets meet, are curved, and there is usually a diagonal stress. Oldstyle letters look better as words, which is why typefaces such as Caslon and Garamond were typically used for book text matter.

Transitional

Transitional Roman typefaces are a remodeling of Oldstyle typefaces. Greater contrast is evident between the heavy and light elements. The characters were also wider than the equivalent Oldstyle characters. John Baskerville improved on the Caslon typeface and produced *Baskerville*, the first typeface used to print on smooth paper. The Oldstyle characters were designed to print *into* thick, rough paper, rather than *onto* the surface of thinner and smoother stock.

Modern

The most distinguishing feature of ***Modern Roman typefaces***, first designed by Bodoni in 1789, is the increased contrast between the very

Garamond
Caslon
Roman Oldstyle

Baskerville
Times New Roman
Transitional Roman

Bernhard Modern
Didot
Modern Roman

Goodheart-Willcox Publisher

Figure 6-5. Roman typefaces are classified into groups of Oldstyle, Transitional, and Modern. The differences in stroke weights and serifs are shown.

thin, light elements and heavy elements, creating a more dramatic form. As seen in **Figure 6-6**, the Bodoni typeface has long ascenders and descenders, and the serifs are straight lines without fillets. More mechanical in appearance, Modern typefaces were created for use on smoother paper. The letters have a vertical stress.

Goodheart-Willcox Publisher

Figure 6-6. Bodoni is an example of a Modern Roman typeface with extreme contrast in strokes.

Egyptian or Slab Serif

Egyptian, or slab serif, typefaces are usually formed with strokes of equal weight, like sans serif types, but with finishing-off strokes added. With little to no transition, the shape of the serif is square or block-like, and the serif has the same weight as the main portion of the letter face, **Figure 6-7**.

Goodheart-Willcox Publisher

Figure 6-7. Slab serif typefaces usually have strokes of equal weight.

Sans Serif

Sans in French means without. Therefore, the classification ***sans serif*** is used for typefaces without serifs. This typeface classification is second only to Roman in popularity today.

The following are categories of sans serif typefaces. See examples in **Figure 6-8**.

Grotesque

Having become popular in the late nineteenth century in printed pieces, this new form was called ***grotesque***. The term got its name because of the dramatic departure from years of traditional serif typography, and should not be misinterpreted to mean something unsightly. As the earliest sans serif typefaces, grotesque typefaces often appear to be similar to their serif brothers with the serifs cut off. The letters had varying stroke weights with awkward weight distribution and many irregular curves.

Neo-Grotesque

Evolved from the grotesque classification, ***neo-grotesque*** type was created by modern designers. This classification has very limited contrast in the strokes, and the terminals are straight. In 1957, Swiss developer Max Miedinger of the Haas Type Foundry released the typeface Neue Haas Grotesk. To market this typeface more effectively, Haas rebranded it in 1960 to what we know today as Helvetica. This is unquestionably the most popular typeface of all time, even sparking

Goodheart-Willcox Publisher

Figure 6-8. Sans serif typefaces are broken into four categories: grotesque, neo-grotesque, transitional, and geometric.

an iconic full-length documentary film, *Helvetica*, directed by Gary Hustwit.

Humanist Sans Serif

As with its serif counterpart, the ***humanist sans serif*** bases its shape on the calligraphic contrast in strokes and axes. Because the proportions are influenced by the Roman serifs, they often have a two-story lowercase *a* and *g*, setting them apart from their neo-grotesque brothers.

Geometric Sans Serif

As their name implies, ***geometric sans serif*** typefaces are built on geometric shapes. Rather than following patterns from early grotesques or calligraphic influences, their characters often share rounded or very rectangular glyphs with little or no stroke contrast.

Display or Decorative

Display typefaces, or ***decorative typefaces***, are used for a wide variety of instances where the primary intent is to command special attention, **Figure 6-9**. Sometimes referred to as *novelty*, these typefaces must be used sparingly and should be carefully chosen to express a mood or provide a specific appearance for a theme or an occasion. Each style has individuality and is suited for a particular situation. These faces are not intended to be used as body copy.

As many of these typefaces often are inexpensive or free, they are not technically as advanced or comprehensive as traditional serif or sans serif typefaces. Display types do not always contain complete sets of characters and are often not drawn well for scaling purposes.

Script or Cursive

Both script and cursive typefaces are designed to simulate handwriting. The distinction between them is whether the individual letters in a word are joined or not. The letters in a ***script typeface*** are joined; letters in a ***cursive*** face are not. See **Figure 6-10**. The contrast of characters varies with the typeface design. Like text typefaces, script and cursive typefaces are used primarily for special effects. They are used for headlines, announcements, invitations, and letterheads. Since they are hard to read when copy length is more than a sentence or two, script and cursive types are seldom used for setting a full printed page or a large block of body copy.

Goodheart-Willcox Publisher

Figure 6-9. Decorative typefaces are intended to draw your attention. They are normally used for headlines in advertisements and similar applications as initial caps or for a special highlight.

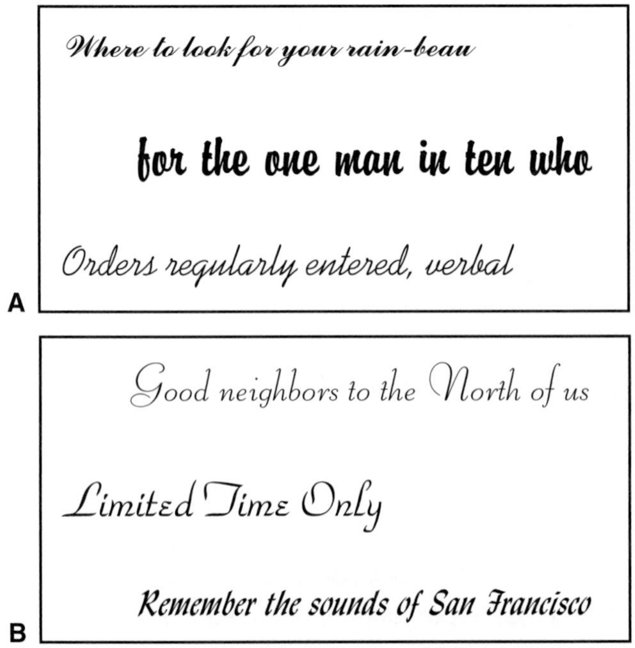

Goodheart-Willcox Publisher

Figure 6-10. Script typefaces have joined letters; cursive letters are separate. A—Examples of script typefaces. B—Examples of cursive styles.

Ornamental

Each and every typeface is comprised of a collection of ***glyphs***, or parts, that together make the details of that particular type unique. Each face contains a set of characters that may include numbers, punctuation, and other symbols.

Some typefaces are made up completely of different symbols. Ornamental typefaces are often referred to as dingbats, pi, pictorial, cartographer, or simply ornaments. These typefaces contain unique and distinctive glyphs. Some are used for specific kinds of documents such as math and maps, and others are simply used for ornamentation. See **Figure 6-11**.

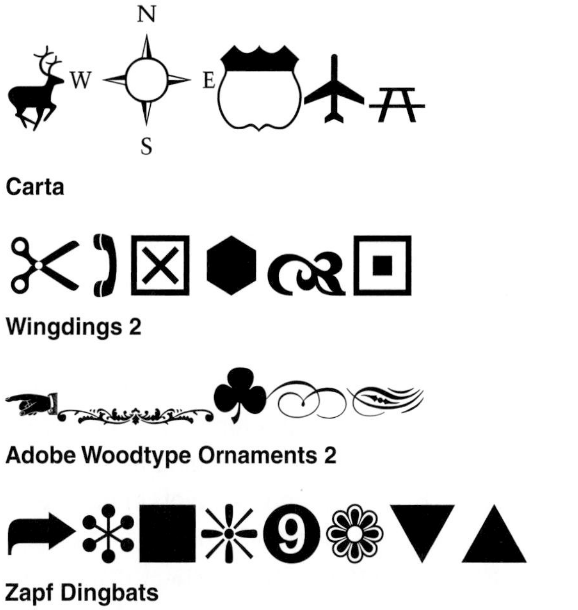

Goodheart-Willcox Publisher

Figure 6-11. Ornamental type consists of characters that are pictorial, iconic, symbolic, or decorative swashes.

Italic or Oblique

Based on the cursive format of calligraphic handwriting, ***italic type*** got its name because it was historically designed in Italy. Italic type is slanted, as opposed to Roman type, which is straight up and down. However, most Roman faces have an italic companion. While true italic characters are slanted to the right, they are also drawn from scratch and have unique details and characteristics separate from their Roman counterpart, **Figure 6-12**. More common in sans serif versions, the slanted version is simply the standard type at a 12° angle. These are called ***oblique***.

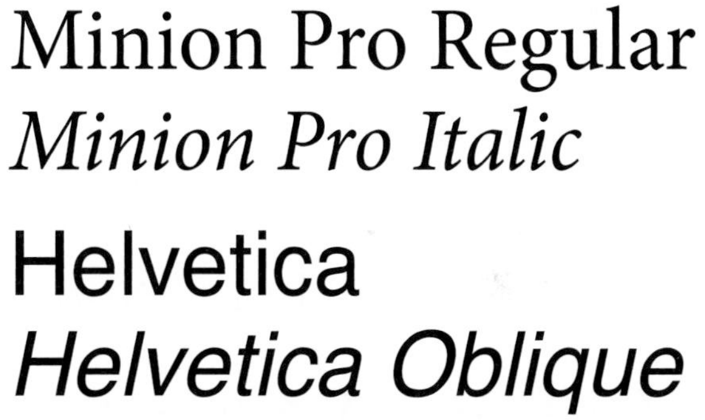

Goodheart-Willcox Publisher

Figure 6-12. An italic is a unique, drawn, and slanted companion version of a Roman typeface, while oblique is the Roman typeface tilted at a 12° angle.

Typeface Families, Series, and Fonts

In addition to the classifications discussed so far, typefaces can be grouped by specific style of type. The term associated with a given style is called *family*. The total range of sizes of one type style of a given font is called a *type series*. A *font* is the complete set of letters, figures, punctuation marks, special characters, and ligatures contained in a typeface.

Typeface Family

A ***typeface family*** consists of the variations of one style of type, **Figure 6-13**. The design elements of the characters set one family apart from another. Even though some typefaces are very similar in appearance, this does not make them part of the

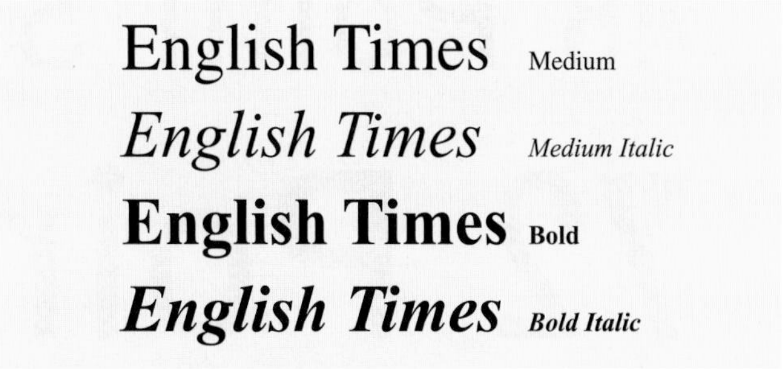

Goodheart-Willcox Publisher

Figure 6-13. A type family is made up of all the variations within one style of type, such as different weights or stresses.

same family. As an example, Garamond is one family, and Caslon is another, even though their design is virtually indistinguishable.

Every variation of the designated typeface style becomes a part of that family. Knowledge of the variations in character widths and weights within a family is important to working effectively with type.

Typeface Series

Historically, a ***typeface series*** is the range of sizes of each typeface in a family, **Figure 6-14**. The common type sizes used in printing are 6, 8, 10, 12, 14, 18, 24, 36, 48, 60, and 72 point. In traditional relief printing, type in sizes 96 points and larger was made from wood rather than metal, **Figure 6-15**.

With the introduction of phototypesetters in the 1960s, a wider variety of sizes previously uncommon to the relief process became available, such as 7-, 9-, and 11-point. Modern software for electronic (computer-based) page assembly has made it possible to generate typefaces in virtually any size needed, even in hundredths-of-a-point increments. This can be a major advantage in design and copyfitting.

Goodheart-Willcox Publisher

Figure 6-15. Type over 96 points used for letterpress printing was traditionally made from wood.

Goodheart-Willcox Publisher

Figure 6-14. A typeface series is a full range of sizes of one typeface.

Type Font

A ***font*** consists of all the characters, such as letters, numerals, punctuation marks, and symbols, that make up a specific typeface in a specific size. For example, Helvetica is a typeface family, Helvetica Bold is a typeface, and 12-point Helvetica Bold is a font.

When applied to foundry type, where each character is on a separate piece of metal, "font" has a somewhat different meaning. As shown in **Figure 6-16**, a foundry type font consists of different quantities of each character in one size and style of type. This is necessary because the individual characters are physically assembled into words, **Figure 6-17**. Enough copies of each character must be available to make up a number of words.

The kinds and total number of characters differ from font to font. While most will include a full set of capital and lowercase letters, the numerals 0 to 9, and the usual punctuation marks, they often will

Goodheart-Willcox Publisher

Figure 6-16. A foundry type font consists of a full assortment of characters for one size typeface. The varying number of characters is based on frequency of use; more *e* characters are needed than *x* or *z* characters.

Goodheart-Willcox Publisher

Figure 6-17. Setting copy in foundry type involves selecting individual pieces of type and assembling the letters in a holder called a *stick*. This method was used by printers for hundreds of years.

Academic Link

Notation and Conversion of Picas and Points

Pierre Fournier le Jeune developed the first standardized system of typography measurement in the early 1700s. This system was further refined in the late 1770s by Françoise-Ambroise Didot with the addition of points as a unit of measure within picas. This measurement standard is still in use today.

- 1 point is 0.01383″, with 12 points in 1 pica.
- 1 pica is 0.166″, with 6 picas in approximately 1 inch.

Layout and design software programs note pica values as a whole number with a lowercase "p," which is followed by the points value. Using this notation style, a measurement of 4 picas and 5 points is presented as 4p5.

Convert each of the following notations to the equivalent measurement in inches.

1. 3p6
2. 10p2
3. 2p3
4. 7p4
5. 11p1

differ in the symbols and special characters they include. For example, some fonts include ***ligatures***, which are joined letter combinations such as *fi*, *ff*, *fl*, *ffi*, and *ffl*. Other fonts might include ***small caps***, which are capital letters smaller than the normal-sized caps of those fonts. See **Figure 6-18**.

In fonts for computer or phototypesetting, such symbols as stars, asterisks, arrows, percent signs, or checkmarks are known as ***pi characters***. In foundry type, such special characters are called *sorts* or *dingbats*.

For more discussion of fonts, see Chapter 9, *Digital Prepress and Production*.

Measuring Type

Measuring type is challenging because of the large amount and variety of typefaces available, and also the very subtle differences in some key elements that have traditionally been used to measure. However, measuring type remains an important part of the

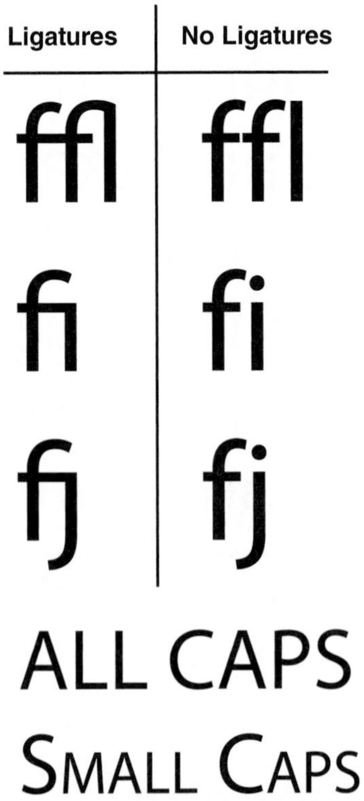

Goodheart-Willcox Publisher

Figure 6-18. Ligatures are two or more characters combined to form one glyph that is more aesthetically pleasing. Small caps use a combination of full size capital letters and a smaller version of the capital letters.

designer's capabilities to match existing type. It is far more efficient and effective to have an idea of the size before you begin a project than it is to guess and use the trial-and-error method.

Points and Picas

The two principal units of measure used in the graphic communications industry are the point and the pica. Points and picas were described in Chapter 5.

Points are used to measure the vertical height of a line of type, while picas are historically used to measure ***line lengths*** and ***composition depth***. The ***point size*** of type is based roughly on the distance from the top of the ascenders to the bottom of the descenders, as shown in **Figure 6-19**. The point size of type should not be confused with the ***x-height***, which is the height of the lowercase *x*.

Goodheart-Willcox Publisher

Figure 6-19. The point size of type is measured from the top of the ascenders to the bottom of the descenders.

The size of type is difficult to distinguish when in print because two typefaces of the same point size may have x-heights that are quite different. The letters of one typeface may appear to be larger or smaller than the letters of the other, but lines set in the two faces would require the same amount of vertical space. See **Figure 6-20**.

Type sizes that range from 4-point through 12-point are usually referred to as ***text*** or ***body type***. Sizes above 12-point are referred to as ***display type***.

Ems and Ens

The em is a unit of printer's measure equal to the height and width of the capital M in the given size of type. For example, in 12-point type, an em would measure 12 points wide and 12 points high; in 18-point type, an em would be 18 points wide and 18 points high. In foundry type, an em quad was used to indent the beginning of a paragraph. Sentences set in foundry type were separated by spaces that were half an em quad in width. That spacing element was called an en quad. See **Figure 6-21**.

Goodheart-Willcox Publisher

Figure 6-20. Typefaces of the same point size may vary greatly in body height, as shown by the lowercase letters here. These typefaces are all set in 36-point.

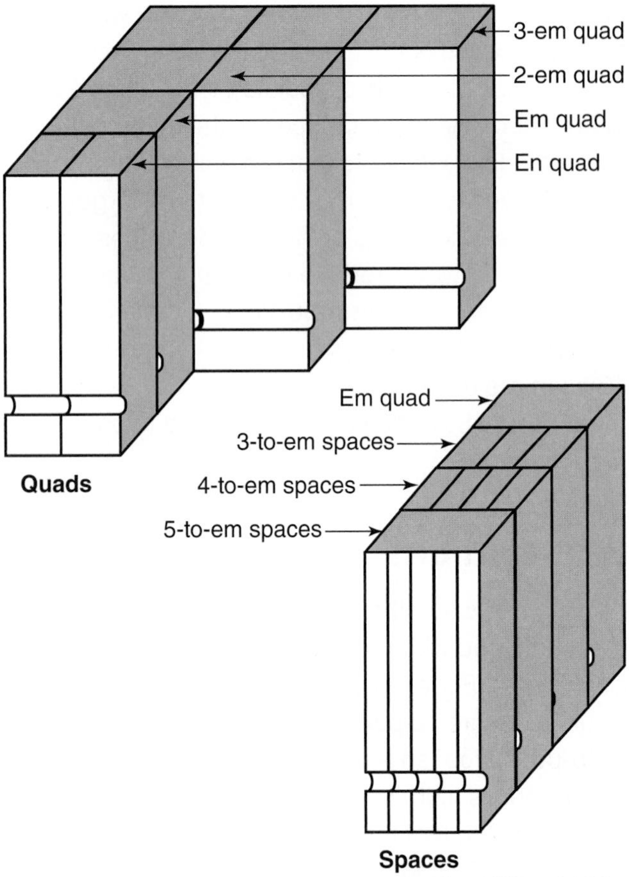

Goodheart-Willcox Publisher

Figure 6-21. Foundry type used blocks called quads for spacing. Blocks narrower than the en quad were referred to as spaces.

Set Size

As you learned, point size refers to the height of the type character. ***Set size***, or set width, refers to the width of a character. Electronic composition has made it possible to change the set width of characters and the words they make up.

When the character is electronically expanded or condensed, the height is not changed, **Figure 6-22**. For example, 12-point type with a 12-set would be normal. If 12-point is programmed as "8-set," the type would be condensed. If 12-point is programmed for a "14-set," the type would be expanded. Although width of the character is changed, spacing between characters remains the same.

THIS IS 12 POINT WITH 8 SET.

THIS IS 12 POINT WITH 12 SET.

THIS IS 12 POINT WITH 14 SET.

Goodheart-Willcox Publisher

Figure 6-22. Set size is a modern term that refers to width of characters. Computerized typesetting allows letters to be condensed or expanded easily.

Letterspacing and Wordspacing

Letterspacing refers to a change of spacing between letters, while ***wordspacing*** involves varying the spacing between words, **Figure 6-23**. When carefully done, increasing or decreasing the space between letters and words can improve the legibility of type. It is also possible to increase or decrease the copy length to fit an allocated space by altering the letterspacing or wordspacing.

Tracking

Tracking is a feature in typography that refers to a consistent amount of increase or decrease in the space between letters to affect the density in a word, line, or block of text.

Kerning

Kerning is the adjustment of the space between certain characters in the alphabet to improve the appearance and readability of the word. Different typefaces require different kinds of spacing to visually even out the optical white space created by the individual characteristics. With especially large type (72-point or larger) or smaller type (7-point and

Goodheart-Willcox Publisher

Figure 6-23. Letterspacing compared to wordspacing. Letterspacing alters amount of space between each character or letter, while wordspacing changes space between complete words.

under), thoughtful, customized kerning can make the difference in whether or not the text is easily readable. See **Figure 6-24**.

Most authentic typefaces for current computer applications should have built-in ***kerning pairs*** or appropriate customized letterspacing for each font.

Tighten Two letters

Normal Spacing

Tighten Two letters

Kerned

Goodheart-Willcox Publisher

Figure 6-24. Kerning is similar to letterspacing, but changes only spaces between specific letters to improve appearance and readability.

Alignment

Alignment refers to the relationship of a block of text with regard to the page or margin. The four most common kinds of alignment are flush left, flush right, centered, and justified. See **Figure 6-25**.

Flush left alignment is the most common default for most word processing or page assembly applications. The text will maintain an even left margin, and each line will end when a word will not fit in the defined area. That word rolls to the next line, creating a ragged right margin.

Aligning the text with a ***flush right*** margin will give you a ragged left margin. Less common because it is harder to read, flush right is often used when text goes to the left side of an image. See **Figure 6-26**.

Centered text is when each line is centered over the other on a common center point, creating the same amount of space on either side of each line.

Flush Left

Mi, samus exerorerum, utemos illorrum ra acepelessedi adit quam accum et intioribusam et quam volore soluptas dolenis mod modis este experendus qui sam quis etus eum fuga. Ignam aliqui debis et doluptatur am quis ente volest abo. Lorum nobitatur alisqu iatum eiciaerci quaeriam, quam sit fugiam vero moluptae voluptum quiae. Nam inventi cus dolorib ercipitas qui dolorpore, conseri buscime venimperiam enis sit ullaut rati ut aute ipsum, antem atur aligenisqui acilluptat.

Flush Right

Mi, samus exerorerum, utemos illorrum ra acepelessedi adit quam accum et intioribusam et quam volore soluptas dolenis mod modis este experendus qui sam quis etus eum fuga. Ignam aliqui debis et doluptatur am quis ente volest abo. Lorum nobitatur alisqu iatum eiciaerci quaeriam, quam sit fugiam vero moluptae voluptum quiae. Nam inventi cus dolorib ercipitas qui dolorpore, conseri buscime venimperiam enis sit ullaut rati ut aute ipsum, antem atur aligenisqui acilluptat.

Centered

Mi, samus exerorerum, utemos illorrum ra acepelessedi adit quam accum et intioribusam et quam volore soluptas dolenis mod modis este experendus qui sam quis etus eum fuga. Ignam aliqui debis et doluptatur am quis ente volest abo. Lorum nobitatur alisqu iatum eiciaerci quaeriam, quam sit fugiam vero moluptae voluptum quiae. Nam inventi cus dolorib ercipitas qui dolorpore, conseri buscime venimperiam enis sit ullaut rati ut aute ipsum, antem atur aligenisqui acilluptat.

J u s t i f i e d

Mi, samus exerorerum, utemos illorrum ra acepelessedi adit quam accum et intioribusam et quam volore soluptas dolenis mod modis este experendus qui sam quis etus eum fuga. Ignam aliqui debis et doluptatur am quis ente volest abo. Lorum nobitatur alisqu iatum eiciaerci quaeriam, quam sit fugiam vero moluptae voluptum quiae. Nam inventi cus dolorib ercipitas qui dolorpore, conseri buscime venimperiam enis sit ullaut rati ut aute ipsum, antem atur aligenisqui acilluptat.

Goodheart-Willcox Publisher

Figure 6-25. Examples of alignment: flush left, flush right, centered, and justified.

The caption
for this proud
giraffe might
go on the left
side of the
image and it
would work
well as a
flush right
to align with
the image.

Goodheart-Willcox Publisher

Figure 6-26. Flush right copy next to an image.

Letterspacing and wordspacing are used to ***justify*** lines of type so the lines are all equal in length. This combination of both flush left and flush right creates even margins on both sides. The last line of a justified paragraph is generally flush left to keep from having large gaps of white space between the words of that line.

Linespacing or Leading

Linespacing determines the vertical distance separating each line of copy. It is measured in points from one baseline of text to the next baseline of text. This spacing is also called *leading* (pronounced ledding), since lines of hand-set foundry type were separated by strips of lead-based type metal. See **Figure 6-27**.

Proper leading helps the reader's eye to readily separate one line from another. The white space gives the eye better access to the top portions of the lowercase letters. The tops of letters are the more unlike portions, and contribute most to word identity.

Leading also unites a line horizontally. Close word spacing will help to achieve unity in the line. Visibility is increased when extra leading is used on paper with low brightness. The extra leading lightens the tone of the page, and tends to make the type seem larger.

It is also possible to fit copy into a designated area by changing leading. By increasing leading, the copy will take up more space. Decreasing leading does just the opposite.

Widows and Orphans

The terms widow and orphan are often used interchangeably. Neither is desired when formatting your text. A ***widow*** is a single line of text at the end or beginning of a paragraph that is separated from the rest of the paragraph by going to the next column or the next page. An ***orphan*** is a very short word, or part of a word, that forms the final line of a paragraph. The rest of the line is empty. There are various ways to avoid this undesirable amount of white space. The line can be lengthened, the previous line can be shortened by adding or deleting words, or the letterspacing or wordspacing can be changed. See **Figure 6-28**.

Legibility Factors

Legibility, sometimes termed *readability*, is a measure of how difficult or easy it is to read printed matter. When selecting a typeface, legibility is one of the most critical factors.

The major consideration when selecting a typeface is *purpose*, or intent. Content should always drive the typeface selection. If the content is a textbook, for example, legibility should be the aim in selecting a typeface. For an advertisement, the aesthetic characteristics of the type should be given more attention, as it has to work with other elements to convey a message and achieve the goal, which, presumably, is to get people to read the text.

The type you are now reading is what a printer calls *straight matter*. Straight matter is usually below 14-point type. Display type is 14-point type or above and is used as headings and focal point material. Examples of products in which straight matter is used extensively are books, newspapers, magazines, and pamphlets.

Good legibility of the straight matter is the result of a proper combination of type, paper, and ink. It can make reading printed material less tiring to the eyes. Many printed pieces will have thousands of readers of varying ages and physical conditions. This makes good legibility a high priority.

Physical factors that contribute to legibility in the printed pages are visibility, letterforms, definition, type size, line length, space, and leading.

10 point type with 11 point leading

Mi, samus exerorerum, utemos
illorrum ra acepelessedi adit quam 11pt
accum et intioribusam et quam volore 11pt
soluptas dolenis mod modis este experendus qui sam quis etus eum fuga. Ignam aliqui debis et doluptatur am quis ente volest abo. Lorum nobitatur alisquiatum eiciaerci quaeriam, quam sit fugiam vero moluptae voluptum quiae. Nam inventi cus dolorib ercipitas qui dolorpore, conseri buscime venimperiam enis sit ullaut rati ut aute ipsum, antem atur aligenisqui acilluptat.

10 point type with 12 point leading

Mi, samus exerorerum, utemos
illorrum ra acepelessedi adit quam 12 pt
accum et intioribusam et quam volore 12 pt
soluptas dolenis mod modis este experendus qui sam quis etus eum fuga. Ignam aliqui debis et doluptatur am quis ente volest abo. Lorum nobitatur alisquiatum eiciaerci quaeriam, quam sit fugiam vero moluptae voluptum quiae. Nam inventi cus dolorib ercipitas qui dolorpore, conseri buscime venimperiam enis sit ullaut rati ut aute ipsum, antem atur aligenisqui acilluptat.

10 point type with 13 point leading

Mi, samus exerorerum, utemos
illorrum ra acepelessedi adit quam 13 pt
accum et intioribusam et quam volore 13 pt
soluptas dolenis mod modis este experendus qui sam quis etus eum fuga. Ignam aliqui debis et doluptatur am quis ente volest abo. Lorum nobitatur alisquiatum eiciaerci quaeriam, quam sit fugiam vero moluptae voluptum quiae. Nam inventi cus dolorib ercipitas qui dolorpore, conseri buscime venimperiam enis sit ullaut rati ut aute ipsum, antem atur aligenisqui acilluptat.

10 point type with 14 point leading

Mi, samus exerorerum, utemos
illorrum ra acepelessedi adit quam 14 pt
accum et intioribusam et quam volore 14 pt
soluptas dolenis mod modis este experendus qui sam quis etus eum fuga. Ignam aliqui debis et doluptatur am quis ente volest abo. Lorum nobitatur alisquiatum eiciaerci quaeriam, quam sit fugiam vero moluptae voluptum quiae. Nam inventi cus dolorib ercipitas qui dolorpore, conseri buscime venimperiam enis sit ullaut rati ut aute ipsum, antem atur aligenisqui acilluptat.

Goodheart-Willcox Publisher

Figure 6-27. Linespacing, usually called leading, is the amount of vertical space separating one line of type from the next, measured from baseline to baseline.

Mi, samus exerorafsderum, utemos illorrum ra acep elessedi adit quam accum et intioribusam et quam volore soluptas dolenis mod modis este experendus qui sam quis etus eum fuga. Ignam aliqui debis et doluptatur am quis ente volest abo. Lorum nobitatur alisqu agfadsiatum eiciaerci quaeriam, quam sit fugiam veasdfdro moluptae voluptum qafdsfuiae. Nam inventi cus dolorib ercipitas

acilluptat. — widow

Necea volum qui omniste voluptas ut la aut que vollore molupti orporent asit odio occ ulpa simpor susapellame velgsswessi vo lorep udipsae natissi mus am inci con conwrtseq uos conem et quidedafbit est, si blab. — orphan

Goodheart-Willcox Publisher

Figure 6-28. Widows and orphans are parts of sentences or paragraphs that are left hanging.

Visibility

With regards to printed material, ***visibility*** results from the contrast of the dark typeface against the light reflected by the paper. This is due to the paper's brightness, smoothness, and opacity, as well as the ink darkness and type style.

The term whiteness is *not* used because ***brightness*** is a property of both white and colored papers. The brightness of paper varies greatly. The smoother the paper, the more light it reflects; therefore, paper ***smoothness*** also affects visibility of the images. A paper with high ***opacity*** does not allow print from the opposite side to show through.

The contrast of the printed material is affected by ***ink darkness***. That term is used rather than *ink color* because both black and colored inks have degrees of darkness. Darkness depends on the ink's covering power; complete coverage hides the surface of the paper.

The type style is also a factor; the thicker the elements of the letter, the more ink will be deposited on the paper for contrast. As type size decreases, this factor gains in importance.

Reverse type usually consists of white characters on a solid black or color background. This is done occasionally and can be done to stress the importance of the message or information in the copy. For example, a small newspaper advertisement might be reversed to make it stand out on the page and be noticed. Care must be used in choosing a typeface and type size for reversing. Many types are difficult to read when reversed, especially in small point sizes. See **Figure 6-29**.

Letterforms

The details and specific characteristics of each individual letter shape of a particular typeface is called the ***letterform***. Each typeface has its own unique combination of variables that comprise its anatomy.

Definition

Definition refers to the sharpness or distinction of the printed image. Sharply defined letter forms are essential for easier reading. The relationship between the typeface and paper is very important. A small typeface requires a smoother paper for good definition. Top-quality pressmanship contributes to sharp images on the page.

Special consideration must be given when placing type over a screened background because poor definition may result. See **Figure 6-30**. The same principle applies when the background for type is a halftone image, such as a photo of clouds or foliage.

Type Size

The legibility of copy, as it relates to type size, increases dramatically up to 10-point type. This increase flattens out with larger type sizes. Straight matter set in 10-point type is considered a norm for comfortable reading by young and middle-aged adults. **Figure 6-31** compares blocks of copy set in three different point sizes.

The x-height of the font also contributes to legibility. A large x-height would increase the size of the letters, and decrease the contrast and optical length of ascenders and descenders. This combination lessens the contrast, which in turn lessens the readability.

Line Length

Line length is the distance from the left to right sides of a line or body of copy. Measured in picas in early typesetting, this length is critical to legibility.

Eye span is the width people can see with one fixation (sweep or adjustment) of the eye muscles. With body copy, the normal eye span is about one and one-half alphabets (about 40 characters). This width will vary with typeface classification and size, however.

When the width of the line corresponds to the eye span of the reader, the physical task of reading is made easier. Longer lengths require extra physical effort when reading (the more eye fixations per line, the more effort required). Horizontal travel of the eye is considered more tiring than moving vertically from one line to the next.

Case

When we read text, we do not actually read each and every word. We scan the words—specifically, the tops of words. Because the tops of lowercase letters have the most variation, copy that

Reverse type can be difficult to read, especially if a small point size is used. Large blocks of reverse type should be avoided.

Reverse type can be difficult to read, especially if a small point size is used. Large blocks of reverse type should be avoided.

Goodheart-Willcox Publisher

Figure 6-29. While reverse type can be effective as an attention-getting device, legibility suffers when the type is too small. Compare these examples on 18-point and 8-point type.

is in all capital letters is much harder to read. When the first word of a sentence is capitalized and the rest is in lowercase (with the exception of proper names), it is called ***sentence case***. ***Title case*** is where each word has an initial capital letter. See **Figure 6-32**.

COAST TO COAST.
$9.25.
Catalina Island
Catalina is only two very relaxing hours from Southern California's coast via Catalina Cruises. Touring, tanning, shopping, snorkeling, it's a paradise getaway for the whole family. With year-round daily departures from Long Beach or San Pedro to Avalon aboard our spacious 700-passenger ships. Each-way fares: adults $9.25, kids (2-11) $4.90, (under 2) $.50.
Brochures: Catalina Cruises, Box 1948-S, San Pedro, CA 90733 (213) 775-6111 (714) 527-7111
CATALINA
CRUISES
Come on over.
The coast is clear.
Southern California

Goodheart-Willcox Publisher

Figure 6-30. Selecting the proper typeface for placement on a screen pattern is very important to legibility.

6 — 6 point, 1point leaded

This linotype method of copy-fitting is based on character count. Systems that rely upon average word count to a given area seldom are accurate. Even character count calculations, although much more accurate than word count methods, should be recognized as approximate, or average, because of the influence of inevitable variables in copy. Obviously the style

8 — 8 point, 1point leaded

This linotype method of copy-fitting is based on character count. Systems that rely upon average word count to a given area seldom are accurate. Even character count calculations, although much more accurate than word count methods, should be

10 — 10 point, 1point leaded

This linotype method of copy-fitting is based on character count. Systems that rely upon average word count to a given area seldom are accurate. Even character count calcu-lations, although much more accurate than

Goodheart-Willcox Publisher

Figure 6-31. Smaller type sizes (those below 10-point) are difficult to read for the average person. The same copy is shown here in 6-point, 8-point, and 10-point type.

This sentence is in sentence case.

This Sentence Is In Title Case.

THIS SENTENCE IS IN ALL CAPS.

THIS SENTENCE IS IN SMALL CAPS.

Goodheart-Willcox Publisher

Figure 6-32. Case refers to whether letters are uppercase or lowercase.

Typography Details

Being a good typographer is about more than selecting the right typeface. Paying attention to the details of proper grammar, spelling, and punctuation will set you far apart from the average person. Most people do not recognize when something is done correctly, but they will notice immediately if it is done incorrectly.

Dashes

There is a difference between ***hyphens***, ***en dashes***, and ***em dashes***. While similar in appearance, they are different lengths, have specific uses, and are not interchangeable. Hyphens are used primarily for breaking long words that do not fit on a specific line length and alignment, or for forming compound words such as state-of-the-art. It is the only dash that has a dedicated key on a standard keyboard.

The en dash is slightly longer than the hyphen and is used to replace the word *through* or *to* for a span of time, dates, or numbers. See **Figure 6-33**. There should be no space before or after an en dash and the content.

The em dash is the longest dash and the most versatile punctuation mark. The goal of the em dash is to add clarity to content. It can take the place of commas, parentheses, or colons—and in each of these instances, it has a different outcome. Em dashes are flexible—they are more emphatic than commas, less formal than parentheses, and more dramatic than colons. Use them to garner the appropriate attention to your content. As with en dashes, no spaces should be placed before or after em dashes.

✓ The information can be found in chapters 3–5.
✕ The information can be found in chapters 3-5.

✓ The 2014–2015 school year was the best.
✕ The 2014-2015 school year was the best.

✓ 6:30 p.m.–9:00 p.m.
✕ 6:30 p.m.-9:00 p.m.

✓ August 10–August 16
✕ August 10-August 16

Goodheart-Willcox Publisher

Figure 6-33. How and when to use an en dash.

Spacing

As we standardly read the tops of words and groups of words, having clear beginnings and endings of sentences is critical to legibility. Early type used individual pieces of lead for each character. When the typewriter was introduced, it was ***monospaced***, or had the same width space for each character. Finding the end of the sentence was more difficult, as there was a lot of extra white space around some characters. See **Figure 6-34**. Since kerning was not available in these early formats, it became a common practice to put two spaces after a period or terminal point to allow the eye to quickly register the sentence structure.

With digital type, not only does each character have its own space, it has built-in kerning pairs that optically make sentence structure obvious and clear. Now two spaces after a period is not only unnecessary, it is distracting and inhibits the flow of the text or readability.

Punctuation

As a general rule, a sentence should end with only one terminal punctuation mark. There are three options for ending a sentence: a period, a question mark, or an exclamation point.

As computers became part of our everyday life, the flagrant misuse of the apostrophe and quotation marks became prevalent. Apostrophes and quotation marks, unique to each typeface, are generally "curly." That is, they are more rounded in the middle, making them quite different from inch marks or foot marks. There are standard keyboard equivalents to both that generally depend on the preference settings in your word processing or page assembly application. ***Typographer's quotes*** are a preference that allows the standard keyboard strike to display the apostrophe and quote marks. If this preference is turned off in the program or application, the standard key becomes straight up and down, or the inch mark and foot mark. See **Figure 6-35**.

Choosing the Right Typeface

Until this point, we have been discussing the history, the specifics, and the technical side of typefaces. While all are important aspects of

Each letter has the same space alloted for the character and the space around it.

monospaced.

not monospaced.

Each letter has its own space unique to the character.

Monospaced without two spaces after a period.

not correct — He ran around the block. The children walked the dog. Everyone liked to play outside on the sunny day in spring.

Monospaced with two spaces after a period.

correct — He ran around the block. The children walked the dog. Everyone liked to play outside on the sunny day in spring.

Non monospaced without two spaces after a period.

correct — He ran around the block. The children walked the dog. Everyone liked to play outside on the sunny day in spring.

Non monospaced with two spaces after a period.

not correct — He ran around the block. The children walked the dog. Everyone liked to play outside on the sunny day in spring.

Goodheart-Willcox Publisher

Figure 6-34. Monospaced type can have unsightly space around the letters, which makes it difficult to find sentence structure without putting two spaces after a period.

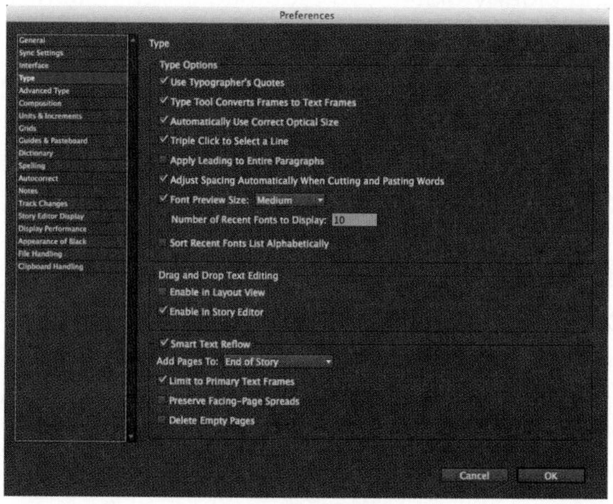

"Let's watch television," he said. ✓

"Let's watch television," he said. ✗

Goodheart-Willcox Publisher

Figure 6-35. Using quote marks and apostrophes correctly makes the copy look professional.

typography and critical to the success of the type selection, we have not yet considered one of the most difficult parts of creating a great design—choosing the proper typeface. Components to consider for typefaces include voice, contrast, and relationship.

Voice

If the typography chosen for a piece does not have the right voice, all of the technical and other considerations will not get the right message conveyed. Some people read words aloud in their head; others do not. Either way, each typeface has its own voice. Using the wrong voice for a message can change the meaning. For instance, which example in **Figure 6-36** has the right voice for the word "quiet"? While the immediate reaction is to

A quiet

B **QUIET**

Goodheart-Willcox Publisher

Figure 6-36. Examples of selecting the right typeface and style for a word's voice.

say *A* because it has a "quieter" voice, it actually depends on the content. If you are using it as a person shouting at a crowd to be quiet, *B* is the obvious choice. The first step in determining the proper voice or typeface is to read the content.

Weight

The weight of a particular typeface has a large impact on its voice. There are a variety of weights for typefaces, including light, regular, semibold, bold, extra bold, and black, with many options in between. Some typefaces have a broad family of choices and some have only one.

If you choose to bold a word in a paragraph of regular type, the bold word will stand out or have more emphasis when you read it. If you overuse bold, you dilute the emphasis. There is a saying: If everything is bold, nothing is bold.

Structure

Structure refers to how a typeface is built. In other words, is it a serif or display, a sans serif or script? Selecting the right typeface structure for a project is important to both its voice and its readability. For instance, if you are creating a wedding invitation, a script might be a good choice. However, if the wedding is an informal, country hoedown, the script's improper voice will send the wrong message to the viewer.

Contrast

Creating a dynamic between parts of a design will establish hierarchy and lead to a clear message. Adding contrast in typography is an easy and effective way to add interest and voice to text.

A standard rule of thumb is to keep it simple. Do not make the viewer struggle to read the content. Keep the number of different typefaces used to a minimum. Multiple typefaces from the same family, however, is effective.

When selecting two typefaces to use together, do not pick two from the same classification. Two serifs together, for example, do not provide as much contrast as using a serif and a sans serif. Keep typefaces the same or make them different. Strengthen the differences and you strengthen the contrast. Make sure it is the appropriate contrast for the message.

Form

Distinct letter shapes are part of the form. An italic typeface has a very different form from a Roman. As with weight, changing the form of a typeface can add emphasis. Contrasting an italic with a Roman typeface will have a stronger statement than keeping it all Roman.

Relationship

Every element you put on a page forms a relationship with the page and with other elements. Three ways to compare the relationship of typefaces on a page are concordant, contrasting, and conflicting. See **Figure 6-37** for a comparison.

Concordant

Concordant type is where you use only one type of family without much variety in size, form, and weight. This creates a very sedate or formal voice and can easily be dull or boring.

Contrasting

Using clearly distinctive typeface combinations can be very exciting. Varying the size, weight, structure, or form can enhance a design. Rarely is only one ***contrast*** effective. Emphasizing the differences and combinations will create visual energy, if that is the voice you need.

Conflicting

Combining typefaces that are similar in size and structure is disturbing. If they are not the same, but they are not different either, a ***conflict*** is created and it looks incongruous.

Web Typography

Studying the time line of web typography shows exponential changes occurred in a relatively short time. It began in 1988, with the ability to display

Concordant

Gauging popular opinion

A recap of the past year's issues and our readers' responses

Contrasting

Gauging popular opinion

A recap of the past year's issues and our readers' responses

Conflicting

Gauging popular opinion

A recap of the past year's issues and our readers' responses

Goodheart-Willcox Publisher

Figure 6-37. Examples of the relationship of typefaces used together.

subpixels (three times smaller than a pixel). This rendered type with much greater definition far easier to read on the screen.

In 1993, the National Center for Supercomputing Applications developed the first graphical web browser, Mosaic, which allowed images to be displayed inline with text.

New additions to web typography in 1996 streamlined the process of defining type for the web. Microsoft® developed a core set of fonts that were legible and covered many languages with a versatile range of weight and style. In addition to this, Cascading Style Sheets (CSS) were released, which made defining font sizes and colors efficient and easy as opposed to the tedious process of embedding the hypertext markup language (HTML) code.

Unfortunately, typefaces and styles displayed on screens were dependent on the browser the viewer was using. Because of the limited choices for fonts, websites all looked very similar. Often, designers would create the text as an image to get the font they wanted to use. This opened the door to other issues, as this limited the use of that typography. Further, it was not accessible for search engine crawlers, which lowered the search engine optimization (SEO), the rankings websites receive based on their number of visitors.

Web-Safe Fonts

Web-safe fonts are a group of common fonts that will likely be present on most computers. If a computer does not have that font, the browser will replace it with a different one specified by the designer as a backup. These backup fonts are called ***font stacks***. See **Figure 6-38**.

Web Fonts

The web typography world was rocked in 2008 when Apple® released Safari 3.1. This allowed their web browser to download OpenType (OTF) or TrueType (TTF) font files. Other browsers followed. Microsoft, however, did not permit this download. Finally, in 2009, the Web Open Font Format (WOFF) was developed specifically for the web, protecting the foundries and their intellectual properties.

Known as ***web fonts***, these files are downloaded from a web server. Then the browser renders them with HTML, allowing the display of fonts that are not on the viewer's computer.

Other Fonts

Now that we have moved into the world of web fonts, there are so many different options for

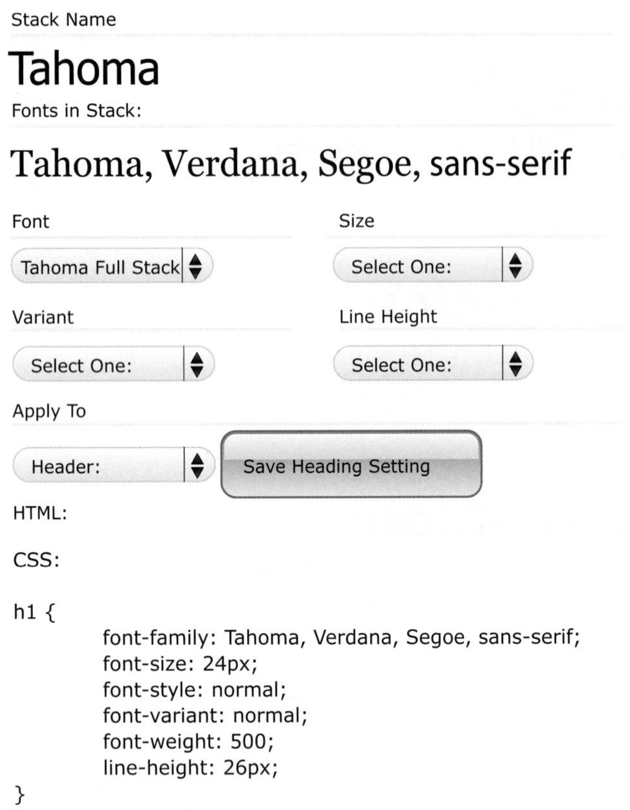

Goodheart-Willcox Publisher

Figure 6-38. A CSS font stack for Tahoma, with substitutions listed in order of preference by the designer.

designers. Getting an interesting and relevant font on your site is now easier than ever.

Many third-party options exist for designers to access hundreds of fonts. They require only a few lines of code that direct the browser back to the source, and many are inexpensive or free.

Designers recognize that typography is a critical part of graphic design, whether it is for print or web presence. As content and usability are keys to successful web design, choosing the right typography is an integral part. Web fonts provide designers with the options they are accustomed to having with print media.

Paper Wings/Shutterstock.com

It is important to choose a typeface with the correct voice for a project. What type of project might you use this typeface for?

Summary

- Typefaces are distinctive visual symbols that are used to compose printed pages on paper or another substrate. Characters are the individual visual symbols in a particular typeface.
- The process of mechanical printing from individual pieces of type was introduced in Europe in the fifteenth century, using type metal and foundry type.
- The seven typeface classifications are Roman or serif, Egyptian or slab serif, sans serif, display or decorative, script or cursive, ornamental, and italic or oblique.
- The term associated with a given style is called *family.* The total range of sizes of one type style of a given font is called a *type series.* A *font* is the complete set of letters, figures, punctuation marks, special characters, and ligatures contained in a typeface.
- Type style selection plays an important role in the design of a printed product, and is critical to a successful design.
- The two principal units of measure used in the graphic communications industry are the point and the pica.
- When selecting a typeface, legibility is one of the most critical factors.
- Web fonts and web-safe fonts became necessary to accommodate web pages.

Review Questions

Answer the following questions using the information in this chapter.

1. What are *characters*?
2. The art of expressing ideas through the selection of appropriate typefaces is called _____.
3. An ascender extends _____ and a descender _____ the x-height letters.
4. What is the baseline?
5. Define the term *x-height.*
6. The finishing-off stroke at the top or bottom of a character is called a(n) _____.
7. Who is credited with designing and cutting the first Roman typefaces?
8. The German black letter type styles gradually were replaced by the _____ typeface.
9. Which designer first developed a typeface with letters designed solely for printing?
10. List and describe the seven basic typeface classifications.
11. What is the most popular typeface?
12. Name the three styles of type for typefaces.
13. A typeface _____ consists of the variation of one style of type.
14. A type _____ consists of the letters, figures, and punctuation marks that are of one size and style.

15. *True or False?* The point size of a typeface is the same as its x-height.
16. Which is the larger unit of measure, the em or the en?
17. Changing the distance between words in a line of copy is called _____.
    A. letterspacing
    B. leading
    C. kerning
    D. wordspacing
18. _____ refers to changing the distance between some letters of a word to improve appearance of the type.
19. Name and describe three physical factors that affect legibility.
20. Which dash is used to substitute for the words *through* or *to*?
    A. Hyphen.
    B. En dash.
    C. Em dash.
    D. Forward slash.
21. The ability to display _____ increased type definition, making it far easier to read type on the screen.

Suggested Activities

1. Select a type style that denotes each of the following factors: decorative, boldness, ancient, modern, delicate, action, and an event.
2. Select a type style and develop its origin.
3. Briefly discuss some of the advantages the computer has brought to typography.
4. Write three words that describe you as a person. Select two typefaces for each that have the right voice for your personality.

Chapter 7

Design and Layout

Learning Objectives

After studying this chapter, you will be able to:

- Summarize the role of the graphic designer.
- Explain the elements of design.
- Draw the color wheel.
- Explain the principles of design.
- Explain the gestalt principles.
- Explain the elements of layout.
- Explain a project brief.
- Differentiate between a passive and active layout.
- Explain what thumbnails are and why they are drawn.
- Explain why a grid is useful.

Goodheart-Willcox Publisher

Important Terms

active layout
additive colors
analagous
body type
closure
color
color wheel
complementary colors
composition
comprehensive
continuation
contrast
contrast pairing
design
dummy
elements of design
elements of layout
formal balance
gestalt
graphics
grid
gutters
harmony
headline dominant
hierarchy
hue
informal balance
layout
line
margins
passive layout
picture dominant
power corner
primary colors
principles of design
process colors
project brief
proximity
rhythm
rough
rule of thirds
saturation
secondary color
shape
similarity
size
spatial zones
specifications
spread
subtractive color
tertiary color
texture
thumbnails
unity
value
visual center
white space

G-WLEARNING.COM

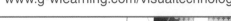

While studying this chapter, look for the activity icon to:

- **Practice** vocabulary terms with e-flash cards, matching activities, and vocabulary game.
- **Reinforce** what you learn by submitting end-of-chapter questions.

www.g-wlearning.com/visualtechnology/

In graphic communications, ***design*** refers to the application of proper methods to create a product that is both artistic and functional. A successful design requires the skillful use of design elements and principles.

This chapter will cover the primary elements and principles of design and layout. Knowledge of common design techniques is critical in producing a layout and evaluating the visual quality of a product.

The Graphic Designer

Graphic design is a problem-solving component of graphic communications. It is the development of a systematic plan designed to communicate a specific message, with a specific objective, to a specific audience in a visually pleasing way using a combination of words, graphics, and images. The distribution of this message can be in a variety of methods including printed material or digital output.

The role of the graphic designer varies greatly within the graphic communications industry. Because the technology and tools change often, the designer's role continues to evolve. Many jobs include combinations of graphic design for print, web design, marketing, mobile marketing, photography, copywriting, and production. See **Figure 7-1**.

Elements of Design

Design involves the selection and arrangement of visual images to make a pleasing presentation. To design is to plan. The text and graphics used in a design will have a tremendous impact on the viewer; therefore, it is essential to develop a strong layout of visual materials.

A successful graphic designer must apply the fundamental elements of design. The basic ***elements of design*** are line, shape, texture, space, size, and color.

Line

Line is a design element that forms the shape of an image. Lines can be used to give the printed image a personality. Lines can be loose and free or they can be straight and sharp. See **Figure 7-2**. Repeating lines create patterns and add emotional impact to the visual image.

Lines can also be used as a form of universal language in communication. Lines represent order and give the eye specific directions as to where to look and how to interpret what it sees. Representing order in design, lines can group related objects together or divide unrelated objects. Often at the edge of where two shapes meet, lines are most

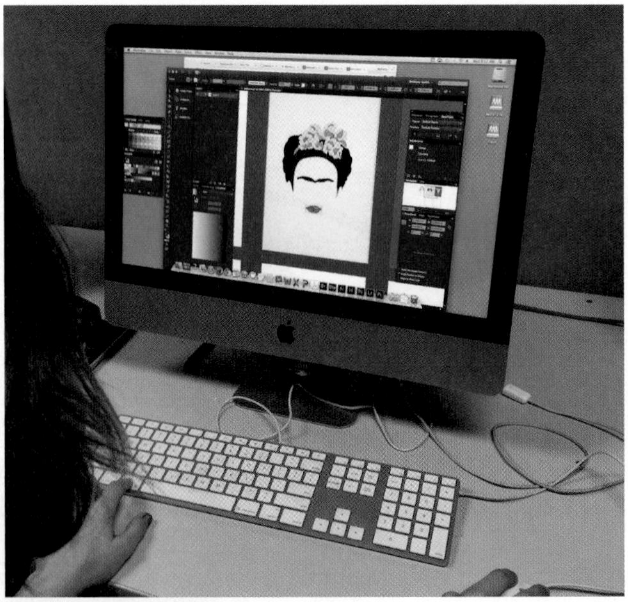

©Bernie Fritts

Figure 7-1. A graphic designer develops a plan to communicate a specific message visually.

Goodheart-Willcox Publisher

Figure 7-2. Lines can be used to denote a specific meaning. Curved, loose lines imply a free spirit. Lines drawn straight imply a more straightforward or disciplined theme.

often functional rather than decorative. Calligraphy, maps, floor plans, and graphs are all practical uses of lines. Arrows and other symbols are examples of lines used as a visual form. See **Figure 7-3**.

Different kinds of lines project different emotions. Horizontal lines suggest a feeling of rest, while vertical lines communicate a feeling of strength and elevation. Architecture in our cities is dominated by vertical lines. See **Figure 7-4**. Diagonal lines suggest motion and direction. They tend to be unstable. Deep, intense curves can give a feeling of confusion, while shallow curves suggest relaxation. See **Figure 7-5**.

Lines are often used to enhance or change the visual quality of styles of type. They can appear very harsh or very delicate. Lines play a highly important role in designing a layout that communicates effectively.

Shape

Shape is an area that is defined by a perimeter. It could be a line, a color change, a value change, or an actual form. Design is the arrangement of

Goodheart-Willcox Publisher

Figure 7-4. Our cities and architecture rely heavily on vertical lines. When viewed on a diagonal, motion and direction are implied.

Goodheart-Willcox Publisher

Figure 7-3. Lines can deliver a visual message when they are drawn as arrows or other symbols.

Goodheart-Willcox Publisher

Figure 7-5. Curved lines can be soothing or create unrest.

these shapes. It is important for the designer to see each element as a shape. Everything has a shape, even emptiness.

Square, Circle, and Triangle

The three basic geometric shapes are the square, circle, and triangle. These structured shapes are associated with a psychological meaning, as shown in **Figure 7-6**.

Do not underestimate the importance of familiarity. The comfort of having square pages and books provides stability. Squares are uniform and symbolize equality.

Circles do not often appear in design outside of logos. They are great for grabbing attention or providing emphasis. They are complete and suggest protectiveness.

The visual attitude portrayed by the triangle is one of conflict or action. Often acting as an arrow or flag to give direction, triangles also have religious significance.

It is not that squares are boring, but unexpected shapes can grab attention better. The fluidity of natural or abstract shapes is good for reinforcing a theme or giving a feeling of impulse.

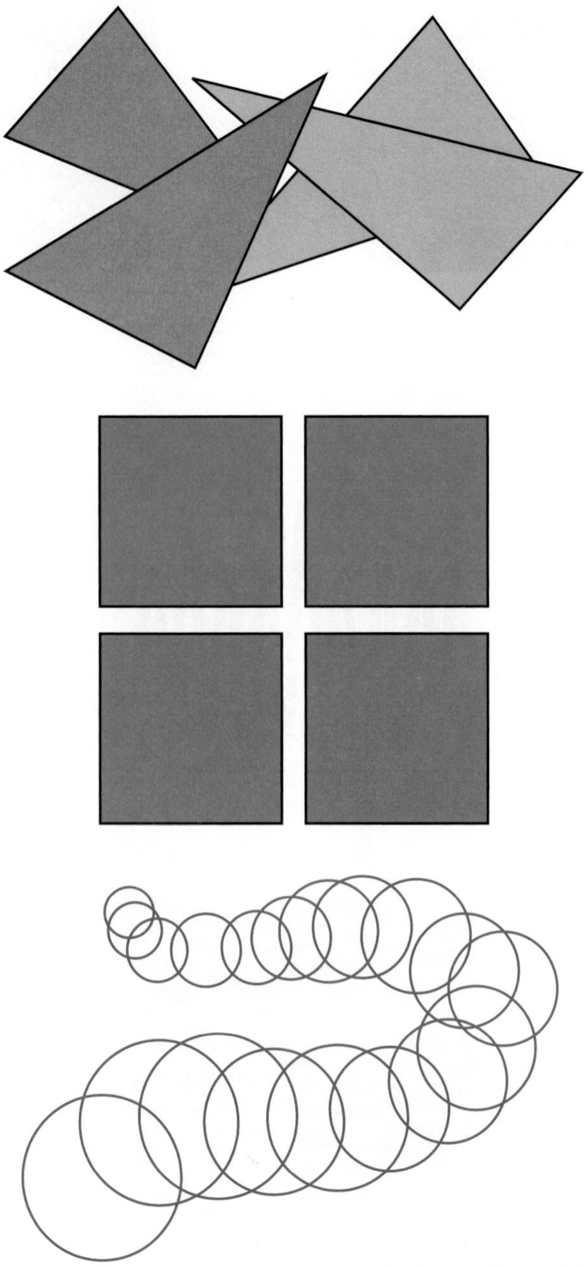

Goodheart-Willcox Publisher

Figure 7-6. Shapes can imply a psychological meaning.

Texture

The ***texture*** of a visual image is a projection of emphasized structure or weight. When gauging the texture of an object, the first inclination is to touch the surface. Most often in graphic communications, texture is visual; there is no feeling gained through the sense of touch. However, new kinds of substrates are becoming popular for publications and advertising collateral that provide an interactively tactile nature. Actual texture for a printed image may also be produced by embossing, which presses a shape or irregular surface into the substrate. See **Figure 7-7**.

Many elements can be used to create texture, including type, line, and shape. Patterns can have a dramatic effect on a design. Texture varies and depends on the structure and weight of the individual letters, the amount of space between lines, and the shapes in a certain space. Type as texture can be a special display font or unique blocks of text. See **Figure 7-8**.

Goodheart-Willcox Publisher

Figure 7-7. Embossing has a raised surface that is tactile as well as visual.

Space

Space should never be considered the leftover area. Space provides relationships for the elements in a design. Each element placed forms a relationship with the page and with other elements. Space is created when this happens and often provides a ground or frame of reference for the content.

Many famous designers and artists are known for their use of space in design. Some of them include M.C. Escher, Saul Bass, Paul Rand, and Alan Fletcher. Many logos and optical illusions rely on space for their effectiveness. White space is covered more thoroughly later in this chapter.

Size

Size is the relationship between elements on a page. The use of proportion helps achieve balance and unity in a layout. However, keeping everything proportional, in the same plane, is unnecessary. Using the unexpected to generate a dramatic response is a good way to get attention. Making an element larger or smaller than anticipated is one of the most effective ways to generate contrast in a design. Some ways to achieve this are through interesting cropping of images, implied action, and use of depth. See **Figure 7-9**.

Goodheart-Willcox Publisher

Figure 7-9. Cropping images in an interesting and unexpected way can create excitement.

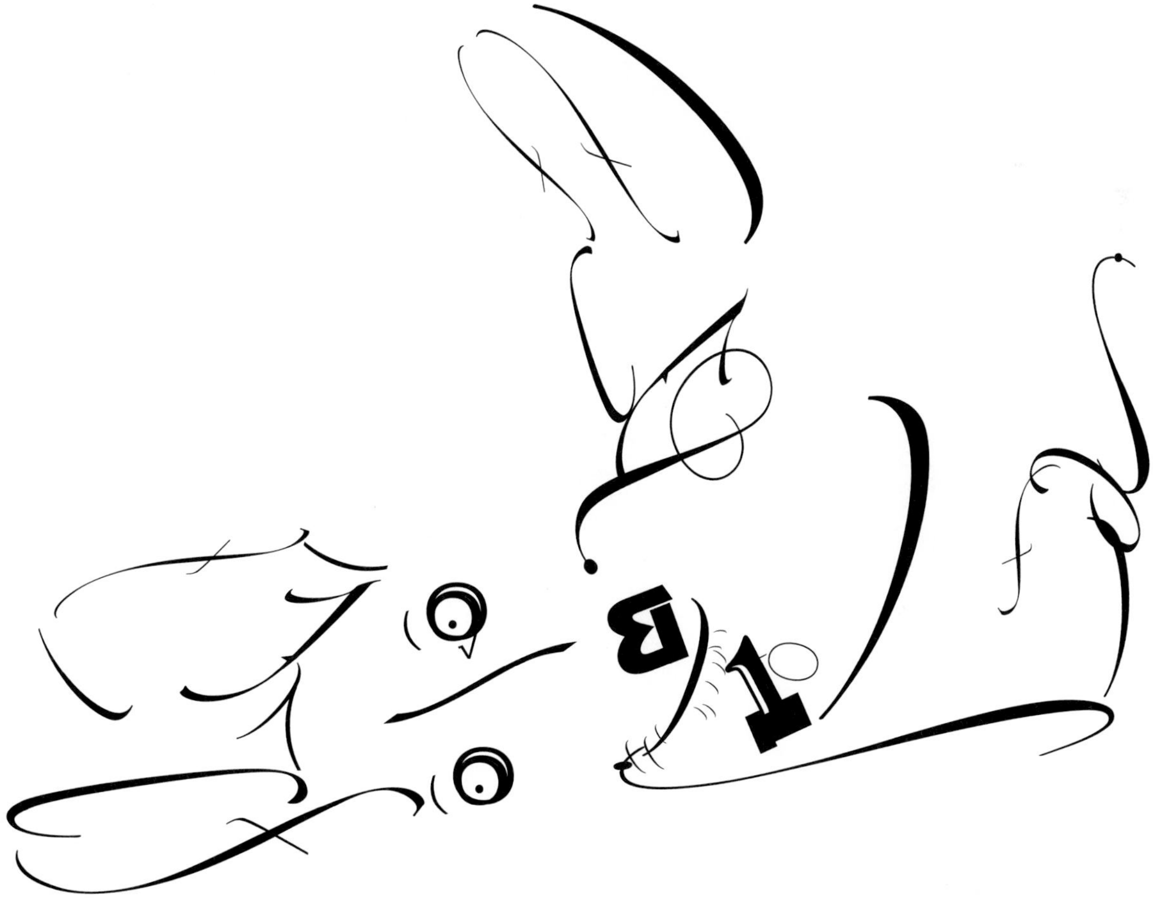

Goodheart-Willcox Publisher

Figure 7-8. Using text as texture to make a portrait from only letters and characters.

When the content is size specific, maintaining the proportional relationship of the elements is important. For instance, in an advertisement for jewelry, a diamond ring and a diamond pendant should be proportional. If the ring is enlarged to show more clearly, the size of the pendant becomes unknown.

Using a frame of reference for an item is very important if the item is not something that can stand on its own. An example would be showing a bottle. Bottles come in all shapes and sizes. Without something else to help determine its relative size, the viewer has to guess. Shoes, on the other hand, do not require a frame of reference. While shoes come in all shapes and sizes, we still know about how big they are.

Color

Color is an important element to be considered when planning or designing a printed product. Color can draw attention and produce a strong emotional and psychological impact. Different colors have traditional and symbolic meanings. A basic understanding of color is essential to creating a good design.

Using color thoughtfully and with a meticulous plan can make a design, while adding color randomly can destroy it. Color in design should be simple. It can be used to organize or highlight, provide direction or make a statement, or add interest and variety to a design. A small amount of color can heighten the visual quality of a page, and it should be part of your original plan. Using many colors with randomness adds clutter and confusion for the viewer. See **Figure 7-10**.

Color does not exist alone. Each color you place on a page is affected by the other elements around it, including the substrate, other colors, shapes, and quantities. Knowing some basic facts about color will help you make good color decisions.

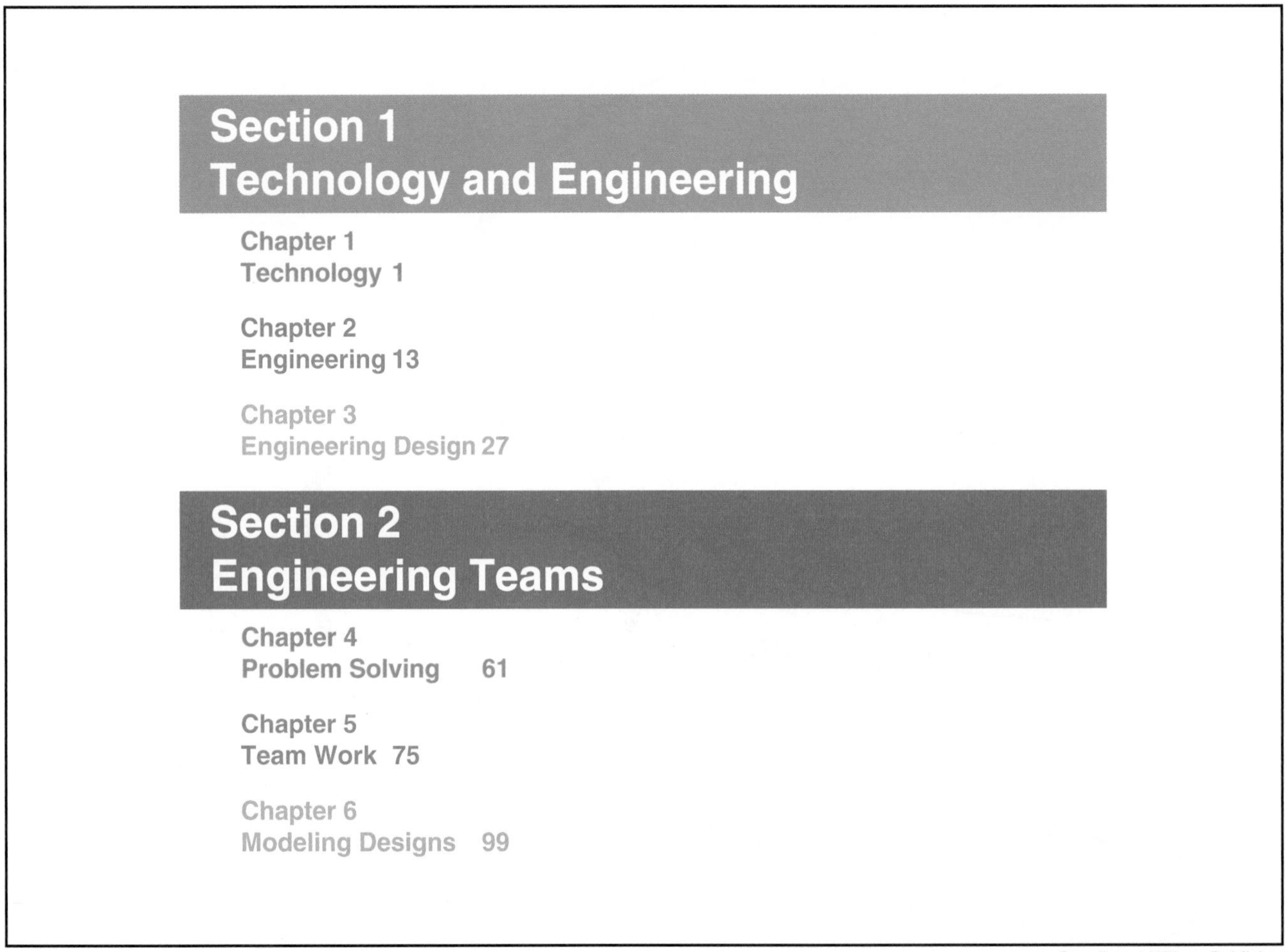

Goodheart-Willcox Publisher

Figure 7-10. Adding color randomly and with no purpose creates a cluttered look.

- Colors appear brighter when placed within a black box, **Figure 7-11**.
- Different color combinations change the appearance, **Figure 7-12**.
- Different proportions of color change the appearance, **Figure 7-13**.
- Dark colors recede; light colors come forward, **Figure 7-14**.
- Warm colors move forward; cool colors move back, **Figure 7-15**.
- Equal proportions of color do not allow for contrast, **Figure 7-16**.

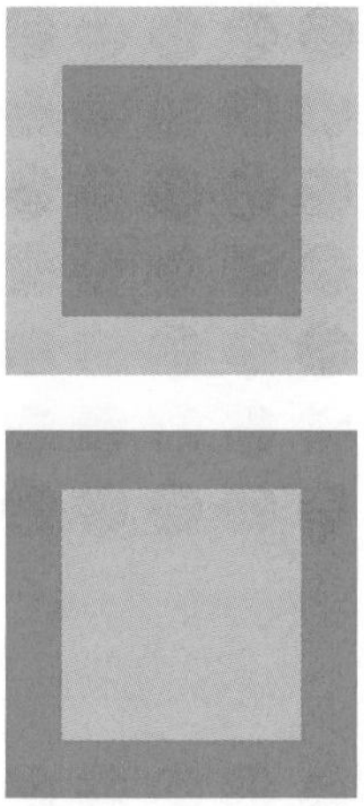

Goodheart-Willcox Publisher

Figure 7-13. Different proportions of color change the appearance.

Goodheart-Willcox Publisher

Figure 7-11. Colors placed on a black background appear brighter.

Goodheart-Willcox Publisher

Figure 7-14. Dark colors recede, while light colors come forward.

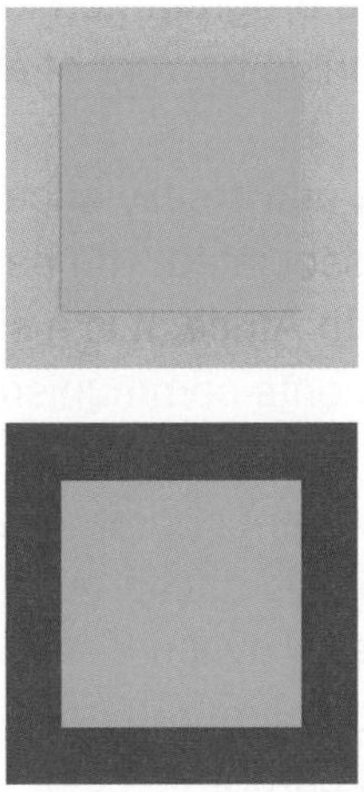

Goodheart-Willcox Publisher

Figure 7-12. Different color combinations change the appearance of the color. The green is the same color in both examples.

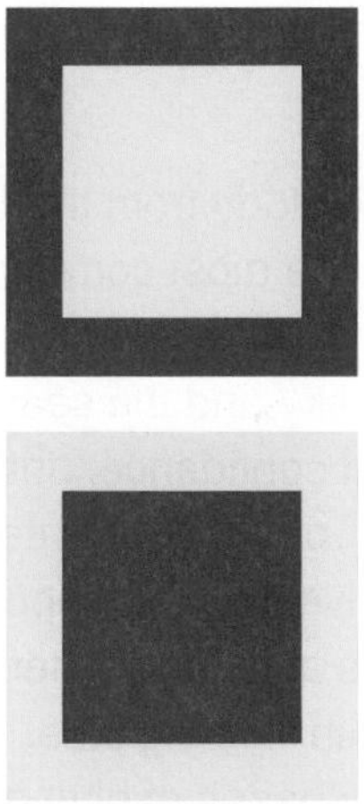

Goodheart-Willcox Publisher

Figure 7-15. Warm colors move forward, and cool colors move back.

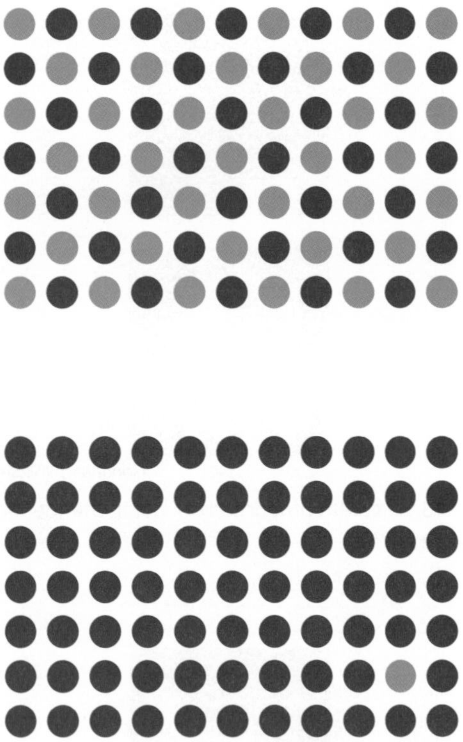

Goodheart-Willcox Publisher

Figure 7-16. Equal proportions of color do not allow for contrast.

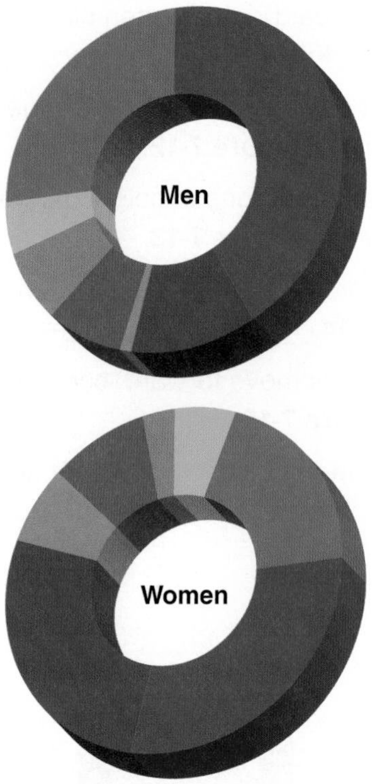

Goodheart-Willcox Publisher

Figure 7-17. These charts show a prefered choice for both men and women.

Culture of Color

Because we are often designing for a global society, the culture of color needs to be given consideration. Colors that work for domestic designs may not be appropriate for another country. Let's look at some basic considerations of common colors.

Blue

According to a study from the University of Maryland, blue is the most common favorite color for men and women, **Figure 7-17**. It is dominant in nature with the sky and the seas. It is a color of importance and confidence, and is the color of the "power suit" of the corporate world. Blue is usually conservative; it is the opposite of strong and energetic. It is also associated with sadness or depression, as in "feeling blue." Because many light and medium shades of blue are soothing and relaxing, it often makes a great background color, allowing items to jump to the foreground using contrast.

Red

Red is a strong color that stands for passion and violence. It can represent temperature (red hot) or be a symbol of anger (seeing red). Flushed cheeks are a natural physical reaction to anger or embarrassment. We roll out the red carpet for celebrities. We are programmed to equate red signs with danger; motorists beware of all kinds of red road signs.

These are not universally accepted signals. In China, red is associated with happiness and prosperity; in South Africa, it is a sign of mourning. In Russia it represents communism, and it is a sign of purity in India.

Use red if you want to grab attention or take action. It is not a good background color because the strength and energy it creates do not stay in the background. A little bit of red goes a very long way. Red is a common corporate color for the food and health industries because of the natural connection to both medical symbols and many food items, including fruits and vegetables.

Green

In the United States, green has historically been associated with money because of the color of the dollar. Using green in a financial statement design signals a positive financial report (red would indicate the opposite). Also a symbol of naiveté or inexperience, it is also the color of jealousy, as in "green with envy." Green has always been a sign of life. Now, with the strong environmental movement, green has become associated with saving energy, nature, renewable resources, and anything that is environmentally conscious. Because of the traffic signal, green means go! Finally, green is often associated with holidays such as Christmas and St. Patrick's Day, and Ireland is known as the Emerald Isle. See **Figure 7-18**.

Yellow

A bright color that generates excitement, yellow is for sunshine and cheerfulness, as well as cowardice and deceit. With such a high visibility, yellow is commonly used in high-profile areas such as construction zones, hazard signs, and school buses. In western countries, yellow is a sign of hope. In Japan, it is a sign of courage, and in Egypt, a sign of mourning.

Orange

Orange is a seasonal color that also signifies good health. It gets noticed without being overwhelming. Interestingly, studies have shown that it stimulates your appetite, which may be why many restaurants use orange in their décor. A playful and creative color, it is common in the food and sports industries.

Purple

A color of royalty, purple is noble and spiritual. Holding a special place in nature, many of our common shades of purple are derived from their plants, such as lavender, orchid, lilac, and violet.

Pink

Pink has always been a feminine color, often associated with little girls. In 1991, the Susan G. Komen® organization began handing out pink

©Jeremy Hamman

Figure 7-18. The Emerald Isle.

ribbons at the NYC Race for the Cure® fundraiser for breast cancer survivors. See **Figure 7-19**.

Black

Black is technically the absence of all color and is associated with elegance and formal sophistication. It is a sign of mourning in the United States and of rebellion among youths. Associated with mystery and authority, black provides contrast with most other colors.

Color Wheel

As color is science and wavelengths that are interpreted by the mechanics of our eyes, to discuss color we must work from the three ***primary colors***: red, green, and blue. A ***color wheel*** is a visual tool that illustrates the basics of color. It is an arrangement of colors that provides a means of identifying colors in a consistent manner. See **Figure 7-20**.

Contrary to what you may have learned in grade school, red, yellow, and blue are only primary colors when it comes to paint. For the color we see and the color we work with in a digital environment, all things come from the ***additive colors*** of red, green, and blue. If you mix all of the primary colors together, you get white. See **Figure 7-21A**.

Subtractive colors are a result of mixing together the additive primary colors next to each other. As shown in **Figure 7-21B**, the middle of the color wheel shows a neutral. Subtractive colors—cyan (C), magenta (M), and yellow (Y)—are also called ***process colors*** because they are the ink colors used in traditional offset printing. Mixing the subtractive colors together results in black (muddy brown). Because inks are not pure, black was added

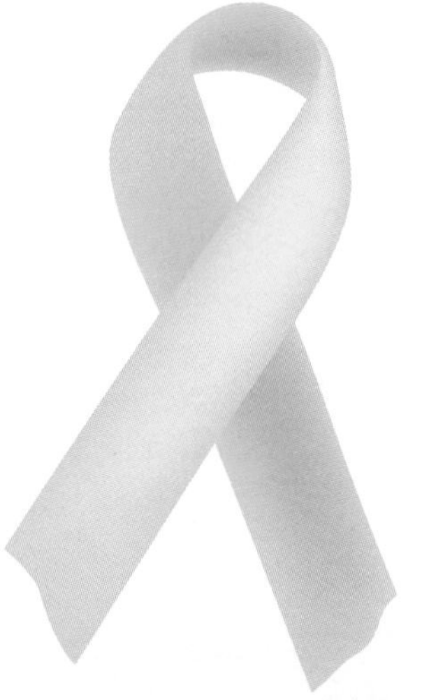

Goodheart-Willcox Publisher

Figure 7-19. Pink has become the international color to represent breast cancer awareness, started by the Susan G. Komen® organization in 1991.

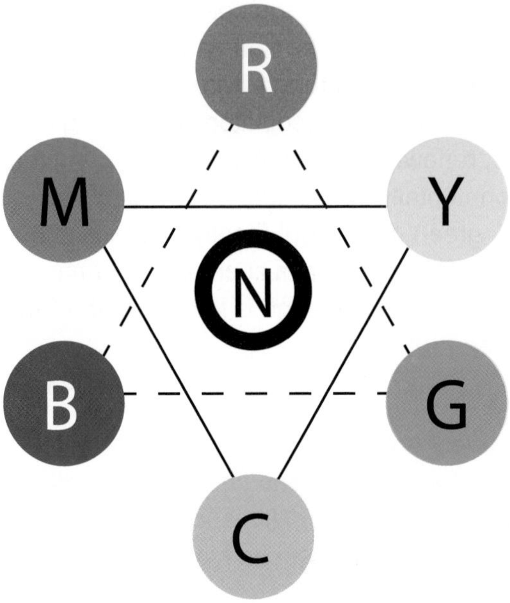

Goodheart-Willcox Publisher

Figure 7-20. The digital color wheel.

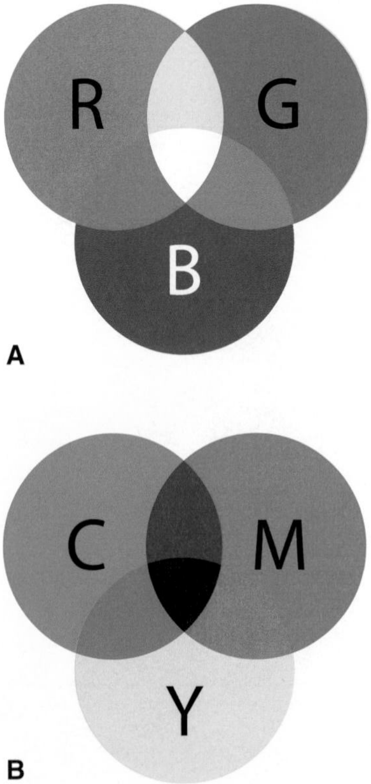

Goodheart-Willcox Publisher

Figure 7-21. A—Additive colors. B—Subtractive colors.

to the printing process to help define shadows and detail. See **Figure 7-22**.

Color must be thought about in three dimensions. As seen in **Figure 7-23**, the three dimensions of color are: ***hue***, the real color on the color wheel; ***saturation***, how close to the neutral middle the color is; and ***value***, the lightness or brightness of the color, or where it hits on the white-to-black axis. While defining color is all about science, using color is more about common sense.

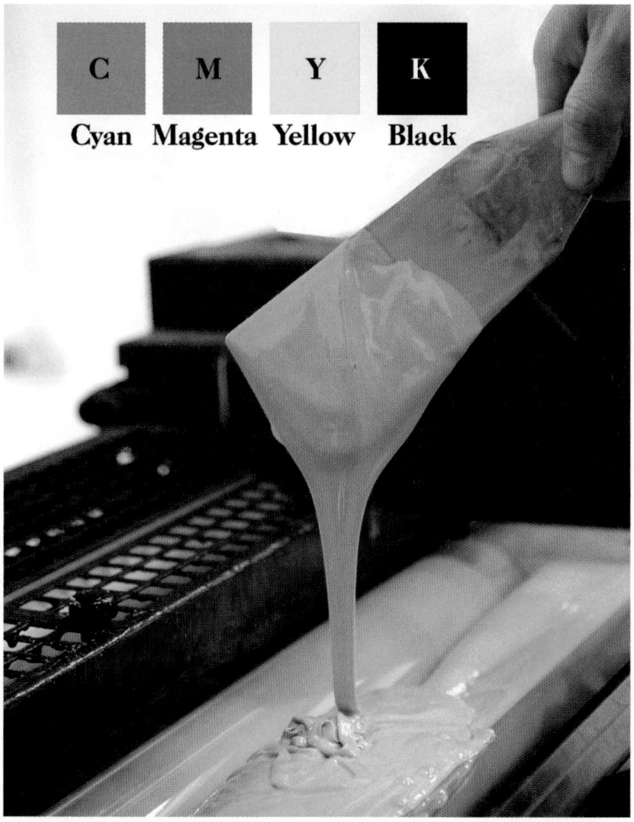

Goodheart-Willcox Publisher

Figure 7-22. The process colors used to generate four-color process printing.

Color Harmony

Harmonious color, or ***harmony***, is a palette that consists of colors that are pleasing when used together. Because color can be very subjective, it is important to select colors that are appropriate for the given problem and meet the general objective of the solution. Below are some basic theories for color harmony.

Complementary

Complementary colors are colors that are opposite each other on the color wheel. See **Figure 7-24**. Using these colors creates maximum contrast and stability. They should not be used in equal portions, however, as they tend to vibrate and can hurt your eyes. See **Figure 7-25**.

Analogous

Colors that are side by side on the color wheel are ***analogous***. To build this palette, extend the color wheel to secondary and tertiary colors. ***Secondary colors*** appear in between the standard

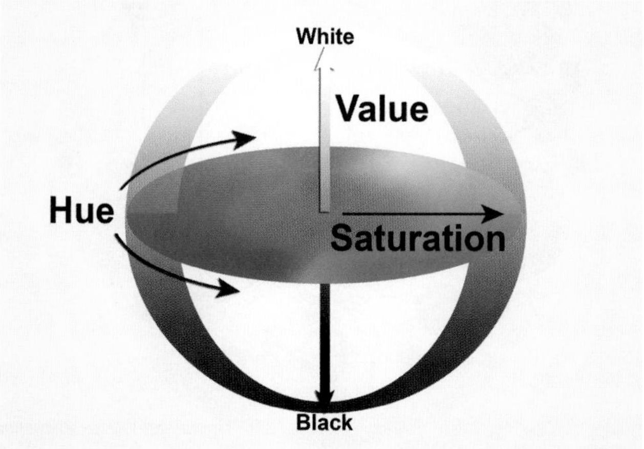

Goodheart-Willcox Publisher

Figure 7-23. The three dimensions of color are hue, saturation, and value.

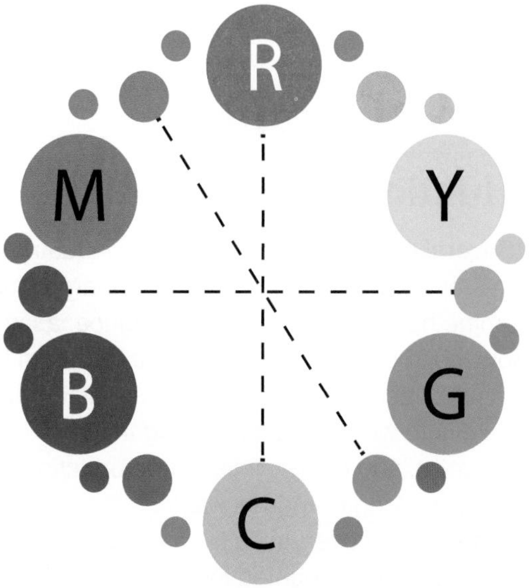

Goodheart-Willcox Publisher

Figure 7-24. Complementary colors are those directly opposite each other on the color wheel.

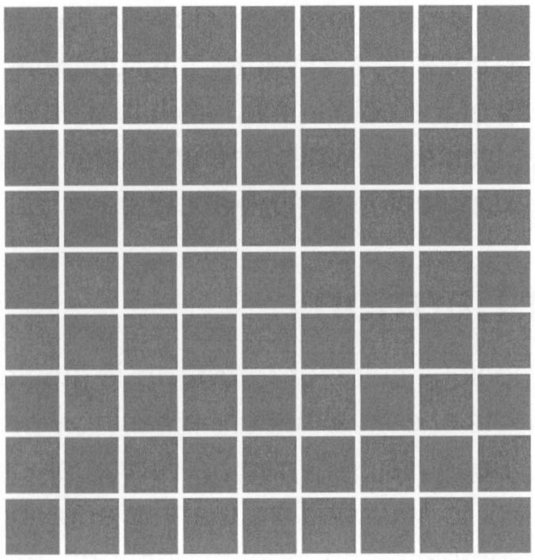

Goodheart-Willcox Publisher

Figure 7-25. Colors used in equal proportions do not create contrast.

colors on the wheel, such as orange, yellow green, turquoise, royal blue, red violet, and carmine red. ***Tertiary colors*** appear in between in the next grouping, which includes red-orange and orange-yellow. See **Figure 7-26**.

Geometrics

One of the easiest ways to pick a color theme that will always work is to place a geometric shape such as a square, rectangle, or triangle on the color wheel. Whatever colors the points touch work together. See **Figure 7-27**.

Think Green

Reduction

Several companies in the printing industry are taking steps toward going green. Companies must determine how much waste they produce, as well as how much carbon dioxide is emitted due to the printing process. One of the first steps a company can take is to work toward reducing the amount of paper, water, and energy it uses in production. A company working to reduce waste is more vigilant, and the status of everything from energy use to VOC reduction will be accounted for. As a result, studies have shown reductions of this nature have had the greatest impact on the environment so far.

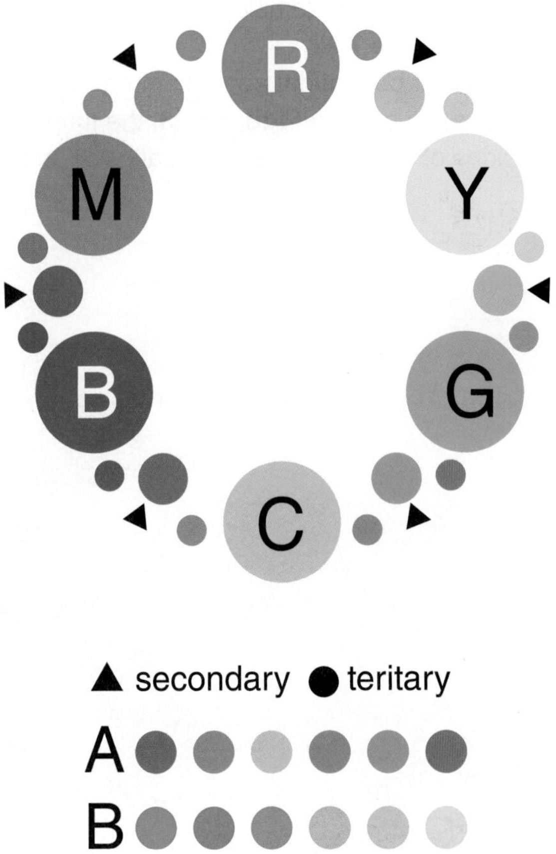

Goodheart-Willcox Publisher

Figure 7-26. Showing secondary colors (marked with triangles), tertiary colors (smallest circles), and analogous color themes.

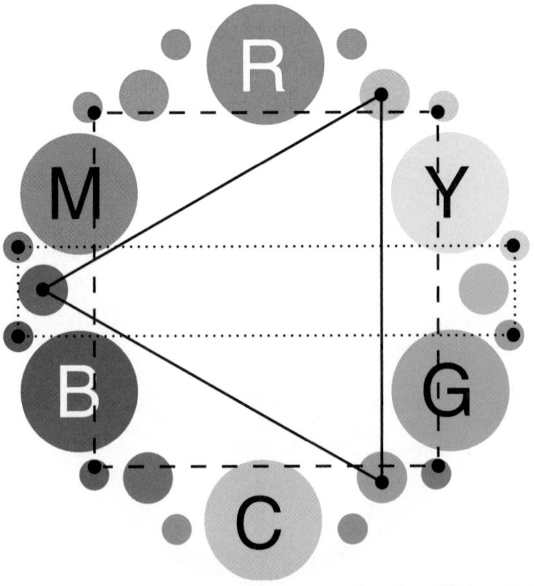

Goodheart-Willcox Publisher

Figure 7-27. Place any geometric shape such as a square, triangle, or rectangle on the color wheel, and whatever colors the corners touch will work together.

Color Temperature

Temperature of a color is a characteristic of the visual perception. Warm colors are magenta, red, orange, yellow, and sometimes green. Cool colors are cyan, blue, purple, and sometimes green. Using the colors in different combinations can create different meanings. See **Figure 7-28**.

Principles of Design

In the process of designing a printed product, many different ideas are generated through the use of design elements. To ensure the images have a pleasing relationship, design principles must be applied to sort out or select the right ideas.

The basic ***principles of design*** are balance, contrast, unity, rhythm, and hierarchy. These principles are used by the design artist to create an image that is both visually pleasing and functional.

Balance

Balance describes the even distribution of images to create a pleasing visual effect. Balance has one of the most important psychological influences on human perception. Consciously and unconsciously, people have a basic need for balance.

This principle can be illustrated by the placement of letters on a scale, as shown in **Figure 7-29**. Visually, a judgment can be made by the value of each image. The type of balance in **Figure 7-29A** is symmetrical and is called formal. The type of balance in **Figure 7-29B** is asymmetrical and is called informal.

Formal balance is achieved when all of the elements on a page are of equal weight and are positioned symmetrically. ***Informal balance*** may be achieved by changing the value, size, or location of elements on a page. The use of various colors and color intensities can also create informal balance. For example, two squares of equal size but different color values, such as pink and dark red, will appear to be unequal in size when placed side by side.

Balance is a guiding principle of design. The layout should be considered as a whole when positioning the elements.

Contrast

Contrast is the most powerful of the design tools and is about nearly everything, including the variation of elements in a printed product. When used, contrast gives meaning and direction to a design, which leads to successful hierarchy and a successful pattern.

Goodheart-Willcox Publisher

Figure 7-28. Warm and cool colors react differently to each other in different proportions.

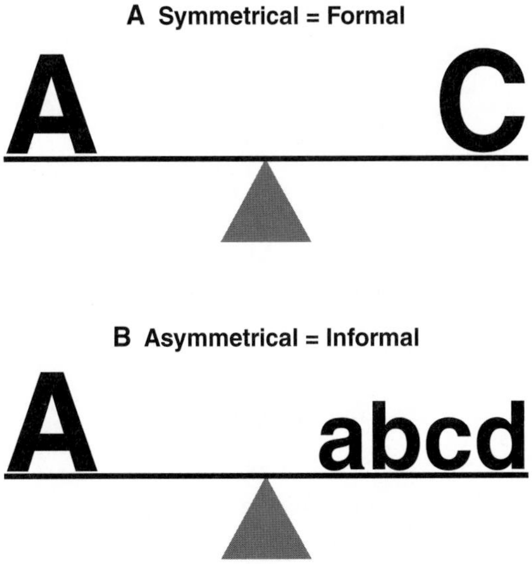

Goodheart-Willcox Publisher

Figure 7-29. Balance in an image is produced through an equal positioning of elements. A—Letters placed symmetrically to achieve formal balance. B—Letters placed in uneven quantities to represent informal balance.

One of the most important skills a designer can have is to choose the level of contrast necessary to achieve the goal of the project. ***Contrast pairing*** is a great way to think about how to introduce contrast into your design. See **Figure 7-30**. Finding the right contrast to achieve unity in your design is the challenge. If everything contrasts, nothing contrasts. However, too little contrast can make your design boring and unattractive. See **Figure 7-31** and **Figure 7-32**.

Styles of type can be contrasted to produce greater legibility and design variation. Some other useful contrasts are round and straight, ornate and plain, and broad and narrow.

The relationship between an unprinted area and a printed area of an image can also be enhanced through the use of contrast. White space, when used effectively, creates contrast and balances an image. See **Figure 7-33**.

CONTRAST PAIRS

SPACE
filled: empty
active: passive
near: far
contained: unrestricted

POSITION
top: bottom
high: low
right: left
in front: behind
centered: off center

FORM/SHAPE
simple: complex
abstract: representational
geometric: organic
symmetrical: asymmetrical

DIRECTION
vertical: horizontal
clockwise: counterclockwise

TYPOGRAPHY
serif: sans serif
light: heavy
regular: italic
condensed: expanded
script: roman

SIZE
big: little
long:short
wide: narrow

COLOR
black: color
light: dark
warm: cool
bright: dull

TEXTURE
fine: coarse
smooth: rough
slippery: sticky

Goodheart-Willcox Publisher

Figure 7-30. Examples of contrast pairs for layout design.

Goodheart-Willcox Publisher

Figure 7-31. Too little contrast can be boring.

Goodheart-Willcox Publisher

Figure 7-32. Too much contrast can be chaotic and difficult to read.

Rhythm

The movement of a reader's eye is often determined by the shapes used in the image. The square reflects horizontal and vertical movement. The triangle reflects diagonal movement, and the circle reflects a curve.

Rhythm in a design results when the elements have been properly used to create visual movement and direction. See **Figure 7-34**. Rhythm can also be achieved through the use of a pattern or repetition. Patterns can be used in contrast with an element to create an effective design. See **Figure 7-35**.

Goodheart-Willcox Publisher

Figure 7-33. Using contrasting typefaces makes a design more exciting.

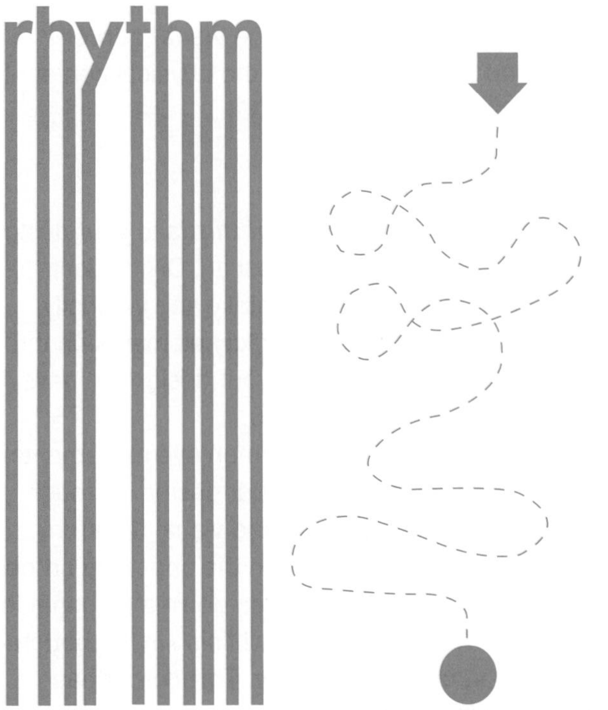

Goodheart-Willcox Publisher

Figure 7-34. Images that imply movement or direction give rhythm to a design.

Hierarchy

Hierarchy is the distribution of elements in a design based on their level of importance to the message or objective. The designer is creating a general road map that tells the viewer where to start, where to go next, and where to finish. Designs that do not have clear hierarchy are either boring and nothing stands out, or they are chaotic and you do not know where to focus. Generally, in an effective design, the most important factor is where you want the eye to start. Visually leading the viewer throughout the piece is based on the structural hierarchy you establish.

Unity

Unity, or harmony, is the proper balance of all elements in an image, resulting in a pleasing whole and an image that is viewed as one piece. Every element must be in proper position to create a harmonious image. The characteristics of a design can be moved and manipulated to create an interesting and functional combination of elements.

Choosing type styles is also important to achieving unity. A unified design is the result of viewing the layout as a whole and not as separate elements. See **Figure 7-36**.

Goodheart-Willcox Publisher

Figure 7-35. A balanced pattern provides rhythm by contrasting with the rest of the image.

Goodheart-Willcox Publisher

Figure 7-36. Unity in design is achieved using balance, hierarchy, contrast, and a clear message.

Gestalt

Gestalt is a psychology term that means "unified whole." The theory of how people tend to organize visual elements into groups or a unified whole was developed by German psychologists in the 1920s. Successful designs use these principles to create unity.

The unity is based on the fact that the whole is viewed independently from its parts. When viewed separately, the parts can take on a completely different meaning from when looked at together.

Gestalt Principles

The gestalt principles include:

- ***Similarity***—The appearance of objects looking alike so that the viewer perceives them to be a group or pattern.
- ***Proximity***—Elements that are placed close together are viewed as a group and become visually tied together.
- ***Closure***—The property of a space that is not completely enclosed (or a specific object is incomplete) but enough is implied that your eye fills in the missing information. The panda in the World Wide Fund for Nature logo is an example of closure.
- ***Continuation***—Continuation is the result of your eye continuing though one element into another. The FedEx® logo shows continuation with the arrow.

See examples in **Figure 7-37**.

Layout

Layout is the road map of elements that shows the visual hierarchy and provides the direction for the viewer. The ***elements of layout*** include all of your assets: the text, the graphics, and the page itself.

Composition

The arrangement of these elements must be pleasing to the eye and easy to read. The designer is responsible for assembling the elements to make a ***composition***.

Because symmetry is the easiest way to achieve balance, if you place the most important element at the visual center of the page, you can add impact to your design. The ***visual center*** is slightly up and to the right of the physical center of a page or area. See **Figure 7-38**.

Rule of Thirds

Applying the basic ***rule of thirds*** to your design makes the layout more interesting. Divide your page into thirds, both horizontally and vertically. Using this layout and placing key elements on the intersections of these lines, your design will have more power. See **Figure 7-39**.

The *Z* layout utilizes common eye movements to direct the viewer though your design. Through placement of key elements and visual hierarchy, you want the viewer to start in the upper-left corner, continue across the page, then down a diagonal to the bottom left. This layout will finish in the bottom-right corner, or ***power corner***. This corner has more visual "weight" than the rest of the page. See **Figure 7-40**.

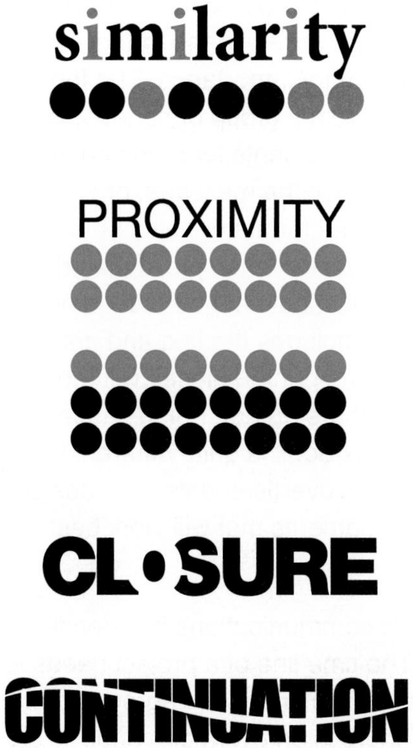

Goodheart-Willcox Publisher

Figure 7-37. Four of the Gestalt principles shown here are similarity, proximity, closure, and continuation.

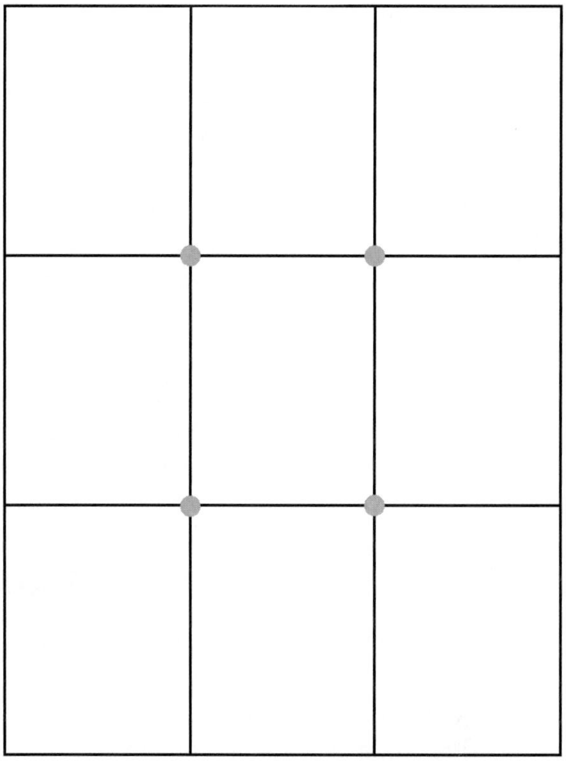

Goodheart-Willcox Publisher

Figure 7-39. Using the rule of thirds adds visual punch to a design.

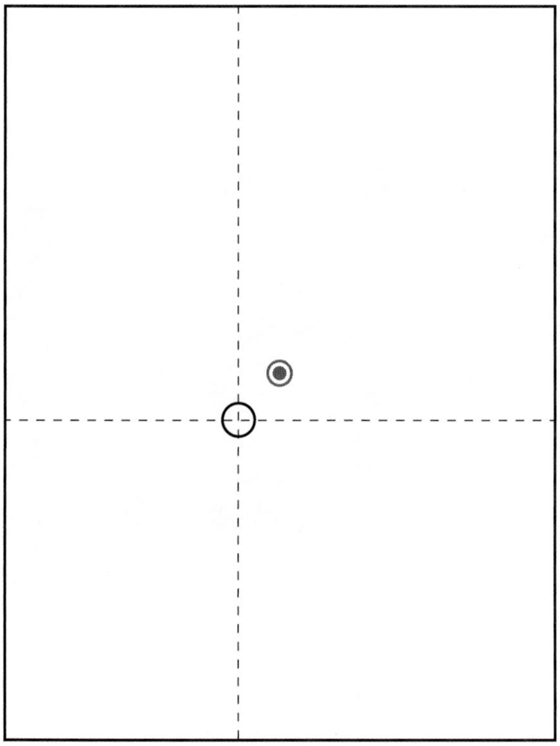

Goodheart-Willcox Publisher

Figure 7-38. The visual center of a page is slightly up and to the right of the actual center.

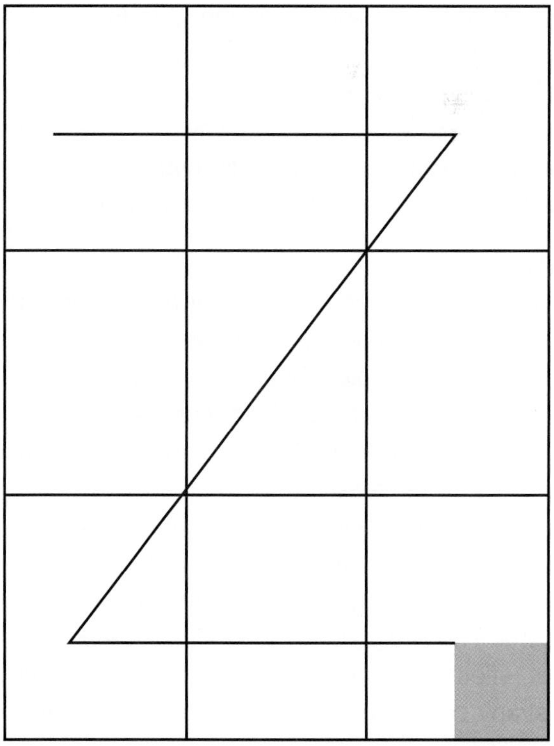

Goodheart-Willcox Publisher

Figure 7-40. A *Z* layout starts in the upper left and progresses through the page to end in the power corner.

Inverted Pyramid

The foundation of a pyramid holds up the rest of the structure. Without a firm foundation, everything would fall apart. In design, however, an inverted pyramid is a basic layout structure. The goal is to visually lead the viewer through our design in a way that provides meaning to achieve the goal of the project. With an inverted pyramid, you lead the viewer from the big end to the point where the key information or call to action is placed. The pyramid acts like an arrow leading us through the page. If it were a traditional pyramid, the top point would lead our eye off the page and we would never see the rest of the design.

The Process of Graphic Design

Graphic design is a process. Embracing the process will not only make your design stronger and more effective, it will make it easier and more efficient. This process is about problem solving. You need to see the problem, define the problem, and then solve the problem.

The process starts with a plan. This plan may be generated through the use of a project brief. A ***project brief*** is a series of questions you need answers to before you can begin. See **Figure 7-41**. Each project will require a different set of questions, but the easiest course of action to remember is who, what, when, where, and why. It is less intense than a full proposal but more than just a simple outline. It is the foundation for your layout.

Who

Defining who the project is for (your client) and to whom it is targeted (your audience) are critical elements of the project brief. One helps you as the designer, and has the backstory on who you are working with. The other helps you determine who you are trying to reach.

Knowing the audience is very important. For example, one ad might be designed for young people, while another might be aimed at senior citizens. The design of each ad should be unique and must reflect the intent of the printed piece, as well as meet any specific needs the audience may have.

What

The specifications of the project are needed at the beginning. Are you creating a brochure, a poster, a website, or perhaps an advertisement? Deciding how to organize the format of the printed piece is of primary importance. The format is the style, size, spacing, group of pages, margins, and all printing requirements for a printed job. Will a single sheet carry the message, or will a booklet do a better job? The format will also be determined by its intended use. For example, if the printed piece is to be posted, it should not be printed on both sides.

The style includes the text and graphic elements. Some printed pieces will require a set style, while others do not. For instance, the style used in this textbook is quite different from the styles used in advertisements. The designer must choose the elements that will work best.

When

Graphic communications is a deadline-driven industry. The time line of a project needs to be determined at the onset and agreed upon by all parties. If there is an event or a specific date that the project needs to meet, work backward through the entire process, including production and delivery, to determine your schedule.

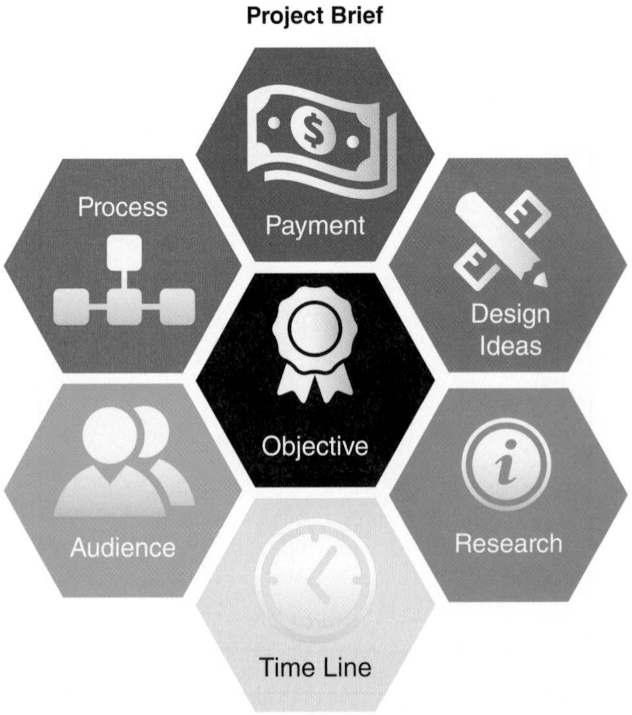

Goodheart-Willcox Publisher

Figure 7-41. Project briefs provide valuable information needed to create a successful design.

Where

Knowing not only how, but where, the final piece will be distributed provides valuable information as to how you will direct your message to reach the audience.

Why

The final and most critical piece of information is to understand the goal. Knowing what your client hopes to achieve with the design is critical to the success of the design. Having the best visual design ever is wasted if the objective is not met. Having and agreeing on a final objective is an important step. For example, an objective might state that the final printed piece should inform the reader, through text and illustrated material, how a piece of equipment will help in a specific production situation.

The objective describes what the information on the printed page is intended to do. Knowing the purpose helps the designer determine which text and illustrations will be best for the job.

Assets

Evaluating your assets—text, graphics, and page—and determining the structure of your layout will guide you in establishing the visual hierarchy of the design. The hierarchy is the order of importance and direction, and it needs to be clear and obvious for the viewer to follow.

Text

Body type is the printed type that makes up the text in a layout. Body type must be chosen to reflect the intent of the message. The text must be clearly legible and must relate to the topic. Typically, a topic aimed at a contemporary audience would use a modern typeface. See **Figure 7-42**. The placement of type requires proper spacing. White space can be just as important as the type itself.

Usually, the body type itself is not the focal point of the layout. The text will contain a message that expands on the other elements. All of the elements, including type, are positioned in a logical progression of importance to meet the layout objectives. Some layout elements will be primary, while others become secondary, according to the objectives of the layout.

Goodheart-Willcox Publisher

Figure 7-42. Body text should be legible and the appropriate style and size but not the focus of the layout.

Display Type

Display type is the type that conveys the main message of the layout. It is intended to draw attention. Newspaper and magazine headlines are typical examples of display type. One kind of layout is called ***headline dominant***. This type of layout makes the display line the most important element on the page and is used when that content is key to the success of a message. If the display type creates interest, the reader will proceed to the body. See **Figure 7-43**.

The display type in an advertisement leads the reader to other information. After reading the display material, the person must be satisfied or directed to continue reading the text.

The style of display type is very important because it must correspond to the visual message. Some type styles can be very dramatic, as illustrated in **Figure 7-44**. In such cases, the topic and type style must be compatible.

Goodheart-Willcox Publisher

Figure 7-43. A layout is headline dominant when the headline generates the first attention to the page.

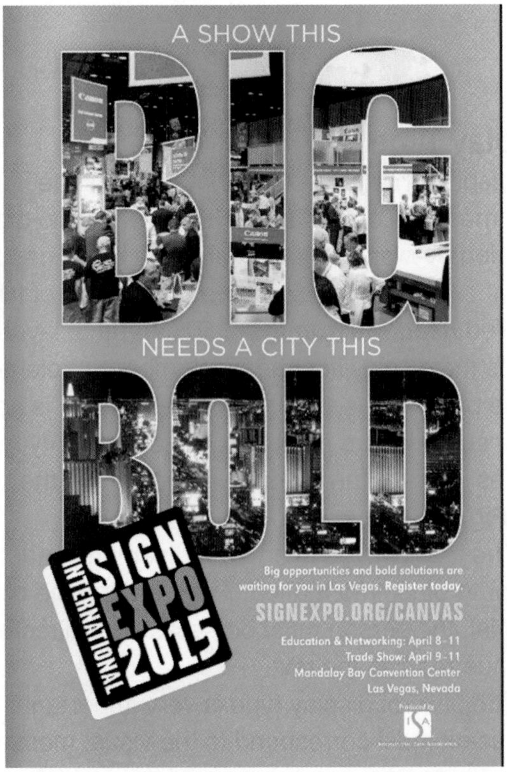

©International Sign Association/CSG Creative (Design Agency)

Figure 7-44. This ad for SignExpo.org shows a dramatic use of type for the headline.

The entire layout must be looked at when choosing a display typeface. The display line must be distinctive and appropriate. To properly select a typeface, the job objective must be fully understood by the designer.

Graphics

The ***graphics*** in a layout include the ornamentation, photographs, and artwork, such as illustrations. When an image or graphic is the dominant, or key, element to a layout, it is called ***picture dominant***.

The message provided by this layout can be very revealing. See **Figure 7-45**. The old saying, "A picture is worth a thousand words," applies to many printed materials. Pictorial images are a very strong way of conveying a message. In some cases, an illustration may convey the message by itself.

White Space

White space includes areas of the layout that are devoid of printed images. Treating the white space as an element makes it thoughtful and can add to the strength of the message and visual quality of a layout. White space is often the most overlooked element. It is important to first see the space to use the space.

©Amanda Hall

Figure 7-45. This image-dominant layout shows how the image has the focus but leads you to the text and message.

White space is often not white. It includes the area that is trapped between elements, the counters in type, negative space, and margins. Never think of white space as empty area. If only the elements on the page are arranged, the white space is ineffective and unused. If the white space is treated as an element and well planned, the design becomes effective. White space can balance another area or element. It has shape and it has mass. See **Figure 7-46**.

One way to increase or add white space to a page is to address the type. Increasing line spacing, paragraph spacing, gutters, and margins, and using flush left alignment all give the illusion of more white space and, in turn, type becomes easier to read.

Passive vs. Active

Two different kinds of layouts to consider are passive and active. While not all layouts fit cleanly into these two categories, it is a good place to start. A ***passive layout*** is very symmetrical. If you divide the page down the middle, you have basically the same information or balance on each side. Passive layouts are good for a clean, corporate, or sophisticated look. ***Active layouts*** are asymmetrical and, while balanced, they do not have the same information on each side. If the content calls for excitement or action, an active layout is a good place to start.

This delineation is especially helpful if you are presenting several concepts to a customer who is unsure what he or she wants. If you present three active layouts and the customer really wanted passive, that customer will not be drawn to any of your choices. If you present a combination of the two, the customer will usually be drawn to one format or the other. See **Figure 7-47**.

Developing a Layout

The first step in determining your layout is to conceptualize. You should always start with a

Career Link

Graphic Designer

Designs of printed products are created by graphic designers. Graphic designers use visual elements to get a message across. Their designs may be used in several different areas, such as book layouts, brochures, posters, annual reports, packaging, or websites.

A company or client will give the graphic designer an idea of the message that must be conveyed. Once the graphic designer has this information and understands the needs of the client, he or she works to develop the visual elements that will convey the message. Graphic designers begin to develop their designs by creating rough sketches of their ideas, either by hand or by using appropriate software. In some cases, graphic designers also help printers by choosing materials such as the proper substrate. Final design copy is approved by the client, who often works with the printer.

While many graphic designers are employed by agencies, publishers, or printers, some are self-employed. However, all graphic designers must have similar education and training to assist them in skill development. Graphic designers use a variety of computer design programs. They must also be familiar with applications of color, layout, type, photography, and printing processes. Graphic designers must have an associate or bachelor's degree to be competitive in the job market. In addition, graphic designers must be skilled at planning, organizing, analyzing, and learning to use the most up-to-date technology.

"Graphic communications remains a strong and viable field today and will continue far into the future."
Mike Chiricuzio
Arizona State University

Goodheart-Willcox Publisher

Figure 7-46. The white space is not "empty." It balances the rest of the text.

Goodheart-Willcox Publisher

Figure 7-47. Active and passive layouts.

pencil and paper. Possessing drawing skills is not necessary to follow the steps of the concept.

Begin with ***thumbnails***. Thumbnails are small, quick, and simple preliminary ideas doodled onto paper. When drawing thumbnails on paper, you will generally explore options that you would not consider on the computer. The size of a thumbnail is not important. The thumbnail sketch is generally smaller than the size of the printed product. The first thumbnail sketch might not be the design selected, but each one will help the artist visualize the end product.

A soft pencil or felt-tip pen is typically used to draw thumbnail sketches. Use boxes for images and lines for text. Never edit while doing thumbnails; start a new one if you want to change something. The purpose of the thumbnail sketch is to evaluate the weight of each element. The thumbnail sketch shows the basic shape and tone of the total piece. See **Figure 7-48**.

A ***rough*** is the next step. It is a thumbnail taken to the right proportions of the final design, preferably at 100% of the size, with slightly more detail. The rough layout has a closer resemblance to the intended printed piece than the thumbnail sketches.

The next step is the ***comprehensive***. This is where you detail the assets more clearly. Block in the display type and add color. This step is often done on the computer and ultimately becomes the final file.

Job Specifications

Before you begin, you need to know all the job ***specifications***, or specs. The size requirements, printing specifications, finishing information, and binding requirement all influence how a layout is developed. Think backward.

How a piece will be bound affects the margins. Saddle-stitching requires different margins from coil-binding. For more information on stitching, see Chapter 17, *Finishing and Binding*. Where text and images are placed is impacted by the binding. Check with your printer to determine how much margin they will need for the final layout.

Most finishing requirements are set up in the file from the beginning. For instance, the width of the panels for a trifold brochure depends on how it folds. A Z-fold has different panel widths from a letterfold. Die-cuts and foils need to be included in the electronic file.

Printing Specifications

Printing specifications include size, quantity, paper requirements, color, and resolution. One important concern is the size of the press required to run the job. The finished size also determines the size of the paper to be used in printing.

The number of pages to be printed and the number of copies required will help determine the printing requirements. Based on the number of pages and the size, the printing company will decide the most economical way of printing the job.

Printing requirements include the kind of stock or paper to use. The necessary stock must

©Randy Burnett

Figure 7-48. Thumbnails are preliminary ideas, very quickly generated with pencil on paper, to show a number of different ideas or options for a particular layout or design.

be available at the designated time for printing. A custom stock may need to be ordered, which may require additional time. Other considerations in ordering stock are the size of the order, paper weight or thickness, and opacity.

The printer should also provide the information necessary for achieving the best color and most accurate representation of the images. Color profiles, file format specifications, and resolution requirements are all details that the designer must have for proper file setup.

File Setup

Choosing the correct software to create your document is an important decision. Just because you can create a document in a particular program does not mean you necessarily should. Software applications have particular functions to perform specific jobs. Examples of page geometry software that meet industry standards are InDesign® and QuarkXPress. Using a word processing application or business software for page layout will limit your capabilities and very likely create problems at printing time.

If you have multiple pages or panels in your document, make yourself a dummy before you start. A ***dummy*** is a small representation of your final piece. The pages may be blank but it should show pagination as well as how the final piece folds. See **Figure 7-49**.

Goodheart-Willcox Publisher

Figure 7-49. A dummy is a small, folded paper example of the final piece showing folding and pagination.

Grid

Using a grid for your layout will give you consistency among pages and make your decision-making process as to where to place text and graphics much easier and more efficient. A ***grid*** is an underlying template that shows where the columns, gutters, and margins are. To determine what grid you want to use, evaluate the content being used. The content drives the grid; the grid should not drive the content. For instance, if you have a lot of long stories or text, you might want to allow for callouts or sidebars to help you break up the look. Images and captions, subheads and charts, and graphics of all kinds are considerations that will help you determine what kind of grid to use.

The grid itself should be invisible, but the effect it has on your design will be apparent. A grid is not designed to be limiting. It provides a foundation for your document that will give it a certain look and streamline your process.

Using a grid does not mean you will have a boring layout. Using ***spatial zones***, or groups of boxes on a grid, allows a mixture of visual spaces that keeps the layout interesting but consistent. See **Figure 7-50**.

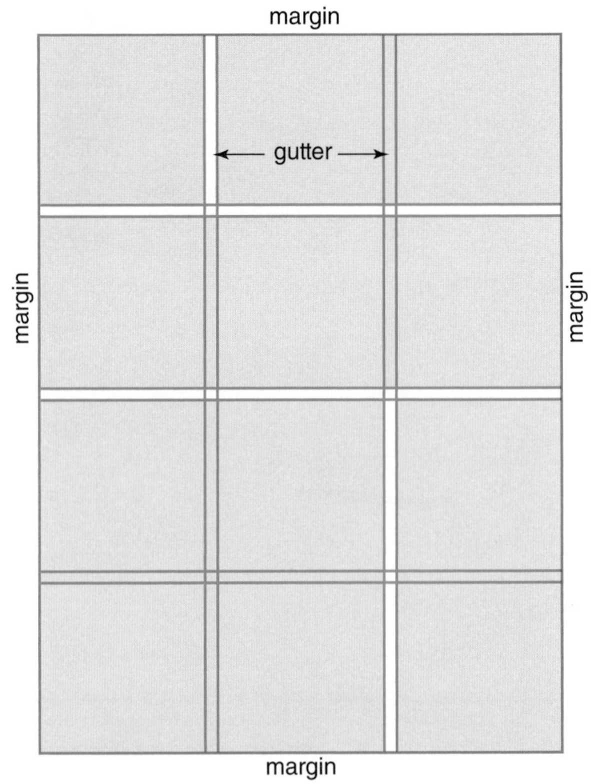

Goodheart-Willcox Publisher

Figure 7-50. A grid showing different spatial zones for optional layouts.

Margins

White space must be defined in a grid as well. The simplest grid is a one-column grid, defined by your ***margins***, or edges of the design. Make sure your margins are big enough to give the eyes a break from the text and to allow for your finishing and binding process.

Using spacious margins gives an importance to the content. Margins in a textbook or workbook are sometimes functional, allowing space for notes. On a ***spread***, or where two pages are always seen side by side, the inner margins might be larger than the outside margins, usually by two-thirds of the size, to accommodate the binding edge and create the illusion of equal margins. See **Figure 7-51**.

When using columns of text, set the ***gutters***, or area between the columns, smaller than your outside margins. This ensures that the text in the columns will visually relate to each other rather than the edge of the page. More margin space may be necessary at the bottom of the page to accommodate footers or page numbers. In most cases, you should not go any closer to the edge of the page than 1/8″.

Goodheart-Willcox Publisher

Figure 7-51. Margins add white space and allow the eye to rest when reading text.

Summary

- Graphic designer responsibilities include graphic design for print, web design, marketing, mobile marketing, photography, copywriting, and production.
- The basic elements of design are line, shape, texture, space, size, and color.
- A color wheel is an arrangement of colors that provides a means of identifying colors in a consistent manner.
- The basic principles of design are balance, contrast, unity, rhythm, and hierarchy.
- Gestalt is a theory of how people tend to organize visual elements into groups or a unified whole. Gestalt principles include similarity, proximity, closure, and continuation.
- The elements of layout include text, graphics, and the page itself.
- A project brief is a series of questions you need answers to before you can begin.
- A passive layout is symmetrical; active layouts are asymmetrical.
- Thumbnails are small, quick, and simple preliminary ideas doodled onto paper.
- A grid is an underlying template that shows the locations of the columns, gutters, and margins.

Review Questions

Answer the following questions using the information in this chapter.

1. In graphic communications, design refers to the use of proper methods to produce a product that is both _____ and _____.
2. Explain the role of the graphic designer.
3. Which of the following is *not* an element of design?
   A. Shape.
   B. Texture.
   C. Size.
   D. Beauty.
4. What are the three basic design shapes?
5. The _____ is a tool that illustrates the basics of color.
6. What are the three primary colors?
7. Colors that are directly opposite each other on the color wheel are called _____.
   A. secondary
   B. tertiary
   C. complementary
   D. analogous

8. Red, red-orange, orange, yellow-orange, and yellow would be what kind of harmony?
9. Name the five principles of design.
10. _____ is the proper balance of all elements in an image so a pleasing whole results and the image is viewed as one piece.
11. Name the four Gestalt principles.
12. List the three elements of layout.
13. Where is the visual center of a page?
14. What are the basic questions that need to be answered in a project brief?
15. *True or False?* White space is the area left over after placing elements on a page.
16. _____ is intended to draw attention to the printed piece.
17. *True or False?* Passive layouts are asymmetrical.
18. A(n) _____ is a quick preliminary idea drawn on paper.
19. Size requirements and printing, finishing, and binding information are all job _____ that will influence how a layout is developed.
20. A(n) _____ gives you consistency between pages of your document.
21. Your _____ should always be bigger than your gutters.

Suggested Activities

1. Select designs in a publication that stress the design elements of lines, shapes, mass, texture, and color.
2. Find a magazine advertisement that you think is well balanced and uses color as contrast. Find another one you think does not have clear hierarchy. What would you do to change it?
3. Create a landscape using only type as texture.
4. Study a magazine and identify the underlying grid.

Chapter 8

Evaluation and Critique

Goodheart-Willcox Publisher

Learning Objectives

After studying this chapter, you will be able to:

- Analyze your design.
- Critique your own work effectively.
- Critique other work effectively.
- Properly accept constructive criticism.
- Comfortably receive feedback.

Important Terms

constructive criticism

critique

design forums

project brief

G-WLEARNING.com

While studying this chapter, look for the activity icon to:

- **Practice** vocabulary terms with e-flash cards, matching activities, and vocabulary game.
- **Reinforce** what you learn by submitting end-of-chapter questions.

www.g-wlearning.com/visualtechnology/

It is easy to look at a design and say, "I like it," or "I don't like it." It is considerably more difficult to look at a design and determine *why* you like it or *why* you do not. When analyzing a design, you need to not only express approval or disapproval, but also describe the reasons behind your assessment. This is known as a ***critique***. Critiques are often misinterpreted as fault-finding exhibitions meant to call out flaws. Awaiting a critique has caused many an artist great anxiety. This is unfortunate because a true critique is impartial and points out the strengths as well as the weaknesses. *Critique* should not be confused with *criticism*, which is disapproving. A critique is a disciplined, educated evaluation that can include positive or negative feedback.

If you are seeking an opinion from someone in particular, presumably this person is important to you or the project, and you value and/or rely on his or her input. Either way, you want to get more from him or her than, "that's fine."

Valuable input or feedback includes information, suggestions, or ideas that you can consider, explore, and evaluate, **Figure 8-1**. There are no rules that say you have to implement any or all of these comments. It would be foolish, however, to ignore the ideas from those you have determined matter to you or the project. Look at their suggestions and evaluate their validity and impact.

©Dana Thelander

Figure 8-1. Before making a final decision, it usually helps to discuss ideas and get feedback from others to get different perspectives.

Analyzing

Paying close attention to all the details of a job or project, including specifications, parameters, and goals, is an important step in successful job completion. It is also critical to check and review all of the design decisions you have made and evaluate them with regard to the end goal.

Critiquing Your Own Work

It is difficult to be objective about your own work. Your judgment may be clouded because you have invested time, effort, and equity into your project. When you have reached a point in your process that you are ready to stand back and see if it works as a viable solution, refer to your project brief. The ***project brief*** is the document you will have developed with the key players in the project, and it contains critical information, such as specifications, goals, research, schedules, costs, and agreed-upon workflow. Review the brief to see if the objectives are met. Literally stand back, away from your screen, and evaluate your work. Squint at the piece. Do not just screen check it; print it out and reevaluate it. Check the hierarchy, making sure that the design relays the message in the right visual order with the right level of impact. See **Figure 8-2**. Ask yourself the following questions:

- What is the first thing my eye sees when I look at the document?
- Does the design lead me through the page clearly?
- Is the message clear?
- Does this appeal to the right audience?
- Is the voice of the typeface correct?
- Is it easily read?
- Do the colors add value to the final design?
- Does the contrast make it interesting?
- Does it have unity?

Goodheart-Willcox Publisher

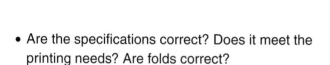

Figure 8-2. The hierarchy should help the design relay the message correctly.

©Dana Thelander

Figure 8-4. Print out your design and evaluate it with someone you trust. Discuss whether it does what you intended it to do.

- Are the specifications correct? Does it meet the printing needs? Are folds correct?
- Are the margins appropriate? See **Figure 8-3**.

Ideally, this self-analysis should be done at various stages throughout the project, to make sure you stay on the right track. See **Figure 8-4**. Each time you evaluate the specifics of your design with regard to the elements and principles of design, you strengthen your ability to make solid and efficient design decisions. This will build your self-confidence and improve your design.

Critiquing the Work of Others

One of the most valuable habits any designer can have is to study visual graphics around him or her. Materials of all kinds that utilize design surround us, whether they are printed items, online marketing messages, or television commercials. Looking closely at the designs other creatives have done can help strengthen your own skills. You can learn as much from something you do not like as you can from something you do. Go back to our series of questions. Figure out what you like specifically in a

Goodheart-Willcox Publisher

Figure 8-3. Evaluate a design to ensure margins are appropriate. Which margins seem more appropriate between these two designs?

great design. Does the color really reach out, or is it the beautiful typography? Look at a design that particularly offends you and ask, "Where did it fail?" The answer is usually in the hierarchy or the contrast. Think about what you would do differently to improve the design. If time permits, try some thumbnails to see if your ideas have merit.

Start a collection of examples you especially like. See **Figure 8-5**. This becomes a great resource from which to draw inspiration when you get stuck. If the typography on a direct mailer looks terrific, you may want to apply that particular technique to a brochure later on. A particular challenge of graphic design is being creative on demand. Sometimes you just do not feel particularly creative, you hit a mental block, or you simply run out of time. Having this collection of ideas can be a lifesaver.

Constructive Criticism

To embrace the benefits of ***constructive criticism***, a goal must be specified for the critique. The goal of any critique should be to enhance or improve upon a design. Effective criticism, whether positive or negative, is always constructive. As long as any comments are well-intentioned, specific, and objective, they are worth considering. Well thought-out and organized comments can lead to valuable discussions with good, interactive feedback that provides new thoughts and views. See **Figure 8-6**. Provided it is from a trusted and objective source, do not take any feedback personally. Instead, take that feedback and use it to improve your design. That is how to ensure constructive criticism is just that—constructive.

Presenting for Feedback

When presenting your work for critique, try to address the following topics:

- The objective of the design
- Why you made specific choices you made
- Your favorite part of the piece

This gives specific talking points for others to give feedback. If you have a particular problem area

©Dana Thelander

Figure 8-5. Start a collection of design samples that you find and that you really like as a resource from which to draw inspiration.

©Dana Thelander

Figure 8-6. Feedback from a trusted and respected source can be beneficial to eliminating design errors and improving your final product.

that you are concerned about, ask about it directly. Consider each critique practice for when you have to present to a client. Practice not only makes perfect, it also thickens your skin. See **Figure 8-7**.

Using Design Forums

Social media provides a great resource for getting feedback on your projects throughout the design process. Many options exist that can help you get other opinions on your designs. There are a number of ***design forums*** that you can join, where you can post your design, see other designs, and give and receive feedback.

Another option is to form your own group of trusted people. With this kind of network, you can show your project at any stage to get feedback on your design decisions. This collaborative process can act as a corrective step in the process and keep you from going in the wrong direction.

Giving Feedback

When issuing feedback, try to avoid the words "good" and "bad" and statements such as, "I don't like the typeface." This kind of feedback is unhelpful criticism. Instead, say something like, "I think a typeface with a different voice would better serve the message." That opens the door to conversations regarding the message and what kind of voice it should have.

Be as specific as possible. For instance, if the design has gone overboard with color, start with a positive statement regarding the bold use of color. Then suggest that perhaps simplifying the color palette and picking two or three of the colors would strengthen the impact of color on the design. This type of feedback identifies the problem, proposes a solution, and suggests the potential outcome.

Pull out your design vocabulary. Using design terms helps keep the focus of the discussion on specifics. Being specific goes for positive feedback as well. Rather than, "I really like what you did with the type," try, "the typeface you chose for the headline has the perfect voice and balance for the audience." The more detail given in a critique, the more likely the comments will take seed and help the designer grow. Always put yourself in the shoes

©Dana Thelander

Figure 8-7. Giving and receiving feedback on your design is a valuable way to gain insight into the success of your final product.

Academic Link

US Currency

In addition to using intaglio or gravure printing processes, the US Bureau of Engraving and Printing makes use of several high-tech processes to thwart the activity of currency counterfeiters. Intaglio and gravure printing add unique patterns and texture to paper currency, but additional identifiers have been added to the redesigned currency in circulation.

- **Watermarks:** Faint images that are part of the paper and are visible from both sides of the paper. Common watermarks on US currency include portraits of historical figures and the numeric value of the currency.
- **Security threads:** A plastic strip embedded in the paper that displays the value of the bill. Depending on the denomination, security threads glow orange, green, or yellow when held under ultraviolet light.
- **Microprinting:** Tiny characters, words, or phrases printed on the bills that are usually not visible to the naked eye. The microprinted words are difficult, if not impossible, to reproduce by counterfeiters.
- **Color-shifting ink:** Images or numbers printed on the bills change from copper to green when viewed at different angles. This effect is created by adding metallic flakes to the ink.

of the one being critiqued. How would you like to hear suggestions? What would make you listen with an open mind to the ideas of others?

Receiving Feedback

Constructive feedback on your design is an important way to increase communication as well as help you grow as a designer. Often a great motivator, feedback can give you different perspectives as to how your work is perceived.

Listening

It is sometimes difficult to hear others talk about your design, especially if the comments are negative. Do not get defensive about what people say. The goal of the critique is to receive input that will enhance or improve your design. Getting the opinion of other creatives gives a new perspective and a "fresh pair of eyes."

Opportunity for Improvement

Getting feedback gives you an opportunity to see aspects of the design that you may have overlooked. Let's say you are designing a brochure for a new exhibit at the zoo. See **Figure 8-8**. Your objective is for a potential tourist to pick up the brochure, see immediately that there is a new exhibit, and then make plans to go see it. Having a critique gives you the opportunity to "test drive" the brochure and see if people respond how you want them to. Finding out why they did or did not react the way you intended will help you strengthen the design.

Keep an open mind. If you are sure your design is the best it can be, and others offer suggestions to enhance your design or clarify the message, do not ignore them. Give thoughtful consideration to all suggestions. Ultimately, you have the power to make the decision as to whether or not you will make changes.

Polite Reception

Even if you are devastated at the end of a critique, be polite and thank your fellow creatives for their input. Again, do not take it personally. Any critique before you present to the client is a great opportunity to receive valuable insight with no risk. Embrace the situation and use the feedback to your advantage.

Goodheart-Willcox Publisher

Figure 8-8. New zoo brochure layout.

Note Taking

If possible, have someone take notes on your feedback. See **Figure 8-9**. Otherwise, as soon as the critique is complete, sit down and note everything you can remember. Critiques sometimes go very quickly and you do not want to miss anything. Often, you will receive conflicting comments. This is not uncommon. Everyone reacts to things differently and you want as many diverse opinions as you can get. Evaluate them all based on your objectives, your project brief, and your own thoughts. Determine which suggestions you want to look at more closely, then apply those that you feel will enhance your design.

Goodheart-Willcox Publisher

Figure 8-9. Feedback notes on the zoo brochure layout in Figure 8-8.

Summary

- Valuable input or feedback includes information, suggestions, or ideas from other creatives that you can consider implementing into your design.
- When analyzing your design, refer to your project brief to see if the objectives are met.
- Constructive criticism is well-intentioned, specific, and objective.
- A bad design usually fails in the hierarchy or the contrast.
- Receiving and accepting feedback will enhance and improve your design.
- A critique offers you a test audience to tell you the strengths of your design and where it falls short.

Review Questions

Answer the following questions using the information in this chapter.

1. An analysis of work is called a(n) _____.
2. Which of the following is a question you should ask yourself when doing self-analysis of your design?
   A. Is there enough contrast?
   B. Is the message clear?
   C. Is the type readable?
   D. All of the above.
3. *True or False?* Constructive criticism is always positive.
4. What is a design forum?
5. What is the goal of receiving a critique?

Suggested Activities

1. Find an example of a printed piece you like and evaluate it. Discuss what you like specifically and why.
2. Find an example of a printed piece you do not like and evaluate it. Create thumbnails and a rough of the changes you would make to improve it.
3. Join a design forum.
4. Compare the changes in how currency has been printed over the last 40 years.

Chapter 9

Digital Prepress and Production

Learning Objectives

After studying this chapter, you will be able to:

- Identify different computer platforms.
- Explain the characteristics of different types of memory and storage devices.
- Differentiate among various output devices.
- Explain the processes used in text and graphics preparation.
- Summarize the features of page composition programs.
- Describe the color gamut and how it affects images.
- Explain the proofreading process.
- Explain the preflighting process.
- Compare types of production proofs.
- Explain digital prepress workflow.

Goodheart-Willcox Publisher

Important Terms

additive color formation
aliasing
anchor points
antialiasing
augmented reality
baseline grid
Bezier curve
binary
bit
bit depth
byte
cable modem
character style
clipboard
cloud-based storage
color management system (CMS)
color space
comparison proofing
contract proof
cross-platform
data center
desktop
digital camera
digital prepress system
digital subscriber line (DSL)
Drupa
dye-sublimation printer
effective resolution
flash drive
flash memory card
font set
gamut
gigabyte
graphical user interface (GUI)
graphics tablet
GREP
halftone dot
hardware
hex colors
hinting
image resolution
ink-jet proof
in port
interpreter
Job Definition Format (JDF)
laser proof
link
linking
lossless compression algorithm
lossy compression algorithm
loupe
master page
menu
modem
monitor
nested style
OpenType font
operating system
out port
output device
overset text
page description language (PDL)
Pantone
paragraph style
pasteboard
pixel
platform
portable document format (PDF)
PostScript®
PostScript® Type 1 font
preferences
preflighting
print engine
printer resolution
proof
proofreader's mark
proofreading
QR code
random-access memory (RAM)
raster
raster image processor (RIP)
resolution
retina display
satellite Internet
screen frequency
soft proofs
software
solid-state drive (SSD)
style sheet
subtractive color formation
tablet computer
terabyte
template
threading
toner
tool palette
TrueType font
two-person proofing
vector graphics
workspace
wysiwyp

G-WLEARNING.COM

While studying this chapter, look for the activity icon to:

- **Practice** vocabulary terms with e-flash cards, matching activities, and vocabulary game.
- **Reinforce** what you learn by submitting end-of-chapter questions.

www.g-wlearning.com/visualtechnology/

Digital systems dominate every stage of the printing process, from formatting the author's manuscript, to running the press, to finishing the product. Maintaining a smooth workflow requires the consistency of digital data throughout the production process. Sustaining consistency, as well as compatibility, requires that everyone involved in the production process have an understanding of current digital media.

In a perfect world, every piece of digital equipment, as well as every computer program and file produced, would be compatible. Unfortunately, this is not the case. For this reason, many organizations, such as the American National Standards Institute (ANSI), the International Standards Organization (ISO), the Joint Photographic Experts Group (JPEG), and International Color Consortium (ICC) created standards to guide manufacturers and consumers of digital media and equipment to improve compatibility. The entrepreneurial and innovative aspect of the graphic communications industry envelops a vast amount of information and products. This chapter covers general information that applies to digital prepress operations and general file production.

©Dana Thelander

Figure 9-1. Computers are used for creating page layouts in page composition software.

Digital Basics

The computer is the focal point of job creation and assembly of text and images into page layouts within the graphic communications industry. The computer and associated devices, in conjunction with the specialized graphics programs, are components in the ***digital prepress system***, **Figure 9-1**.

A computer uses a ***binary*** system to process and store information in digital form. This means that the computer recognizes only two numbers, or digits: 1 and 0. These digits represent two states, on (1) and off (0). The individual 1s and 0s are called ***bits***, or binary digits, and can be combined into groups of eight digits to create a binary word, or ***byte***. Since there are 256 possible combinations of 1s and 0s in an eight-digit byte (from 11111111 to 00000000), a special code was devised to assign a specific meaning to each combination.

The American Standard Code for Information Interchange (ASCII) provides a way to digitally store and process letters, numbers, punctuation marks, and symbols. When the letter *c* is pressed on a keyboard, for example, it is converted to a specific combination of 1s and 0s. Different combinations are assigned for the capital and lowercase forms of each letter. Once in digital form, the information can be processed by the computer's circuits and stored as digital or magnetic charges.

Regardless of size or complexity, a computer system has three major functions: input, processing, and output, **Figure 9-2**. Computer systems also have some means of storing information, either within the system, in a portable form, in a cloud-based system, or all three. There are a number of different methods and devices used for input, storage, and output. They are described in the following sections.

Computer Platforms

The ***platform*** of a digital prepress system comprises a computer ***hardware*** device and an ***operating system*** used to run various applications. The operating system is the interface between the user and the computer, as well as the computer and the application. The hardware (laptop, tablet, desktop) contains a processor, memory, storage, and an operating system. Common operating systems include Microsoft® Windows®, Mac OS X® from Apple®, Linux OS for standard computers, and Symbian OS, Android™, Apple iOS, Blackberry® OS, and Windows® OS for mobile devices.

©Dana Thelander

Figure 9-2. This computer system configuration illustrates the three main functions of input (scanner, keyboard, and mouse), processing (CPU built into the monitor), and output (monitor and printer).

Computer platforms include the elements necessary to create, assemble, and output data in the finished pages, **Figure 9-3**. While all individual computers are personal computers, or PCs, the term has become widely accepted to mean the computer platforms based on the Microsoft® Windows® operating system. The major platforms used in graphic communications are PC and Apple® Macintosh®. Once the platform is defined, software developers design and install corresponding software applications. ***Software*** is a computer program that initiates a specific function of the computer. Types of software include word processing, page composition, and graphics programs.

©George Deal

Figure 9-3. Desktop publishing allows graphic designers to create and edit both text and art.

Some file formats and devices are ***cross-platform***, which means they can operate on or be used with different platforms. For example, a cross-platform word processing program allows users to create and modify documents using different operating systems, if necessary. While Apple is considered the industry standard for graphic communications, the software functions virtually the same on both PCs and Macs.

Macintosh®

The Macintosh® computer was introduced in 1984 and quickly became popular because of its ease of use and ability to generate high-quality graphic images. The Macintosh® system was designed around the concept of a ***graphical user interface (GUI)***, which allowed for easy-to-understand, on-screen graphic representations of computing tasks. At that time, competing platforms were based on the more difficult method of typing commands to perform tasks. This platform was central to the development of Desktop Publishing (DTP) Systems and continues to play a major role.

In 1999, Apple introduced OS X. OS X is a Unix-based operating system that provided more stability. In 2005, Steve Jobs announced the transition to Intel processors for all Apple computers, and in

2011, the use of the Thunderbolt I/O interface was announced. This PCI Express technology allows the connection to high-speed peripherals as well as high-resolution displays with double the bandwidth and transfer speeds of 20 GB/s in both directions.

Personal Computers (PCs)

The PC is the platform most often used in business environments. In the early 1990s, the original command-based operating system for PCs was replaced by Microsoft® Windows®, which was GUI-designed to give the PC the same ease of use as the Macintosh®. The introduction of versatile word processing programs, sophisticated illustration and graphics software, and powerful page composition software made this platform a strong competitor to the Macintosh® for the graphic communications industry.

Memory

When data is input into a computer, it is stored as memory. There are two kinds of memory associated with a computer: temporary and permanent.

Temporary Memory

In addition to having a computer system capable of running programs, there must be some means of storing and transmitting data. Every computer system is equipped with a certain amount of physical memory, usually referred to as ***random-access memory (RAM)***. See **Figure 9-4**.

wavebreakmedia/Shutterstock.com

Figure 9-4. RAM is temporary memory.

RAM is the short-term, or temporary, memory the computer uses to store information in process. When a computer is turned on, the operating system is loaded into RAM. Any applications that are subsequently opened are also loaded into RAM. The functionality of the application is working in the short-term memory. When you save a file, it writes that information to permanent memory, known as storage. RAM requires power to store information. When the power is removed, so is the information. That is why it is recommended to save active files periodically to protect against data loss from a power outage. Systems can be updated and memory capabilities can be increased to enhance computing speed and efficiency.

Permanent Memory

Because most page composition files, images, and illustrations are very large, there are many types of storage devices available that accommodate large files. Storage devices vary in terms of capacity, physical size, access capabilities, speed, reusability, and integrity. Storage capacity, historically measured in kilobytes (1024 bytes) and megabytes (1024 kilobytes), is now considered in ***gigabytes*** (1024 megabytes) and ***terabytes*** (1000 gigabytes).

A number of different types of devices have been developed to store and reuse digital files. Examples of permanent storage include removable hard drives, portable hard drives, flash drives, solid-state drives, and cloud storage. These options make it possible to back up data, store and retrieve it remotely, and carry it with us wherever we go. See **Figure 9-5**. Both external and internal hard drives are common today, **Figure 9-6**. An internal hard drive contains one or more rigid, non-removable aluminum disks coated with a magnetic material. When the computer is operating, the drive motor spins the disk and a read/write head moves over the disk surface, which contains densely packed magnetic tracks. The head is used to write, or magnetize, information to portions of the tracks as they spin past the head. The head can also read, or play back, previously stored information. The single most critical occurrence for any hard drive is when it becomes inoperable, or crashes. The adage "It isn't *if* your hard drive is going to crash, but *when*" should be taken very seriously. Optimizing the drive for operational efficiency and regularly backing up the data should be part of standard operating procedures. External hard drives add additional storage capability to your computer and are connected and networked through your computer. Although removable, they are not designed to be transported around. A portable hard drive is usually connected through a Universal Serial Bus (USB) port and has more shock resistance than an internal hard drive.

Flash memory cards are small, removable storage devices that have high storage capacity with fast access and retrieval speeds. With all of our mobile media options, these cards have become a critical part of our digital lives. There are a variety of options including Secure Digital (SD) card, microSD, SDHC (high capacity), CompactFlash, and more. They differ in size, physical format, and speed, and compatibility among assorted devices varies. It is best to read your device's manual to determine what type of card it requires.

©George Deal

Figure 9-5. External, portable storage and flash drives.

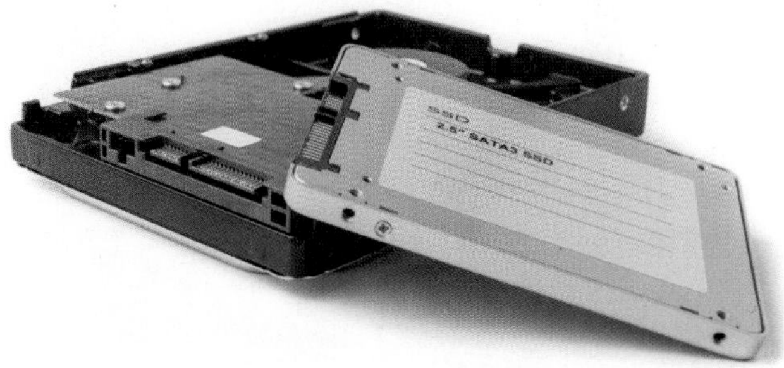

Evgenii Mironov/Shutterstock.com

Figure 9-6. Internal hard drives are used to back up, store, and retrieve data.

Flash drives, or memory sticks, are storage devices that use a USB interface. These USB flash drives are physically much smaller than other options and are relatively inexpensive.

Solid-state drives (SSDs) are an alternative type of storage device. Both traditional hard drives and solid-state drives perform the functions of booting your system and storing your applications and files. Different from traditional hard drives that have platters that spin, solid-state drives do not have moving parts and process and transfer data at faster speeds than other storage devices mentioned. As a result, they are far more stable. Although more expensive than hard drives, SSDs are often the choice of graphic communications professionals because of their speed and durability.

Cloud-based storage offers many advantages over physical storage devices. A cloud-based system is an offsite storage system maintained by a third party where you can save and access your data. Connecting to this server via the Internet provides access to the data from any web-based device and connected location. Many options exist with different capabilities and capacities. ***Data centers*** of these third party sources build redundancy into their storage, making them very secure. You can also access your data at any time.

Input Devices

There are a number of ways in which text or graphic information can be entered into the computer system. Methods range from manual entry such as keyboarding, to electronic transmissions and mobile devices.

Keyboard

The computer keyboard is the most common way of entering text into a computer system. In addition to standard typing tasks, the keyboard may also be used to perform special functions through dedicated keys (such as the delete and insert keys). Special function keys carry out different tasks, depending on the program being used.

Mouse

Many computer systems rely extensively on input from the mouse. This navigation device is especially necessary for user interfaces and graphics. Mice can be wireless or connected by a cable and can be simple point-and-click devices or accommodate complex gaming formats. See **Figure 9-7**.

Internet Connection

Several options exist for Internet connection. A ***digital subscriber line (DSL)*** requires a ***modem***, an electronic device that converts digital signals into a form that uses a 2-wire copper telephone line. ***Cable modems***, devices that offer broadband connections that operate over radio frequency channels, provide faster access because of the greater bandwidth of the coaxial cable.

Wi-Fi, although technically a product that is based on standards from the Institute of Electrical and Electronics Engineers, has become a common term to define any wireless network that uses radio frequency bands that provide an always-on connection. As long as you are in an area with network coverage, you can access the Internet. With ***satellite Internet***, you connect via a small satellite dish with a Network Operations Center (NOC) that transmits and receives information with the orbiting geostationary satellite.

Scanner

Handheld scanners are small devices that are moved across the image area by hand. Flatbed scanners process images that are positioned on a flat glass surface or scan area that is stationary. Document scanners can quickly convert entire pages of type or printed material into digital form, **Figure 9-8**.

Voice Recognition System

The premise of voice recognition technology is to use voice commands to control devices and to enter data simply by speaking into a microphone. Some of the major challenges in using this type of system include:

- Recognizing the voices of multiple users on the same system.
- Distinguishing homonyms, such as "there," "their," and "they're."

Tablets

Many types of tablets are available as input devices. A ***graphics tablet*** or digitizer lets the user draw images, animations, and graphics by hand, much like you would use a pencil and paper. Another kind of tablet is a ***tablet computer***. These utilize touchscreen displays and options

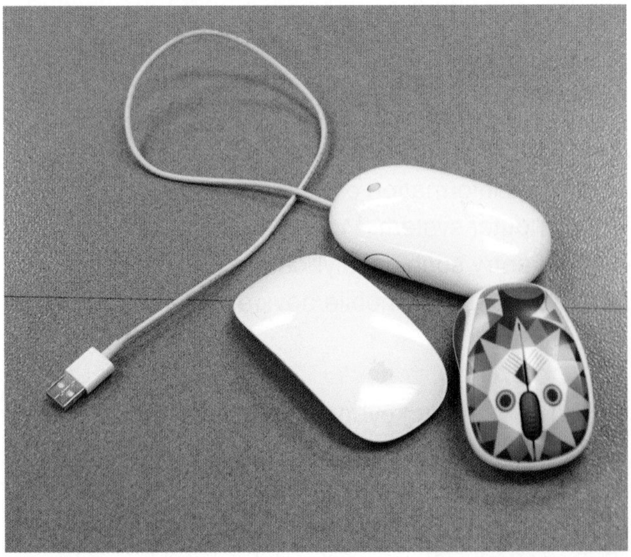

©Dana Thelander

Figure 9-7. Wired and wireless mice are used as input devices.

©George Deal

Figure 9-8. Desktop flatbed scanners can convert type or images into digital form.

such as cameras, microphones, and ports for network connections. Basically a mobile computer, tablet computers usually feature pop-up virtual keyboards for typing, and some utilize a stylus for drawing.

Digital Cameras

A ***digital camera*** takes an image or video and stores the information for later reproduction. These cameras are available in a variety of options and quality, offer extensive zoom ranges, traditional controls, high-end features, and some are even waterproof. By contrast, smartphone cameras allow you to take the image, edit it, and then upload it to share globally, all within a couple of minutes.

Mobile Devices

Mobile devices, such as smartphones, provide a number of ways to input information. The variety of mobile applications that are used for input extend from voice recognition and handwriting converters to QR (Quick Response) code readers and augmented reality.

A ***QR code*** is an optical label that uses a matrix barcode. The codes can contain data that users access with a reader app on their smartphones. Used primarily as inventory control or in advertising campaigns, these codes can extend a new level of value to a consumer. See **Figure 9-9**. Not only are they used as automatic links to websites, QR codes also work as vCard electronic business cards. The retail and restaurant industries utilize them to present special deals or discounts, and movie studios use them to generate hype for movie openings. The key to success with QR codes is putting them in accessible locations.

Augmented reality is a real-world environment or item that has extended value from computer-generated sensory input, such as sound, video, graphics, and GPS data, through a marker or tag that is read by a device and proprietary software. Used in children's books, for example, characters can jump off pages. See **Figure 9-10**. Some catalogs include pages with 360° views of their products. With Autodesk® software, 3D CAD models are transformed into interactive presentations.

Output Devices

Most computer systems are connected to a variety of ***output devices***, including monitors, a wide range of printers, and external processing devices. Some output devices produce physical material, often referred to as *hard copy*. These include ink-jet and laser printers of all sizes and quality that produce copies on different substrates, and higher-end devices that produce printing plates.

Monitors

As content is entered using a keyboard or other input device, it is almost instantly processed by the computer and displayed on a monitor. A ***monitor*** is a visual display device that connects to and transmits data from a computer to the viewer. The software used in graphic communications provides a WYSIWYG (what you see is what you get) display on the monitor, **Figure 9-11**. As monitor sizes

Goodheart-Willcox Publisher

Figure 9-9. QR codes can be used by consumers to find additional information about products or services.

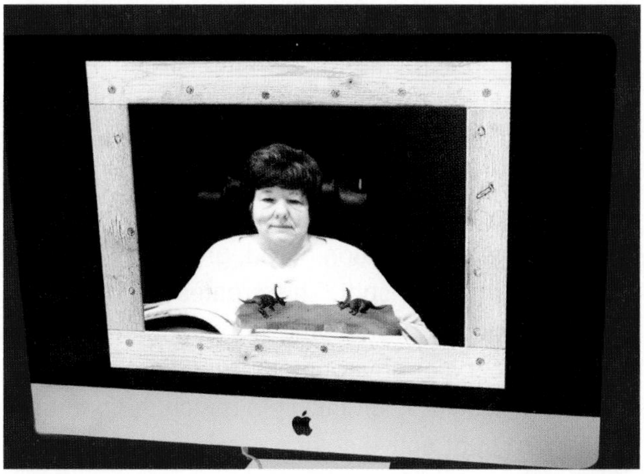

©George Deal

Figure 9-10. Augmented reality helps material jump off pages.

©George Deal

Figure 9-11. The WYSIWYG monitor display provides the user with a very close approximation of how material will appear when printed out. The screen in this figure is displaying an edited image. This image can later be exported to a page layout program, where it may be altered further, as needed.

©Dana Thelander

Figure 9-12. A retina display has a higher pixel density.

continue to grow, if space allows, try to stay above a 20″ screen for page layout display.

Many monitors use a light-emitting diode (LED) flat panel display. They are also common on billboards and illuminated outdoor signage. Liquid-crystal display (LCD) monitors do not emit light directly. Some monitors use an LCD with an LED-backlit display.

In-plane switching (IPS) is improved technology for LCD that provides higher quality color reproduction. ***Retina display*** is an Apple® brand for a monitor with a higher pixel density. See **Figure 9-12**.

In addition to display size, resolution is an important characteristic to consider when choosing a monitor. The ***resolution*** is a monitor's ability to show fine detail and is stated in the number of pixels lined up across and down the screen. A common resolution for monitors is 1920 × 1080. Also known as 1080p, it offers the right number of pixels to watch high-definition Blu-ray Discs™. A color monitor uses the ***additive color formation***, based on the combination of red, green, and blue (RGB) to form white light. This creates a problem for the desktop publisher who is trying to achieve a WYSIWYG color environment. Since colors are displayed in RGB, it is difficult to match the printed results of a subtractive color environment. In the ***subtractive color formation***, cyan, magenta, yellow, and black (CMYK) inks are combined to produce the printed image. This means that full-color representations of images on a monitor and on a printed sheet are achieved through different principles. To overcome this problem, a ***color management system (CMS)*** is installed to provide a monitor display that is closer to a CMYK representation of the final printed product. This software provides a ***wysiwyp*** (what you see is what you print) display.

Printers

For proofing text, graphics, and page layouts, a printer is used to produce a hard copy on paper. The resolution of a printed image is measured in dots per inch (dpi) and ranges from 300 dpi (or less) to 1200 dpi (or higher), depending on the type and quality of printer. In some cases, final copy or page layouts can be output by a high-resolution laser or ink-jet printer to achieve quality sufficient for short-run reproduction.

Ink-Jet Printers

Ink-jet printers form images by using a print head that projects tiny droplets of ink onto the paper surface and provide a resolution of 300 dpi or more. Positioning the droplet is carefully controlled. Ink-jet printers are often used to make color proofs of graphics and page proofs as a color-accurate representation of the final printed product, **Figure 9-13**. Ink-jet printers

©Dana Thelander

Figure 9-13. Ink-jet printers can be used to make color proofs and page proofs.

range from low-end devices using the four process colors, CMYK, to higher-end digital proofers, many using extended inks such as light, light black; light black; light cyan; light magenta, and more, to better simulate the gamut of final offset printing process colors. Larger format and higher-end ink-jet printers are used for contact proofing and as final product generators.

Laser Printers

Laser printers operate much like photocopy machines. A photocopy machine uses reflected light to create an image on a drum, while a laser printer uses a laser beam to create an image on the drum, **Figure 9-14**. The laser printer has a ***print engine*** that translates the output of the computer into a bitmapped image for printing. A laser transfers the page image to a light-sensitive drum that has a positive electrical charge. As the laser light moves across the rotating drum, it emits the image drawn from printer memory. The polarity of the drum changes in the areas where the laser has transferred the image to be printed. ***Toner*** is a positively charged powder that is attracted only to the negatively charged areas on a page to create an image. The paper with toner applied passes between heated rollers that fuse the powder onto the paper and produce a permanent image. Laser printers can produce images of 300 dpi and higher, and they are typically available in both color and black-only models.

ekkapon/Shutterstock.com

Figure 9-14. Laser printers work similarly to photocopiers.

Dye-Sublimation Printer

A ***dye-sublimation printer*** uses heat to transfer dye onto various substrates, such as plastics, cards, papers, or fabrics. Often used to print on novelty items, apparel, signs, and banners, this process uses the combination of time, temperature, and pressure to produce a nearly permanent and high-resolution print.

Computer-to-Plate Devices

When high-resolution images must be output for commercial printing, the server with the raster image processor (RIP) outputs directly to plates or a digital printing press.

The ***raster image processor (RIP)*** converts all elements of a page or image into a bitmapped image at the resolution of the selected output device. The RIP interprets the page composition information for the marking engine of the output device. Output problems are most likely to occur during the *ripping* process. It is usually the responsibility of the operator to troubleshoot these problems. However, if the files have not been properly prepared, they may need to be returned to the point of origination for correction.

Page Description Languages (PDLs)

A ***page description language (PDL)*** serves as the interface between the page composition workstation and the RIP. PDLs are used to identify all the elements to be placed on the page, their respective positions on the page, and the page's position within the larger document, in a manner that the output device can understand. PDLs enable digital output devices developed by different companies to interpret digital files from any number of personal computers and software programs. Common PDLs include Adobe® ***PostScript***®, Adobe® ***portable document format (PDF)***, and Hewlett-Packard PCL (printer control language).

An ***interpreter*** is a computer program used with output devices that receive the PDL page descriptions and translates them into patterns of dots for a printer or pixels for monitor display. After receiving a page description, the interpreter constructs a representation of the page to suit the output device. For example, the interpreter can determine whether the output device is a black-only or color printer, an RGB video monitor, or a 2400 dpi platesetter. Once these parameters are defined, the interpreter modifies its instructions accordingly.

Preparing Content

Software used with digital imaging systems is classified by its role in the digital prepress process. This process essentially consists of preparing content, composing pages, and outputting the finished file. The software used in prepress work consists of word processors, vector drawing programs, photo manipulation programs, and page geometry programs. Once the file gets to the printer, proprietary ripping software is used to properly prepare the file for press, including preflight, trapping, profiles, and ink densities.

Warning

It is important to maintain the original text and image files when preparing content; make a copy of the original material and work from the copy. This ensures that the original material is available if data is lost or destroyed during prepress production, or if graphics must be drastically resized or modified.

Text

There are several options available when preparing text for the digital prepress process. The simplest method is to enter copy directly onto the page, while using page composition software. Text may also be imported from other electronic sources.

Word processing software is an efficient tool for creating and editing text. Although it was originally designed for correspondence and similar tasks in the business environment, many word processors have the capability of formatting both text and graphics. Do not use a word processor for anything other than text entry and editing. Word processing software does not have the extensive capabilities for page layout and final file preparation for output that page geometry software does.

Word processors typically include proofing tools that allow the operator to detect and correct errors in spelling, punctuation, and word division. These proofing tools go beyond mere spell-checking, as they are usually capable of detecting incorrect, extra, or missing punctuation; incorrect hyphenation; improper abbreviation; missing or incorrect capitalization at the beginning of a sentence; doubled words; and much more. Page geometry software includes many of these same proofing and editing tools.

Industry standard software for page geometry is InDesign® and QuarkXPress®. In 1990 Quark, had a 95% market share. Adobe took on the giant by embracing the new technology changes with operating system upgrades, specifically OS X for the Macintosh. InDesign® also took digital typography to a new level. Combined with bundling packages with other applications, such as Photoshop and Illustrator, InDesign® became the dominant software.

There are several ways you can add text to a document:

- Type directly into the document
- Paste or place text from another application
- Drag-and-drop text, provided the word processing program supports that functionality

With InDesign®, if you have the cursor set at the insertion point in a text box on your page when you place text from another document, the text will populate that box. If you do not have anything selected, simply click, and the text will automatically create a filled box. By adjusting your program's preference settings to **Show Import Options**, you can control whether the text maintains or discards any previous formatting, including styles.

When importing rich text format (RTF), Microsoft® Word text, Excel text, or tagged text, there are specific options to address if you select **Show Import Options**.

A detailed list of choices is displayed, including how to handle table of contents text, index text, quotes, styles, tables, manual line breaks, and tracked changes, to name a few. See **Figure 9-15**.

Adjusting preferences allows you to control how the text comes into the document. The text can enter with formatting or as plain text.

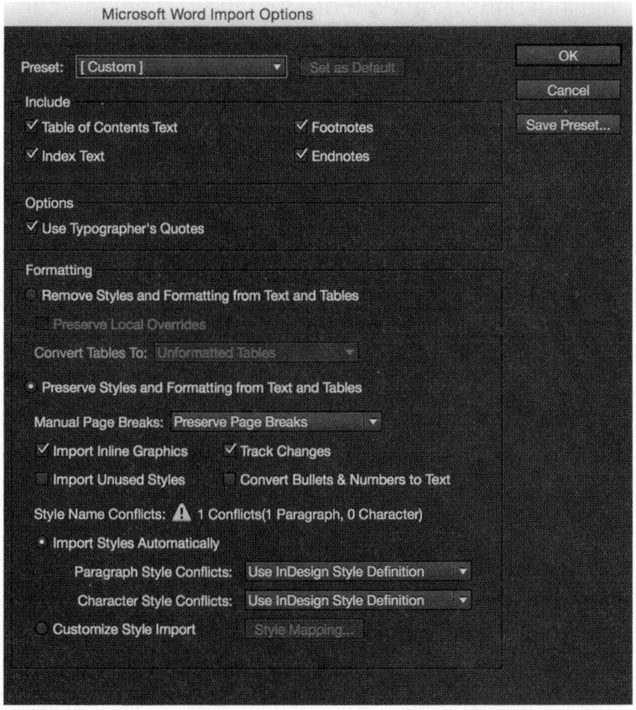

Goodheart-Willcox Publisher

Figure 9-15. Import options when placing text into a document in a page layout program.

There are two options for editing text in InDesign®. You can write or edit in the document on the layout page, or in the story editor window. This window allows tracked changes and does not show any formatting. Editing in story editor will automatically update the text in the document layout.

Many other text-handling and advanced options are available in InDesign® for complex and long documents. You can create books with chapters and automatically generate tables of contents and index files from document text. Other options include documents using text variables, data merge, and hyperlinks.

Typing on a Path

Text can be formatted to follow the edge of a shape or an open path. Select an existing path or draw one with the pen tool, and select the type on a path tool. Click on the edge of the path and you may begin typing. If you run out of room on the path, the overset text box will appear. Either edit the path or the content to make it fit.

To move the text on the path, select the insertion line and move it along the path, or grab the middle point (which is sometimes hard to see) and move the text to the other side of the path. The path may be edited independently by selecting it with the direct selection tool (open arrow). See **Figure 9-16**.

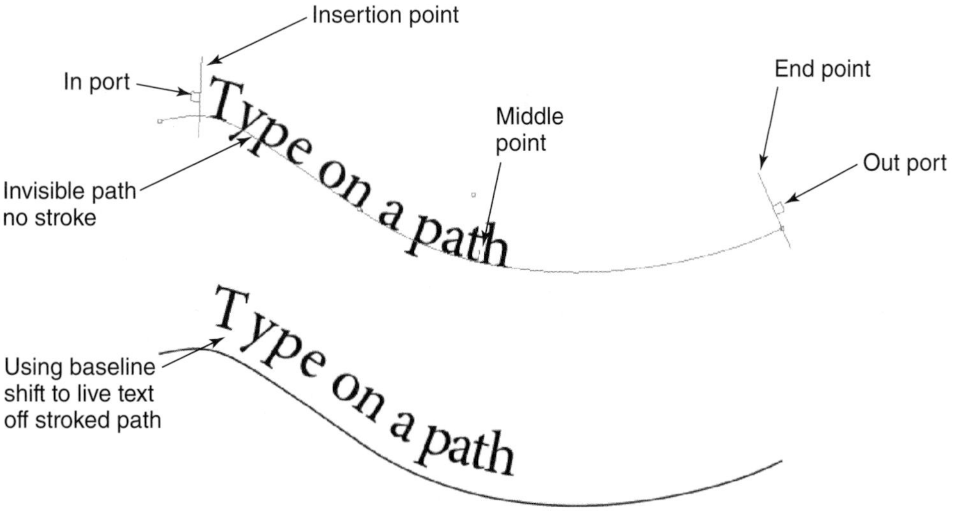

Goodheart-Willcox Publisher

Figure 9-16. Text can be placed on a path by first creating the path and then typing along the edge.

Text Flow

Text boxes can either stand alone, or they can be linked together so the text will flow from one box to the next. This is called ***linking***, or ***threading***, text. Each text box has a small box at the top left of the frame called an ***in port***, and one at the bottom right of the frame called an ***out port***. See **Figure 9-17**. By clicking on the out port of one frame and then selecting the in port of another, the boxes become linked and the text will thread from one to the next. See **Figure 9-18**. If text is already in the first box, when the out port is selected, the cursor becomes a "loaded text icon." See **Figure 9-19**. This icon allows you to select another frame to unload it into, click and drag to create a text box, or just click the icon and it will automatically create a text frame the width of the margin, which you can then populate.

When there is more text in a frame than will fit, the out port becomes a red square with an *x*, called the ***overset text*** symbol. See **Figure 9-20**. This indicates there is more text there than you can see. Each overset text sign needs to be addressed before a file goes to print. Either make the text box bigger to accommodate the text, edit the text, or thread it to another box. Sometimes the overset is a return after the last line. Because of the leading, the extra line (which contains no content, only an invisible paragraph return symbol) does not fit, so the overset symbol shows. If the paragraph return is deleted, the overset will correct.

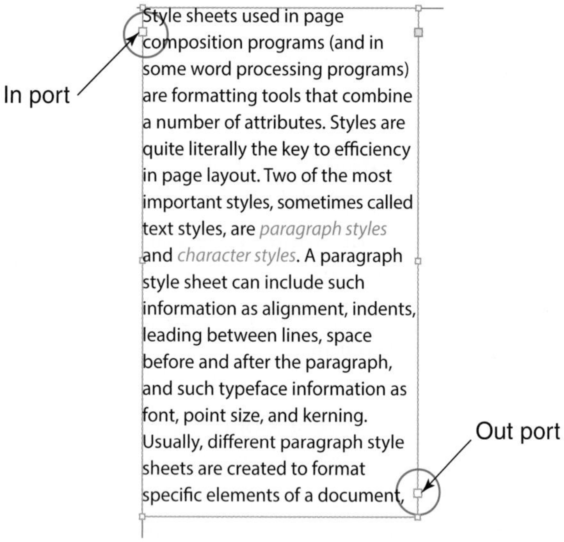
In port
Style sheets used in page composition programs (and in some word processing programs) are formatting tools that combine a number of attributes. Styles are quite literally the key to efficiency in page layout. Two of the most important styles, sometimes called text styles, are paragraph styles and character styles. A paragraph style sheet can include such information as alignment, indents, leading between lines, space before and after the paragraph, and such typeface information as font, point size, and kerning. Usually, different paragraph style sheets are created to format specific elements of a document,
Out port

Goodheart-Willcox Publisher

Figure 9-17. In ports and out ports are used to link boxes.

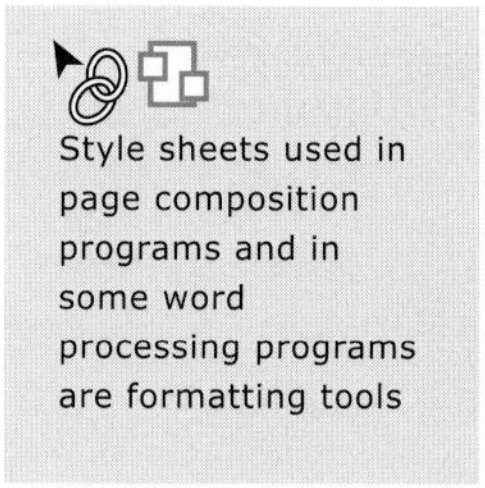
Style sheets used in page composition programs and in some word processing programs are formatting tools

Goodheart-Willcox Publisher

Figure 9-19. Loaded cursor ready to drop into another text box to create a threaded path.

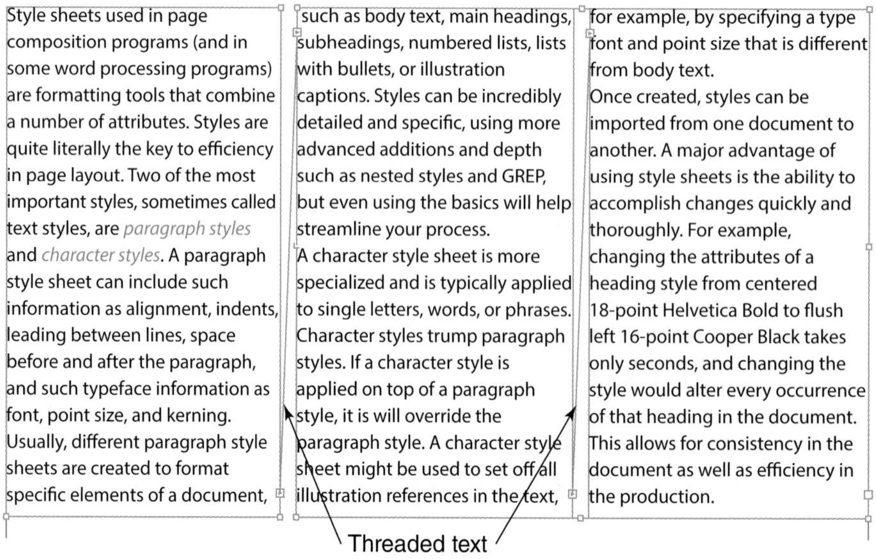

Goodheart-Willcox Publisher

Figure 9-18. Threaded text blocks can be created by clicking out ports and in ports.

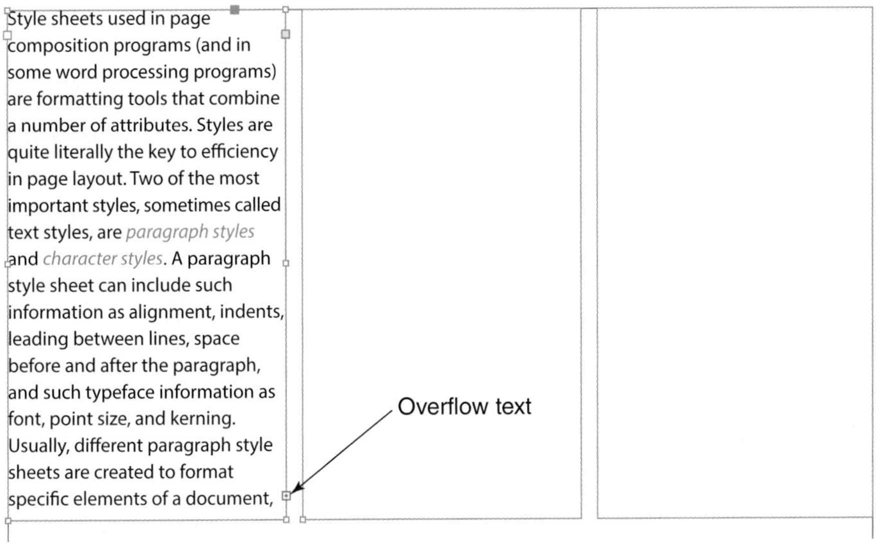
Style sheets used in page composition programs (and in some word processing programs) are formatting tools that combine a number of attributes. Styles are quite literally the key to efficiency in page layout. Two of the most important styles, sometimes called text styles, are paragraph styles and character styles. A paragraph style sheet can include such information as alignment, indents, leading between lines, space before and after the paragraph, and such typeface information as font, point size, and kerning. Usually, different paragraph style sheets are created to format specific elements of a document,
Overflow text

Goodheart-Willcox Publisher

Figure 9-20. The red box indicates there is more text than will fit into the text box.

Graphics

While graphics are often a combination of text, illustration, color, and images, they can generally be broken into two different categories: vector and raster. To understand how the graphics are defined and the difference in the two, we have to understand the basics of a binary computer system.

Bits

A bit is the smallest unit of information a computer can store. Coming from the term *BInary digiT*, a bit is either black or white, on or off, 1 or 0. Eight bits equals a byte of information. As discussed earlier, it takes eight bits, or one byte, to make a character. A byte might look like 01100111. If you add up all of the possible combinations of eight 0s and 1s, you get 256. This is a magic number in computers. See **Figure 9-21**.

Because we want to work with and see color on our computers, and they only crunch the 0s and 1s of a binary system, our bits of information are considered to have depth. ***Bit depth*** is the number of bits used to indicate the color of a single pixel. A one-bit color is either black or white. If a pixel is eight-bit color, it still works with the two colors, black and white, but it has eight options for each. This equates to 2^8, or 256, which gives us the option of 256 colors of black and white, or a grayscale image.

An image in the RGB format is 2^{24}. The equation comes from two colors, black and white, with the eight options for each of the three colors: red, green, and blue. So, $8 \times 3 = 24$. If you do the math, 2^{24} equals 16 million color options. These are called 8-bit graphics because each color has eight-bit depth. See **Figure 9-22.**

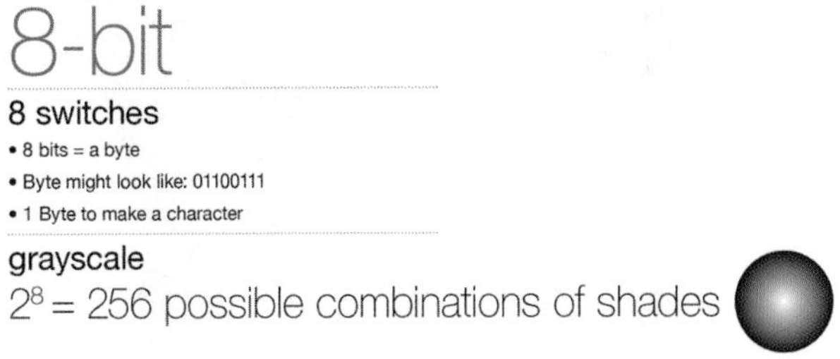
8-bit
8 switches
• 8 bits = a byte
• Byte might look like: 01100111
• 1 Byte to make a character
grayscale
2⁸ = 256 possible combinations of shades

Goodheart-Willcox Publisher

Figure 9-21. A bit is the smallest unit of information a computer can store.

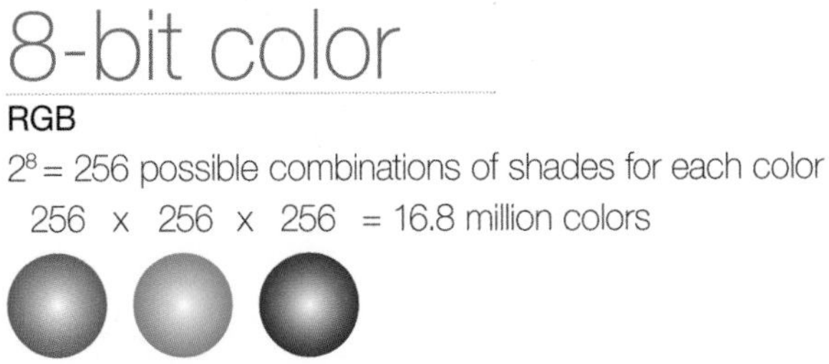
8-bit color
RGB
2⁸ = 256 possible combinations of shades for each color
256 x 256 x 256 = 16.8 million colors

Goodheart-Willcox Publisher

Figure 9-22. 8-bit graphics utilize binary data and 8 switches for each of the three colors, RGB.

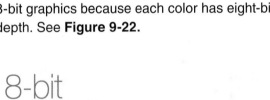

Vector

Vector graphics are represented as mathematical formulas or algorithms that define all the shapes in the image, as well as their placement in a document. Sometimes called *object-oriented*, vector graphics are resolution independent and can be scaled without any loss in quality. In computer graphics, a vector is a line that is defined by its start point and endpoint. A piece of line art generated by a drawing program is a vector graphic, **Figure 9-23**. A drawing program gives the designer control over shape, placement, line width, and object pattern.

A ***Bezier curve*** is a vector graphic named after French mathematician Pierre Bezier. It is defined mathematically by two endpoints and two or more other points that control its shape. Nearly all drawing programs support Bezier curves. The two endpoints of the curve are called ***anchor points***. The other points that define the shape of the curve are called *handles*, *tangent points*, or *nodes*. Attached to each handle are two control points. The shape of the curve can be modified by moving the handles or the control points. See **Figure 9-24.**

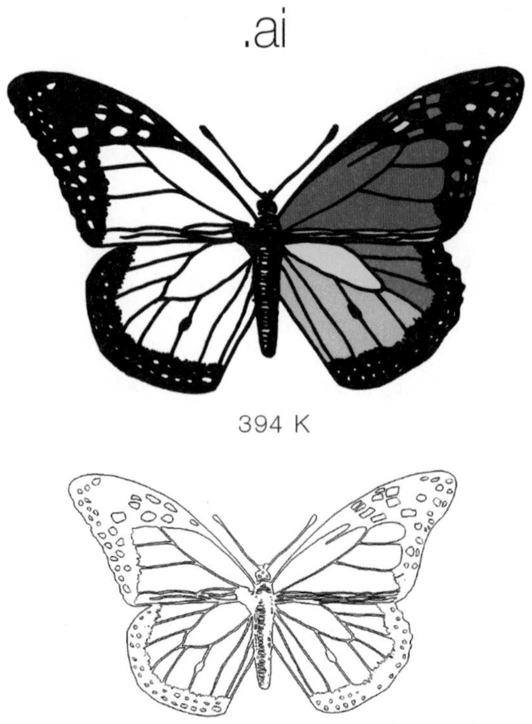

Goodheart-Willcox Publisher

Figure 9-23. Object oriented graphics use mathematical algorithms rather than pixels, which makes them resolution independent.

There are several advantages to using vector images:

- Shapes can be resized without degradation because objects are defined geometrically.
- The images print the same, even when scaled to different sizes, and can be represented at any resolution, which makes them more flexible than bitmapped images.
- A computer can store vector images efficiently, making them ideal for high-resolution output.

Raster

A ***raster*** graphic is a representation of an image on a grid of pixels of predetermined size and depth and is, therefore, resolution dependent. A ***pixel*** (short for *picture element*) is the smallest amount of displayable information for a digital image. Each image has a grid of pixels on the *x* and *y* coordinates that are viewable on a display device. The number of pixels and their size are determined by the resolution of the image. The resolution is defined when the pixel is first generated by the application, a scanner, or a digital capture. Scaling this information after it has been established may cause a loss in quality.

Every pixel has a numeric value, even if that number is zero. This data is stored for each pixel in the grid for each image. The pixel is characterized not only by its size but also by its depth. The color gamut (explained later in this chapter) defines the bit depth. All raster images are bitmapped images because they have an underlying bitmap of pixels.

When working with bitmap images, the individual pixels, rather than whole objects or

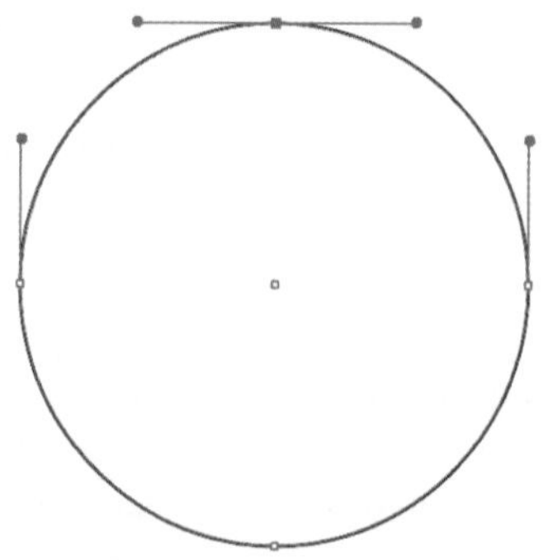

Goodheart-Willcox Publisher

Figure 9-24. Anchor points are data stacks that contain the data for the vector graphics.

shapes, are edited. Through these actions, the image size, shape, or colors may be modified.

Bitmaps are composed of a grid of pixels that does not allow for smooth curves. As a result, when bitmaps are enlarged or reduced, the edges can become ragged. This process is referred to as aliasing. ***Aliasing*** is the process by which smooth curves and other lines become jagged due to the reduced resolution of the graphics device or file. ***Antialiasing*** is a software technique for diminishing jagged lines, or *jaggies*. These stairstep-like lines occur because the output device is not equipped with high enough resolution to represent a smooth line. Antialiasing reduces the prominence of jaggies by surrounding them with intermediate shades of gray or color, **Figure 9-25**. Shades of gray are used for gray-scaling devices, and color is used for color output devices. Although this reduces the jagged appearance of the lines, it also makes them fuzzier or softer.

Raster images can be created and saved in a variety of ways. Digital images can be created using raster programs, digital photography, and electronic scanning. The electronic images created are saved in one of many file formats. The file format used for graphics is a very important consideration because it determines how much an image may be manipulated and how well it will reproduce. Digital camera and digital scanner operation are covered in detail in Chapter 10, *Image Capture*.

Other applications, such as drawing and page layout programs, have some image editing capabilities, but these alterations are best done by the software designed for that purpose.

Page Layout

The assembly of text and graphic images into the final page is accomplished using a page layout program. Page layout software is built to handle both text and graphics with extensive controls and print settings effectively and efficiently. The most widely used page composition software packages today are InDesign® and QuarkXPress®. Although the specific operations are somewhat different, an experienced operator can use either program to combine text and graphics to create a file for final output. Most of the examples shown are from InDesign®.

Desktop

The ***desktop*** is the entire background of your monitor that is shown when your computer starts up. On the desktop of a PC, there are icons for applications, stored folders or files, the **Start** menu, the task bar containing pinned applications, and the system tray. See **Figure 9-26**. A Mac's desktop has a menu bar across the top with the application menu, the **Apple** menu, the current user, the **Spotlight** menu, and icons for the connected hard drives. The dock, usually located at the bottom, shows icons of frequently accessed apps for easy launch. See **Figure 9-27**.

Preferences

When you launch a page layout application, a menu bar shows up across the top. Below the menu bar is an application frame and a control bar. See

Goodheart-Willcox Publisher

Figure 9-25. Antialiasing gives the illusion of a rounded edge using pixels.

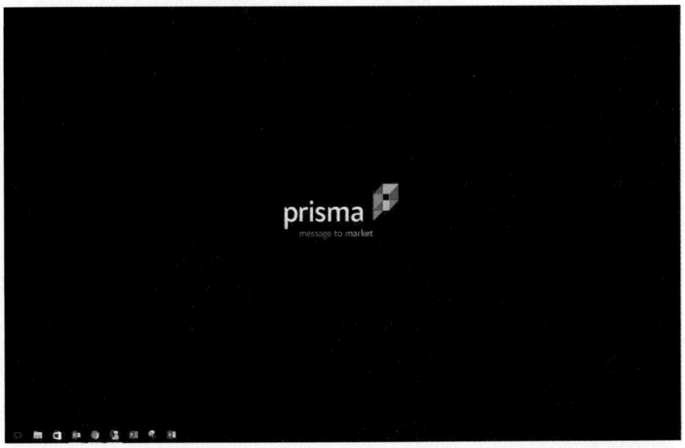

©Nathan Deal

Figure 9-26. Windows® desktop.

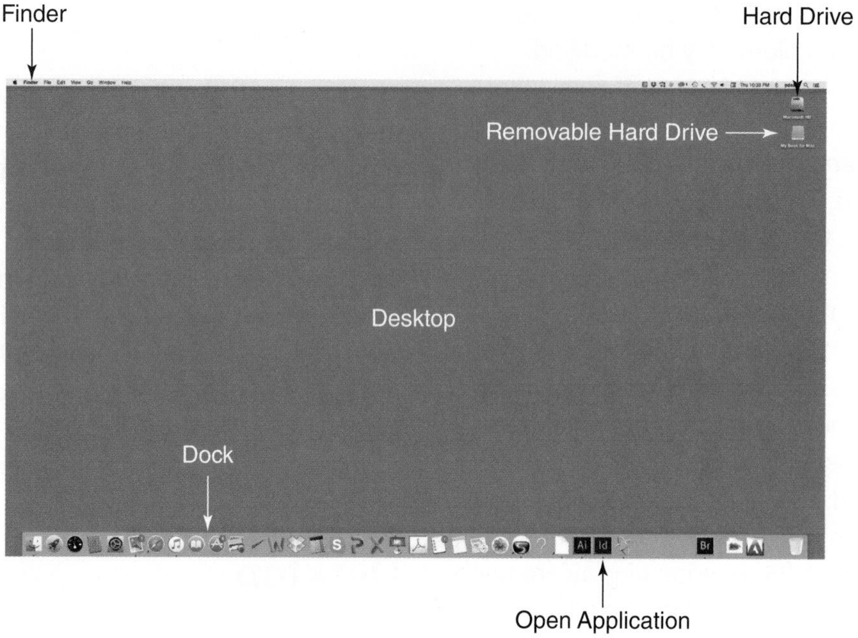

Goodheart-Willcox Publisher

Figure 9-27. Macintosh® desktop.

Figure 9-28. There are vertical and horizontal scroll bars used to shift the screen view up and down or left and right.

Applications are controlled by ***preferences*** that can be changed by the user. If you change preference settings with the application open but no document open, the preferences will apply to any document you open from then on, until you change the preferences again. If you open a document and then change the preferences, they will only apply to that document. Likewise, if you alter any settings in your tool bar or control panel with no document open, they will become your default settings.

There are preference settings for panel positions, display options, graphic and type options, and general settings. The default settings are

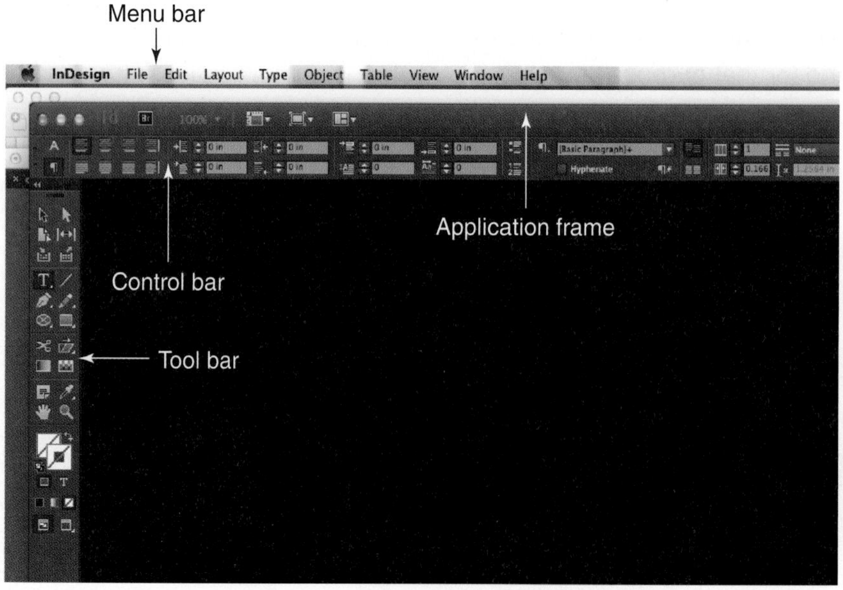

Goodheart-Willcox Publisher

Figure 9-28. Application frame is shown when you launch a page layout application.

generally intuitive but not necessarily what you want for every document. See **Figure 9-29**.

New Document

To create a new document, go under the menu bar and select **File > New > New document**. Decisions are made now regarding the specifications for your file. Some can be changed later on, but it is best to set them correctly from the inception. See **Figure 9-30**. The size of the document, the orientation, number of pages, columns, gutter size, margins, and bleed are all settings you can select. If your document will use variations on margins and columns, for example, set the margins to 0 and the columns to 1, then utilize master page settings, which will be covered later in this chapter. Note that you cannot set the columns to 0 as that would not allow for any work area in your document.

Menus and Workspaces

Your ***workspace*** is the arrangement of your menus for your document and pasteboard area. The ***pasteboard*** is the area within the application frame that is beyond the document edges. This setting is customizable. If you want to use a default, there are several to choose from, depending on the type of document you are working with. If you arrange your menus in a way that is comfortable or job specific, that workspace can be saved by selecting **Window > Workspace > New workspace**, and then naming the setting. It will then appear in the workspace drop-down menu. See **Figure 9-31**.

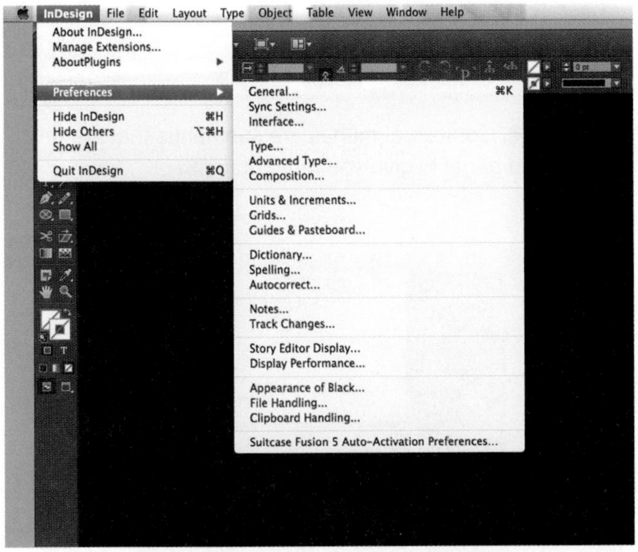

Goodheart-Willcox Publisher

Figure 9-29. Preferences are where you customize settings for an application.

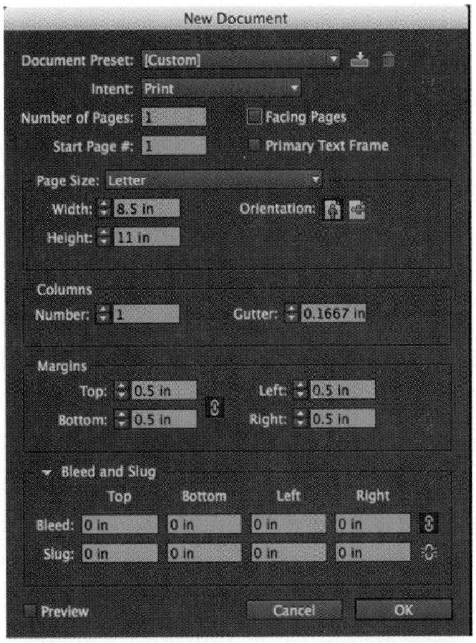

Goodheart-Willcox Publisher

Figure 9-30. New document window to set beginning parameters.

Goodheart-Willcox Publisher

Figure 9-31. Your workspace can be customized for multiple projects or documents.

Menus are panels that are selectable from the menu bar under Window. The Page menu, for example, is used to insert, delete, or move pages within a document, and provides choices for quickly moving from page to page. The main menu is the panel that shows when you select the menu or pull it from the side bar of your workspace. If you select the icon at the top right of the menu, the panel menu will appear with different options. If you right-click (Windows®) or control-click (Mac OS) on an area of the menu, you get a contextual menu. Clicking in different areas of the menu panel gives you different contextual menus that apply to that item. You may specify an action, input measurements, select colors, or apply a style. Some contextual menus include drop-down lists, similar to submenus, which can be used to make a selection. See **Figure 9-32**.

Tools

The ***tool palette*** is a modified form of menu that can be resized and positioned on the screen to suit the operator's preferences. A palette can also be set to display or be hidden. When displayed, it always remains visible, overlaying any other images on the screen.

The tool palette is the most often used because it allows the operator to perform many different layout functions. The tool palette displays icons for the different tools available, and is divided into four categories of tools: selection, drawing and type, transformation, and modification and navigation. Some tools have a little arrow at the base of the icon. This arrow indicates that there are additional tools hidden underneath. See **Figure 9-33** for a visual breakdown and the keyboard shortcut that will access that tool.

Selection Tools

Here is a list of selection tools and their functions.

- **Selection.** The solid arrow selects a box, line, or other item on the screen to be moved, resized, or reshaped.
- **Direct Selection.** Selects the contents of a box or individual points on a path.
- **Page.** Allows you to create multiple page sizes within the same document.
- **Gap.** Adjusts the space between objects.
- **Content Selector.** Saves text to a sub window for later placement.
- **Content Placer.** Places previously saved text from a sub window into your document.

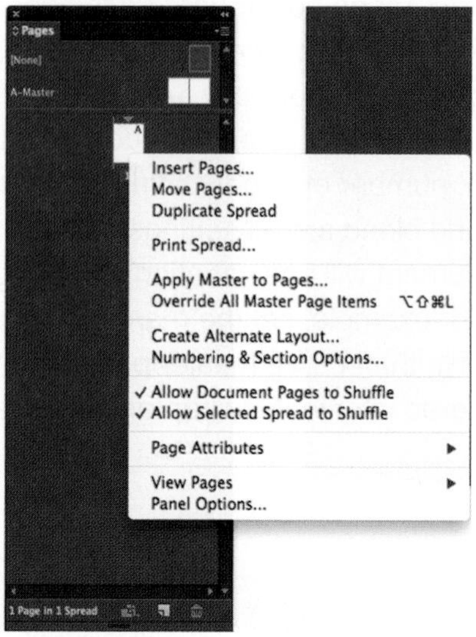

Goodheart-Willcox Publisher

Figure 9-32. Contextual menus are submenus that are part of the menu panel to give you more options.

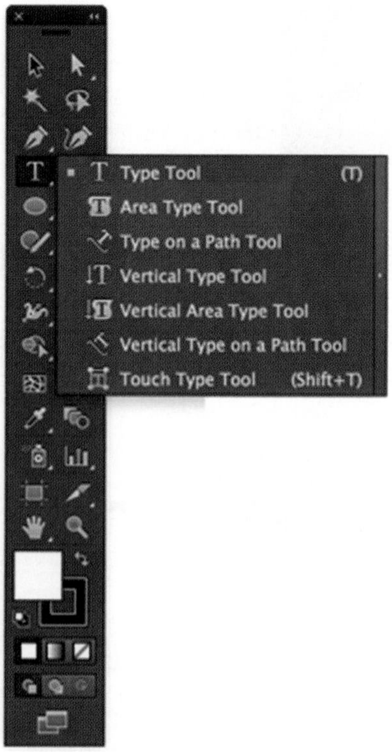

Goodheart-Willcox Publisher

Figure 9-33. A small triangle next to a tool in a tool palette indicates that more variations of the tool or other related options are available if you select the marker.

Drawing and Type Tools

Here is a list of drawing tools and how to use them.

- **Type.** Create a text box and select text. Click to begin typing.

  Plus: Type on a path. Vertical type.
- **Line.** Draw a line segment.
- **Pen.** Draw straight or curved paths or shapes.

  Plus: **Pen+**. Add an anchor point to a path.
  Pen-. Delete an anchor point from a path.
  V. Convert an anchor point.
- **Pencil.** Draw a freestyle path.
- **Rectangular frame (with an x).** Create a rectangular frame.

  Plus: **Ellipse frame**. Create a circle or oval frame.
  Polygon frame. Create a multiple-sided frame.
- **Rectangular frame.** Create a rectangular frame.

  Plus: **Ellipse frame**. Create a circle or oval frame.
  Polygon frame. Create a multiple-sided frame.

Transformation Tools

Here is a list of transformation tools and how to use them.

- **Scissors.** Cut a path.
- **Free Transform.** Rotate, shear, or scale an object.

  Plus: **Rotate**. Rotate an object around a fixed point.
  Scale. Enlarge or reduce an object from a fixed point.
  Shear. Skew or angle an object from a fixed point.
- **Gradient Swatch.** Define the path of a selected gradient.
- **Gradient Feather.** Feather a fill to transparent.

Modification and Navigation Tools

Here is a list of modification and navigation tools and how to use them.

- **Notes.** Add a note to a text box.
- **Eyedropper.** Sample and copy attributes from an object.

  Plus: **Color theme**. Create a color palette from a selected area of an image or object.
  Measurement. Measure the distance between two points.
- **Hand.** Moves the page inside the document window to change where you are looking.
- **Zoom.** Increase or decrease the magnification of the selected area of the document window.

At the base of the tool palette are squares that show "fill" and "stroke" attributes for each selected object or text. Change the characteristic of an element by selecting it and redefining these attributes. Whichever box is in the front is the active box. The arrow in the upper-right corner of these boxes is a switch arrow to flip the attribute, not the active box. If you have a "fill" of white and a "stroke" of black and you click the arrow, the "fill" becomes black and the "stroke" becomes white. The one that was active is still active.

The tiny replica of the two boxes in the lower-left corner is a button to reset the selection to the default setting. Under these boxes are two icons to show an active element. If a box is selected and the left icon is highlighted, the attributes displayed refer to the box itself. If the **T** icon is selected, the attributes refer to the text inside the frame. The next three icons are apply color, apply gradient, and apply none. The last two boxes are normal and preview modes. See **Figure 9-34**.

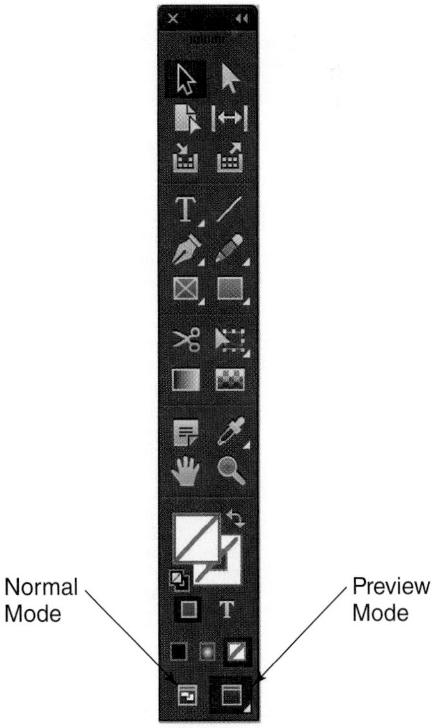

Goodheart-Willcox Publisher

Figure 9-34. Boxes at the bottom of the tool palette allow you to have a normal and preview mode of your document.

Master Pages

Using master pages is a way to streamline your layout process and keep a consistency to your document. A ***master page*** is set up in the pages menu and will contain elements that repeat, such as page numbers, headers and footers, and logos. Any page that is defined as that master page will have those elements in the exact position. Because the document has a stacking order, the items on the master page appear behind everything else. See **Figure 9-35**.

A single document may have many master pages. By changing an element on a master page, any document page using that master will automatically update with the change. Changing a document page to a different master is as simple as dragging the icon of the new master over the document page.

Master pages provide extensive and dynamic options. For example, master pages can be set up based on other master pages. An element on a document page can be detached from the master by overriding it, using keyboard commands.

Styles

Style sheets used in page composition programs (and in some word processing programs) are formatting tools that combine a number of attributes. Styles are quite literally the key to efficiency in page layout. Two of the most important styles, sometimes called text styles, are ***paragraph styles*** and ***character styles***. A paragraph style sheet can include such information as alignment, indents, leading between lines, space before and after the paragraph, and such typeface information as font, point size, and kerning. Usually, different paragraph style sheets are created to format specific elements of a document, such as body text, main headings, subheadings, numbered lists, lists with bullets, or illustration captions. Styles can be incredibly detailed and specific, using more advanced additions and depth such as ***nested styles*** and ***GREP***. But even using the basics will help your process be more efficient. See **Figure 9-36**.

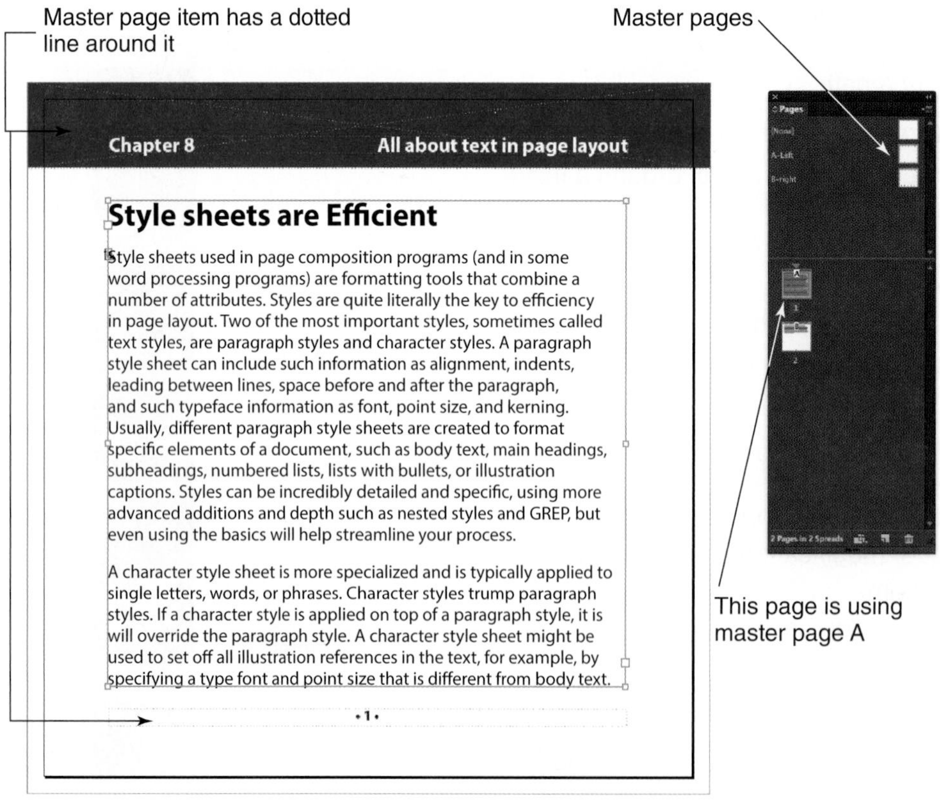
Master page item has a dotted line around it
Master pages
Chapter 8
All about text in page layout
Style sheets are Efficient
Style sheets used in page composition programs (and in some word processing programs) are formatting tools that combine a number of attributes. Styles are quite literally the key to efficiency in page layout. Two of the most important styles, sometimes called text styles, are paragraph styles and character styles. A paragraph style sheet can include such information as alignment, indents, leading between lines, space before and after the paragraph, and such typeface information as font, point size, and kerning. Usually, different paragraph style sheets are created to format specific elements of a document, such as body text, main headings, subheadings, numbered lists, lists with bullets, or illustration captions. Styles can be incredibly detailed and specific, using more advanced additions and depth such as nested styles and GREP, but even using the basics will help streamline your process.
A character style sheet is more specialized and is typically applied to single letters, words, or phrases. Character styles trump paragraph styles. If a character style is applied on top of a paragraph style, it is will override the paragraph style. A character style sheet might be used to set off all illustration references in the text, for example, by specifying a type font and point size that is different from body text.
•1•
This page is using master page A

Goodheart-Willcox Publisher

Figure 9-35. Master pages contain repeating elements in a design.

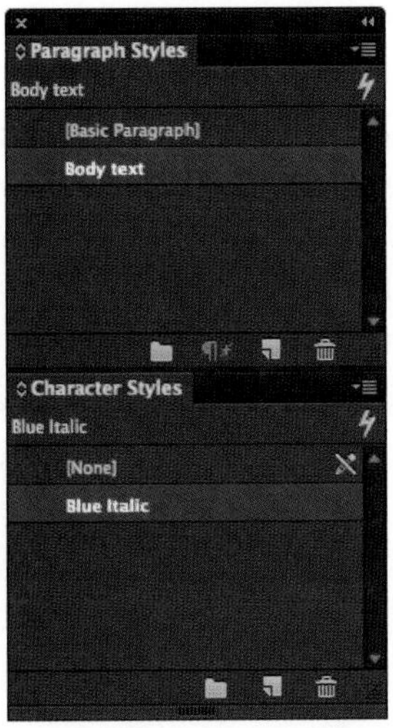

Goodheart-Willcox Publisher

Figure 9-36. Paragraph styles allow consistency in your document.

A character style sheet is more specialized and is typically applied to single letters, words, or phrases. Character styles override paragraph styles. If a character style is applied on top of a paragraph style, it will override the paragraph style. A character style sheet might be used to set off all illustration references in the text, for example, by specifying a type font and point size that is different from body text. See **Figure 9-37**.

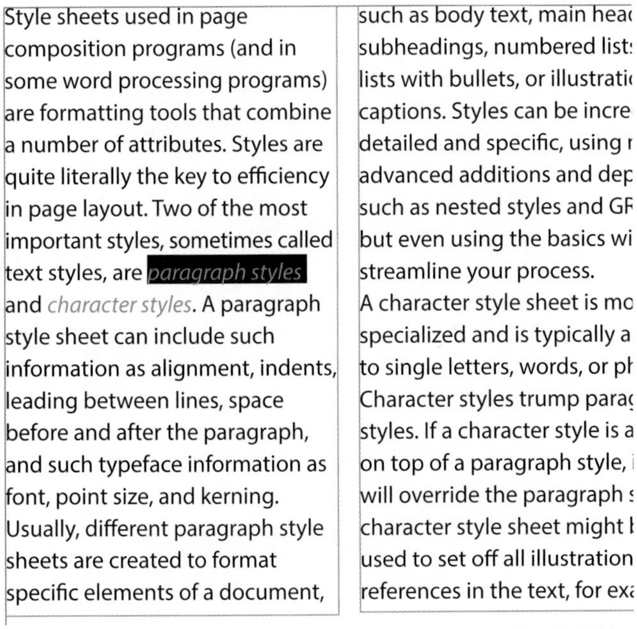
Style sheets used in page composition programs (and in some word processing programs) are formatting tools that combine a number of attributes. Styles are quite literally the key to efficiency in page layout. Two of the most important styles, sometimes called text styles, are paragraph styles and *character styles*. A paragraph style sheet can include such information as alignment, indents, leading between lines, space before and after the paragraph, and such typeface information as font, point size, and kerning. Usually, different paragraph style sheets are created to format specific elements of a document,

such as body text, main head subheadings, numbered list lists with bullets, or illustrati captions. Styles can be incre detailed and specific, using r advanced additions and dep such as nested styles and GR but even using the basics wi streamline your process.
A character style sheet is mo specialized and is typically a to single letters, words, or ph Character styles trump parag styles. If a character style is a on top of a paragraph style, i will override the paragraph s character style sheet might b used to set off all illustration references in the text, for exa

Goodheart-Willcox Publisher

Figure 9-37. Character styles override the paragraph style setting

Once created, styles can be imported from one document to another. A major advantage of using style sheets is the ability to accomplish changes quickly and thoroughly. For example, changing the attributes of a heading style from centered 18-point Helvetica Bold to flush left 16-point Cooper Black takes only seconds, and changing the style this way alters every occurrence of that heading in the document. This allows for consistency in the document as well as efficiency in the production.

Templates

A ***template*** can be created that incorporates all the master pages and other formatting attributes. A new publication or page can easily be set up by opening the reusable template and customizing the page formats as necessary. The main advantage of using a template is the increased productivity and less time spent recreating the same page information, as well as protecting the original file. For example, a monthly publication can start with a base template that includes the grids, master pages, styles, layers, and colors. Prepare the file the same way a traditional document would be until it comes time to save it. Then, instead of choosing **Save**, choose **Save As**, which allows you to create a new file, leaving the template intact.

Baseline Grid

The ***baseline grid***, sometimes called a *frame grid* or *page grid*, is a nonprinted set of guidelines on each layout page. Guidelines for margins, columns, gutters, and other basic page elements are included in the grid. One important function of the grid is to align type horizontally when the page is arranged in two or more columns. The operator may choose to display or hide the grid lines. See **Figure 9-38**.

Importing Graphics

Both bitmapped graphics created with image programs and vector graphics created with drawing or illustration programs can be imported and placed in a picture box. Photographs are captured with a digital device, such as a camera or scanner, which converts them to a digital format. The digital file may then be imported to a picture box.

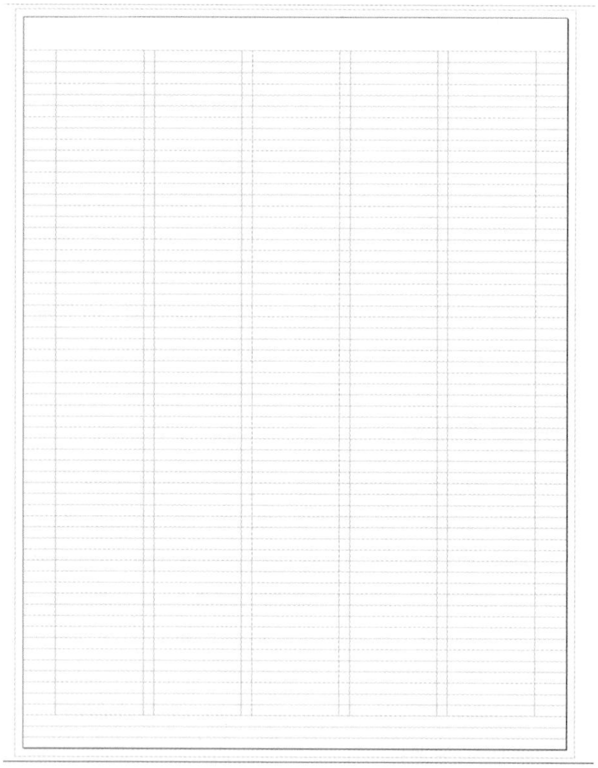

Goodheart-Willcox Publisher

Figure 9-38. A baseline grid serves as guidelines for a designer.

Once an image is in a picture box, it can be manipulated in various ways to suit the page layout. The image can be enlarged or reduced, cropped, moved around on the page, changed in color, or edited and altered using a variety of methods. The amount of successful manipulation is affected by the format in which the graphic was imported. For example, bitmap images do not enlarge very well—as the image size increases, the pixels also increase, which gives the image a jagged-edged look. When this occurs, the image is said to be "pixeled," **Figure 9-39**. Graphic file formats are covered in detail later in this chapter.

There are three ways to import a graphic into a page layout program: place, paste, or drag. The **Place** command is the suggested method because it gives the most support for the resolution, the file format, the color, and handling PDFs.

Under the **File** menu, select **Place** and navigate to the folder where the original image resides. This will prompt a loaded cursor that can be unloaded into an existing picture frame, dropped on the page, or dropped while you click and drag to create the size box desired.

Placing the image creates a ***link***. The high-resolution information in the image is not part of the document file. A preview of the image shows on the page. There is an electronic link to the original file with the preview. If the original file is moved or deleted, the link is broken and the image will not print correctly. Check the **Links** panel to make sure all of the graphics are linked and updated. If the panel indicates the graphic needs to be updated, it means that the original was altered in some fashion after it was placed in the document. Select the **Link** icon and it will update the placed image. See **Figure 9-40**.

Goodheart-Willcox Publisher

Figure 9-39. Jaggies or a stairstepped appearance of pixels show when the resolution is too low.

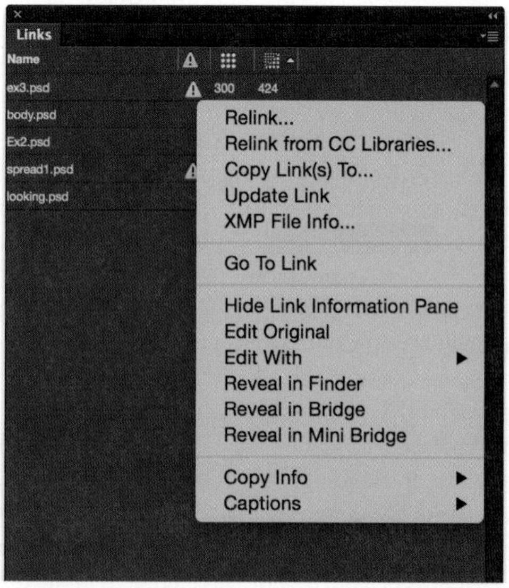

Goodheart-Willcox Publisher

Figure 9-40. The links panel shows detailed information about an image that has been placed in a document, including whether the image path is linked to the original image.

If an image is in a frame and you want to replace it with a different image, select the frame before you select the new image. Double-click on the new image file and it will automatically place into the existing frame and replace the previous image.

Another way to import a graphic is to paste it into the document. Select the original image and copy it to the clipboard. The ***clipboard*** is a temporary holding area in RAM. Only one thing can be on the clipboard at a time. When you copy something else, it replaces the previous item. Navigate to your document and paste into a frame, or onto the page itself, creating a frame. This will embed the image into the page layout document. This, however, limits future handling of the image.

A third way to import an image is to drag the image from its location onto the page. Dragging the image onto the page produces a loaded cursor. The image can be placed by dropping onto the page or by clicking and dragging to create a frame the size needed. If you drag onto the page over an existing frame, you can drop and it will go into that frame. This method also creates a link to the original graphic.

Fonts

Most applications that support text also provide a variety of fonts to choose from. The printer should use the same fonts as the original page composition, provided they can support them. The entire page composition can change if fonts are substituted. Font substitution can cause document reflow, bad word or line breaks, and loss of kerning and tracking. The fonts must be included in the project files if the production house or printer is expected to use them.

Fonts have long been a frequent source of trouble for the printer and are one of the most common interruptions in any workflow. Understanding fonts will help eliminate problems down the road. For a digital font to work, it needs four components:

- Bitmapped or screen data for the screen to have a preview of what it will look like.
- Mathematical algorithms or vector information for the printer to print (so the letters are crisp and round).
- Metrics that make up the unique details of the font.
- A process to utilize the algorithms for a more accurate display on the monitor, called ***hinting***.

Font Formats

There are three basic font formats graphic designers deal with: PostScript® Type 1, TrueType, and OpenType. ***PostScript® Type 1 fonts*** are the oldest form. The first to bridge the gap at the onset of the desktop publishing revolution, these fonts utilize PostScript® information. PostScript® is the page description language that enabled typeset quality text. The downside was they were expensive and you needed multiple pieces kept together for them to work. The screen fonts resided in suitcases, with one for each font style: bold, italic, etc. Then there were printer fonts for each style as well. All of these files had to be kept together or they simply did not work. PostScript® fonts were proprietary to Adobe®. To support multiple platforms, they had to buy the same fonts twice, in two different formats. Printers and designers invested heavily in font libraries.

TrueType fonts were developed by Apple® and Microsoft® to compete with PostScript® fonts. Although TrueType support is built into all Windows® and Apple® operating systems, they do not always translate well. All of the font information was stored in one suitcase, so they were much easier to handle, and they were less expensive to purchase. Unfortunately, they did not use PostScript®, which was the page description language of the RIPs. TrueType fonts were unreliable at the printer. Many printers refused to take files that used them. After several upgrades to PostScript®, TrueType fonts started working more smoothly. However, because the format is easier to work with, many TrueType fonts have been created by simply drawing an alphabet rather than truly developing a font with depth and details, such as accurate scalability and built-in kerning. Many of these are available as free downloads online and do not include complete character sets. More importantly, they are often not supported by the PDF format, which is the most common workflow for printing.

OpenType font was released in 1996 and was trademarked by Microsoft®. These fonts utilize the best of TrueType and the sophistication of Type 1, but add a huge array of flexibility. They are open-source technology and embrace many of the diverse behavior of all the world's different writing systems. These fonts support a much larger character set, including 65,536 glyphs. Perhaps their most significant advantage is the ability to use the same fonts on multiple platforms.

All of these formats are used, but check with your printer before using TrueType to verify they will not have any problems. Also make sure the fonts will embed when being saved in a PDF format.

Typekit®

Typekit® is a subscription-based font service from Adobe® that allows you to sync fonts to your computer or to a website. Developed to allow creatives to have a larger font library (especially for web design), Typekit® has brought fonts from many major foundries to a broad customer base. Be especially wary when using these fonts and make sure they have the necessary attributes and licensing for your specific output.

Font Management

There are more than 100,000 digital fonts. Realistically, you will never use the vast majority of them, but they are available. Managing digital fonts is a critical part of being a designer. Fonts are stored on computers in a number of different places, and they are not always easy to find. Depending on where they are stored affects the access that software has to use them. Some fonts are accessed directly by the application and are not available to other applications. To have fonts available to all applications on the computer, they must be stored together.

Font utility programs are designed to assist in font management. Many programs allow fonts to be stored in a folder on the hard drive, then accessed through the font software so that only the fonts needed are activated. This provides a simple way to control project or customer font folders. Creating ***font sets***, or font lists, grants immediate access to the fonts. See **Figure 9-41**. It is very important to maintain fonts and keep them organized in a manner that suits your personal workflow.

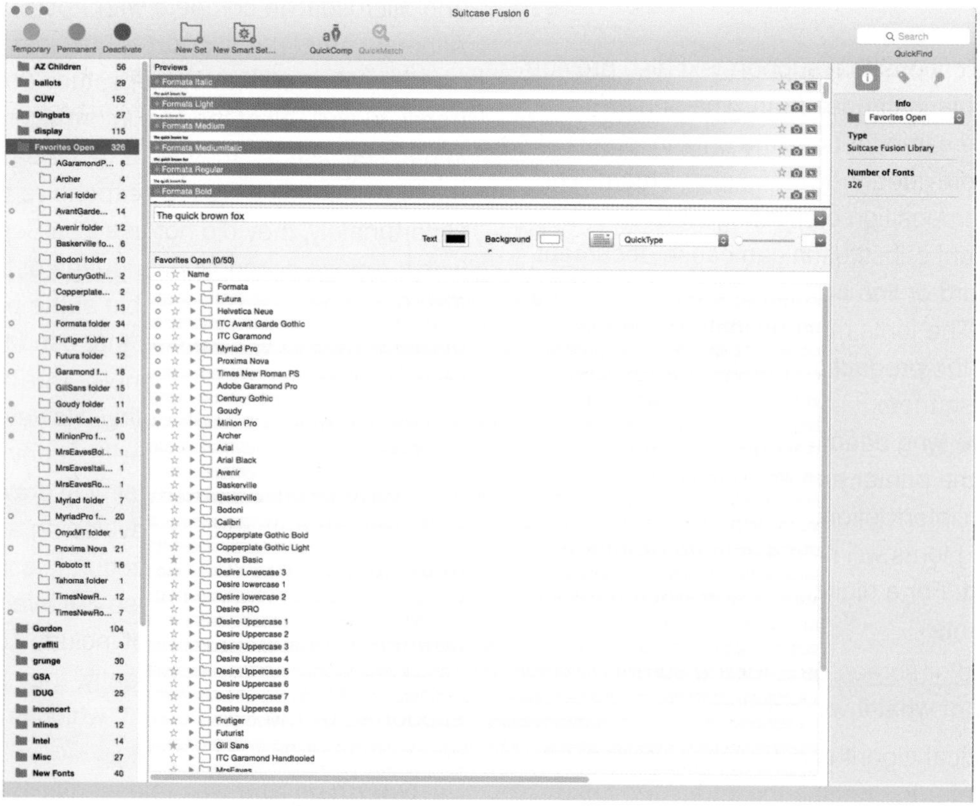

Goodheart-Willcox Publisher

Figure 9-41. Sets are an effective way to organize your fonts in a font management program.

Problems also occur when fonts in a document have the same name as the printer's fonts but are actually different fonts. Computers cannot distinguish between fonts that are named the same, but originate from different publishers. It may not always be possible to substitute one publisher for another. Avoid mixing publishers within the same typeface family because it complicates and slows the workflow.

Warning

Fonts are software and are subject to strict software licensing agreements. The user is responsible for maintaining licensed versions of the fonts used at their location.

Color of Images

Dealing with color from a prepress perspective is covered in great detail in Chapter 11, *Color*. The following section looks at the color gamut and what it means to the image.

Gamut

A color ***gamut*** refers to a subset of colors within a ***color space***. See **Figure 9-42**. On a computer, a color can only be defined in one color space at a time. For instance, if an image is in RGB format, a pixel in that image cannot be a combination of red and cyan, by definition. These color spaces are defined in different ways and have different gamuts. The image can be converted from one space to another but they cannot coexist. Some examples of color spaces are RGB, CMYK, LAB, Pantone®, spot color, and hex colors. The LAB color space is device-independent, and it communicates color on a three-axis system. Measured with a spectrophotometer, the color is considered absolute, or exact. ***Pantone*** is a global brand that uses a formula-based system to provide specific ink colors for printing. A spot color refers to any color or finish that requires its own plate for printing. ***Hex colors*** are colors defined using a hexadecimal system for display on the Internet.

Traditional offset, four-color process printing uses CMYK as the color space. Each of these colors is put down separately on the paper as it goes through the press. There is one unit for each of the four colors. Tiny dots work together in a rosette pattern to create the optical illusion of a continuous tone image when we look at a printed page. However, looking through a ***loupe***, or magnifier, the rosette is apparent and you can see the individual color dots. See **Figure 9-43**. It is important to know that the inks do not "mix." The dots overlap to create colors, and the size of the dot changes to vary the visual saturation of the color, but the ink itself is always 100% of the CMYK color. For instance, a light blue sky uses the same cyan that a dark blue car would use. They just have a different-sized dot and other colors surrounding them. See **Figure 9-44**. This is covered in detail in Chapter 11, *Color*, and Chapter 12, *Color Management*.

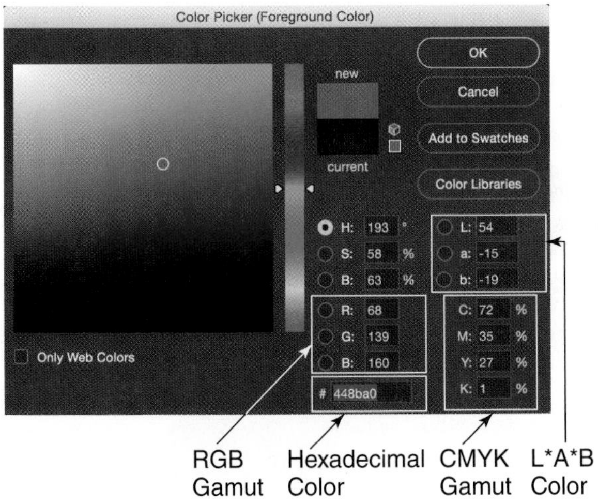

A

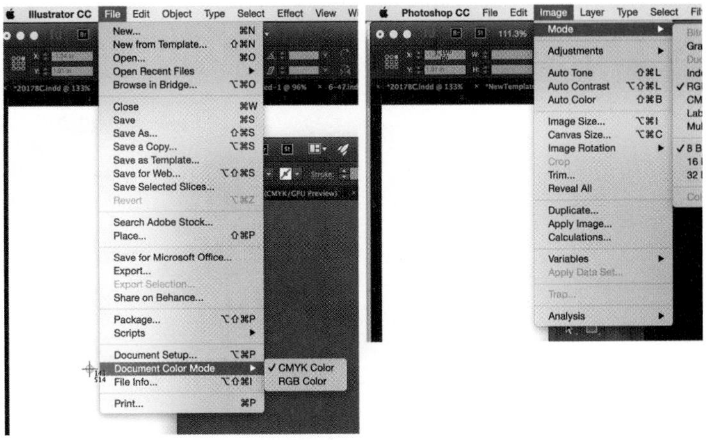

B

Goodheart-Willcox Publisher

Figure 9-42. A—Color mode is where you set the gamut for a document. B—Color picker shows the variety of color gamuts available for a color.

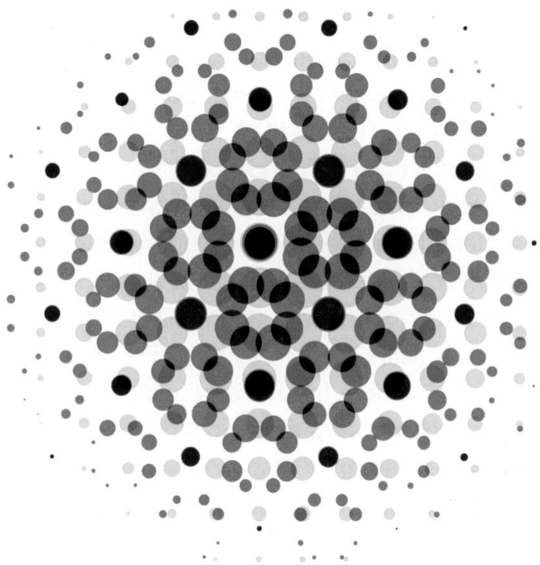

Goodheart-Willcox Publisher

Figure 9-43. The rosette is a pattern created by multiple screen angles for process colors determined by the line screen setting.

Goodheart-Willcox Publisher

Figure 9-44. Different types of the color blue use dots of different sizes.

If a customer requires a special or specific color, such as a metallic or logo color, another unit on the press is used and the ink is specified using the Pantone Matching System (PMS). This is a proprietary color system that utilizes spot colors of specialty inks, or a separate unit on the press. See **Figure 9-45**. Some colors are not within the CMYK gamut, but customers might require it for their logo. Many big name corporations traditionally have their own PMS color. If you were printing a letterhead, for example, and it only needed the PMS color and black, it would print as a two-color job. This would then use only two units on the press, and the dots would be varying sizes and combinations of the PMS color and black. If a customer requires four-color process plus a PMS, they will use five units and print offset on at least a five-color press.

Hex colors are the colors that were used for displaying web pages. Based on a hexadecimal system, these colors were specified using code. See **Figure 9-46**.

As a designer, it is important to set the file up correctly for the colors being used in printing. If a job is printing as process, you do not want your file to consist of more than four separations. It is easy to check in your page layout program to see if it is set up correctly. In InDesign®, go to **Window > Output > Separations Preview**. A menu will appear that will allow you to turn the separations on. It will also show you how many colors are being used. See **Figure 9-47**.

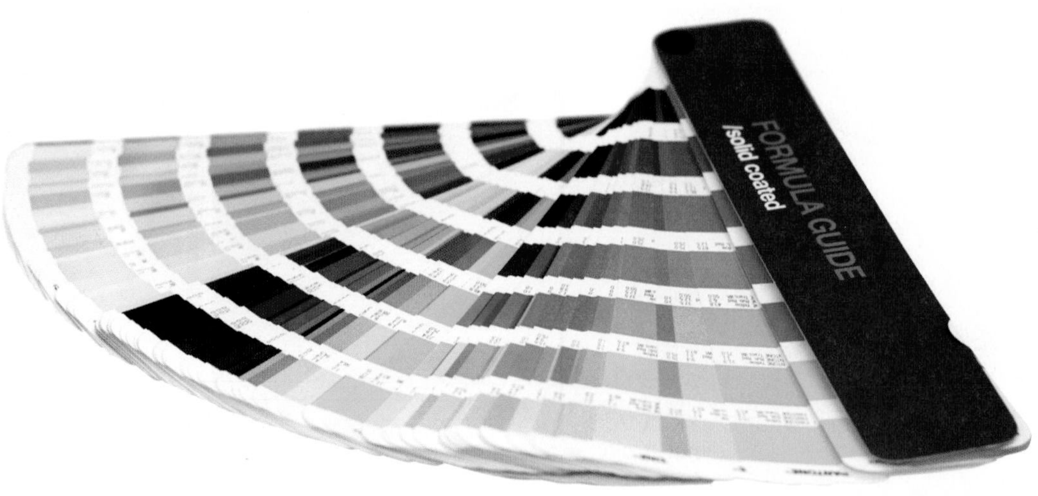

Goodheart-Willcox Publisher

Figure 9-45. Pantone is an industry standard spot color that requires a separate plate and unit on the press.

Red	FF 00 00	
Green	00 FF 00	
Blue	00 00 FF	
Cyan	00 FF FF	
Magenta	FF 00 FF	
Yellow	FF FF 00	
Black	00 00 00	
White	FF FF FF	

Goodheart-Willcox Publisher

Figure 9-46. Hexadecimal colors are defined by a hexadecimal code and are commonly used for web color settings.

Color Management

Managing the color in your images is critical to the success of your final output. Covered in detail in Chapter 12, *Color Management*, we will just touch on the high points here. Images should stay in the RGB color space as long as possible. Using color profiles for a specific output device is the only insurance that the color you see and want is the color you will get. To apply a color profile, the image must be in RGB format. Because the RGB gamut is larger than the CMYK gamut, there is more information to work with.

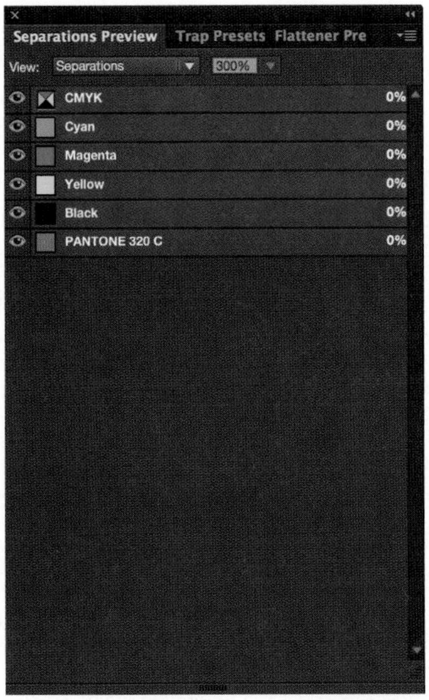

Goodheart-Willcox Publisher

Figure 9-47. The Color Separation Preview panel shows the number of channels or plates required to print a job as it is set up.

Resolution

Resolution is a measurement of the detail in a bitmapped or raster image. It is all about how many and how big the pixels are in an image. Each kind of resolution refers to something unique and is measured in different ways. The resolutions that are important to the designer and the creation of a successful file are image resolution, screen frequency, and output resolution.

Image resolution is all about the pixels: how many and how big. It is measured in ppi, or pixels per inch. The resolution of the image is determined when the pixel is captured or created. The determining factors should be quality requirements, enlargement or reduction requirements, and output requirements.

The resolution goal should be to have just enough pixels to produce a high-quality reproduction. Too few pixels will result in a jagged appearance and less detail, and too many will slow down the process and not enhance the image. The resolution of an image should be twice the line screen (explained later) used to print, at 100% of the image size. Arguably, (this is not an absolute), a one-to-one ratio should technically be sufficient. Because this formula will usually give you a high-quality file, it is a simple way to remember it.

The key part of that phrase is "at 100%." You can print a 72 ppi image if the image is large and the reproduction is small. The key to successful resolution is knowing the ***effective resolution*** as it appears in the document. If your original image has a resolution of 200 ppi and you place it in your document at 50% of its original size, the effective resolution is twice the size, or 400. If you place the same image at 200%, the effective ppi is half the original, or 100 ppi. The easiest way to check in InDesign® is to open the **Links** panel, select your image, and show the **Info** panel. The important number is under **Effective ppi**. This is the actual resolution of that image in that file. See **Figure 9-48**.

Screen frequency, or line screen, is measured in lpi, or lines per inch. The line screen refers to the number of halftone dots printed in a linear inch. The ***halftone dot*** is designed to simulate a continuous tone image, and it is the dot you see when you look through a loupe. The dot size is based on the grid created by the line screen mesh. See **Figure 9-49**.

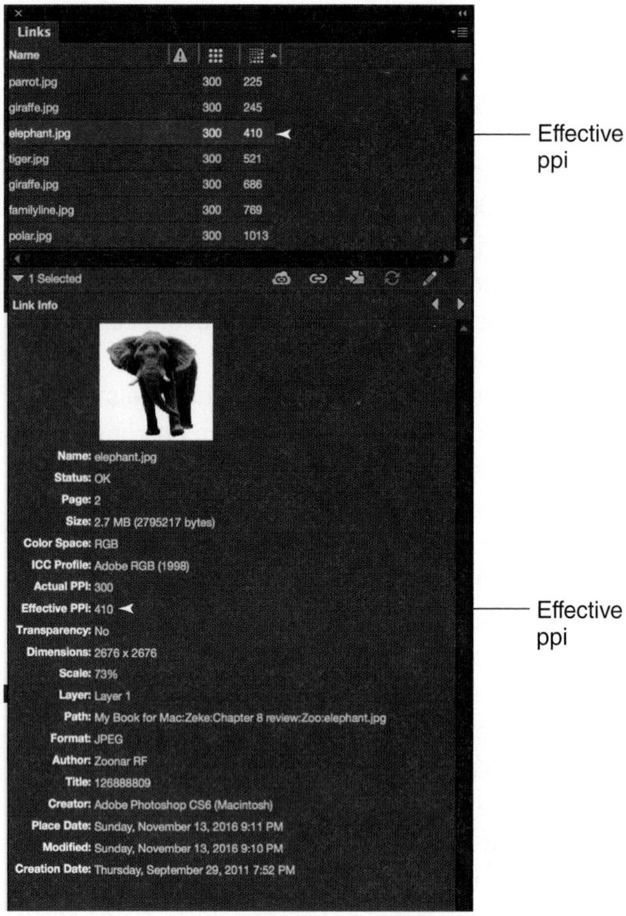

Goodheart-Willcox Publisher

Figure 9-48. The effective ppi is the true resolution of an image based on the pixels and the final output size.

Goodheart-Willcox Publisher

Figure 9-49. Halftone dots simulate a continuous tone image.

If a printer is using a 150 line screen, there are 150 × 150 lines in an inch, which creates a small halftone dot. Newspapers and screen printers use a bigger line screen (smaller number), such as 85 × 85, which creates bigger dots.

Dots happen when the file with pixels and vector information goes through the RIP (raster image processor), or ripping process. This process takes the file information through the page description language PostScript, and converts the data to halftone dots using the line screen.

Printer resolution is known as dpi, or dots per inch. However, only the printer or output device deals with dots. The resolution of the output device is a measure of how many printer dots are used to create the halftone dot. Each halftone dot is made up of tiny printer dots. See **Figure 9-50**. The more dots used to create the halftone dot, the smaller these printer dots can be and the crisper the edges in the output.

There is a trade-off. The higher the screen frequency, the smaller the halftone dot. The smaller the halftone dot, the fewer printer dots, which results in fewer possible shades of gray. Another formula is dpi divided by lpi squared. This will give you the maximum number of shades of gray (or of each color) that can be reproduced. For example, if you are printing with a 2400 dpi output device and a 150 line screen, the formula would be $(2400 \div 150)^2 = 16^2$, or 256. This is an optimal situation. However, many printers output with much higher lpi and dpi. If they print a 3600 dpi and a 250 lpi, they get 204 shades of gray, which will not reproduce the image to its fullest possible quality. Have the discussion with your printer prior to building your file to achieve the best results.

File Formats

Many different image file formats exist; each varies in the way images are saved, how images can be modified, and how well images will reproduce. File formats contain a number of important aspects, including image placement, resolution, color, and background.

Tagged Image File Format (TIFF or TIF)

The tagged image file format (TIFF or TIF) is a raster graphic file used for exchanging bitmapped

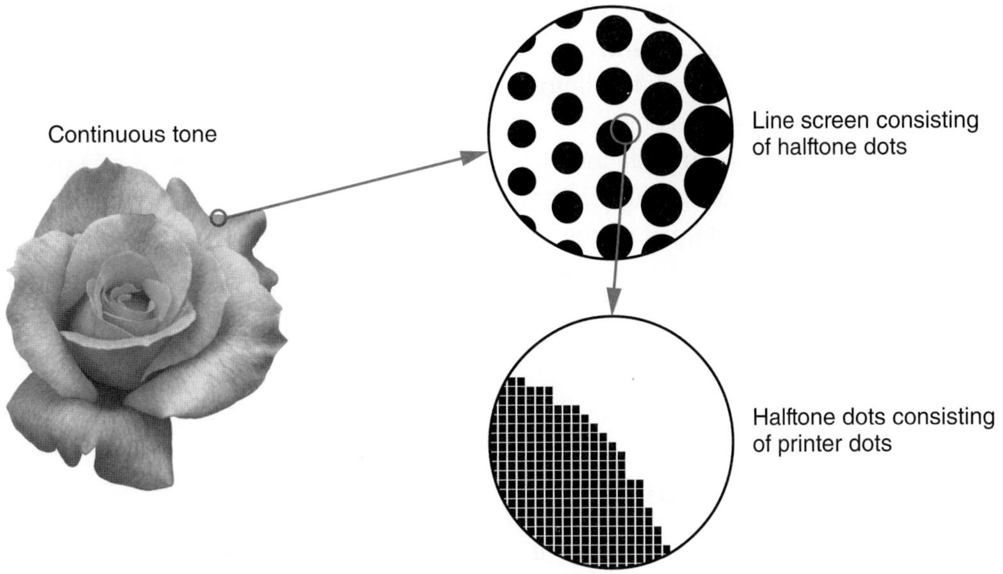

Goodheart-Willcox Publisher

Figure 9-50. Printer dots are the microscopic dots that compile each halftone dot, determined by the output resolution of the device.

images between applications. Depending on the source application, a TIFF file can allow lossless or JPEG compression. Compression is discussed later in this chapter. The format supports bitmap, grayscale, RGB, CMYK, and indexed color models. TIFF grayscale files can also be colorized in a page layout program without affecting the original file.

Encapsulated PostScript (EPS)

Encapsulated PostScript (EPS) was one of the most stable file formats used in delivery to a digital output device because it handles both vector and raster images. Although it is still usable, this format has been widely replaced with the native formats for vector and raster files, and with PDF for page files.

Graphics Interchange Format (GIF)

The graphics interchange format (GIF) supports raster images and handles only up to 256 colors. GIF files offer lossless data compression, which makes them particularly effective for drawn images, animations, and images used on the Internet. Lossless data compression will be discussed later in this chapter.

Portable Document Format (PDF)

The Adobe® portable document format (PDF) has become a standard for electronic document distribution throughout the world. It is a universal file format that preserves all aspects of a native file, regardless of the application or platform used to create the PDF file. Anyone using Adobe® Reader® (a free downloadable application) can view, navigate, and print the file exactly as the author intended.

Portable document format files are easy to make. Unfortunately, they are so easy that without careful consideration of the print requirements, the files are useless in a prepress environment. Here are several factors for consideration that will impact the success of the file:

- Page size.
- Version of Adobe® Reader®.
- Compression.
- Fonts.
- Transparency.
- Color management.

Page layout programs will allow you to export the native files as a PDF, which keeps transparency. If a printer is using a PDF workflow, ask them for the PDF settings or the settings file. Presets can be set up for any situation with all of the appropriate selections for individual printers or output devices.

Designed to reduce the extreme redundancy of PostScript, PDF files process quickly and can be sent across the Internet or a network for remote proofing or printing. PDF files are also page-independent, so single pages can be replaced or altered without reprocessing the other pages. Page independence also allows the printing of pages in any order from a single file. The PDF file is self-contained, meaning that the file has all the fonts and other resources needed to image it.

JPG or JPEG (Joint Photographic Experts Group)

The JPEG file format was created by the Joint Photographic Experts Group, in collaboration with the International Standards Organization (ISO) and the Consultative Committee for International Telegraphy and Telephony (CCITT). The JPEG format was designed to establish an international data compression standard for continuous-tone, digital still images. JPEG compression is an open-system, cross-platform, cross-device standard that can reduce files to about 5% of their normal size.

JPEG is based on the discrete cosine transform (DCT) algorithm, which analyzes each pixel block, identifies color frequencies, and removes data redundancy. This algorithm requires the same amount of processing to either compress or decompress an image. JPEG compression can incorporate other algorithms, including quantization algorithms and one-dimensional, modified Huffman encoding.

As a file utilizing lossy compression, JPG, or JPEG, files are suitable for transferring files over the Internet or for websites. They are not good for text or detail, as crisp lines will blur and colors will shift.

JPEG 2000 (Joint Photographic Experts Group)

The latest file format, JPEG 2000, is a wavelet-based method of compression. Wavelets transform data in a way that makes it mathematically reversible and also possible to compress different parts of the same image using different levels of quality. Developed by the Joint Photographic Experts Group committee in 2000, it was designed to replace the original JPEG format. Still not widely supported by web browsers, mobile devices, and digital cameras, this format is rarely used.

PNG (Portable Network Graphics)

Developed to be a web graphics replacement for GIF, PNG files support transparency and utilize a lossless compression format, explained later in this chapter.

File Names

File naming conventions are often overlooked, or even ignored. However, carefully naming files helps keep work organized. Whether creating a standard in-house convention or following recommendations from a printer, the file format must be consistently applied.

Computer platforms and programs are subject to their own conventions. Even though some of the latest operating systems allow file names up to 255 characters, file names should be limited to fewer than 20 characters with a three-character extension. Other general rules for file naming include:

- Use *only* alphanumeric characters; symbols should be avoided.
- File names should *not* begin with a space.
- Each file name should be unique.
- Use the appropriate file extension to identify file type, such as .tif, .eps, or .pdf.

To avoid confusion, revised files should not be submitted with the same name as the original file. Updated files can contain a number at the end, with the number increasing to indicate the latest version.

File Compression

Before sending digital data to a printer, most publishers compress, or reduce, the size of the files. Some programs automatically compress the file when it is converted and decompress when it is viewed. Compressed files require less storage space, allow more efficient data management, and can be transmitted faster because redundancies and other unnecessary elements are eliminated from the original file.

Lossless Compression

A ***lossless compression algorithm*** refers to a data compression process in which no data is lost. The PKZIP compression technology is an example of lossless compression. The files are often referred to as ZIP files and typically have .zip as the file extension. PKZIP files with an .exe extension are self-extracting files, which can be unzipped simply by opening the file. Decompressing either of these types of files is called *unzipping*.

For most types of data, lossless compression techniques can reduce the file size by about 50%. Lossless algorithms used for image compression assume that the likely value of a pixel can be inferred from the values of surrounding pixels. Because lossless compression does not discard any of the data, the decompressed image is identical to the original.

Other common lossless compression methods are the Huffman method, Lempel-Ziv-Welch (LZW), and run-length encoding (RLE). Both the Huffman and LZW methods of compression are techniques where adjacent bits are replaced with codes of varying lengths. For example, this technique would encode the fact that zero occurs 20 times, rather than using 20 zeros. This information would use 4 bytes instead of 20. Run-length encoding encodes digital data to reduce the amount of storage needed to hold the data without any loss of information. Each coded item consists of a data value and the number of adjacent pixels with the same data value. In other words, strings of the same character are encoded as a single number. This is a very efficient way of encoding large areas of flat color used in linework and text.

Lossy Compression

A ***lossy compression algorithm*** refers to data compression techniques in which some data is lost. Lossy compression methods attempt to eliminate redundant or unnecessary information. Most video compression technologies use a lossy compression. This improves the speed of data transfer, but causes slight degradation when the image is decompressed.

Lossy compression techniques include quantization, Delta Pulse Code Modification (DPCM), and JPEG. Quantization is a filtering process that determines the amount and selection of data to eliminate, so data can be encoded with fewer bits. DPCM measures one set of bits and then measures differences from that set. The differences are then encoded into fewer bits.

Lossless compression is preferred for printed images because each time a lossy compression is applied, more information is lost. The loss of data may not be noticeable on screen, but will be very noticeable in high-resolution printed output.

JPEG is a popular standard for images used on the Internet due to its extreme compression capacity and ability to support 24-bit color. The JPEG file format allows the compression ratio and reproduction quality to be controlled at the point of compression, **Figure 9-51**. JPEG files contain bitmap information only and support grayscale, RGB, and CMYK color models.

A major goal of JPEG is to maintain the appearance of an image, rather than the actual data contained in the original. This works because we are visually less sensitive to high-frequency color. JPEG is a lossy compression, and therefore deletes some image information, but the decompressed image remains visually whole.

Goodheart-Willcox Publisher

Figure 9-51. JPEG images allow for different types of control.

JPEG functions best for color and grayscale, continuous-tone images. Compressing images with high-contrast edges (such as line graphics or text) to significantly reduce the file size adversely affects the portion containing the text. Selective compression enables users to specify different compression levels for the various elements within a single image. For example, EPS color image files embedded in a digital document result in a very large file. EPS-JPEG compression creates files for page composition software that are significantly smaller than standard EPS files. Images vary in the amount of data that can be compressed without affecting the visible quality. Experiment with quality settings to determine the maximum compression settings that do not perceptibly alter appearance. Since data is lost in each compression/decompression cycle, use JPEG compression at the maximum quality setting and only on final images.

Proofreading

A ***proof*** is any copy or art that is checked before going into print. In traditional typesetting, the proof is a galley pulled (printed) from the metal type or a printout on phototypesetting paper. In today's electronic production systems, a proof is typically a printout from a laser or ink-jet printer.

In traditional typesetting situations, a manuscript was edited and marked for type size and style before being sent to the compositor. The compositor followed all editing instructions and set the copy exactly as it was written. After the copy was set, the ***proofreading*** process was carried out to detect and mark any typesetting errors. The marked proof would then be sent back to the compositor for correction, and a corrected proof would be produced and checked.

In digital composition methods, the author and editor create the final copy. This does not eliminate the need for proofreading, but changes the method and approach. The designer is often the producer of the text and must read the proof carefully for errors and mark for corrections. After corrections are made, the copy must be checked again.

Proofreading Skills

A proofreader has the very important job of making sure the final product meets the standards of expected quality and professionalism. In larger publishing and printing facilities, people are hired with expertise in proofreading. In smaller facilities, a variety of people may have this responsibility. Every printer, especially in a small plant, should be able to read proofs.

The proofreader must be a meticulous person and have the ability to accurately check individual letters in words, as well as look for combinations of letters. Proofreaders cannot scan a page, but must study each word separately. If proofreading is done poorly, the highest quality paper, best printing methods, excellent content, and other favorable aspects of the product will be ruined. It is critical that care and time is taken for this very important step.

Proofreader's Responsibilities

The typical duties of a proofreader include:

- Checking the spelling of all words.
- Ensuring word divisions or hyphenations are correct.
- Verifying that the style is consistent.
- Checking that copy has not been omitted or repeated.

Proofreader's marks are widely used symbols that single out and explain copy changes or errors, **Figure 9-52**. The symbols are used to show when something should be taken out, added, or changed.

The appropriate proofreader's mark is placed in the margin of the page to indicate the type of correction to be made. This system is an efficient means of showing the location of the fault and the desired correction. Proofreading marks must be written clearly and should be exaggerated so they are not overlooked. When needed, the proofreader can write special notes pertaining to the marks in the border. Sometimes, an extra sheet of instructions may be attached to the copy or page layout.

Proofreading Methods

Comparison proofing, or one-person proofing, is done primarily to find such major problems as copy deletion, incorrect sequence, or copy duplication. It is most suitable for small jobs with little copy. Using this method, the proofreader scans through the proof once to check for obvious errors or changes. The proof is then placed next to the manuscript, and the proofreader traces along the lines of the proof with a pen while reading. Placing a straightedge across the copy and moving it slowly down the page is also helpful. To be consistent, the proofreader must always compare the proof with the copy, not vice versa.

Two-person proofing requires the reader to work with an assistant. This is the most common proofreading method when accuracy and speed are important. It is frequently used with larger jobs, such as a textbook. The two people are referred to as the reader and the copyholder. The reader follows the

Goodheart-Willcox Publisher

Figure 9-52. Proofreaders marks are symbols used to convey changes to a designer or layout artist.

printed design proof (or computer screen display) to check closely for errors. The copyholder follows the original manuscript. Usually, the two take turns reading to each other. Each word must be carefully pronounced and the reading pace must not be too fast. The reader must have time to scan the letters of each word, and check punctuation, style, and other items.

A special jargon or language often develops between the reader and copyholder. For instance, some readers pronounce each capital letter as "cap" and each period as "peer" to denote the beginning and end of a sentence.

Spell Check Programs

A spell check program, also called a spellchecker or proofing program, is incorporated into the majority of graphic communications software. Depending on the operator's preference and the program, it automatically checks the spelling of each word as it is typed, or all the words in a document when keyboarding is complete.

A spell check program compares words in the document with those in the program dictionary. If a word is spelled incorrectly, a correction is suggested, **Figure 9-53**. The suggested spelling can be accepted or the proper spelling may be entered and applied to the document. Spell check programs also permit unusual spellings or technical words to be added to the program dictionary.

Spell check programs can be very helpful to production speed and quality. When properly used, they can greatly reduce typos and make the correction cycle much more efficient. However, spell check is only the first step in proofreading, not the only step. Copy must still be reviewed. Fewer typing errors allows more attention to be given to checking style, illustration references, sequence, and other important content aspects.

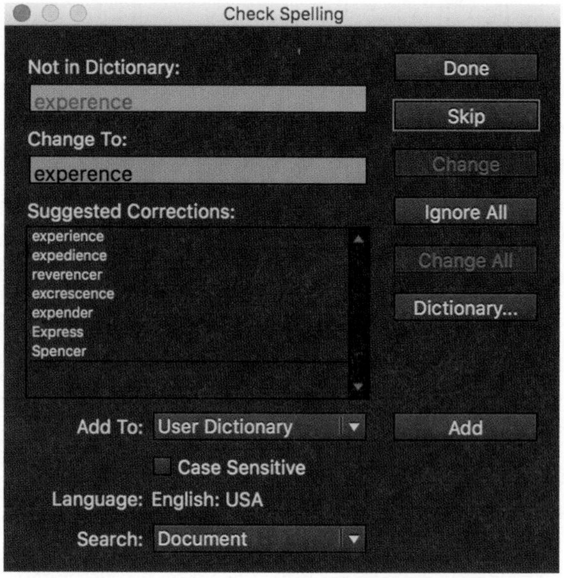

Goodheart-Willcox Publisher

Figure 9-53. Spell check is a great tool for first look at proofreading for spelling error. The panel will show you the suspect word and give you recommended options for correction.

Preflighting

Just as a pilot performs a list of preliminary system checks before taking off, a designer must make sure the file does not contain any errors that could cause problems at output. Preflight is about checking all of the components in the file. A basic list of things to look for is built in to most page geometry programs, with the ability to create specialized presets from detailed specifications unique to each printer. To make sure ***preflighting*** goes smoothly, discuss file format and preparation with the printer while the project is still in the design stage. Knowing their requirements ahead of time will save both time and money.

According to the Printing Industries of America (PIA), some of the most common problems with the files customers provide are:

- Missing or incorrect fonts.
- Incorrect color management.
- Scans supplied in wrong file format.
- Graphics not linked.
- Incorrectly defined or underdefined bleeds.
- No laser proofs supplied.
- Missing graphics.
- Resolution too high or too low.
- Incorrect PDF settings.

Both native files and PDF files have the ability to preflight within the applications. There are a number of diagnostic tools built into the software. Print Production lets you check the file for items such as transparency and outlined text. Output

Preview not only shows how many colors the file is set up to print with, but it also shows ink limits. By setting the maximum ink limit number in the output preview window, areas that exceed the value will be highlighted to easily see where problems could occur on press. See **Figure 9-54**.

In Acrobat®, checking properties will give you size information to evaluate bleed settings, embedded font information, and number of pages. The preflight option will allow extensive checks and analysis. See **Figure 9-55**.

Preflighting software and diagnostic tools are comprehensive. However, there are still elements in the file that need to be checked that requires a thorough examination by the designer. See the checklist of items in **Figure 9-56**.

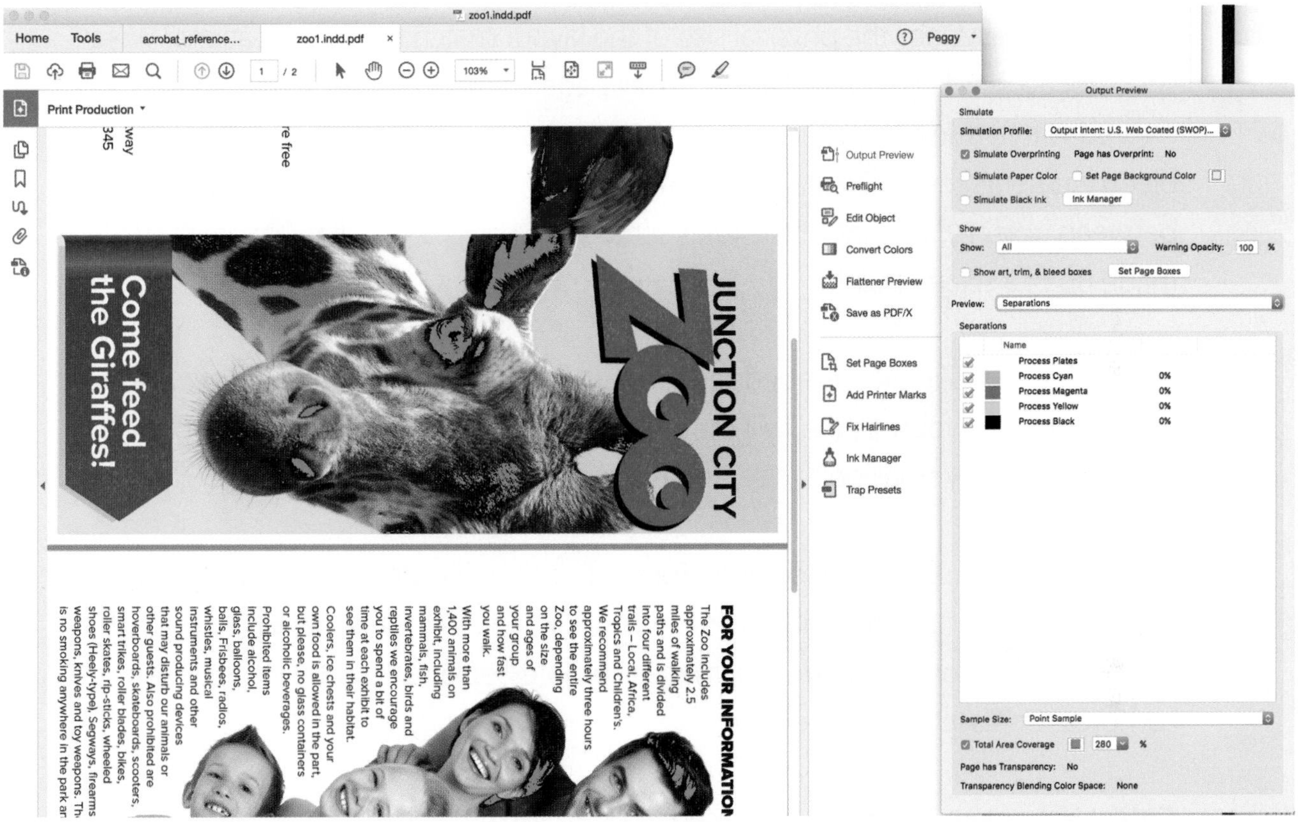

Goodheart-Willcox Publisher

Figure 9-54. Ink limits are shown as a part of the pdf output preview.

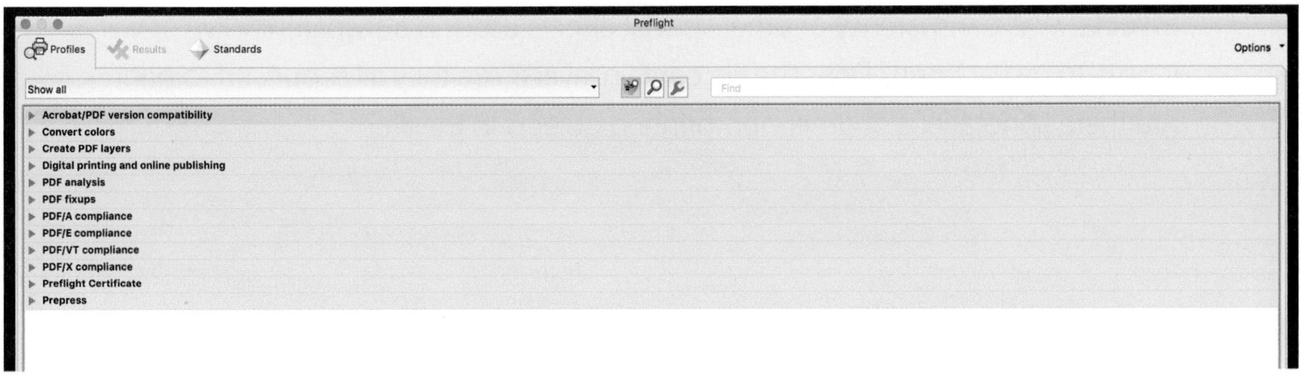

Goodheart-Willcox Publisher

Figure 9-55. The Acrobat® preflight option allows you to analyze files.

THE CHECKLIST

A checklist is the basis of preflight, whether it's done with the assistance of a piece of software or by "hand." Some of the things the typical checklist helps you to examine:

Layout issues: Does the physical size of the layout match the specifications? Were specs (or a job ticket) supplied at all? Are all page elements there? Was the job created with a true DTP appliction? What version(s) of the file(s) are supplied? Are bleed elements there? Do graphic elements abut properly (will there be white gaps between objects)? Are any of the rules set to a thickness of "hairline," or are they made up of a screen build?

Fonts: Are they supplied/embedded properly? What type of fonts are they? Are they from a valid foundry (i.e., will they RIP)? Were they menu-styled? Has any type been set to a very small point size, and is small type made up of a screen build?

Images: Is there sufficient resolution for the printing or output method? Do the images contain unsightly artifacts? Is the TAC/ink density of shadow areas too high for the printing condition? Are the images compressed and, if so, by what type of compression? Is retouching required?

Color: How many colors are supposed to print? What color space are the images/layout objects? Are DeviceN colors used? Are ICC profiles used? Are spot colors indicated consistently? Which color swatch library was used?

Effects: Was transparency or other special effects used? Is transparency live or will it have to be flattened? Does the file contain layers? Are they all supposed to print? Are there annotations or other non-printing objects in the file?

Goodheart-Willcox Publisher

Figure 9-56. A standard preflight checklist endorsed by industry specialists.

Sending Files to the Printer

At the beginning of the production process, a dialog with the printer should occur to get all the necessary specifications for final output. Printers have their own workflow and requirements, and they all impact the basic file setup.

If the printer wants the native file to print from, the designer must prepare it accordingly. Page layout software has a handy feature under the file menu called **Package**. Selecting this brings up a menu of options. After entering the contact information and instructions, a new folder is created in the determined location. More options at the bottom of this dialog box must be addressed. It is critical to the success of the file that all links, fonts, and specialty settings, if applied, be included. Files using the latest version of InDesign® cannot be opened by previous versions of the software. If your printer is using an older version of the software, an IDML, or InDesign® Markup Language, file needs to be generated. The IDML format allows older versions to open newer files but can be risky as new versions may use attributes unavailable in older versions, and there could be changes. A PDF can be generated at this time with appropriate settings for that printer. When you package, a warning about font licensing appears. Read this carefully to comply with copyright laws. See **Figure 9-57**.

The new folder contains a copy of the document file, a **Links** folder with all graphics, a **Fonts** folder, the **Summary** file with contact information, and whatever else you selected. This is the folder that is sent to the printer. They will have all of the necessary items to reproduce your file accurately.

Many printers use the PDF workflow. To create your file correctly, use the specifications or settings they provide. It is always best to include a hard (paper) copy of your file with the electronic folder. The hard copy provides actual proof that serves as an accurate representation of the file. It does not have to show approved color, but should indicate any special requirements for folding, pagination, finishing, or binding.

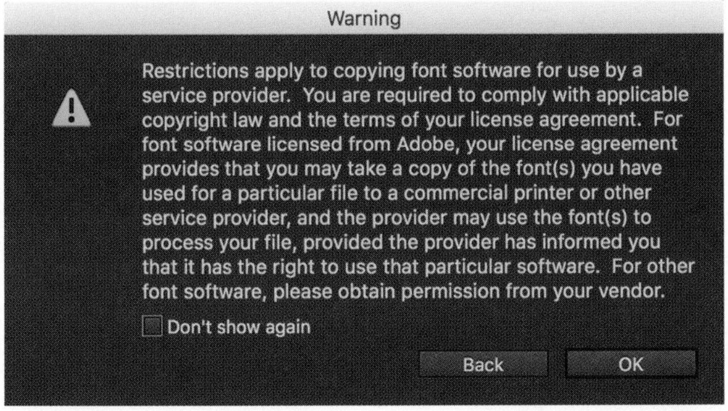

Goodheart-Willcox Publisher

Figure 9-57. Check for restrictions when packaging fonts.

Think Green

Soft Proofs

With the growing use of technology in the graphic communications industry, as well as the increased concern for environmental issues, soft proofs are becoming more widely used than digital proofs. Soft proofs reduce the use of paper in multiple rounds of checking proofs. They eliminate the use of ink and the creation of any VOCs in the production of printing proofs. There is also no transportation involved since soft proofs are sent over the Internet. While some companies are concerned about the quality of soft proofs, others have found that with monitor calibrations, the on-screen page should match the printed page. Companies have found soft proofs to be a more efficient alternative to hard copy proofs because of the turnaround time and ease of use.

Production Proofs

Depending on the complexity of a project and previous arrangements with the printer, a number of proofs must be reviewed before the job goes to press. Proofs serve as samples for the customer and guidelines for the press operators. Proofs can be made directly from digital files, viewed online, or run off on a proof press. Cost variations often determine the type of proofs requested at different stages of prepress production. The most commonly used proofs today are soft proofs and digital proofs.

Career Link

Preflight Technician

The preflight technician uses digital imaging technology to achieve the planned requested job. When using this technology, the preflight technician takes the electronic files that are given to him or her by the customer and checks them for all aspects of completeness. It is very similar to the checklist a pilot goes over before the plane takes off; the formalized preflight manual checklist makes sure everything is in order. Therefore, the preflight technician tasks are critical to the elimination of output problems of the electronic files. Preflighting software can speed up the process. Sometimes checklists and software are both used by the preflight technician.

Some of the responsibilities of the preflight technician include making sure submitted discs are not damaged, ensuring discs are readable, checking in-house font availability, checking for missing material on submitted discs, checking for correct size indications, checking for proper trapping and adequate bleeds, and checking for font problems. All these preflighting tasks ensure the digital job is ready for the intended output device. The ability to work closely with the customer and other departments is an imperative attribute.

The preflight technician should have formal postsecondary graphic communications training in digital technology; an associate degree is often stated as a requirement in the job description. It is also beneficial to be familiar with the printing process and production workflow. Preflight technicians must have good communication and basic problem-solving skills, be comfortable with the pressure of deadlines, and be proficient with computer applications.

"Students entering the graphic communications discipline need to have a variety of skills for employment in our ever-changing industry. They need to be versed in the practical application of traditional web and offset printing, digital printing, prepress and prepress software, print management, and to have a firm understanding of the Internet and how it relates to the printing industry."

Tony Mancuso
Typography Unlimited, Inc. (TUI)

Soft Proofs

Soft proofs are electronic files that represent what the final printed page will look like. These proofs may be press-ready files created using the project composition files submitted to the printer. Soft proofs may be delivered via e-mail or accessed on the Internet, and are most often saved as PDF files. Soft proofing jobs has become a common industry practice, as it takes advantage of information technology to save the time and expense involved in producing printed proofs. Additionally, the client is able to review proofs in a significantly shorter time frame and may instantly approve pages or send comments through e-mail or a secure website.

Online soft proofs are posted and managed using web-based applications specifically developed for electronically proofing documents. While each printer may not use the same interface, the functions and tools available to proof a job are similar from one application to the next.

Digital Proofs

The two most common types of digital proofs used today are laser proofs and ink-jet proofs. ***Laser proofs*** are printed onto paper using electronic files. They are produced by an industrial laser printer and may be in black and white or use process colors. They are an inexpensive type of proof. However, the quality is said to be less than that of ink-jet proofs.

Ink-jet proofs are produced by a printing process that generates four-color proofs directly from the digital files. Ink-jet proofing is often used as a ***contract proof***, replacing the press proof. The color simulates what will be produced on a press. A contract proof is the agreement between the customer and the printer as the final proof before going to press. It represents the acceptable quality in color, text, images, and pagination. However, there is often no halftone dot, so conventional screening problems such as moiré patterns cannot be predicted. Ink-jet proofs can be presented early in the proofing process because they are very inexpensive.

Digital Prepress Workflow

The changes resulting from the transition of conventional prepress methods to digital have brought about many workflow enhancements and radically changed the processes in the prepress department.

PDF Workflow

In a PDF workflow, the PDF file is used to create the film or plates needed by the print production facility. The PDF file contains all of the necessary information, such as the fonts, graphics, images, text, and document layout. No further prepress steps remain to be completed by the production department. Portable document software typically saves a document bitmap, the ASCII text, and the font data. Even with compression, most PDF files may be many times larger than the native file.

The PDF file is practically an ideal preflighting tool. If all the necessary elements are not present at the time of file creation, the user is warned. PDF files also provide a single file for viewing, distributing, archiving, editing, and printing small file sizes, and a built-in preview.

Job Definition Format (JDF)

The ***Job Definition Format (JDF)*** is a file format that automates the printing workflow, from design to production, and was developed through a partnership between Adobe®, Agfa, Heidelberg®, and Man Roland. The International Cooperation for the Integration of Processes in Prepress, Press, and Postpress Organization (CIP4) began managing JDF at Drupa 2000. ***Drupa***, held every four years in Düsseldorf, Germany is the largest printing expo in the world. This file format is based on JMF, a job messaging format based on Extensible Markup Language (XML), and provides a standard format that is compatible with any JDF-enabled equipment.

JDF files are similar to an embedded electronic job ticket, in that they can contain information on the document designer, fonts used, images contained, stock type and size, ink colors, bindery instructions, and other static data. In addition, the file may contain instructions for JDF-enabled devices used in the production process, including ink fountain settings on a press and the configuration of bindery equipment. Throughout the production process, the information and instructions contained in a JDF file may be manually amended to allow for adjustments or additions, such as completion dates, delivery schedules, and client contact information. This technology expedites production, reduces errors that occur in the processes, and automates the workflow of print production.

Summary

- The computer and associated devices, and specialized graphics programs are components in the digital prepress system.
- Computer platforms include hardware devices and operating systems.
- Components for Microsoft PC and Apple Macintosh computers include memory, storage, input devices, and output devices.
- The digital prepress process consists of preparing content, composing pages, and outputting the finished file.
- Graphic sizes are represented in bits. Vector graphics define all the shapes in the image; raster graphics are resolution dependent. A pixel is the smallest amount of displayable information for a digital image.
- Page layout software is built to handle both text and graphics.
- A color gamut refers to a subset of colors within a color space.
- The printer should use the same fonts as the original page composition.
- Resolution is a measurement of the detail in a bitmapped or raster image.
- File formats include TIFF, EPS, GIF, PDF, JPEG, JPEG 2000, and PNG.
- A proof is any copy or art that is checked before going into print.
- Proofreaders detect and mark any typesetting errors.
- Preflighting checks all components in a file and creates specialized presets unique to each printer.
- Proofs must be reviewed before the job goes to press.

Review Questions

Answer the following questions using the information in this chapter.

1. List the three major functions of a computer system.
2. Explain the function of computer software.
3. What is the difference between memory and storage?
4. List three different storage devices.
5. What do the letters WYSIWYG represent?
6. *True or False?* Additive colors are also called process colors.
7. What is the function of a raster image processor?
8. What are the advantages and disadvantages of PostScript?
9. Flowing text from one box to another is called _____.
   A. rolling
   B. streaming
   C. threading
   D. flowing
10. A computer processes and stores information using the _____ system, which is a series of 1s and 0s.
11. Explain *bit depth*.
12. Vector graphics are represented as _____, and raster graphics or bitmapped images are _____ dependent.
13. A vector is a line that is defined by its _____ and _____.

14. Which of the following is *not* a common feature of the computer screen display for a page composition program?
    A. Scroll bars.
    B. Pasteboard.
    C. Scanner port.
    D. Menu bar.
15. The arrangement of menus, control bars, palettes, etc., for a document and pasteboard is called _____.
16. What are the four categories of tools available in the tool palette?
17. *True or False?* The "fill" and "stroke" switching arrow swaps the definition but *not* the active window.
18. Style sheets are _____ tools that combine a number of attributes.
19. *True or False?* Pasting an image into a frame creates a link.
20. Name three advantages of OpenType fonts.
21. A color _____ refers to a subset of colors within a(n) _____.
22. What does a color profile do?
23. Name three resolutions that are important to the designer and the creation of a successful file.
24. Which dot is designed to simulate a continuous tone image, and is the dot you see when you look through a loupe?
25. Printer resolution is measured in _____.
    A. lpi
    B. dpi
    C. ppi
    D. tpi
26. Name three image file formats.
27. What are the general rules to follow when naming files?
28. What is the difference between lossless compression and lossy compression?
29. A(n) _____ is any copy or art that is checked before going to print.
30. What are proofreader's marks?
31. What is *preflighting*?
32. What should you include when you send your file to the printer?

Suggested Activities

1. Prepare a workflow chart of a typical digital prepress department.
2. Select a product you want to print that includes line work and photographic images. Choose the computer platform to operate the software you will use to prepare the prepress project documents. Explain your equipment selection.
3. List the computer programs commonly used in your school and explain the unique features of each program.
4. Research various printing facilities and make a list of the job titles found in the prepress department.
5. Place an image on a page at 50%, 100%, and 200%. Print the page and describe the differences you see.

Chapter 10

Image Capture

Learning Objectives

After studying this chapter, you will be able to:

- Recall the difference between analog format and digital format.
- Identify the various types of light sensors used in imaging devices.
- Identify differences between point-and-shoot cameras and digital single lens reflex (DSLR) cameras.
- Summarize the function of each component on a digital camera.
- Explain the advantages and disadvantages of shooting in JPEG and RAW format.
- Understand the importance of proper lighting and its effect on the captured image.
- Recall the specific characteristics of each type of scanner.
- Recall the different types of resolution.
- Explain how spatial resolution and tonal resolution affect the performance of digital imaging devices.
- Identify the use of common image manipulation program tools.

Goodheart-Willcox Publisher

Important Terms

A/D converter
analog charge
analog format
bit depth
charge-coupled device (CCD)
CMOS
digital format
effective ppi
exposure latitude
filter
flatbed scanner
gray card
histogram
layers
mask
mottling
Newton's rings
optical character recognition (OCR)
paint effects
quantizing
retouching tools
scan area
scanner
screen ruling
spatial resolution
tonal resolution
unsharp masking (USM)
well sites
white balance

G-WLEARNING.com

While studying this chapter, look for the activity icon to:

- **Practice** vocabulary terms with e-flash cards, matching activities, and vocabulary game.
- **Reinforce** what you learn by submitting end-of-chapter questions.

www.g-wlearning.com/visualtechnology/

Since its introduction, digital imaging has had a steadily increasing impact on the printing industry. Computer software allows images to be quickly modified by changing or adding colors, removing unwanted components, and combining multiple images.

Print production requires digital images. These images are a result of scanning or digital photography. While some images are scanned, most are coming from digital photography as the cameras become more and more popular. Regardless of how the image is captured, many require some form of manipulation to gain optimal results on press.

Analog and Digital Images

Photos taken with older film-based cameras are in ***analog format***. The principal feature of something in analog format is that it is continuous. Just as the volume control on a TV increases the sound in smooth increments from soft to loud, the image on a film negative has smooth gradations of tone from light to dark. In contrast, something in ***digital format*** consists of values measured at distinct points or positions, **Figure 10-1**. When an image in analog format is converted to digital format, each of the distinct points represents variances in brightness and image color. These points are recorded as pixels (picture elements). Pixels are arranged in rows and columns to form a grid. An analog image is recorded into a digital format by assigning each pixel a set of numbers that designate position, brightness, and color.

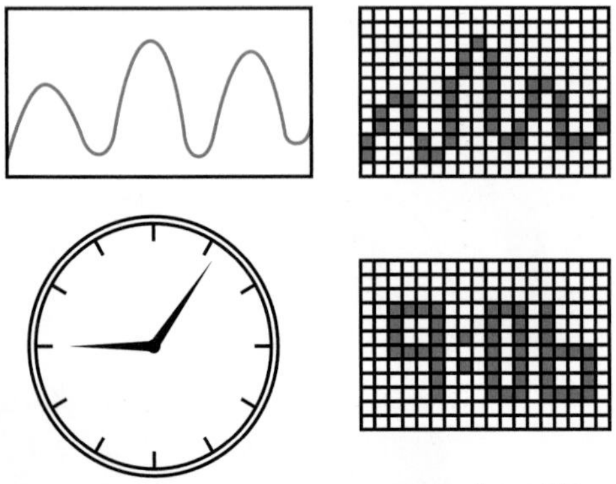

Goodheart-Willcox Publisher

Figure 10-1. The curved line and time on the left represent analog format. The same curved line and time displayed on the right represent a digital format.

When digitizing an image, using a large number of pixels produces more detail in the image, or better resolution. Additionally, setting a high ***bit depth*** results in smoother color gradations. The greater the bit depth, the more colors or grayscales are represented. For example, an 24-bit color image comprises 16.8 million colors. But a 48-bit color image can portray 281 trillion colors. A large color range is only useful if light sensors within the imaging device are capable of detecting a great number of distinct colors. See **Figure 10-2**.

All digital imaging input devices function approximately in the same way: they expose the original with light and measure the amount of red, green, and blue light reflected back or transmitted through the object. These measurements are converted into digital data, which is then recorded. The type of light-gathering sensors used by the imaging device determines both the pixels per inch (ppi) and bit depth. This is the key difference among various types of digital cameras, camera backs, and scanners.

Light Sensors

Both flatbed scanners and digital cameras use light-gathering sensors to gather information about an image. Just as film in a conventional camera records an image when light strikes it, these sensors use light to record an image electronically.

CCD Sensors

Charge-coupled devices (CCD) are solid-state chips composed of hundreds or even thousands of separate photosensitive elements known as ***well sites***, or photosites. Each of the well sites in an array has a slightly different sensitivity from every other site.

The CCD converts light reflected from the subject matter into an ***analog charge***, or series of electrical impulses. The charge is converted from analog to digital form through an ***A/D converter***, and stored as pixels using binary code to represent the tonal values and detail of the subject. The A/D converter creates the digital image by converting the analog charge into a series of steps. This process is called ***quantizing***. The need for

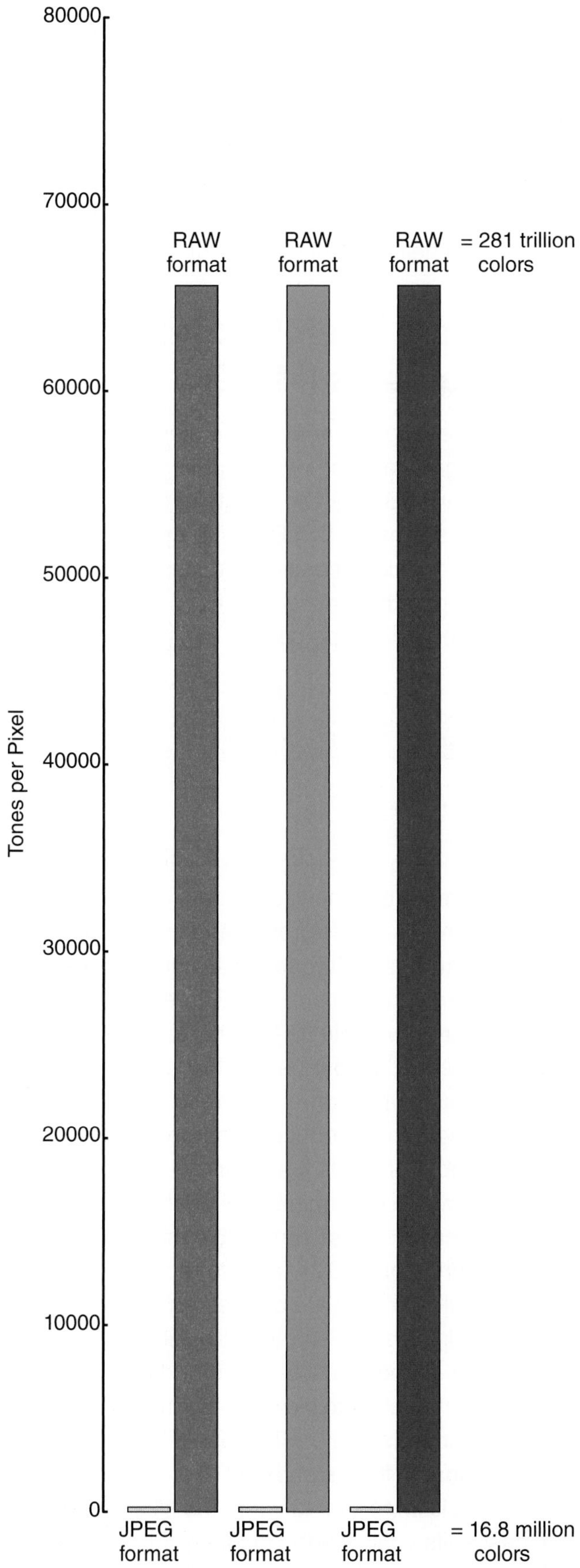

Figure 10-2. This chart shows dramatic differences between 8-bit color and 16-bit color.

special production processes for these mainly analog devices has kept the prices high and the technological advancements slow.

CMOS Sensors

Because the cost of digital cameras has come down significantly, their popularity has exploded. Instrumental to the cost reduction has been the introduction of complementary metal oxide semiconductor active pixel sensors, or ***CMOS***, which are inexpensive to manufacture. Previously used only in low-end point-and-shoot cameras, the quality has increased steadily, and they were also introduced in DSLR cameras.

Advancements to digital technology have allowed CMOS sensors to improve image quality as high as 50 megapixels and greater. Although they are more susceptible to noise than the CCD sensors, CMOS sensors consume very little power. Each pixel has several transistors next to it, which lowers the light sensitivity. In addition, because their speed is fast enough to shift pixel data in nearly real time, they can be used with a mechanical shutter.

Digital Cameras and Camera Backs

Camera backs are digital connections for analog cameras. While some high-end cameras still use these devices, most people have opted for digital cameras, eliminating the need for camera backs.

Point-and-Shoot Cameras

A point-and-shoot type of camera comes in a variety of sizes and features, **Figure 10-3**. Originally designed for the casual user, the camera phone has risen to market preeminence because of its quality and convenience. Even professional photographers recommend camera phones now.

Camera phones and traditional point-and-shoot cameras utilize an LCD screen to view the image being taken. Because you are not looking through the lens, what you are seeing is not the exact picture you are taking. There is a shift in the perspective. This anomaly is called parallax.

Peter Bernik/Shutterstock.com

Figure 10-3. The most common point-and-shoot digital camera is the smartphone.

Holding the camera away from your face to focus on the screen increases the chance for movement.

DSLR

A digital single lens reflex (DSLR) camera is most often used by serious and professional photographers. These digital cameras allow lenses to be interchanged, **Figure 10-4**. For example, this allows a macro lens to be removed and replaced with a lens that has greater distance capabilities. DSLR cameras use a mirror to reflect the actual image being taken. Light goes through the lens, hits the mirror, and is bounced back through the viewfinder. Because you look through the viewfinder, you can use your face to steady the camera and help control movement.

©George Deal

Figure 10-4. Digital SLR cameras allow lenses to be interchanged to meet the needs of any shooting environment and subject matter.

Mirrorless Interchangeable Lens Cameras (MILC)

Mirrorless digital cameras are stepping up to bridge the gap between point-and-shoot cameras and standard DSLRs. The quality of these cameras rivals that of DSLRs. With mirrorless interchangeable lens cameras (MILCs), you look directly through the lens to the LED screen on the back. This eliminates parallax.

Digital Camera Considerations

When buying a digital camera, it is important to select a camera that fits your needs. The size and price of cameras varies greatly and model changes come with surprising frequency. Cameras have many features and options that differentiate various models. Carefully evaluate the characteristics of the cameras that fit your needs. For example, if you desire pictures with high-quality resolution, you will want a camera that produces high-pixel pictures. A high number of pixels means increased picture resolution, which determines the printing quality.

Digital cameras use removable memory cards called secure digital (SD) cards to record picture data. Not all SD cards are created equal. The cards vary in size and storage capacity, and are divided into speed classes. The four different speed classes, from fastest to slowest, are 10, 8, 4, and 2. Different cameras and devices use different sizes of cards ranging from standard SD to miniSD and microSD. It is important to verify the size and speed that best suits your needs, and fits your camera, before you buy. Storage media can be formatted and used over and over again, and the cost of the card increases with the capacity.

File Formats

As you shoot photos, your images are saved to your camera's memory card. These files are then transferred to a computer or printer. There are different types of file formats available depending on the camera. The settings may be changed before you begin to use your camera. Two of the most commonly available file formats are JPEG and RAW.

JPEG

When shooting an image, the sensor can capture wavelengths beyond what the human eye can see. Camera settings determine the data captured by the sensor. The data must then be reproduced for the computer or editing system by recombining the RGB information into a compressed file. The standard 8-bit sRGB model, which is the default for most JPEG images, can reproduce 16.8 million colors. This is derived from the binary system, which has only two positions (on and off) with 8 possible switches. This means there are 256 (2^8) tints or shades. Because you have these shades for each channel of the RGB image, there are 16.8 million (256 x 256 x 256) color possibilities. While this seems like a lot, the reality is that when the image data is recombined, the sRGB uses only whole integer data, which eliminates many of the 10 million colors and shades that the human eye *can* see. It is then compressed using a lossy compression, which gets rid of data to reduce the file size as well as the number of colors.

As with most decisions made in the graphic communications industry, it is important to look at the specific end use and requirement before deciding if JPEG is the right file choice. While there is a loss of data and quality with JPEG, this might be offset by the speed in shooting and large numbers of images processed.

Consider a sports photographer at a professional basketball game. He or she is looking for the best shot for the publication and may take hundreds of images that need to be processed quickly and on deadline. The end use does not require high-end color and detail, so JPEG might be the best choice. Have all the information for the final output and use of the image to make an educated decision as to what settings, format, and resolution you will need.

RAW

Shooting in RAW format has many advantages. First, it does not eliminate, combine, process, or compress any information. All of the data read by the sensor is stored directly into memory. Any setting or decision made at the time of capture can be undone in the photo editing process since all of the data is there.

RAW shoots as 12- and 14-bits, and goes to 16-bits for the editing software. As you can imagine, the file size is larger and slower to process. But when quality and color is of the essence, RAW gives you everything to work with each and every time.

Digital Camera Components and Features

Though the main components of a camera typically remain the same from model to model, the capabilities and features may differ greatly. Be aware of the different options available on various camera models.

Lens

Some lenses are permanently attached to the camera, while others can be detached and replaced with other lenses. Lenses on digital cameras have two types of zoom options: optical zoom and digital zoom. Optical zoom is a true function, which uses the camera's optics to change the closeness of the photographed object. This is an important feature to evaluate before purchasing a digital camera. Digital zoom is a software feature that does not rely on the abilities of the lens. When using digital zoom, some of the detail in a picture is almost always lost. The lens aperture determines the speed of the lens. The lower the f-stop setting, the faster the lens (f/1.8 or f/2.8). A fast lens can capture low-light images by giving more exposure to the sensor.

Viewfinder and LCD

Optical viewfinders on digital cameras serve the same purpose as those on film cameras, which is to frame the scene and shoot the picture. For photographers who wear glasses, an optical viewfinder equipped with an adapter allows the focus of the viewfinder to be adjusted.

Most digital cameras also have a liquid crystal display (LCD) screen on the back of the camera that displays the exact image being photographed. Look for a sharp LCD screen that shows an excellent image in both bright and dim light. The size of the LCD screen does *not*, however, determine the size of the final image. The LCD screen also allows in-camera review and editing of images, which may be accomplished before downloading the photos to a computer.

Batteries

Batteries vary depending on the type of camera. Point-and-shoot cameras tend to have a shorter battery life than DSLRs because the image sensor, LCD screen, flash unit, and microprocessor are all powered at the same time. DSLR cameras have a more efficient battery and will last considerably longer.

Flash

Lighting conditions may often require additional illumination, **Figure 10-5**. A flash unit on the camera addresses that need. When shooting people or animals, it is recommended that the camera have a red-eye-reduction flash. Many cameras have a built-in flash, while others are equipped with a *hot shoe* (attachment point) for an external flash unit. The hot shoe allows the flash to be secured to the camera and electronically connects it to the camera.

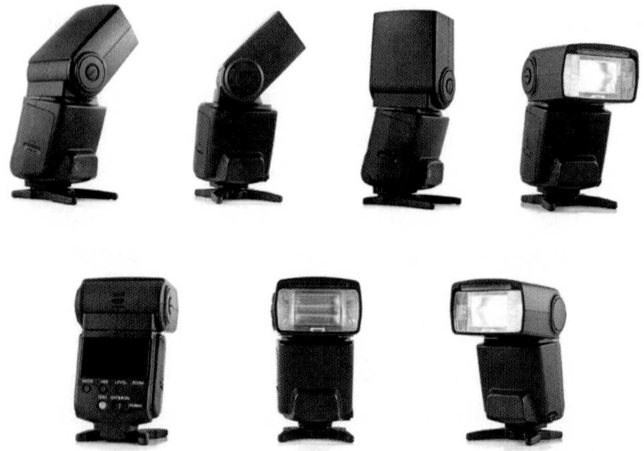

Arsgera/Shutterstock.com

Figure 10-5. To compensate for different lighting conditions, various flash units may be attached to a camera or be added to the shooting environment.

Image Stabilization

Image stabilization is a camera feature that detects and counteracts camera movement. This feature is particularly useful when handheld shots are taken at slower shutter speeds or with long focal-length lenses. Knowledge of this feature is imperative to eliminate blurred images caused by camera shake.

Image stabilization can be built into the camera body or the camera lens. Point-and-shoot cameras do not have removable lenses; they are built into the camera body. Most DSLRs have lens-specific image stabilization built into the lens.

Exposure Modes

Digital cameras are programmed with a fully automatic mode, which allows the operator to point the camera and shoot an image. When reviewing a camera's exposure control, look for aperture and shutter priority modes. The full manual mode allows the operator total control of the camera's settings.

Even though digital point-and-shoot cameras do not completely rival their conventional counterparts, the introduction of affordable, higher-quality point-and-shoot cameras has increased their use by nonprofessionals. Many lower-end cameras now offer advanced features originally found only on professional equipment.

Image Capture Time

The amount of time required to write image-capture files to disc limits the performance of all digital cameras and digital camera backs. Even though image capture by an area array requires only a fraction of a second, the size of the camera's internal buffer determines how many sequential exposures can be made before the camera must pause to write the files to an internal or external storage device.

The buffer is a temporary storage area that enables the manipulation of data before it is transferred for internal or external storage. With a small buffer or with high-resolution files, the camera may need to pause after every exposure. More sophisticated designs may permit up to a dozen sequential exposures before a pause is required to write to disc.

Lighting Considerations

The key to lighting considerations with cameras is ***white balance***. White balance is making the objects that are actually white appear white in your image by considering the color temperature of a particular light source.

There are two questions to ask when considering lighting. Do I have enough light to capture the exposure? Is the quality or color of light correct? The standard color temperature reference for digital cameras is 5500 K, **Figure 10-6**. This reference corresponds to lighting conditions under a clear blue sky with unobstructed sunlight (roughly between 10:00 a.m. and 2:00 p.m.). These qualifications are necessary because daylight, being subject to the movement of sun, clouds, and weather fronts, is extremely variable. For instance, if the sun is obscured by clouds, color temperature rises because the proportion of warm, direct light is decreased.

The direction of daylight and how the light falls on the subject being photographed affects the color temperature. If the light is from the north sky with the sun obscured, the color temperature may rise to 10,000 K or higher. This results in very cool, bluish light. In early morning or late evening, when the sun is low on the horizon, the color temperature may fall to 2500 K to 3500 K.

Before the advent of electronic flash, 3200 K was the standard for tungsten lighting used by studio photographers and cinematographers. During the last few decades, the widespread use of electronic flash has decreased the use of tungsten lighting. However, certain digital camera designs have caused a resurgence in the use of tungsten lighting.

Cameras that use trilinear scanning arrays depend on constant and steady lighting conditions because RGB exposure times often extend from three to ten minutes. Scanning backs record pixel information three rows at a time as they step across the image-capture plane. Slight variations in light intensity can cause banding in certain regions of the image, instead of an even tone.

The most commonly used lighting for commercial studio photography is an electronic flash or tungsten. Daylight is not usually used because of its variability and the additional lighting controls required to maintain consistent color temperature. In addition to freezing motion, an advantage of electronic flash is its consistent color temperature. It simulates the effect of shooting under constant daylight conditions, which lends a consistent visual appearance to ongoing projects, such as shooting for product catalogs.

When a digital camera uses multiple exposures to gather RGB data, it is important for the color temperature to be constant throughout the exposure cycle. Most manufacturers build their electronic flash equipment to deliver a color temperature of

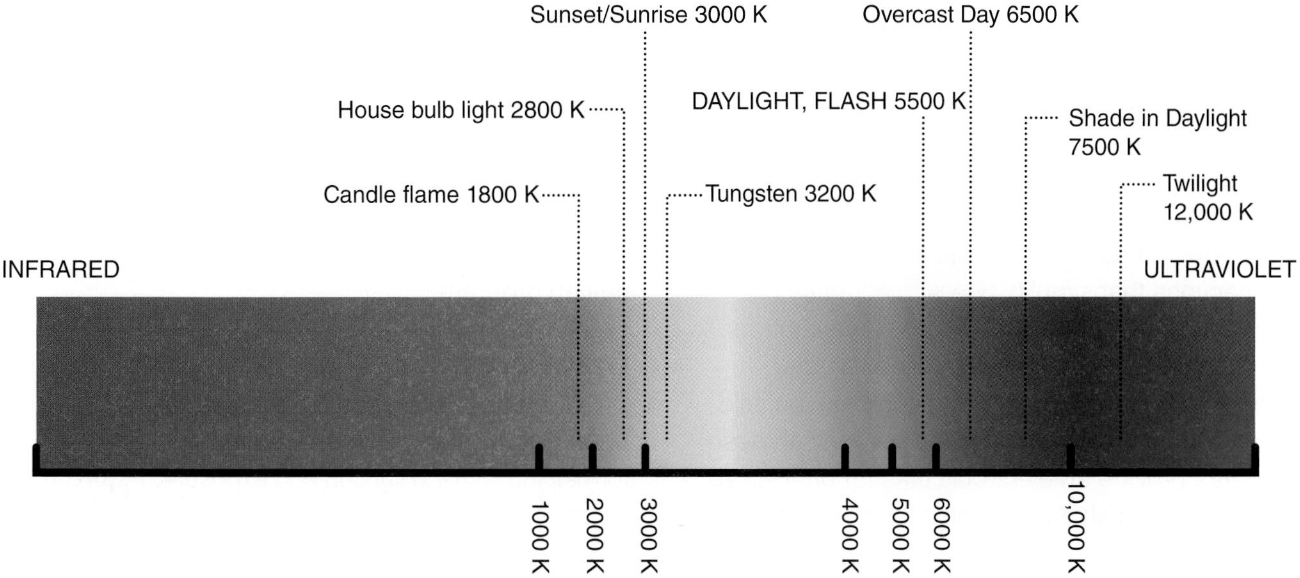

Goodheart-Willcox Publisher

Figure 10-6. Standard Color Temperature Guide.

Career Link

Digital Photographer

Each camera operator has a desired outcome when shooting an image. It may be to record an event, tell a story, or create a picture. This requires the operator to select the proper equipment to accomplish the desired goal. Achieving the proper effect, such as subject enhancement, is essential. Lighting is often a major consideration. Some of the common positions of camera operators are portrait photographers, commercial and industrial photographers, news photographers, and studio camera operators.

The operator must be technically proficient. There is a great emphasis on creativity, imagination, and self-expression. When using a digital camera, the images are saved onto memory cards and then transferred to a computer or the cloud. The operator must be familiar with editing software. While the photographer can manipulate digital images to create the desired outcome, using the proper settings when taking the shot is more efficient and effective.

The operator must have a technical understanding of photography and camera operation. The training for the necessary skills may be acquired at technical schools, colleges, universities, and specialty schools. On-the-job training is a possibility at some firms.

"Advancements in the prepress area have had a profound effect on graphic designers, illustrators, and photographers, all of whom now work on computer screens instead of drawing boards. From the creative stages to the print-ready file, our world is now digital."

Frank Romano
Rochester Institute of Technology

5500 K regardless of flash duration or intensity. If the color temperature shifts during exposure, it affects the gray balance of the resulting image. When this occurs, color correction may be necessary using image-editing software. For this reason, it is not practical to shoot with three- or four-exposure RGB image-capture cameras under variable daylight conditions.

Handheld digital cameras designed for single-exposure use have much more flexibility in terms of their lighting requirements. Moderately expensive field cameras have built-in flash-synchronized connections that simplify use with a variety of electronic flash equipment. Focal plane shutters permit a range of flash-synchronized shutter speeds and make it possible to combine multiple light sources for a single exposure. Many of these cameras provide an electronic bias for often-used light sources such as electronic flash, daylight, tungsten, and fluorescent.

Less expensive point-and-shoot digital cameras include built-in electronic flash capability. This feature enables them to provide greater consistency under variable shooting conditions including daylight, tungsten light, and fluorescent light. Since the flash is designed to be the primary light source, off-color secondary lighting is less detrimental to good grayscale.

When shooting in JPEG format, you must calculate and compensate for white balance. White balance cannot be corrected using in-photo editing software. On the other hand, RAW format does not have white balance issues. Because all of the data is captured, this can easily be adjusted in the photo editing program.

Gray Cards

Used as a reference for middle gray in photography, the ***gray card*** serves as a great tool for helping with the lighting and exposure, **Figure 10-7**. When shooting in RAW, if you take a shot with the gray card in each lighting setting of a shoot, the images can be batch processed by correcting that image in the photo editing software.

Scanners

A ***scanner*** is an electronic device that measures the color densities of an original image, stores those measurements as digital information, manipulates or alters the data, and uses the data to create a digital file, **Figure 10-8**.

A scanner's imaging quality is affected by many variables, including dynamic range, resolution, quality of optics, the light source used, the number of bits per color, and aperture. Differences in any of these variables explain why the sharpness of an image of 4000 ppi resolution can vary from one scanner to another. ***Unsharp masking (USM)*** is the increase of tonal contrast where light and dark tones come together at the edges of an image. USM is accomplished electronically on a color scanner by comparing readings taken through two different-size apertures, and adding the signal difference between the two readings to the signal from the larger aperture. This signal reduces density in the lighter areas of the original and increases density in the darker areas, creating a sharper picture.

Depending on the type of scanner, almost any type or size of original material can be scanned. This includes film negatives or positives (transparencies), photographic prints, printed media, drawings, graphs, and text. Text scanning requires the use of an ***optical character recognition (OCR)*** system. Scanners do not distinguish text from illustrations and represent all images as bitmaps. Therefore, you cannot directly edit text that has been scanned. To edit text read by an optical scanner, you must use an OCR system to translate the image into ASCII characters.

©George Deal

Figure 10-8. Flatbed scanner.

Portable Scanner

Portable scanners are lightweight and small. They can often be powered by battery or USB, and many come with built-in Wi-Fi for easy transfer to your computer or mobile device. Able to scan multiple sizes and kinds of substrates, these portable devices can scan at resolutions up to 1200 ppi.

Flatbed Scanner

Flatbed scanners process images that are placed on a glass bed, or ***scan area***, **Figure 10-9**. The scan area varies in size from machine to machine, and can be as small as 8.5″ × 11″ (216 mm × 280 mm) or larger than 13″ × 18″ (330 mm × 457 mm). Once the image

©George Deal

Figure 10-7. A gray card is a reference tool for neutral middle gray to help set white balance.

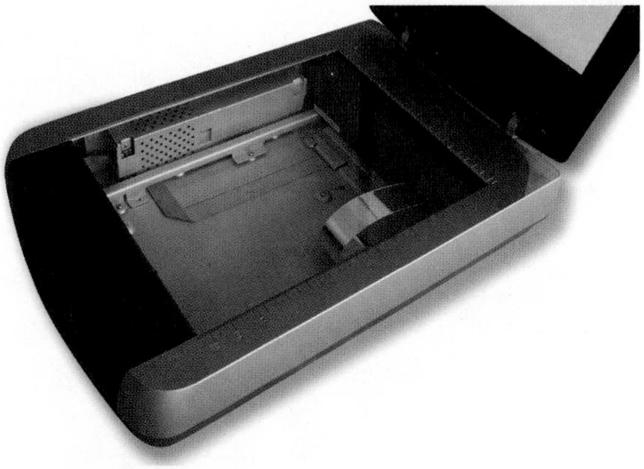

©George Deal

Figure 10-9. This desktop scanner uses a stationary bed, so the scanning head moves across the scan area of a flatbed scanner.

is on the bed, it is illuminated by light as multiple CCD arrays read the information and convert the data into pixels.

With the use of a magnetic image holder, some manufacturers have eliminated the glass between the image and the optics. This helps preserve sharpness, and reduce distortion and ***Newton's rings***, **Figure 10-10**. These rings are undesirable color patterns caused by interference between the exposure light and its reflected beam from the closest adjacent surface. Newton's rings may reproduce as unwanted ***mottling*** of halftones or tint areas.

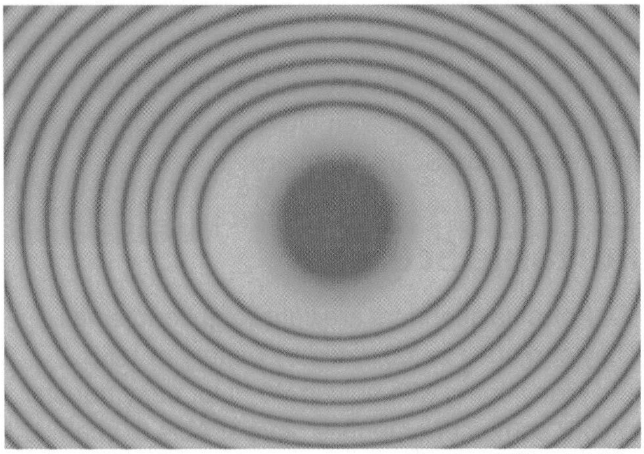

Goodheart-Willcox Publisher

Figure 10-10. An example showing Newton's rings.

The versatility of flatbed scanners determines the kinds of jobs and volume of work they can perform. Flatbed units can scan original materials that vary in thickness; many units can even scan three-dimensional objects. Flatbeds are adaptable to automation features, such as page feeders. Templates can be used to set up work with bar codes that specify size, location, and resolution requirements.

Image Resolution

The resolution of a digital image, measured in ppi, determines the reproduction size possible within a specific screen ruling, **Figure 10-11**. The ***screen ruling*** is the number of ruled lines per inch (lpi) on a halftone screen.

Each captured image, whether by scanning, camera, or software creation, has a resolution.

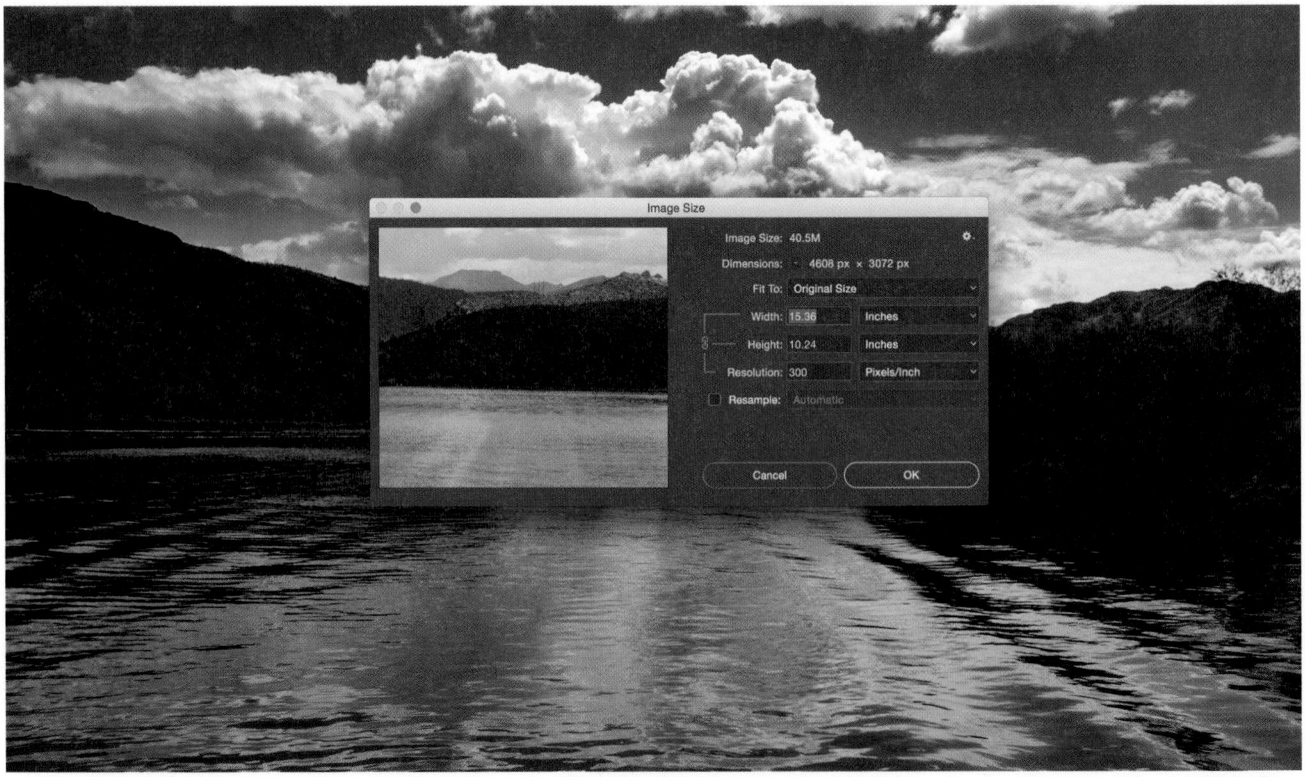

©George Deal

Figure 10-11. This is a screenshot of the image size menu showing resolution.

Ideally, you want to have just enough pixels to reproduce your image at the proper size for your high-end output. Because your image is measured in pixels and the output is actually measured in dots, the conversion relies on the screen ruling, which is the number of ruled lpi used to create the halftone dot, **Figure 10-12**. Many printers use the equation lpi multiplied by 2 (two pixels for every halftone dot) is equal to resolution at 100%. The lpi is determined by the printer based on paper and press quality. Since for years the standard lpi for high-end output was 150, 300 ppi became an industry favorite. Better technology has allowed the line screen to increase for many presses. It is critical to ask your service providers what their specifications are before you capture the image.

When you scale an image in your page layout software, the resolution is altered. Therefore, it is important to know what the "real" resolution of the image in the document is. Page layout software has a menu that displays ***effective ppi***, which is what the resolution of that image is at the scale used in the document. See **Figure 10-13**. In the end, this is the only resolution that matters.

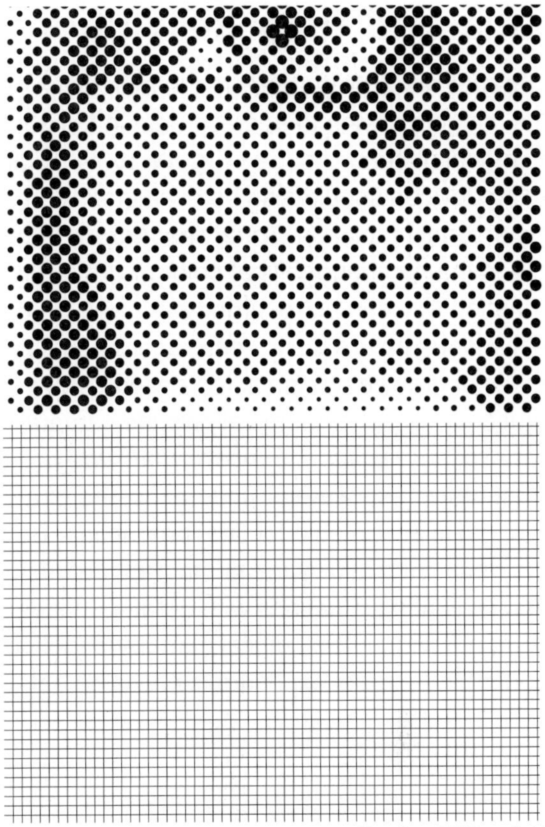

Goodheart-Willcox Publisher

Figure 10-12. Halftone dots.

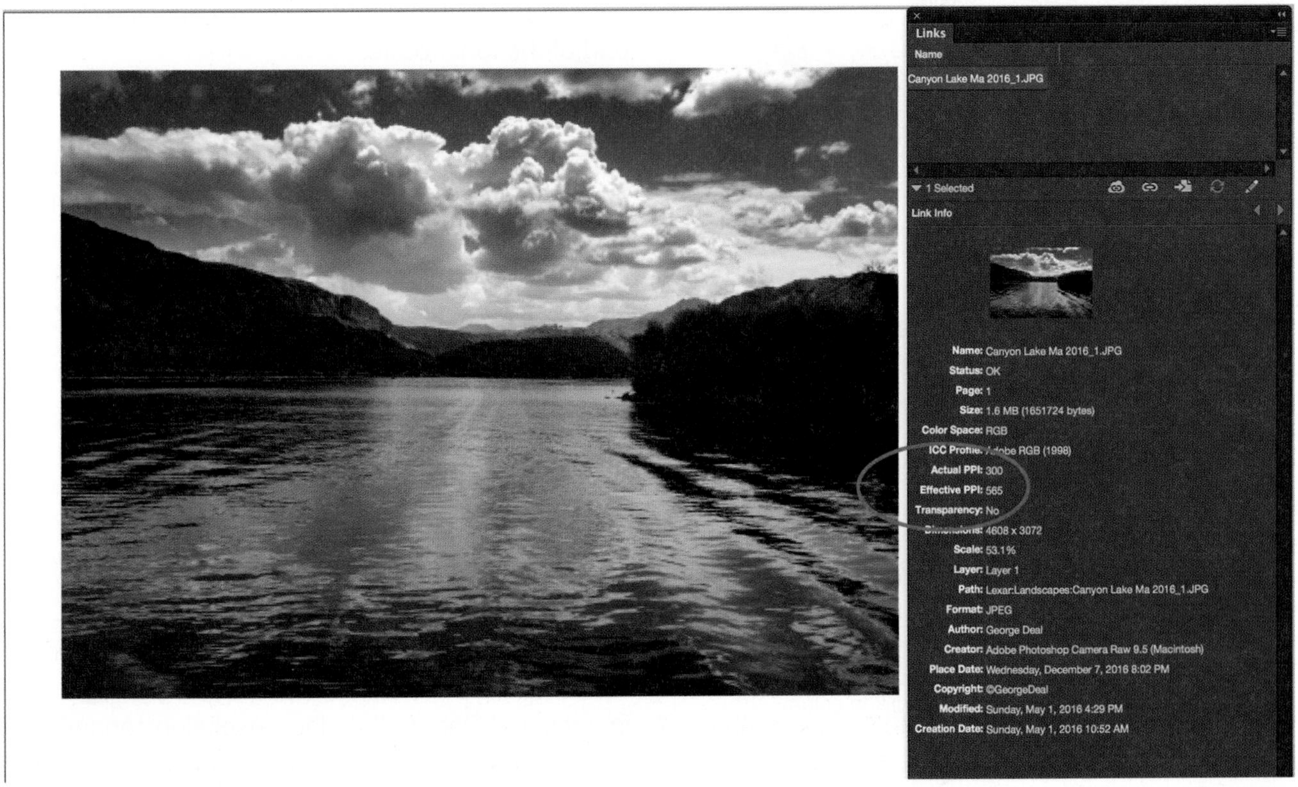

©George Deal

Figure 10-13. The effective ppi of an image is the resolution of the image at the size it is being printed.

Spatial and Tonal Resolution

Spatial resolution refers to the ability of a digital imaging device to address data in horizontal and vertical dimensions. See **Figure 10-14**. Digital imaging devices should also be evaluated in terms of tonal resolution. ***Tonal resolution***, or bit depth, is the number of bits of color or grayscale information that can be recorded per pixel. An 8-bit digital image capture device can record 256 colors or levels of gray per channel. Increased tonal resolution in digital cameras allows the camera better exposure latitude. ***Exposure latitude*** is the amount of overexposure or underexposure of an image that is acceptable for final production. Better exposure latitude allows the photographer to shoot in difficult lighting situations with greater confidence.

When using an 8-bit digital camera, shooting a subject at the correct exposure is critical to obtain good highlight and shadow rendition. In many lighting situations, an 8-bit tonal scale is just long enough to provide good highlight and shadow detail, but only if the midtone is placed exactly in the correct position.

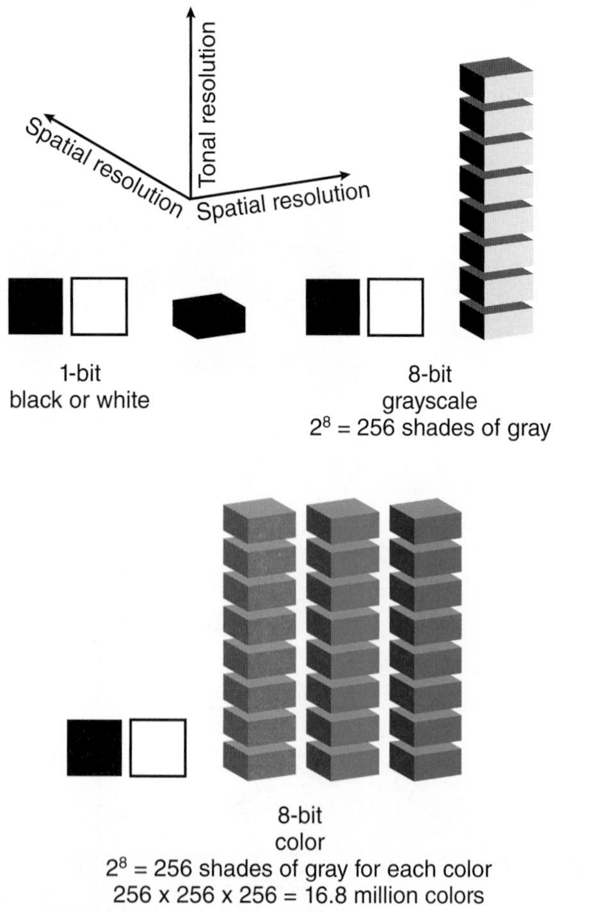

Goodheart-Willcox Publisher

Figure 10-14. Spatial resolution refers to the ability of a digital imaging device to address data in two dimensions—horizontal and vertical.

The exposure latitude is similar to what photographers experience when shooting fine grain transparency films. If it is not within 1/3 f-stop of the correct midtone position, the image will be either underexposed or overexposed. Overexposure results in the loss of highlight detail; underexposure results in the loss of shadow detail.

When using digital cameras with 12 bits or more of tonal resolution per channel, the increase in exposure latitude means the photographer has a greater margin for error. Midtone placement may be off by as much as one full f-stop in some cases. The longer tonal range resulting from increased bit depth permits the camera to render good highlight and shadow detail, despite difficult lighting situations or exposure miscalculation.

To properly evaluate image capture files, it is necessary to open them in an image-editing software program that provides a ***histogram*** display of the pixel information, **Figure 10-15**. In graphic form, the histogram appears as a horizontal display of highlight, midtone, and shadow values that correspond to the number of pixels affected in each part of the tonal scale.

A good exposure is characterized by smooth tapering of the highlight and shadow values at opposite ends of the scale. If the display of pixel values appears cut off at either end, the highlight or shadow information has been lost due to incorrect exposure. To ensure correct highlight, midtone, and shadow detail, it is best to make a new image capture of the subject using the predetermined exposure adjustment.

Image File Storage and Transfer

Ongoing advances in digital technology have made it possible to deal with increasingly larger images and files. With higher resolution capabilities, the captured image files continue to steadily grow in size. Storage devices, such as flash drives, portable hard drives, and internal/external hard drives, are used to store the larger image files. See **Figure 10-16**. Because digital cameras are often used to capture images "on the fly," they require unique transfer speed and storage capabilities. Many online servers offer cloud storage, or online storage, as well as file sharing and transfer options.

Data Transfer

Most serial and parallel ports have been replaced by the Universal Serial Bus (USB). The USB is designed to allow various peripherals to be connected to a standardized socket. The three most common types of USB plugs are Type A, Type B, and Type Mini-B. Type A plugs are found on various types of storage devices and peripherals, such as keyboards and computer mice. Type B plugs are commonly found on printer cables. Type Mini-B plugs can be found on devices such as digital cameras. The speed of USB cables depends on their specifications. For example, a USB 1.1 cable transfers data at a rate of 1.5 megabits per second, while a USB 2.0 transfers data at a rate of 480 megabits per second.

©George Deal

Figure 10-16. Common types of storage for file transfer.

The FireWire device was designed as a high-speed serial bus to connect hard disks and audio and video equipment. FireWire accommodates the higher performance required by audio and video applications, which cannot be handled by USB.

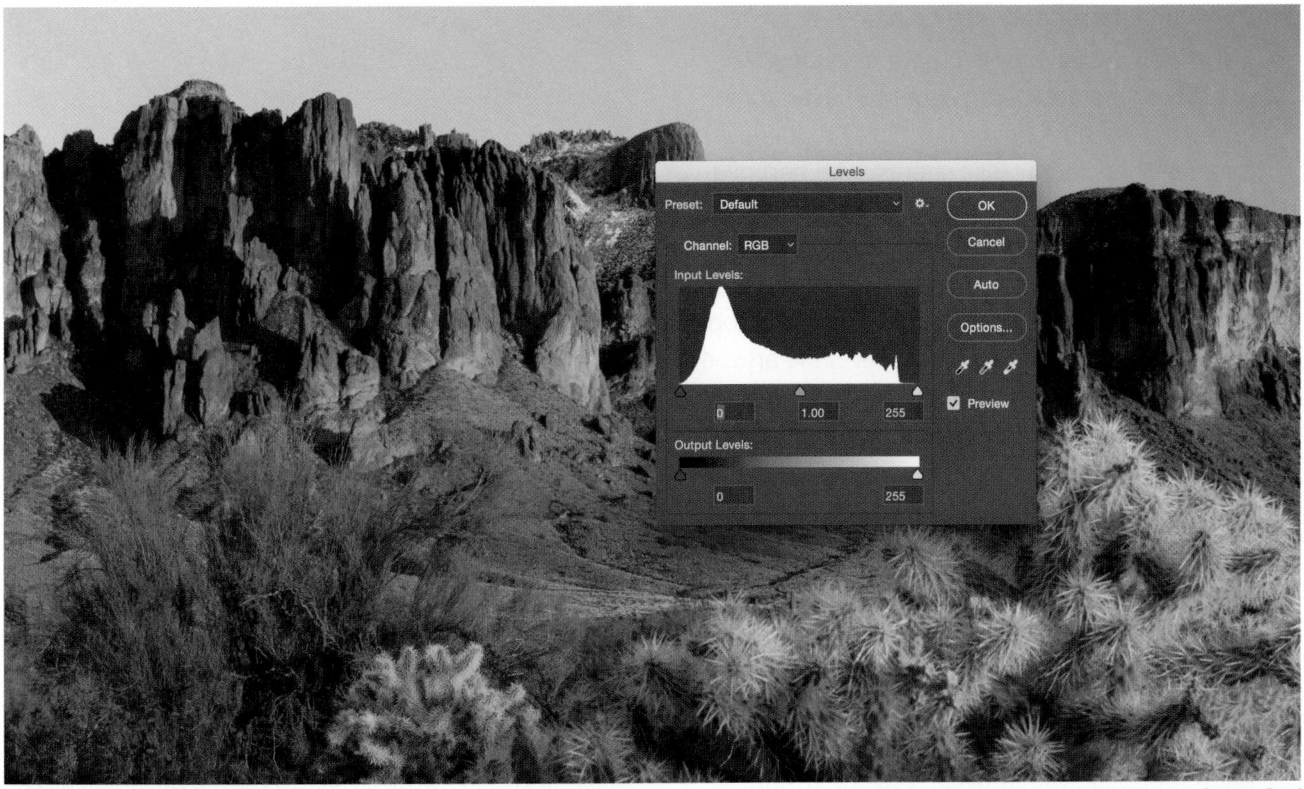

©George Deal

Figure 10-15. A histogram provides a graphic display of how the pixel values in an image are distributed.

Image Manipulation

Once an electronic image has been captured and transferred, editing can be done through an image manipulation program. Some of the most commonly used manipulation programs are Adobe Photoshop™, Adobe Lightroom, and Adobe Bridge. The type of program that can be used depends on the computer platform and image format.

For color correction, the best software to use are nondestructive applications. Adobe Bridge and Lightroom both work in a nondestructive environment. This means that while working in Camera Raw, you can make your alterations and color edits without affecting the original data in the image.

With full-featured image editors, the user can manipulate any aspect of the image. This includes cropping, adjusting color and contrast, adding or removing visual information, and even combining images. Background clutter can be eliminated, and unwanted elements in the picture can be erased. See **Figure 10-17**. Most image editing programs offer similar tools and applications, and allow changes to be made in a single area, multiple areas, or the entire image. Most programs also allow work to be done in layers, the application of filters and masks, paint effects, and retouching.

- ***Layers*** allow the user to create multiple levels of artwork that reside on separate, overlapping layers in the same document. Think of the layers as a stack of clear plastic sheets, with part of an illustration on each sheet. On the portions of the sheets with no illustration, the layer is transparent and you can see through to the layer below. By creating and working in layers, it is easier to modify objects without affecting all aspects of the artwork, **Figure 10-18**. Separate layers take up additional storage space, so they should be merged or flattened when editing is complete.
- ***Filters*** are used to apply special effects to bitmap images, including textures and patterns, **Figure 10-19**. For example, a color halftone filter simulates the effect of using an enlarged halftone screen on each channel, or color separation, of the bitmap image. For each channel, the halftone filter divides the image into rectangles and replaces each rectangle with a circle, **Figure 10-20**. Applying filters to large bitmap images can be time-consuming. To save time, some filters allow you to preview the effect that they create.
- The ***paint effects*** feature in most image manipulation programs performs the same functions as a paint or draw program. Various tools allow the user to fill in and erase colors, create and add color, and assign and adjust color values and gradations.
- ***Retouching tools*** allow the user to "dodge" areas that are too dark and lack detail, while burn tools increase exposure to areas that are too light. Retouching tools also include features for adjusting color, contrast, hue, and saturation, **Figure 10-21**.

©George Deal

Figure 10-17. Image manipulation can be used to alter an image. In the bottom image, the man in the canoe has been removed.

Goodheart-Willcox Publisher

Figure 10-18. Using layers allows the compositing of several images.

Goodheart-Willcox Publisher

Figure 10-19. When applying filters, you can preview the effect and make a variety of adjustments, including the direction of light.

Goodheart-Willcox Publisher

Figure 10-20. Halftone pattern is a filter option.

Goodheart-Willcox Publisher

Figure 10-21. The dodge and burn tools are for retouching an image that is too dark or too light.

- ***Masks*** are used to isolate an area to protect it from the effects and changes applied to the rest of the image. When a part of an image is selected, the remaining area (not selected) is masked and protected from editing. Semitransparent masks allow an area of an image to be partially affected by changes. Masks can consist of a single path or a compound path, **Figure 10-22**.

Image manipulation software has become very sophisticated, and you can achieve some unique and creative results. Combining images, correcting in proper perspective, and adjusting for wide angle lens distortion are just a few of the complex alterations you can make.

Future Trends

Digital imaging devices have become a driving force in redefining the traditional boundaries that separate the disciplines of photography and printing. Personal computer technology and desktop publishing innovations have transformed prepress processes. Today, original artwork is likely to be a digital file produced in an imaging software application, or captured with a scanner or digital camera.

With advances in digital imaging technology, the role of the photographer as a member of the creative team is evolving. Color separators long ago realized that the full tonal range of a photographic transparency could not be transferred to ink on paper. The transparency color gamut, using high-quality dye pigments, far exceeded what could be reproduced with a CMYK ink set on a lithographic press. Photographers were not necessarily concerned with these production complications until digital photography provided the ability to control how an RGB-to-CMYK conversion affects the appearance of their images.

Just a few years ago, the photographer's job was finished when the art director signed off on the transparency film. The transformation from film to digital image file was in the hands of the color separator. Today, using the digital camera, the photographer is compelled to take on new responsibilities.

Goodheart-Willcox Publisher

Figure 10-22. The mask applied in the image allows the user to modify the display without affecting the rest of the image.

Summary

- An analog image is recorded into a digital format by assigning each pixel a set of numbers that designate position, brightness, and color.
- CCD sensors and CMOS sensors gather and record images electronically.
- DSLR cameras are used more by professionals, while amateurs prefer point-and-shoot cameras.
- Digital camera components include lenses, viewfinders, LCDs, batteries, flash, and image stabilization.
- Photographers and artists must know the differences between JPEG and RAW file formats.
- White balance is making the objects that are actually white appear white in your image by considering the color temperature of a particular light source.
- Handheld scanners are moved across paper by hand, while flatbed scanners process images placed on a glass bed.
- Types of resolution include image, spatial, and tonal.
- Spatial resolution is the imaging device's ability to address data in horizontal and vertical dimensions. Tonal resolution is the number of bits of color or grayscale information that can be recorded per pixel.
- Most programs allow work to be done in layers, the application of filters and masks, paint effects, and retouching.

Review Questions

Answer the following questions using the information in this chapter.

1. The colors and lines of an image in _____ format are continuous. The colors and lines of an image in _____ format consist of values measured at distinct points.
2. Explain how *CCD sensors* operate.
3. What are the three types of digital cameras?
4. Printing quality is determined by the number of _____.
5. What are the advantages and disadvantages to shooting in JPEG?
6. What are the advantages and disadvantages to shooting in RAW format?
7. Name the most commonly used types of lighting for commercial studio lighting.
8. What is *unsharp masking*?
9. When scanning text, you must use a(n) _____ system to translate the bitmapped image into ASCII characters.
10. What is *spatial resolution*?

11. Explain the use of a *histogram*.
12. List some typical storage devices used for images captured by common point-and-shoot cameras.
13. What purpose do *layers* serve in an image manipulation program?
14. _____ are used to apply special effects, such as patterns and textures, to bitmap images.
15. Which image manipulation tool would be used to protect an area of an image from changes and effects applied to the rest of the image?

Suggested Activities

1. Select two different digital cameras and make a comparison chart of the features and capabilities of each. Identify a typical user for each camera.
2. Visit a camera or electronics store and ask for a recommendation for the best storage card for a camera you own. Ask why one specific storage card is better than others available.
3. Take a picture of an image using three cameras with different megapixel ratings. Reproduce each image to 12″ × 18″. Make note of and describe any visible difference in resolution.

Chapter 11

Color

Learning Objectives

After studying this chapter, you will be able to:

- Explain the basic principles of visible light.
- Recall various color space and organization methods.
- Draw a standard color wheel using the primary colors of light.
- Summarize the characteristics of both additive color formation and subtractive color formation.
- Explain the basic principles of color separation.
- Recall various color measurement instruments and explain the use of each.
- Identify the parts of the human eye and recall the function of each.

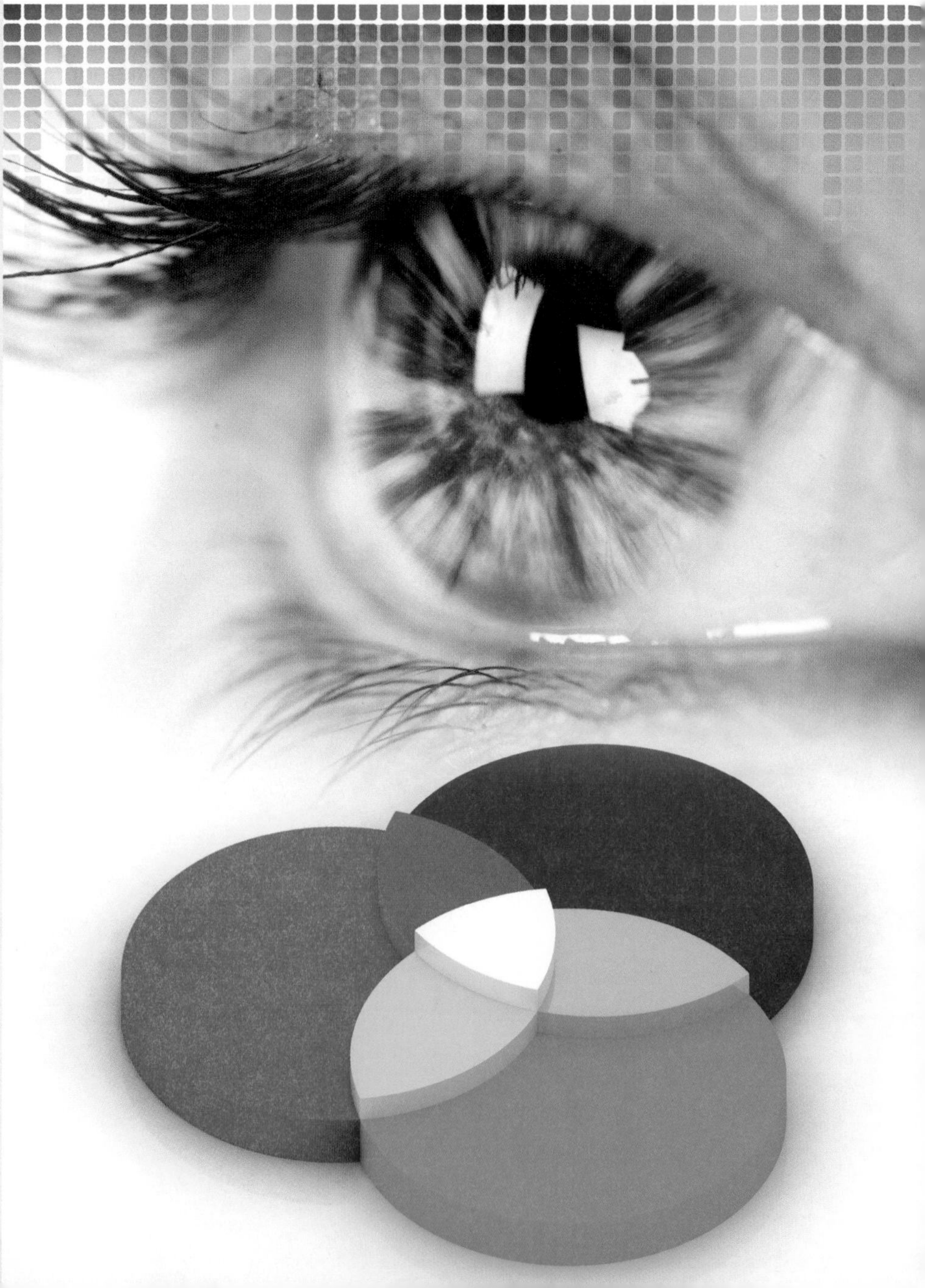

Goodheart-Willcox Publisher

Important Terms

achromatic vision
adaptation
additive color formation
adjacency
afterimage
brightness
chroma
chromatic adaptation
chromatic induction
chromaticity
chromaticity coordinates
colorants
color constancy
color gamut
colorimeter
color separation
color space
combination densitometer
complementary colors
cone
constructive interference
continuous spectrum
cornea
densitometer
destructive interference
dichromatic vision
diffraction grating
dye
electromagnetic spectrum
fovea
hue
incident beam
iris
macula
monochromatic colorimeter
near-complementary color
opacity
photopigments
pigment
primary colors
process color printing
reflected beam
reflection densitometer
retina
rod
saturation
shade
spectrodensitometer
spectrophotometer
spectrum locus
subtractive color formation
successive contrast
tint
transmission densitometer
trichromatic colorimeter
tristimulus values (X, Y, Z)
value
viewing booth

G-WLEARNING.COM

While studying this chapter, look for the activity icon to:

- **Practice** vocabulary terms with e-flash cards, matching activities, and vocabulary game.
- **Reinforce** what you learn by submitting end-of-chapter questions.

www.g-wlearning.com/visualtechnology/

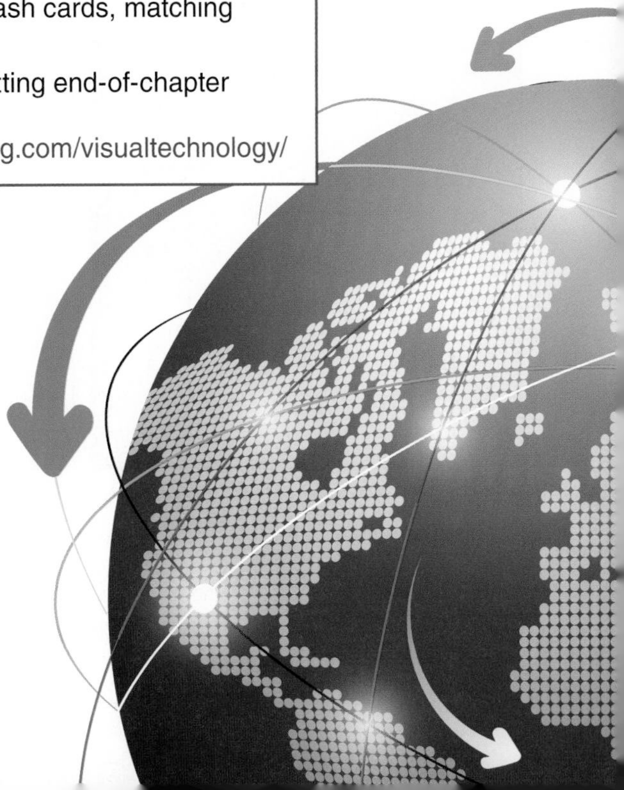

Color plays many important roles in our daily lives. Aside from the aesthetic benefits to our surroundings, the use of color on any medium can greatly enhance communication. Color can be used to grab attention, set a mood, or clarify images.

Colors should maintain consistency throughout the production process. This is especially true when so many products are recognized simply by the colors on their labels or logos. To accomplish this type of consistency, everyone from the graphic designer to the press operator should have a basic understanding of color.

Color Science

Without light, there is no color. Therefore, you must understand a few principles of light before understanding color science.

Principles of Light

The ***electromagnetic spectrum*** consists of bands of different wavelengths, ranging from radio waves to gamma rays, **Figure 11-1**. The wavelengths are usually measured in nanometers (nm). A nanometer is equal to one billionth of a meter. Another unit used to measure the wavelength of light is the Angstrom (Å). Ten Angstroms are equal to 1 nm.

Our eyes can detect only a very small part of the electromagnetic spectrum known as visible light, which includes wavelengths ranging from 400 nm–770 nm. Each wavelength is seen as a different color. Red light has the longest visible wavelength (630 nm–770 nm) and violet has the shortest (410 nm–440 nm).

Most light sources, including the sun, emit light that appears to be white. However, that light is

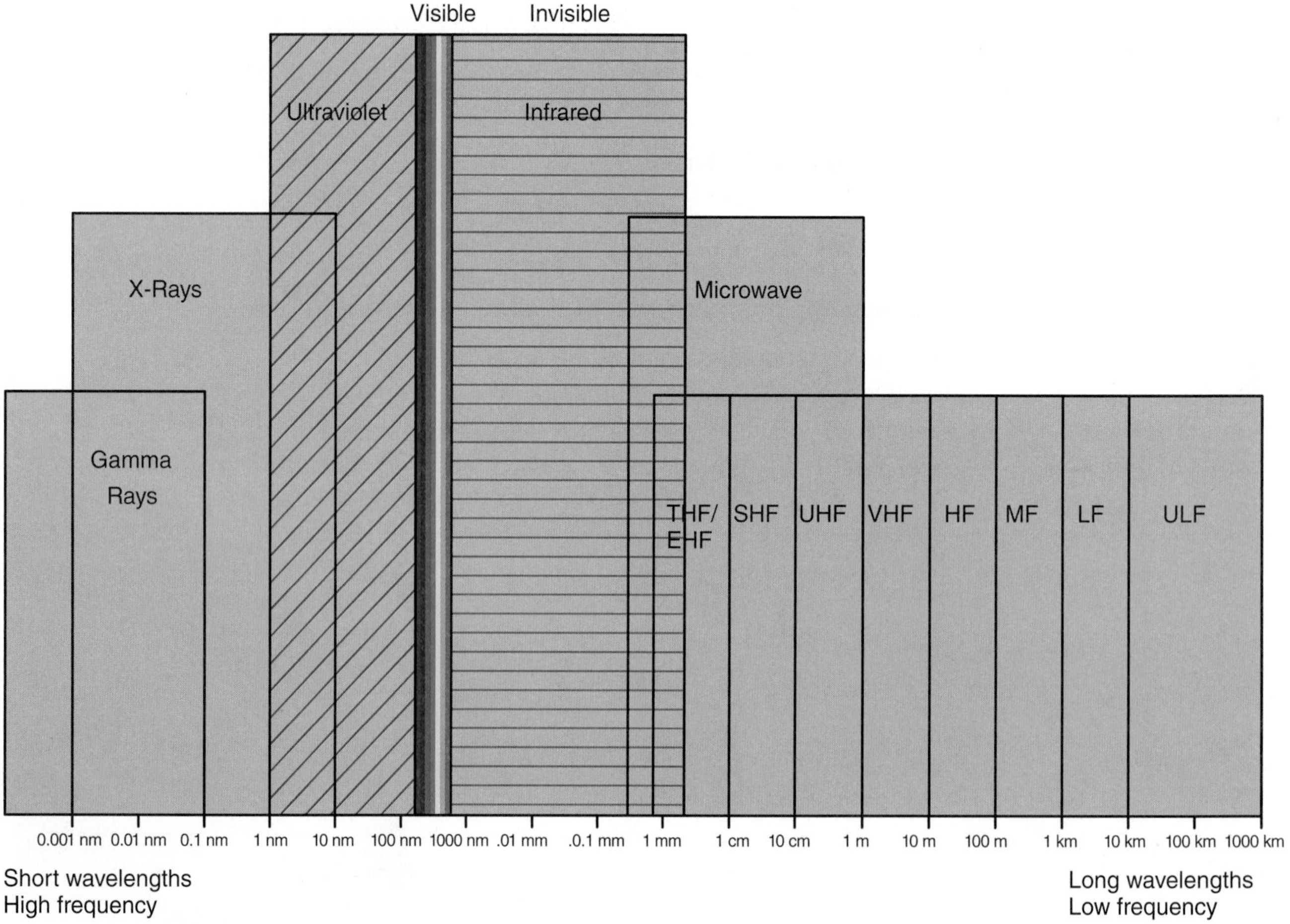

Goodheart-Willcox Publisher

Figure 11-1. This illustration of the electromagnetic spectrum shows how small the range of visible light actually is. Each color has its own wavelength or frequency.

actually a combination of roughly equal parts of all the visible wavelengths. Using a prism, **Figure 11-2**, white light can be broken down into six major colors: red, orange, yellow, green, blue, and violet. When sunlight is passed through a prism, a ***continuous spectrum*** is created that blends smoothly from one color to the next. Many other sources of light do not produce a continuous spectrum. A sodium-vapor streetlight, for example, may produce bright yellow and blue, and also has dark regions in its spectrum. This difference in light sources greatly influences individual perception of colors.

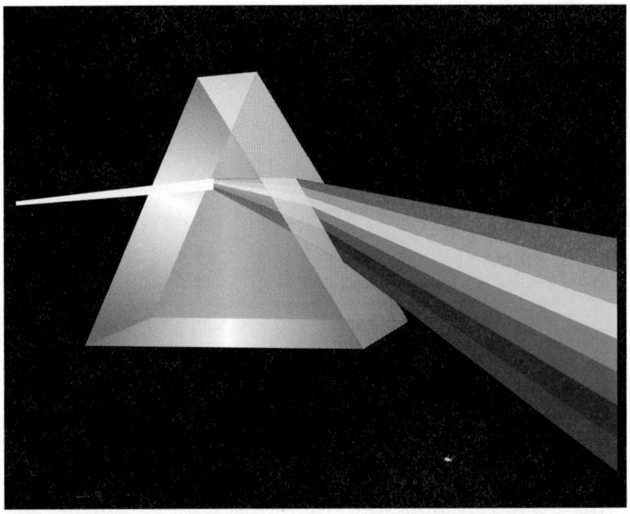

Goodheart-Willcox Publisher

Figure 11-2. A prism disperses the light that passes through it, so our eyes can perceive individual wavelengths. The shorter waves are more dispersed than the longer waves. Because of this, the violet wavelength is always positioned at the bottom and the red wavelength is always at the top.

Temperature of Light

The color of light is measured in degrees Kelvin (K). In terms of color temperature, blues and violets are the warmest colors; reds and oranges are the coolest, **Figure 11-3**. This range of colors can be demonstrated by heating a piece of metal called a *black body*. As the black body is heated, it emits light in a range of colors. Beginning with dull red, it moves through orange, yellow, and white. If no chemical or physical change occurs, the metal eventually emits blue light. The color of light emitted from the black body can be described by its temperature.

COLOR TEMPERATURE	
Blue skylight	10,000 K–18,000 K
Overcast sky	6250 K
Electronic photo flash	6000 K
Evening light	5000–6000 K
Morning light	5000–6000 K
Midday sunlight (direct)	4500 K–5500 K
Studio lights	3200 K–3400 K
Household bulb	2500 K–3000 K
Candlelight	1800 K–2000 K

Goodheart-Willcox Publisher

Figure 11-3. Approximate color temperatures of some common light sources.

Behavior of Light

When light travels through a continuous medium, it travels in a straight line. However, when light reaches a surface or boundary between two types of material, such as air or water, several things can happen. Some of the light may reflect from the surface, while some may pass through it. The light that passes through the second material may refract, or bend. In addition, some of the light may be scattered or absorbed.

Reflection

A beam of light coming toward a surface is called the ***incident beam***. After the beam is reflected, it is called the ***reflected beam***, **Figure 11-4**. Depending on the type of material causing light to reflect, the reflected beam may contain a different mixture of light waves than the incident beam. If the mixture is different, the new combination of wavelengths gives the material its color. For instance, a red book exposed to white light appears red because the surface absorbs all other wavelengths of color in the

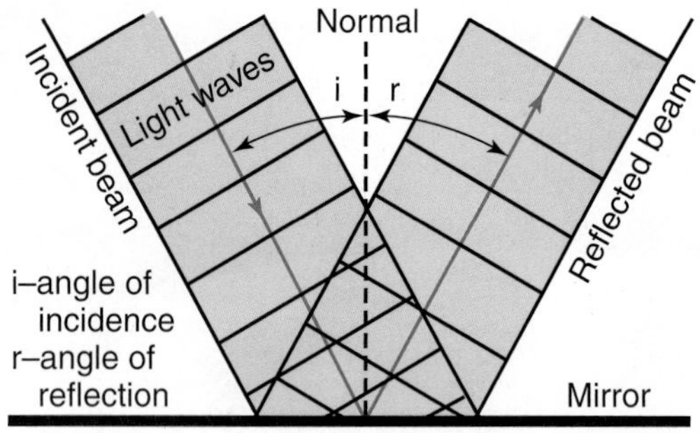

Goodheart-Willcox Publisher

Figure 11-4. The angle of an incident beam (right angles to a surface), is equal to the angle of the reflected beam.

light. Only red wavelengths of the light spectrum are reflected off the red cover.

Refraction

When light passes through a surface at any angle other than a right angle, the speed of the light changes and its direction is altered, **Figure 11-5**. In other words, the light refracts. The type of material affects how much the light bends. Refraction can be demonstrated by placing a pencil in a glass of water. The pencil appears to be bent at the surface of the water. Light from the top of the pencil comes directly to your eyes, while the light from the bottom passes through the glass and water.

Scattering

Scattering occurs when light waves strike the molecules of another substance. The molecules cause the waves to scatter. A clear sky appears blue because air molecules scatter a greater amount of shorter wavelengths (blue) than longer wavelengths in white sunlight.

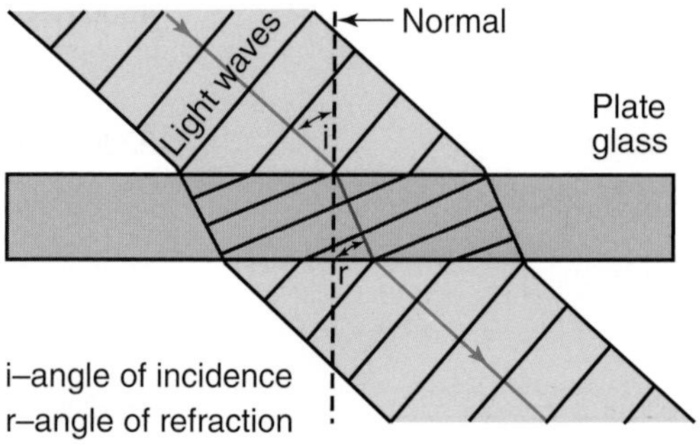

Goodheart-Willcox Publisher

Figure 11-5. Refraction causes a beam of light to bend and slow down as it passes through a substance. The angle of refraction is less than the angle of incidence.

Interference

When two light waves cross through the same spot, they interfere with each other. The interference between light waves occurs as constructive interference or as destructive interference. To illustrate interference, think of light as a wave with crests and troughs. ***Constructive interference*** occurs when the crests of multiple light waves pass through the same point at the same time. At this point, the light is brighter than any one wave can emit alone. ***Destructive interference*** occurs when the crest of one wave crosses the same point as the trough of another wave. The trough reduces the height of the crest, which leaves the spot very dim or even dark.

Diffraction

Light waves usually travel in straight lines. However, light waves diffract, or spread out, into curving waves when passing through an opening or slit, around a small object, or beyond an edge, such as the outline of a person or a building.

The diffraction of light is useful when studying colors in a light beam. For instance, scientists are able to separate the colors of light from a star using a ***diffraction grating***. The grating uses thousands of thin slits to diffract light. Each color in the light diffracts by a slightly different amount, and the spread of colors can be large enough to make each color visible. Astronomers use this color information to determine the makeup of the star.

Diffraction can also be a hindrance. As the magnifying power of a high-quality microscope is increased, for example, the edges of the object being viewed begin to blur. The edges blur because the light diffracts when passing over the edge on its way to the eye.

Color Space

Both science and the graphic communications industry require precise color definition and classification. Words are imprecise in distinguishing and describing color. What one person identifies as yellow-green might be described by another as light green or "greenish." For this reason, various systems have been devised to establish universal terms for color classification.

The various color systems and color models describe colors through numerical or coordinate means. The numerical values or coordinates allow the colors to be defined within the system's parameters. These parameters define the system's ***color space***. The term *space* is used because color data occur in three dimensions. The color space defines the limits by which the color model can be used. The full range of colors that can be defined by a color model is called a ***color gamut***. To better define color space, many color models are triaxial. A triaxial system involves three axes (vertical, side-to-side, front-to-back). This section addresses the various color spaces in common use today.

Color organization begins with two small groups: pure chromatic colors and achromatic colors (white, grays, and black). All other colors exist within these two extremes.

The Color Wheels

A color wheel consists of a range of colors in the form of a circle and is useful for demonstrating the relationships among colors. The colors can be described as primary, secondary, or tertiary.

Painted Color Wheel

Coming after many years of discussion, revision, and scientific study dating back to Sir Isaac Newton in 1672, the color wheel has long been based on the color spectrum composed of the seven colors of the rainbow: red, orange, yellow, green, blue, indigo, and violet (ROYGBIV). For centuries, artists have utilized this color wheel as defined by the use of pigments with the main colors, or ***primary colors***, of red, yellow, and blue. Secondary colors are orange, green, and violet. Other colors on the wheel, known as tertiary, or intermediate, colors are yellow-green, blue-green, blue-violet, red-violet, red-orange, and yellow-orange. See **Figure 11-6**.

Primary colors are defined as colors, that when combined, create all other colors; and a color, in its purest form, that cannot be created by any combination of colors. Secondary colors are created by mixing equal amounts of two primary colors. For example, orange is made by mixing yellow and red pigments. Green is made by mixing yellow and blue. Violet is made by mixing blue and red. The secondary colors are positioned between the primaries on the color wheel.

Tertiary colors are made by mixing a primary color with a secondary color. These colors are named after the two colors used to make them, with the primary color listed first. For example, yellow-orange is created by mixing the primary color yellow with the secondary color orange. Although not the true color wheel, this works for fine artists and for mixing pigments.

True Color Wheel

Color as we see it is based on science and the way our eyes function. The red, green, and blue cones in our eyes allow us to see in color. This additive color system of light is based on the true primary colors: red, green, and blue. See **Figure 11-7**. As creatives work almost exclusively within the digital environment using computers and digital cameras, it is critical to embrace the additive color wheel.

Color Triads

Any three colors that are an equal distance apart on the color wheel compose a color triad. The colors in a triad often go well together, so color triads are important design tools. The primary, secondary, and tertiary colors on the color wheel all form triads, **Figure 11-8**. Placing almost any

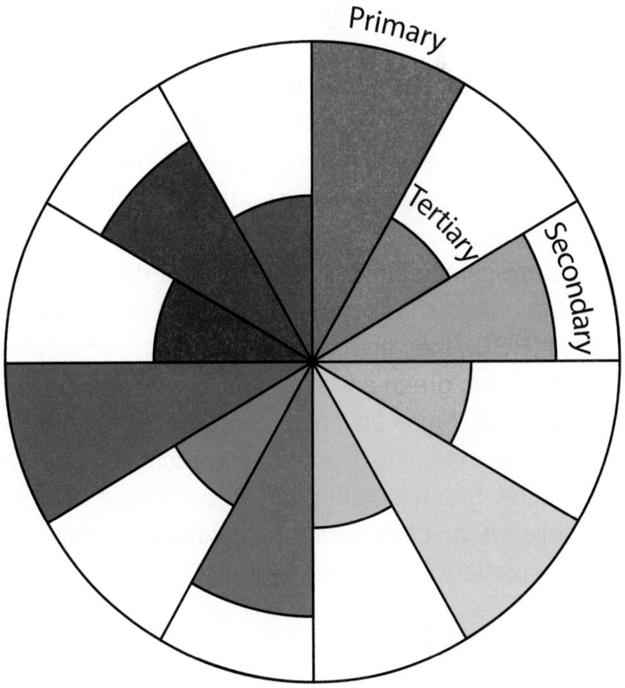

Goodheart-Willcox Publisher

Figure 11-6. This color wheel presents the primary, secondary, and tertiary colors of the color wheel as determined by the use of pigments.

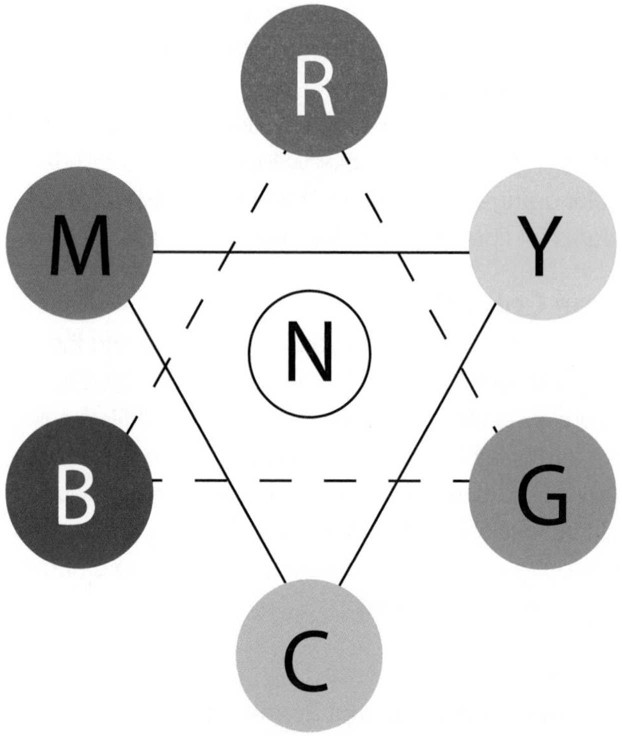

Goodheart-Willcox Publisher

Figure 11-7. The true color wheel or additive color wheel as determined by the use of light. This is the color wheel that should be utilized in the graphic communications industry.

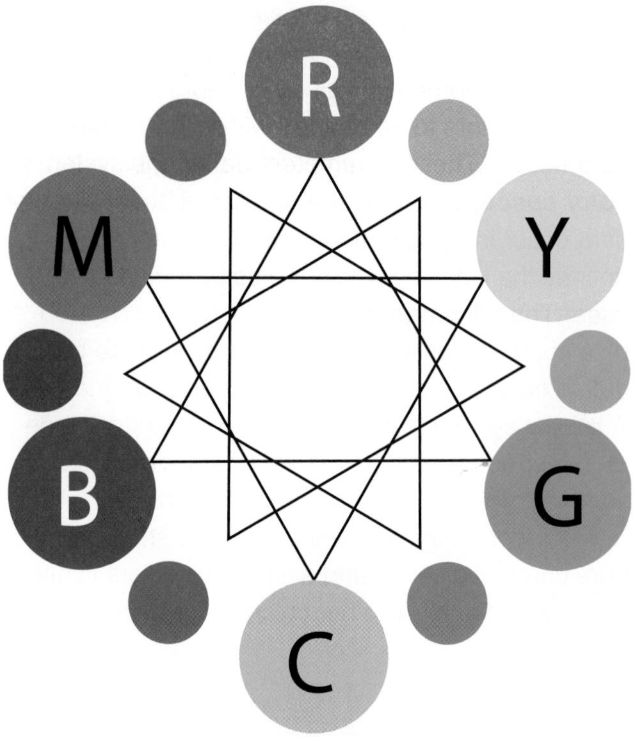

Goodheart-Willcox Publisher

Figure 11-8. Triangles drawn in the center of the color wheel identify different triads.

geometric shape on the color wheel will give you pleasing color combinations. See **Figure 11-9**.

Complementary Colors

In color theory, two colors mixed in exact proportion to produce a neutral color (white, gray, or black) are ***complementary colors***. On the HSV (hue, saturation, and value) color wheel, opposite colors are complementary. When properly mixed, they become a shade of gray. In the additive color model (RGB), they are paired in the following way: red and cyan, green and magenta, and blue and yellow. A color may also harmonize with colors that lie on either side of its complement, such as magenta with yellow-green or with green-cyan. These colors are called ***near-complementary colors***, or split-complementary colors. See **Figure 11-10**.

Shades and Tints

Monochromatic color schemes are comprised of the shades and tints of a single color.

- ***Shades*** are created by lowering the saturation of the color selected, **Figure 11-11**.

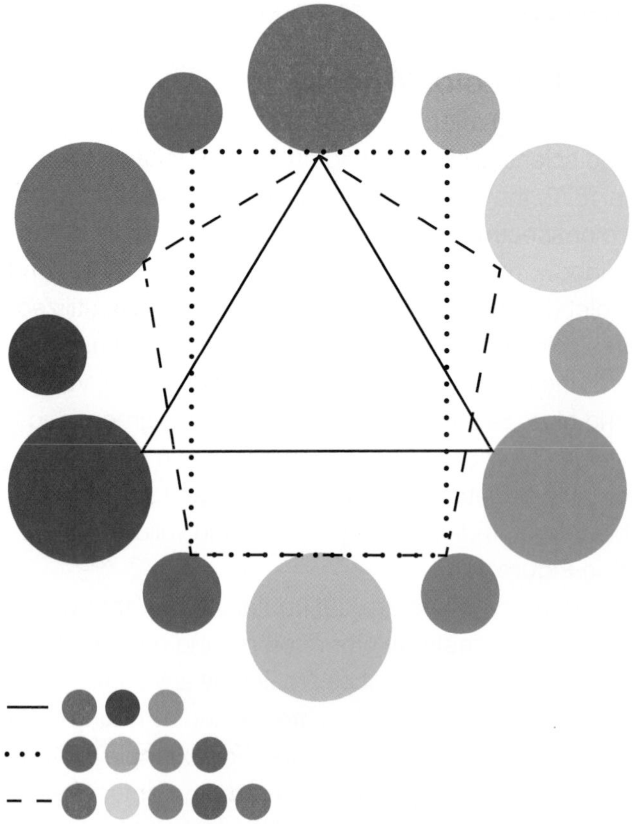

Goodheart-Willcox Publisher

Figure 11-9. Geometric shapes drawn on the color wheel to show color palette selection options.

- ***Tints*** are created by increasing the saturation of the complementary color, **Figure 11-12**.

Computer software allows for the alteration of a color's ***opacity***. This creates the illusion of a tint when placed on a white background because the white shows through the color as you adjust the transparency. It is important to note this is *not* the correct way to create a tint, **Figure 11-13**.

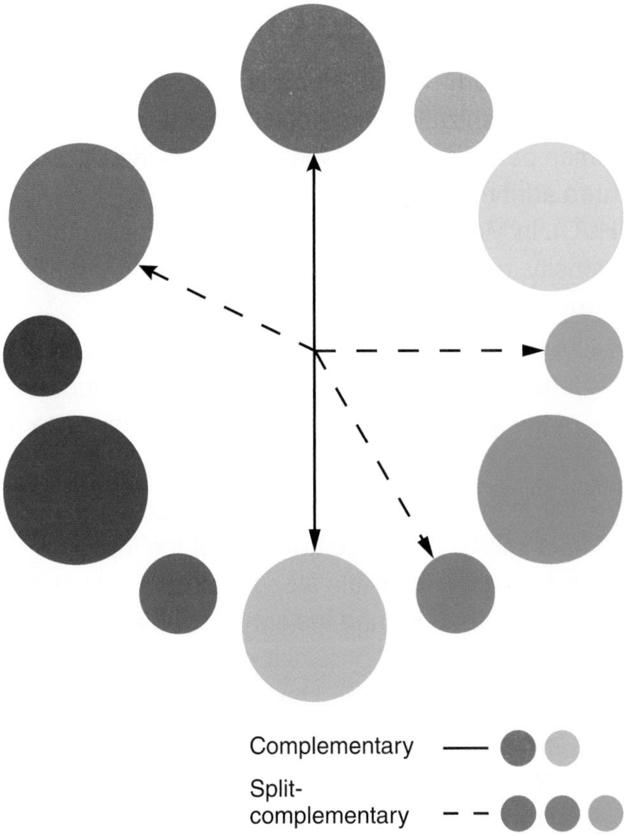

Goodheart-Willcox Publisher

Figure 11-10. Color wheel with complementary and split-complementary color options.

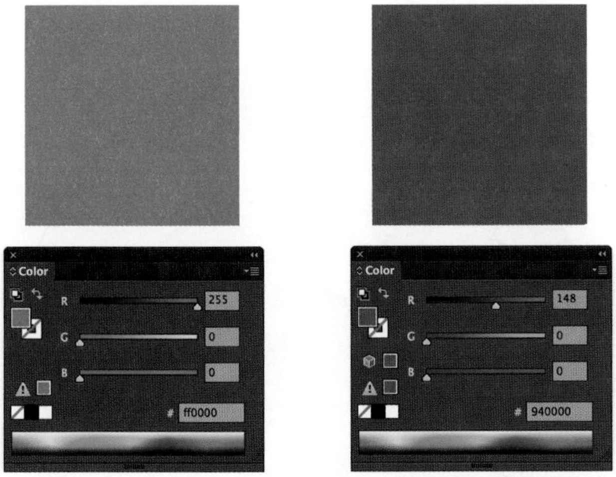

Goodheart-Willcox Publisher

Figure 11-11. Shades are created by lowering the saturation of the color selected.

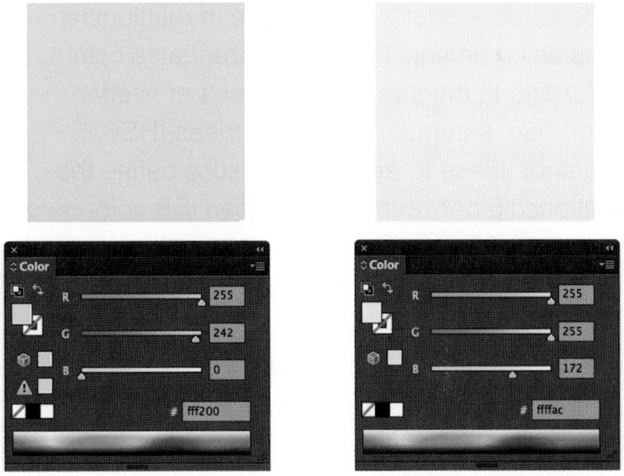

Goodheart-Willcox Publisher

Figure 11-12. Tints are created by increasing the saturation of the complementary color.

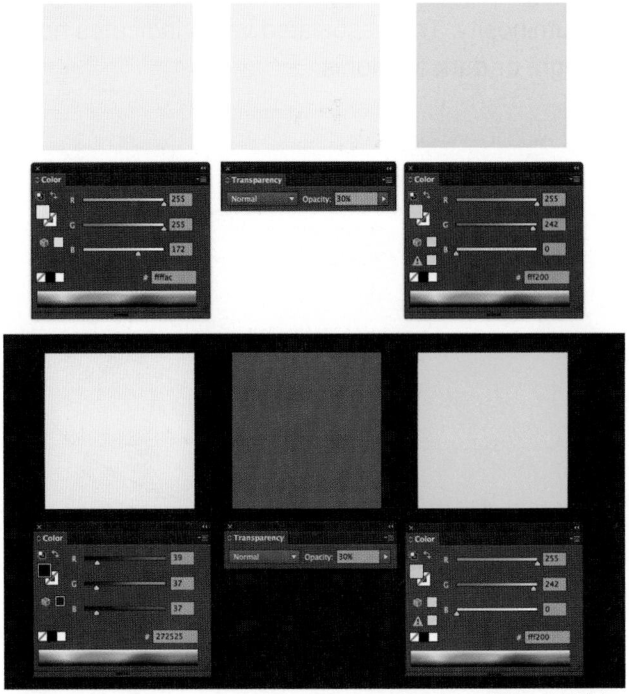

Goodheart-Willcox Publisher

Figure 11-13. These examples illustrate why adjusting opacity is not the correct way to create a tint.

The number of pure chromatic and achromatic colors is small compared to all color possibilities. The human eye can differentiate about 300 colors and about 150 shades of gray.

Hue, Saturation, and Brightness (HSB)

It is impossible to definitively describe the appearance of a color. However, it is possible to describe a color's appearance in relationship to its environment. The eye differentiates colors according to the three basic criteria of every color: hue, saturation, and brightness (HSB). Together, these three characteristics define the relationship between colors in the HSB color model, **Figure 11-14**.

- ***Hue*** is the color of an object perceived by the eye, determined by the dominant light wavelengths that are reflected or transmitted. It is the color in its purest form as it sits on the edge of the color wheel.
- ***Saturation*** defines a color's degree of strength or difference from white. It can also be defined as the predominance of one or two of the three RGB primary colors.
- ***Brightness*** is often referred to as lightness or luminosity. The associated value indicates how light or dark a color is.

Hue, Value, and Chroma (HVC)

In the early 1900s, Albert H. Munsell developed a color organization and definition system based on human perception. The Munsell system identifies the three attributes of color as hue, value, and chroma (HVC). In Munsell's system, chroma indicates the intensity, or strength, of a color and its saturation, **Figure 11-15**.

- *Hue* is the color name and is indicated by the letter H, followed by a fraction. The top number of the fraction represents the value. The bottom number indicates the chroma.
- ***Value*** is the lightness or darkness of a color. It is shown on the central axis of the Munsell model as nine visible steps. The darkest value is at the bottom and the lightest value is at the top. The value of pure black is designated as 0/, pure white as 10/, and middle gray as 5/.
- ***Chroma*** is shown by the horizontal band extending outward from the value axis. The chroma value shows the amount that a given hue deviates from a neutral gray of the same value. The number of chroma steps varies because hues vary in saturation strength.

Munsell's color system continues to be popular in the fine arts area because it separates

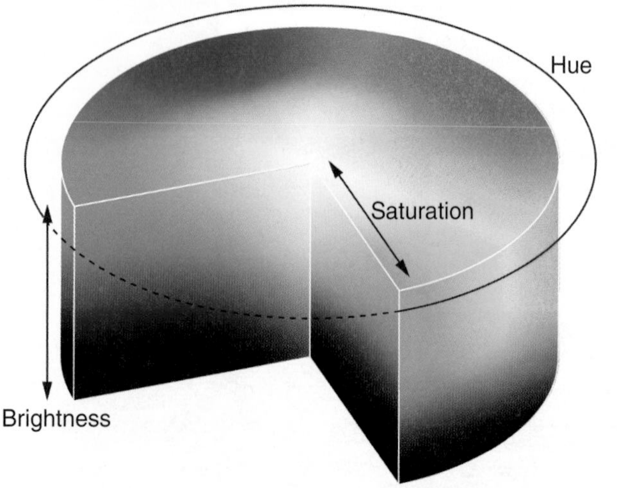

Goodheart-Willcox Publisher

Figure 11-14. The HSB diagram showing hue, saturation, and brightness.

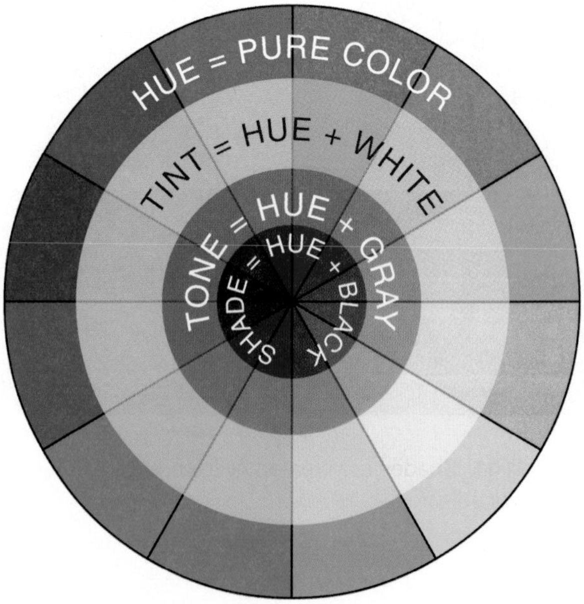

Goodheart-Willcox Publisher

Figure 11-15. Hue, tint, tone, and shade are all defined in this image according to the Munsell system.

the color-independent component, brightness (Munsell's value), from hue and saturation (Munsell's chroma). This enables two-dimensional color representation. In addition, it is perceptually uniform. Color distances on the model correspond to perceived differences between the colors. Every color has a specific location with this system. While this may be an effective method of definition when dealing with pigments, working with and reproducing colors digitally requires a much more scientific and consistent system.

The International Commission on Illumination (CIE)

To precisely match colors in the graphic communications industry, most ink and paper manufacturers have adopted the CIE system of color specification. CIE stands for Commission Internationale de l'Eclairage, or the International Commission on Illumination. In 1931, the CIE established a worldwide color measurement standard. The CIE system is a mathematical model of human color perception, **Figure 11-16**. Numerical values quantify the responses of the average human eye to different wavelengths of light.

The CIE defined several standard light sources, a standard observer, and standard viewing conditions. See **Figure 11-17**. The standard observer was chosen to have color vision representing that of the average person. Standard viewing conditions were determined using a dark background and only foveal vision. Foveal vision covers only about a 2° angle of vision. The CIE's angle of vision is 10°. The wider angle provides a more accurate correlation with the visual perception for larger samples.

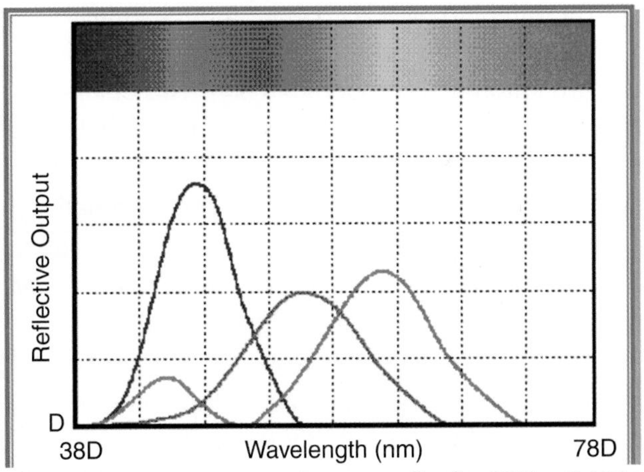

Goodheart-Willcox Publisher

Figure 11-16. Responses of the average human eye to different light waves were used to establish the CIE color standard. As illustrated above, the human eye does not perceive color as equally spaced. Human perception of color is much greater in the center of the spectrum than on the ends.

Illuminant	Temperature
CIE source A, tungsten	2856 K
CIE source B, sunlight	4870 K
CIE source C, daylight	6770 K
CIE source D_{50}, daylight	5000 K
CIE source D_{55}, daylight	5500 K
CIE source D_{65}, daylight	6500 K

Goodheart-Willcox Publisher

Figure 11-17. The CIE Standard Illuminants. D_{65} is the most widely used to represent average daylight conditions. D_{55} and D_{50} are other commonly used daylight sources.

The CIE Uniform Color Space (CIE XYZ)

Determining accurate color measurements requires information from three variables: the light source, the color sample, and the receiver. After this information is gathered, a sample's ***tristimulus values (X, Y, Z)*** can be determined. The X, Y, and Z stand for red, green, and blue (RGB), respectively. Any color may be specified on the CIE XYZ color model by listing the amounts of the three primary colors (red, green, and blue) required to match it. Certain methods are used to manipulate the data graphically or mathematically. These values can be quickly determined using measurement devices, computers, and computer software.

The CIE XYZ color space is the parent system for nearly all color standards. Variations such as the CIE Yxy, CIELAB, and CIE Luminance Y models serve different scientific and technical purposes.

The CIE Chromaticity Diagram

The CIE chromaticity diagram (CIE Yxy color space) is a two-dimensional graph of hue and chroma, **Figure 11-18A**. ***Chromaticity*** refers to a quality of color that includes hue and saturation, but not brightness.

As with Munsell's HVC color model, the CIE Yxy separates the achromatic component (Y) from the two chromatic components (xy). Two colors that are the same except for luminance would have the same chromatic definition, and therefore the same ***chromaticity coordinates***. The chromaticity coordinates are represented by the x and y values. The color's brightness (Y) is specified by a number, not a location on the graph, **Figure 11-18B**.

The CIE chromaticity diagram has a horizontal x axis and a vertical y axis. When the chromaticity coordinates of visible light (380 nm–770 nm) are converted and plotted, the resulting points fall on a horseshoe-shaped curve known as the ***spectrum locus***, **Figure 11-19A**. Since all visible colors are comprised of mixtures of light wavelengths, all visible colors must occur within the boundary

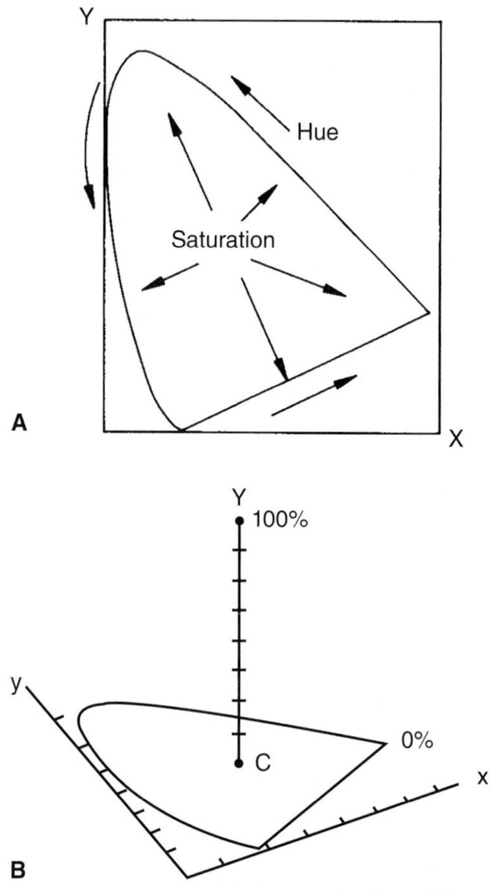

Goodheart-Willcox Publisher

Figure 11-18. A—The CIE chromaticity diagram represents the hue and saturation of a specific color or the chromaticity coordinates of that color. B—The luminance value (Y) is seen as a vertical axis, rising up from a neutral position of the illuminant or light source.

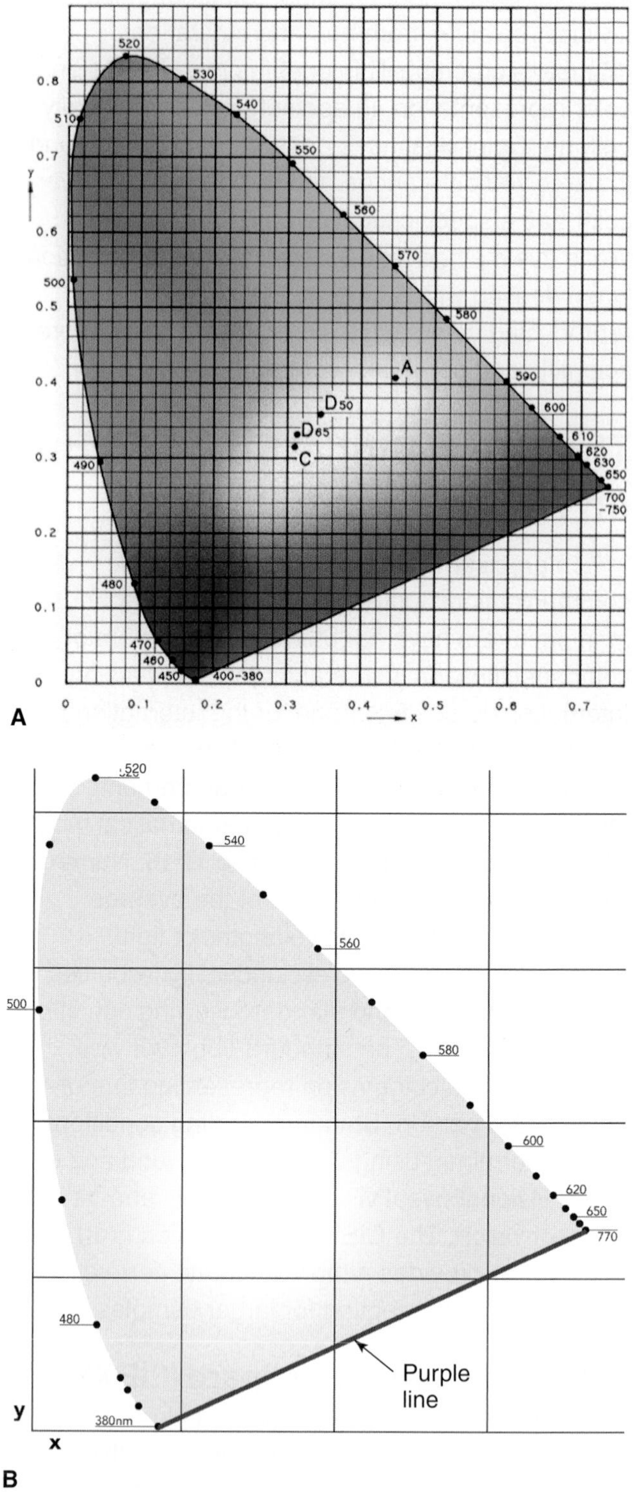

Thomas Detrie

Figure 11-19. A—The CIE chromaticity chart. B—The bold line between 380 nm and 770 nm represents the purple boundary at the base of the spectrum locus.

formed by this curve. Connecting the spectrum locus curve endpoints forms a line called the purple line, or the purple boundary. Colors on this line are mixtures of pure violet (380 nm) and red (770 nm) light, **Figure 11-19B**.

The colors plotted on the chromaticity diagram are relative to the light source used. The A, C, D_{50}, and D_{65} labels in **Figure 11-19A** represent the location of the CIE standard light sources. The CIE values of dominant wavelength, purity, and luminosity are dependent on the color temperature of the light source used in making the measurements. In the CIE system, dominant wavelength relates to hue, and purity relates to chroma or saturation.

CIELAB

In 1976, the CIE revised the standards to create a more even distribution of colors. The result is the CIELAB model, **Figure 11-20**. The distance between colors corresponds to perceived color differences. The CIELAB model is the current standard for measuring the color of light and is very similar to Munsell's color model.

The CIELAB color space separates color and luminance into discrete color space dimensions. These dimensions are represented by the designations *L*, *A*, and *B*.

- **L.** The first dimension, which represents lightness. All colors of the same lightness lie in a plane. Lightness varies vertically.

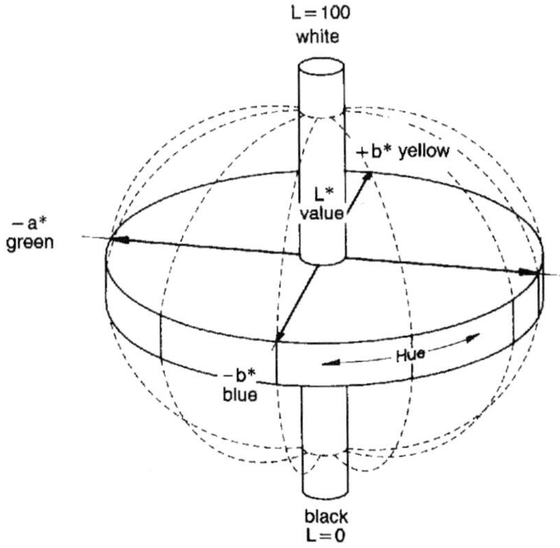

Goodheart-Willcox Publisher

Figure 11-20. The CIELAB color space defines color based on our visual system's perception of color.

- **A.** Indicates the red to green value. Positive a* values (+a*) appear reddish and negative a* values (–a*) appear greenish.
- **B.** Represents the yellow to blue value. Positive b* values (+b*) are yellowish and negative b* values (–b*) are bluish.

The a* and b* designations both represent a two-dimensional color subspace.

The human visual system is more sensitive to the L dimension, so digital systems allocate more data space to it than to the color components. This allows even more efficient coding of the color values. Using the LAB color gamut is the only true way to accurately describe color that is device-independent.

The Pantone® System

The Pantone system of color specification is widely used in the graphic communications industry. Unlike the HVC or HSB color models, the Pantone system is not based on equal visual differences in color. The colors used are based on ink colors common to the printing industry.

Manuals and swatchbooks provide Pantone color representations, names, and mixing formulas, **Figure 11-21**. The colors are usually presented on both coated and uncoated paper. Using the manuals or swatchbooks, designers, clients, and printers can effectively communicate color selections. The swatchbooks and the accuracy of their color depend on the paper, the press, and the age of the book itself.

For years, displaying the Pantone inks on your monitor and printing to your desktop printer were unreliable ways to represent the inks. The libraries in the software programs that defined the colors used different lookup tables, all in CMYK format, which made proofing inconsistent. The newer Pantone Plus series has changed how they define the colors. Using LAB values to define the colors, these spot colors provide a more accurate representation of the actual Pantone inks, and are consistent throughout applications and devices, including desktop and mobile. It is important to make sure you have properly communicated with all parties involved in a project when using Pantone colors.

©George Deal

Figure 11-21. Pantone® offers printers, designers, and color professionals a variety of materials for choosing and using the Pantone colors.

Printed Color

Creating colors can be accomplished using either additive color formation or subtractive color formation. ***Additive color formation*** is based on mixing primary colors of light; ***subtractive color formation*** is based on mixing colorants. ***Colorants*** are chemical substances that give color to such materials as ink, paint, crayons, and chalk. Colorants that dissolve in liquids are called ***dyes***. Colorants that do not dissolve but spread as tiny solid particles through liquids or other substances, such as ink, are called ***pigments***.

In today's world of digital hardware and software, color remains a hot topic of discussion. Modern technology enables a more accurate and consistent reproduction and definition of color than ever before.

Additive and Subtractive Color Formation

In additive color formation, the primary colors of light (red, green, blue) combine to form other colors. Red, green, and blue are called the additive primary colors and are usually referred to as RGB. The human vision system, which is sensitive to red, green, and blue light, uses additive color mixing. Television sets and computer monitors create images in a full range of colors by combining dots of red, green, and blue light.

In subtractive color formation, color is seen by reflected light. Each of the subtractive primary colors—cyan, magenta, and yellow (CMY)—absorbs (subtracts) other colors from the white light and reflects only its own. For example, a spot of cyan printed on a page absorbs red wavelengths of light, and reflects back only blue and green wavelengths that form the color cyan. A spot printed with black ink (or a black spot made by combining equal parts of cyan, magenta, and yellow) absorbs all the wavelengths and does not reflect any color. In the same way, a white paper surface reflects all the wavelengths, producing white light. Colorants of the subtractive primaries can be mixed together in equal proportions to form the additive primaries.

In ***process color printing***, where only subtractive primary colors and black are used, the same principle applies. However, colors are mixed visually rather than physically. Varying combinations of tiny, closely spaced dots of cyan, magenta, and yellow ink absorb and reflect the different wavelengths of light to produce different colors.

The two color formations act almost as opposites. On our color wheel, the additive colors are the result of mixing the subtractive colors together. While the combination of all three additive colors equals white, the combination of the three subtractive colors equals black. See **Figure 11-22**.

Because inks are not as pure as light, the black is muddy and would require a heavier ink deposit on the paper, resulting in an increased drying time. Adding black as the fourth color is not only more cost-effective since it is less expensive than color inks, it also enhances imagery on press. Black allows greater and crisper detail, and deeper, more well-defined shadow areas in imagery. In the descriptions of the subtractive color system, black is designated with the letter *K*. Thus, the four process colors are described in abbreviated form as CMYK.

Color Separation

Color separation is the process of dividing the colors of a multicolored original into the subtractive, or printing, primaries (CMY) and black (K). The CMYK color separations are used to prepare printing plates, **Figure 11-23**. For years, color separations were created using three different methods: direct screen photographic, indirect screen photographic, and electronic.

Image manipulation, page geometry, and drawing software either show or create the separations automatically. In Adobe® Photoshop®, the separations are shown in the **Channels** panel. Each file will show the separations based on the color space of the image. Using the color separations panel under the output window in page layout software, each file shows the separations or plates necessary to reproduce the document. By clicking on the eye next to the separation, the individual colors can be turned off or on to show custom views and ensure that the proper data is on the proper color. See **Figure 11-24**.

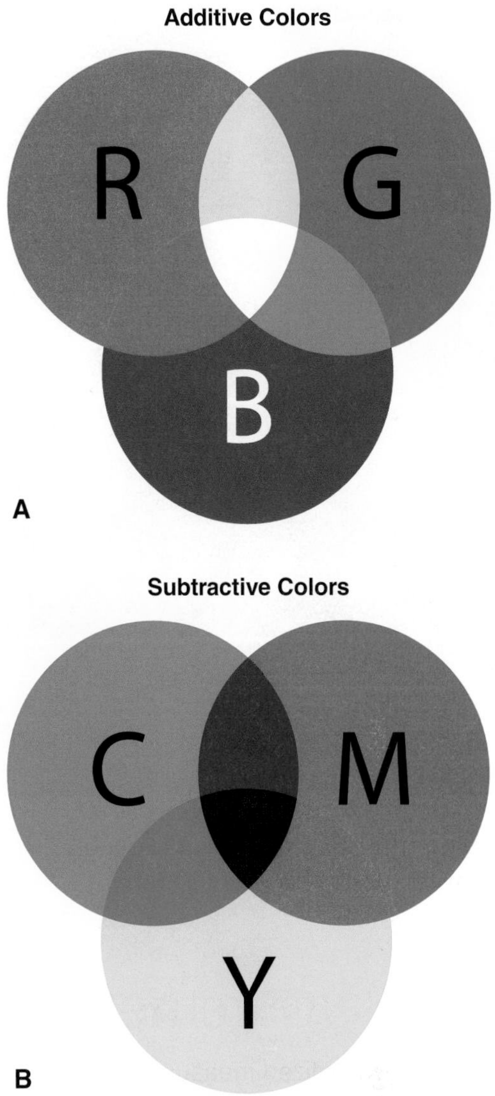

Goodheart-Willcox Publisher

Figure 11-22. Additive color formation. Red, green, and blue additive primaries can be mixed in pairs to form magenta, yellow, and cyan. Mixing all three results in white light.

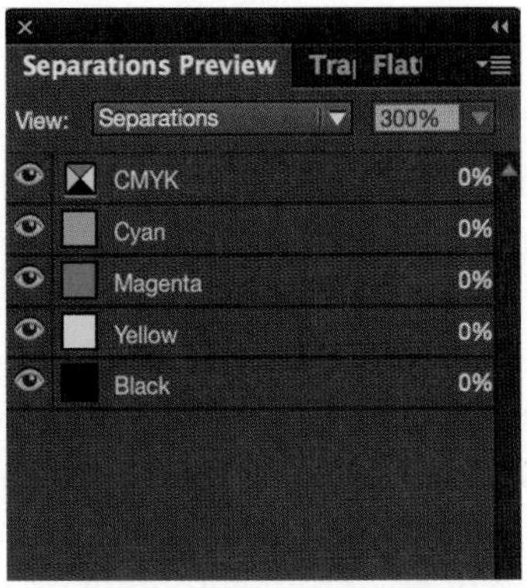

Goodheart-Willcox Publisher

Figure 11-23. The **Separations Preview** panel in a page layout application shows the number of colors in the document needed to print.

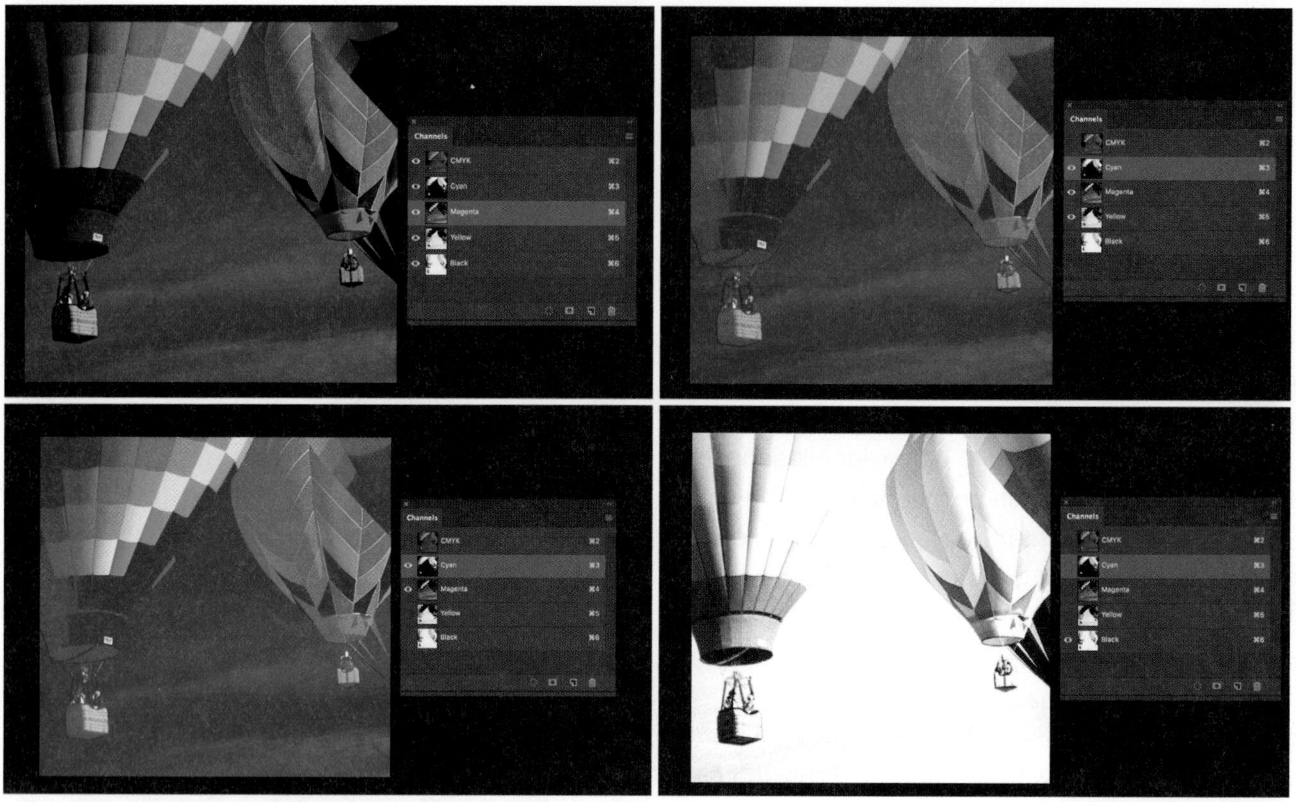

Goodheart-Willcox Publisher

Figure 11-24. The **Channels** menu in an image manipulation application shows all the data on each color channel. You can show them individually or in any combination.

Color Measurement

Precise standardized measurement is also part of color evaluation. Measuring instruments vary in both design and function. Some measure density, some measure color values, and others measure light waves. The most common color measuring instruments are spectrophotometers, densitometers, colorimeters, and spectrodensitometers.

Spectrophotometers

A photometer is used to measure light intensity. Adding the prefix *spectro-* indicates that the instrument is capable of measuring light of different colors or wavelengths. When used for measurement in the graphic communications industry, a ***spectrophotometer*** converts this data to CIE color specifications. A spectrophotometer is the most accurate type of color measurement device.

The readout system of a spectrophotometer either plots spectrophotometric curves or provides the data from which the curves can be plotted. Spectrophotometric curves provide a contour or envelope that describes the reflection or transmission characteristics of a sample. The sample may be the image area on printed media, a color negative, or a positive color transparency.

Spectrophotometric curves describe the physical characteristics of viewing samples. They do *not* describe the colors as perceived by a person viewing the samples. For example, the curves for skin colors show that human skin has the lowest reflectance in the blue region and the highest in the red region of the spectrum. See **Figure 11-25**. Light skin has the highest reflectance at all wavelengths, but the curve is not very smooth. The reflectance for any specific wavelength is easily obtained from the curves. In the example at 700 nm, light skin has a reflectance of 70%, dark skin 45%, and very dark skin 15%.

Most spectrophotometers used in the graphic arts industry are limited to reading light waves in the visible spectrum. When reading light waves in the visible spectrum, the samples must be placed as close to the detector as possible to reduce the problem of light scattered by the system, **Figure 11-26**.

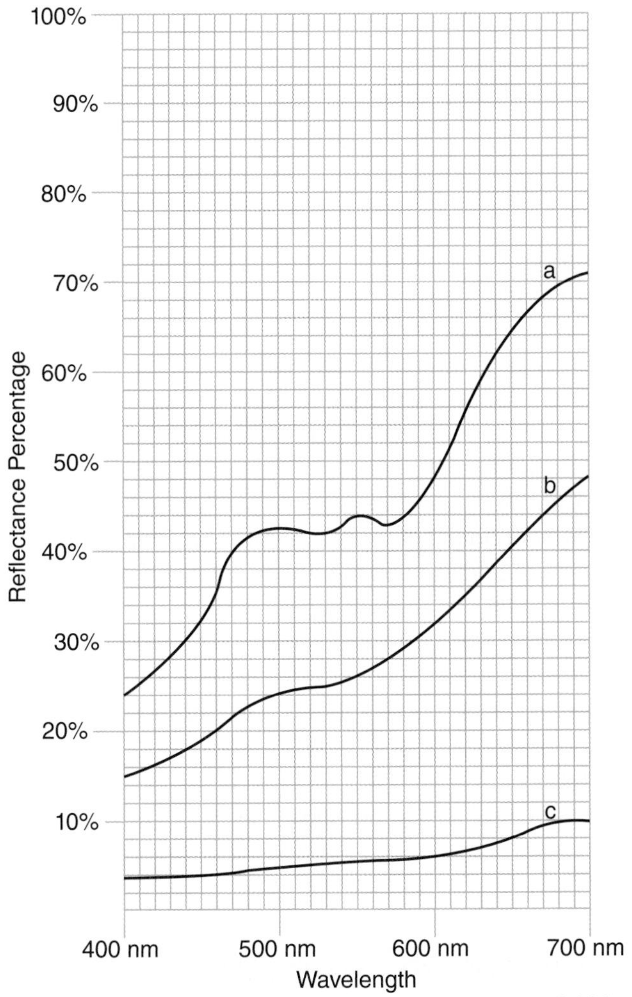

Goodheart-Willcox Publisher

Figure 11-25. Spectrophotometric curves of an image.

Densitometers

Densitometers compute optical density, the light-stopping or light absorption ability of an image or surface material. The fundamental difference between a densitometer and a spectrophotometer is the bandwidth of light used. A densitometer uses red, green, and blue filters to isolate broad bands of light, which are about 55 nm wide. A spectrophotometer uses a prism or diffraction grating to spread the light, and a slit to isolate narrow bands of light between 1 nm and 10 nm. The densitometer uses numbers, not curves, to express density. Depending on the type being used, densitometers can be used on negative or positive transparencies, photographs, or printed images.

- ***Reflection densitometers*** measure the amount of light that bounces off a photographic print or printed sheet at a 90° angle. It can be configured to make direct measurements of halftone values on printing plates.
- ***Transmission densitometers*** measure the fraction of incident light conveyed through a negative or positive transparency, without being absorbed or scattered.
- ***Combination densitometers*** measure both reflection and transmission densities.

©George Deal

Figure 11-26. Strip reading spectrophotometer.

Career Link

Color Specialist

A high percentage of the jobs that are printed today have some color as a part of the finished product. The customers know what they want or like. When someone says the red is not red enough, the color specialist must work with that customer to meet the needs so the images are accepted. Customer approval of color images is a very critical step in the process of creating the finished printed product.

The color specialist must be an expert in understanding color theory. The end results of the specialist's work must ensure accurate color reproduction. Therefore, the color specialist must be competent in working with color calibrations, color separations, and color management. This expertise requires the application of color to types of media as well as to all printing processes. The ability to communicate clearly with customers and technicians is imperative. This person must be able to process, comprehend, and follow detailed written and verbal instructions.

A college education degree in graphic communications is recommended. Experience in the prepress area is imperative. Many of the high-quality printers require that the color specialist be a G7 certified GRACoL expert. The G7 certification is a way of defining visual appearance. Belonging to this group classifies the specialist as an elite professional.

"Starting in 2000, the full-sized heatset web-fed presses were able to upgrade to closed loop color, presetting of inks, and registration that really worked."

Pam Carritt
Courier Graphics Corporation

Colorimeters

Colorimeters measure and compute XYZ color values in a way that models vision. The results are usually reported in a CIE color space. Colorimeters record all visible colors, but generally are not as precise as densitometers or spectrophotometers. Two types of colorimeters are the trichromatic colorimeter and the monochromatic colorimeter.

Used for quality control and calibration, colorimeters are effective at measuring color and creating profiles to ensure color accuracy across a range of electronic devices, such as your monitor, printer, projector, and camera.

A ***trichromatic colorimeter*** allows the user to match a patch of light by combination of the three primary colors. Even though this instrument relies on the perception of the eye, it is a useful device for color measurement.

A ***monochromatic colorimeter*** does not measure types of color, but measures the intensity of a particular color. Unlike the trichromatic colorimeter, it does *not* depend on the perception of color by the eye.

Spectrodensitometers

Spectrodensitometers serve all the functions of a spectrophotometer, densitometer, and colorimeter in a single instrument. In addition to measuring color value and optical density, including ink density, dot gain, and dot, they also measure paper attributes and special colors.

Computer-to-plate technology now requires a tool to read the microscopic details on the plate substrate. These spectrodensitometers use powerful graphic signal processors for imaging. See **Figure 11-27**.

The Human Visual System

A photomechanical reaction that occurs in the eye when light stimulates retinal receptors allows us to see. The retinal receptors supply electrical impulse patterns to the brain. Images are formed in the mind and take on meaning for the viewer.

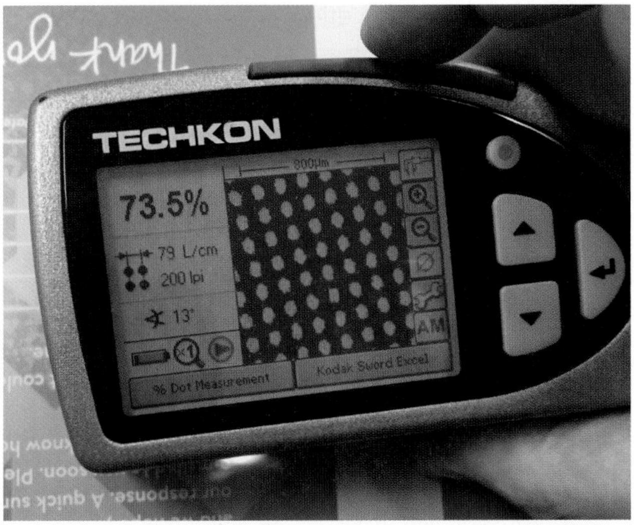

©George Deal

Figure 11-27. Newer spectrodensitometers read very small details on plates.

Exactly how the brain makes us aware of colors is still much of a mystery.

Anatomy of the Eye and Vision

When light reaches the eye, it is focused onto the ***retina***, a layer of light-sensitive cells at the back of the eye. See **Figure 11-28**. This occurs mainly by refraction at the front of the ***cornea***, a transparent window at the front of the eye. A special lens behind the pupil and the eye's muscles control adjustments needed for focusing. The ***iris*** controls the amount of light entering the eye by altering the size of the pupil—from 0.08″ (2 mm) in bright sunlight to 0.3″ (8 mm) at night.

Our perception of light and color is determined by the light-sensitive nerve cells of the retina, known as ***rods*** and ***cones***. There are about twelve million rods and seven million cones in the human eye. The rods detect light intensity and are most sensitive to black, white, and shades of gray. Very little light is needed to stimulate the rods, so they are particularly important for night vision.

The retina has three types of cones that detect both intensity and wavelength (color). The cones contain light-sensitive chemicals called ***photopigments*** that respond to red, green, or blue. All colors are mixtures of signals from these three types of cone receptors. In other words, colors are perceived according to which cones are stimulated by wavelengths of light entering the eye. This color-mixing ability allows us to perceive a multitude of colors derived from the three primaries. For

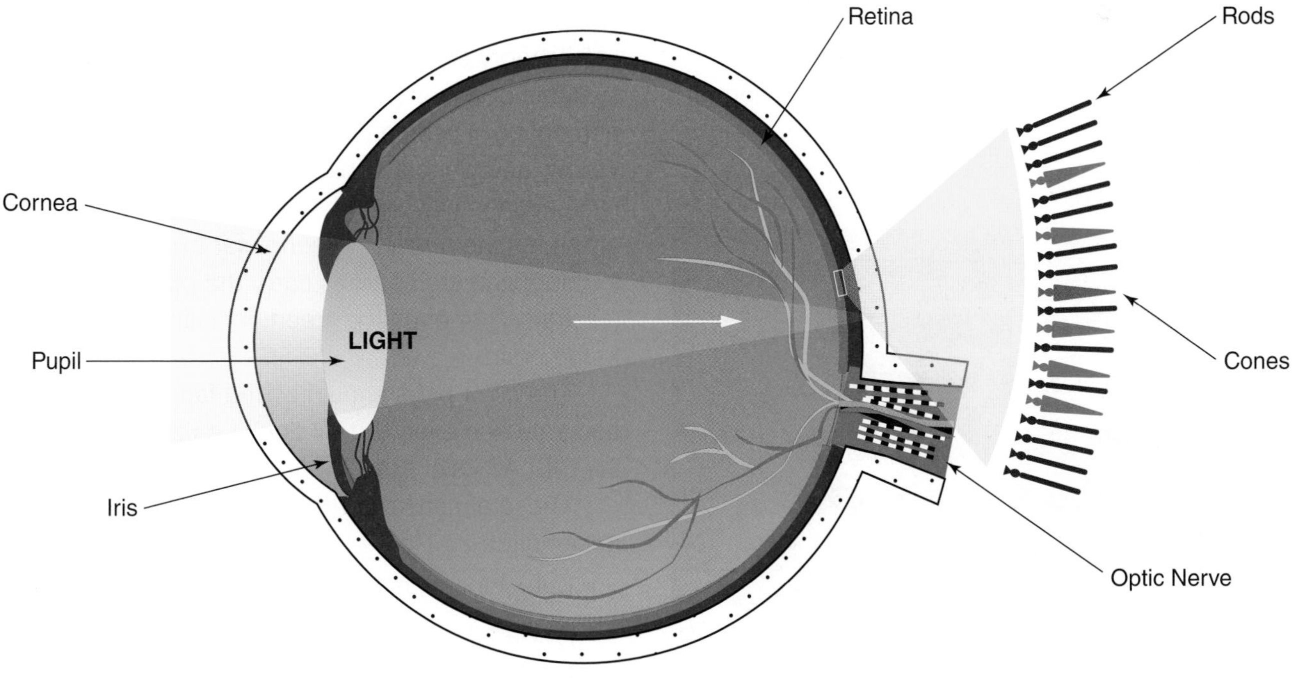

Goodheart-Willcox Publisher

Figure 11-28. The rods and cones are located in the retina of the human eye.

example, despite yellow's pure appearance, it is not a pure color. There is no retinal receptor sensitive to the yellow frequency. The color yellow is perceived through the combined activity of the red-sensitive and green-sensitive cones.

With three colors—red, green, and blue—it would seem logical that the cones would have an even distribution of 33% for each color. The reality is that we have 64% red cones, 32% green, and only 2% blue. The missing 2% accounts for damaged cones. Using red and green for stoplights is not an arbitrary decision.

The ***macula*** is a small hollow in the middle of the retina. The cones are concentrated in the macula and diminish in concentration toward the edges of the retina. At the center of the macula is the ***fovea***, the most sensitive part of the retina. The fovea is packed with cone cells and is the area of sharpest vision. Unlike rods, the cones need high levels of light. This is why colors often appear muted or absent at night.

Brightness and Intensity

The cones and rods of the retina are extremely sensitive light detectors. Even the smallest amount of radiant energy stimulates them. The intensity of light entering the eye causes the sensation of brightness.

Bright light bleaches the color-sensitive cones of the retina. This bleaching stimulates the nerves. After exposure to bright light, it takes time for the photochemical activity of the eye to return to normal.

Goodheart-Willcox Publisher

Figure 11-29. To see an afterimage, stare at the center of this flag for about 30 seconds. Then, look at a white sheet of paper. You will see an image of the flag with its proper colors.

A good example of this effect is when a person is temporarily blinded by a camera flash. During the time a region of the retina is bleached, that region is less sensitive than surrounding regions. This can cause both positive and negative afterimages. ***Afterimages*** are created when the eye attempts to restore equilibrium. Gazing for some time at a green square and then closing your eyes causes a red square to appear as an afterimage. If the square is red, a green square will be the afterimage. This experiment demonstrates that, with any color, the afterimage is always the complementary color, **Figure 11-29**. The technical name for this color-vision effect is ***successive contrast***.

Opponent Color Theory

Scientists have established how additive and subtractive colors work and how they have solidified the additive color wheel. Referring to Figure 7-20, note that magenta is the opposite or complementary color to green. Yet magenta is the only color that does not appear in the prism and does not have a wavelength. The only way to get magenta is to eliminate all traces of green. Magenta is the "anti-green." So when there is no green, rather than seeing actual magenta, our brains merely perceive magenta.

Afterimages are a perfect example of Ewald Hering's opponent-process theory of color vision, first proposed in 1878. The opponent-process color theory suggests that there are three basic systems of opposing neurons that define our color perception. These pairs are red and green, blue and yellow, and white and black. See **Figure 11-30**. Our eye sees the wavelengths. It sees more red and green, as the number of cones far exceeds those for blue, and the neurons carry the positive red (excitatory) or negative green (inhibitory) responses to the brain.

The color pairs should sound familiar. The most accurate and even distribution of colors comes from the CIELAB color space, which is device-independent.

These dimensions are represented by these designations:

- **L.** Lightness, black and white.
- **A.** Red to green values where positive a* values (+a*) appear reddish, and negative a* values (–a*) appear greenish.

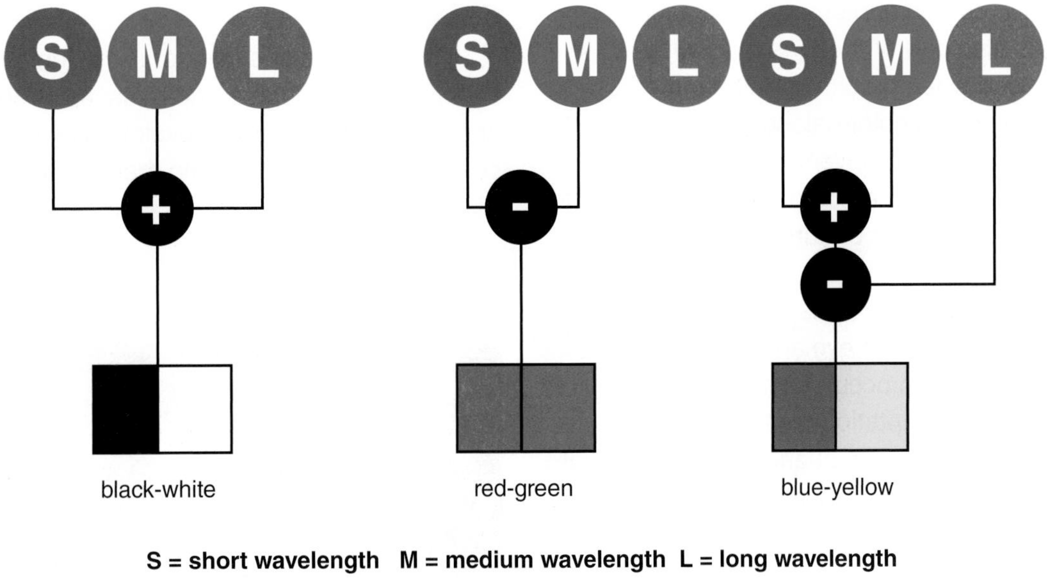

Goodheart-Willcox Publisher

Figure 11-30. The opponent color theory shows one method of how light is seen and perceived by the brain.

- **B.** The yellow to blue values where positive b* values (+b*) are yellowish, and negative b* values (–b*) are bluish.

Metamerism

Metamerism is a phenomenon where two colors appear the same using one light source but are different under a different light source. While this happens regularly in the real world with clothing and other items, it presents a unique problem for those in the graphic communications industry. Especially relevant for web designers and online stores, the general public wants to know what color an item is that they are purchasing. Designers can control the color they use with profiles, and embed that information into a graphic they upload to the site. Web browsers are becoming much better at color accuracy and profile representations. Metamerism occurs on mobile devices as well, **Figure 11-31**.

Because of the number of variables that are out of our control, minimizing metamerism by viewing color under the proper or expected lighting is sometimes the best that we can do.

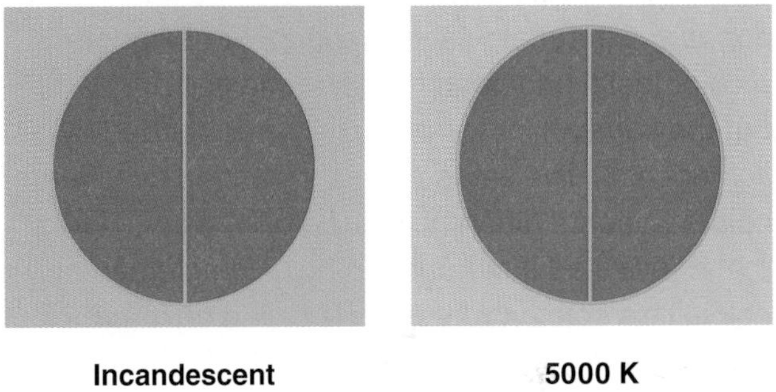

Goodheart-Willcox Publisher

Figure 11-31. Metamerism is a color phenomenon in which colors appear the same in one light and different in another.

Adaptation

The adjustment eyes make to lighting conditions is called ***adaptation***. If the eyes experience low light for some time, the cones and rods grow more sensitive and light appears brighter. This is dark adaptation. Just as a photographer increases exposure time in a dim lighting situation, the dark adaptation of the eyes increases vision "exposure time" to raise sensitivity. Your eyes adapt to the color of light in much the same way. This is called ***chromatic adaptation***. A good example of this effect is reading at night using a tungsten lamp that emits light with a yellow cast. The reader's eyes quickly adapt to the yellow color to the point that it is not even noticeable. If the reader steps outside and looks in through the window, he or she would clearly see that the light has a yellow cast.

Adaptation makes it difficult to use your naked eye to determine such things as the amount of light needed in certain photographic situations. Adaptation is also part of the reason viewing booths are used when proofing printed materials. A ***viewing booth*** has color-balanced lighting (5000 K illumination), so anyone viewing the same printed materials sees them under identical lighting conditions. The light temperature used in a viewing booth appears clear and color-balanced, and is ideal for making color comparisons, **Figure 11-32**.

Cones and rods in the eye adapt at different rates. Cone adaptation occurs in about seven minutes, while rod adaptation continues for an hour or more. Decreased light and increased visual sensitivity also reduce the ability to make out fine detail.

Adjacency

Adjacency is a change in color perception that is caused by colors adjacent to or surrounding a subject, **Figure 11-33**. If you place the same color against different background colors, the color appears different in each scenario. For example, a color looks brighter if the surroundings are dark, but the same color looks darker if surrounded by a lighter color. The same color surrounded by different colors appears different. Additionally, a color looks more saturated if surrounded by a complementary color. This color-vision effect is called ***chromatic induction*** or simultaneous contrast.

Color Constancy

Color constancy is the tendency to perceive the color of an object to be the constant, even when environmental conditions (such as lighting) are changed. Skin tones are also commonly misperceived. When viewing the printed image of a person, for example, his or her skin color may appear correct due to the color maintained in the viewer's memory. The actual difference in color is apparent when the person is compared to the printed image.

Color Viewing Variables

Although the human vision system is both highly sensitive and accurate, it is also very subjective. Visual perception varies among individuals for many reasons and can even be affected by changes in emotional and physical states.

Color Blindness

The ability to see in color is not inherent to all animals. Although some birds, fish, reptiles, and insects have highly-developed color vision systems, it is almost certain that very few mammals below the primates possess color vision. Among

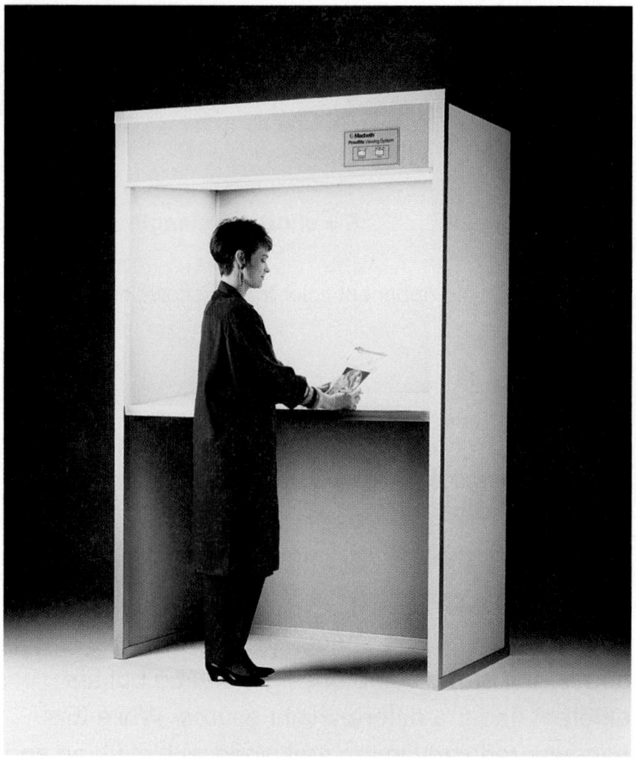

Photo courtesy of GretagMacbeth, New Windsor, NY

Figure 11-32. Standardized viewing conditions are necessary to properly evaluate color reproduction. This viewing booth emits 5000 K illumination.

Goodheart-Willcox Publisher

Figure 11-33. When a color is viewed against a light background, it appears darker. When the same color is viewed against a dark background, it appears lighter. Surrounding a color with different colors makes it appear different.

humans, approximately 10% of males and about 1% of females experience some degree of color blindness. Color blindness is the inability to tell colors apart. Knowing these statistics can help with the decision-making process regarding color.

A person with normal vision has cones that respond to all three of the additive primary colors (RGB). A color-blind person lacks one, two, or all three types of cones. Most color-blind people have ***dichromatic vision*** and can see only yellows and blues. They confuse reds with greens, and some reds or greens with some yellows. Very few people are truly blind to all colors. Those who are completely color blind see only in shades of white, gray, and black, and are said to have ***achromatic vision***.

Vision Fatigue

Random retinal impulses and involuntary rapid eye movements are essential to vision and keep the vision system perpetually active. Vision soon fades when an image becomes optically fixed on the retina. Movement of the eye sweeps the light pattern over receptors to continually signal the brain that the image is present. However, overuse fatigues the system and can impair color judgment. For example, viewing a saturated color for an extended period of time causes a second color to appear different because vision fatigue subtracts some of the first color from the image.

Aging

Even with the complete absence of light, random retinal impulses reach the brain. This continuous background of random activity creates a problem for the mind. The mind must decide whether the activity is "noise" or information. Internal visual noise increases with age and is partly responsible for the gradual loss of visual discrimination. Aging also impacts visual accuracy and adaptation.

Viewing Conditions

In addition to vision deficiencies and variations, external conditions also affect color judgment. External variables include diverse lighting types, different substrates, disparate viewing angles, unconventional illumination angles, the size and shape of the color area, the paint color on walls, and even the color of clothing, **Figure 11-34**. Because color vision requires sensory data, it is impossible to actually remember color; we can only compare color. However, accurate color comparison is almost impossible unless items are viewed under identical viewing conditions.

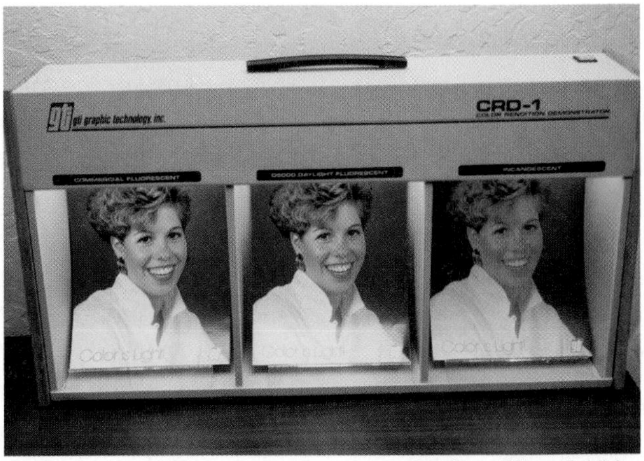

Goodheart-Willcox Publisher

Figure 11-34. Differences in viewing conditions under 2500 K, 5000 K, and 6500 K illumination.

Summary

- The electromagnetic spectrum consists of bands of different wavelengths. Our eyes can detect only a very small part of the electromagnetic spectrum known as visible light.
- The various color systems and color models describe colors through numerical or coordinate means. The numerical values or coordinates allow the colors to be defined within the system's parameters.
- We are taught in art and with paint that the primary colors are red, yellow, and blue. Secondary colors are orange, green, and violet. Tertiary colors are yellow-green, blue-green, blue-violet, red-violet, red-orange, and yellow-orange.
- Color is a science. The true primary colors are red, green, and blue, based on the way our eyes perceive color as light.
- Additive color formation is based on mixing primary colors of light; subtractive color formation is based on mixing colorants.
- Measuring instruments include spectrophotometers, densitometers, colorimeters, and spectrodensitometers.
- Parts of the human eye include the retina, cornea, iris, rods, and cones.

Review Questions

Answer the following questions using the information in this chapter.

1. Our eyes are sensitive to only a small part of the electromagnetic spectrum. What is this range called?
2. A beam of light coming toward a surface is called the _____ beam.
3. How does light become refracted?
4. Explain the difference between the *constructive interference* of light and the *destructive interference* of light.
5. What is a *diffraction grating*?
6. What is a *color triad*?
7. How are shades and tints produced?
8. Identify and define the three criteria used in the HSB color model.
9. Explain the properties of Munsell's HVC color organization system.
10. What do the letters *LAB* represent in the CIELAB color model?
11. Which color specification system is based on ink colors common to the printing industry?
12. Draw the true color wheel based on light.
13. Describe the process of *additive color formation*.
14. Identify the *subtractive primary colors*.
15. Explain why black is used as the fourth process color.
16. Name four color measurement instruments.
17. Which parts of the eye determine our perception of light and color?
18. Why is a viewing booth necessary to accurately compare colors?
19. Define *adjacency* and give an example of the effect.
20. What is the difference between *dichromatic vision* and *achromatic vision*?

Suggested Activities

1. Visit the physics lab of your school, if it has one. Observe the visible light through a prism and identify the wavelengths.
2. Ink up the press with red ink, cut several different types of substrates, and run the substrates through the press. Once printed, notice the appearance of the red ink on the various types of substrates. Describe the differences in appearance.
3. Using a reflection densitometer, measure the density of several printed control strips. Explain your findings.
4. Select several color-printed pieces and view them under different types of light sources, including bright sunlight, fluorescent lighting, incandescent lighting, and natural indoor light. Describe the color variation in each situation.
5. Create a document using Pantone color swatches. Print it out and compare the screen version and the printed version to a Pantone swatchbook.

Chapter 12

Color Management

Learning Objectives

After studying this chapter, you will be able to:

- Give several examples of color standards adopted by the graphic communications industry and explain how they are used.
- Explain how a color management system (CMS) regulates color conversion through the workflow.
- Explain how International Color Consortium (ICC) profiles work.
- Explain several methods used for color separation and correction.
- Explain trapping and list conventional and electronic methods.
- Explain the various screening methods used in graphic arts.
- Explain how color may be affected in the preflighting stage.
- Recall proofing methods used in the graphic communications industry.
- Explain the importance of ensuring ink colors are used correctly.

Goodheart-Willcox Publisher

Important Terms

absolute intent
additive color formation
automatic trap
brightness
calibration
characterization
choke trap
color control bar
color correction
color gamut
color management module (CMM)
color management system (CMS)
contrast
conversion
digital blueline proofs
digital proofs
dot gain
dot pitch
error-diffusion screening
gamma levels
gamut alarm
gamut compression
gray component replacement (GCR)
grayscale
hinting
ICC color profile
International Color Consortium (ICC)
IT8 reflective target
knockout
lookup tables
maximum resolution
overprinting
perceptual intent
press proofs
relative intent
rendering intent
saturation intent
soft proofs
spot screening
spread trap
stochastic screening
stroke
subtractive color formation
trapping
undercolor addition (UCA)
undercolor removal (UCR)
video card
white point

G-WLEARNING.com

While studying this chapter, look for the activity icon to:

- **Practice** vocabulary terms with e-flash cards, matching activities, and vocabulary game.
- **Reinforce** what you learn by submitting end-of-chapter questions.

www.g-wlearning.com/visualtechnology/

Color management in graphic communications describes the systematic approach to color conversions from input to output devices. The conversions can involve output to monitors, to digital color printers or presses, to plate material, or to mobile devices. The primary issue is getting the color transformation correct to ensure consistent and accurate color reproduction, regardless of the number or types of devices involved.

Computer monitors, digital proofing devices, and printing presses all render color differently. Documents viewed on-screen and output to different devices will have widely varying results. With an effective color management system, images can be scanned accurately, displayed on-screen correctly, and output as close to the original colors as possible.

Standards, Regulations, and Color Models

Numerous means of regulating, testing, and reproducing color have been adopted by the graphic communications industry. Because ink and toner composition, printing presses, and substrate quality also affect the accuracy of color reproduction, their design and operation are also covered under many of the same standards.

The International Commission on Illumination (CIE)

Many computer, ink, and paper manufacturers have adopted the CIE system of color specification. CIE created the three-dimensional, device-independent CIELAB color model.

The CIELAB color model is an ideal color space for performing ***color correction***. Instead of representing a color as a percentage of other colors, the CIELAB model puts the grayscale information into the L channel and uses the A and B channels for color information.

Grayscale is a means of showing the shades of gray that represent the image. When an image is converted to grayscale, all color information is discarded. The gray levels, or shades, of the converted pixels represent the luminosity of the original pixels. Because the grayscale channel is isolated in the CIELAB model, the user is able to apply sharpening and tonal settings without distorting the relationships of colors.

Although many image-editing programs allow the user to enhance the crispness of an RGB or CMYK image, halos and other distortions often occur when sharpening commands are applied. If possible, images should be captured in RAW mode, modified in the CIELAB color space, and then converted to RGB or CMYK, depending on their final purpose. The CIELAB mode is also recommended for moving images between systems.

The color gamut of a device is usually displayed using the CIE chromaticity diagram, **Figure 12-1**. The CIE chromaticity diagram shows just two dimensions of the CIE Yxy color space: hue and chroma. The achromatic component, or color's brightness, is represented by *Y* and is specified by a number, not a location on the graph.

The degree of inability of a device to display or print color is called its ***gamut compression***. If the color plot of a computer monitor is superimposed on the CIE chromaticity diagram, it can be seen

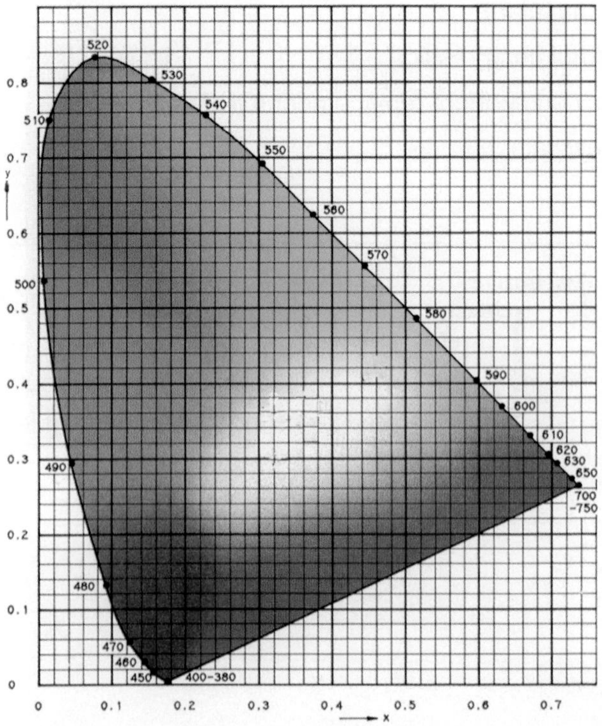

Goodheart-Willcox Publisher

Figure 12-1. The horseshoe-shaped CIE chromaticity diagram contains the colors of the visible spectrum.

that the monitor can display only a fraction of the visible spectrum, **Figure 12-2A**. If the plot of printable colors is superimposed on the same chart, it is clearly visible that the gamut of most printing presses is even more limited, **Figure 12-2B**.

Rendering Intents

An ICC profile, discussed below, is a specific set of data for a device that serves as a translator from one color space to another. Another bit of information, the ***rendering intent***, is needed to tell the color management software how to map the colors from one space to another and what to do with any colors that fall out of the device's gamut. There are four basic rendering intents: perceptual, relative, absolute, and saturation.

Perceptual intent changes the color data but keeps the same "feel" when the image is viewed by maintaining the relationship between the colors. If your image has a lot of out-of-gamut colors, this intent will change all colors, even those that were originally correct. This can produce some major color shifts.

Relative intent, or colorimetric rendering intent, maintains the color relationships for the in-gamut colors. It also adjusts the out-of-gamut colors to the closest possible match of the final destination color space. This produces a more accurate rendering.

Using ***absolute intent*** preserves the white point. While this sounds positive, it will actually create very harsh and unsightly image color shifts.

Brightly colored graphics might use ***saturation intent***. Photographers do not, however, because it does not maintain color realism. Keeping the color saturation can jeopardize the hue and lightness.

Warning

No matter what type of color mode is used, some quality is lost each time an image is converted. To preserve image quality, use conversions sparingly and apply them once, only to the final image.

The International Color Consortium (ICC)

Until 1993, the formats used to describe the color behavior of particular devices varied by

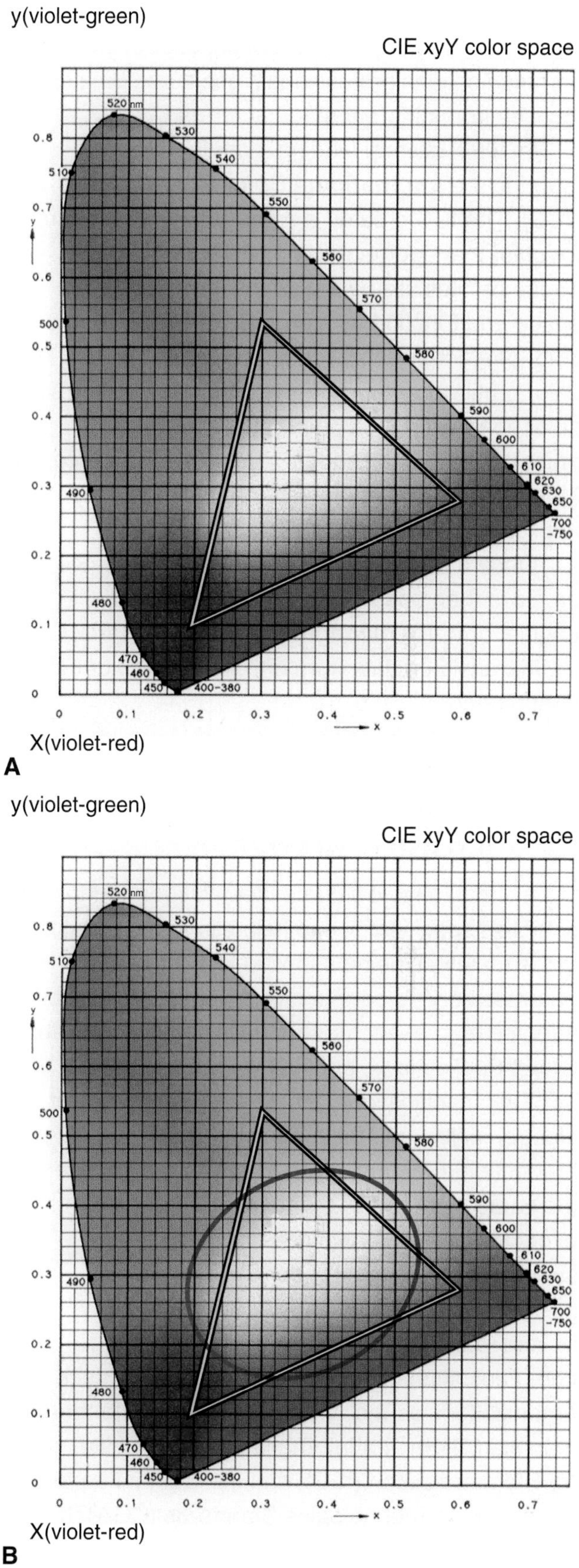

Goodheart-Willcox Publisher

Figure 12-2. Gamut compression. A—The triangle represents the color space of a computer monitor. B—The oval represents the CMYK space of a printer.

manufacturer. These multiple color standards were extremely impractical because most graphic communications professionals use a combination of devices from different manufacturers.

In 1993, several leading manufacturers founded the ***International Color Consortium (ICC)***. The ICC created a cross-platform standard for color management using ***ICC color profiles***. These profiles are based on the CIELAB color space and function as standards for describing color characterizations of different devices. ICC color profiles contain information on the device's color space and the compensation required to bring the device to its ideal level of performance. Most graphic arts manufacturers have developed applications that support ICC color profiles.

Once a device profile has been created, the profile is then used by a color transformation engine, or ***color management module (CMM)***. The CMM translates data from one device's color space to another.

Specifications for Web Offset Publications (SWOP)®

In 1975, a review committee was formed to establish specifications to help eliminate variations in the materials being supplied to printers by prepress service bureaus. In 1976, the committee adopted its present name, Specifications for Web Offset Publications, or SWOP®.

The specifications concentrate on the use of electronic files and their impact on publication production. Electronic files are expected to meet the same high-quality standards that had been expected of the graphic arts films and proofs supplied to the printer under SWOP.

SWOP developed its specifications in accordance with many of the graphic communications standards established by such organizations as the American National Standards Institute (ANSI), the International Organization for Standardization (ISO), and the Committee for Graphic Arts Technologies Standards (CGATS).

Areas covered under the specifications included standard lighting for viewing proofs, electronic file formats, register marks, film requirements, ink measurement and control, and proofing, both on and off press. The specifications were also adopted for gravure publications.

IDEAlliance

In 1996, the IDEAlliance Committee was formed as a task force challenged with developing a series of guidelines, recommendations, and specifications that the industry could utilize as a basic reference tool for printing color. The goal was set forth to have these guidelines reflect new technologies, and improve communication and education within the graphic communications industry. Originally, the new specification called the General Requirements for Applications in Commercial Offset Lithography, or GRACol®, incorporated adjustments for ink densities, dot gain, and print contrast for ISO-defined inks and papers, while focusing on neutrality and shared color appearance.

Rather than having each printer develop profiles for each press, the GRACol profile became a standard that many printers adopted and maintained. As long as the printer held to the GRACol standards, the designer could utilize the profile to ensure color consistency.

G7™

As technologies continue to improve, the necessary profiles and standards must keep up. G7™ is a certified process from IDEAlliance that incorporates the principles of digital imaging, spectrophotometry, and ISO 2846-1 defined inks. *G* stands for grayscale, and *7* is for the subtractive colors, CMYK, and the additive colors, RGB. This process relies on the gray balance in mid-tones and inks that measure as closely as possible to CIELAB values. Designed to eliminate the subjectivity and uncertainty in color evaluation, G7 strives to keep consistency during the entire process, from proofing through the pressroom. The certification process is comprehensive and monitored closely. Printers must adhere to quality control standards to maintain their standing.

SWOP2006_Coated 3v2 and SWOP2006_Coated 5v2

Newer SWOP profiles have been developed by IDEAlliance for modern technologies rather than the legacy film-based information from US Web SWOP coated v2 that was the industry standard for so long.

Color Rendition Charts

Color changes with time and environmental conditions. Many professionals use color test charts to make objective measurements. Charts such as the X-Rite/Pantone ColorChecker are useful to the graphic communications professional, **Figure 12-3**.

The ColorChecker chart is composed of twenty-four 2″ (5 cm) square color patches made of matte paint applied to a smooth paper. The patches are selected Munsell colors that closely match real-object colors, such as dark and light human skin, foliage, and blue flowers. The additive and subtractive primary colors and a six-step neutral scale are also included.

Each patch can be identified by number; name; its CIE Yxy chromaticity coordinates; Munsell's hue, value, and chroma; an ISCC-NBS standard name (Inter-Society Color Council-National Bureau of Standards); and an assigned name, **Figure 12-4**. Subjective evaluations can be made by comparing the reproduction to the chart, or by comparing the reproductions of different systems. Comparisons should be made under the proper viewing conditions.

The Pantone® System

The Pantone® System of color specification is a widely used system in the graphic communications industry. It is a universal color language that helps ensure color consistency throughout production. The Pantone System is based on ink colors common to the printing industry.

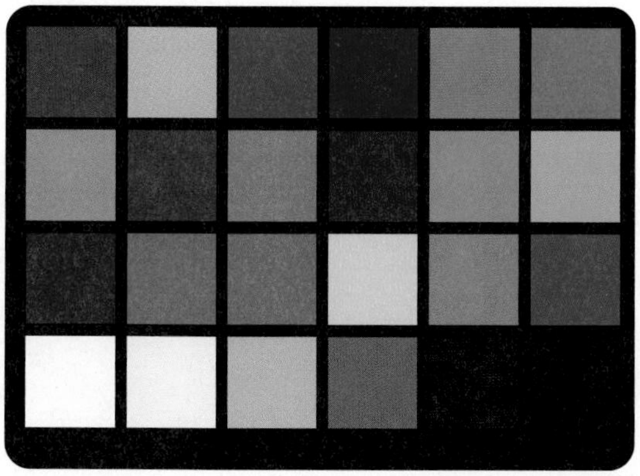

Goodheart-Willcox Publisher

Figure 12-3. The ColorChecker chart has twenty-four 2″ (5 cm) square color patches that closely match real-object colors, such as dark and light human skin, foliage, and blue flowers.

Designers, clients, and printers can communicate color selections using manuals or swatchbooks containing representations of the Pantone colors. The manuals and swatchbooks provide color simulations, names, and mixing formulas.

Pantone has developed software programs that allow the users of most computer systems to specify Pantone colors, **Figure 12-5**. The Pantone Matching Guide and the Pantone 4-Color Process Guide provide color control for solid color printing and process color printing.

The designer can select from one of more than 1000 Pantone colors in the solid color range when using the Pantone Color Formula Guide. With the Pantone 4-Color Process Guide, the user can specify any one of more than 3000 process tints. The colors are viewed with a fan guide displaying the colors in a spectrum, **Figure 12-6**.

Pantone has also developed chromaticity values for both Pantone colors and monitor phosphors. These values allow monitors to display Pantone colors that accurately represent the ink on paper. A color calibrator that compensates for monitor drift and phosphor decay is also available. The white balance can also be adjusted so the white screen on the monitor looks more like a press sheet illuminated in a printing plant.

The results of printing with Pantone colors and the accuracy of the printed Pantone guides and swatch books are relevant to and dependent on the paper choice and press options. Many printer manufacturers have been licensed to produce Pantone colors, but results vary with the resolution of the printer as well as the purity of the cyan, magenta, and yellow inks.

Using Spot and Process Colors

Defining spot and process colors correctly is essential for proper color separation. Most page composition programs provide editing features that allow the user to indicate the desired separation, **Figure 12-7**.

If spot colors are used in imported graphic files, the same colors must be defined in the page composition files. Illustration or image editing programs may name colors differently from page composition programs. Therefore, it is necessary to change the name in one file so that it matches the other exactly. If the names do not match, spot colors may separate as their

		CIE (1931)			Munsell Notation		ISCC/NBS Name
No.	**Name**	**x**	**y**	**Y**	**Hue**	**Value/ Chroma**	
1	Dark skin	.4002	.3504	10.05	3.05YR	3.69/3.20	Moderate brown
2	Light skin	.3773	.3446	35.82	2.2YR	6.47/4.10	Light reddish brown
3	Blue sky	.2470	.2514	19.33	4.3PB	4.95/5.55	Moderate blue
4	Foliage	.3372	.4220	13.29	6.65GY	4.19/4.15	Moderate olive green
5	Blue flower	.2651	.2400	24.27	9.65PB	5.47/6.70	Light violet
6	Bluish green	.2608	.3430	43.06	2.5BG	7/6	Light bluish green
7	Orange	.5060	.4070	30.05	5YR	6/11	Strong orange
8	Purplish blue	.2110	.1750	12.00	7.5PB	4/10.7	Strong purplish blue
9	Moderate red	.4533	.3058	19.77	2.5R	5/10	Moderate red
10	Purple	.2845	.2020	6.56	5P	3/7	Deep purple
11	Yellow green	.3800	.4887	44.29	5GY	7.08/9.1	Strong yellow green
12	Orange yellow	.4729	.4375	43.06	10YR	7/10.5	Strong red
13	Blue	.1866	.1285	6.11	7.5PB	2.90/12.75	Vivid purplish blue
14	Green	.3046	.4782	23.39	0.1G	5.38/9.65	Strong yellowish green
15	Red	.5385	.3129	12.00	5R	4/12	Strong orange yellow
16	Yellow	.4480	.4703	59.10	5Y	8/11.1	Vivid yellow
17	Magenta	.3635	.2325	19.77	2.5RP	5/12	Strong reddish purple
18	Cyan	.1958	.2519	19.77	5B	5/8	Strong greenish blue
19	White	.3101	.3163	90.01	N	9.5/	White
20	Neutral 8	.3101	.3163	59.10	N	8/	Light gray
21	Neutral 6.5	.3101	.3163	36.20	N	6.5/	Light-medium gray
22	Neutral 5	.3101	.3163	19.77	N	5/	Medium gray
23	Neutral 3.5	.3101	.3163	9.00	N	3.5/	Dark gray
24	Black	.3101	.3163	3.13	N	2/	Black

Goodheart-Willcox Publisher

Figure 12-4. This table provides the names and specifications of color patches in the X-Rite ColorChecker chart.

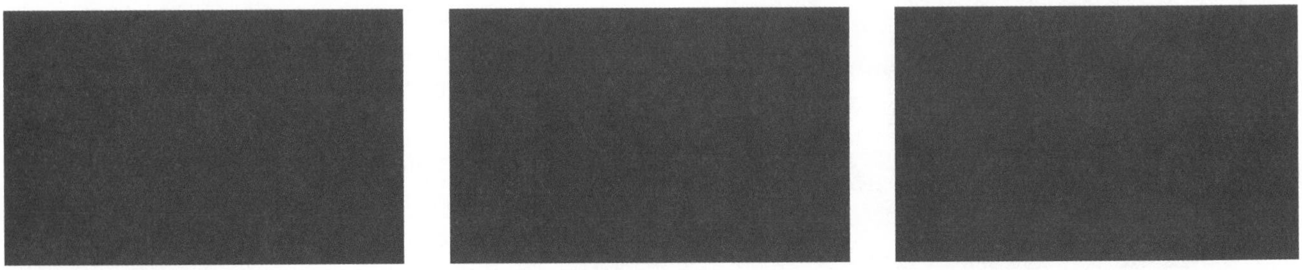

PMS285 InDesign **PMS285 Illustrator** **PMS285 Photoshop**

Goodheart-Willcox Publisher

Figure 12-5. Many page composition and illustration programs allow the user to specify Pantone colors. Each program may render a color differently on-screen, as shown, even though the printed color would be as specified.

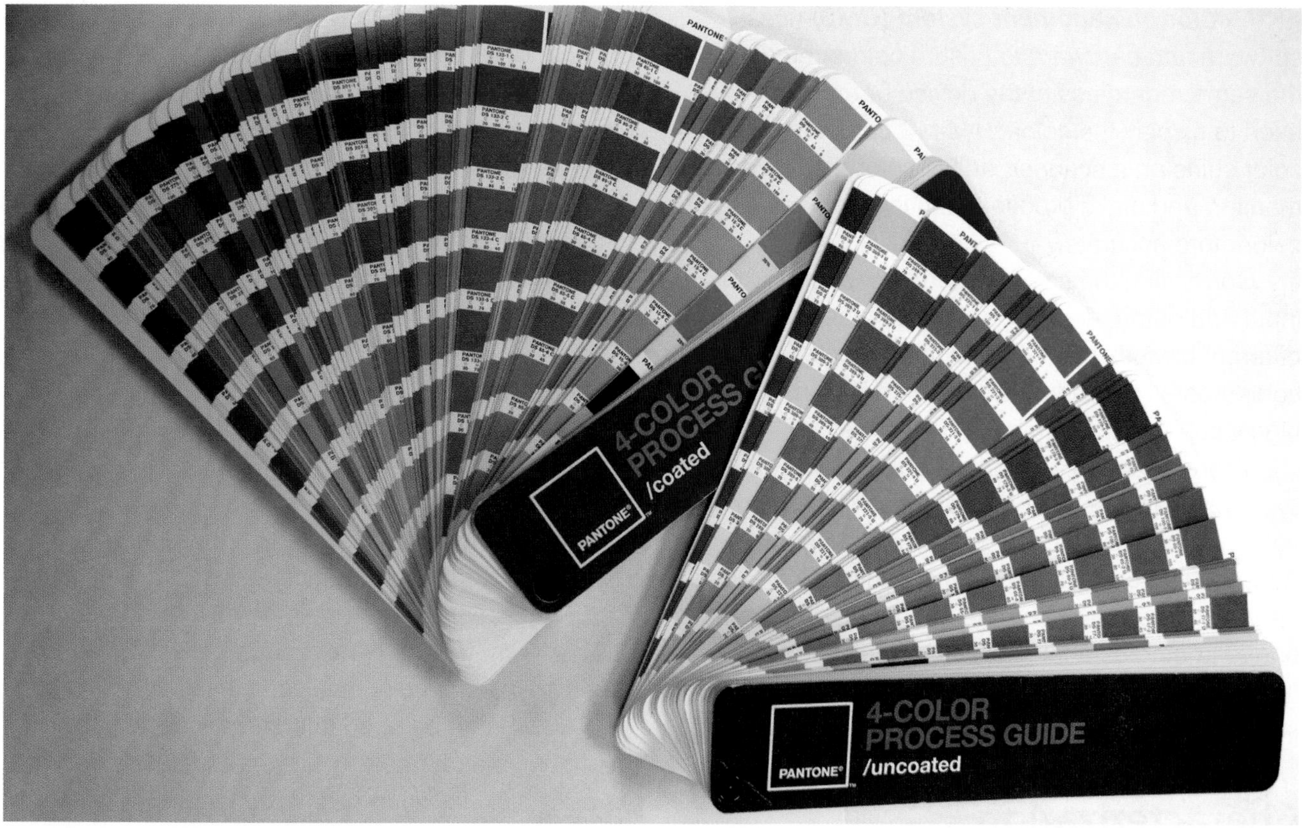

©Dana Thelander

Figure 12-6. Pantone Color System.

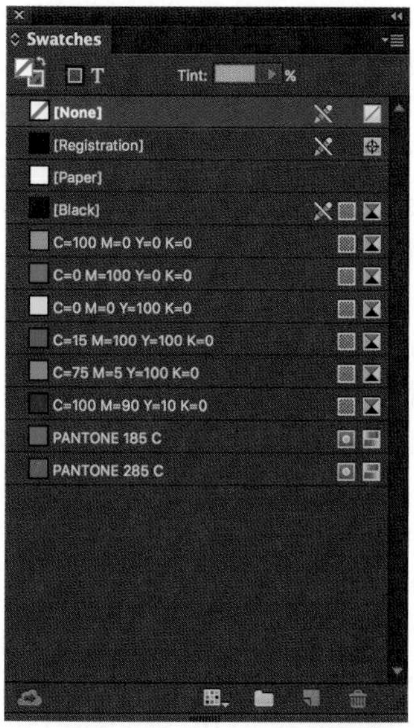

Goodheart-Willcox Publisher

Figure 12-7. Color swatches defined as CMYK and Pantone spot colors in the page layout application.

CMYK equivalents. Some page composition programs automatically add the spot color to the color palette when importing graphics using that color, but do not automatically change the name.

When building process colors for output on a press, you should keep in mind that it is better to avoid ink coverage that is too heavy. Maximum densities for the process colors vary for different types of presses, and colors should be created with these values in mind.

Color Management Systems (CMS)

Color management for electronic imaging and reproduction involves more than the management of color separations and ink composition. Electronic color reproduction requires a system of color management that will enable operators throughout the production process to maintain and produce accurate color reproduction.

A ***color management system (CMS)*** uses software and hardware to ensure colors remain the same regardless of the device or medium used to display the colors. A CMS can correct for color shifts on a scanner; adjust color display on a monitor; and make proofing, printing, and viewing of color more accurate.

Correlating the color-rendering capabilities of input and output devices is a difficult task because different devices use different technologies and color models to produce colors. In addition, color is highly subjective.

There are quite a variety of color management systems available; the type you use will depend on your operating system as well as your output needs. As with most computer systems, similar applications operate in a similar manner, and changing from one to another is a fairly simple process. Color management can be divided into three primary steps: characterization, calibration, and conversion.

Characterization

Characterization describes the color limitations, or profile, of a particular device. The profile defines how the device's specific color space relates to a device-independent color space. The profile can also be used to define the ***color gamut*** of a device.

A CMS depends on the device profiles that store the color characteristics of the devices being used. As a means of standardization, most device profiles are described with the device-independent CIELAB color space.

Some color management systems have a generic device profile describing the manufacturer's specifications for the product. However, if the device is not performing to those specifications, the profiles will not be accurate.

Calibration

One of the most important steps when setting up a CMS is calibrating the input device(s). The ***calibration*** process allows the user to understand the small color changes to an image that a particular device introduces each time the device is used. Regular calibration is necessary to bring the device in line with its intended specifications.

The calibration of any device requires the use of a standard. The device can then be calibrated by first determining its deviation from the standard. Once the deviation has been determined, the proper correction factors can be identified and applied. In graphic communications, it is necessary to calibrate everything from the scanner through the monitor, the proofing device, and the actual press and paper on which the job will run.

Monitors

It is important to understand that the colors displayed on a computer monitor are different from those printable on a press. This is obvious when you look at the superimposed color gamut of a monitor on the CIE chromaticity diagram. Refer to **Figure 12-2A**. A monitor can be calibrated, but it will never match the printed page perfectly because of the physics of color involved.

A CMS can be used to ensure your monitor provides as accurate a color representation as possible. Before the CMS can begin characterization, four calibration elements must be set on the monitor to characterize it properly. These elements are the monitor's brightness, contrast, gamma levels, and white point.

Brightness is the attribute of light-source colors by which emitted light is ordered continuously from light to dark in correlation with its intensity. ***Contrast*** is the relationship between the lightest and the darkest areas of an image. Brightness and contrast levels are set manually with the controls on your monitor.

The ***gamma levels*** of a monitor are the degrees of contrast of the screen image. Gamma levels affect the distribution of tones between highlight and shadow areas of the original. The ***white point*** is the color that results when red, green, and blue channels are operating at full intensity. The white point defines the lightest area in an image. It is a movable reference point that, when changed, causes all other areas to be adjusted accordingly.

White point temperature defines the coolness (bluish) or warmness (yellowish) of video white. In some monitors, the white point will tend toward blue; in others, toward a warmer color. The white point can be set to match the light under which proofs will be viewed to help standardize color at different stages of production.

The gamma levels and white point temperature of your monitor are set within the monitor's software and are typically adjustable from the control panel within the system software. Both the gamma level and white point of your monitor may vary according to the computer's age and operating temperature.

The next step involves the use of a colorimeter or spectrophotometer. When used for color measurement on a monitor, these devices use a rubber suction cup or other device that affixes directly to the monitor, **Figure 12-8**.

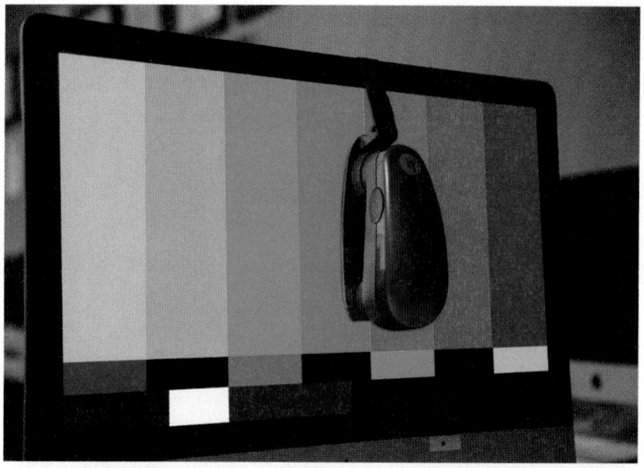

Goodheart-Willcox Publisher

Figure 12-8. A color calibration device hangs over your monitor to determine white points and color settings.

Once prompted, the CMS commands the monitor to broadcast different colors on the screen. The device measures the colors emitted and sends the data back to the CMS. The CMS creates a profile of the monitor's performance by relating the color values measured to ideal colors. If the monitor tends slightly toward blue, the CMS will know that it will need to subtract that percentage of blue from every color it processes.

It is not necessary to perform a complete measurement procedure every time the white point or gamma level setting is altered. Some color management systems can automatically adapt to a new white point and gamma level.

Along with regular monitor calibration, you should eliminate light glare from windows, skylights, and overhead lighting. This can be done by constructing a glare hood for your monitor and placing egg-crate diffusers on overhead lighting.

Monitor Limitations

It is not easy to accurately reproduce color on a computer monitor, and it is practically impossible to display the exact colors of a printed image on a monitor. This problem exists because monitors and printing devices produce color through two entirely different processes. Monitors use additive color formation, and printed images are formed by subtractive color formation.

In ***additive color formation***, the primary colors of light (red, green, blue) combine to form other colors. Since liquid crystal display (LCD) screens and light-emitting diode (LED) screens have millions of pixels, each of these pixels has an LCD or an LED. The pixels become tiny lightbulbs capable of lighting up as colors.

Some monitors are analog devices and must translate an image's binary data before being able to display it. Computers use a ***video card*** to translate and generate the corresponding electrical voltage levels needed to produce the colors on the monitor. For a monitor to display at its optimum resolution, the video card must be able to operate at the proper level.

The video card uses color ***lookup tables*** and a digital-to-analog converter to coordinate the digital and analog color information. Lookup tables store the dot sizes needed to produce given colors. The type of video card used and the accuracy of the lookup tables will determine the quality of the conversion process.

In ***subtractive color formation***, color is seen by reflected light. Each of the subtractive primary colors (cyan, magenta, and yellow) absorbs other colors from the white light and reflects only its own. In process color printing, colors are mixed visually, rather than physically. Tiny, closely spaced dots of cyan, magenta, and yellow ink absorb and reflect the different wavelengths of light to produce different colors.

Monitors vary by size and resolution quality. They should be chosen based on the tasks they are to perform. The overall size of the monitor should be considered. For example, a 15″ screen may be the most cost-effective for RIP stations, but a 17″ screen would be more suitable for a scanning station. Designers working on page composition need monitors with screens measuring at least 21″–27″, **Figure 12-9**.

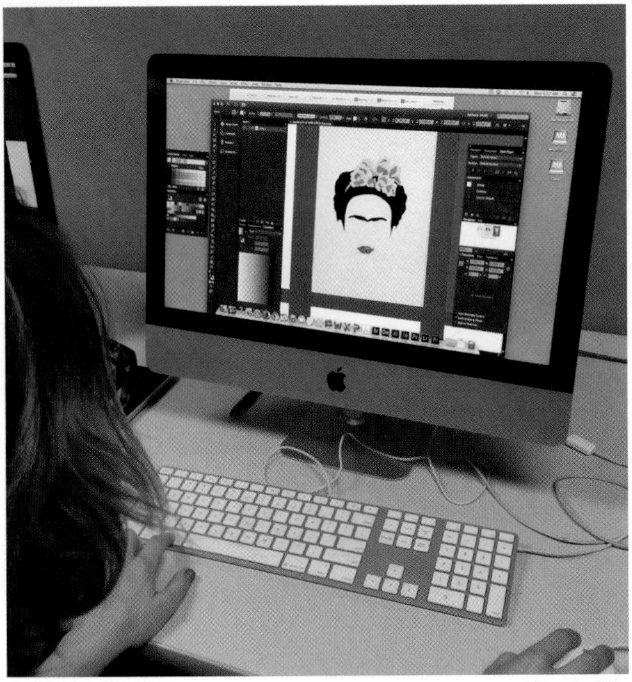

©Bernie Fritts

Figure 12-9. Graphic designers prefer larger monitors for page layout.

Other criteria to consider are dot pitch and maximum resolution. ***Dot pitch*** is the size of the pixels that make up the screen matrix. ***Maximum resolution*** is the maximum number of pixels that the screen can represent in both horizontal and vertical dimensions. Higher resolution provides a clearer image and allows the user to have more windows open on the screen at the same time.

New monitors and mobile devices are measured in pixel density, not the overall number of pixels. Smartphones, tablets, laptops, and desktop computers all calculate the required pixel density based on a typical viewing distance. The numbers change and increase with each new device offering and upgrade.

Scanners

Most digital imaging equipment provides a means of performing characterization and calibration. For example, to assist in determining the characterization of a scanner, manufacturers will include a reference image and a set of reference values for that image. The reference image contains well-defined color patches and will typically be the IT8 reflective target or pattern, or some type of similar target, **Figure 12-10**.

IT8 Reflective Target

The ***IT8 reflective target*** is a standard color reference tool used to calibrate input and output devices. It is also known as a color target. Samples from the CIELAB color space are used to create the IT8 reference targets.

These targets are used to measure the values of transmissive color being read by the input device. The IT8 is also used for input scanner calibration, but it is used to measure reflective color. Transmissive color is light conveyed through a negative or positive transparency without being absorbed or scattered. Reflective color is color that is seen by reflected light. The reference image is scanned and the measured results are related to the ideal values measured in the manufacturer's lab.

An ideal scanner would allow the user to scan images directly into an independent color space, such as CIELAB. However, most scanners are limited to the RGB and CMYK color spaces. All scanners start with an RGB signal and many allow conversions to CMYK as the scan is being made. If the CIELAB color space is not available, RGB should be used because it provides greater flexibility for the scanned image.

Some scanners convert from the RGB scan signal to CMYK on the fly, automatically creating a color-separated file from the original image. This is a less desirable approach to scanning in RGB because it makes the file device-dependent and limits the potential uses of the image. CMYK files are locked into the color gamut of the output process for which they are separated. This

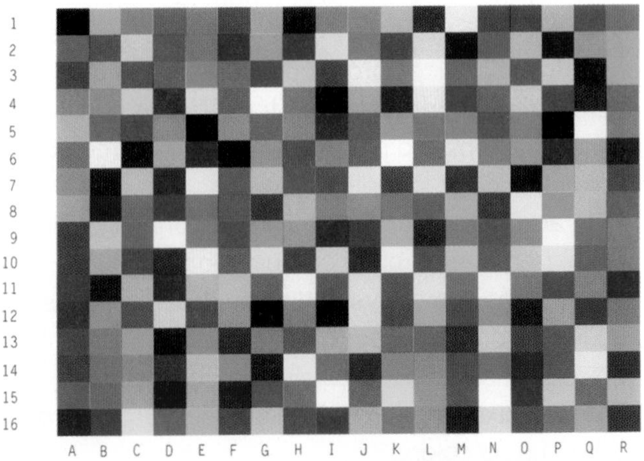

Goodheart-Willcox Publisher

Figure 12-10. IT8 targets are available for various uses and from many different manufacturers.

makes the conversion to other spaces difficult or impossible, and causes the conversion back to RGB to result in a less-than-optimum image for RGB purposes. A CMS is usually capable of making CMYK to RGB conversions, but the color quality is reduced because the original scan was made to a reduced-gamut CMYK space. Therefore, scans should be saved in the original CIELAB or RGB format to preserve the maximum amount of color, and to ensure the image can be used for a number of different purposes.

Color correction and modification are easier to perform in the CIELAB or RGB mode than in CMYK. An RGB or CIELAB image file is also about 25% smaller than the same image saved in CMYK. Some imaging programs allow the user to preview an image in CMYK and still keep the file in RGB or CIELAB color. H8.7/3 or 7/4 and EC12002 targets are often used for CMYK profiling.

Calibration Schedules

Most circumstances do not warrant daily equipment calibration. However, some situations warrant device calibration on at least a monthly (if not weekly) basis. An example would be a printer that deals with large amounts of work.

Current calibration devices come with their own tools to use for setting the calibration on electronic devices. Different methods are used to calibrate scanners, printers, monitors, and cameras, and the process depends on the specific calibration device. Ranging from hundreds to thousands of dollars, each device has specific benefits and should be selected based on the user's specific requirements.

Printers

Characterization and calibration of printing devices is also important to the accurate reproduction of color. The first step, generally, is to output a target file that is appropriate for the final printing process. This is usually provided with the calibration device. After the target file is printed, it should be measured with a color spectrophotometer, **Figure 12-11**.

After the target is evaluated, profiling software can be used to create the printer's color profile. This profile is used by the CMS to adjust color inaccuracies in the printer as files are output.

©George Deal

Figure 12-11. X-Rite/Pantone scanning table generates accurate profiles.

The time needed to establish color management standards depends on the complexity of the operation. The calibration of monitors takes just a few minutes, while the calibration of scanners can require more time. However, the procedure does not need to be repeated often because most scanners are stable performers. Printing presses and proof printers take longer because the number of color spot readings needed to build a profile is high. For larger operations, however, automated color measurement instruments are available and are capable of making hundreds of readings in seconds.

Profiles

Making sure your color settings are correct is the first step in using profiles. The default color setting for Adobe® products is a generic sRGB. If you read the description carefully for what this setting is appropriate for, you will discover it "Reflects the characteristics of the average CRT display. This standard space is endorsed by many hardware and software manufacturers, and is becoming the default color space for many scanners, low-end printers, and software applications. Ideal space for Web work, but not recommended for prepress work (because of its limited color gamut)." See **Figure 12-12**. Unless this setting has been specifically changed, it is the default used by many professionals, and is obviously not intended for high-end printing.

Color settings or profiles should be created in Adobe® Photoshop® and applied in Adobe® Bridge. Using Bridge to apply the settings makes sure that the Adobe® applications such as Illustrator®, InDesign®, and Adobe® Photoshop® are all using the same color settings. This is shown by having solid "pie." See **Figure 12-13**. A broken pie icon indicates that the settings are not consistent from application to application. Having consistent color requires the use of the same settings in all applications for a project. Applying the profile for the

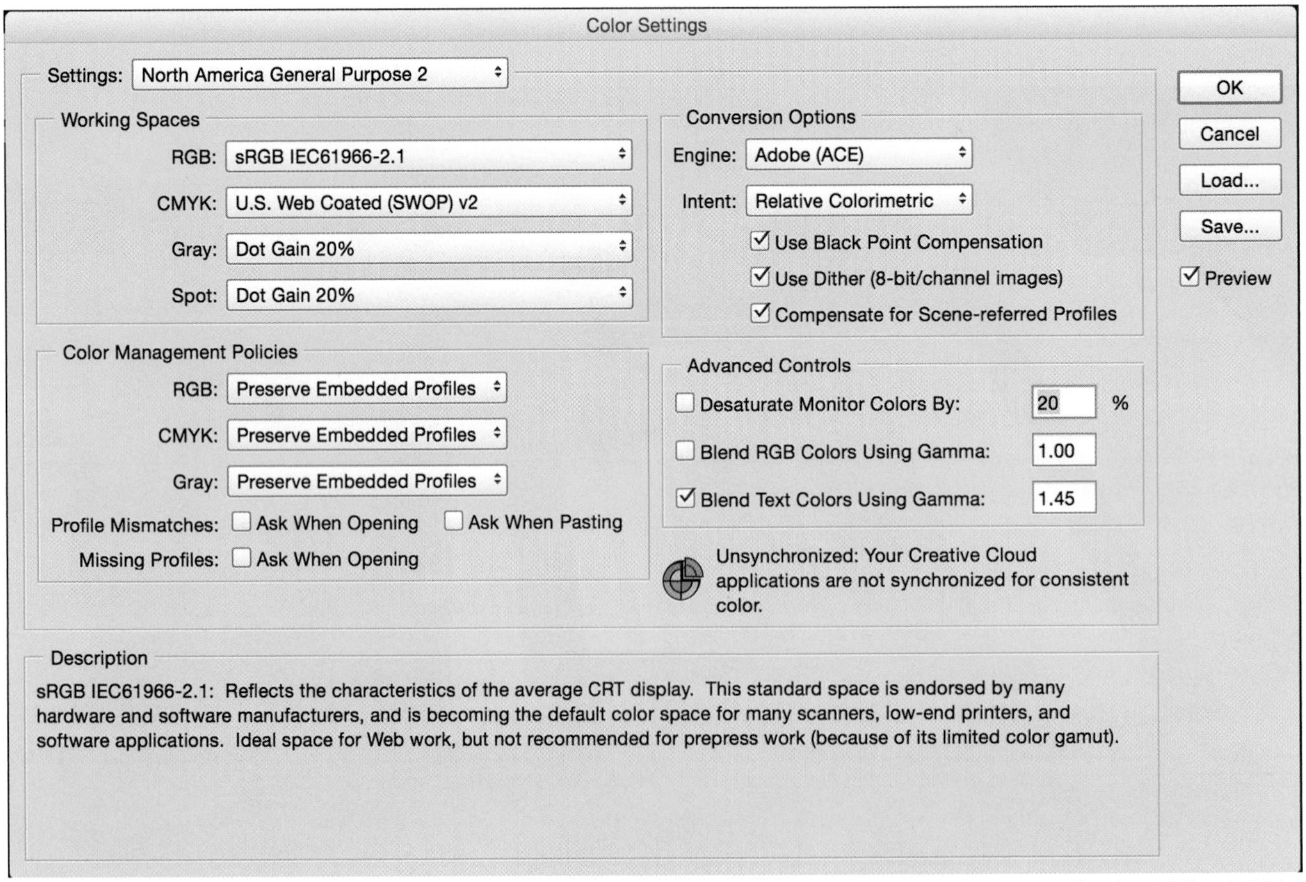

Goodheart-Willcox Publisher

Figure 12-12. Color settings profile showing the sRGB default selection.

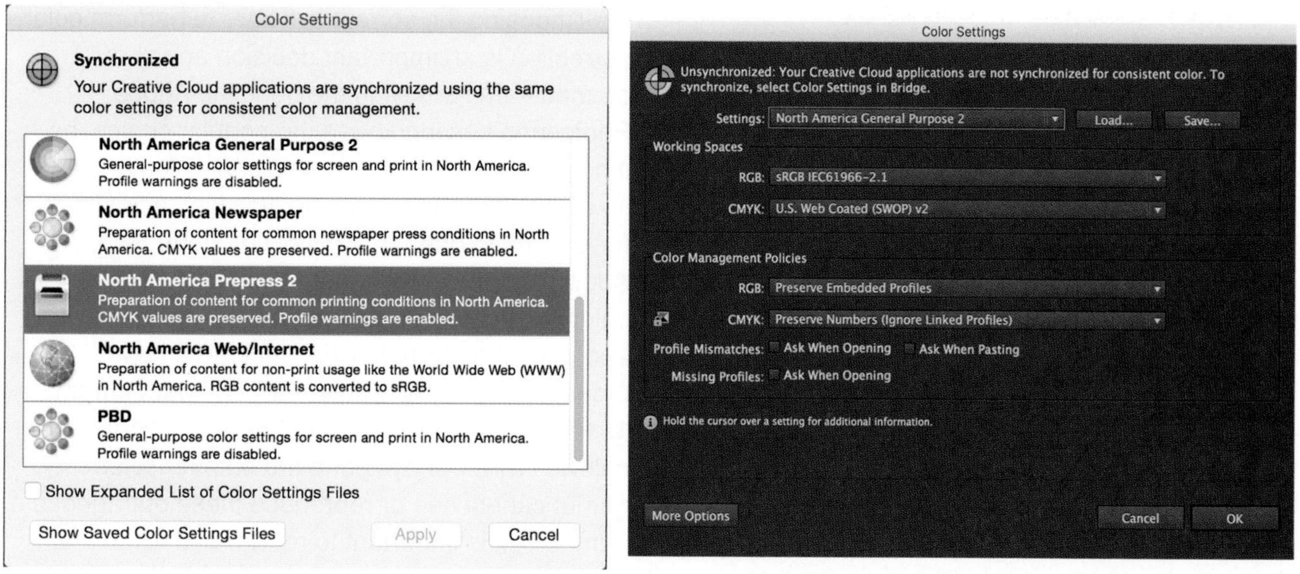

Goodheart-Willcox Publisher

Figure 12-13. Adobe applications show the difference between consistent color settings and inconsistent settings.

final output device will adjust the data for a more accurate color reproduction of what you are seeing on your calibrated monitor.

Implementing a color-managed workflow and using ICC profiles require special equipment, software, and an education process with experimentation to be successful. It is critical to make sure all persons are following the same procedures. To reach your desired goals, speak with your service provider to ensure communication is clear and the options are correct.

Color Conversion

The ***conversion*** step performs color correction between imaging devices. Color management systems are used to compensate for and select from the possible range of colors available on each device. In most imaging programs, images can be converted to, displayed in, and edited in eight image modes. These eight modes are bitmap, duotone, indexed color, grayscale, multichannel, RGB, CMYK, and CIELAB, **Figure 12-14**.

Your system and output needs determine which image mode best suits your work. For instance, if a publication is to be printed in black and white, the grayscale mode can be used to convert color images into high-quality black-and-white images.

When converting images from one mode to another, the conversion creates a permanent change to the color values in the image. For example, the four-channel CMYK space contains far fewer colors, a narrower dynamic range, and a much smaller color gamut than the three-channel RGB space. Therefore, colors must be compressed to fit into the smaller color gamut. The gamut compression gives the illusion that all color chroma, saturation, and value are present, but there is always a loss of color.

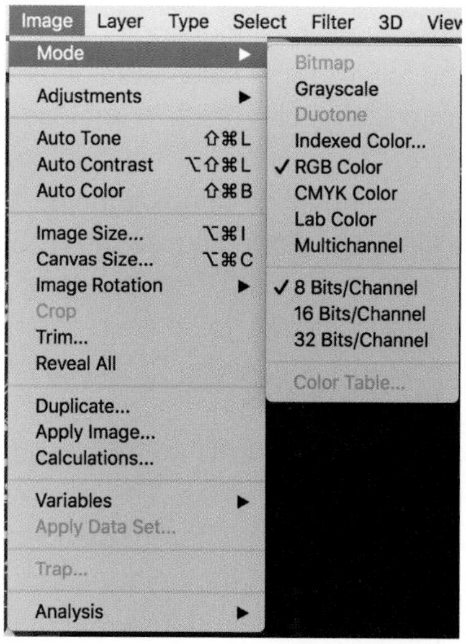

Goodheart-Willcox Publisher

Figure 12-14. This drop-down menu shows different color mode selections for image manipulation programs.

Warning

Each conversion changes data, so you should always save a backup copy of the original file.

Color Correction

One of the biggest challenges in graphic communications is getting color to reproduce the way it should or even to predict what the printed colors will look like. Color correction is complex because color functions are interconnected. For example, in an RGB system (such as a computer monitor or television set), a change in value changes chroma. For a brighter, more saturated red, the percentages of red, green, and blue must be adjusted. The percentage of red cannot simply be increased because that would increase lightness as well. To achieve a brighter red in a CMYK system, the cyan and black would need to be reduced and the yellow and magenta would need to be increased.

What used to be the job of prepress technicians is now often the responsibility of the designer. Before the advent of computers in prepress production, methods such as photographic masking and dot etching were used for color correction and manipulation.

Controversy has surrounded the topic of color correction since the beginning of the electronic age. Because many designers do not understand or utilize the full extent of color management, the conversion to CMYK can result in unpleasant surprises to the color quality. Many printers feel this conversion should be done by the designer before the file is sent for output so the results can be studied prior to proofing. Unfortunately, as soon as you convert to CMYK, you have rendered the further use of profiles useless. Profiles do not alter data that is already in CMYK mode.

Working in RGB or LAB mode allows the application of printer profiles. The same image can be printed on many different devices and maintain the integrity of the color as long as the correct profile is applied for each printer. If necessary, wait until the final minute to convert to CMYK using the correct profile, then save as a copy of your original.

Choosing the correct software to perform color correction is an important decision and should be made after studying the benefits. Adobe® Photoshop has long been the popular choice, as it has become more and more sophisticated in its capabilities. Two other applications actually have more to offer in terms of color correction. Adobe® products Lightroom® and Bridge allow color correction in a nondestructive environment and have the ability to work in camera Raw mode, increasing the potential color gamut from 16.8 million colors of the jpg format to 281 trillion colors. While our eyes and the output device gamut cannot see or reproduce these outrageous numbers, it is important to realize that when the software makes color choices, the more choices you have to choose from, the better the end results.

Shadow Clarity

In theory, by combining equal parts of cyan, magenta, and yellow, you can produce black. However, due to impurities present in all printing inks, a mix of these colors actually yields a muddy brown. To compensate, some cyan, magenta, and yellow is removed from areas where the three colors overlap, and black is added. Printing black ink over the three primaries improves and enhances shadow details of the reproduction.

The effect of having full colors with the primaries can be achieved in a number of ways, but prepress operators typically use undercolor removal, gray component replacement, and undercolor addition.

Undercolor Removal (UCR)

Undercolor removal (UCR) is a process of color correction typically associated with high-speed web printing. UCR can be accomplished in an image editing program, **Figure 12-15**.

The shadow details of a four-color separation will typically be represented as the three process colors overprinted with black. When printing with high-speed presses, it is not desirable to overlap layers of ink that are too heavy. Problems with drying and ink trapping can occur with saturated ink layers.

The theory of UCR is to reduce the amount of magenta, yellow, and cyan in shadows and neutral areas of an image, and replace them with an

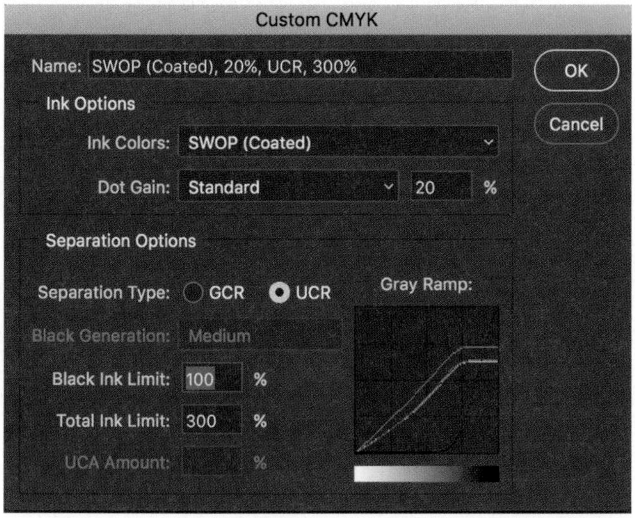

Goodheart-Willcox Publisher

Figure 12-15. Undercolor removal settings are used to replace overlapping values of cyan, magenta, and yellow to make up a dark neutral with one color—black.

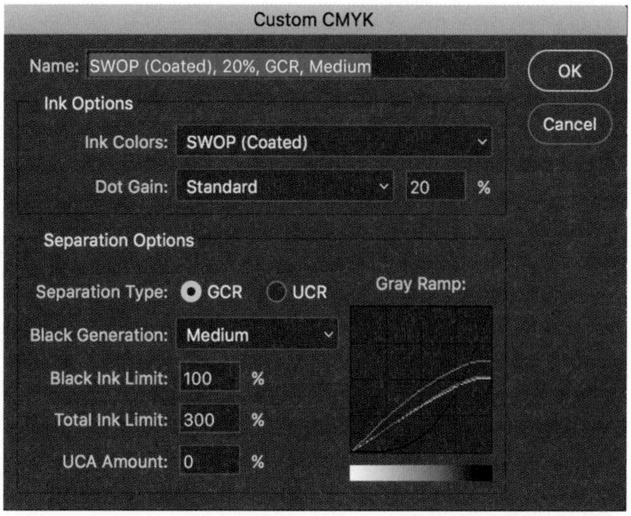

Goodheart-Willcox Publisher

Figure 12-16. Gray component replacement settings replace common amounts of cyan, magenta, and yellow values throughout the document with black.

appropriate amount of black. This is accomplished by reducing the shadow dot structure in the overlapping areas of the yellow, magenta, and cyan inks. UCR produces good shadow densities by using the black printer to its fullest capacity.

Gray Component Replacement (GCR)

Gray component replacement (GCR) is an electronic technique used to substitute black ink for calculated amounts of cyan, magenta, and yellow inks, **Figure 12-16**. Substitutions occur mainly in the neutral tones and in gray components of desaturated colors. When applying GCR, the black printer is used to replace a proportionate amount of cyan, magenta, and yellow anywhere the three colors overlap.

GCR separations tend to reproduce dark, saturated colors better than UCR separations. GCR separations also maintain better gray balance on press. Other advantages include better detail and contrast within the reproduction, reduced ink costs, reduction of ink offset (unwanted ink transferring to adjoining sheet of paper), and reduced drying time.

Many scanner and electronic prepress equipment manufacturers have developed specific software packages for GCR. The type of separation you should use will depend on the substrate and requirements of the printer.

Undercolor Addition (UCA)

Undercolor addition (UCA) is the inverse function of undercolor removal. UCA is used to add cyan, magenta, and yellow after removing some of the black in the shadow areas. Undercolor addition is applied with gray component replacement because 100% GCR does not produce a good saturated black in print.

UCA helps produce rich, dark shadows in areas that might appear flat if they were printed with only black ink. The color added to the shadow or black areas will determine the warmth or coldness of the black.

The amount of undercolor addition is set with the same control used for GCR. Increasing the UCA amount increases the amount of cyan, magenta, or yellow added to the shadow areas. Check with your service bureau or printer for the appropriate values.

Trapping

When colors printed from separate plates border one another, the slightest amount of misregistration can cause gaps between printed objects (graphics and type). Printers use a method called ***trapping*** to create a small area of overlap between colors to compensate for potential gaps. Trapping can be defined as how well one color overlaps another without leaving a white space between the two or generating a third color.

When responsibilities for color separation shifted from trade shops to electronic page-production artists, trapping needed to be incorporated into the electronic page assembly process, **Figure 12-17**. Trapping must be considered any time two colors meet. Methods used to set traps include spread, choke, and automatic.

A ***spread trap*** is created by spreading the foreground over the background color, **Figure 12-18**. Spread traps are used when a lighter object knocks out of a darker background. Illustration programs that are limited to one type of trapping usually use spread traps.

Choke traps are performed by spreading the background under the foreground object. The object may appear to be squeezed or reduced in size.

Automatic traps, sometimes called process bridges, are set by building art with common colors. As long as a ***knockout*** is not specified and common colors are used, the shared component compensates for the space between the objects. For example, if two overlapping objects contain cyan as part of their CMYK values, any gap between them is covered by the cyan content of the object underneath. In **Figure 12-19**, no background shows through because both the letter and the background contain a percentage of cyan.

Some illustration programs allow the user to perform trapping automatically by applying a trap filter. This type of trapping is intended for simple objects where parts can be selected and trapped individually. It does not work with gradients or patterns, however. Fortunately, most illustration programs provide an alternative trapping method that allows more complex work to be performed.

It is best to scale graphics to their final size before adding a trap. Otherwise, the amount of trapping will increase or decrease if you scale the object. For example, if you create a graphic that has a 0.5-point trap and scale it four times its original size, the result will be a 2.0-point trap for the enlarged graphic. Trapped files should also be imported into the page composition program at the same size. If they are scaled after they are imported, the traps will also be scaled and will need to be recreated.

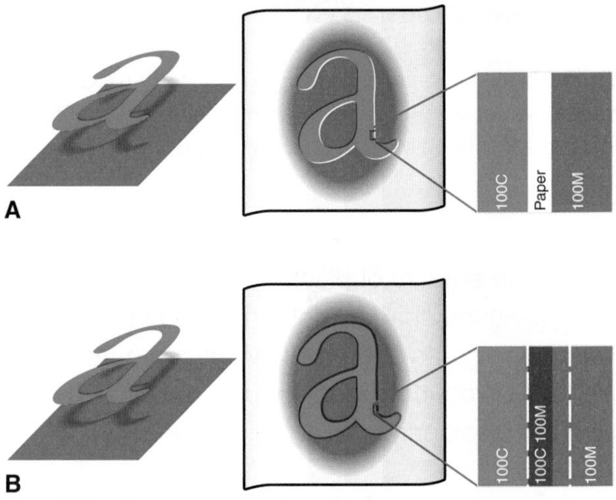

Goodheart-Willcox Publisher

Figure 12-18. Spread trap. A—If no allowance is made for misregistration (i.e., trapping), the paper will show through as white lines around the image. B—When trapping with uncommon colors, the stroke should be the same color as the object being trapped. Half the width will fall outside the edge and blend with the other color.

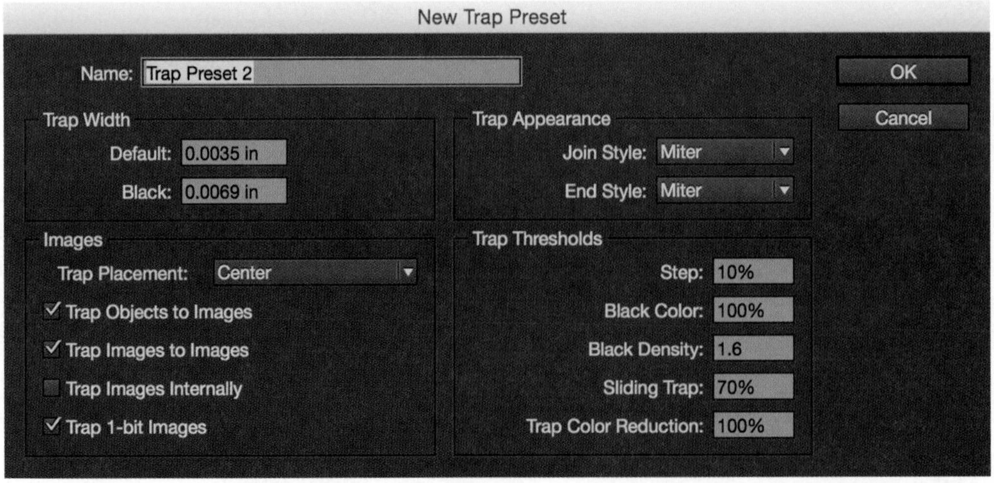

Goodheart-Willcox Publisher

Figure 12-17. Standard preset for trapping in page layout software.

Trapping Type

There are a variety of factors that must be considered when setting traps. They include everything from the type of paper used to pressroom conditions. These variables are extremely important when applying traps to type because spreading or choking may cause character distortion.

Applying process colors to type at small point sizes should be avoided because any amount of misregistration can make the text difficult to read. Trapping type at small point sizes can also result in hard-to-read copy. However, if it is necessary to trap type, always remember that smaller type requires a smaller trap to prevent distortion, **Figure 12-20**.

Goodheart-Willcox Publisher

Figure 12-19. A process bridge is created when two items share a common process color, so trapping is not necessary.

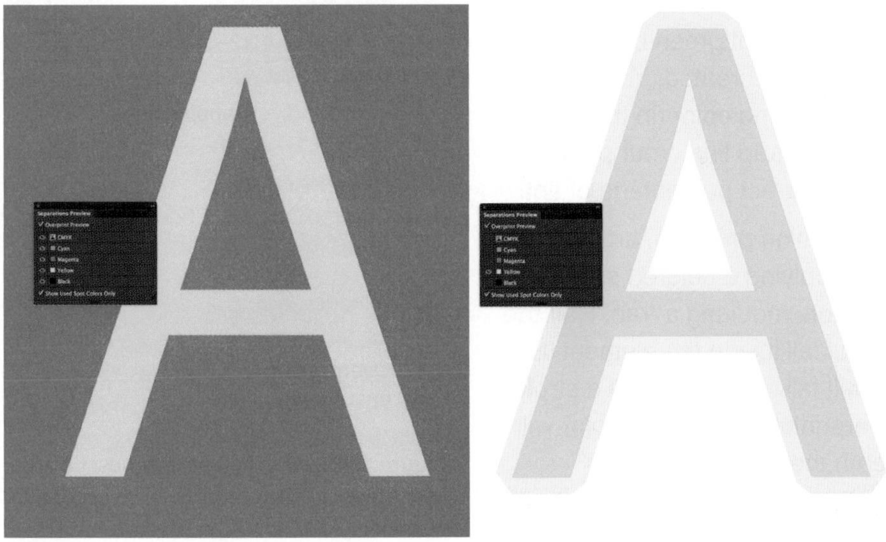

Goodheart-Willcox Publisher

Figure 12-20. As the size of the trap is increased, the letter elements thicken and the character loses some of its integrity. The light yellow shows the trap.

Text can also be trapped by first converting it to outlines and then placing a copy behind the original. A trap could then be created as with any other graphic object. However, when type is converted to outlines, ***hinting*** is lost. Hinting optimizes how type prints at small point sizes on printers with a resolution of 600 dpi or lower. Text can no longer be edited when converted to outlines because it becomes a graphic instead of type. You should contact your printer for recommendations.

Special Considerations

Trapping tools and capabilities vary with each illustration program, so you should refer to the user's guide for detailed instructions. However, there are several points that should be considered when creating traps, regardless of the program being used.

- In general, the lighter color is spread into the darker color. If there is no obvious lighter or darker color, then content is considered when determining the trap. For example, if text is one of the elements, it probably would not be spread over the background. However, it is okay to spread type over the background if the type is a very light color against a dark background. The dark background will hold the character shapes.
- When trapping two light-colored objects, the trap line may show through the darker of the two colors, resulting in an unsightly dark border. For example, if you trap a light blue object into a light yellow object, a bright green border is visible where the trap is created. You can specify a tint of the trapping color (in this case, yellow) to downplay the trap line. Your printer can recommend the correct percentage of tint.
- When using an illustration program, artwork can be trapped by applying a colored ***stroke*** or outline to the elements requiring a trap. Half the width of a stroke will fall inside the element it outlines and half will fall outside. When a stroke is specified to overprint, the adjoining color will be trapped beneath the outside half.
- Color gradations are difficult to trap because the best trap would be a gradation of colors. When trapping a gradation to a solid color, a common color between the background and gradation should be selected. After a common color has been selected, a trap can be created.
- To trap lines electronically into a background of a different color, create two lines, one directly on top of the other, **Figure 12-21A**. The first line should be wide enough to create a trap.
- The need for trapping is eliminated if ***overprinting*** of colors is specified, **Figure 12-21B** and **Figure 12-21C**.
- Trapping is intended to correct misalignment of solid tints in CMYK images and should not be created for continuous-tone images. Excessive trapping may generate a keyline effect or even crosshair lines in C, M, and Y plates. These problems may not be visible in the on-screen composite image and might show up only when output to film or plates.
- If photos are to be printed on a color background, they should always be choked by the surrounding background color.

Trapping can be an extremely complex process. Besides layout considerations, factors such as the type of paper, printing process, pressroom conditions, and expected ***dot gain***

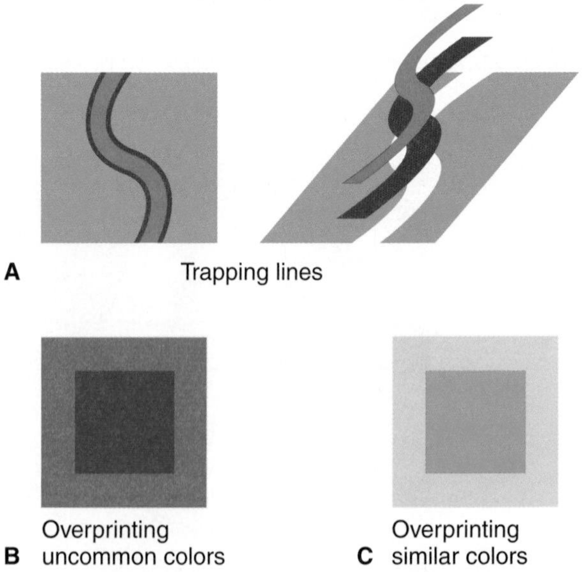

Goodheart-Willcox Publisher

Figure 12-21. A—The trap line must be wider than the original line in order to overprint it. B—The overprinted image adds its color completely to the background. C—The background color contains 30% cyan, and the image has 8% cyan. The largest percentage of color is used for the overprint, so the overprinting area contains 30% cyan instead of 38%.

must be considered. Many printers do not want the designer to perform the trapping on the document. In fact, they will often strip out the trap built into the document and use their own preflight and ripping software that automatically does a more sophisticated and accurate trapping. Ask your service provider which way they prefer to receive the file.

Screening

Proper screening is vital to producing a halftone of high quality for reproduction. This gives the full tonal range of pictorial materials. A screening pattern is the strategic placement of dots to create the illusion of a continuous-tone image. Conventional printing uses variable-sized dots in fixed spacing to reproduce photos, **Figure 12-22**.

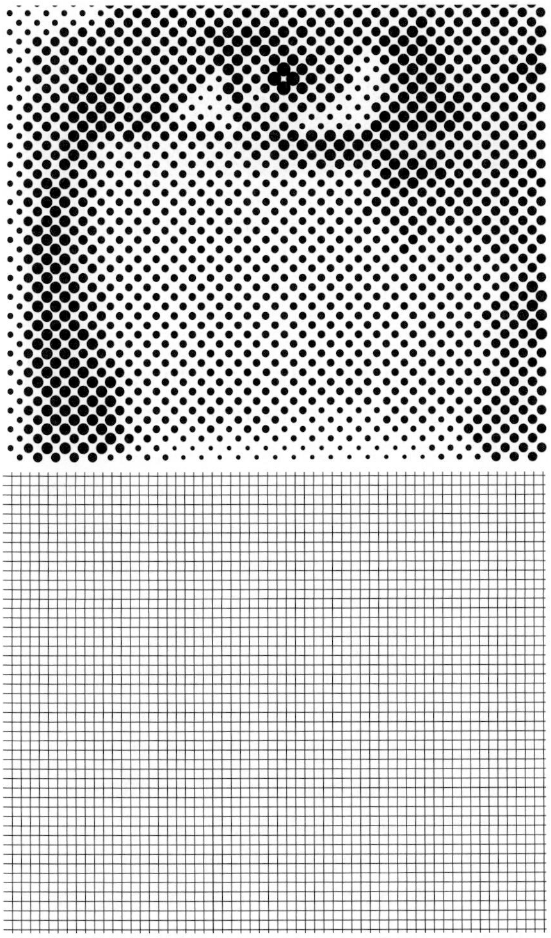

Goodheart-Willcox Publisher

Figure 12-22. Closeup to show the the halftone dots and the invisible grid or line screen used to produce them.

Digital printing uses smaller, fixed-size dots to create photorealistic images.

Screening options allow the user to do such things as eliminate moiré patterns while holding rosettes across the page, and apply higher screen frequencies at lower resolutions. Features often include the ability to shift angles to accommodate gravure, screen printing and flexography, and to render dots in a variety of shapes. The printers know which methods and choices work best on their presses, so let them determine which selections to make.

Academic Link

Printer's Math

Basic math skills are essential in performing daily tasks in a print shop. Calculating the amount of paper needed for a job, the correct proportions for ink and solution mixtures, and the per-item cost of supplies are necessary for the efficient and successful operation of a printing business. The following are examples of how math is regularly applied in the print production process. Use your knowledge of basic math operations to solve each of these problems.

1. The finished pages of a printed book are 7.5″ wide. There is a 1/2″ margin around the type on both the left and the right side of each page. Additionally, the customer wants the pages to be perforated 1/4″ from the left edge. What is the total margin on the left side of the page? How much room is left on the page for printed material?
2. One hundred sheets of cover stock measures 1.25″. How many sheets of cover stock are in a stack that is 34.75″ high?
3. A skid of 100 lb of coated stock contains 7,750 sheets of paper and costs $2,400. What is the per-sheet cost of the paper?
4. One hundred-fifteen lb of black ink is needed to stock the supply shelves of the shop. The ink is available in 5-lb cans. How many cans need to be ordered?
5. How many full-sized sheets of 23″ × 35″ paper must be ordered to print a job that involves 1,200 pieces of 8.5″ × 11″?

Spot Screening

Spot screening is a screening method in which dots are laid in a grid pattern based on the color tone. The spacing between the dot centers is held constant, but the dot size is varied to produce different shades or tones. Because the grids for different colors are offset at angles, a distinctive rosette pattern is created in the image. Stochastic screening attempts to overcome the rosette pattern that frequently mars images created with spot screening.

Stochastic Screening

Stochastic screening is a halftoning method that creates the illusion of tones by varying the number of micro-sized dots in a small area. Unlike conventional halftones, the spots are not positioned in a grid-like pattern. The placement of each spot is determined as a result of a complex algorithm that evaluates and distributes spots under a fixed set of parameters. In stochastic screening, the spacing of dots varies, **Figure 12-23**. Stochastic screening is also referred to as frequency modulation (FM) dots or FM screening.

Stochastic screens can provide greater definition and detail in irregular shapes and expand the range of tones that can be reproduced through increased ink densities and improved color saturation. The disadvantage of stochastic screens is that tints or solid-color areas can sometimes appear grainy because the tiny dots are not really replaced in a random pattern. The random pattern helps with moiré issues that are induced by screen angles and their overlap.

To correct this problem and maintain the image's photographic attributes, most raster image processors (RIPs) provide additional screening options. Multiple screening options allow the prepress operator to select the best screening method for the type of image used. For best results, photos, line art, and vector graphics may each require different screening methods.

Goodheart-Willcox Publisher

Figure 12-23. Closeup to show the random nature of stochastic screening.

Error-Diffusion Screening

Error-diffusion screening places dots more randomly than stochastic screening. It uses data from surrounding cells to determine dot placement. The difference between the color tone requested and that printed for a cell is fed through a filter and carried to other cells as they are processed, diffusing the error across surrounding cells. Although this reduces graininess in solid areas, it can also cause the loss of image sharpness. However, error diffusion can create smoother transitions of colors or tones for certain types of images and result in better printed output. The type of screening method used will depend on the output device and the intended use of the image.

When RIPs were first introduced, they were designed for use with 200-dpi electrostatic printers. Variations of stochastic and error-diffusion screening between different manufacturers had an obvious impact on the visual appearance of printed images. RIP software developers have since developed screening patterns to the point that it is almost impossible to detect the difference.

Screening patterns can affect file processing speed. If one pattern adds more dots for image sharpness, the file size will be larger and take longer to process. On the other hand, to process blends more quickly, the screening pattern on some RIPs will eliminate the top 5% and bottom 5% of the data.

Preflighting

During the design process, many colors may be defined, tested, and rejected. Rejected colors may remain in the files and should be removed from the color palette to speed printing and to ensure they are not accidentally used.

Ideally, the color palette in a page composition program would display *only* the colors used in the job. Unfortunately, this is not usually the case and unused colors will often be left in a layout. If an unused color is present, a ***gamut alarm*** will appear when preflighting the files and you will need to find and delete the color. If you cannot delete a color, it is probably an extra spot color from an imported graphic file. You will have to go back to the imaging program to delete the stray color. If a stray color is not deleted, it will increase the chance that an incorrect color will be applied to the text or to a graphic.

Special colors, such as metallics or fluorescents, are not always available in an application's color palette. When using a special color, it should be defined as a spot color and given a unique name. You should contact your printer for detailed instructions.

Proofing

Depending on the complexity of a project and the arrangement you have with the printer, you will review a number of proofs before the job goes to press. Proofs are generated for performing corrections (text, layout, and color), and to provide a means for confirming a contract. Besides confirming that layout, fonts, and other design elements were not lost or deformed before reaching the output stage, proofs should be generated for checking color accuracy and resolution, **Figure 12-24.**

Proofs are usually made directly from digital files. Cost variations will often determine what type of proofs you will request at different stages of prepress production. ***Soft proofs*** are the electronic files that represent the final pages.

Timof/Shutterstock.com

Figure 12-24. Many proofs are produced for a printed job to ensure the quality and accuracy of the type, images, color, and pagination.

Digital Proofing

Press proofs may still be one of the best verification proofs, but the digital proof is fast becoming the standard. ***Digital proofs*** are generated by outputting files on a high-resolution, high-quality printer, **Figure 12-25**. Technological advancements have allowed many types of digital output devices to meet industry color standards for prepress proofing.

Color management systems can be used to compensate for all factors affecting the printing process. A quality CMS will compensate for such factors as ink hues, color contamination, press gains and losses, plate gains and losses, and the paper's color and absorptivity.

Depending on the system's capabilities, digital proofs can simulate results from any type of printing press. Most dye-sublimation printers and ink-jet printers are able to simulate both process inks and spot colors. These machines produce dotless color images that closely simulate the press sheet, at a reasonable cost.

Many digital proofing systems can also simulate dot patterns and the dot gain expected on final output. This is especially useful when customers insist on seeing the halftone dots or screen pattern before accepting the proof as a true indication of color and quality.

Some electrostatic printers and high-quality printer/copiers can also simulate the printing inks of a press. They are commonly used for proof production, as well as short-run impressions of finished color printing. The same process used to calibrate printers is used for calibrating proofing devices.

Digital Blueline Proofs

Computer-to-plate workflows originally lacked a proof for checking final imposition before output to the platesetter. Several manufacturers have designed and produced two-sided signature proofs that are referred to as ***digital blueline proofs***.

The digital blueline can be defined as a two-sided digital position proof for eight-page impositions (sixteen-page signatures). These proofs are usually printed on wide-format ink-jet proofers. In some proofers, after imaging on one side of the ink-jet media, the paper is flipped and repositioned. Other systems print both sides at once. Most systems allow proofs

©George Deal

Figure 12-25. High-end proofer for printing customer proofs for approval.

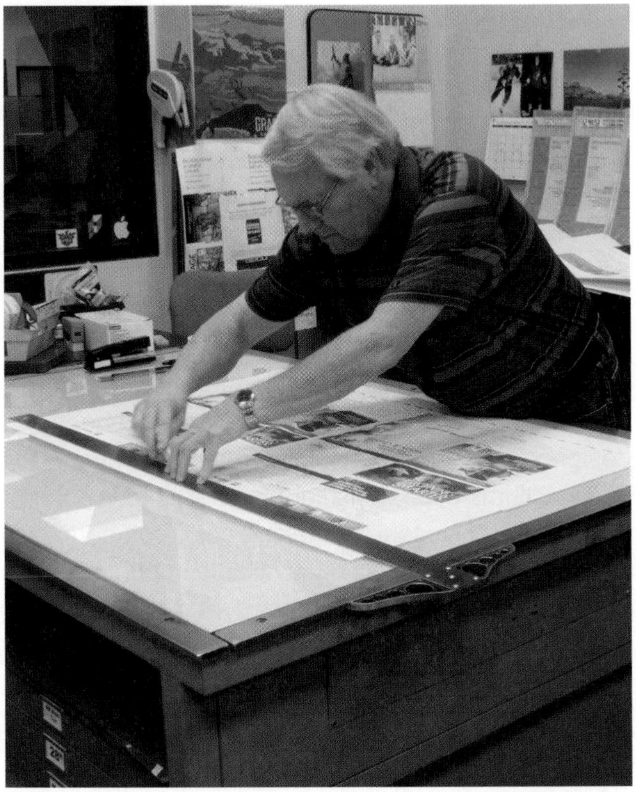

©George Deal

Figure 12-26. Final proofs are cut down and booked into their final configuration to show an accurate representation of the final product.

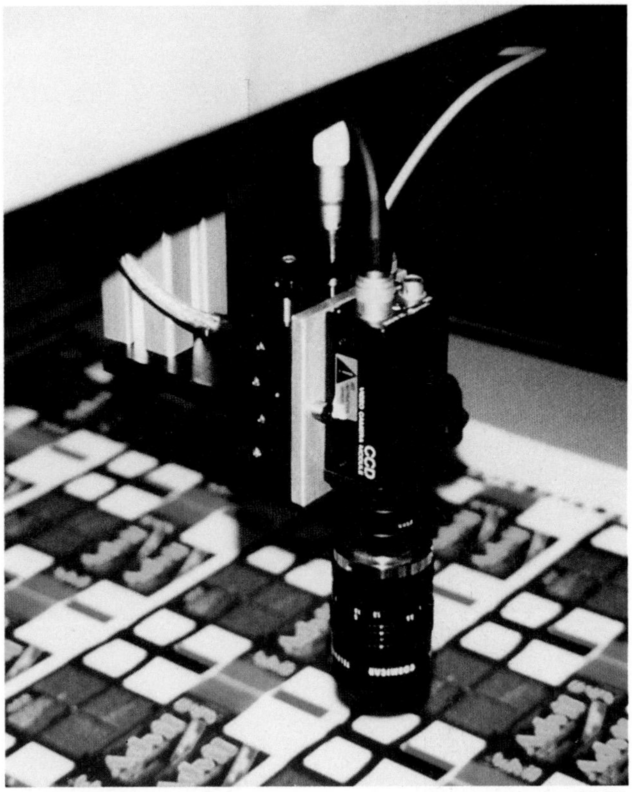

GSMA

Figure 12-27. Automatic proofreading systems are able to complete their proofreading process in as little as three percent of the time required for traditional proofreading.

to be output in full color or in a single color to check basic layout and imposition. It is unlikely that this type of digital proof will eliminate the need for contract color digital proofs, **Figure 12-26**.

Automatic Proofreading Systems

Automatic systems can be used for proofreading plates, film, carton stock, stuffer sheets, label stock, textbooks, and a variety of other printed material. Some systems are capable of detecting details as fine as missing or partially missing periods in 3-point type, **Figure 12-27**. Sensors are mounted at various press stations to identify and warn the operator of defects such as streaking, stains, and under- or over-inking.

A database of pixels that make up the text and graphics of each sheet is generated by the system. During the inspection process, charge-coupled devices (CCDs) are used to inspect printed sheets by searching for missing or unwanted pixels. Therefore, any combination of different languages, symbols, and graphics can be accurately proofread at the same speed as simple text. The operator can call up the file of inspected images that is made during proofreading and magnify any highlighted discrepancies.

Color Control Bars

A ***color control bar*** is a strip of colors printed outside the trim area of a press sheet. It is used to monitor printing variables such as trapping, ink density, dot gain, and print contrast. It usually consists of overprints of two- and three-color solids and tints; solid and tint blocks of cyan, magenta, yellow, and black; and additional aids such as resolution targets and dot gain scales, **Figure 12-28**. Color control bars may also be referred to as color bars, color control strips, or proofing bars. Color control bars are reliable and convenient quality-control devices that pressmen use to regulate the consistency and accuracy of color.

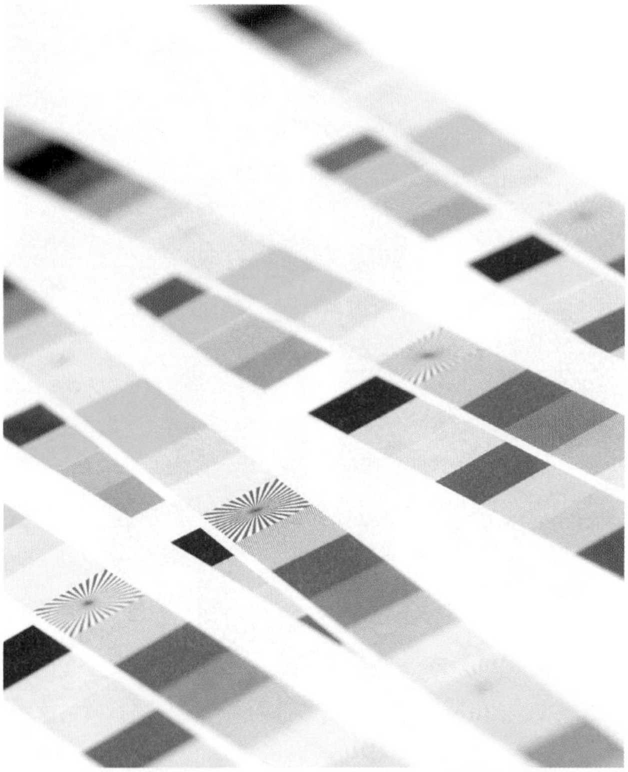

Today ago kids/Shutterstock.com

Figure 12-28. Color control bars are added to every plate for quality control at the press.

Calibration and Characterization

Just as the calibration of scanners and monitors is vital to accurate color reproduction, proper characterization and calibration of proofing devices is vital to the production of accurate digital proofs. Before outputting a job to any type of digital output device, an output profile should be created. The output profile can be used to correct color inaccuracies in the printer, or it can be combined with a printing press profile to simulate the effect of the press on the proof printer.

The first step is to create a target file that is appropriate to the printing process. A four-color file is made for a printing press. The target file is printed and then measured with a color spectrophotometer.

After the target is printed and evaluated, the profiling software creates a profile that describes the color capabilities of the device. This profile then becomes the output profile, which adjusts the color of the file as it is output. Using this output file, the proofing system can output proofs that will accurately depict what the job will look like when printed on the printing press.

Viewing Variables

There are many variables to consider when viewing or judging color. In addition to inherent human variables (color blindness, vision fatigue, aging), viewing conditions must also be considered.

Accurate color comparison is almost impossible unless items are viewed under exactly the same viewing conditions. For this reason, the graphic communications industry has established an illumination standard. Viewing booths have been designed with a neutral color environment and 5000 K illumination. This light temperature is color-balanced and is ideal for making color comparisons. Viewing booths are usually available in printers. Unfortunately, many customers do not have standardized viewing areas and cannot view proofs under the same lighting conditions as printers.

Ink Colors

Color reproduction systems should be engineered from the pressroom back to the point of creation. One of the first steps in the engineering of a color reproduction system is the analysis of process inks.

Process inks differ from one ink manufacturer to another. To evaluate the set of inks used in a specific printing facility, a set of color bars is printed under normal printing conditions. Most printers will furnish test patterns for comparison purposes.

Ink film density is read with a reflection densitometer. The densities recorded can be used to determine the working characteristics of a set of process inks. The four factors that best describe the working characteristics or impurities of the inks are strength, hue error, grayness, and efficiency.

Ink strength is important because it will identify the range and depth of colors that can be produced from a set of inks. This factor can be determined by visually comparing the density readings, and selecting the highest reading for the yellow, magenta, and cyan inks.

Ink hue error determines the percentage of the reflection of colored light from a specific color of ink. A hue is determined by the eye in terms of cone stimulation to colors of light. For example, the color or hue of magenta ink should absorb and prevent green light from reflecting off the paper surface, and allow all of the blue and red light to reflect. The ink impurities in the magenta ink pigmentation that distort this normal reflection ratio can be measured as a percentage of hue error.

The grayness factor of a set of process inks identifies the purity of the process colors. A color is considered grayed when it reflects less light of its predominant color than the white sheet of paper on which it is printed. For example, cyan should reflect 100% blue and green light, but is considered grayed in percentage because it reflects less blue than the white paper.

Ink efficiency is similar to hue error, but instead of measuring the percentage of error in the reflection of light, a positive percentage is expressed. The ability of the ink's color to filter out its complementary additive color and reflect the other two-thirds of the spectrum is the measurement of its efficiency. The higher the percentage of an ink's efficiency, the greater the gamut of possible colors, and the less color correction will be required. For additional information on inks and their formulation, see Chapter 16, *Ink*.

Summary

- Many computer, ink, and paper manufacturers have adopted the CIE system of color specification.
- Grayscale is a means of showing the shades of gray that represent the image.
- A color management system (CMS) uses software and hardware to ensure colors remain the same regardless of the device or medium used to display the colors.
- Undercolor removal (UCR) color correction is typically associated with high-speed web printing. Gray component replacement (GCR) is used to substitute black ink for calculated amounts of cyan, magenta, and yellow inks.
- Trapping is how well one color overlaps another without leaving a white space between the two or generating a third color if there is any misregistration on press.
- Screening options include spot screening, stochastic screening, and error-diffusion screening.
- If an unused color is present when preflighting files, a gamut alarm will appear.
- Proofs are usually made directly from digital files. Soft proofing is the proofing of images on-screen.
- Ink strength identifies the range and depth of colors that can be produced from a set of inks.

Review Questions

Answer the following questions using the information in this chapter.

1. What is the primary purpose of color management in the graphic communications industry?
2. Describe how the CIELAB color space is used to perform color correction.
3. What are the four rendering intents?
4. Why shouldn't color conversions be applied more than once to an image?
5. What areas of graphic communications are covered under SWOP?
6. What does G7 stand for, and what is it?
7. What are the three primary steps of color management?
8. Before a color management system can begin characterization, what four calibration elements must be set on the monitor?
9. The _____ is a standard color reference tool used to calibrate scanners and printers.
10. Why does scanning an image into a CMYK color space limit its potential uses?

11. *True or False?* With gamut compression, there is always a loss of color.
12. _____ replaces measured amounts of magenta, yellow, and cyan in shadows and neutral areas of an image with black.
    A. GCR
    B. UCR
    C. UCA
    D. RGB
13. When must *trapping* be considered?
14. Graphics should be scaled _____ (after/before) adding a trap.
15. What is the disadvantage of the stochastic screening method?
16. What makes a gamut alarm appear during the preflighting process?
17. What is a *digital blueline*?
18. Color control bars are used to monitor _____.
    A. dot gain
    B. print contrast
    C. trapping
    D. All of the above.
19. What four factors describe working characteristics or impurities of inks?

Suggested Activities

1. Request printed samples of various screening techniques from printers in the area. Examine the copies and write your observations of variations existing between the screening techniques.
2. Visit a printing plant, and identify the color management system used by the plant.
3. Look for printed products that required the use of spreads and chokes. Were the printed results of high quality?
4. Compare the quality of color reproduction on the following: a newspaper retail insert, a cereal box, a clothing catalog, and a new car brochure.

Chapter 13

Digital Printing

Learning Objectives

After studying this chapter, you will be able to:

- Explain how digital processes have affected the graphic communications industry.
- Compare digital printing technologies.
- Explain the practical uses of variable data printing and distributed printing.
- Recall the purpose of digital asset management systems.
- Summarize the advantages and disadvantages of digital printing.

Goodheart-Willcox Publisher

Important Terms

aqueous inks
continuous ink-jet printer
digital asset management (DAM)
digital printing technology
direct imaging (DI)
distributed printing
dye sublimation
electrophotography
electrostatic printing
ink-jet printing
ionography
magnetography
makeready
piezoelectric ink-jet printer
software-as-a-service (SaaS)
solvent inks
thermal ink-jet printer
thermal transfer
UV inks
variable data printing
wide format printers

G-WLEARNING.com

While studying this chapter, look for the activity icon to:

- **Practice** vocabulary terms with e-flash cards, matching activities, and vocabulary game.
- **Reinforce** what you learn by submitting end-of-chapter questions.

www.g-wlearning.com/visualtechnology/

Digital Printing Overview

Digital printing technology is any reproduction technology system that receives electronic files and uses dots for replication without the need to create physical static printing plates to apply ink, toner, dye, or pigment to the final substrate. This type of printing eliminates the time-consuming and costly preparation of film and plates. Though not without limitations, digital printing provides customers with options that bring professional printing closer to the desktop with quick turnaround, flexibility, and cost-effective short-run color printing.

Prior to digital printing technology, the production of printed materials did not lend itself to complete integration. However, the application of digital technology to all aspects of the workflow has reduced the number of steps and made the process simple and more productive, **Figure 13-1**.

Digital technology is now used to create text, capture or create images, create printing plates for analog printing processes, and even apply ink or toner directly to pages. Computer applications and digital presses have made possible many printing options that were once unimaginable. See **Figure 13-2**. Jobs of four or more colors can be produced within hours or even minutes. Technology has increased the range of print runs on digital presses. Runs in the thousands are available for "static" printing, where all copies are the same. Runs now can go even into the millions, where all or some portion of the content is unique or versioned specifically to a particular recipient to make the communication personalized.

The major digital printing technologies include electrostatic and ink-jet printing technology. Both technologies have been available for many years, but recent advances in their speed and print quality have made them more competitive with conventional printing technology. There is a wide variety of applications for digital printing technology, including business cards, flyers, brochures, calendars, coupons, greeting cards, invitations, postcards, short-run printing, and variable data printing. See **Figure 13-3**.

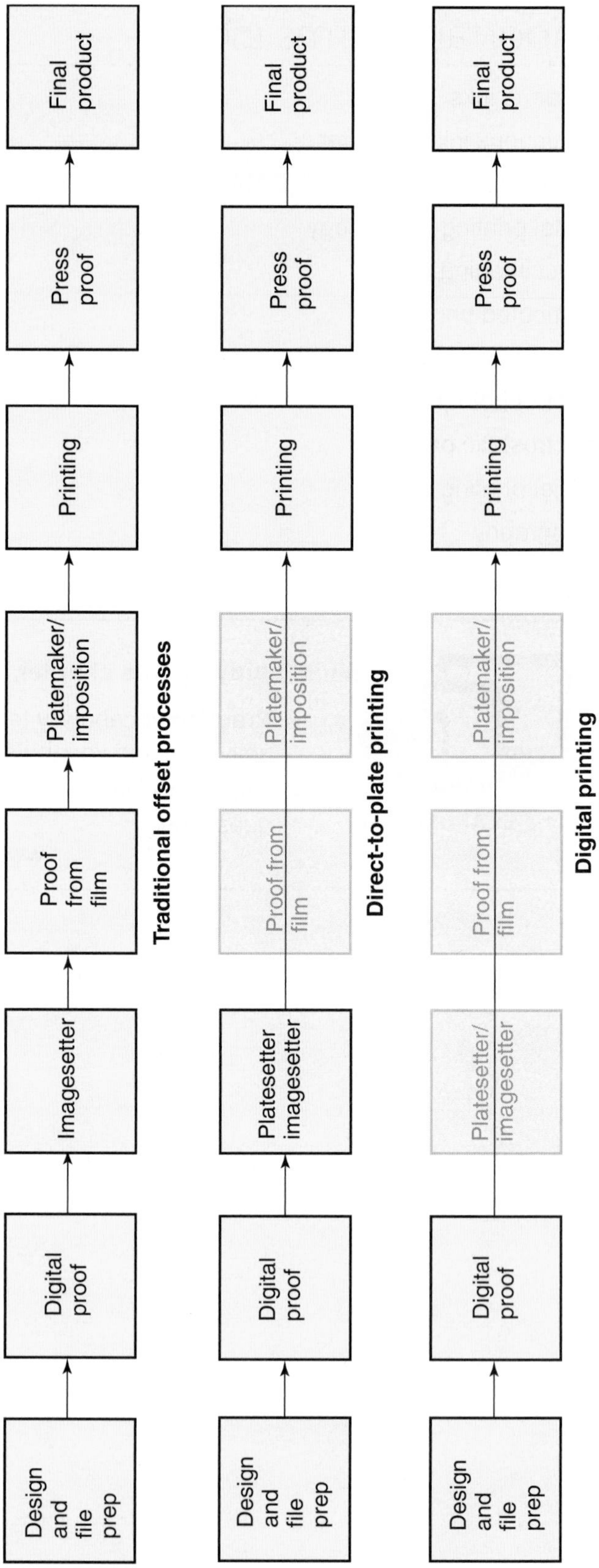

Goodheart-Willcox Publisher

Figure 13-1. Comparing traditional offset processes with digital printing technology.

©George Deal

Figure 13-2. This four-color digital press can print over 110 pages per minute.

Goodheart-Willcox Publisher

Figure 13-3. Digital printing technology can be used to print several different products, including business cards, postcards, flyers, and personalized material.

Process of Direct Imaging

Direct imaging (DI) is a variant of digital printing that is used for short- to medium-run lengths where all copies remain the same. DI essentially involves the process of sending a digital file directly to a specialized press. This press can image its own static plates onboard the printing press without the use of traditional standalone, offset, or computer-to-plate devices, processes, or chemistry. DI presses eliminate the production steps and variables normally associated with offset platemaking processes.

Today's DI presses combine the versatility of offset with the convenience and ease of use of digital while delivering a high degree of speed, quality, and automation to the four-color printing market. DI presses provide good image quality and a significantly reduced environmental footprint because of the chemistry-free plates.

The DI press, **Figure 13-4**, reduces makeready time and improves productivity. ***Makeready*** is the process of preparing a press for printing a job. The prepared digital files are sent via a high-speed network directly to the press, where plates are automatically advanced and mounted on the press plate cylinder and imaged simultaneously and in register. DI presses have found their niche in short- to medium-run lengths. Run lengths are determined by page size and turnaround time, **Figure 13-5**.

Digital Workflow

The printing workflow consists of the various steps to create, prepare, and print materials. As discussed in Chapter 9, *Digital Prepress and Production*, many changes have been made in the process of prepress

Heidelberg, Inc.

Figure 13-4. This direct imaging press prints four colors in a single pass.

workflow. Manual tasks are now done using various types of software. The preparation of text, graphics, and layout is completed on a computer. The general steps of a digital workflow, **Figure 13-6**, can be summarized as the following:

1. The creation of text and images.
2. Importing text and images to create page layouts.
3. Imposition and sheet assembly of final pages.
4. Platemaking and printing, for either traditional or DI presses.

PDF workflows are now commonly used in industry. PDF files allow users to include necessary pieces of a job in one file. With all the document information, such as fonts, text, and graphics, PDF files may be quite large. They are, however, more compact than sending native files and all their support graphics, fonts, etc., as separate items. Additionally, job ticket information, including everything from customer information to shipping information, can be incorporated into a PDF file, making it a versatile tool of the printing industry.

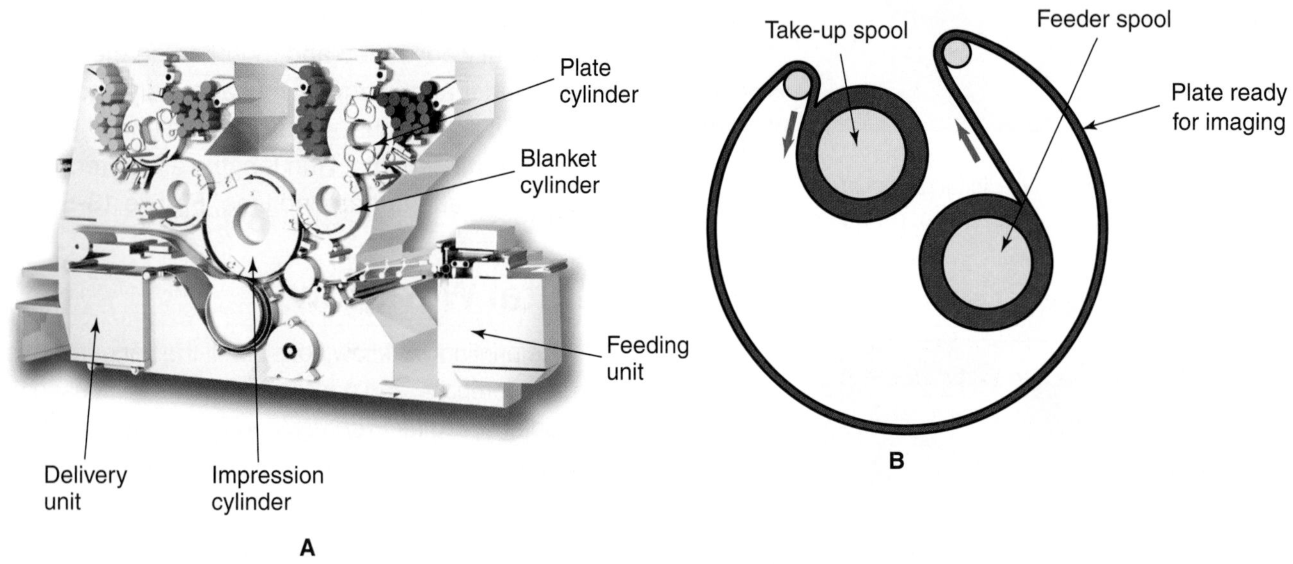

Presstek, Inc.

Figure 13-5. The workings of a direct image press. A—A cross section reveals a common impression cylinder. B—One method of automatic plate loading is to place both the feeder and take-up spools within the plate cylinder.

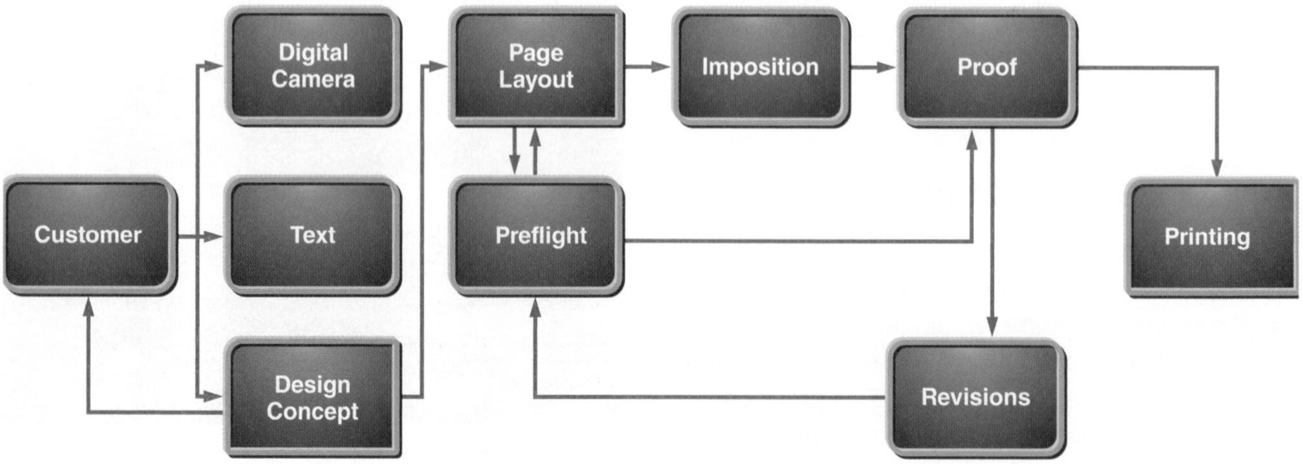

Goodheart-Willcox Publisher

Figure 13-6. The general steps of a digital workflow.

Goodheart-Willcox Publisher

Figure 13-7. Ink-jet printers can be used for variable data printing in various sizes.

Digital Printing Methods

Digital printing is done using various methods. The most common is ink-jet printing due to its scalability and desktop versions used in offices and homes. Some techniques, such as electrophotography, are types of electrostatic printing. ***Electrostatic printing***, which is responsible for producing more pages than any other digital technology, uses electrical charges to cause toner or ink to fuse onto a page. Typically, this involves a dynamic plate surface created "on the fly" during the printing process, which then transfers the image to a blanket surface and then onto the actual printing substrate. Other less-common types of digital printing are iconography, magnetography, dye sublimation, and thermal transfer.

Ink-Jet Printing

Ink-jet printing is a direct-to-paper technology that typically has no intermediate image carrier. It uses digital data to control streams of very fine droplets of ink or dye to produce images directly on paper or other substrates. In some cases, the droplets go to a blanket-type material and then onto the substrate. While the majority of commercial ink-jet printing is static, digital printing allows for the option of variable data printing of single or spot colors, such as direct mail advertising or large format posters, banners, or signage for limited distribution, **Figure 13-7**. Variable data printing is discussed later in this chapter.

Ink-jet printers are classified as either desktop, large format, or grand format based on the size of the reproduced image. Desktop printers are typically those that can produce images up to 13″ × 19″.

Wide format printers, or large format printers, are those that typically produce images from paper rolls larger than 13″ in width and technically limited in length only by the length of the roll of substrate material, often 100′ or more. Some of the more common products produced by wide format printers include wallpaper, banners, image and car wraps, posters, architectural plans, duratrans, signage, and graphics.

The ink transfer systems of the wide format ink-jet printer include:

- **Aqueous.** Water based.
- **Solvent.** Uses petroleum product liquids.
- **Dye sublimation.** Uses diffused inks to produce superior quality.
- **Ultraviolet (UV).** Uses ***UV inks*** that are polymer-made and UV-curable.
- **Pen/plotter.** Uses pens to draw on the substrate.

There are some large format specialized printers that print on speciality substrates (such as canvas), especially in the world of art reproduction, sometimes referred to as Giclée (a French term for a spray of liquid, pronounced *zhee-clay*). Large format ink-jet printers, **Figure 13-8**, are used extensively within the graphic communications industry for critical proofing applications, as well as for indoor signage and decorative graphics. Ink-jet printers beyond the classification of large format are called superwide or grand format printers. They are commonly used to create outdoor signage using solvent, resin, and latex-based inks.

Types of Ink-Jet Printers

The three main technologies used with ink-jet printers are thermal, piezoelectric, and continuous. The way the ink is dispersed onto the substrate is what makes the technologies different.

In a ***thermal ink-jet printer***, the ink cartridges have an ink chamber with a heater and a nozzle.

©George Deal

Figure 13-8. Large format ink-jet printers may be used for posters, banners, and signs.

Electrical current is sent to the heater for a few microseconds to generate heat. This heat is transferred to the ink, which is superheated to form a bubble. The bubble expands through the firing chamber, and the ink is forced out of the nozzle, **Figure 13-9**. The ink then refills in the chamber. Thermal ink-jet printers use aqueous inks, which are discussed later in this chapter.

In a ***piezoelectric ink-jet printer***, the piezocrystal is charged by an electric pulse. The electric pulse causes pressure, which forces droplets of ink from the nozzle, **Figure 13-10**. Piezoelectric ink-jet printers may use a wide variety of inks.

The ***continuous ink-jet printer*** is used commercially for marking and coding of products and packages, **Figure 13-11**. A continuously circulating flow of ink through the printhead is maintained while the power is on. In all other respects, it behaves like a thermal ink-jet printer. The printhead and the ink storage reservoir are separate components, and the ink storage reservoir also contains an area to store waste ink.

Types of Ink-Jet Inks

Several special inks are needed to create an image on a substrate using the ink-jet method of printing. The most commonly used inks are aqueous, solvent, and UV-curable.

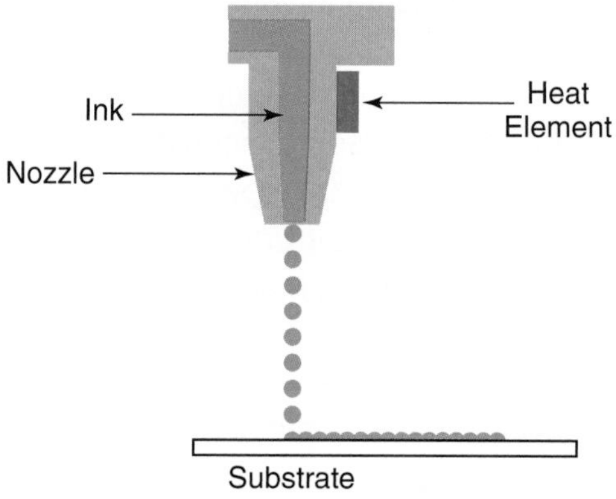

Goodheart-Willcox Publisher

Figure 13-9. Exploded diagram of a typical thermal ink-jet printer.

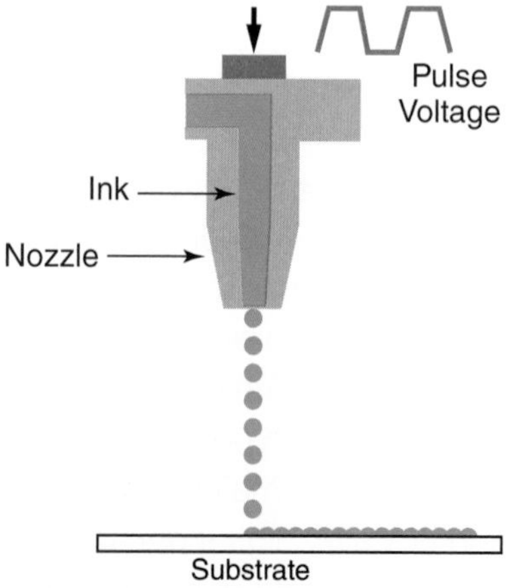

Goodheart-Willcox Publisher

Figure 13-10. Process of a piezoelectric ink-jet printer.

Domino Printing Sciences plc

Figure 13-11. Continuous ink-jet printers are used to mark and code products.

Many of the desktop ink-jet printers use ***aqueous inks***, based on a mixture of water, glycol, and dyes or pigments. Aqueous inks are able to withstand high temperatures that are needed to form a bubble without affecting the chemical makeup of the ink.

In ***solvent inks***, the main ingredient used as the carrier of the dyes or pigments is considered to be high in volatile organic compounds (VOCs). Environmental concerns must be taken into consideration to meet government standards. When this ink is placed onto the paper, the solvent evaporates very rapidly, sending the VOCs into the atmosphere while the colorant remains on the substrate.

There are no VOCs in UV-curable inks. After the UV ink droplets are forced onto the substrate, they are subjected to UV light. The ink is polymerized. The result of the curing process is the instant hardening of the ink. The image produced by UV-curable inks is very sharp in appearance.

With latex and resin-based inks, there is a major reduction in VOCs and odor compared to water-based inks. They are suitable for a wide variety of applications, including outdoor usage. As with other ink-jet technologies, significant pre- and post-heating of the substrate is required. Some newer technologies now in development, including Nanography® from Landa Digital Printing, are using particle-sized ink droplets and an intermediate blanket surface to allow removal of the liquid from the ink. This eliminates the need to heat or specially

Academic Link

Volatile Organic Compounds

Volatile organic compounds (VOCs) are chemical compounds that emit vapors at normal room temperatures. These compounds are found in many common items, such as paints, varnishes, adhesives, aerosol sprays, household cleaning products, and air fresheners. Some common VOCs include:

- Formaldehyde: Found in liquid adhesives.
- Butyl acetate: Found in adhesive caulk, dry erase markers, and nail polish.
- Methylene chloride: Found in aerosol spray paint and paint stripping agents.
- Perchloroethylene: A chemical used in dry cleaning.

Short-term exposure to VOCs can cause irritation of the eyes, nose, and throat; headaches; dizziness; and nausea. Long-term exposure to some VOCs may cause damage to the liver, kidneys, and central nervous system, or may cause cancer.

It is recommended that products containing VOCs be avoided. If it is necessary to use products containing VOCs, follow all the safety instructions on the product label and use the product outside or in well-ventilated areas.

Research common VOCs and evaluate your daily environment. What are the sources of VOCs around you every day? What steps can you take to reduce your exposure to VOCs?

treat the substrate, making it possible to print on virtually any substrate at a higher rate of speed and quality than current forms of ink-jet printing.

Types of Ink-Jet Printheads

The two main ink-jet printhead designs are fixed-head and disposable head. The fixed-head ink-jet printer design has a built-in printhead that is expected to last the life of the printer. When the ink runs out, the printhead can be refilled with ink. In the disposable head ink-jet printer, the cartridge is replaced when the ink runs out.

Electrophotography

Electrophotography is the most widely used commercial printing technique. It is seen most often in photocopiers and digital printing presses from companies such as HP® Indigo, Xerox®, Kodak®, Konica Minolta, and Ricoh. In the electrophotographic process, an original image is reflected onto a drum or dynamic plate surface coated with chargeable photoconductors that discharge in the nonimage areas after exposure to light. See **Figure 13-12**. The image receives dry or liquid toners or ink in the charged area, and it transfers either onto an impression blanket or directly onto a substrate. The substrate is charged by the corona assembly, and the image is fused by heat, solvent vapor, or other fixing method. Most electrophotographic systems accommodate a wide range of paper finishes, weights, and sizes, **Figure 13-13**.

A common type of printer that uses an electrophotographic process is a laser printer. Many laser printers and copiers use one system that contains a scanning bed and an imaging system. Software to connect the printer to the computer and the step of using a raster imaging processor (RIP) are added to the process. Multiple mirrors and a laser beam are used to expose the image on the drum or dynamic plate surface, **Figure 13-14**.

Electrophotographic printing has become more systemized by connecting the device to a network and viewing the output device as part of a

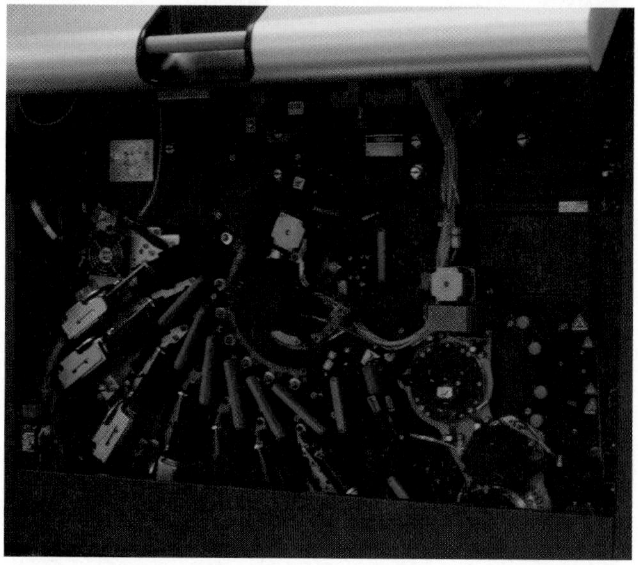

©George Deal

Figure 13-13. This digital press from HP uses a proprietary liquid electrophotgraphy (LEP) technology.

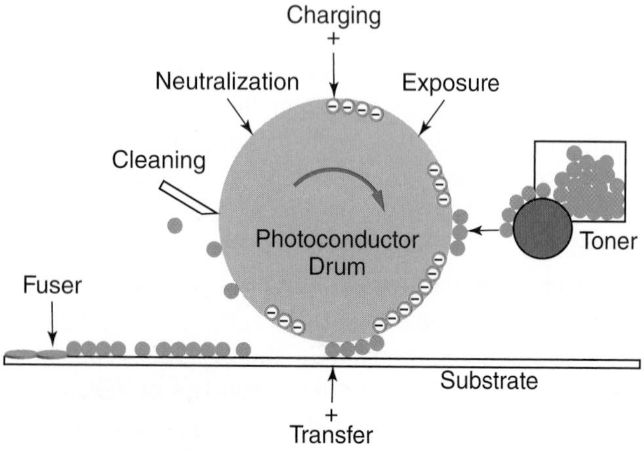

Goodheart-Willcox Publisher

Figure 13-12. Diagram of an electrophotographic printer.

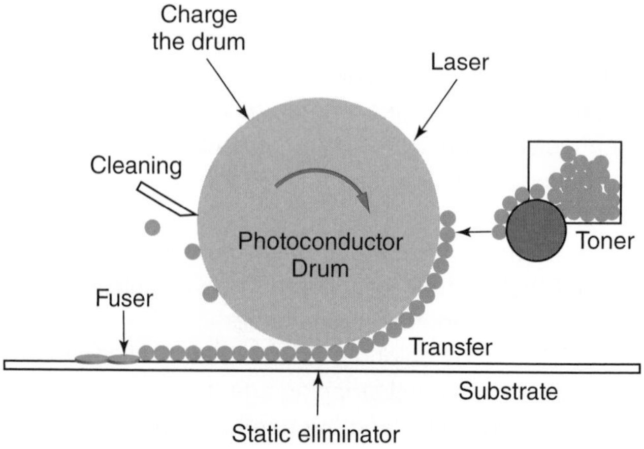

Goodheart-Willcox Publisher

Figure 13-14. Diagram of a laser printing system.

system consisting of a page layout workstation, a scanner, an RIP, and a printer. In some instances, electrophotographic printing systems are being used to produce content and contract proofing, including final output copies. See **Figure 13-15**.

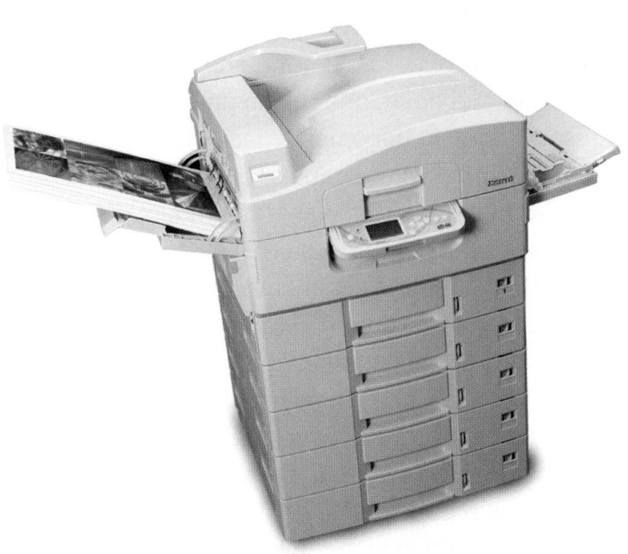
Xanté Corporation

Figure 13-15. This electrophotographic printer is capable of printing high-quality, four-color printing jobs.

Ionography

Ionography is similar to electrophotography. The difference is instead of using mirrors to expose the image onto the drum, ionography uses an electron cartridge, or ion generator. A negative charge is dispersed from the electron cartridge. The charge is then transferred onto a heated nonconductive surface covered with a magnetic toner. The image is then fused onto the substrate. See **Figure 13-16**.

Misregistration, or the misalignment of colors, may occur because of the pressure of the image transfer. Therefore, ionography is used mainly for single- or spot-color printing. Ionography systems are used for high-volume and variable data printing. Variable data printing is discussed later in this chapter.

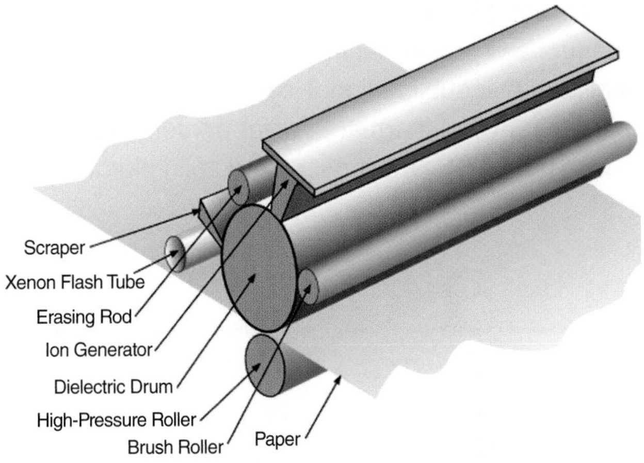

www.PrintingTips.com, owned by Austec Data Inc. dba Tecstra Systems

Figure 13-16. Diagram of an ionographic printer.

Magnetography

In ***magnetography***, the image is converted to a magnetic charge on a drum that then attracts magnetized toner. Similar to ionography, magnetography exposes an image onto a drum and then uses high pressure to fuse the toner onto the substrate.

As with ionography, magnetography is commonly used for single- or spot-color printing. The iron oxide contained in the core of the magnetic toner causes the toner to be darker on paper. One advantage magnetographic systems have over other digital printing systems is that they are faster than other types of systems. Magnetographic systems are commonly used for printing bar codes and other types of variable data printing. Variable data printing is discussed later in this chapter.

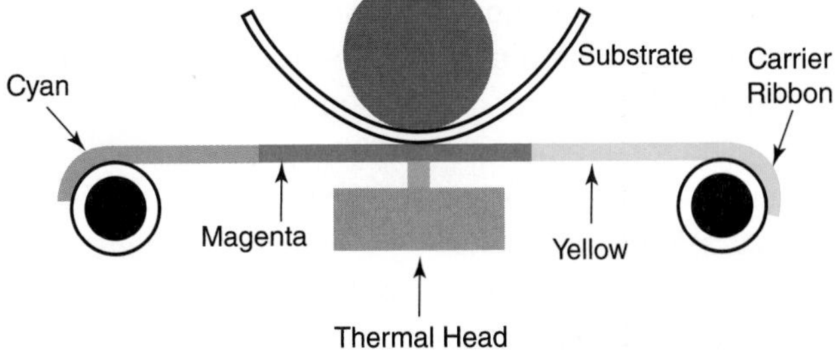

Goodheart-Willcox Publisher

Figure 13-17. Diagram of a dye sublimation printer.

Dye Sublimation

Dye sublimation is a type of thermography. Dye sublimation is the process of using heat and pressure to change solid dye particles to a gas, which vaporizes as it permeates the surface of the substrate. See **Figure 13-17**. In dye sublimation printers, a ribbon is made up of cyan, magenta, and yellow panels of solid pigment. The ink panels pass over a thermal head, and as the panels are heated, the solid pigment becomes a gas, which transfers to the paper below the panels. The thermal head changes temperature to vary the amount of ink dispensed on the substrate. This makes dye sublimation a type of continuous tone printing process. After the three colored panels have been printed onto the substrate, a lamination is applied to prevent smudging caused by warmth, **Figure 13-18**.

An advantage of dye sublimation is that the ink is dry as soon as it is done printing. A disadvantage is that once a panel has been used, it cannot be reused, resulting in higher ink costs than other methods of printing. Dye sublimation is commonly used to print digital photographs and plastic cards. It is also used to print on polyester.

Thermal Transfer

Thermal transfer is a type of thermography. The process of thermal transfer printing is very similar to dye sublimation. However, the ink panels are different in a thermal transfer printer. Rather than a ribbon of panels of colored solid pigment, thermal transfer printers use a different ribbon for each color. Thermal transfer printers have been used mainly for one-color printing, but newer systems with multiple ribbons of different colors are also used. The type of ink used for thermal transfer makes it difficult to control the amount of ink transferred to the substrate. This technique is commonly used for color proofing on larger offset printing processes.

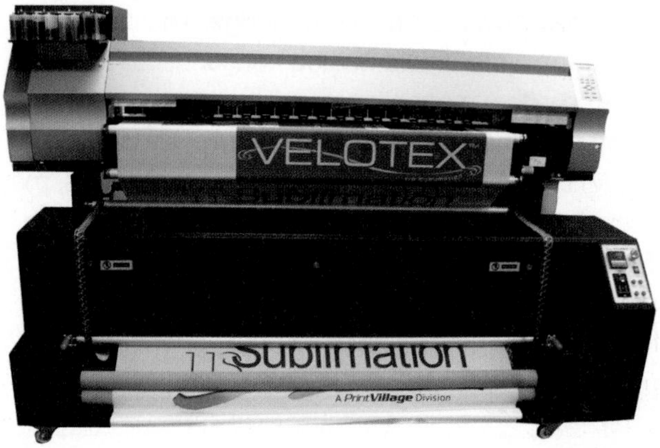

US Sublimation

Figure 13-18. An example of a dye sublimation textile system with on-board curing.

Career Link

Digital Press Operator

Digital press operators are found in small printing shops, as well as larger printing plants. The operator works with digital printing presses and computerized systems to produce printed material, and is generally required to troubleshoot and maintain the press. Also, press output must be monitored for optimum image quality.

The requirements of a digital press operator include knowledge of various merge applications, multitasking and prioritizing skills, and possessing mechanical and technical skills that apply to the operation of computerized systems. Following safety rules and practicing safe work habits are essential characteristics for an operator, as well. Necessary skills to be a digital press operator may be acquired at technical schools, colleges, and universities. On-the-job training may also be offered by some printing establishments.

"At a time when methods of communicating are becoming increasingly digital, printing on paper and countless other substrates has consistently proven to be the most reliable medium to convey ideas and images."

Michael Makin
Printing Industries of America

Digital Printing Applications

Digital printing allows for more flexibility in the printing process. This flexibility and electronic workflow permit materials to be easily shared and customized. Many of the items people receive in the mail are the products of digital printing processes.

Variable Data Printing

Variable data printing is a printing process that is unique to digital printing systems. It enables quick and easy content changes at several points within a print run. The "on the fly" imaging device in all true digital printing presses allows customized and personalized materials to be produced. Printed materials that are customized typically target a specific audience or group but not a particular individual. Personalized printed materials are unique and intended for a specific person.

Printing variable data items begins with the designer's work: a basic template of the printed material. Within the design, certain sections are designated as changeable fields. The data for these fields are held in a database or separate file and are applied during the digital printing process. The results of variable data printing include direct marketing mailers, area-specific sales flyers, and product mailings that include customer-specific messages.

Distributed Printing

Distributed printing is a system of digital printing in which the electronic files for a job may be sent anywhere in the world through a wide area network (WAN) and printed near the point of distribution. For example, a brochure can be sent electronically to a digital printing operation near a trade show location prior to the event. The brochure can be printed and delivered to the convention center or hotel, saving time and shipping costs. Also, national newspapers and magazines use distributed printing technology to print regional editions of the publications. A central or home office sends an electronic file to all its regional offices for the addition of area merchant ads and articles of local interest. The regional offices may then send the completed file to a local digital printing facility for production and distribution.

Distributed printing has limitations. Using color management systems at both ends of the process helps ensure color consistency, but it may still be necessary to send hard copies to clients if color fidelity is critical. Many companies prefer to proof the printed documents prior to a press run, either for their own proofing/approval purposes or to get final approval from a customer. Businesses using distributed printing on a regular basis may be able to provide local representatives for on-site approval.

Digital Asset Management

Digital asset management (DAM) consists of the protocol and resources established to handle all digital files and data. Common management tasks include downloading, processing, organizing, storing, and transmitting data. The types of data typically involved in digital printing processes include design files, templates, images, font files, and databases. An effective data asset management system streamlines the business processes that involve handling digital data.

There are a number of applications where digital asset management systems are essential in managing a large amount of necessary digital information. For example, data libraries use asset management systems to manage the storage and retrieval of large amounts of infrequently changing media assets, such as archival documents, photos, and videos. Digital supply chain services that push digital content (music, videos, and games) out to digital retailers are another example of a business where digital asset management systems are essential.

Effective large-scale digital asset management solutions involve scalable, reliable, configurable hardware and software products that can handle a great number of files, as well as many simultaneous users, workflows, or multiple applications operating on the system. Some management systems are offered as installed software with web-based access, called ***software-as-a-service (SaaS)***. SaaS systems manage and maintain data externally and provide clients with system-specific software to facilitate data access through an Internet

Think Green

Electronic Media Waste

Although digital technology is helping reduce the damage from existing threats to the environment, its continuing use and constant growth comes at a price. When computers and other types of electronics are replaced, the older machines that are thrown out become e-waste. E-waste is the fastest growing cause of toxic waste in the United States. The toxic chemicals found in e-waste can consist of lead and mercury. While these toxins can damage the environment, they are also harmful for your health. Exposure to lead can cause neurological damage and cancer. Mercury poisoning can cause damage to the nervous and endocrine systems. Recent policies regarding the disposal and recycling of e-waste have been adopted in several countries. Several electronics manufacturers have initiated recycling programs for their products.

connection. Industry-focused systems, such as AGFA's Apogee or Kodak's InSite, combine automated publishing workflows with digital asset management in a web-enabled environment that supports multiple-user collaboration. For small-scale applications or individual use, some image viewer applications offer management capabilities, including backing up, organizing, and reading/writing metadata and keywords.

Advantages and Disadvantages of Digital Printing

There are certain areas in which digital and conventional printing each have distinct production and economic advantages. There are also many areas where they overlap, as emerging and conventional technologies adapt to meet the short-run market demands.

Conventional color printing requires long runs to absorb the high makeready costs. However, computer-to-plate technology has eliminated many of the time-consuming and expensive steps involved in traditional printing. The quality of digital printing has become comparable to traditional offset printing, leaving speed and sheet size as the only real disadvantages. See **Figure 13-19**.

The term "on-demand printing" is often used solely to describe digital-to-paper printing. This, however, is a misnomer, because all printers print on demand. If a customer "demands" an order, the printer will print it. On-demand printing is better described as short-run, distributed, or just-in-time printing, no matter how it is produced.

Digital presses offer quick turnaround times, a great deal of flexibility, and cost-effective printing for short color runs. Depending on finishing requirements, an experienced print shop using a digital press can typically turn around digital printing runs in 24–48 hours. With the proper full-color digital printers, digital printing can also provide a means to produce quick, cost-effective, high-quality proofs for gravure and offset printing.

The flexibility of digital printing exists because there are no static plates or drums; digital presses are imaged on the fly. Last-minute changes can be made with little or no extra cost. Digital printing allows individual pages to be customized during print runs and enables electronic files to be transmitted almost anywhere in the world for printing. Digital printing provides a cost-effective

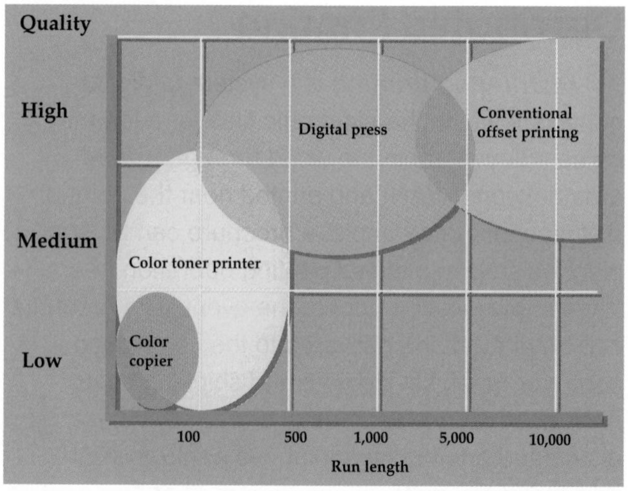

Goodheart-Willcox Publisher

Figure 13-19. Color printing technology is available with various levels of quality and all types of run lengths.

means for printing out-of-print titles and short runs of manuals, books, and textbooks, **Figure 13-20**.

By eliminating much of the traditional press preparation, digital presses make the overall cost of short color runs affordable. Short-run, process-color printing includes very short printing runs that can range from one to several thousand copies. The unit cost may be higher with digital printing, but the overall cost is less expensive than on a traditional press. A short run on a traditional press would be prohibitively expensive due to the setup costs involved.

The quality produced on digital presses has made leaps since being introduced 20 years ago. To most people, and even many experts, the printed documents are on a par with traditional offset printing. In fact, in the case of some substrates such as uncoated papers and specialty substrates, the quality of digital can even surpass traditional printing.

Limited sheet size is one of the disadvantages of digital printing, unless you go to a large format output. Traditionally much smaller than offset lithography, sheet sizes are generally large enough for an 11″ × 17″ spread with bleed, or a bit larger. This area is one of growth, and the sizes are growing with each new update. As the quality of digital graphic arts technology continues to improve, the advantages it promises are certain to grow. These include lower costs, greater flexibility, and faster production time. Today's fastest digital printing presses can produce 20,000 full-color pages per hour. New technology will also require the mastery of new skills for every step of the production process.

The trend toward all-digital design, storage, production, and reproduction is very exciting. However, this trend also involves the expansion of complex input and output options and application of consistent standards for product creation, transmission, and reproduction. As with all technology, you must continually update your knowledge and equipment to remain competitive.

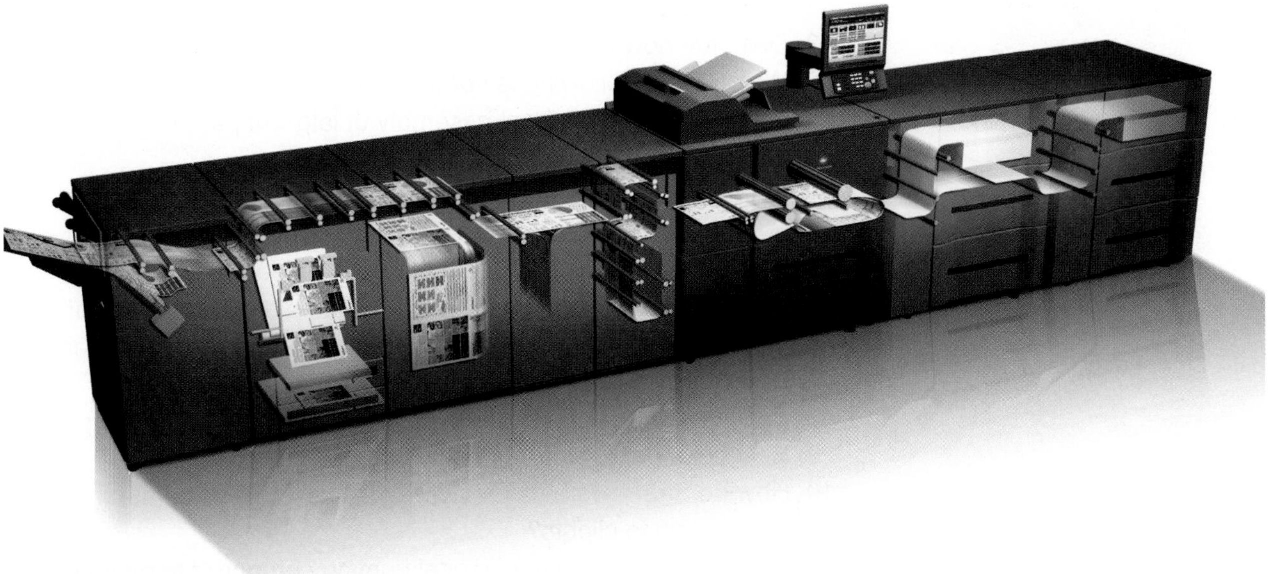

©*Konica Minolta*

Figure 13-20. Digital printing may provide a variety of finishing options, including binding, punching, and booklet making.

Summary

- Digital technology is now used to create text, capture or create images, create printing plates for analog printing processes, and even apply ink or toner directly to pages.
- The most common types of digital printing are ink-jet, electrophotography, ionography, magnetography, dye sublimation, and thermal transfer.
- Digital printing allows for variable data printing.
- Distributed printing is a system of digital printing in which the electronic files for a job may be sent anywhere in the world through a wide area network (WAN) and printed near the point of distribution.
- Digital asset management systems are used to manage digital files and data.
- Digital technology has eliminated many of the time-consuming and expensive steps involved in traditional printing.
- The only disadvantages of digital printing compared to offset printing are speed and limited sheet size.

Review Questions

Answer the following questions using the information in this chapter.

1. _____ is any reproduction technology that receives electronic files and uses dots for replication.
2. Describe how a DI press works.
3. Which of the following is *not* a step of a digital workflow?
   A. Imposition and sheet assembly of laid-out pages.
   B. Creation of text and images.
   C. Paste-up to produce a mechanical.
   D. Importing text and images to create page layouts.
4. List three main technologies used with ink-jet printers.
5. What type of commonly used ink contains a great amount of VOCs?
6. _____ is the type of printing technology used by laser printers.
7. Name two common types of thermography.
8. Explain how materials are customized using variable data printing.
9. How does distributed printing save time and money?
10. How do SaaS systems provide digital asset management capabilities to clients?
11. List some advantages of digital printing compared to offset printing.

Suggested Activities

1. Visit a printing plant and determine what digital applications are being used in the facility.
2. Compare color digital printed images with conventional printed images for detail, color, dot structure, sharpness of image, and other selected factors.
3. What types of applications are appropriate for variable data printing?

Chapter 14

Printing Processes

Learning Objectives

After studying this chapter, you will be able to:

- Describe the offset lithographic printing process.
- Explain the relief printing process.
- Describe the gravure printing process.
- Describe the screen printing process.

Goodheart-Willcox Publisher

Important Terms

blanket
blanket cylinder
brake mechanism
brush system
burned edge
cell distortion
cell size
color correction
dampening system
delivery pile
delivery system
double-sheet detector
electrostatic assist
electrotype
filament
flexography
flying splicer
former board
gravure
impression cylinder
inking system
mesh count
offset lithographic printing
percent open area
perfecting press
pH scale
pH value
photopolymer plates
plate cylinder
platen press
printing system
register unit
retarder
rubber plates
screen printing
sheet-fed press
squeegee
sucker feet
tensiometer
thinner
undercut
warp thread
washup solvent
web-break detector
web-fed press
web splicer
weft thread
zero-speed splicer

G-WLEARNING.COM

While studying this chapter, look for the activity icon to:

- **Practice** vocabulary terms with e-flash cards, matching activities, and vocabulary game.
- **Reinforce** what you learn by submitting end-of-chapter questions.

www.g-wlearning.com/visualtechnology/

The printing process has various methods of transferring an image to some type of surface we call a *substrate*. Usually, the first substrate that comes to mind is paper. Each method makes it possible to reproduce numerous copies of the same image. This chapter will explain the processes of offset lithographic, relief, gravure, and screen printing.

Offset Lithographic Printing

Offset lithographic printing is a process of printing directly from a flat surface. Lithographic printing is based on the principle that oil and water do not readily mix. The plate has a nonimage area that receives water and repels oil- or grease-based ink. The image area accepts ink and refuses water. **Figure 14-1** illustrates how ink and water act in lithographic printing.

The operation of an offset lithographic press involves the transfer of images from one surface to another. The image is offset from the plate to a ***blanket*** and is then transferred to the paper. After the blanket receives the image in reverse form from the plate, the image transfers back to its original form on the substrate. Electronic platemaking and desktop publishing systems are used extensively throughout the graphic communications industry.

Lithographic Press Systems

Different types of presses and press operations are used in the lithographic printing operation. Lithographic presses are classified as either sheet-fed or web-fed presses, based on how paper is fed through the system. See **Figure 14-2**.

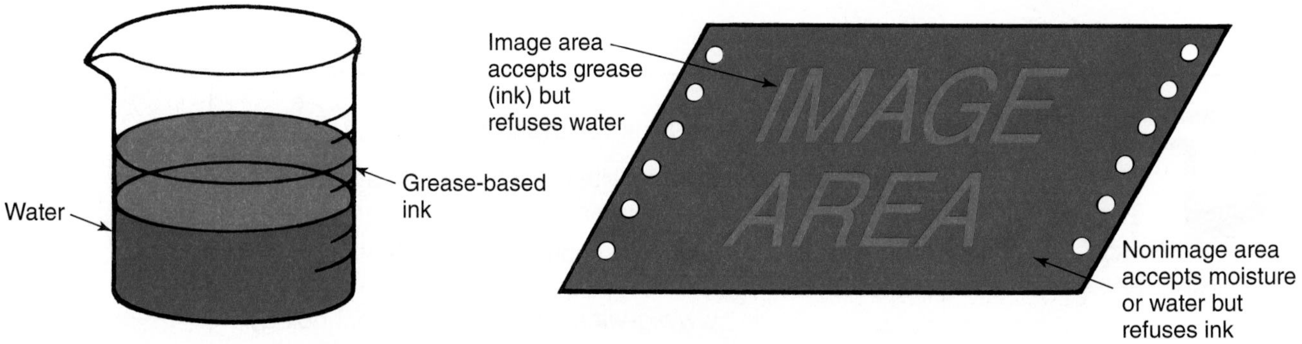

Goodheart-Willcox Publisher

Figure 14-1. Lithography is a printing method based on the principle that oil or grease and water do not readily mix. The image area accepts ink but rejects water, while the nonimage area accepts water but rejects ink.

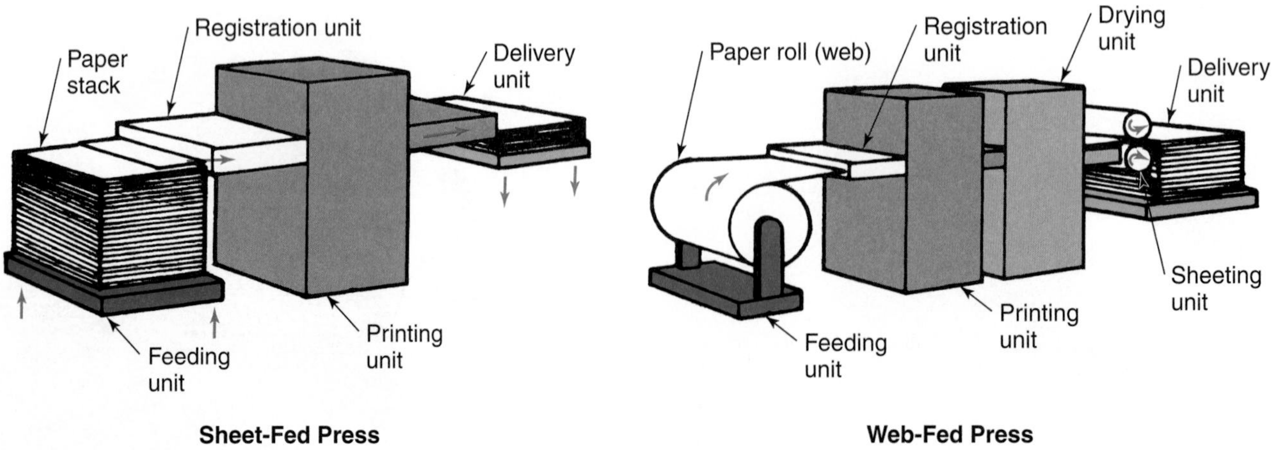

Goodheart-Willcox Publisher

Figure 14-2. A comparison of sheet-fed and web-fed press designs.

A ***sheet-fed press*** prints on individual sheets of a substrate (paper) as they are drawn through the system. Sheets are removed from a stack, one at a time, and fed through the press. See **Figure 14-3**.

A ***web-fed press*** prints on one long, continuous web of paper that is drawn into the press from a roll. As the roll unwinds, images are printed on the web and the entire length of paper winds through the press, **Figure 14-4**.

The operation of a lithographic press is divided into five systems, each of which performs a basic function. The five basic press systems are the feeding system, printing system, dampening system, inking system, and delivery system, **Figure 14-5**.

Feeding Systems

Feeding systems are classified as sheet-feeding systems or web-feeding systems. Paper is fed, printed, and delivered differently depending on the type of press used. See **Figure 14-6**.

Sheet-Feeding System

On a sheet-fed press, sheets of paper are typically stacked on a feeding platform and removed one at a time by the press. The automatic press feeders operate at high production speeds. To assist in separating sheets, air-producing separators are positioned along the upper edges of the paper stack. Each sheet is then transported to the register unit, which positions, or registers, the paper for insertion into the press. When the press

©George Deal

Figure 14-4. A web-fed press prints on a continuous roll of paper, called a web, that feeds through the entire system.

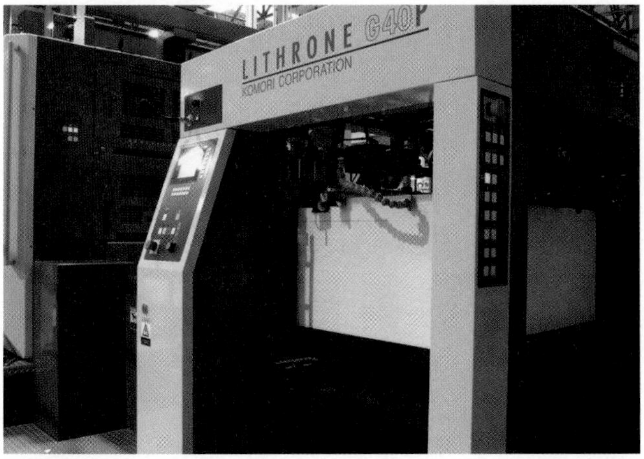

©George Deal

Figure 14-3. A sheet-fed press feeds and prints paper one sheet at a time.

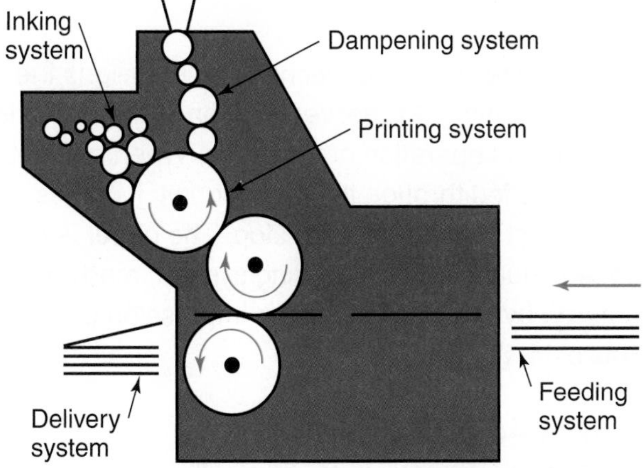

Goodheart-Willcox Publisher

Figure 14-5. Five basic systems are used in the operation of a lithographic press.

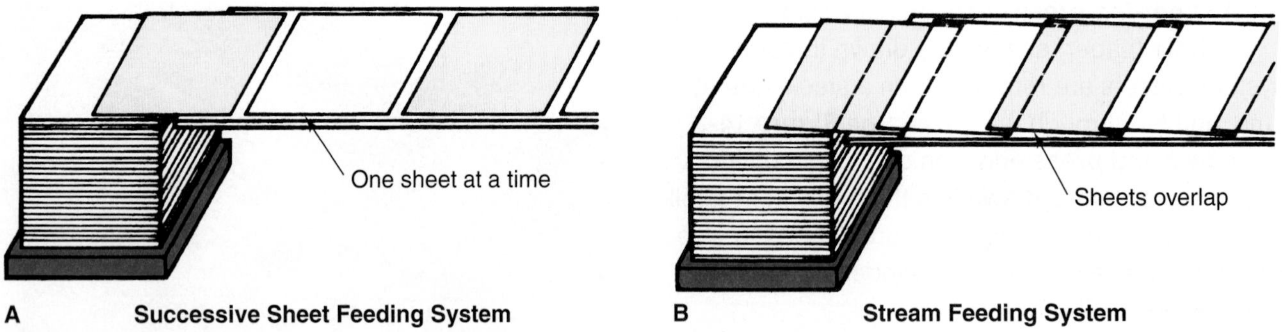

Goodheart-Willcox Publisher

Figure 14-6. Sheet-fed presses can use a successive sheet feeding system or a stream feeding system. A—In successive feeding, one sheet at a time is fed through the press. B—Stream feeding allows sheets to partially overlap when they are fed, resulting in faster press speeds.

is running, the paper stack must remain at a certain height on the platform. Operating height is generally monitored with a control device.

Sheet Transfer

Sheets are commonly transferred from the stack and fed to the press by ***sucker feet***. Sucker feet create a vacuum that removes sheets and positions them for access to the press-feeding pullout rollers. On many smaller presses, the sucker feet are positioned at the leading edge of the sheet, **Figure 14-7**. On larger presses, the sucker feet may be located at the rear edge of the sheet. The rear feet draw the paper forward to the pullout rollers, **Figure 14-8**. An example of a press equipped with sucker feet is shown in **Figure 14-9**.

To ensure that only one sheet passes through the press, the press is equipped with a control device called a ***double-sheet detector***, **Figure 14-10**.

Register Unit

A ***register unit*** is a mechanism that aligns the sheet for printing. Proper registration of the paper is critical to the operation of the press. When a sheet of paper is fed through the register unit, it comes into contact with the register stop. The paper is then aligned square with the printing system, ready to be captured by the grippers on the impression cylinder, **Figure 14-11**.

Web-Feeding Systems

Printing on a web-fed press is done on a continuous roll of paper that winds through a series of rollers, **Figure 14-12**.

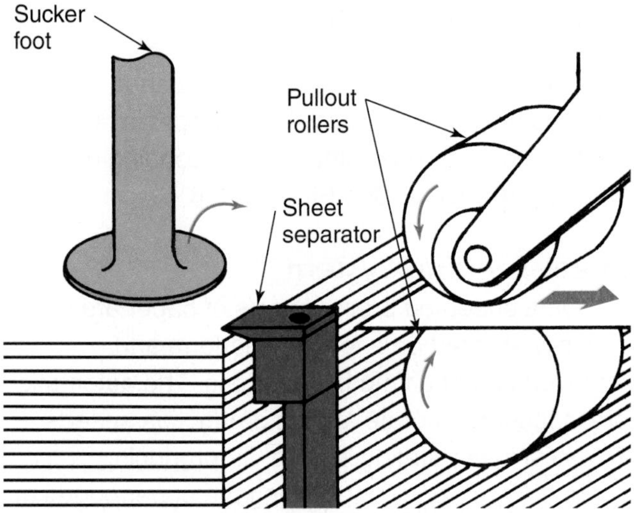

Goodheart-Willcox Publisher

Figure 14-7. Sucker feet are used to lift and guide sheets of paper to the pullout rollers in a feeding system.

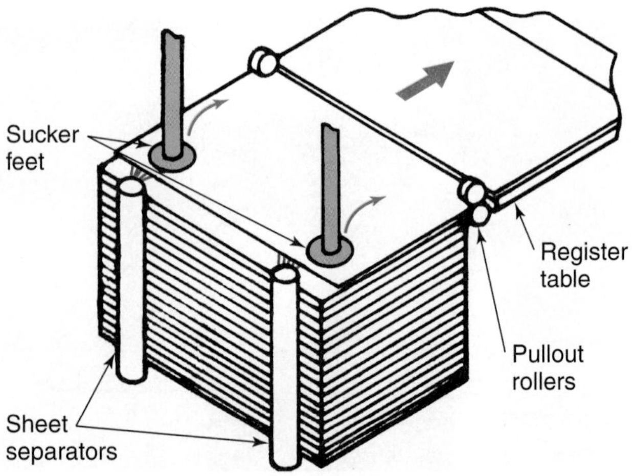

Goodheart-Willcox Publisher

Figure 14-8. Sucker feet located at the rear edges of the paper draw sheets forward from the stack.

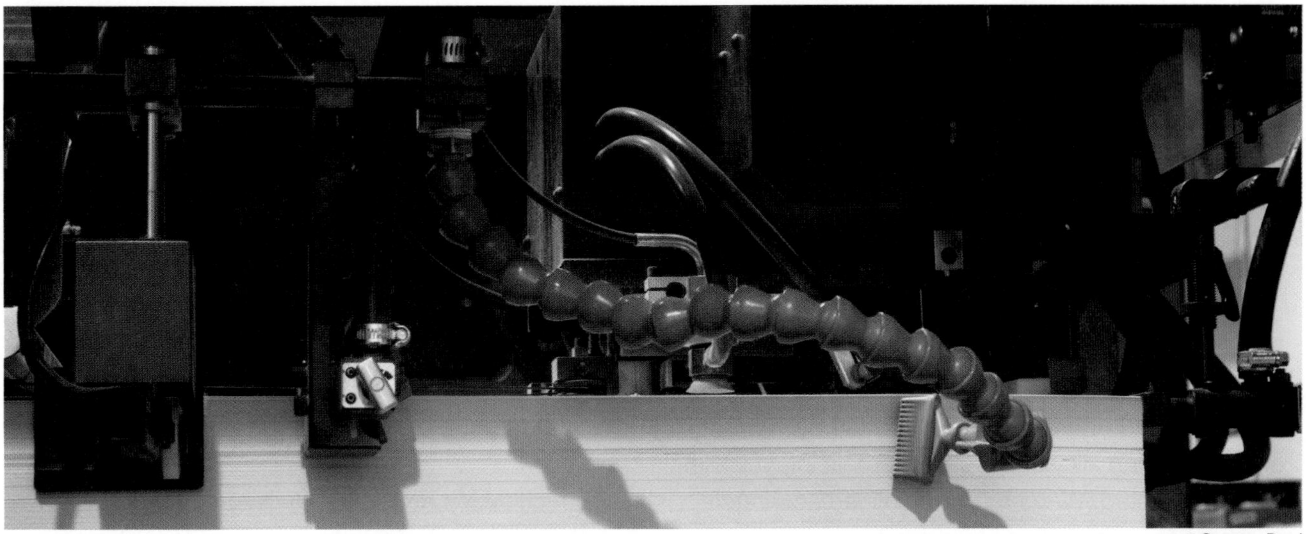

©George Deal

Figure 14-9. A typical sheet-fed press equipped with sucker feet to feed paper for printing.

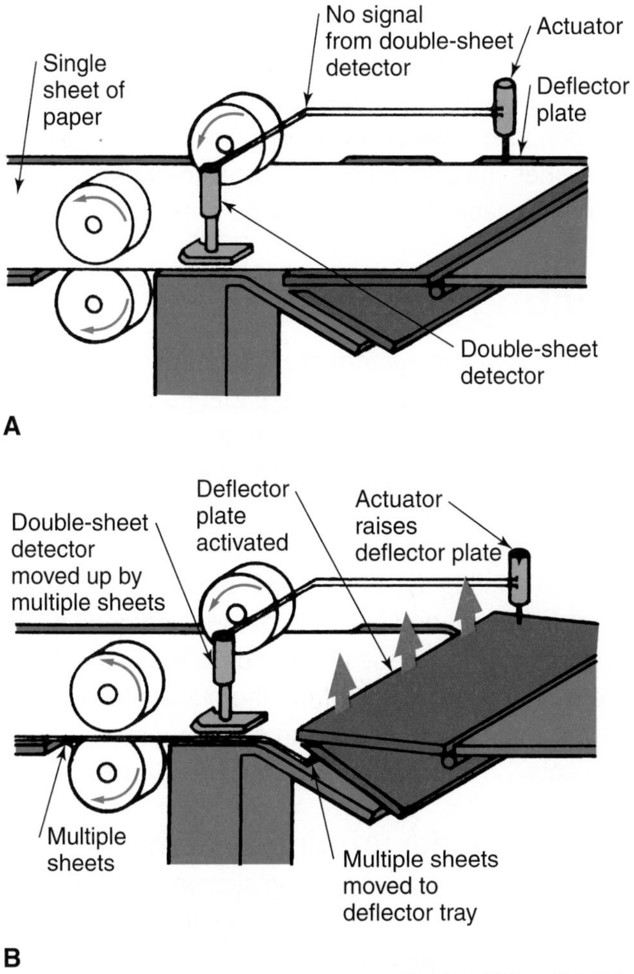

Goodheart-Willcox Publisher

Figure 14-10. A double-sheet detector senses paper thickness as sheets are fed through the system. A—When a single sheet is fed, the detector remains inactive. B—When it senses excess thickness, the detector activates the deflector plate for removal of the paper.

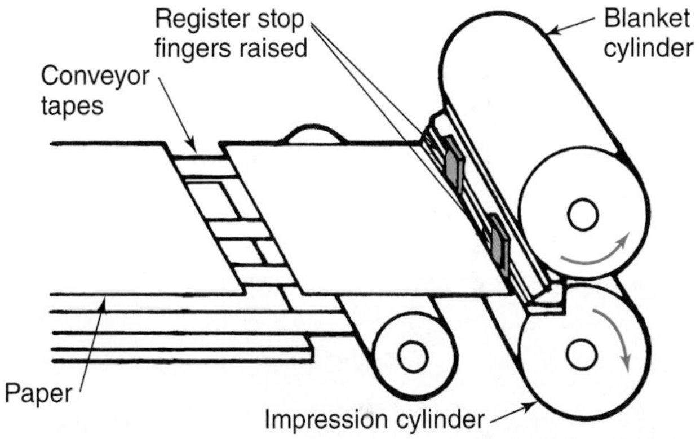

Goodheart-Willcox Publisher

Figure 14-11. The register stop places paper in register, ready to pass through the printing system.

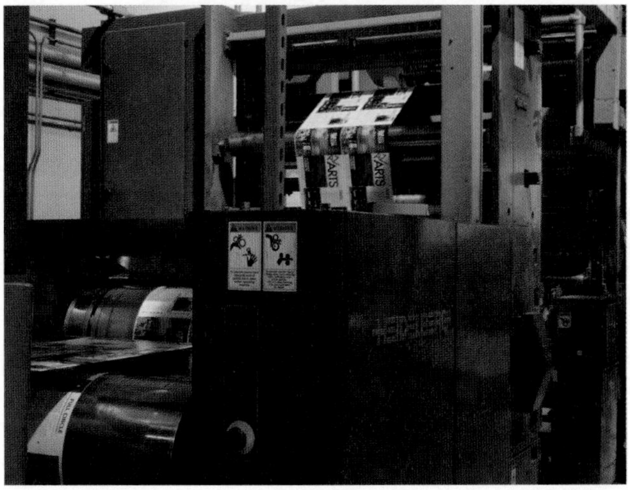

©George Deal

Figure 14-12. Paper travels through a web-fed press as one continuous web. The web winds through a series of rollers as it is printed.

The movement of paper through a web-fed press is controlled by a paper tension device. A ***brake mechanism*** is one of the most commonly used tension control devices on a web-fed press, **Figure 14-13**. The brake mechanism is attached to the paper roll and is designed to produce a slight amount of friction, or drag, on the web.

Web Splicer

When a new roll of paper replaces an existing roll while the press is running, a ***web splicer*** splices, or bonds, the end of the existing roll to the start of the new roll. Splicing allows the web to remain intact while it is being printed. Webs must be spliced accurately; an improper paper splice could cause a web break.

A ***zero-speed splicer*** uses a set of rollers called a festoon to draw out slack from the web before a splice is made. The festoon unit allows the new roll to be spliced to the old one while the press uses up the slack.

A ***flying splicer*** is a device that bonds a new roll of paper to the existing web without stopping any operations on the press. Neither web roll is stopped while the splice is made. An adhesive, such as double-sided tape, is applied to the end of the new web to make the splice.

When the existing web roll is nearly empty, the splicing unit rotates the new roll toward the existing roll and accelerates it to match the speed of the moving web. When the new web meets the moving web, the two ends are spliced together and the old web is cut. The new web becomes the moving web and is rotated into the running position previously occupied by the old web.

©George Deal

Figure 14-13. A brake mechanism provides the correct tension as the web is fed from the roll on a web-fed press unit like this one.

Web-Break Detector

A ***web-break detector*** is a device that automatically shuts down the press if the web snaps or tears. Modern web-fed presses operate at tremendous speeds.

A web-break detector uses a sensor to detect a break in the web. If a break occurs, the detector will kill power to the press instantly. It will also activate a mechanism that cuts off the incoming web before it reaches the printing system, preventing any incoming paper from entering the press.

Printing Systems

The ***printing system*** of a lithographic press consists of a group of cylinders that transfer images from the printing plate to the substrate. The components of a printing system are the plate cylinder, the blanket cylinder, and the impression cylinder, **Figure 14-14**.

The printing system accepts paper from the feeding system and uses the dampening and inking systems to print images from the plate. On an offset press, images are offset from the plate cylinder to the blanket cylinder, and then offset again as paper contacts the impression cylinder. See **Figure 14-15**.

Three-Cylinder Printing System

The three-cylinder printing system has a plate cylinder, a blanket cylinder, and an impression cylinder. Each cylinder has a specific task. The purpose of each cylinder is discussed next.

Plates and Plate Cylinder

The ***plate cylinder*** holds the printing plate on the press. The components of a plate cylinder

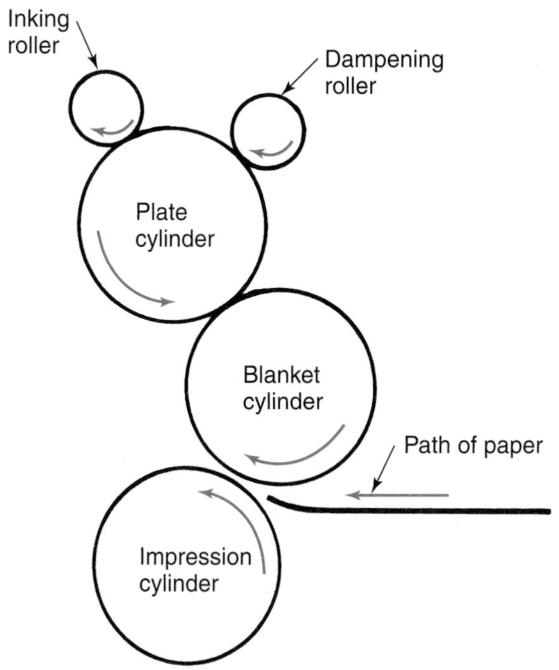

Goodheart-Willcox Publisher

Figure 14-14. The three components that make up a printing system are the plate cylinder, the blanket cylinder, and the impression cylinder.

©George Deal

Figure 14-15. An open view of the blanket and the impression cylinder.

include the body, bearers, bearings, and a gear that drives the cylinder, **Figure 14-16**.

Plates are made of many different materials, but the most common base is aluminum. Aluminum is widely used because it is flexible, lightweight, and more receptive to water than grease. See **Figure 14-17**.

Often, lithographic plates have three parts: the base or plate grain, the plate covering, and plate coating. The plate grain of the lithographic plate is the surface texture of the plate base. It can appear very smooth or quite rough when magnified. Plate coverings are layers of material bonded to the base of the plate, while plate coatings are the surface layers of light-sensitive material that harden when exposed to light. Automatic plate processors are generally used to process the plates. Carefully follow the manufacturer's suggested plan.

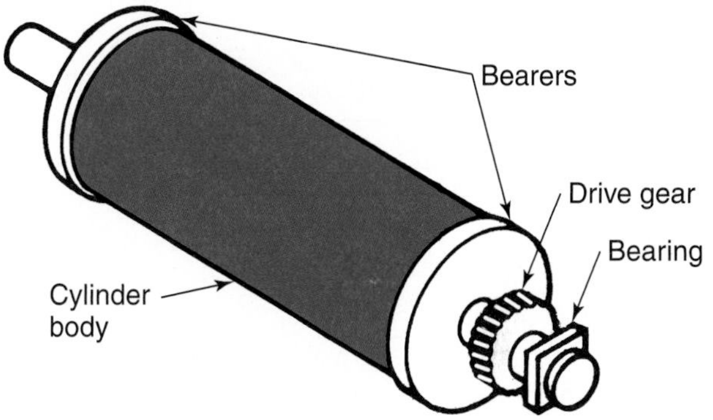

Goodheart-Willcox Publisher

Figure 14-16. The basic parts of a plate cylinder.

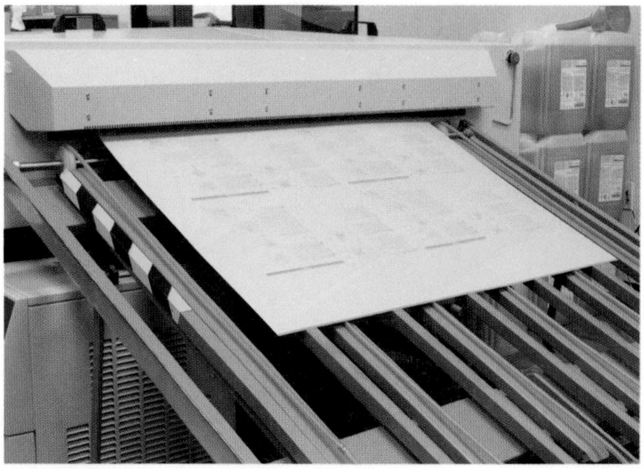

©George Deal

Figure 14-17. A metal plate being imaged.

Computer-to-plate technology uses platesetters to accept digital files from computers, and then image light-sensitive or heat-sensitive plates. The system is an electronic network that eliminates the use of film as an intermediate, producing plates with high resolution.

A plate cylinder has a series of clamps that hold the plate in place. Plates are classified as serrated, straight, or pin bar, **Figure 14-18**. The cylinder clamps are used to tighten or loosen the plates. Proper tension must exist between the plate and the plate cylinder. Excessive tension can place too much stress on the plate and cause it to crack or tear. Insufficient tension can affect registration and print quality.

The vertical space that lies between the surface of the plate cylinder bearers and the cylinder body is known as the ***undercut***, **Figure 14-19**. The undercut allows for the thickness of the plate and packing. The size of the undercut can be determined by measuring the difference between the diameter of the cylinder bearers and the diameter of the cylinder body, **Figure 14-20**. Undercut can also be measured with a cylinder packing gauge.

Computer-to-Press System

This system eliminates the need for a plate, as it places an image directly onto the cylinder. Once printed, the image can be removed and the cylinder can be reimaged.

Blanket Cylinder

The ***blanket cylinder*** holds the image-receptive blanket on the press and acts as an intermediate between the plate cylinder and the impression

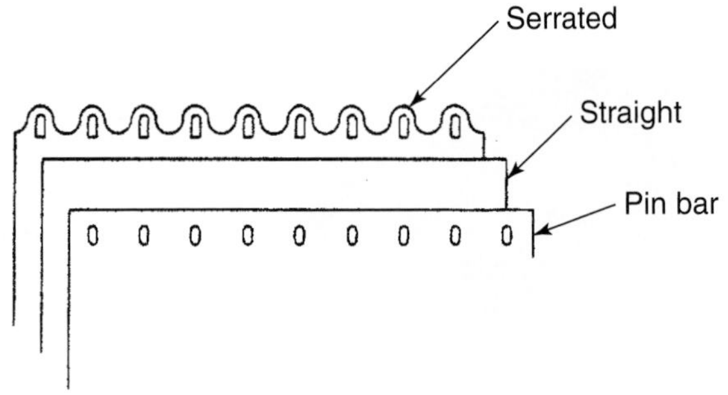

Goodheart-Willcox Publisher

Figure 14-18. Different attaching methods for plates.

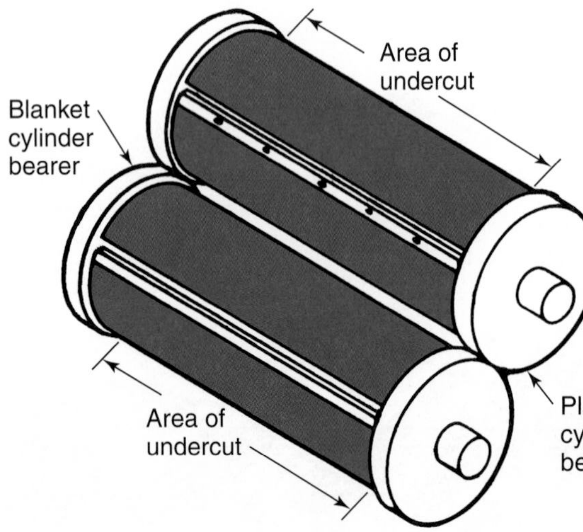

Goodheart-Willcox Publisher

Figure 14-19. Cylinder surfaces are undercut from the bearers to allow for plate and blanket thickness and packing.

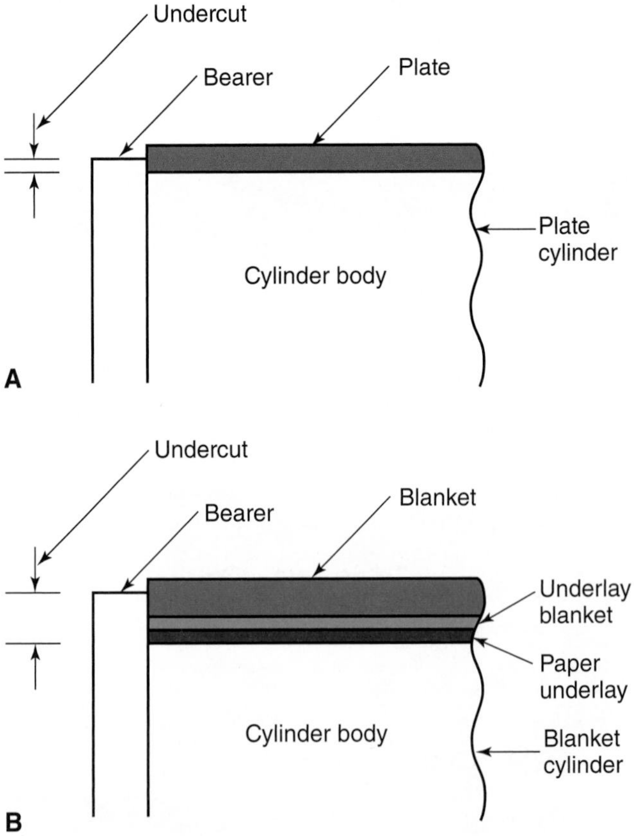

Goodheart-Willcox Publisher

Figure 14-20. The undercut of a plate or blanket cylinder is equal to the difference between the diameter of the bearers and the diameter of the cylinder body. A—The plate cylinder body is undercut to allow for the thickness of the plate and packing. B—The blanket cylinder is undercut to allow for blanket thicknesses and packing.

cylinder. During printing, the blanket receives the image in reverse from the plate and then offsets the image to the substrate in its original orientation.

The blanket cylinder consists of the same components as the plate cylinder. The blanket cylinder body holds the blanket in place with a set of clamps. Blankets are elastic and are designed to stretch around the cylinder. Blanket surfaces are commonly made of rubber and supported by a woven cloth base, **Figure 14-21**.

©George Deal

Figure 14-21. Press blankets stretch to fit the blanket cylinder. The resilient surface of the blanket accepts the inked image from the plate.

Impression Cylinder

The ***impression cylinder*** brings the stock to be printed into contact with the blanket cylinder. As paper travels between the impression cylinder and the blanket cylinder, the image is transferred from the blanket to the paper. The impression cylinder carries the substrate from the feeding system to the delivery system, **Figure 14-22**.

The impression cylinder serves as the base component of a three-cylinder system. It applies the pressure needed to transfer the image from the blanket cylinder to the substrate. As the substrate passes between the cylinders, the impression cylinder must provide the correct amount of gap between the paper and the blanket to make the impression.

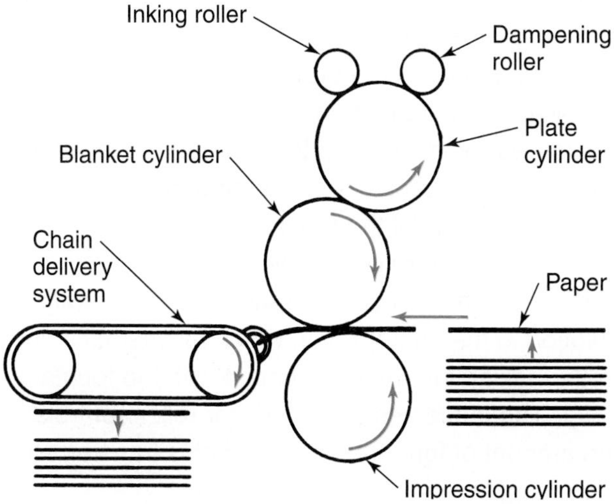

A.B. Dick Company

Figure 14-22. The impression cylinder brings the paper into contact with the blanket cylinder and provides the pressure needed to offset the image.

Perfecting Press

A ***perfecting press*** is a printing system that prints both sides of the substrate simultaneously. As shown in **Figure 14-23**, the perfecting press consists of two plate cylinders and two blanket cylinders. The pairs of cylinders are arranged above and below the path of the substrate. As the substrate comes into contact with both blanket cylinders, the upper cylinder prints one side of the substrate, while the lower cylinder prints the other side.

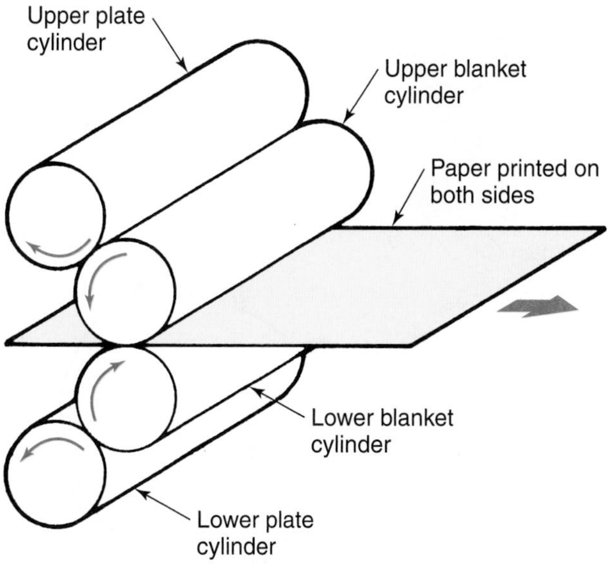

Goodheart-Willcox Publisher

Figure 14-23. One kind of perfecting press is equipped with two plate cylinders and two blanket cylinders to print both sides of the substrate simultaneously.

Dampening Systems

A ***dampening system*** is a group of rollers designed to apply moisture to the nonimage area of the plate. Before the plate is inked, the nonimage area is coated with fountain solution to separate it from the image area. When the plate is inked, only the image area is receptive to ink; the nonimage area repels ink.

The two most common types of dampening systems used on a press are the conventional dampening system and the continuous dampening system.

Conventional Dampening System

A conventional dampening system uses a series of rollers to distribute fountain solution from the fountain to the plate when the plate is positioned on the press. The basic components of a conventional dampening system are a dampening fountain, a fountain roller, a ductor roller, a distributor roller, and a form roller, **Figure 14-24**.

During the printing process, fountain solution is supplied to the dampening fountain by a bottle or similar reservoir. To keep the solution at the same level, many presses use a container that works by gravity feed to refill the fountain.

The fountain roller revolves in the fountain to draw out the solution. It transfers the fountain solution to the ductor roller, which moves back and forth, making intermittent contact with the fountain roller. The movement of the ductor roller controls the amount of fountain solution that is transferred to the rest of the system.

As the ductor roller rotates, it carries the fountain solution to the distributor roller. The distributor roller is used to spread the solution evenly across the rollers and prepare the solution for distribution on the plate. The distributor roller transfers the solution to the form roller, which applies the solution to the plate. Different systems may use one or more form rollers and typically use a fabric cover to retain moisture.

Dampening system rollers should be regularly cleaned and adjusted to ensure the correct levels of pressure exist between each roller. Covers must also be cleaned and rinsed thoroughly on a regular basis to remain effective.

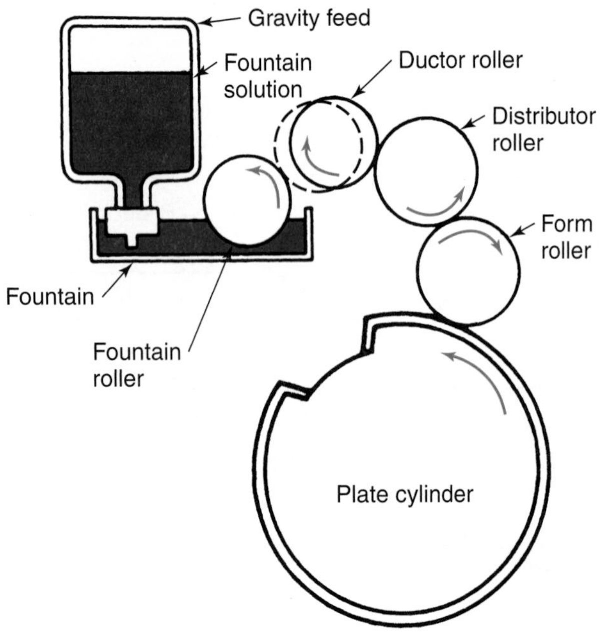

Goodheart-Willcox Publisher

Figure 14-24. In a conventional dampening system, rollers are used to carry fountain solution from a fountain to the plate.

Continuous Dampening System

A continuous dampening system is a system of rollers that distributes a continuous flow of fountain solution to the plate. This system eliminates the ductor roller, **Figure 14-25**. A transfer roller used in place of the ductor roller makes direct contact with the fountain roller to distribute the solution.

A metering roller is commonly used in a continuous dampening system. It serves the same purpose as the fountain roller but can be adjusted to control the flow of solution when it makes contact with the transfer roller. This presents an advantage over other dampening systems by allowing the system to respond quickly to changes in fountain settings. When the press is in operation, the operator can adjust the flow of solution if there is not enough reaching the plate.

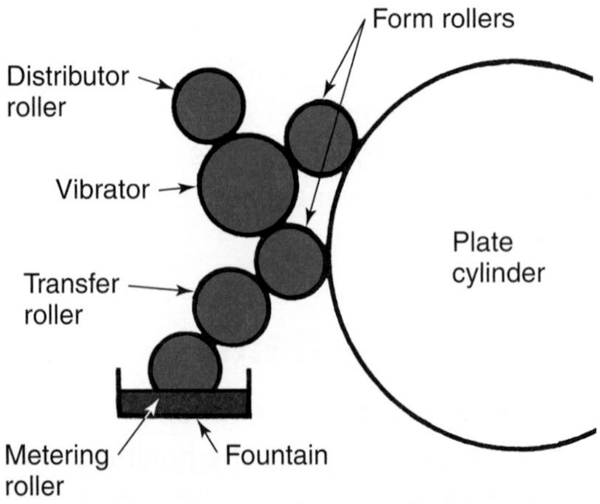

Goodheart-Willcox Publisher

Figure 14-25. A continuous dampening system applies moisture to the plate with a continuous alignment of rollers. A transfer roller carries fountain solution from a metering roller to the rest of the system.

A ***brush system*** is a continuous dampening system that uses a brush roller to transfer solution from the fountain roller to the rest of the system. The brush roller is used in place of a transfer roller to control the flow of solution, **Figure 14-26**. The brush roller draws solution from the fountain roller and spreads it accurately to a distributor roller, which transfers the solution to the form roller.

Fountain Solution

The fountain solution used in a dampening system must be properly mixed to provide a consistent dampening solution for the plate surface. Fountain solutions are commonly identified by their ***pH value***, a measurement that indicates the acidity or alkalinity of the solution. A ***pH scale*** provides numeric pH values ranging from 0 to 14, with 7 designated as neutral, **Figure 14-27**. A pH value less than 7 is an acidic solution, with a value of 0 representing the highest acidity. A pH value above 7 is an alkaline solution, with a value of 14 representing the highest alkalinity. Each successive pH value is 10 times the previous value. For example, a solution with a pH reading of 3.0 is 10 times more acidic than a solution with a pH reading of 4.0.

Plates have a recommended pH value that is used when mixing the fountain solution. Most plates are designed to use solutions with a pH reading between 4.0 and 5.5. Some presses are equipped with devices that automatically monitor the pH value of the fountain solution.

Inking Systems

An ***inking system*** consists of a set of rollers that carries a thin film of ink to the image area of a plate, **Figure 14-28**. The inking system, also known

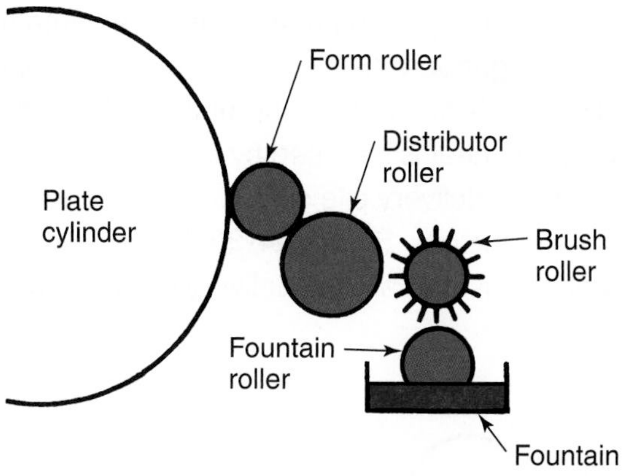

Goodheart-Willcox Publisher

Figure 14-26. In a brush system, a brush roller spreads the fountain solution and is part of a continuous series of rollers.

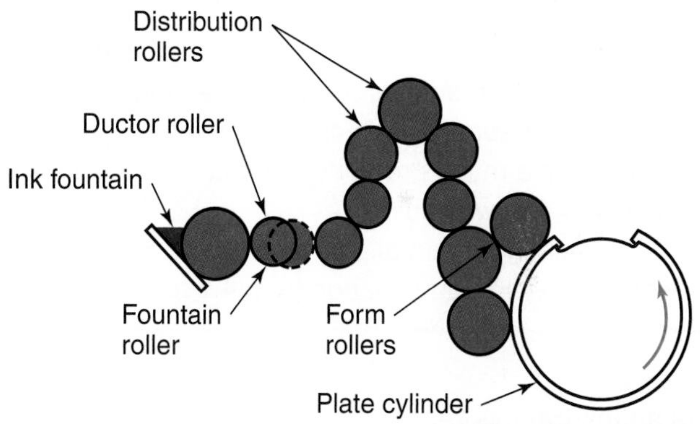

Goodheart-Willcox Publisher

Figure 14-28. Ink is applied to the plate by a series of rollers that make up the inking system.

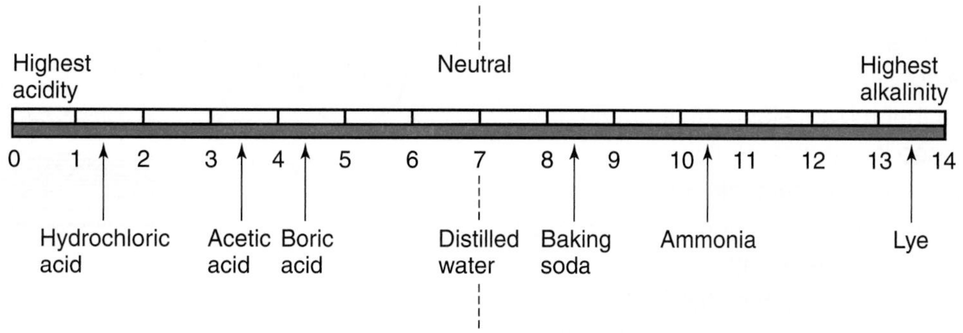

A.B. Dick Company

Figure 14-27. A pH scale measures the acidity or alkalinity of a solution. The scale ranges from 0 to 14, with 7 indicating a neutral solution. A value above 7 indicates an alkaline solution; a value below 7 represents an acidic solution.

Academic Link

Acidity/Alkalinity

The fountain solution used on printing presses keeps ink off areas on the plate that do not contain an image. To ensure that the solution performs optimally, it is important to regularly measure the pH of the solution. Maintaining the proper pH level impacts the quality of the printed material, as well as the wear on the printing plate.

As mentioned in this chapter, the pH scale contains measurement values from 0 (acid) to 14 (alkaline), with 7 being neutral. Typically, the fountain solution pH reading for sheet-fed work is around 4.0. It is best to follow the manufacturer's directions when adjusting a solution's pH.

A change in pH by one unit of measure is actually a difference of 10 in the pH of the solution. For example, a change in pH from 7 to 8 is an increase of one unit of measure, but represents a 10-point jump in pH. This solution has gone from neutral (7) to alkaline (8). A practical example is lemon juice with a pH around 2 and stomach acid with a pH of about 1. The change in one pH unit represents a much greater difference in the actual acidity of the two liquids.

If each incremental pH value is a change of 10, what is the pH value change from 4.5 to 5?

as an ink train, is responsible for maintaining a consistent flow of ink to the plate surface. A typical system includes an ink fountain, a fountain roller, a ductor roller, and a combination of distribution rollers and form rollers.

Ink is supplied to the system by an ink fountain. On larger presses, an ink agitator may be used to help maintain a consistent ink flow. An agitator is a revolving device that moves along the fountain and stirs the ink to keep it at the same flow level.

The fountain roller transfers ink from the fountain to the ductor roller. The ductor roller makes intermittent contact with the fountain roller and the distributor roller. The ink is then distributed by one or more distributor rollers to the intermediate rollers or directly to the form rollers. The form rollers place the final film of ink on the plate.

Delivery Systems

A ***delivery system*** removes the printed substrate from the printing system of the press and prepares it for finishing operations. Delivery systems on sheet-fed presses are designed differently from those used on web-fed presses.

Sheet-Fed Delivery Systems

A sheet-fed delivery system removes sheets after they are printed and stacks them onto an outfeed table or tray. Sheet-fed delivery systems vary in design and use.

The most common delivery system used on a sheet-fed press is a chain delivery system, **Figure 14-29**. As a sheet of paper leaves the printing system, it is directed to the ***delivery pile*** by a pair of chains that serve as conveyor belts. Two delivery bars extending between the chains contain grippers that grasp the sheet and guide it through the system. The gripper bars are positioned along the length of the chains so one set of grippers pulls a sheet from the printing unit at the same time the other set of grippers delivers a sheet to the delivery pile. The pile is stacked on top of the outfeed table.

When a sheet is released by the gripper bars, it is aligned in the delivery pile by guides positioned along the sides of the pile, **Figure 14-30**. Proper alignment of the sheets is critical. The delivery pile must be

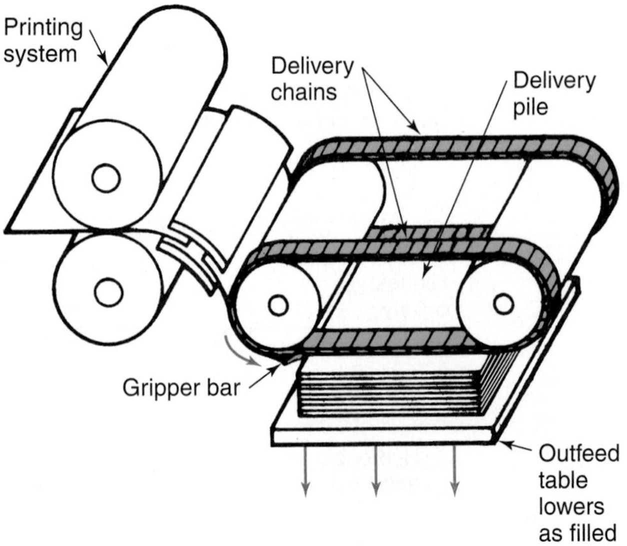

Goodheart-Willcox Publisher

Figure 14-29. A chain delivery system driven by a pair of chain conveyor belts directs printed stock to a delivery pile.

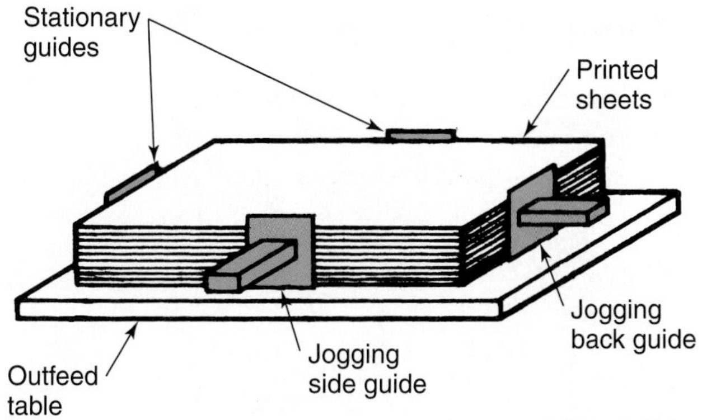

Goodheart-Willcox Publisher

Figure 14-30. Guides are positioned to align delivered paper on the outfeed table.

uniformly arranged so the paper can be trimmed or folded after it is stacked. Two stationary guides and two jogging guides place each sheet in position and straighten the stack. The stationary guides are on two sides of the paper. The jogging guides are adjustable and move or jog the paper into place as it is fed to the pile. As the sheets build up, the outfeed table slowly drops under the weight of the pile.

Web-Fed Delivery Systems

A web-fed delivery system is designed to provide a series of finishing operations in addition to the actual delivery of paper. The feeding and delivery systems used with web-fed presses are designed much differently from those used with sheet-fed presses. After the paper is printed, it is transferred to a group of units that make up the delivery system.

Different delivery systems are used on various web-fed presses. A typical system includes a dryer, chiller, and folder, **Figure 14-31**.

The dryer unit dries the ink printed on the web. The dryer operates at high temperatures and removes much of the moisture from the ink through evaporation. The web is then cooled by the chiller unit, which lowers the temperature on the web surface and hardens the ink. The system may also include a moisturizing unit to restore web moisture that is lost in the drying and chilling processes.

Once the web passes through the dryer and chiller units, it is transferred to the folder, where it is trimmed and folded into signatures. A signature is a folded sheet that is commonly printed on both sides and trimmed. A typical folder folds sheets using a ***former board***, a curved or triangular plane that serves as the folding surface.

Relief Printing

Relief printing, also known as letterpress, is a traditional printing method in which images are printed from a raised surface. Elements making up the image are raised (in relief) above the surface.

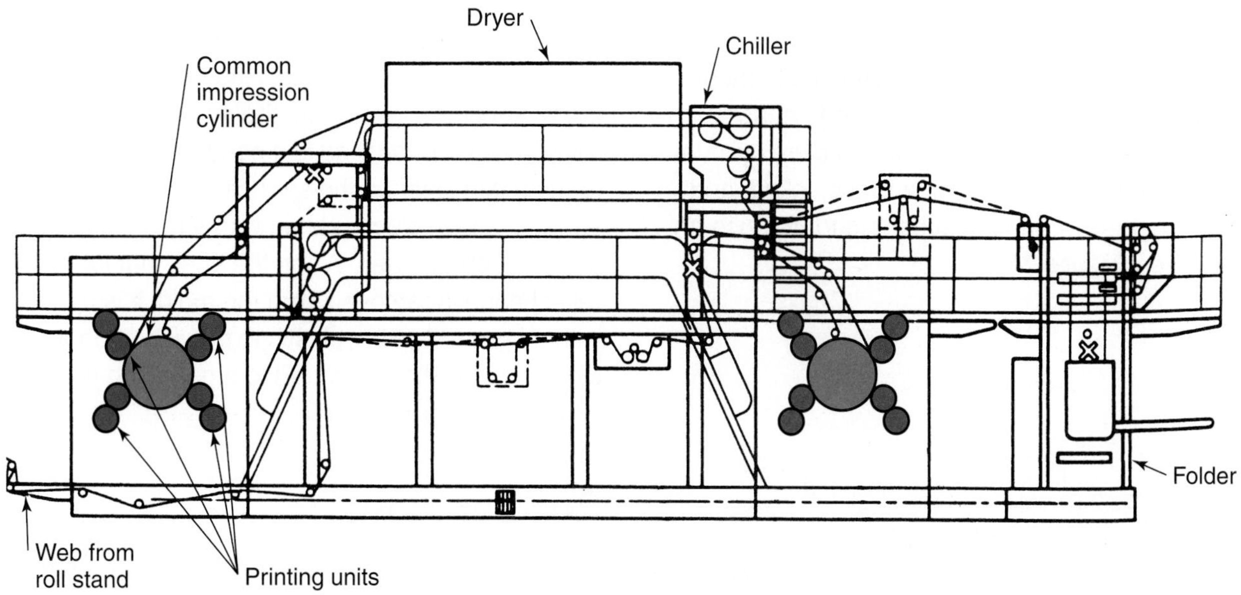

Baker Perkins Limited

Figure 14-31. The delivery system of a web-fed press is commonly equipped with separate dryer, chiller, and folder units.

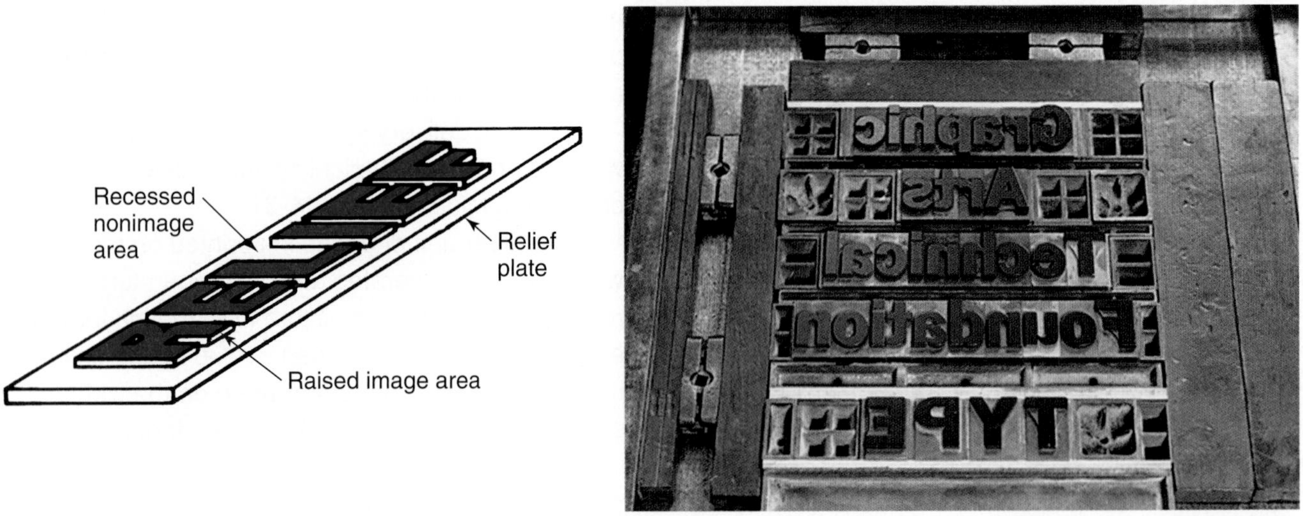

Goodheart-Willcox Publisher; ©PIA

A B

Figure 14-32. A—The relief process prints images from a raised surface that accepts ink. The nonimage area is recessed and lies below the raised image. B—Letterpress tray.

The nonimage area is recessed and lies below the surface, **Figure 14-32**. After the image carrier or plate is inked, the raised surface is pressed against paper to print the image.

Traditional relief printing methods have limited use today in commercial operations. They are used to some extent in printing packaging materials and in finishing operations such as embossing, ticket numbering, perforating, and die cutting. After paper is printed, it can be diecut into a special design using letterpress equipment. The printed material is trimmed to a final shape by pressing it against a die mounted on a press.

Flexography is a type of relief process. Flexography uses a curved or flexible plate made from rubber or plastic. When mounted on the press, the plate is wrapped around a plate cylinder. The plate is then mounted on a press, inked, and pressed against a printing substrate to produce an image. See **Figure 14-33**.

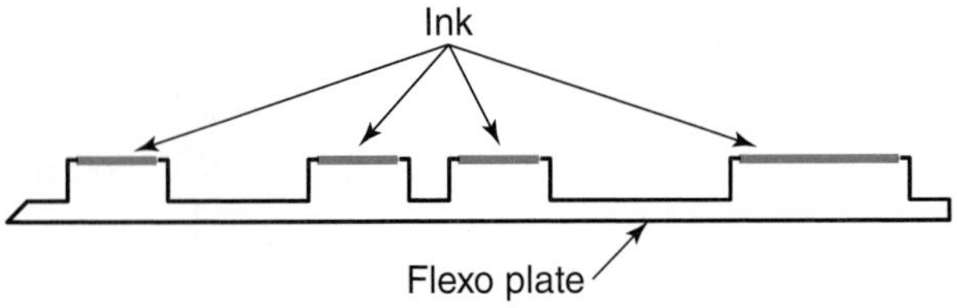

Goodheart-Willcox Publisher

Figure 14-33. The flexographic process is a type of letterpress relief that uses a flexible plate.

Relief Plates

Plates used in traditional relief printing are designated as either original or duplicate plates. Original plates can be used for direct printing or to make a duplicate plate. Duplicate plates are used for long press runs when one plate is expected to wear out before the printing is completed. Duplicates made from a master can also be sent to different locations for printing.

Electrotypes

An ***electrotype*** is produced from a mold through an electrochemical process. After a mold is made from the original type form, the image is sprayed with silver. The silver coating is a conductive material that forms a thin layer on the surface of the mold. The surface is then electroplated with a layer of copper or nickel to form a shell. When the shell that forms the relief image is removed from the mold, it is backed with a layer of lead or plastic to provide support. The electrotype is then attached to a base and ready to be printed, **Figure 14-34**.

Rubber Plates

Rubber plates are flexible relief plates commonly used in flexographic printing. They have a raised image area that is formed from a mold or matrix. As

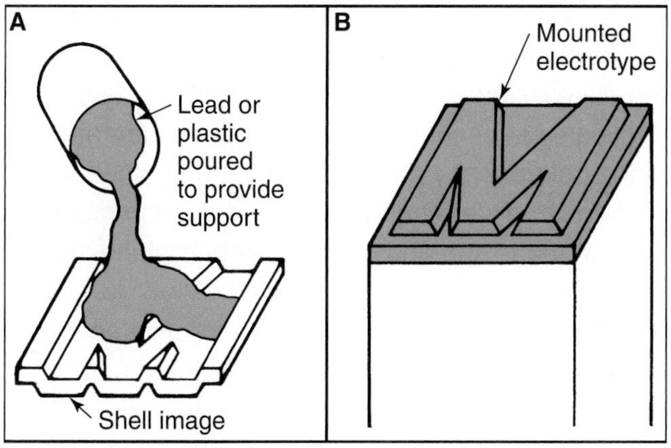

Goodheart-Willcox Publisher

Figure 14-34. Electrotypes are duplicate plates that are formed through an electrochemical process. A—The shell containing the image is produced from a mold of the original form and is backed with a layer of lead or plastic. B—The newly formed plate is mounted on a base for printing.

discussed earlier, rubber plates are designed to wrap around the plate cylinder of a press.

Photopolymer Plates

Photopolymer plates are light-sensitive plastic image carriers that are widely used in flexographic printing. The plate surface contains a hard, sensitized plastic coating or polymer that is bonded to a backing or base, **Figure 14-35**. Photopolymer plates are flexible and designed for long use.

Photopolymer plates can be imaged directly by lasers using computer-to-plate (CTP) technology. An image is scanned and transferred directly to the plate by the computer and then the plate is automatically processed by washing out the nonimage area.

Relief Presses

Three types of relief presses are commonly used in the relief printing process: a platen press, a flatbed cylinder press, or a rotary press, **Figure 14-36**.

Platen Press

A ***platen press*** produces printed materials by pressing a locked-up form or plate containing the image against a platen, the printing surface that holds the paper. Platen press designs vary, but

Think Green

Recycled Plates

Lithographic plates can be coated with a variety of metals. Some of the most commonly used are plastic, stainless steel, and copper. One that is becoming used more and more is aluminum. There are many advantages to using aluminum, but it is important to note that aluminum plates can be recycled. Several lithographic printing plants are going green. A common attribute among them is that they use recyclable aluminum plates so the waste does not go to landfills. Recycling programs for aluminum plates are offered by multiple platemaking companies. Most of these services also provide tracking for printers so they can verify that their plates have been properly handled and recycled.

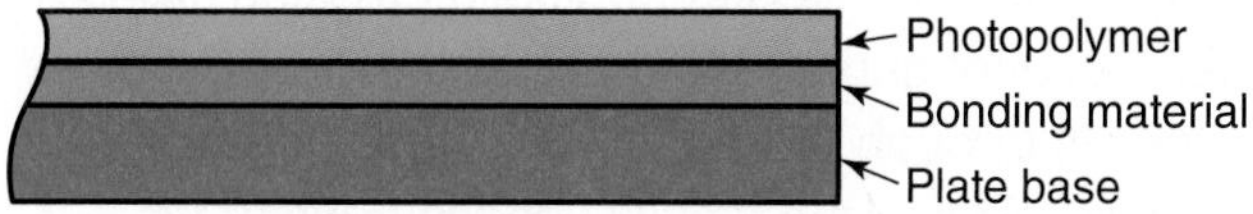

Goodheart-Willcox Publisher

Figure 14-35. Photopolymer plates have a sensitized plastic surface layer that hardens after exposure to ultraviolet light.

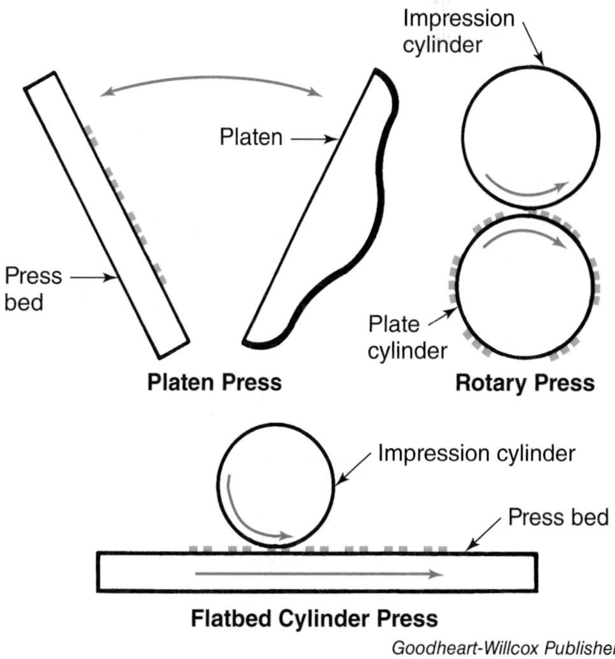

Goodheart-Willcox Publisher

Figure 14-36. The three types of presses most commonly used in relief printing are the platen press, the flatbed cylinder press, and the rotary press.

components used include a feedboard, a bed, a platen, bails, grippers, and a delivery board.

Hand-fed platen presses use gauge pins to align the paper on the drawsheet. The location of the gauge pins is determined by printing a test impression on the drawsheet and placing a sheet of paper over the image. The pins are inserted to fit the dimensions of the paper, typically at the top and left sides. When paper is placed on the platen, the gauge pins are used to hold each sheet in the desired position for printing. After the gauge pins are set, the test impression can be removed from the drawsheet with solvent.

Flatbed Cylinder Press

A flatbed cylinder press prints by producing contact between a flat surface or bed supporting the plate and a revolving impression cylinder that carries sheets of paper. The chase holding the plate or type form is mounted onto the bed. The paper on the cylinder then rolls over the bed and receives the image from the inked form. The impression cylinder uses a set of grippers to grasp and deliver paper as it travels through the press. The pressure between the cylinder and the type is used to transfer the image. Many of the same devices and techniques that are associated with platen presses are used to operate flatbed cylinder presses.

Rotary Press

A rotary press prints the substrate as it travels between an impression cylinder and a plate cylinder, **Figure 14-37**. The impression cylinder draws paper into the printing unit and releases it after it is printed. The image carrier used by a rotary press is a curved plate that is mounted onto the plate cylinder. Rotary presses typically use duplicate plates for long press runs and operate at high speeds. They are designed as both sheet-fed systems and web-fed systems and are commonly used in magazine and newspaper publishing, where longer runs are required.

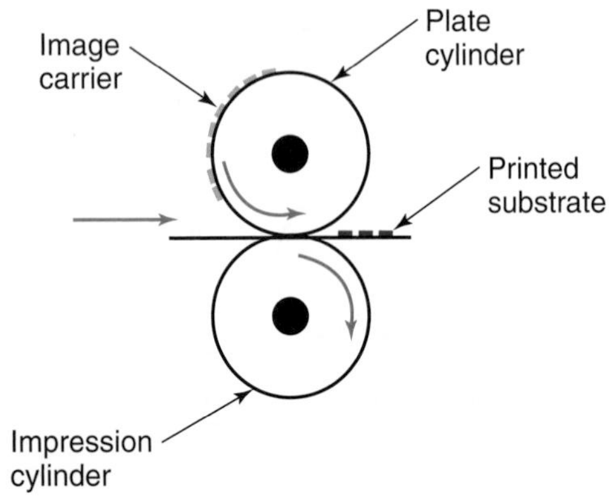

Goodheart-Willcox Publisher

Figure 14-37. A rotary press is designed to print paper as it passes between a plate cylinder and an impression cylinder.

Rotary presses used in multicolor printing are equipped with several printing units. Each unit contains a separate plate cylinder that prints a single color. In this design, a common impression cylinder is surrounded by several printing units. The common cylinder provides the pressure needed to transfer images from each plate to the paper as it is fed through the system.

Like other web-fed presses, web-fed rotary presses are designed to print high volumes of materials on a continuous roll of paper. The web winds through each system during operation of the press, **Figure 14-38**. Rotary presses are equipped with individual feeding, printing, drying, and delivery systems.

Gravure Printing

Gravure creates prints from images that are etched below the surface of the image carrier. Images are etched onto the printing plate or cylinder with electronically controlled cutting devices or with laser imaging technology. See **Figure 14-39**.

The dominant gravure process uses a metal cylinder as the image carrier. The engraved image area is recessed below the nonimage surface. The press rotates and prints continuously, at high speed, on both web-fed and sheet-fed stock.

The gravure process has four basic steps, as shown in **Figure 14-40**.

1. Ink is deposited onto the surface of the image carrier and collects in microscopic ink cells below the surface.
2. Excess ink is removed from the nonimage area.
3. The substrate is pressed against the image.
4. The substrate absorbs or attracts the ink to produce a printed image.

The paper, usually fed by a web traveling about 30 mph (48 km/h), acts like a blotter, absorbing the

Goodheart-Willcox Publisher

Figure 14-38. This web-fed rotary press prints on a continuous web (roll) of paper and is designed to operate at high speeds.

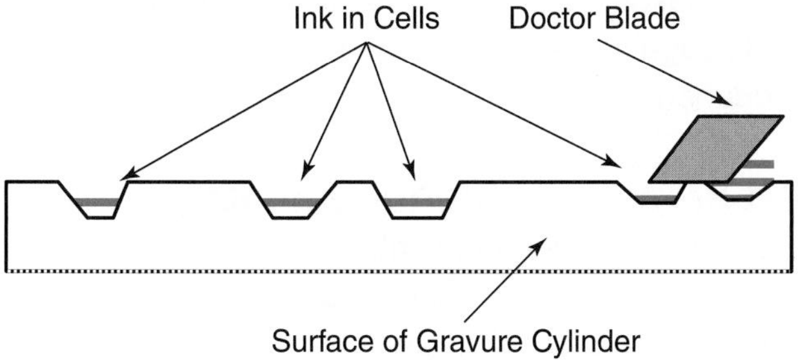

Goodheart-Willcox Publisher

Figure 14-39. The cells for the ink and the doctor blade that removes excess ink in the gravure process.

ink from the microscopic ink cells. The cylinder can have as many as 22,500 ink cells per square inch. The amount of ink absorbed into the surface of the substrate depends on the size and depth of the ink cells, **Figure 14-41**.

Gravure Industry

The gravure industry is divided into three major markets: publication/advertising, packaging, and specialty products. Products typical of the publication/advertising market are magazines,

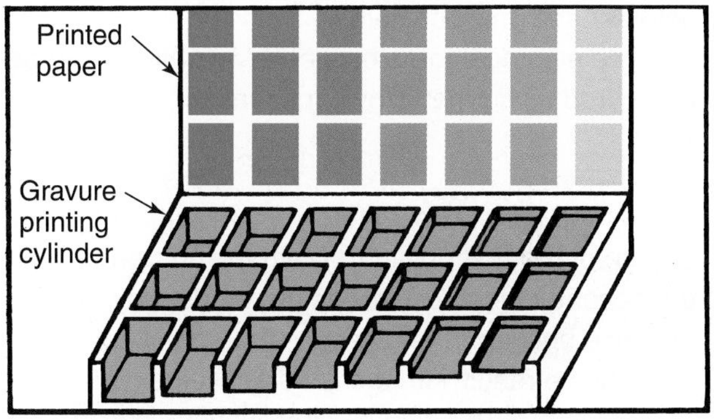

Goodheart-Willcox Publisher

Figure 14-41. Magnified ink cells. Deep cells produce darker, denser image areas. Shallow cells produce lighter, less dense image areas.

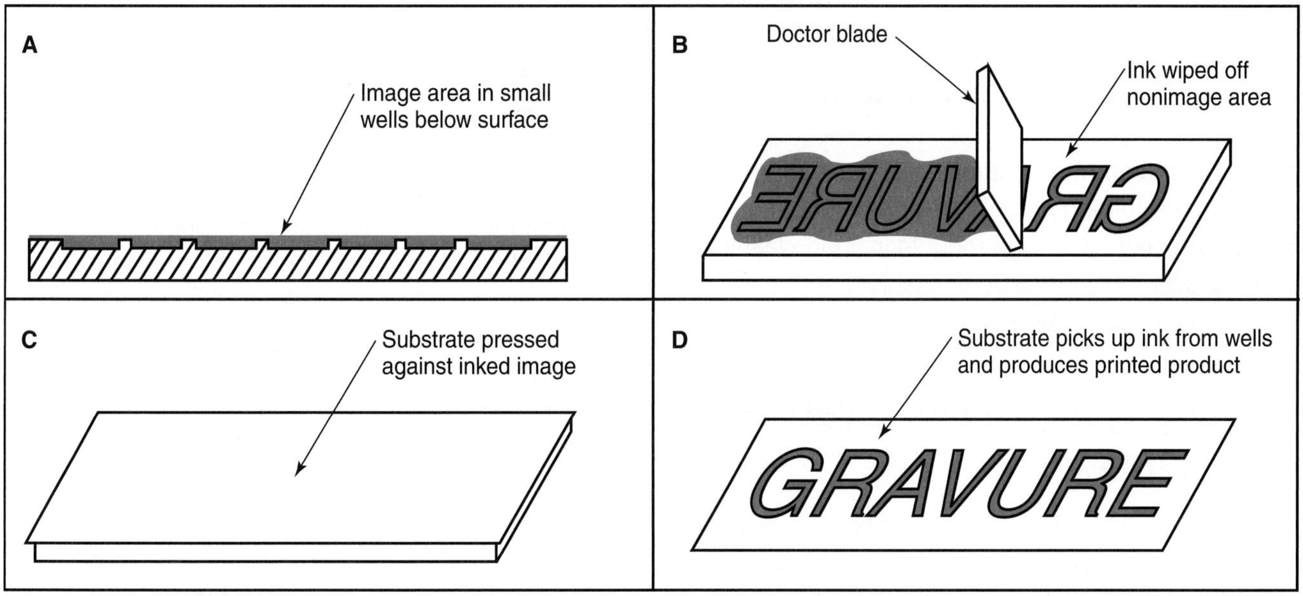

Goodheart-Willcox Publisher

Figure 14-40. Basic steps for printing with gravure. A—Side view of an image carrier shows ink collected in tiny ink wells recessed below the nonimage surface. B—A doctor blade is slid across the image carrier to remove excess ink. C—The substrate is pressed against the inked image. D—The substrate absorbs the ink for a printed image.

Academic Link

Coulomb's Law

In the field of electrostatics, Coulomb's law is one of the principle foundations. French physicist Charles Augustin de Coulomb published some of his research and experiments in 1785, which included electrostatic forces. The force between positively and negatively charged items will either repel (two positives or two negatives) or attract (one positive and one negative) and is affected by the distance between the charged items.

The electrical force between two objects can be measured using the following equation:

$$F = k (q_1 \times q_2) / r^2$$

To find the electrical force (F), multiply the charge of the first object (q_1) with the charge of the second object (q_2), divide the product by the distance between the objects squared (r^2), and multiply the result with the constant value (k).

Coulomb's law also has applications outside the field of electrostatics. Because protons have a positive charge and electrons have a negative charge, Coulomb's law explains how atoms bind together to form molecules. Coulomb's law also applies when studying crystal structures. Crystals are composed of charged particles called *ions*, which arrange themselves in such a way that the charges are balanced.

catalogs, and stamps. Examples of packaging products are folding cartons, wrapping paper, and labels. Specialty printing products include wall and floor coverings, automobile windshield and glass tints, and plastic containers.

Advantages and Disadvantages of Gravure

The main advantage of gravure printing is its simplicity. Gravure is a direct printing process, so it can run at higher speeds. Gravure is capable of consistent, high-quality reproduction at a low per-unit cost on extremely long press runs. The microscopic cell structure of the image carrier results in the appearance of nearly continuous tone on the press sheet. Furthermore, the long life of the gravure cylinder sustains high-quality reproduction. The inks used in gravure printing dry rapidly, allowing for faster press speeds.

The main disadvantage of gravure is inherent in the printing cylinder. If an engraved gravure cylinder is damaged during shipping or production, the entire cylinder or set of cylinders may have to be re-engraved.

Gravure Prepress Considerations

Several factors must be considered at the prepress stage. These include art preparation, page makeup, color reproduction, film preparation, and image carrier configuration. Most artwork is produced digitally.

Art Preparation Requirements

Both line work and continuous tone images are reproduced with a screen pattern. Because the screen pattern disrupts fine lines, medium- or bold-faced styles are recommended for 8-point or smaller type. Small sans serif type styles reproduce better than small type in styles containing a hairline serif structure.

Continuous Tone and Color Requirements

Continuous tone photographs or copy selected for reproduction should have average contrast and good tonal separation. Reflection copy includes, such items as color photographs, watercolor or oil paintings, or any other opaque copy. In reproduction, white light is reflected from the copy and passed through filters before striking unexposed film. When reflection is a problem because images are not on the same plane, as with oil paintings, a color transparency can be made for reproduction.

Color correction should be done before reproduction to compensate for impurities in the printing ink. Color evaluation and viewing of both originals and reproductions should be performed under uniform lighting conditions. The gravure industry uses the ANSI standard of 5000 K for viewing.

Image Carrier Configurations

The three basic gravure image carrier configurations are flat, split cylinder, and cylinder, **Figure 14-42**.

The flat image carrier is used on sheet-fed presses. It is used for limited runs requiring high-quality results, such as printing stock certificates and limited editions of fine art originals.

A split cylinder, or wraparound plate, is thicker than an offset plate. However, like the offset plate, it is flexible and designed to bend around a cylinder. In the United States, sheet-fed gravure is used primarily for limited runs. Some wraparound presses have as many as six printing units. They cannot produce an edgeless or continuous design because they use a clamping gap to hold the plate onto the cylinder.

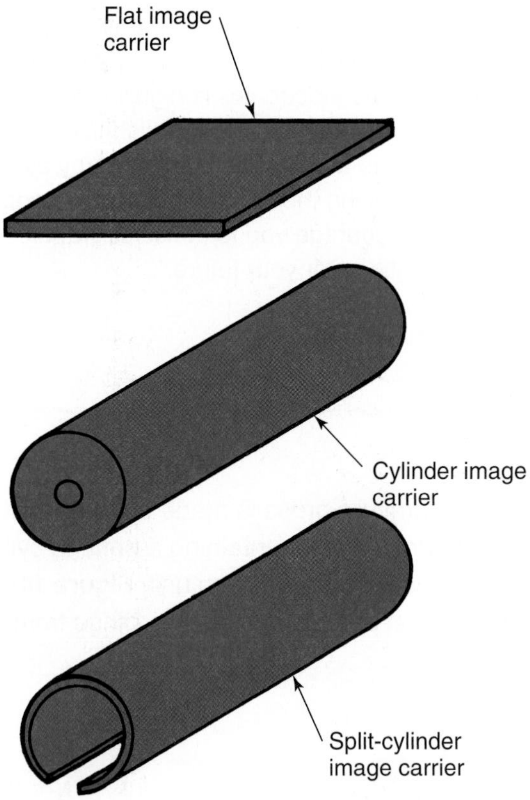

Goodheart-Willcox Publisher

Figure 14-42 Basic image carrier configurations. The cylinder is able to produce a continuous image.

Gravure cylinder engraving is done almost exclusively by direct digital input to electronic and laser cylinder production devices. The image is engraved by a cutting mechanism or a laser beam. The quality of gravure cylinders has increased considerably. See **Figure 14-43**.

The quality of the final image depends on the construction and preparation of the cylinder. Base cylinder refers to the gravure cylinder before it is imaged. If the base is made of steel or aluminum, it is ground and polished to a tolerance of 0.001″ (0.025 mm).

Transferring the image to the cylinder is accomplished using an electromechanical engraving machine or laser beam.

Electromechanical Engraving Method

In direct digital engraving, electronic circuits feed the digital information, stored in the computer file, to the engraving unit. A computer-controlled engraver receives the electronic pulses that are generated by the computer file, prompting a diamond stylus cutting tool or a laser device to form tiny ink wells on the image carrier surface.

Copper was originally used for laser engraving. However, copper did not prove to be a suitable metal for use with the laser. Later research has shown that zinc is a more suitable metal base for laser engraving.

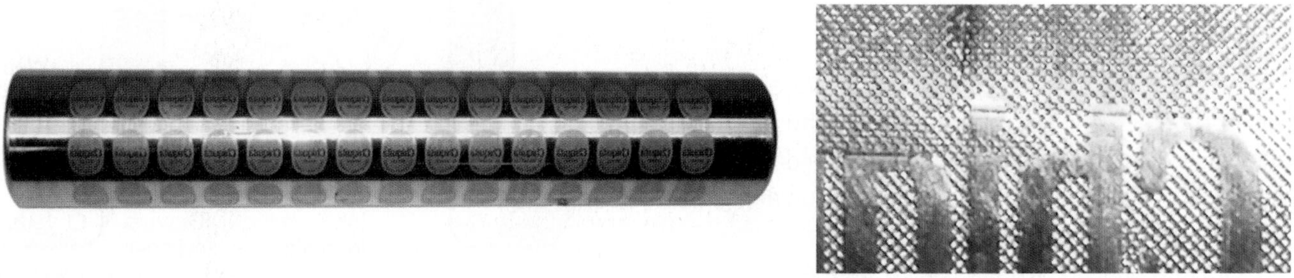

A B

©PIA

Figure 14-43. A—Gravure cylinder showing the etched image area. B—Closeup view.

Career Link

Lithographic Press Operator

Lithographic press operators run many different types and sizes of printing presses found within the industry. On any type or size press, the operator must produce a product that is of high quality, is completed on time, and matches the job specifications to meet the customer needs. In addition to press operation, the operator must perform regular maintenance on the press and other printing equipment. Keeping equipment in excellent condition helps to ensure optimum output.

Other responsibilities of a lithographic press operator include preparing stock for printing, maintaining a clean and organized production area, monitoring product quality during production, observing all shop and equipment safety guidelines, and working closely with other team members to assure customer satisfaction. Operators are expected to have adequate knowledge of substrates and production processes. Mechanical knowledge of machines and tools is also considered beneficial.

Most of the lithographic press operator positions require a minimum of a high school diploma. Many operations require technical school or certification program training. Equipment-specific training is typically provided on the job or through manufacturer-sponsored training sessions. Knowledge in basic mathematics, chemistry, computers, and electronics is highly desirable.

"Whether your interests are technical in nature, or based in the areas of marketing or any aspect of communicating thoughts, ideas, or philosophies, I strongly encourage you to consider graphic communications for your future."

Mike Chiricuzio
Arizona State University

Cylinder Evaluation and Finishing

Once the gravure cylinder is engraved, it must be closely inspected. Under 12× or greater magnification, the ink cell structure is checked for flaws. Cylinder correction can be accomplished by spot plating, burnishing with charcoal, lacquering, or other methods.

Once any necessary corrections are completed, the cylinder is plated in chrome to increase the life of the image carrier. Plating is typically 0.0003″ (0.008 mm) thick. Chromium is harder than copper and can better withstand the friction of the doctor blade.

Gravure Printing Press

After the flexographic press, the gravure press has one of the simplest reproduction methods. Unlike offset, the gravure press does not require a dampening system. Cheaper grades of paper can be run at higher press speeds without the threat of web tear.

Gravure printing typically uses a web-fed or rotary press. A press running at 2000 to 2500 fpm has a web that is traveling around 30 miles per hour (mph).

The gravure press is made up of a number of printing units, each containing a printing cylinder. The web is fed through each unit, **Figure 14-44**. The combination of printing units can range from 4 to 16

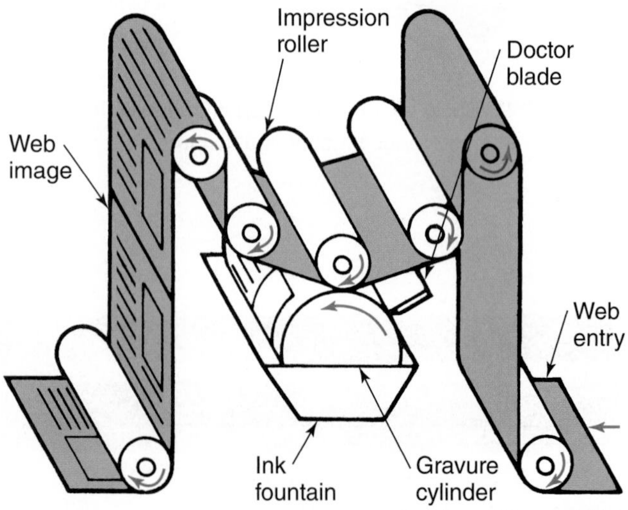

Goodheart-Willcox Publisher

Figure 14-44. Movement of the web through a gravure printing unit.

or more. The number of units depends on the number of pages being printed and the amount of color work being produced.

At each unit, the cylinder is immersed in the ink fountain. As the cylinder turns, its tiny ink cells fill with ink. Modern gravure printing presses can have cylinders over 12′ (3.6 m) wide.

Doctor blade thickness is typically 0.006″ (0.15 mm), with a set angle of 20°. The blade can be stainless steel or plastic, but is usually made of blue-spring steel. Both thickness and set angle can vary.

An impression roller usually applies pressure at 100 lb–200 lb per linear inch at the printing nip point. Impression rollers are made of rubber, neoprene, and other synthetic products. Impression rollers should be tested for the degree of hardness as determined by the printing substrate. Resilience and solvent resistance are important to the continued quality of printing.

Gravure printing is done on a wide variety of substrates, including inexpensive paper stocks. Paper should be evaluated by strength and ink absorption. Packaging and specialty products typically use such substrates as film, cellophane, cloth, plastic, and corrugated board.

Many gravure printing presses use a process known as ***electrostatic assist*** to improve ink transfer to the substrate, especially when the surface is hard or has poor ink receptivity. If ink transfer is incomplete or inconsistent, highlights or light tone values will have a speckled appearance, or color reproduction may shift in hue. In electrostatic assist, electrical charges between the impression roller (negative) and the printing cylinder (positive) create a force that achieves a nearly complete release of ink from the etched cells, **Figure 14-45**.

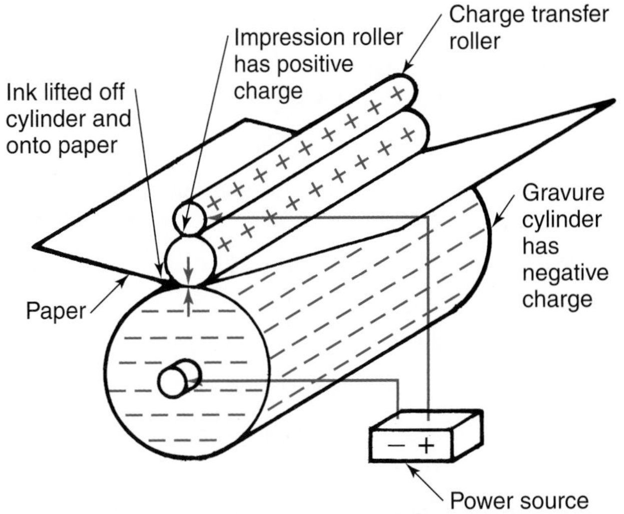

Goodheart-Willcox Publisher

Figure 14-45. In electrostatic assist, a power source feeds a positive charge to the transfer roller which, in turn, transfers the charge to the impression roller and the paper. The gravure cylinder receives a simultaneous negative charge. A magnetic force is created, helping to pull ink out of the wells onto the substrate.

Warning

Fires can occur on the gravure press when electrical charges are exposed to volatile solvent-based inks. Take all necessary precautions to prevent this from happening.

Gravure Process Inks

The process color inks used in gravure printing differ in both hue and composition from the average offset lithography and letterpress inks.

Classification of Gravure Inks

Figure 14-46 shows a general guide only. It cannot cover all technologies and technical variants used to address the needs and demands of an ever-changing gravure market. It is important to use technical information and proper handling information furnished by the manufacturer.

Screen Printing

Screen printing is the process of forcing ink through a porous fabric and the open areas of a stencil to produce an image. It is known by two names: *serigraphy* in the field of fine arts, and *screen printing* in the graphic communications industry.

Screen printing can be a very simple process, requiring only a few inexpensive tools and materials, or it can be extremely complex, requiring an array of sophisticated equipment and production techniques. The deciding factors are the complexity and level of quality required in the finished piece. See **Figure 14-47**.

Type	Function
Type A	This type of ink is mostly used for newspaper supplements, catalogs, advertising inserts, and similar publication work.
Type B	This ink is formulated mainly for publication printing on coated stock.
Type C	These inks are primarily used for package printing on foil, paperboard, coated and uncoated paper, metallic paper, and some types of fabrics.
Type D	These inks work well when printing on plastic film.
Type E	These inks are often used on paper and paperboard, shellac or nitrocellulose-primed foil, and many coated papers and boards.
Type M	These inks are made from polystyrene resins that are used to produce low-cost top lacquers.
Type T	High gloss type of ink, but the health and safety hazards associated with chlorinated rubber has almost eliminated its use.
Type V	These inks are used to print on vinyl. Decorative products, which include labels, cartons, shrink sleeves, and wall coverings, are typical examples.
Type W	These are water-based inks that are primarily used in package printing and product gravure.
Type X	Inks not associated with any of the listed types are classified as Type X, Miscellaneous.

Goodheart-Willcox Publisher

Figure 14-46. General classification of inks.

©Caryn Butler

Figure 14-47. Students using the screen printing process on T-shirts.

Screen Printing Applications

The hallmark of screen printing is its diverse applications. It can be done on a wide variety of materials, including metal, glass, and wood. Images created using screen printing include posters, clothing, and printed circuit boards. Finished products are as diverse as a football jersey or a traffic sign. Screen printing is frequently the only process that can do the job.

Images are created in much the same way as other printing processes. Handmade stencils are still used in the industry, but many are now created on the computer. Drawing and page composition programs are used to create the images. Existing digitized images may also be used. These images are commonly output on an imagesetter.

Screen Printing Process

First, porous fabric is stretched across the frame. Next, a stencil is adhered to the fabric, blocking out portions of the fabric and leaving open the desired image areas. Ink is poured onto the fabric and forced through the image areas using a rubber or plastic blade called a ***squeegee***. The ink is deposited onto a substrate below, producing an image of the cut stencil. Additional prints are made by repeating the squeegee action on a new substrate. See **Figure 14-48**.

Squeegees

A handheld squeegee has a smooth wooden or aluminum handle and a rubber or polyurethane blade. Squeegee blades are usually 3/16″ (4.7 mm) to 3/8″ (9.5 mm) thick and 2″ (5.1 cm) high.

Squeegee blades are rated by hardness. Blades are also distinguished by material used. Always keep squeegee edges sharp.

Different substrates require different blade edges. Six squeegee blade shapes are shown in **Figure 14-49**. The squared-edge blade is used for flat surfaces and general-purpose printing. The squared-edge with rounded corners provides extra-heavy ink deposits on flat substrates and is used when a light color will be printed on a dark substrate. A rounded-edge blade is used primarily in textile printing where an extra-heavy ink film is required. Single-sided beveled edge blades are used for printing on glass. The double-sided beveled edge with flat point is used for printing on ceramics, and the double-sided beveled edge, is used for printing on cylindrical objects such as bottles and containers.

Machine squeegees are similar to hand squeegees. The machine squeegee handle is rectangular and has a thicker profile, **Figure 14-50**.

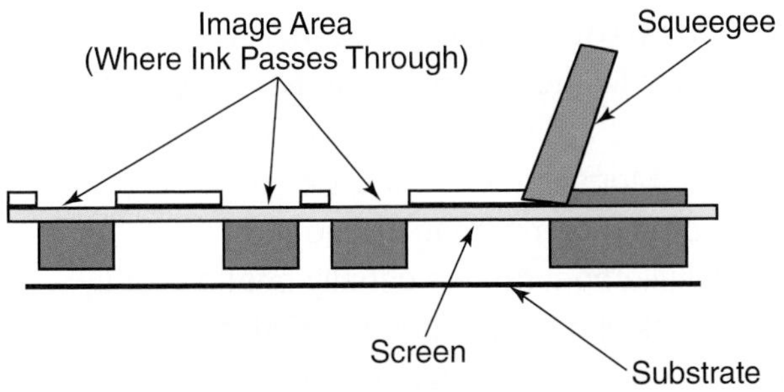

Goodheart-Willcox Publisher

Figure 14-48. The screen printing process.

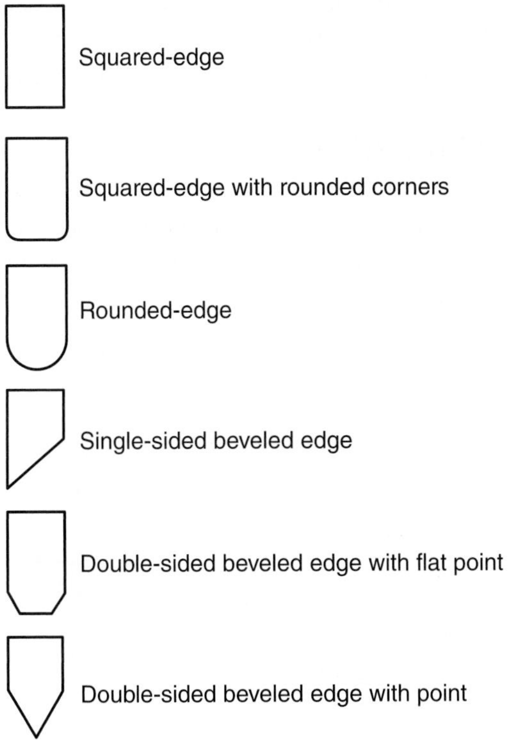

Goodheart-Willcox Publisher

Figure 14-49. Squeegee blade shapes used for printing on various substrates.

Screen Solvents

Screen printing solvents are classified as thinners, retarders, and washup solvents. ***Thinners*** are solvents added to ink to change the viscosity (thickness) of the ink. ***Retarders*** are solvents added to ink to thin the viscosity and slow the drying time. Retarders are necessary with some fast-drying inks that may clog mesh openings in the screen fabric. This is an especially important factor in warm climates, where solvent evaporation and drying is accelerated. ***Washup solvents*** are used to remove ink from the screen. They are inexpensive and their only function is to dissolve ink.

Warning

Prolonged exposure to solvent fumes can be harmful. Provide adequate ventilation and air exchange.

Drying Systems

Oven drying systems provide fast drying times. Three oven drying methods used often are conduction, convection, and radiation.

burnel1/Shutterstock.com

Figure 14-50. A squeegee on a screen printing press is automatically pulled across the image.

Conduction occurs when heat is generated within an object by contact with a heat source. Convection heating uses warm air to transfer heat to the object. Radiation heating occurs when heat is generated within an object through exposure to radiation.

Screen Frames

The screen frame:

- Provides a means of attaching fabric at the proper tension.
- Provides rigidity and dimensional stability.
- Resists mechanical stress and warpage.
- Resists chemical action and corrosion.
- Provides a means for register.

Frame Materials

Materials used to manufacture screen frames include wood, metal alloy, steel, and plastic. Wood and metal alloy are the most common.

Wood frames are still popular for general screen printing applications. A hardwood such as maple is ideal, but pine is most frequently used because of its low cost. Frames and fasteners are under a constant deluge of water. Avoid metal fasteners when possible. Rust and corrosion will cause the frame joints to loosen and weaken. Wood frames should be glued using an adhesive that is waterproof. Apply a waterproof sealer before the frame makes contact with moisture.

Metal alloy frames provide greater rigidity and dimensional stability than wood frames and are essential in commercial screen printing. While not susceptible to chemical attack from water, these frames have poor resistance to acids and soda solutions. Metal alloy frames are available in a variety of styles and sidewall dimensions. Most have built-in mechanical clamps for attaching and stretching the screen fabric.

Frame Profiles

If fabric tension causes the frame to bend inward, the fabric tension will be varied, causing the image to lose register or become distorted. To compensate for the inward pull, some screen printers intentionally deflect frame sidewalls inward when attaching fabric, **Figure 14-51**. After the tensioned fabric is attached, the frame automatically relaxes, resulting in an outward pull of the frame sidewalls to balance the inward pull of the tensioned fabric.

Classifying Screen Fabrics

Screen fabrics are classified according to filament, mesh count, strength, and weave pattern. A filament refers to the selected type of thread. The mesh is the number of threads per inch. The strength is designated by the diameter of the thread. The weave determines the pattern of the vertical and horizontal threads to make the screen.

Filament

A ***filament*** is a single thread. A fabric may be either multifilament or monofilament. Multifilament means there are several strands of material per filament. Monofilament means each filament is a single strand of material, or one thread.

Multifilament fabrics usually print a slightly uneven ink film. Monofilament fabrics provide better ink film thickness uniformity and dimensional stability than multifilaments.

Mesh Count

Fabric ***mesh count*** is specified by the number of threads per linear inch. The higher the mesh count, the better the reproduction of fine details. As mesh count increases, fabric strength and durability decrease.

Fabric Strength

Fabric strength is directly related to thread diameter. The strength of multifilament fabrics is specified by X, XX, or XXX. X has the smallest

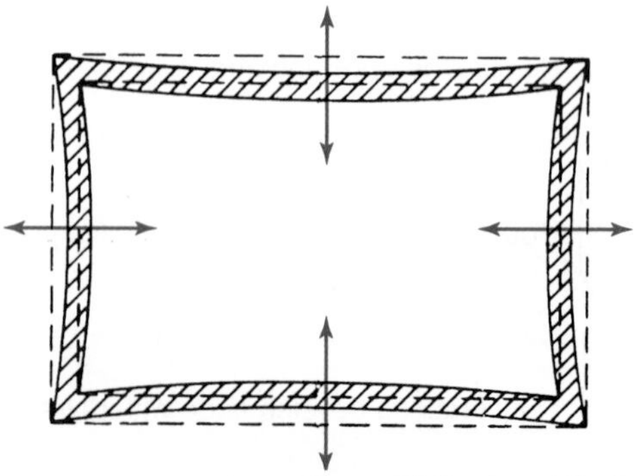

Screen Printing Association International

Figure 14-51. An inward deflection of the frame causes an outward pull on the fabric, which produces fabric tension.

diameter, and XXX has the largest diameter and yields the strongest fabric. As mesh count increases, thread diameter must decrease or no porous areas (open cells) will exist.

Weave Patterns

Weave pattern determines how the vertical and horizontal threads are woven into the fabric. Threads that run horizontally are called ***weft threads***. Threads that run vertically are called ***warp threads***.

Three weave patterns used for screen fabrics are shown in **Figure 14-52**. The plain or taffeta weave is a general-purpose weave used in most situations requiring good strength and sharp detail. The gauze weave is strong, so it is generally selected for extremely long runs. The twill weave causes uneven ink film thickness and poor edge definition, resulting in a more pronounced sawtooth effect. Twill weave fabrics are not capable of producing fine details.

Percent open area is the percentage of area per square inch through which ink can pass. The greater the percent open area, the thicker the ink film and the weaker the fabric. ***Cell size*** is the distance across individual open areas between adjacent threads. It is specified in thousandths of an inch. As cell size increases, the percent open area increases, and fabric strength decreases.

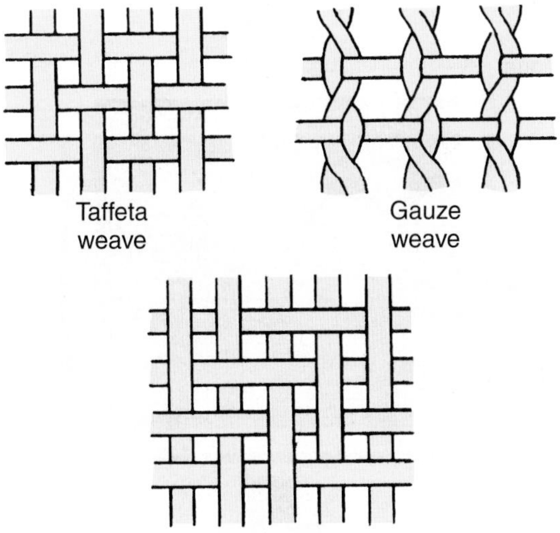

Screen Printing Association International

Figure 14-52. Three types of fabric weaves used for screen printing.

Types of Screen Fabric

Three types of fabric are used as screens: natural, synthetic, and metal mesh. Natural fabrics are always multifilament. Synthetic fabrics may be either multifilament or monofilament. Metal mesh is always a monofilament. Most screen printers prefer synthetic and metal fabrics.

Silk is a natural fabric that has good durability and dimensional stability. It cannot be used with certain chemicals.

Polyester is a synthetic fabric available as a multifilament or monofilament. Monofilament polyester has better ink film uniformity and the best dimensional stability of any natural or synthetic fabric.

Nylon is a synthetic fabric available only as a monofilament. Nylon is the most durable of the natural or synthetic fabrics and adapts well when printing on rough-textured or uneven substrates.

Metal mesh is a monofilament. It is used for printing with heated inks on plastic or when excellent dimensional stability is required. Metal mesh is durable but fragile. Any kinks or deformities usually require replacement of the mesh.

Metalized polyester is a hybrid monofilament fabric with a nickel-plated coating. The coating increases dimensional stability for printing critical tolerances, as with electronic circuit board printing. Metalized polyester is more durable than metal mesh and not as susceptible to kinks or deformities.

Fabric Attaching and Tensioning

The practice of attaching and tensioning fabric to a frame is known as stretching. Despite the fact that it requires two actions, it is considered one operation. Fabric can be attached to the frame using one of four methods: stapling, cord and groove, mechanical clamping, or adhesive bonding.

Stapling

Staples are the least desirable means for attaching and tensioning fabric. A continuous piece of staple tape is placed over the screen before stapling to help keep the screen from tearing. However, staple tape does not solve the basic problems associated with stapling.

Staples are placed in the center of each side of the wood frame with the fabric. Stretch the fabric to a near corner and staple. Gradually pull and tension the fabric while installing the staples. Finish the side by placing the staples at an angle, about 1/8″ (.3175 cm) apart. Then, pull the opposite side and staple. The remaining side is finished in the same way.

Cord and Groove

The cord and groove method is popular in small screen applications where printing requirements are not critical. A cotton or plastic cord is forced into a groove in the frame, **Figure 14-53**. As the cord moves down into the groove, the fabric is stretched across the frame.

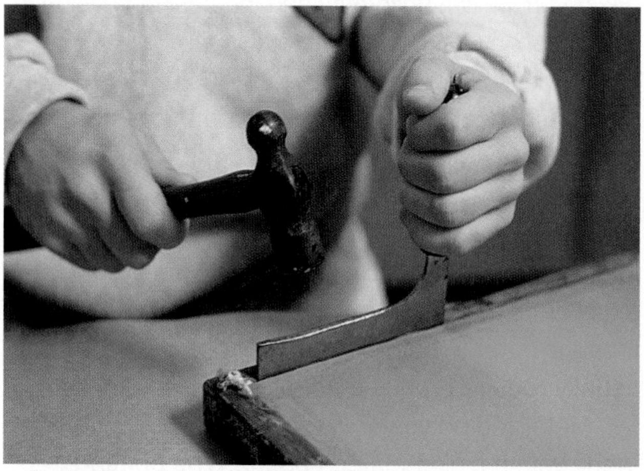

Bowling Green State University, Visual Communication Technology Program

Figure 14-53. Fabric is being stretched using the cord and groove method. As the cord and fabric are forced into the groove, tension is placed on the fabric.

Mechanical Clamping

Mechanical clamps are available on many aluminum frames. The fabric is clamped in position on all four sides. Screws are then turned, forcing the movable clamps outward and resulting in fabric tension.

With mechanical clamping, the fabric may be tensioned to exact specifications. The screw threads should be lubricated periodically to prevent corrosion and wear.

Adhesive Bonding

To attach fabric to a frame with adhesive, a stretching machine is necessary. With a stretching machine, fabric may be tensioned to exact specifications without cell distortion. ***Cell distortion*** is the result of tensioning the fabric in one direction without stretching it equally in the other direction, **Figure 14-54**. Cell distortion is always present when using any method of stretching other than a stretching machine.

Measuring Fabric Tension

Screen tension, or tightness, can be accurately measured using a ***tensiometer***. Tension is expressed in *percent stretch*. Proper tension

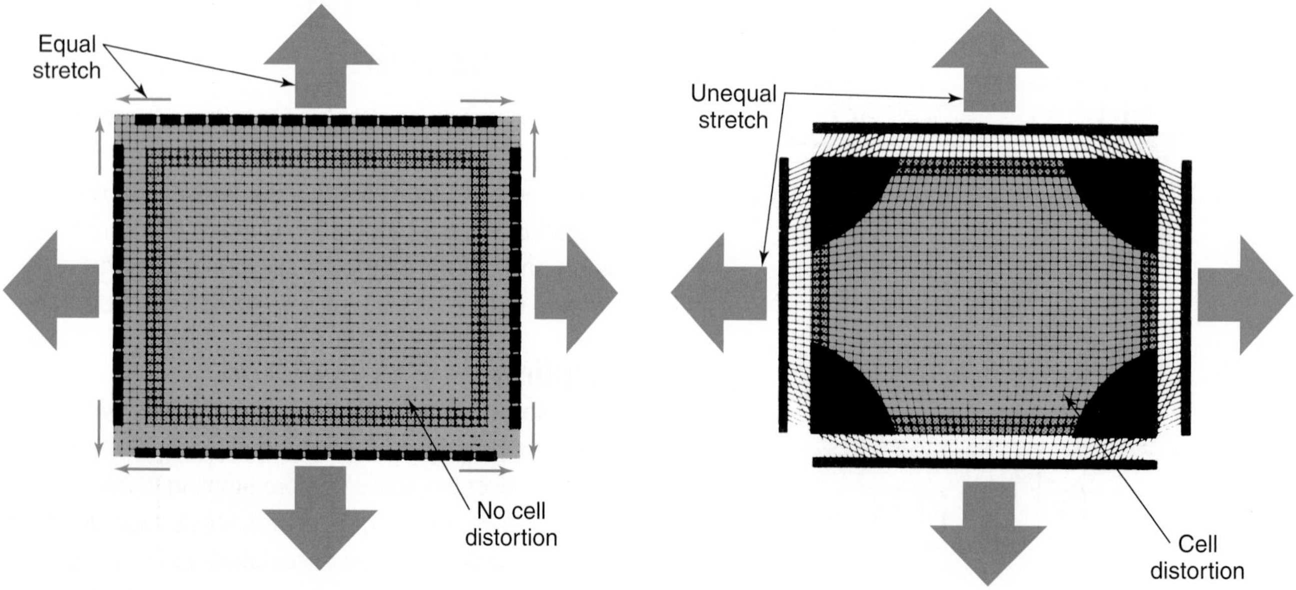

Tetko, Inc.

Figure 14-54. With equal tension applied, cells or openings in the fabric are not distorted.

ensures the screen will create a quality image on the substrate.

When using a tensiometer, measurements are taken from all areas of the fabric. A tensiometer measures tension in Newtons per centimeter. The reading is compared to other areas of the fabric and to the manufacturer's specifications, **Figure 14-55**.

Fabric Treatment

For the stencil and fabric to adhere to each other, the fabric must be cleaned chemically, mechanically, or both. Proper cleaning removes surface grease, airborne contaminants, and residue.

Chemical treatment alters the adhesion characteristics of the fabric and allows for better bonding between the stencil and fabric. Mechanical treatment changes the physical properties of the fabric to enhance the bond between stencil and fabric. Usually, chemical and mechanical treatments are done only once with new fabric. Repeated use of these treatments will degrade the fabric and cause premature fabric failure. Cleaning the fabric, or degreasing, should be done just before a new stencil is adhered to the fabric.

Warning

Always wear skin and eye protection when handling and using chemicals. Follow all safety precautions indicated on chemical containers.

Stencils

Proper selection and tensioning of fabric determines whether images will have quality edge definition, image resolution, ink film thickness, and ink uniformity. The stencil, however, determines whether the quality available in the selected fabric will be maintained. No matter how fine the fabric mesh or accurate the tension, an incorrect or improperly processed stencil will not produce the desired results.

Knife-Cut Stencils

The three types of knife-cut stencils are paper, water-soluble, and lacquer-soluble. Paper stencils are cut from thin, durable types of paper, such as vellum. Generally, paper stencils are used for simple designs, especially if the production run is limited, **Figure 14-56**. Water-soluble stencils consist of a plastic support sheet coated with a water-soluble gelatin. The gelatin is cut and removed from the image area to produce a stencil. Lacquer-soluble stencils are essentially the same as water-soluble stencils, except they are adhered to the screen using a lacquer-based solvent.

Both water-soluble and lacquer-soluble stencils can produce imperfect images if ***burned edges*** are present. Burned edges are the result of poor cutting or adhering techniques, **Figure 14-57**. If the backing sheet is cut, solvent will collect in the cut and burn the cut edge.

Bowling Green State University, Visual Communication Technology Program

Figure 14-55. A tensiometer measures fabric tension.

Bowling Green State University, Visual Communication Technology Program

Figure 14-56. A paper stencil on a screen press.

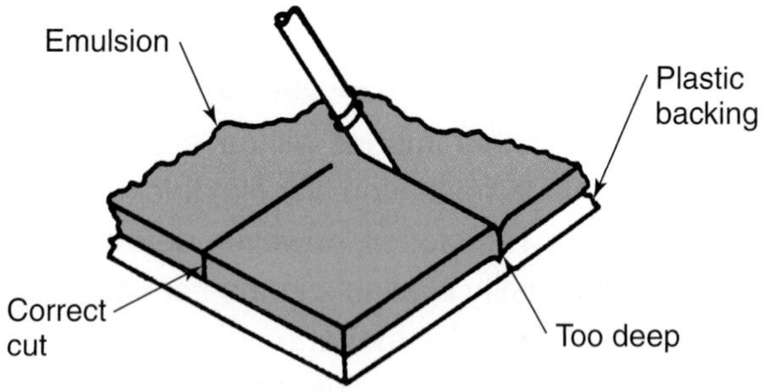

Goodheart-Willcox Publisher

Figure 14-57. Cutting too deeply may groove the backing sheet. Solvent can collect in the groove and burn the stencil.

Photographic Stencils

Photographic stencils are classified as indirect, direct, or direct-indirect. Indirect stencils are exposed off the screen fabric. Indirect water-soluble stencils are used for relatively short production runs, and they reproduce fine detail well. Direct stencils are exposed after a light-sensitive emulsion has been applied to the screen frame. Direct stencils, or photographic emulsions, are favored for their durability on long runs. Direct-indirect stencils are a combination of the two stencil techniques and materials. Direct-indirect stencils can be either emulsion-adhering or water-adhering.

All photographic stencils require a specific exposure. With any change in fabric, mesh count, stencil, or exposure device, a new exposure time needs to be determined. Whenever a colored screen fabric is used to reduce light scatter within a direct or direct-indirect stencil, the exposure time must be increased by 1/3 to 1/2. **Figure 14-58** lists some common problems associated with improper stencil exposure.

The computer-to-screen system produces a high-resolution screen stencil without film. First,

Indirect Stencil	
Underexposed	**Overexposed**
Stencil becomes too thin after washout. Excessive pinholes. Early failure of stencil. Images spread.	Stencil fails to adhere to fabric. Images choke. Stencil is difficult to remove.
Direct Stencil	
Underexposed	**Overexposed**
Stencil is soft in nonimage areas. Stencil becomes too thin after washout. Images spread. Early failure of stencil. Excessive sawtoothing at edges of image (poor mesh bridging).	Stencil is difficult to wash out. Loss of details (such as serifs). Images choke. Stencil is difficult to remove.
Direct-Indirect Stencil	
Underexposed	**Overexposed**
Stencil is soft in nonimage areas, or washes away completely. Squeegee side of stencil becomes too thin. Images spread. Early failure of stencil. Excessive sawtoothing at edges of image (poor mesh bridging).	Stencil is difficult to wash out, or washes out completely due to high pressure required. Loss of details (such as serifs). Images choke. Stencil is difficult to remove.

Goodheart-Willcox Publisher

Figure 14-58. Common exposure problems for three types of stencils.

the screen is coated with an emulsion. A positive image is then placed on the emulsion. This is accomplished by using wax rather than ink from an ink-jet setup. The imaged screen is exposed by using a standard exposure system.

Fabric and Stencil Compatibility

The fabric and stencil must be compatible to get the best image resolution and edge definition. Indirect stencils are best suited to a multifilament polyester fabric, although they can be used successfully with any fabric. Direct stencils and direct-indirect stencils work well with any fabric, but are typically used with a dyed monofilament polyester when printing critical detail.

As light strikes each fabric thread, rays scatter to adjacent areas of the stencil. As a result, small, detailed images can be lost. Ruby, orange, or yellow fabrics reduce the chance of exposure in the image areas due to light refraction. The threads of dyed fabrics act as a safelight filter, refracting wavelengths of light to which the stencil is sensitive. Colored monofilament polyester should always be used when printing halftones or processing color reproductions.

Screen Images

Whenever a screened image is to be printed, the screen fabric tension, frame stability, and stencil processing become even more important in producing an acceptable product.

Using conventional process color angles, the fabric mesh count should be five to six times higher than the screen ruling of the halftone dots. This ratio should eliminate a moiré pattern between screen and fabric mesh. The angle between the screen ruling and the fabric mesh should be 22.5° for the least noticeable interference pattern between lines of halftone dots and fabric mesh.

Screen Printing Presses

Screen printing requires specialized equipment. The most commonly used are the flatbed press, the cylinder press, and the rotary press. The degree of equipment automation is determined by the type of substrate used. Semiautomatic presses require the operator to hand-feed the substrate into the printing position. After printing, the substrate may or may not be removed automatically. Once adjusted, the machine carries out all printing functions. Automatic presses infeed and outfeed automatically.

Summary

- Offset lithographic printing is a process of printing directly from a flat surface. Lithographic printing is based on the principle that oil and water do not readily mix.
- Traditional relief printing is used in printing packaging materials and in finishing operations, such as embossing, ticket numbering, perforating, and die cutting.
- Gravure creates prints from images that are etched below the surface of the image carrier. Images are etched onto the printing plate or cylinder with electronically controlled cutting devices or with laser imaging technology.
- Screen printing is the process of forcing ink through a porous fabric and the open areas of a stencil to produce an image. It is known as serigraphy in the field of fine arts, and screen printing in the graphic communications industry.

Review Questions

Answer the following questions using the information in this chapter.

1. Explain the process of offset lithographic printing.
2. What are the three types of printing plates?
3. Which type of platemaking system scans images as digital data and transfers them directly to the plate?
4. What is the most common base for printing plates?
5. Relief printing creates images from a(n) _____ surface.
6. List three finishing applications of traditional relief printing equipment.
7. *True or False?* Flexography is considered to be a relief process.
8. Name two types of relief presses.
9. List the four basic steps in gravure printing.
10. List three advantages of gravure printing.
11. Both line work and continuous tone images are reproduced with a(n) _____.
12. What are some typical applications of screen printing?
13. Describe the basic process of screen printing.
14. What produces burned edges?
15. Relief printing creates images from a(n) _____ surface.
16. What is the purpose of a duplicate plate?
17. In what printing process are images engraved onto a printing plate?
    A. Gravure.
    B. Rotogravure.
    C. Intaglio.
    D. Offset lithography.
18. *True or False?* An engraved gravure cylinder damaged during shipping or production may have to be re-engraved.
19. Both line work and continuous tone images are reproduced with a(n) _____ pattern.

20. What is the purpose of electrostatic assist?
21. *True or False?* The classification of gravure inks is only a guide, not a standard.
22. _____ are solvents added to screen ink to alter viscosity and slow drying time.
23. Fabric mesh count is specified by the number of _____ per inch.
24. Distinguish between weft threads and warp threads.
25. What type of fabric is used for printing heated inks or when the ultimate of dimensional stability is needed?
    A. Organdy.
    B. Nylon.
    C. Polyester.
    D. Metal mesh.
26. What is the *least* desirable way of holding fabric on a wooden frame?
    A. Staples.
    B. Adhesive.
    C. Mechanical clamp.
    D. Cord and groove.
27. Chemical treatment alters the _____ characteristics of the fabric.
28. What type of photographic stencil is used for long runs because of its durability?
    A. Indirect.
    B. Direct.
    C. Direct-indirect.
    D. None of the above.

Suggested Activities

1. Choose one of the many types of printing plates, and write a paper describing, in detail, the method used to create images on a carrier.
2. Print a two-color close register letterhead using register marks.
3. Visit a plant and write a paper describing safety devices found on a sheet-fed and a web-fed press.
4. Select 10 major magazines and determine if any of them are printed by the gravure process.
5. Research and list technological changes that are taking place in gravure cylinder preparation.
6. Locate at least 10 different products that were printed by the screen printing process.
7. Print the image of a class student design on a T-shirt. Make the image at least two colors.

Chapter 15

Substrates

Learning Objectives

After studying this chapter, you will be able to:

- Explain how paper is manufactured.
- Identify the basic characteristics of various types of paper.
- Describe the applications of coated and uncoated papers.
- Explain the basic size and basis weight of paper.
- Determine various paper weights.
- Summarize the characteristics of plastic substrates.
- Explain the changes occurring with substrates based on environmental issues.

Goodheart-Willcox Publisher

Important Terms

basic size
basis weight
bleaching
calendering
cellulose
chain of custody
chipper
coated paper
de-inking
elemental chlorine
equivalent weight
fillers
Fourdrinier machine
furnish
grades
grain
grain long
grain short
lignin
opacity
paper flatness
petrochemicals
postconsumer paper waste
preconsumer paper waste
printability
print strength
pulpers
ream
recycled paper
show-through
sizing
substance weight
substrate
supercalendering
tensile strength
thermoformed
totally chlorine-free (TCF)
trim
uncoated paper
watermark

G-WLEARNING.COM

While studying this chapter, look for the activity icon to:

- **Practice** vocabulary terms with e-flash cards, matching activities, and vocabulary game.
- **Reinforce** what you learn by submitting end-of-chapter questions.

www.g-wlearning.com/visualtechnology/

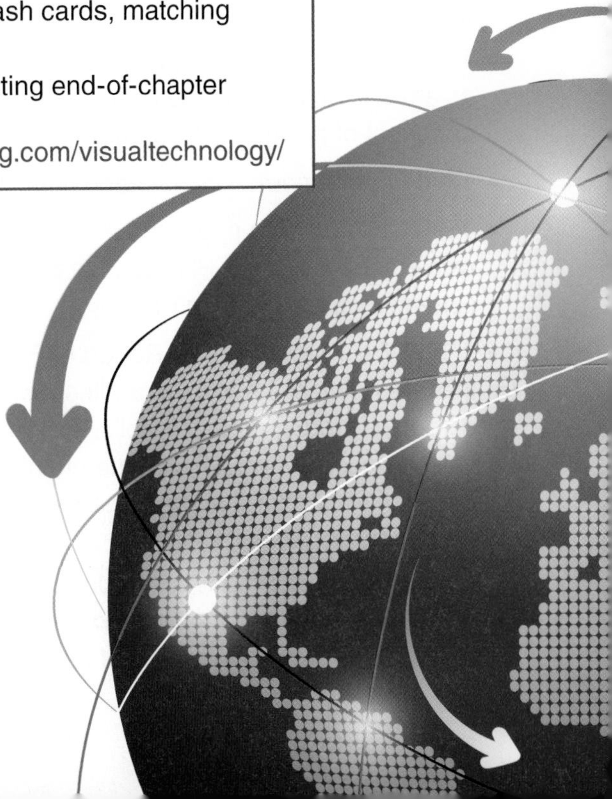

Substrates include any material with a surface that can be printed or coated. Although the most common printing substrate is paper, substances such as plastic, metal, and wood are also classified as substrates.

Matching the substrate to the job is critical. A high-quality layout, plate, ink, and printing technique will be wasted if a low-quality substrate is used. On the other hand, expensive stock should not be used to print low-quality products such as newspapers or sales flyers. Salespeople, designers, press operators, and finishing and binding personnel must have knowledge of the characteristics of paper and its applications. Its misuse can be very costly. More than one thousand different grades of paper are listed in paper merchants' catalogs.

Papermaking History

Most paper is manufactured using machine technology, although some paper is still handmade. The use of handmade papers is usually limited to special applications, such as fine art reproductions, or limited editions of books printed and bound by craftworkers using hand methods.

Some historical highlights of papermaking are:

- 105 CE—Ts'ai Lun, a Chinese official, mixed the bark of the mulberry tree with linen and hemp to make a crude form of paper.
- 500 CE—The Mayans produced paper using fig tree bark.
- 751 CE—Papermaking spread to Europe as a result of the Crusades and the Moorish conquest of northern Africa and Spain.
- 1400 CE—Papermaking by hand flourished.
- 1690 CE—The first paper mill in America was established near Philadelphia by William Rittenhouse and William Bradford.
- 1798 CE—Nicholas Louis Robert of France invented a machine with an endless wire screen to produce paper in rolls. The machine was financed by two English merchants, the Fourdrinier brothers, and was named the American Fourdrinier machine.

Most of the paper manufactured in the United States today is made on the ***Fourdrinier machine***. It can produce continuous sheets of paper up to 33′ (10 m) wide at speeds faster than 3000′ (900 m) per minute. Some Fourdrinier machines are more than 350′ (110 m) long. The mechanical principles of the original machine have remained nearly unchanged. Other inventions have occurred, but many are simply refinements.

Significant improvements in papermaking in recent years include thermomechanical pulping, synthetic wires and felts, twin-wire machines, and the use of computers to control pulping and papermaking operations. Paper manufacturers have also worked to improve pollution control and energy conservation in the industry.

Making Paper

For centuries, the principle raw materials used in papermaking were cotton and linen fibers obtained from rags. Some cotton and linen fibers are still used for high-quality writing papers, business letterhead papers, art papers, and documents that will be kept for years. However, ***cellulose*** is the raw material used to make most paper today.

Pine, fir, spruce, aspen, beech, birch, maple, and oak are typical species harvested for papermaking. The length of the tree fibers varies and determines, among other characteristics, the strength of the paper.

Papermaking is a complex manufacturing process. It uses both chemical and mechanical means to reduce wood fibers to pulp, which is the material used to ultimately produce paper in sheet form. See **Figure 15-1**.

Chipping

Harvested logs are cut to uniform length, debarked, **Figure 15-2**, and sent to a chipper or grinder. The ***chipper*** cuts the logs into 3/8″ to 3/4″ chips. The chips are sized so the digester is able to separate the cellulose fibers. After the chips are screened for size, they are put in a huge cooking kettle called a *digester*.

Making Pulp

In the chemical pulpmaking process, chemicals in the sealed, pressurized digester break down the ***lignin*** present in the cellulose fibers. The cellulose fibers,

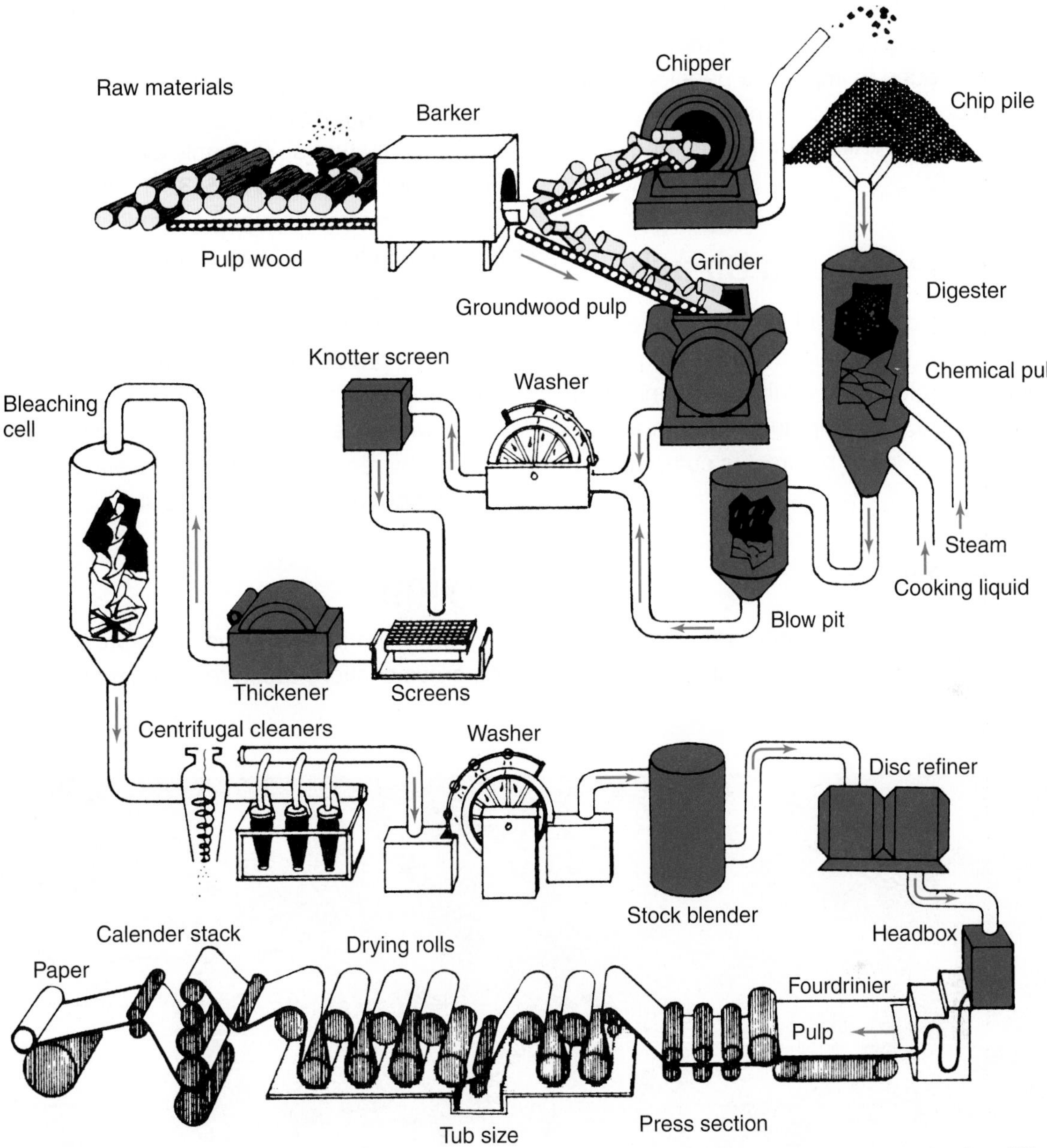

Goodheart-Willcox Publisher

Figure 15-1. Major steps in the manufacture of paper. A modern papermaking operation requires a large investment in equipment and raw materials.

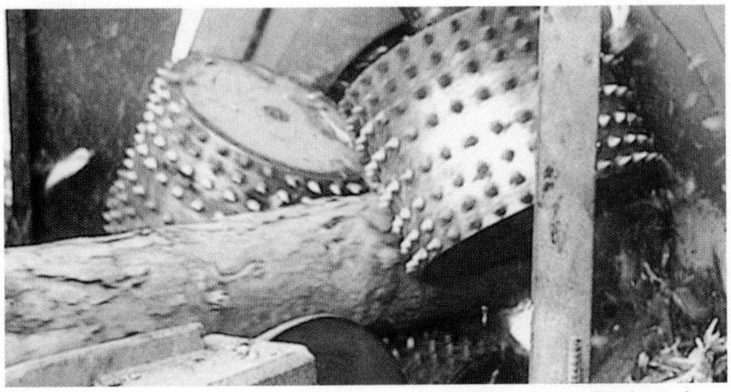

Southern Forest Products Assn.

Figure 15-2. This huge machine rotates logs inside a toothed chamber to remove the bark.

which once resembled soda straws, become pulp, a mass of soft, spongy matter. The pulp is blown into a pit where the chemicals are washed away.

The mechanical pulpmaking process (groundwood process) uses grinding wheels to reduce the logs to fiber. The by-product is pulp with high opacity but relatively low strength.

Sizing and Fillers

Sizing is added to the pulp slurry to make the paper more resistant to moisture. Rosin is a common sizing material. Alum is added as a binding agent. Binding is a part of the sizing process.

Fillers are needed to improve a paper's opacity, brightness, smoothness, and ink receptivity. Three common fillers are clay, titanium dioxide, and calcium carbonate.

Dyes, Pigments, and Bleach

Dyes and pigments are added to produce colored substrates, while bleach makes the pulp white. Coloring or bleaching additives are mixed in vats called ***pulpers***. The pulp goes through a final beating and refining stage before it is pumped to a stock chest.

Removing Water

A jordan machine is a beater or refiner of the fibers. A jordan machine refines the fiber slurry until it is about 99% water and 1% fiber and other solids. At this point, the paper is known as ***furnish***. The solution is pumped into the headbox of the papermaking machine.

The pulp furnish is evenly dispersed on the Fourdrinier wire, **Figure 15-3**. The wire screen vibrates as it travels along an endless belt, aligning the fibers in the direction of travel. A continuous web of paper is formed in the process. Gravity and suction remove about 35% of the water.

Some papers are given a ***watermark***, a translucent identifying design impressed in the paper while it is still wet. The symbols or images are created by rearranging the fibers with a tool known as a dandy roll. See **Figure 15-4**.

Drying

When the furnish leaves the screen, it enters the press section, which removes more water. Then,

Mead Publishing Paper Division

Figure 15-3. The Fourdrinier wire section of the papermaking process. Wet paper fibers ride on an endless wire screen. This is known as the "wet end" of the machine. Water drains off as the fibers move toward the dryers.

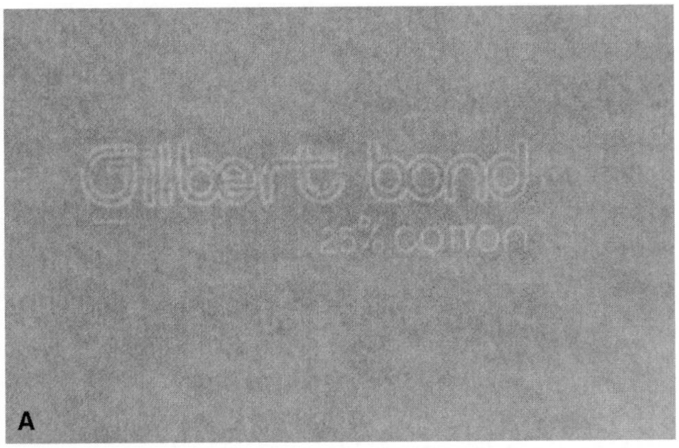

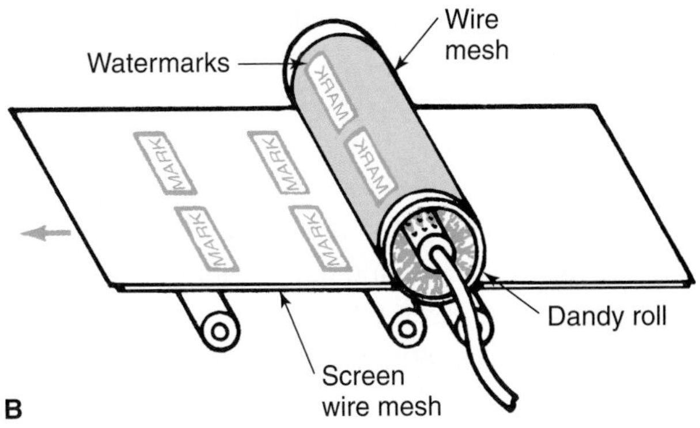

Goodheart-Willcox Publisher

Figure 15-4. Creating a watermark. A—The watermark is simply a rearrangement of paper fibers. It identifies the grade of paper or the trademark of a company. B—A dandy roll is used to place the watermark on the paper.

the paper enters a dryer section consisting of large temperature-controlled rollers. More moisture is removed. Coatings are applied as the paper moves through the machine, **Figure 15-5**.

At some stage of the drying process, the paper must be calendered. ***Calendering*** is the process of flattening and smoothing the paper surface by passing it between a series of rollers.

Mead Publishing Paper Division

Figure 15-5. Many of the papers used today for magazine and book publishing are coated for better reproduction of color and fine-screened halftones. Coating is applied on the papermaking machine.

Supercalendering uses heated steel rollers and pressure to form a very smooth, high-gloss finish, **Figure 15-6**.

Rolling

The untrimmed paper is wound into rolls. Some rolls are rewound, slit, and cut into lengths to make flat packages of paper. Others remain as rolls for use in web-fed presses, **Figure 15-7**.

Paper Types

Adhesive-coated, safety, bond, carbonless, offset, duplicator, cover, ledger, index, newsprint, and recycled are some of the many types of paper. A general understanding of the characteristics and applications of various papers is important.

Coated and Uncoated Papers

Coated paper is a broad classification of paper that has layers of latex, pigments, and adhesives applied to its surface. Coated papers typically have a smoother, stronger surface than uncoated papers. Finishes may be high-gloss, dull-coated, or matte-coated. They are more expensive than uncoated papers but yield better reproduction of images.

Coated papers are rated by brightness. A No. 1-rated paper is suitable for high-quality jobs, such as sales literature. Material intended to convey a prestigious image might use a matte finish, while high gloss might be used to convey a bright and exciting image. No. 1 paper produces very bright color through the use of transparent inks. Printed material, such as catalogs or posters, is typically printed on No. 2 or No. 3. Groundwood-processed sheets are of lower-grade stock, often No. 4 or No. 5.

Mead Publishing Paper Division

Figure 15-6. Heated supercalender rolls are used to smooth and polish the paper surface to a high gloss.

Uncoated paper does not have a layer applied over the surface and tends to have a textured feel. Uncoated paper textures include laid, woven, and linen. These textures are suited to printed pieces that will be written on, such as stationery. Uncoated papers also enhance legibility, making them good choices for text-intensive printed material, such as textbooks or novels.

Adhesive-Coated Paper

Adhesive-coated stock is coated with an adhesive material that is permanently tacky or activated by water or heat. Labels are a common product that use this type of substrate. The heat-seal type of paper uses heat to melt the coating so it will stick to another surface. Stock with a coating that is permanently tacky is commonly called pressure-sensitive. These stocks require contact and pressure to make them adhere to another surface.

Mead Publishing Paper Division

Figure 15-7. On the machine in the background, rolls of paper are being rewound after being slit to different widths. Some of these rolls may later be cut into sheets and packaged; others will be used on web-fed presses.

Safety Paper

Safety stock is typically used for printing checks. The specifications are very rigid because the stock must expose any attempted alteration of the document. If someone tries to alter it by erasure or by using chemicals, the paper automatically displays a change in the design or color. Some other documents using safety paper include bonds, deposit slips, coupons, tickets, certificates of title, warranties, and legal forms.

Bond Paper

Bond paper is a broad classification of quality paper used for business forms, letterheads, stationery, and many other products. Characteristics of bond paper include strength, good ink receptivity, and erasability.

Bond paper is used extensively for printers connected to desktop computers. Laser printers can provide acceptable quality using the same paper designed for photocopying machines. Paper for use in ink-jet printers has a coating formulated to accept the dye-like inks used by these printers.

Bond paper is made from cotton or rag fiber, or from chemical wood pulps. It has an even, hard finish on both sides. Rag bond is the most expensive type of paper and often has a watermark.

Carbonless Paper

Carbonless paper is used to make multipart business forms that will be written on or used in some type of impact printer (a device, such as a typewriter, that makes a physical impression by striking the paper). Carbonless paper starts with a base stock similar to ordinary bond. The paper is coated with encapsulated colorless dyes and a receptor coating that reacts with the dye to produce an image. The capsules are broken when pressure is applied, releasing the dye onto the sheet below. The receptor coating develops the image.

Carbonless business forms have a variety of applications. Checks, vouchers, shipping labels in clear plastic envelopes, and continuous forms for impact-type printers are common uses.

Offset Paper

Offset paper is designed specifically for use on offset printing presses. It has good opacity, rapid ink absorption, and permanence. It can be coated or uncoated. Offset paper is used for a wide variety of products, such as books, form letters, magazines, manuals, and advertisements. See **Figure 15-8**.

Offset paper is sometimes called book paper because both have similar properties and construction methods. Offset papers are made from various materials, including chemical wood pulp, mechanical wood pulp, recycled papers, and even straw. Frequently, two or more of these raw materials are combined to make offset paper.

Impregnated offset paper receives a mineral film to smooth and strengthen the surface for better image reproduction. It is sometimes called pigmentized offset paper.

Text paper is an expensive grade of offset or book paper. Depending on its surface smoothness, it can be both attractive and functional. Smooth text paper is used for accurate reproduction of halftones. Rougher surfaces are used when halftone reproduction quality is not important.

Grant Blankman/Shutterstock.com

Figure 15-8. Books and many other printed products are produced using offset paper, often on web-fed presses like this one.

Cover Paper

Cover paper is a thick or heavy paper, typically used for the covers of books, catalogs, brochures, manuals, and similar publications. Sometimes, two layers of cover paper are bonded together to produce double thickness. When pasted together, it can be sold by caliper or thickness.

Ledger Paper

Ledger paper has a smooth, matte finish that resists erasing. It easily accepts pen and is both strong and durable. Ledger paper is used for accounting notepads, bookkeeping forms, business ledger sheets, and financial statement forms.

Index Paper

Index paper is a thick, stiff, smooth paper, frequently two-ply or greater. Index stock may be coated or uncoated. Its most common uses are index cards and postcards, so it must be sturdy enough to withstand frequent handling. Bristol paper is not as smooth as index paper, but the thickness and use is similar.

Newsprint Paper

Newsprint is one of the lowest grades of printing paper. It is made by the groundwood or mechanical method of papermaking. Newsprint has very short fibers that enable the paper to be folded easily in any direction. When new, it has a grayish-white color, but it turns yellow and becomes brittle with age. Since newsprint absorbs ink readily, a drying system on the press is not needed.

Zink Paper

Zink™ stands for Zero Ink. This product is a very unusual substrate. It is made of composite materials composed of different layers. Embedded between the top layer and the polymer base are dye crystals

Think Green

Paper Recycling

Recycling paper is one of the easiest ways to help protect the environment from the dangers caused by paper waste. There are multiple organizations dedicated to helping the graphic communications industry be less harmful to the environment. One example already discussed is the Forest Stewardship Council. Others include the Sustainable Forestry Initiative and the Green Press Initiative. These organizations ensure pulp for paper comes from recycled material or from approved forests. In order to be considered recycled, the paper must contain at least 30% recycled materials. Recycled paper comes in the forms of preconsumer waste or postconsumer waste. Preconsumer waste includes scraps or other types of leftover paper. Postconsumer waste is paper that has been printed on, used, and recycled. Recycled paper must be de-inked before it can be reused. In order to make recycled paper usable, it must be bleached. The most environmentally friendly process is elementally chlorine-free bleaching. Organizations such as those mentioned offer assistance and certify the paper used by printers is environmentally safe.

of cyan, yellow, and magenta. The paper is colorless and appears as a regular sheet of paper stock. The printer uses heat to activate the embedded crystals, which in turn colorizes the stock.

Recycled Paper

Several environmental issues, such as depleting resources and landfill space, have contributed to the trend toward buying and using recycled paper. ***Recycled paper*** is made from old or used paper products, **Figure 15-9**. There are different grades of recycled paper. High grades can be made into quality printing paper. Low grades can be made into newsprint, cartons, and other products.

The recycled paper arena is dynamic. Guidelines relating to the manufacture of recycled paper are continually being reviewed by the US Environmental Protection Agency (EPA). The

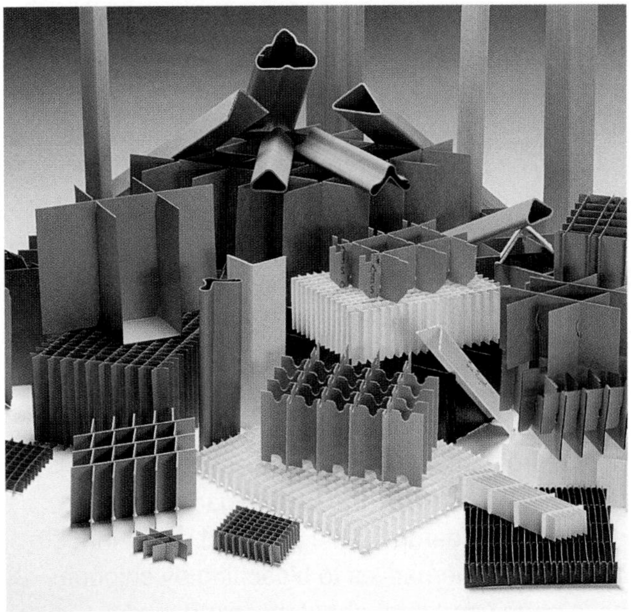

Sonoco Products Co.

Figure 15-9. Corrugated packaging is a major user of fiber from recycled paper.

federal government has established minimum-content standards for the paper it purchases.

Recycled papers may contain preconsumer waste, postconsumer waste, or both. Waste material created by manufacturing processes that would otherwise be disposed of is called ***preconsumer paper waste***. Used materials that have served a purpose and may be recycled into new paper is called ***postconsumer paper waste***.

Guidelines were issued by the Federal Trade Commission for the use of labeling products as recycled in a way that is clear and truthful for consumers. The label must consist of the percentage and type of recycled content, **Figure 15-10**.

Goodheart-Willcox Publisher

Figure 15-10. A product must be labeled to indicate the percentage of recycled matter it contains. The recycled content of this product came entirely from postconsumer waste.

Before paper can be reused, it is subjected to chemical and mechanical processes to return it to a pure condition. ***De-inking*** is the process of removing inks, fillers, and coatings from waste paper. The mixture is reduced to cellulose fibers suspended in a water slurry.

After the waste paper is de-inked, the fibers are bleached. ***Bleaching*** is the use of chlorine bleach to give paper a bright white appearance.

Elemental chlorine was used to bleach paper. However, the waste given off from chlorine was linked to the creation of dioxin, which can cause health problems, including cancer. Once this discovery was made, the EPA began to develop emission standards for the pulp and paper industry. Since then, alternatives to bleaching by chlorine have been used throughout the world.

Elementally chlorine-free (ECF) bleaching uses safer chemicals, such as chlorine dioxide or sodium hypochlorite, instead of chlorine gas. Using oxygen or other nonchlorine bleaching processes is another alternative to eliminate the formation of dioxins. Another alternative is to use unbleached (slightly brown) paper products known as ***totally chlorine-free (TCF)***.

Paper Applications

Some papers are adaptable to different applications, while others are very limited in their use. The applications of paper to various printing processes will be discussed next.

Paper for Gravure

Newsprint produced for gravure printing typically contains mineral fillers and a calendered surface. Mail-order catalogs are a good example of this type of stock. When high-quality gravure printing is desired, the paper used contains mineral filler, but also a larger percentage of short-fiber chemical pulp.

Paper surfaces may be relatively soft, since gravure ink is not tacky. This eliminates the problem of ink picking fibers from the surface of the paper. Coated surfaces are widely used in gravure. Compressibility of paper is important because the gravure cells must make contact with the paper surface.

Because gravure is used in packaging, the stock must have dimensional stability, thickness must be controlled, and moisture content must be considered. The reaction of the stock to the process is critical in the high-production speeds required of gravure.

Paper for Offset Lithography

In offset lithography, fuzz, lint, and dust must be strictly limited. See **Figure 15-11**. A wide variety of papers can be printed by the lithographic process, but any paper must have sufficient fiber-bonding strength to prevent the pulling of fibers from the stock by tacky ink. Because of the surface contact and tackiness of the ink, special coatings are applied to the paper.

Moisture is another consideration. The paper surface must not become weakened by moisture, or fibers will pick off with each successive impression.

©George Deal

Figure 15-11. Papers used for offset lithography, whether printed on a small duplicator or a large web-fed press, must have a surface resistant to having fibers pulled loose by tacky ink. Loose fibers can cause specks and other defects in the printed product.

Surface irregularity is not critical in offset lithography. The blanket is resilient and should return to its original shape, even if the paper has an irregular surface. Of course, limitations do exist. Halftones and solids do not print well on irregular stock.

Paper for Flexography

Flexography is ideal for printing packaging materials because the soft plates can transfer ink to almost any kind of substrate. Kraft linerboard and coated kraft are used in corrugated boxes. The ink is unable to be absorbed into kraft papers. Other paper and paperboard substrates include folding cartons, labels, gift wrap, and paperback books. Newsprint, corrugated linerboard, and paperboard are relatively rough and very absorbent. Calendered and coated papers are the smoothest and least absorbent. They also exhibit high ink holdout.

Paper for Laser Printing

In digital printing, errors in paper selection can cause such problems as misregistration and ink rub-off. The high speeds and temperatures of digital printing equipment require specially formulated papers, some of which are laser-compatible or laser-guaranteed, as well.

For medium- and high-speed black-and-white or color digital printers, smooth-finished laser papers have superior toner adhesion and excellent performance at high speeds and high temperatures. These printers typically print on papers ranging from 16-lb bond to 60-lb cover and 110-lb index.

Dry-toner digital presses run well with smooth, bright papers from 24-lb bond to 80-lb cover stock, coated or uncoated.

Wet-toner digital presses require a special coating on substrates for optimal toner adhesion. A variety of substrates will work, from 50-lb text to transparencies to labels, as long as they are coated.

Paper Characteristics

The directions of fibers in a sheet or web of paper must be a consideration in all printing processes. Another important factor is the stability of the sheet. Will it curl or have wavy edges? Paper also comes in a variety of weights and sizes.

Grain Direction

Paper made by the machine method has ***grain***, which is determined by the direction in which the pulp fibers lie. Direction of grain becomes important when feeding the paper through the press and during some finishing procedures.

The underlined dimension on a package of paper specifies the direction of the grain. Another way to find grain direction is to tear a sheet of paper in one direction and then the other. The straightest tear is parallel to the grain, **Figure 15-12**.

A third means of finding grain direction is to cut two strips of paper, each in a different direction. Lay the strips over a rod or straight surface. The sheet that curves the most is across or at right angles to the grain.

Grain may also be found by dampening one side of the sheet. The dampened paper will curl with the grain. Usually, a sheet of paper will fold easier and form a more even edge with the grain.

In most cases, sheets are fed through a press with the grain parallel to the cylinder of the offset press. The stock is referred to as ***grain long***. During binding, the grain should be parallel to the binding edge so the fibers will not break. ***Grain short*** is a quality that indicates the grains run across the paper.

Paper Flatness

Paper flatness refers to how well the paper remains straight or unwarped. Flatness is a basic

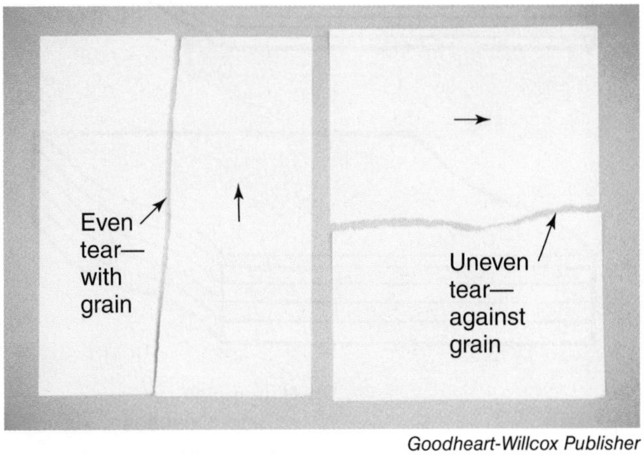

Goodheart-Willcox Publisher

Figure 15-12. An easy way to tell paper grain direction is to tear two sheets in different directions. The straightest tear is parallel to the direction of the grain.

requirement if the stock is to feed through a sheet-fed press without problems.

Paper is naturally hygroscopic, meaning the cellulose fibers seek the moisture in the surrounding area. Most paper is shipped with 4% to 6% moisture content. In a facility with an air temperature of 70°F to 75°F (21°C to 24°C), that equates to 42% to 48% relative humidity.

Wavy paper edges indicate a greater amount of moisture in the edges than inside the sheet, **Figure 15-13**. Sometimes the opposite occurs, resulting in tight edges and a sheet that curls up or down.

Paper handling must be closely supervised. Relative humidity and paper moisture are critical to smooth operation of the press. Packages of paper should be kept closed until needed to keep moisture out. Also, paper must be square and free of dust, lint, and dirt.

Paper Size and Weight

All paper has a grade, a basic size, and a basis weight. The types of paper are also known as ***grades***. Each grade has certain characteristics and uses. The choice of paper grade depends on the intended use.

Basic size, specified by length and width, varies with grade, **Figure 15-14**. The basic size of bond paper is 17″ × 22″. One ream weighs 16 or 20 lb; 16-lb stock is thinner than 20-lb stock. The basic size of book paper is 25″ × 38″. The substance weight of book paper is 2 1/2 times the weight of bond with 2 1/2 times the surface area.

Cover paper has a basic size of 20″ × 26″. It is a durable stock with many textures. It comes in 60-lb to 80-lb weights. The basic size of index stock is 25 1/2″ × 30 1/2″. It is a heavy stock and often identified by the number of plies. One-ply equals 90-lb stock; two-ply equals 110-lb stock; three-ply equals 140-lb stock.

Basis weight is the weight in pounds of one ream of basic-sized stock. A ***ream*** has 500 sheets. Usually, paper is referred to by its ream weight, as in 20-lb bond or 70-lb book. A 20-lb bond means that 500 sheets of 17″ × 22″ writing paper weighs 20 pounds.

If the letter M appears after the weight, it means per 1000 sheets. For example, 25 × 38 – 140M means 1000 sheets of 25″ × 38″ book paper weigh 140 pounds, **Figure 15-15**.

Substance weight is the actual weight of the ream. Papers have many basic sizes and basis weights. Therefore, the thickness of a ream of stock can vary based on its substance weight.

Equivalent weight is the weight of one ream of paper that is of a size larger or smaller than the basic size. Use the following formula to find the

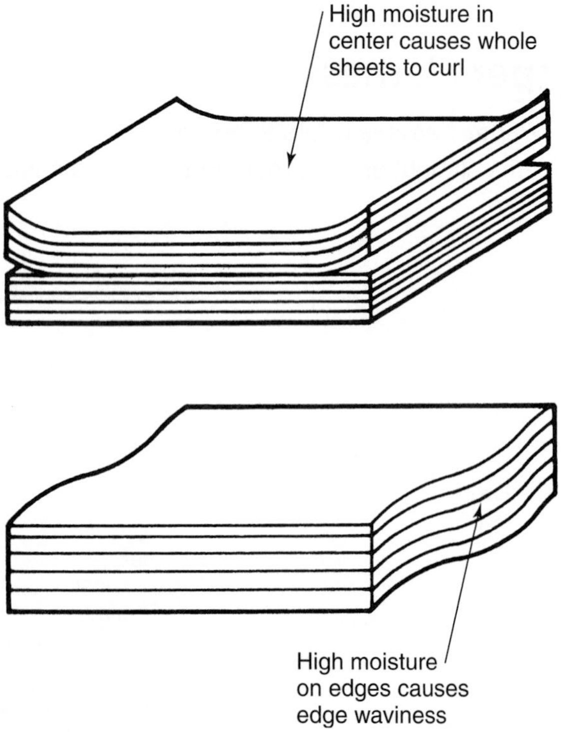
High moisture in center causes whole sheets to curl
High moisture on edges causes edge waviness

Goodheart-Willcox Publisher

Figure 15-13. High moisture content can make paper warp or become wavy.

Kind of Paper	Square Inches	Basic Size
Bond, ledger, writing	374	17″ × 22″
Cover	520	20″ × 26″
Newsprint	864	24″ × 36″
Book, offset, text	950	25″ × 38″
Index, bristols	778	25 1/2″ × 30 1/2″

Goodheart-Willcox Publisher

Figure 15-14. Some common types of paper and their basic sizes.

equivalent weight of paper, referring to **Figure 15-15** for the basic size.

$$\frac{\text{Length} \times \begin{matrix}\text{Width of}\\ \text{sheets}\end{matrix} \times \begin{matrix}\text{Basis}\\ \text{weight}\end{matrix}}{\text{Basic size}} = 81.4 \text{ lb}$$

Example: What is the equivalent weight of a ream of 28″ × 34″ ledger paper, 32-lb stock?

$$\frac{28 \times 34 \times 32}{17 \times 22} = 81.4 \text{ lb}$$

To find the *total weight* of a number of sheets, use the following formula:

Type	Basic Size	Weights
Writing	17″ × 22″	26 32 40 48 56 64 etc.
Cover	20″ × 26″	100 120 130 160 180 etc.
Book	25″ × 38″	60 70 80 90 100 120 140 160 etc.
Index bristol	25 1/2″ × 30 1/2″	117 144 182 222 286 etc.

Goodheart-Willcox Publisher

Figure 15-15. Some typical weights of paper for common sizes.

$$\frac{\begin{matrix}\text{Weight of}\\ \text{1000 sheets}\end{matrix} \times \begin{matrix}\text{Number of}\\ \text{sheets}\end{matrix}}{1000} = \text{Total weight}$$

Example: What is the total weight of 1475 sheets of 17″ × 22″—56M, 28-lb stock?

$$\frac{56 \times 1475}{1000} = 82.6 \text{ lb}$$

To find the *basis weight* (when the sheet size and ream weight are known) use the following formula:

$$\frac{\text{Basic size} \times \text{Ream weight}}{\text{Length} \times \text{Width of sheet}} = \text{Basis weight}$$

Example: What is the basis weight of a ream of book paper 23″ × 29″, with a ream weight of 56 pounds?

$$\frac{25 \times 38 \times 56}{23 \times 29} = \frac{53{,}200}{667} = 80 \text{ lb}$$

The length and weight of paper in rolls can be calculated by applying the factors shown in **Figure 15-16** to the appropriate formula.
To find the *length* of paper in a roll of known width and net weight (not including wrapper and core), use the following formula:

$$\frac{41.67 \times \text{Roll weight} \times \text{Factor}}{\text{Roll width} \times \text{Basis weight}} = \text{Length}$$

Example: How many feet of paper are in a 1000-lb roll of 35″-wide offset book, 75-lb stock?

$$\frac{41.67 \times 1000 \times 950}{35 \times 75} = 15{,}080$$

To find the *approximate weight* of rolls on a 3″ inner-diameter core, use the following formula:

$$(\text{Roll diameter})^2 \times \text{Width} \times \text{Roll factor}^* = \text{Approximate weight}$$

*Roll factors:

Bond	0.021
Smooth Finish Offset	0.022
Vellum Finish Offset	0.018
C2S Web Offset	0.032

Example 1: What is the approximate weight of a 34 1/2″-wide, 40″-diameter roll of coated web paper?

$$(40 \times 40) \times 34.5 \times 0.032 = 1766 \text{ lb}$$

Paper Computation Factors		
Type	Basic Size	Factor
Business papers	17″ × 22″	374
Book papers	25″ × 38″	950
Cover papers	20″ × 26″	520
Printing bristols	22 1/2″ × 28 1/2″	641
Tag, news, conv.	24″ × 36″	864
Index bristols	25 1/2″ × 30 1/2″	778

Inter-City Paper Co.

Figure 15-16. A factor is derived by multiplying the dimensions of the basic size of a type of paper. For example, the basic size of business papers (bond) is 17″ × 22″, which equals 371.

Example 2: What is the approximate weight of a 17 1/2″-wide, 40″-diameter roll of vellum offset?

$$(40 \times 40) \times 17.5 \times 0.018 = 504 \text{ lb}$$

Sometimes it is necessary to figure out how many pieces of paper can be cut out of a large sheet.

To figure the number of pieces per sheet, the dimensions of the desired cut piece are written below the dimensions of the uncut sheet. First, each dimension of the cut size is divided into its corresponding full-sheet dimension. The resulting whole numbers (fractions are dropped) are multiplied to find the number of pieces that can be cut from the sheet. The computation is done two ways. In the vertical method, the dimensions are divided vertically; in the cross method, division is done diagonally.

An example of the two methods is shown in **Figure 15-17**. Stock size is 25″ × 38″, while the desired cut size is 6″ × 9″. The result would be that 16 pieces can be obtained using the vertical method and 12 pieces using the cross method.

It is more economical to cut the short dimension of the piece out of the short dimension of the sheet, which is the number obtained using the vertical method. However, this is true only if it is satisfactory to have the grain run the long way on the piece.

If the grain had to run parallel to the short (6″) dimension of the piece, it would yield only 12 pieces (as determined using the cross method).

Sometimes, it is possible that the ***trim*** can be used for another job. To find out, utilize the same type of formula.

Metric Paper Sizes

In many countries, the SI Metric system is used for specifying paper size. The letters A and B each designate a different series. The sizes in each series are numbered 0 to 8 and represent the number of times a sheet can be folded to obtain a particular size. The sizes in a series are proportionate; any smaller size is always half the next larger size.

In the A series, A0 has an area of 1 m^2. The sheet is not a true square but has a proportion of 5:7, **Figure 15-16**. Using 1 m^2 as a starting point, the subsequently smaller sizes are determined by halving the larger size, **Figure 15-19**.

In the B series, the sizes fall between the A series measurements and are used for unusual situations. Standard metric sizes of paper are listed in **Figure 15-20**. The nearest metric equivalent to the 8 1/2″ × 11″ standard sheet used in the United States is the A4 size. It is 210 mm × 297 mm (8.27″ × 11.69″).

Qualities of Paper

There are several physical qualities that can be used to make judgments about which paper is most well-suited for a particular printing job. These are color, smoothness, strength, brightness, and opacity.

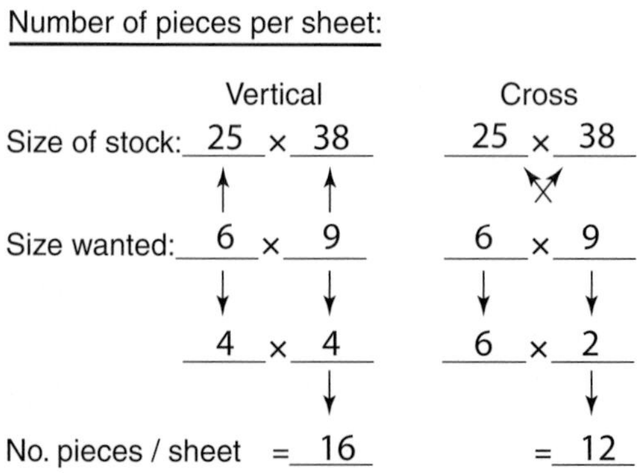

Goodheart-Willcox Publisher

Figure 15-17. How to determine the number of pieces per sheet.

Color

Paper color and ink color must be compatible. White paper is essential for full- or four-color printing. It reflects all the colors of the spectrum, while colored paper does not. Colored paper can create a process color value that is undesirable, producing a finished piece that may not be what the customer expected.

Smoothness

Smoothness and texture both greatly affect ***printability***, or how well images show fine detail. Smoothness varies with paper type. A smooth sheet requires a very thin film of ink to produce sharp images. The opposite is true for rough papers.

Strength

The ***tensile strength*** of paper is determined by how well the inner fibers are bonded together. A roll of paper that cannot feed through a web-fed press without breaking easily has loosely bonded fibers and low strength.

Print strength is determined by how well the surface of the paper is bonded together. A low print strength could allow bits of fiber to be lifted off the paper surface by high-tack inks. Hickeys would appear on the printed image. Coated stock normally has higher print strength than uncoated stock.

Brightness

Brightness is determined by how well the paper surface reflects light. Paper brightness affects the

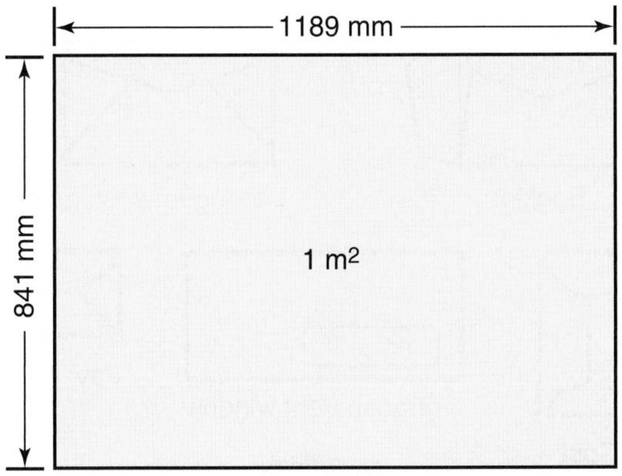

Goodheart-Willcox Publisher

Figure 15-18. Size A0 is the basis for metric paper sizes. It is 1 m^2 in area, with a rectangular shape in a 5:7 proportion.

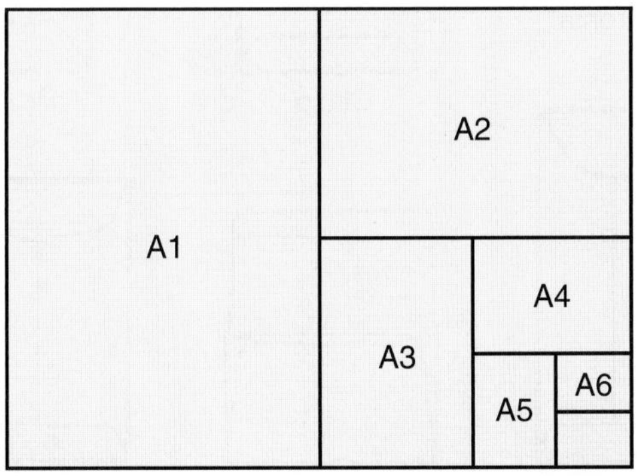

Goodheart-Willcox Publisher

Figure 15-19. Metric paper sizes are simply halves of larger sizes.

Designation	mm	Index
A0	841 × 1189	33.11 × 46.81
A1	594 × 841	23.39 × 33.11
A2	420 × 594	16.54 × 23.39
A3	297 × 420	11.69 × 16.54
A4	210 × 297	8.27 × 11.69
A5	148 × 210	5.83 × 8.27
A6	105 × 148	4.13 × 5.83
A7	74 × 105	2.91 × 4.13
A8	52 × 74	2.05 × 2.91
B0	1000 × 1414	39.37 × 55.67
B1	707 × 1000	27.83 × 39.37
B2	500 × 707	19.68 × 27.83
B3	353 × 500	13.90 × 19.68
B4	250 × 353	9.84 × 13.90
B5	176 × 250	6.93 × 9.84
B6	125 × 176	4.92 × 6.93
B7	88 × 125	3.46 × 4.92
B8	62 × 88	2.44 × 3.46

Goodheart-Willcox Publisher

Figure 15-20. Alphanumeric designations, sizes, and indices for the metric-size paper sheets. An index is the decimal equivalent in inches.

Academic Link

Acid-Free Paper

The acid found in manufactured paper occurs naturally in wood pulp and may also be absorbed from the environment, printing processes, and human hands. This acid causes the paper to turn yellow and physically deteriorate. To ensure longevity, acid-free, or alkaline, paper has become the standard substrate used for archival and historical documents and projects.

During production, acid-free paper is treated with an alkaline compound, usually calcium carbonate, to neutralize the acid and bring the pH of the paper to 7 or slightly more. Acid-free paper also contains a reserve of the alkaline compound to neutralize any acids the paper may encounter once in use or that develop as the paper ages. The integrity of acid-free paper is expected to last hundreds of years. The life span of paper that has not been treated with an alkaline compound may only be a couple of decades.

What are some other common uses of calcium carbonate?

contrast of the printed image. A bright paper makes colors, particularly black, stand out more.

Transparent ink on a bright paper also produces exceptional color rendition. More light reflects up through the ink layers to produce stronger colors.

Opacity

Opacity refers to the ability of light to pass through a sheet of paper. It is also the ability to see through the sheet. Poor opacity produces an undesirable result called ***show-through***. The image on the back side of the sheet can be seen through the paper, and is a distraction to the reader. Examine stock carefully to make sure show-through will not occur. A heavyweight paper has high opacity, whereas a thin paper tends to have low opacity.

Envelopes

Envelopes come in many styles and sizes for a variety of applications. Envelopes used for postal purposes have a minimum size requirement of 3 1/2″ × 5″. Any size over 6 1/8″ × 11 1/2″, or thicker than 1/4″, is subject to additional postage fees. **Figure 15-21** illustrates common envelope styles.

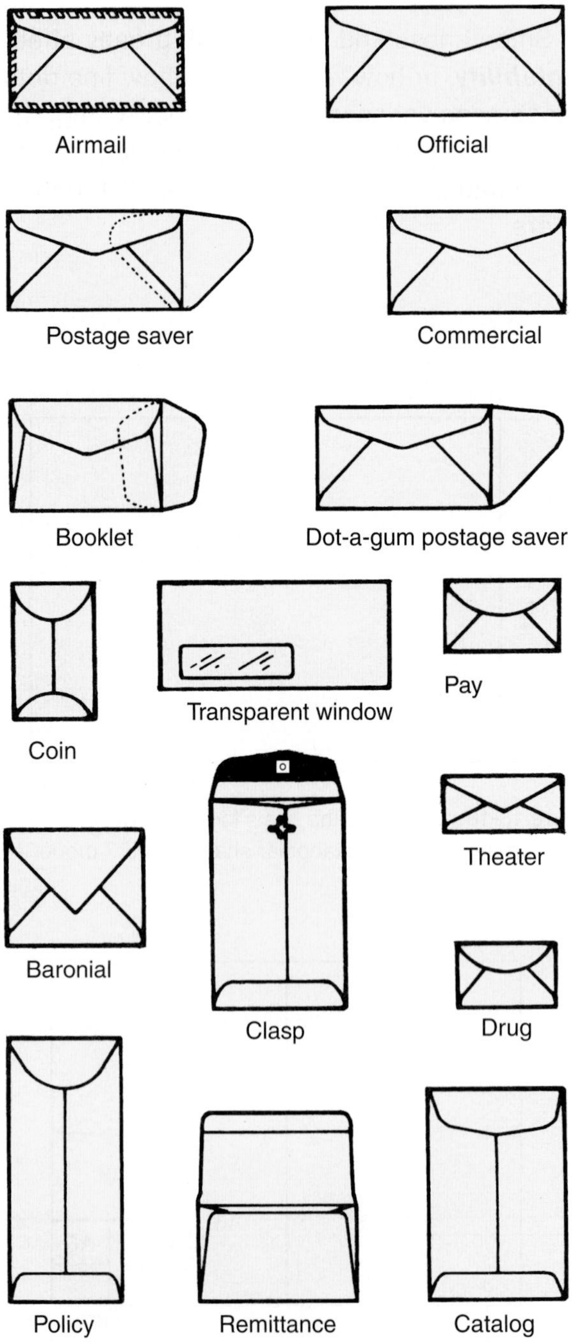

Carpenter-Offutt Paper Co.

Figure 15-21. Typical envelope styles.

- The commercial envelope is typically used to send correspondence. The No. 10 size (4 1/8″ × 9 1/2″) is the most-widely used.
- The window envelope has an opening that allows the address to appear through the clear opening. This is a time-saving and convenient feature.
- The baronial envelope is used mostly for invitations, announcements, and greeting cards.
- The booklet envelope, with its opening on the side, is used to hold house publications and direct-mail pieces.
- The clasp envelope is used to mail bulky materials. The manner of fastening will vary, but it is strong and can take abuse.

Figure 15-22 lists common envelope sizes. Envelope company catalogs provide more detailed information.

Size	Dimensions (inches)	Size	Dimensions (inches)
Office and Commercial		**Office and Commercial**	
5	3 1/6 × 5 1/2	10	9 1/2 × 12 5/8
6 1/4	3 1/2 × 6	**Clasp**	
6 3/4	3 5/8 × 6 1/2	0	2 1/2 × 4 1/4
7	3 3/4 × 6 3/4	5	3 1/8 × 5 1/2
7 3/4	3 7/8 × 7 1/2	10	3 3/8 × 6
8 5/8	3 5/8 × 8 5/8	15	4 × 6 3/8
9	3 7/8 × 8 7/8	11	4 1/2 × 10 3/8
10	4 1/8 × 9 1/2	25	4 5/8 × 6 3/4
11	4 1/2 × 10 3/8	35	5 × 7 1/2
12	4 3/4 × 11	14	5 × 11 1/2
14	5 × 11 1/2	50	5 1/2 × 8 1/4
Baronial		55	6 × 9
4	3 5/8 × 4 11/16	63	6 1/2 × 9 1/2
5	4 1/8 × 5 1/8	68	7 × 10
5 1/2	4 3/8 × 5 5/8	75	7 1/2 × 10 1/2
5 3/4	4 5/8 × 5 15/16	80	8 × 11
Booklet		83	8 1/2 × 11 1/2
2 1/2	4 1/2 × 5 7/8	87	9 3/4 × 11 1/4
3	4 3/4 × 6 1/2	90	9 × 12
5	5 1/2 × 8 1/8	93	9 1/2 × 12 1/2
6	5 3/4 × 8 7/8	94	9 1/4 × 14 1/2
6 1/2	6 × 9	95	10 × 12
7	6 1/4 × 9 5/8	97	10 × 13
7 1/2	7 1/2 × 10 1/2	98	10 × 15
9	8 3/4 × 11 1/2	105	11 1/2 × 14 1/2
9 1/2	9 × 12	110	12 × 15 1/2

Goodheart-Willcox Publisher

Figure 15-22. Common envelope sizes and dimensions.

Plastic Substrates

Plastic has many variations. Sometimes it is a thin film. Other times it is a sturdy yet flexible material. Another plastic might be stiff or even rigid. Plastic substrates are blended from various ***petrochemicals*** and other compounds. Most plastic substrates are available in both roll and sheet form.

Polyester

Polyester is one of the strongest plastic films used as a printing substrate. It has high clarity, toughness, durability, and good dimensional stability. It must be treated to prepare its surface for offset printing. Polyester substrates are used for decals, labels, and signs. They cannot withstand high heat.

Copolyester

Copolyester is an extruded and dull-finished plastic substrate. It has a high degree of dimensional stability, clarity, and formability. It is available in matte finish or transparent colors. Copolyester is a comparatively inexpensive plastic substrate. Book report covers, overhead projector overlays, and flip charts are a few of its applications.

Polycarbonate Film

Polycarbonate film is a high-gloss substrate with good dimensional stability, good heat resistance, and excellent light transmittance. Low-haze polycarbonate film can be printed on offset presses without pretreatment. It is easily die-cut and embossed. Polycarbonate film is used for decals, nameplates, membrane switch panels, overlays, and product identification.

Rigid Vinyl

A rigid vinyl substrate has good stability and is available in calendered gloss or matte finish. It comes in white translucent, white opaque, and standard opaque colors. Rigid vinyl is commonly used for identification cards or credit cards, but it is also used for shelf signs or labels, danglers, wall signs, and pocket calendars. Rigid vinyl is easily die-cut and ***thermoformed*** into shapes.

High-Impact Polystyrene

High-impact polystyrene is a versatile and economical plastic substrate. It is offset-printable and available in translucent and opaque colors. It is used for point-of-purchase display signs and toys.

Cellulose Acetate

Cellulose acetate is a plastic film. It provides outstanding clarity but poor dimensional stability and tear-resistance. Its soft surface is receptive to a wide variety of inks. Cellulose acetate is used for folders, book jackets, and overhead projector transparencies.

Clear-Oriented Polyester

Clear-oriented polyester is the cheapest plastic substrate available. It tears and scratches easily but provides good clarity. It is used for short-term display signs, labels, visual aids, and similar products.

Yupo®

Yupo® is a white opaque or translucent polypropylene film substrate. It serves as a "synthetic paper" that has been treated for offset printing. It is tough and durable, and can withstand repeated folding. Yupo® has good dimensional stability and a waterproof printing surface. It is used for posters, brochures, catalogs, children's books, outdoor maps, globes, menus, and instructional manuals.

Tyvek®

Tyvek® is a strong spunbonded polyolefin plastic substrate. It has a smooth surface, good dimensional stability, resistance to ultraviolet light and moisture, and excellent opacity. Tyvek® is treated with an antistatic agent to facilitate sheet handling. For printing purposes, it is commonly used for envelopes, tags, labels, maps, and book coverings.

Environmental Issues

The paper industry is trying diligently to be good stewards of the earth's natural resources. Reforestation is taking place. Programs are ensuring that perpetual planting, growing, and harvesting of trees is taking place while protecting the environment. The driving force behind recycling advocacy is to keep paper out of landfills. Another benefit of recycling is the saving of trees. It also takes less energy to make pulp out of a sheet of paper than a log.

Chain of Custody

The ***chain of custody*** is the process of tracking and recording the possession and transfer of wood and fiber from forests of origin, through the different stages of production, to the end user. This means that the responsibility now includes paper merchants, printers, agencies, and independent designers. The Sustainable Forestry Initiative (SFI) and the Forest Stewardship Council (FSC) are two programs that authenticate that the fiber source comes from responsibly managed forests.

Standards

Professionals and biologists are managing the forests to be in compliance with the standards of the SFI program. The FSC was established to create an honest and credible system for identifying well-managed forests. The Chlorine Free Products Association (CFPA) is a not-for-profit accreditation and standard-setting organization. The standards relate to the reduction of energy and water consumption, eliminating harmful toxins, providing a chain of custody for all fibers, and reviewing social, environmental and financial responsibility of their products and services.

Summary

- Cellulose is the raw material used to make most paper today.
- Paper types include adhesive-coated, safety, bond, carbonless, offset, duplicator, cover, ledger, index, newsprint, and recycled.
- Coated papers are rated by brightness and may be high-gloss, dull-coated, or matte-coated. Uncoated paper does not have a layer applied over the surface and tends to have a textured feel.
- Basic size of paper varies with grade. Basis weight is the weight in pounds of one ream of basic-sized stock.
- Plastic substrates include polyester, copolyester, polycarbonate film, rigid vinyl, high-impact polystyrene, cellulose acetate, clear-oriented polyester, Yupo®, and Tyvek®.
- Recycling paper helps the environment by keeping paper out of landfills, saving trees, and using less energy.

Review Questions

Answer the following questions using the information in this chapter.

1. List three common materials used as printing substrates.
2. Most paper manufactured in the United States is made on what machine?
3. What is the raw material used to make paper?
4. _____ is added to the pulp to make paper moisture-resistant. _____ are added to improve opacity, brightness, smoothness, and ink receptivity.
5. The process that impresses a translucent design in paper is _____.
   A. watermarking
   B. calendering
   C. furnishing
   D. embossing
6. _____ paper is smoother, stronger, and yields a better image than _____ paper.
7. What are two elementally chlorine-free (ECF) chemicals used as alternatives to using chlorine gas to bleach paper?
8. What characteristic is contained by machine-made papers?
9. How many sheets are in a ream of paper?
10. What is the formula for determining basis weight?

11. What color of paper is essential for true process color reproduction?
12. Print _____ is an important factor affecting hickeys or specks on the printed image.
13. The _____ of paper affects whether the paper will exhibit an undesirable problem called show-through.
14. Which plastic substrate is typically used to make identification cards and credit cards?
15. Explain the role of the chain of custody.

Suggested Activities

1. Explore the possibility of making handmade paper.
2. Using a rubber stamp, place the stamp image on seven different substrate surfaces. Analyze the effect of the stamp on each surface of the various substrates.
3. Visit a paper storage facility and list the paper classifications as well as the paper sizes associated with that classification.
4. As a group project, request the specifications for an actual job from a printing plant. Do all of the calculations necessary to determine how much paper is necessary for the job. Then visit the plant and find out if your calculations were correct.

Chapter 16

Ink

Learning Objectives

After studying this chapter, you will be able to:

- Summarize the various ingredients and properties of ink.
- Identify the characteristics of ink formulations used for different printing processes.
- Summarize the characteristics of some specialized inks.
- Explain how to mix and match ink.
- Give examples of ways ink challenges affect the printed product.
- Identify methods used to analyze process inks.

Goodheart-Willcox Publisher

Important Terms

additives
binders
brayer
chalking
colorant
color diagram
color strength
dispersants
drawdown test
dry
flooding
flush
ink
ink body
ink fineness gauge
ink formulation
ink length
ink mileage
inkometer
ink sticking
ink tack
ink thickness gauge
livering
off color
pigment
plate wear
reflection densitometer
scumming
set
setoff
specking
spectrophotometer
strike-through
thixotropy
tinting
vehicle
viscosity

G-WLEARNING.COM

While studying this chapter, look for the activity icon to:

- **Practice** vocabulary terms with e-flash cards, matching activities, and vocabulary game.
- **Reinforce** what you learn by submitting end-of-chapter questions.

www.g-wlearning.com/visualtechnology/

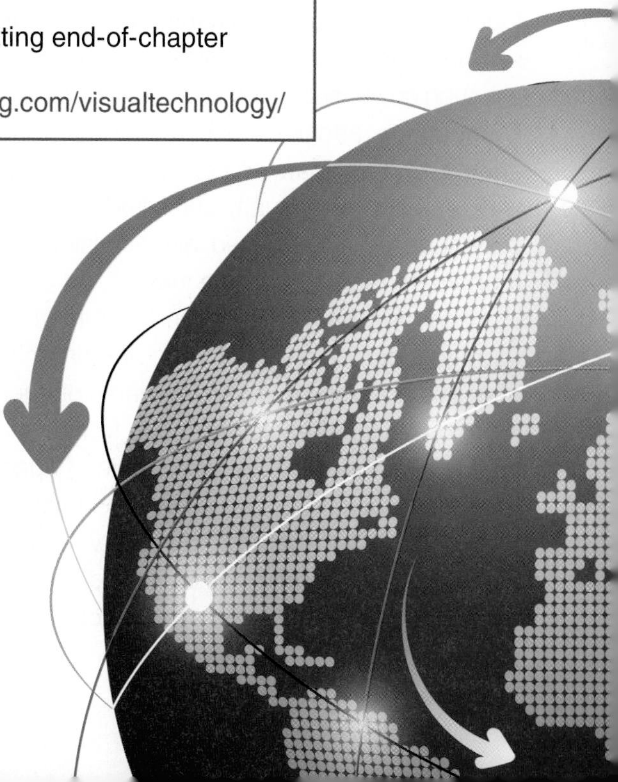

Ink is the most common coating used to place a printed image onto a substrate. Various inks are manufactured for use with the many printing processes and substrates available today. Inks have several properties that can affect printing quality. They must flow properly, have the correct stickiness, be permanent, dry properly, and have a workable consistency for the press rollers. This chapter will discuss the characteristics of printing inks and summarize how ink can affect a print job.

Ink Ingredients

The Egyptians and the Chinese first manufactured ink by binding soot with gums. The mixture was formed into rods and then dried. Moisture was added just before it was used. Many years later, the Chinese used the earth and plants as colors for pigments. Gums were still used as the binding agents. Around the time of Gutenberg, soot was mixed with varnish or linseed oil to make ink.

Ink formulation refers to the amount and type of ingredients used in a particular ink. A few dependent factors are the printing process; the type of substrate used; the drying method; the quality of print; the requirements for appearance; and the meeting of environmental, health, and safety requirements. Three ingredients are essential to the formulation of printing inks: vehicle, pigment, and additives.

The ***vehicle*** is a binding agent that holds the ink together. It also acts as a carrier for the pigment. A vehicle is often a solvent-resin or oil-resin combination, although soy-based paste inks are also widely used. Compounds, additives, oxidant agents, wetting agents, and antifoaming agents may be added, as well. Vehicles are usually classified as oil-based, solvent-based, water-based, and acrylatedoligomers/monomers (energy-curable inks).

The ***pigment*** provides the color in an ink. Pigments can be either organic or inorganic. Natural minerals are used to make inorganic pigment, while organic pigments are made from synthetic chemical compounds. A wide range of opaque and transparent pigments is available. Pigments are usually used dry and ground into a vehicle. They can also be used ***flush***, as a paste dispersed in a vehicle. Dyes also may be used as coloring agents, particularly in flexographic inks.

Additives are ingredients added to ink to impart special characteristics. For example, certain additives reduce body tack, while others help make ink water-resistant. Driers, waxes, plasticizers, and antioxidants are common additives. The oxidation or polymerization time of the drying oils is decreased by the use of driers. Waxes are used to provide rub and scuff resistance, as well as resistance to water, solvents, and alcohol, after printing. Plasticizers give flexibility to the dried ink film. Antioxidants retard surface drying of oil-based inks, a process known as anti-skinning.

Driers accelerate drying, which permits the stacking of printed sheets without causing ***setoff***, the transfer or smearing of ink. See **Figure 16-1**. The most common drier is metallic salts. Metallic soaps and organic derivatives of various metals are also used as driers. Various devices or systems can assist with drying. Infrared (IR) radiation is used to accelerate oxidation. Ultraviolet (UV) radiation assists in curing. Spray powders are sometimes dispersed over the surface of the printed sheet to eliminate direct contact with the next printed sheet.

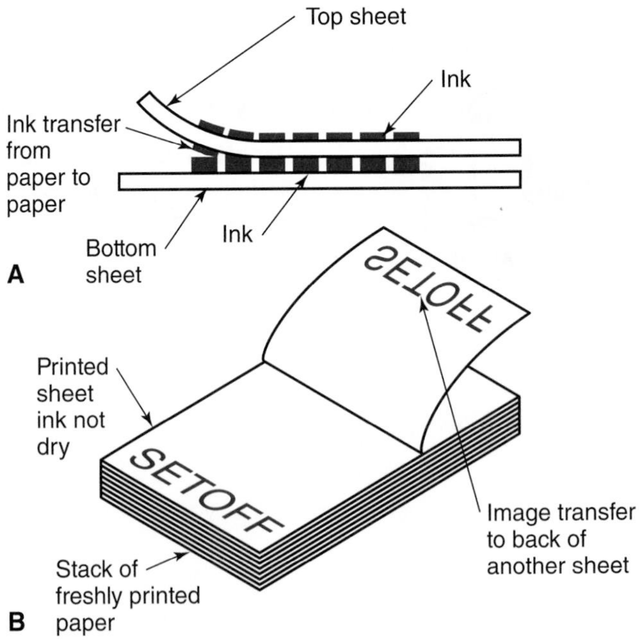

Goodheart-Willcox Publisher

Figure 16-1. Setoff occurs when printed sheets output from a press are stacked on top of each other. Setoff is usually caused by improper drying of ink, but it can also be caused by excessively thick ink film, paper stacked too high, or an improper substrate and ink combination. A—How setoff occurs. B—The result of setoff.

Warning

Ink is a chemical product and must be handled properly. Certain inks require special handling. Always follow the manufacturer's instructions.

Ink Properties

Color strength, body, stability, length, tack, and drying are common properties of ink. These properties relate to the optical, structural, and drying characteristics of ink.

Color Strength

Color strength is the ability of an ink to cover a substrate. Strong ***colorants*** produce vivid, sharp images and give good coverage. Weak colorants are generally not desirable. Pigments or dyes must be compatible with the ink base and carefully selected for the end use. Metallic, fluorescent, and pearl pigments are used to create special effects.

A transparent ink has weak color strength and is used when it is desirable for an image to show through the ink. Transparent inks are used in four-color printing where all colors of the spectrum are produced by overprinting the four process colors.

Ink Body

Ink body refers to an ink's consistency, thickness, or fluidity. The technical term is *rheology*, defined as the study of the deformation and flow of matter under the influence of an applied stress. ***Viscosity*** relates to ink flow. Viscosity of ink is different for each of the printing processes. Some inks are stiff and thick, while others are thin and fluid. The thickness of an ink can affect press operation considerably.

Inks used in relief or offset lithographic printing are very stiff but flow more freely after being mixed by the press rollers. Gravure inks are formulated to be thin so they flow easily onto the substrate from the microscopic ink wells of the gravure cylinder.

With lithography, high ink body tends to thicken the deposit of ink on the substrate. A thinner ink does the opposite. High-speed presses use soft-bodied (more flowing) ink, while slower presses use heavy-bodied (less flowing) ink. Ink must be formulated for a specific printing process.

An ***ink thickness gauge*** is a device used to measure the thickness of the ink film on the press. Ink film is the thickness or depth of coating. The measurement is taken on the steel roller of the ink train of the press. The ink film gauge measurements are in mils (thousandths of an inch). An ***ink fineness gauge*** measures the pigment particle size in the ink with a very high degree of accuracy.

Ink Stability

Ink stability, or ***thixotropy***, is the tendency of an ink to flow more freely after being worked. In relief printing, the press rollers work the ink by squeezing and depositing it onto the press rollers before printing. Stirring ink tends to break down its internal cohesiveness. Ink that is agitated in the fountain flows more easily and distributes more evenly on the press rollers.

Many large presses have agitators to work the ink. The motion of the agitators helps keep the ink stable and fluid while it is in the fountain. Lack of motion causes the ink to become stiff and unable to transfer properly.

Ink Length

Ink length refers to the elasticity of an ink and its ability to form a filament or strand. The filament can be long or short, **Figure 16-2**.

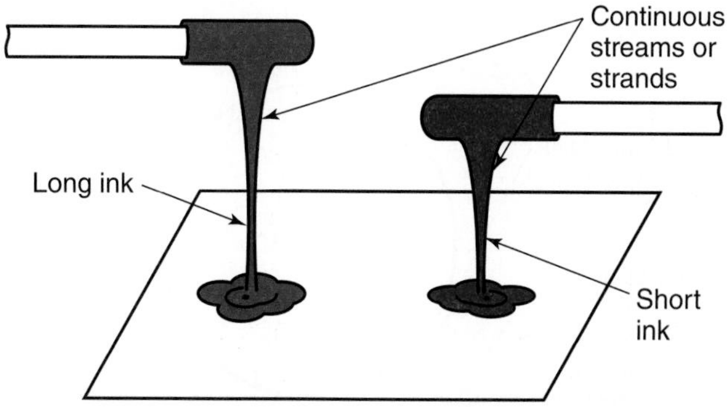

Goodheart-Willcox Publisher

Figure 16-2. To form filaments, a rod is placed in ink, tapped on a surface, and then lifted. An ink that produces long filaments is called a "long" ink. "Short" inks produce shorter filaments.

If the ink forms a long filament, it will have a tendency to fly out on a high-speed press. Long inks, such as those used on newsprint, flow more rapidly than short inks. Short inks flow poorly and have the consistency of butter.

Ink Tack

Ink tack refers to stickiness of the ink. It is a measurement of cohesion between the ink film and the substrate. The term is generally used when describing paste inks, such as those used in lithographic and some relief printing. When the ink is transferred from one roller to another or from one surface to another roller, the ink must split. A portion stays on the first roller, but another portion must transfer to the next roller. If ink does not split, or has too much tack, it cannot be transferred from one roller to another, to the plate and blanket, or from the roller to a surface of the substrate.

An ***inkometer*** measures the tack of an ink to determine if it is too great for the surface strength of the paper. Too much tack can cause the paper to rupture, resulting in picking, splitting, or tearing. See **Figure 16-3**. Ink tack can be reduced. Liquid tack reducer cuts an ink's tack and body. It can be used to correct problems such as picking and linting. Paste tack reducer cuts tack but does not affect ink body. The type of ink, substrate, press design, and press speed establish the tack specifications.

Ink Drying

An ink's ability to dry is important to the quality of the final product. Some common methods ink can use to dry are absorption, evaporation, oxidation, polymerization, and precipitation, **Figure 16-4**.

- Absorption-drying ink, also called penetrating ink, dries when the solvent is drawn into the paper. The ink does not dry hard but remains on the surface as a powder-like substance. Newspapers are a good example of inks that dry by absorption or penetration. If you rub your fingers over newsprint, a black powder will deposit on your skin.
- Evaporation-drying inks dry as the solvent is evaporated into the surrounding air, leaving a solid film of resin on the paper. Evaporation-drying inks are used in flexography, gravure, web-fed offset, and other processes where fast drying time is important. Solvent-evaporative inks consist of resins, solvents, and additives. Specific types include poster inks, lacquers, and textile dyes.
- Oxidation-drying inks dry by absorbing oxygen from the surrounding air. Letterpress and offset printing commonly use oxidation-drying inks.

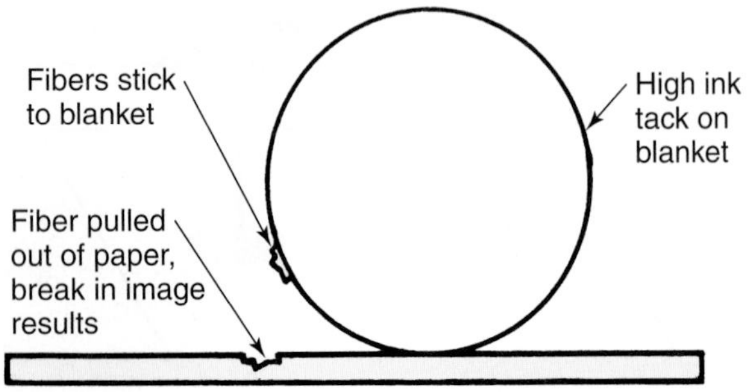

Goodheart-Willcox Publisher

Figure 16-3. Picking can result when ink tack is not matched to stock. High tack can pull off fibers of paper.

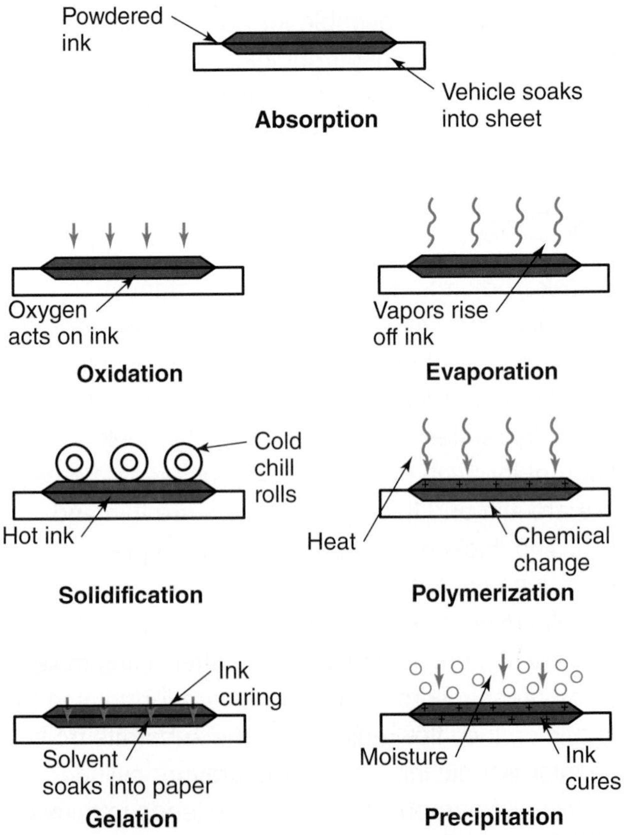

Goodheart-Willcox Publisher

Figure 16-4. Inks dry in a number of ways.

- Polymerization-drying inks dry by a chemical reaction that causes molecules in the ink to combine. Oxygen thickens the ink to a gel-like consistency, allowing the printed product to be handled without smearing before it is fully dried. Polymerization-drying inks can be used to print on metal.
- Precipitation-drying inks, also called moisture-set inks, dry by reacting with water. Steam or water is sprayed onto the ink after printing, causing the ink to set quickly. Glycol in the ink combines with the water and is absorbed into the paper.
- Chemical-reaction inks consist of resins, solvents, additives, and a drying-oil catalyst. These inks cure and dry by evaporation of the solvent and by oxidation. Specific types of ink include enamel, vinyl, epoxy, and polyester.

Other Ink-Related Terms

Other important ink-related terms you should know include:

- *Permanent ink* or *colorfast ink* maintains its color with exposure to sunlight. It will not easily fade and is suitable for posters, signs, and other similar applications.
- *Resistant ink* is very stable and can withstand exposure to forces that would fade other inks. It can tolerate sunlight, chemicals, heat, moisture, and gases without fading.
- *Fugitive ink* will fade and lose its color after prolonged exposure to sunlight. It is useful for temporary signs and posters.
- *Lake* is an ink colorant formed when a soluble dye is converted to a pigment in a white base.
- *Toner* is a strong, concentrated ink colorant. Toner primarily consists of pure pigment ground and mixed into linseed oil.
- *Job black* refers to normal black ink used for a typical press run of average quality.
- *Halftone black* is a higher quality black ink designed for reproducing fine detail in halftone screen images.
- *Watercolors* are inks with a very flat or dull finish. They are water-based and do not contain varnish or oil.

Think Green

Volatile Organic Compounds (VOCs)

As you have learned throughout this text, volatile organic compounds (VOCs) are toxic substances that evaporate into the atmosphere. They are most commonly found in blanket and roller washes, fountain solutions, plate cleaners, glaze removers, degreasers, and film cleaners. The evaporation of VOCs contributes to the development of such environmental hazards as smog. There are also health concerns associated with VOCs. VOCs are generally found in ink solvent. There are now several different types of ink available that contain little or no VOCs. UV-curable inks cure instead of dry, so there are no evaporating solvents. Vegetable oil–based inks, or soy inks, are an alternative to using inks with petrochemical solvents. Vegetable oil–based inks dry very slowly, but they are still commonly found in green printing facilities.

- *Metallic inks* contain metal powders, such as aluminum or bronze, blended with an appropriate vehicle.
- *Cleaning white* is used to wash a press before changing from a dark to a light color.
- *Liquid tack* reducer cuts an ink's tack and body. It can be used to correct problems such as picking and linting.
- *Paste tack reducer* cuts tack but does not affect ink body.
- *Gloss/matte finishes* are the visual effect of ink formulation. Gloss is achieved by the smoothness of the ink deposited onto the substrate as well as the volume of dried ink the substrate retains. The surface of the substrate also contributes to gloss. Matte ink is achieved by the addition of flattening agents. The agents create microscopically irregular surfaces, which the eye sees as matte.
- *Slow-dry additive* can be used to lengthen ink drying time or skinning time in the fountain.

- *Spray powder* can be placed onto ink after printing to prevent setoff. A special press attachment sprays the powder onto the printed images.
- *Ink mill* is a machine with steel rollers for crushing the ink ingredients into a fine substance.
- *Nontoxic compounds* must be used when dried ink has direct contact with food or edible materials.
- *Fluorescent inks* are special colored ink pigments that glow under black light.
- *Opaque inks* are capable of hiding the color of the stock on which an image is being printed.
- *Vegetable oils* have replaced mineral oils, mostly for environmental reasons. Petrochemical solvents and oils emit environmentally toxic volatile organic compounds (VOCs). In addition, ink wastes must be classified as "hazardous waste" and disposed of according to strict federal and state regulations.

Ink Types

Special formulas are used to produce inks that are compatible with certain printing processes. The characteristics of ink formulation are determined by the plates, press units, and type of substrate. The types of ink used in producing images using the four basic printing processes are discussed next.

Relief Inks

Several types of inks are used to place an image onto a substrate by raised surfaces, or relief. Letterpress inks for covering the face of electrotypes, foundry type, and similar printing surfaces are generally quite tacky and thick. High-viscosity ink is thick and resists flow. Low-viscosity ink is fluid and flows more easily. See **Figure 16-5**. Letterpress inks usually dry by oxidation. However, the inks used to print on substrates, such as newsprint, dry by evaporation if heat is applied to the inked surface. Drying oils are used as vehicles to support the pigment. The pigment is often purchased in paste form.

Flexographic inks are fast-drying and used for printing on a variety of substrates, including paper, cloth, plastic, and metal. Alcohol-based flexographic inks dry by evaporation, while water-based flexographic inks dry by evaporation or absorption.

Typical kinds of relief printing ink include rotary, quick-set, precipitation-drying, water-washable, news, and job. The inks are formulated for various types of presses and stocks for printing books, magazines, labels, packaging, or other commercial applications. Job ink is found in many commercial letterpress facilities, since it can be used on a wide variety of presses and papers. The quality of the ink varies with the types of images being printed.

Gravure Inks

Gravure inks are very fluid and dry rapidly, mainly by evaporation. The printing substrate must be capable of absorbing the ink from the recessed cells of a gravure plate or cylinder. Ink must be pulled from the cells and deposited onto a substrate. Inking the cells is known as ***flooding***. A doctor blade removes the ink from the surface of the nonimage areas of the cylinder or plate. Gravure ink must have the right rheology, surface tension, and evaporation rate.

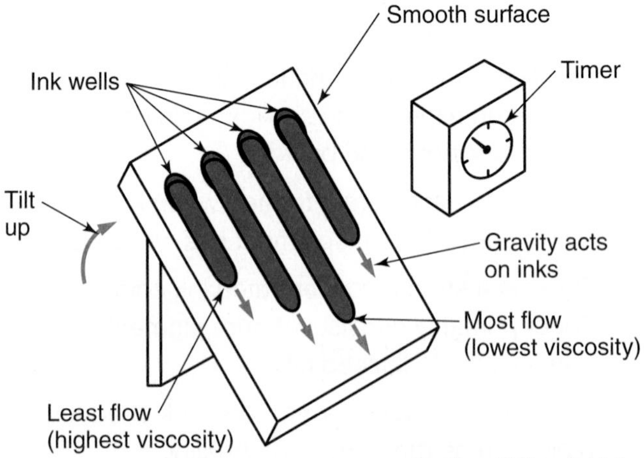

Goodheart-Willcox Publisher

Figure 16-5. Viscosity is a measure of the thickness or fluidity of an ink. A basic method for comparing viscosity is to place the inks in small wells hollowed out of a flat surface. Tilt the surface upward so the inks flow out of the wells. The ink with the most (fastest) flow has the lowest viscosity; the ink with the least (slowest) flow has the highest viscosity. Flows can be timed to get accurate viscosity readings.

Warning

Many gravure inks are highly volatile and require certain precautions against fire. The area must be properly ventilated. Local, state, and federal requirements for pollution control, including solvent drainage, must be strictly followed. Solvent-recovery systems are commonly found in the industry.

Screen Printing Inks

Screen printing inks are thicker than inks used for other processes. They are formulated to flow evenly when forced through the screen by the squeegee. Screen clogging can be a problem with screen printing inks; therefore, the solvent must not evaporate too quickly.

Conventional screen process inks contain pigments, binders, and solvents. The pigment is held together by the binder, which also assists in adhering the ink to the substrate. The solvents dissolve the resins and form a pliable material. The general classifications of screen inks are energy-curable, solvent-based, two-part catalyzed, oxidative, and plastisol inks.

Screen ink formulas vary greatly, since substrates are numerous. Typical substrates include paper, cloth, plastics, metal, and glass. It is important to communicate clearly with ink suppliers and vendors to select the screen ink that best meets the product's requirements.

Lithographic Inks

The image area of a lithographic plate is neither raised nor recessed. It is a flat surface with an image area that accepts ink. The nonimage areas are receptive to moisture.

Inks formulated for offset lithography must have high color strength. In lithography, the ink film placed onto the substrate has less thickness than the ink film used in relief printing. A balance between ink and moisture is essential for complete and even ink transfer to the plate and substrate, **Figure 16-6**.

Lithographic inks dry by oxidation; therefore, it is essential that the ink set quickly. Moreover, the pigment must not bleed in water. Formulation of lithographic inks varies greatly since many types of substrates are used in sheet-fed and web-fed presses. Vehicles must be oxidative. Additives include soluble resins, drying and semidrying oils, and varnishes. Factors that determine ink formulation of lithographic ink include press roller train design, press speed, type of plate, dampening system design, fountain solution, blanket, and the substrate used.

American Roller Company

Figure 16-6. A compressible inner layer on these offset ink rollers eliminates roller distortion throughout the nip and distributes ink more evenly.

Inks that dry by ultraviolet radiation (UV-curable inks) are used in lithographic facilities. Thermal-curing inks also are used. The thermal technique uses low amounts of solvents and requires heat and a catalyst, such as drying oil or any other substance that assists in change.

The amount of moisture absorbed by the ink is critical. The vehicle for lithographic ink must be water-resistant, although the ink may accept 20% to 25% moisture before it emulsifies. Once emulsified, or mixed together, the surface will no longer distribute the ink throughout the inking system of the press. Too much moisture eliminates the tack needed for ink to transfer from one roller to another. The ink must split at the nip point of the press rollers, **Figure 16-7**.

A number of ink problems are associated with offset lithographic printing. Lithographic ink mixes with moisture to form an ink-in-water emulsion. This results in a problem known as ***tinting***, in which a slight tint of ink is left on the nonimage area of the printed sheet.

Scumming is a problem that arises when the nonimage area of the plate accepts ink. There are two main causes of scumming: too much ink or too little fountain solution reaching the plate.

Most inks today contain a combination of vehicles that prevent the ink from scumming in the can or drying overnight if left on the press. Automated ink-dispensing systems also reduce costly ink waste by measuring the precise amount of ink going into the fountain, **Figure 16-8**.

Non-Impact Printing Ink

The image created by non-impact printing (NIP) is transferred to the substrate by *not* applying pressure, a process known as digital printing. The data and images can be printed from digital files.

The inks used in non-impact printing can be liquid, solid, or dry powder. The ink formulation depends on the process, method of drying, substrate used, and end use application.

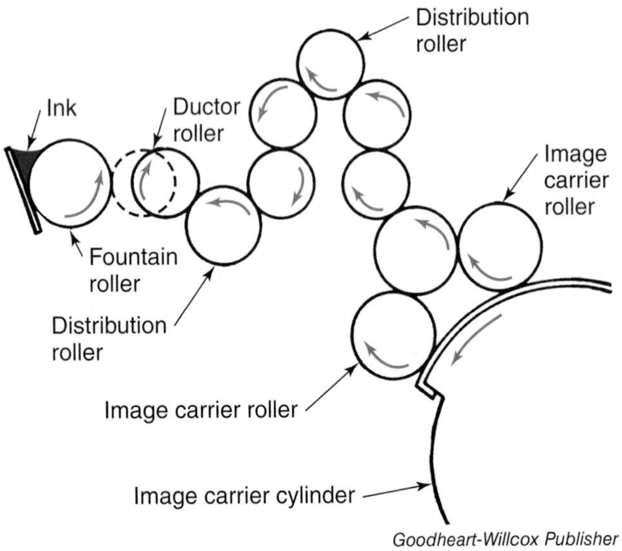

Goodheart-Willcox Publisher

Figure 16-7. Ink formulation is critical to how well an ink splits and transfers from one press roller to the next.

The inks are made up of pigments or dyes, binders, and additives. The liquid inks may consist of solvents, water, oil, or UV-curable components. The pigments or dyes are the same as those used in other printing processes. The binding resins include vinyl, polyester, epoxy, polycarbonate, and styrene copolymers. A wide number of additives are used.

The intermediate carrier inks are usually called *toners*. Toners come in liquid dispersions or dry powders. The dry toner particle size, in the 5–30 micron range, determines the print quality. The liquid toner is made up of sub-micron particles in highly insulated isoparaffin oil. Different resin ***binders*** and ***dispersants*** are used as part of the composition.

©George Deal

Figure 16-8. Vacuum-sealed tubes in this ink-dispensing system prevent oxygen from contacting the ink and causing scumming.

Specialized Inks

While the majority of inks used are process colors in the basic ingredients in ink formulations, many specialized inks have been developed to satisfy specific needs.

Vegetable Oil–Based Inks

A substantial portion of color inks in use now are vegetable oil–based inks, **Figure 16-9**. Vegetable oils have replaced mineral oils for environmental reasons. Petrochemical solvents and mineral oils emit environmentally toxic VOCs. The level of VOCs must be controlled to meet local, state, and federal standards.

National Soy Ink Information Center

Figure 16-9. Soy and other vegetable oil–based inks, which are free of environmentally harmful substances, are replacing solvent-based inks.

Apart from environmental benefits, vegetable oil–based inks have several technical benefits, such as cleaner and sharper printing and brighter colors. Transfer of ink in the system, rub resistance to surface damage, and the amount of ink needed has improved, as well.

Sheet-Fed Inks

Sheet-fed inks contain a high proportion of vegetable oil, most commonly linseed oil. They contain about 5% to 10% petroleum distillates to allow acceptable press speeds. Sheet-fed inks are suitable for use on eight-color perfecting machines, which require an ink that sets at exactly the correct speed.

Laser-Proof Inks

Electrostatic printing uses laser-proof inks for printing on laser printers and copiers. The image is fixed on the paper by heating up to 410°F (210°C) and applying pressure. The inks must be formulated to withstand intense heat without evaporating and to resist softening and transfer to the drum.

Hexachrome Inks

Conventional yellow, magenta, and cyan have been brightened by the addition of fluorescent colors to produce a specialized ink called Hexachrome™ by Pantone. It is suited for six- and seven-color process printing. Colors are brighter than are possible with standard four colors; however, press performance is compromised because of the presence of fluorescent pigments. Fluorescent pigments can have transfer problems because they are difficult to remove from ink rollers.

Metallic Inks

Metallic inks contain metal powders, such as aluminum and bronze, blended with an appropriate vehicle. New gold and silver inks are free of heavy metals, a concern in food and toy packaging. Water-based metallic inks that deliver superior brilliance have been developed for use on multicolor presses.

UV-Curable Inks

Ultraviolet-curable (or UV-curable) inks consist of resins, monomers, additives, and photoinitiators.

These inks do not dry; instead, they cure with no solvent evaporation. As ultraviolet light strikes the ink, a chemical reaction called polymerization occurs, which converts the ink from a liquid to a solid. Specific types of UV-curable inks are available for paper, plastic sheets, plastic bottles, and other substrates.

UV curing is comparable in cost to solvent- and water-based systems. The environmentally friendly aspect of UV technology may be the most important factor in the growth of UV inks. UV-curable inks contain less than 1% VOCs, and UV-printed papers can be repulped and recycled.

Waterless Inks

Higher color density and good adhesion to nonabsorbent plastic substrates make waterless inks attractive. Waterless inks have high viscosity and thickness. Raising the temperature during printing allows a waterless ink to flow more readily. See **Figure 16-10**.

Hybrid Inks

The development of hybrid inks came about because printers wanted a material with the qualities of UV ink at a lower cost. It is very expensive for a printer to dedicate one press to UV inks unless a printer's entire business requires the use of UV ink. Hybrid inks can be used on conventional presses, which are then retrofitted with UV lighting stations. These energy-cured inks can perform as well or better than conventional inks. Most conventional inks do not dry quickly, but when hybrid inks are used, the image is dry when it arrives at the delivery end of the press.

Solid Inks

There are different ways of using ink to produce images on paper. So far, you have learned about such types as aqueous inks used in ink-jet printers, as well as ribbons containing pigments used in thermography. Technology using solid ink substitutes four sticks of process-colored ink for liquid ink. Ink from the sticks is melted to be put onto paper. Once the ink produces an image on the paper, it dries almost instantly. Because the sticks use vegetable oils, they are safe to handle and better for the environment than some liquid inks.

Mixing, Matching, and Proofing

Mixing systems are available for all types of printing inks. These systems are used to blend basic inks. The inks are weighed to a prescribed amount based on information on a cataloged color selector.

The basic equipment for manual color mixing and matching consists of a hard, smooth surface;

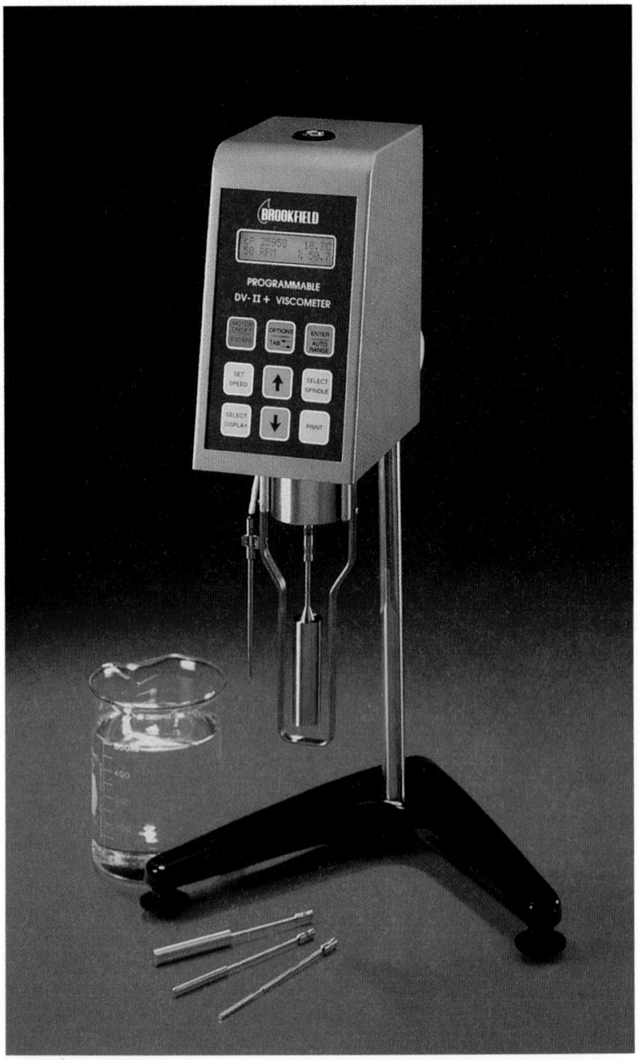

Brookfield Engineering Laboratories, Inc.

Figure 16-10. A viscometer is useful in determining the effect of temperature on the viscoelastic properties of ink used in waterless printing.

mixing knives or spatulas; scales; a color chart; and a record card. See **Figure 16-11**.

Another color matching technique is to read the color values of a sample using a ***spectrophotometer***, **Figure 16-12**. This computer-controlled instrument measures the relative intensity of radiation through the spectrum based on the sample.

Proofing of relief or lithographic ink is accomplished by a variety of instruments found in an ink manufacturing facility. Some are sophisticated, custom-built presses that simulate certain equipment and are able to determine the volume of ink used. Some are small hand-operated presses, while others are manual applicators.

©George Deal

Figure 16-11. Spatulas or mixing knives are used to mix ink by hand.

©George Deal

Figure 16-12. Accurate matches between digital color proofs and color samples can be made using a spectrophotometer.

Custom-built presses are available for flexographic proofing. Proofs can also be done manually using a ***brayer***, a small, handheld roller used to spread ink with both a rubber plate–type roller and a metering steel roll. It simulates the "squeegee" application of ink on a full-size flexographic press. Gravure can be proofed very successfully on custom-built proofing presses and press-simulating instruments.

Mixing and Matching Procedures

Color manuals or charts are available from ink manufacturers, **Figure 16-13**. The charts contain samples of ink on coated and uncoated stock.

Before manual mixing, make sure the work area is clean. Weigh out the designated amount of each ink on a scale, according to the manufacturer's specifications. Be sure to include the weight of the paper placed on the scale pan. Place the inks on a glass plate or smooth surface, and thoroughly mix them with an ink spatula until the color is uniform. Tap some of the ink onto the stock to be used, and compare the color with the sample. Continue selecting and weighing the ink according to the color system until the color matches the sample perfectly.

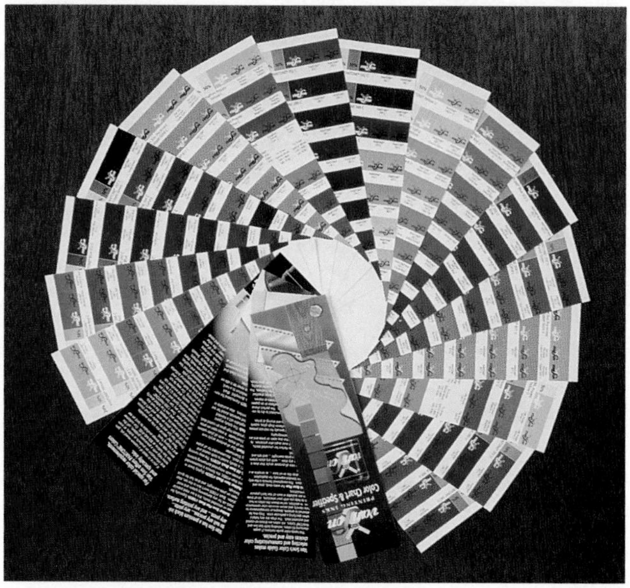

Van Son Holland Ink

Figure 16-13. Color matching charts or manuals are used to match inks with sample colors.

Ink Mileage

How much ink is needed for a specific job? Finding the ***ink mileage*** is not easy, but it is crucial. Running out of ink can be disastrous. Tables can provide the approximate number of square inches that a given amount of ink will cover. For example, full-strength lithographic inks cover between 350,000 in^2/lb and 450,000 in^2/lb on coated, sheet-fed stock. On uncoated sheets, coverage is between 280,000 in^2/lb and 360,000 in^2/lb. Absorption may result in a mileage loss of 20% or more.

When calculating the amount of ink needed, include the ink for makeready as well as the amount left in the ink fountain and on the rollers.

Several factors govern the amount of ink needed: specific gravity and color strength of the ink, stock surface, work to be printed, ink needed to prepare the press, type of press, and thickness of the ink film.

Ink can be purchased in tubes, cartridges, cans, pails, drums, and tanks, **Figure 16-14**. Ink containers should be stored in a cool, dry place and covered tightly to prevent contamination and drying. ***Livering***, a chemical change that takes place during storage, is not reversible. Livering causes a hardened coating on the surface. When removed, the coating breaks up into flakes. Flakes of dried ink cause contamination and should be kept out of the ink fountain.

©George Deal

Figure 16-14. Today's inks are engineered to meet the high-speed requirements of technologically advanced printing presses.

Ordering Ink

Consider the following questions when ordering ink:

- What colors will be used for the job?
- What printing process will be used?
- What are the product requirements? For example, must the ink be long-lasting and weather-resistant?
- What substrate will be used?
- Is ink cost a consideration?
- How many copies are to be printed for the job?

Asking these questions will help you and your ink sales representative select the appropriate ink for the job.

Ink-Related Challenges

Inks can cause a wide variety of printing problems. Sometimes ink *is* at fault; other times, the ink is blamed for what is, in fact, a press or a paper problem.

Setting and Drying

Set is the point at which an ink is dry enough to be lightly touched without smudging. ***Dry*** is the point at which the ink is free of volatile substances and has polymerized to a total solid state. Ink will dry relative to the substrate. On nonabsorbent substrates, ink must dry strictly by oxidation. This may take from 6 to 24 hours.

Chalking

Chalking is an ink-adherence problem that occurs when dried ink rubs off the substrate. Newspaper ink chalks by nature. Since a newspaper is only used once and then discarded, chalking does not pose a serious problem. Chalking would be unacceptable with a more permanent product, such as a textbook. Chalking can be prevented by applying a nonpenetrating varnish to the substrate surface to hold the pigment.

Adhesion in ink is relative to the printing process. Lithographic inks adhere best on porous substrates, while gravure and flexographic printing allow the use of solvents and resins that readily adhere to nonporous substrates, such as foils, vinyl, and polyester.

Strike-Through

Strike-through is an ink-penetration problem that occurs when the ink soaks into the paper too deeply and shows through the opposite side of the sheet. Usually, strike-through is caused by an excessively long ink-drying time. The long drying time allows the ink to soak into the paper. A highly absorbent paper can also cause strike-through.

Strike-through should not be confused with *show-through*. Strike-through is caused by excessive ink absorption. Show-through is a paper problem caused by thin or insufficiently opaque stock.

Setoff

As mentioned earlier, setoff occurs when wet ink transfers onto the back of a sheet that is stacked on top of the previously printed sheet. It is often incorrectly referred to as *offset*. Setoff can also be caused by an excessively thick ink deposit on the paper, improper ink, paper stacked too high, or a drying system problem.

Ink Sticking

Ink sticking can occur if two layers of ink film, on two different sheets, bond together. The problem is similar to setoff; both can be caused by improper drying.

Plate Wear

Plate wear can be caused by pigments that are not fully ground to a fine powder. The unground particles in the ink act as an abrasive, wearing away the surface of the plate. Excessive pigment can also cause plate wear. Always check the ink grind when plate wear is excessive. Excessive roller pressure or an abrasive substrate are two more reasons for plate wear.

Off-Color Problem

When the color of the printed job does not match the intended color, the job is said to be ***off color***. Off-color problems have many causes. A dirty press can alter the colors of the ink. If the substrate is not a true white, its color can affect the printed color. Thickness, opacity, translucence, or other ink qualities can all affect the color of the printed product. Improper ink mixing can also result in an off-color problem.

A ***drawdown test*** can be used to check for proper ink mixing. A standard ink and the newly mixed ink are placed on the stock. Then, a thin blade is used to spread the inks down over the surface of the stock, **Figure 16-15**. After drying, the standard ink is compared to the newly mixed ink for proper color match, tone, and strength.

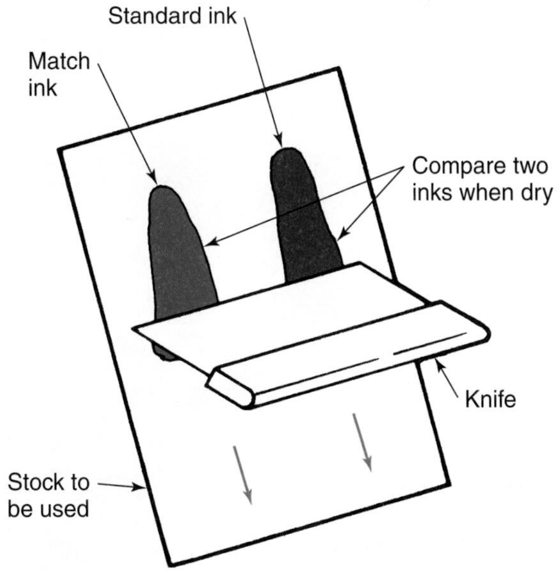

Goodheart-Willcox Publisher

Figure 16-15. In a drawdown test, a standard ink and a mixed ink are placed on the chosen stock. A sharp blade is used to spread the inks onto the stock. After drying, ink qualities are compared.

Specking

Specking is the appearance of tiny dots next to halftone dots or line art. Specking occurs when the ink is contaminated with paper fibers or other foreign material, or when it is not properly ground. Ink film that is too thick can also cause specking.

Process Ink Analysis

Process inks (yellow, magenta, cyan, and black) differ from one ink manufacturer to another. Color bars printed under normal printing conditions may be used to evaluate a particular set of inks used in a printing facility. Most service bureaus or printers furnish test patterns, **Figure 16-16**.

A ***reflection densitometer*** is used for taking density readings from the printed control bars. This instrument measures the amount of light reflected from an object. Record the density readings on a process ink data sheet, **Figure 16-17**. The density readings can be used to determine the four principle working characteristics of a set of process inks: strength, hue, grayness, and efficiency.

Ink strength identifies the range and depth of colors that can be produced from a set of inks. Strength can be determined by visually comparing the density readings and selecting the highest reading for the yellow, magenta, and cyan inks.

Ink hue error identifies the percentage of reflection of colored light from a specific color of ink. A hue or color is determined by the eye in terms of cone stimulation to colors of light. The color or hue of magenta ink should absorb green light, preventing it from reflecting off the paper surface, while allowing all of the blue and red light to reflect. The ink impurities in the magenta ink pigmentation that distort this normal reflection ratio can be measured as a percentage of hue error.

To determine the hue error for one color of ink and its red, green, and blue filter readings, use the equation:

$$\text{Hue Error} = \frac{\text{Medium filter reading} - \text{Low filter reading}}{\text{High filter reading} - \text{Low filter reading}}$$

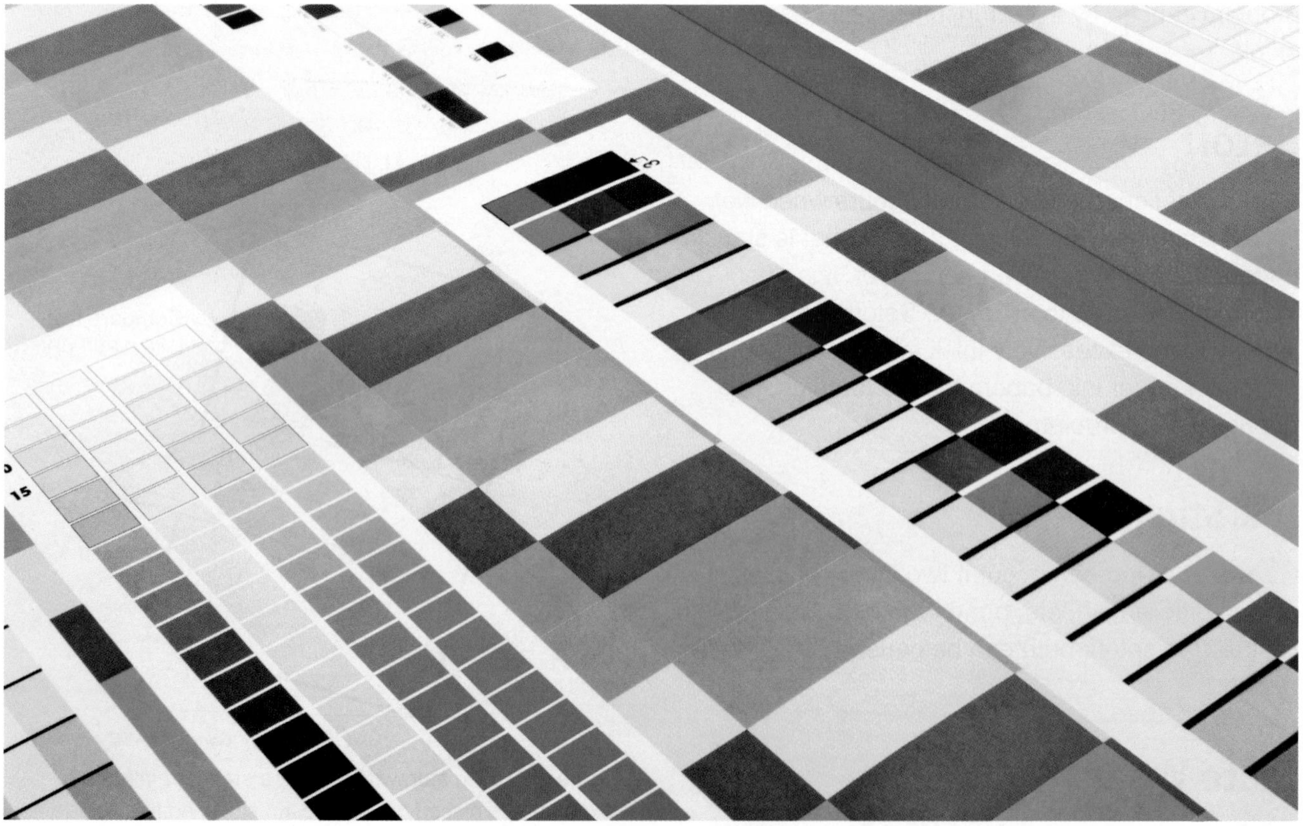

©George Deal

Figure 16-16. An ink analysis test pattern.

The purity of a process color is identified by a *grayness* factor. A color is considered gray when its predominant color reflects less light than the white sheet of paper it is printed on. For example, cyan should reflect 100% blue and green light, but it is considered gray in percentage because it reflects less blue than the white paper.

The lower the percentage factor, the higher the purity level. To determine the grayness factor for a given color of ink, use the equation:

$$\text{Grayness factor} = \frac{\text{Low filter reading}}{\text{High filter reading}}$$

Ink efficiency is similar to hue error, but instead of measuring the percentage of error in the reflection of light, a positive percentage is expressed. Each color of process ink filters out its complementary additive color and reflects the other two-thirds of the spectrum. This is the measurement of efficiency: the higher the percentage of an ink's efficiency, the less color correction will be required and the greater the gamut of possible colors that it can produce.

To determine a specific ink color efficiency percentage, use the equation:

$$\text{Ink efficiency} = \frac{1 - \text{Low filter reading} + \text{Medium filter reading}}{2 \times \text{High filter reading}}$$

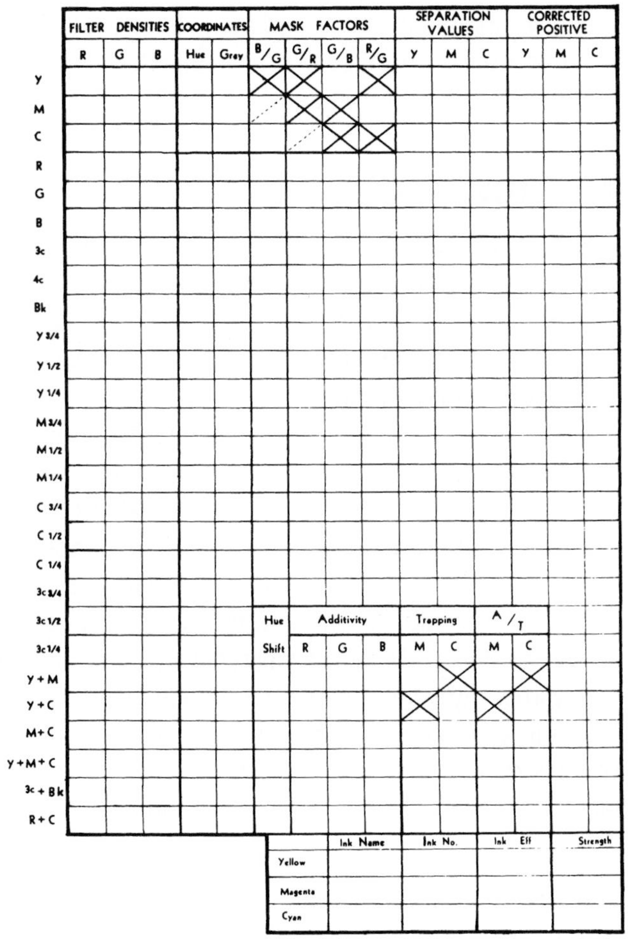

	FILTER DENSITIES			COORDINATES		MASK FACTORS				SEPARATION VALUES			CORRECTED POSITIVE		
	R	G	B	Hue	Gray	B/G	G/R	G/B	R/G	Y	M	C	Y	M	C
Y															
M															
C															
R															
G															
B															
3c															
4c															
Bk															
Y 3/4															
Y 1/2															
Y 1/4															
M 3/4															
M 1/2															
M 1/4															
C 3/4															
C 1/2															
C 1/4															
3c 3/4															
3c 1/2															
3c 1/4															
Y+M															
Y+C															
M+C															
Y+M+C															
3c+Bk															
R+C															

Hue	Additivity			Trapping		A/T	
Shift	R	G	B	M	C	M	C

	Ink Name	Ink No.	Ink Eff	Strength
Yellow				
Magenta				
Cyan				

Goodheart-Willcox Publisher

Figure 16-17. A process ink data sheet can be used to record information concerning methods used to produce separations.

Color Diagrams for Ink Evaluation and Color Correction

When performing process ink analysis, it is beneficial to plot the information on a ***color diagram*** for the purpose of visual evaluation or comparison. Data such as hue error or grayness factor can be calculated and plotted on one of three types of diagrams: the hexagon, circle, or triangle. The ink data, represented by the plots, can then be visually compared to ideal colors on the diagram.

The color hexagon is one of the only diagrams that requires no major computations or formulas. It is one of the easiest and quickest diagrams used to plot color strength and hue differences. The hexagon is best suited for quality control or press control of primary printers and overprints, **Figure 16-18**.

The color circle is designed for visualizing the hue error and grayness factor of actual colors in relation to ideal colors. It is also valuable in determining the color correction system requirements for different inks and substrates. See **Figure 16-19**.

The subtractive color triangle is designed to illustrate the gamut of pure color that is possible with a set of process inks. The plots of ink data can also identify under- or over-trapping and predict overprints. Mask percentages are located along the sides of the triangle to identify masking requirements for color correction of the specific inks. See **Figure 16-20**.

The subtractive color triangle has two additional applications. It can be used to analyze new batches of process ink for hue and grayness by comparing the batches to successful proofs. The triangle can

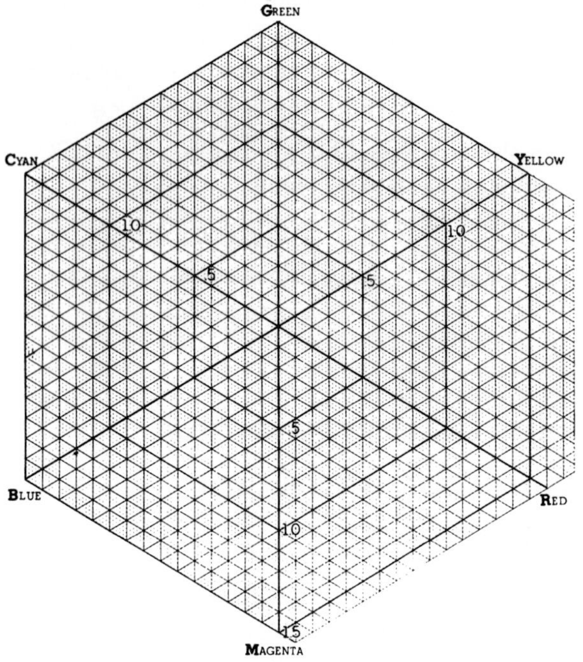

Graphic Arts Technical Foundation

Figure 16-18. A color hexagon is used to plot color strength and hue differences to improve quality control.

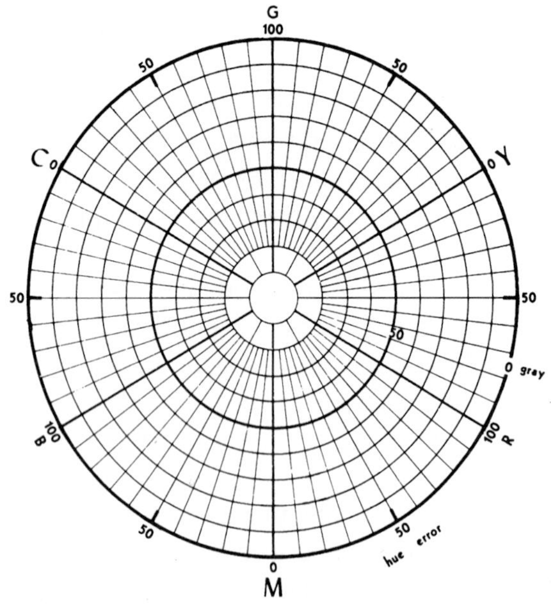

Graphic Arts Technical Foundation

Figure 16-19. A color circle can be plotted so that hue error and grayness can be visualized and compared to ideal colors.

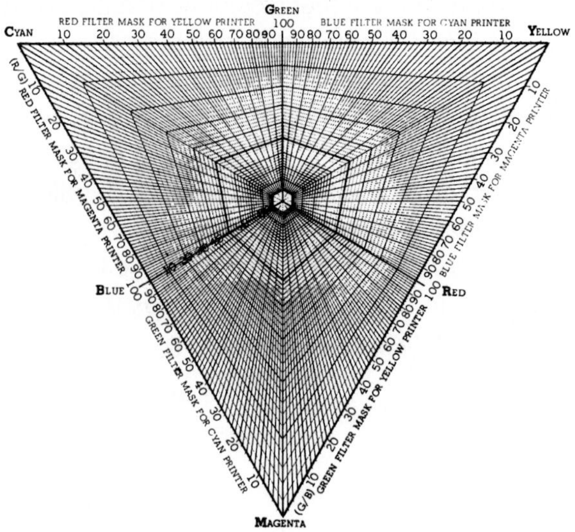

Graphic Arts Technical Foundation

Figure 16-20. A color triangle indicates the gamut of color possibilities for a set of process inks. Mask percentages for color correction are located on the sides of the triangle.

also be used to plot readings from the customer's reflective original art to immediately determine whether the important colors fall within the gamut of the process inks' capabilities.

Ink Impurities

The raw materials of a pigment used in making ink contain metals that appear naturally. Once they have been refined and qualify for printing pigments, they still contain impurities that cannot be removed. The processing operations are not capable of producing purity. Therefore, all inks have impurities.

The data derived from the analysis of a set of process inks will determine the exact masking or color correction requirements. When printing color, masking relates to the ink coverage and the density or reflection of ink film. Usually, the yellow pigment will be the purest. Magenta will typically contain a yellow impurity. Magenta ink can be either rubine or rhodamine in color. Rhodamine is a blue-magenta, which is more expensive and produces good fleshtones. Rubine magenta is more red.

Cyan ink contains the most impurities and will usually have a major impurity of magenta. If the cyan appears to have a magenta impurity, it will also contain a certain amount of yellow that is already in the magenta. Then the cyan ink is said to have a major impurity of magenta and a minor impurity of yellow.

During color correction, the cyan printer separation will receive the least amount of correction. Because the magenta impurity or yellow ink impurity in the cyan ink cannot be removed, less magenta and even less yellow must be printed. The yellow impurity is in both the cyan and magenta ink; therefore, it requires the most reduction, masking, and correction. Reduction is the process of bringing the image to a point where it looks as closely like the original as possible. It is accomplished by removing everything that conflicts with false appearance. The percentage of color correction is best determined by actual ink density readings and evaluation of the four basic ink characteristics.

Summary

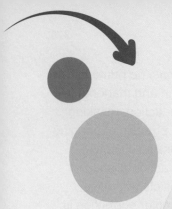

- Three ingredients are essential to the formulation of printing inks: vehicle, pigment, and additives.
- Color strength, body, stability, length, tack, and drying are common properties of ink.
- Types of ink include relief inks, gravure inks, screen printing inks, lithographic inks, and non-impact printing inks.
- Charts from ink manufacturers contain samples of ink on coated and uncoated stock.
- Ink-related challenges include setting and drying, chalking, strike-through, setoff, ink sticking, plate wear, off-color problems, and specking.
- Reflection densitometers are used for taking density readings from test patterns. Color diagrams plot information for visual evaluation or comparison.

Review Questions

Answer the following questions using the information in this chapter.

1. Explain the three main ingredients of ink.
2. _____ is the ink's ability to cover the substrate.
3. _____ refers to the ink's thickness or fluidity.
4. What type of press uses soft-bodied inks?
5. Define *thixotropy.*
6. Which ink quality would tend to make the ink fly out on a high-speed press?
   A. Short ink.
   B. Long ink.
   C. High tack.
   D. Low tack.
7. Low ink tack could cause which of the following problems?
   A. Paper tearing.
   B. Picking.
   C. Splitting.
   D. None of the above.
8. Describe the six ways ink can dry.
9. _____ viscosity ink is thick and resists flow, while _____ viscosity ink is fluid and flows more easily.
10. _____ can be found in many commercial letterpress facilities since it can be used on a wide variety of presses and papers.

11. Why are screen printing inks thicker than inks used for other processes?
12. Name two common problems associated with lithographic inks.
13. Give two advantages of using vegetable oil–based inks.
14. What is the most important factor in the growth of UV-curable ink use?
15. What is the function of a spectrophotometer?
16. What six factors should you consider when ordering ink?
17. *True or False?* Strike-through is an ink-penetration problem that is caused by thin stock.
18. What instrument is used to measure the amount of light reflected from an object?
19. What are the four principle working characteristics of a set of process inks?
20. What three types of color diagrams are used for process ink analysis?

Suggested Activities

1. Place a small amount of two kinds of ink on a sheet of glass. Tap the ink and check the length of each kind of ink by measuring the breaking point. What information is gained from this activity?
2. Mix ink to match a specified color requirement. What technique will you use to check the ink's color and strength?

Chapter 17

Finishing and Binding

Learning Objectives

After studying this chapter, you will be able to:

- Explain terms related to printing.
- Recall the types of folding processes.
- Explain different types of finishing operations.
- Summarize the processes needed for different binding techniques.
- Recall different types of packaging used in the graphic communications industry.

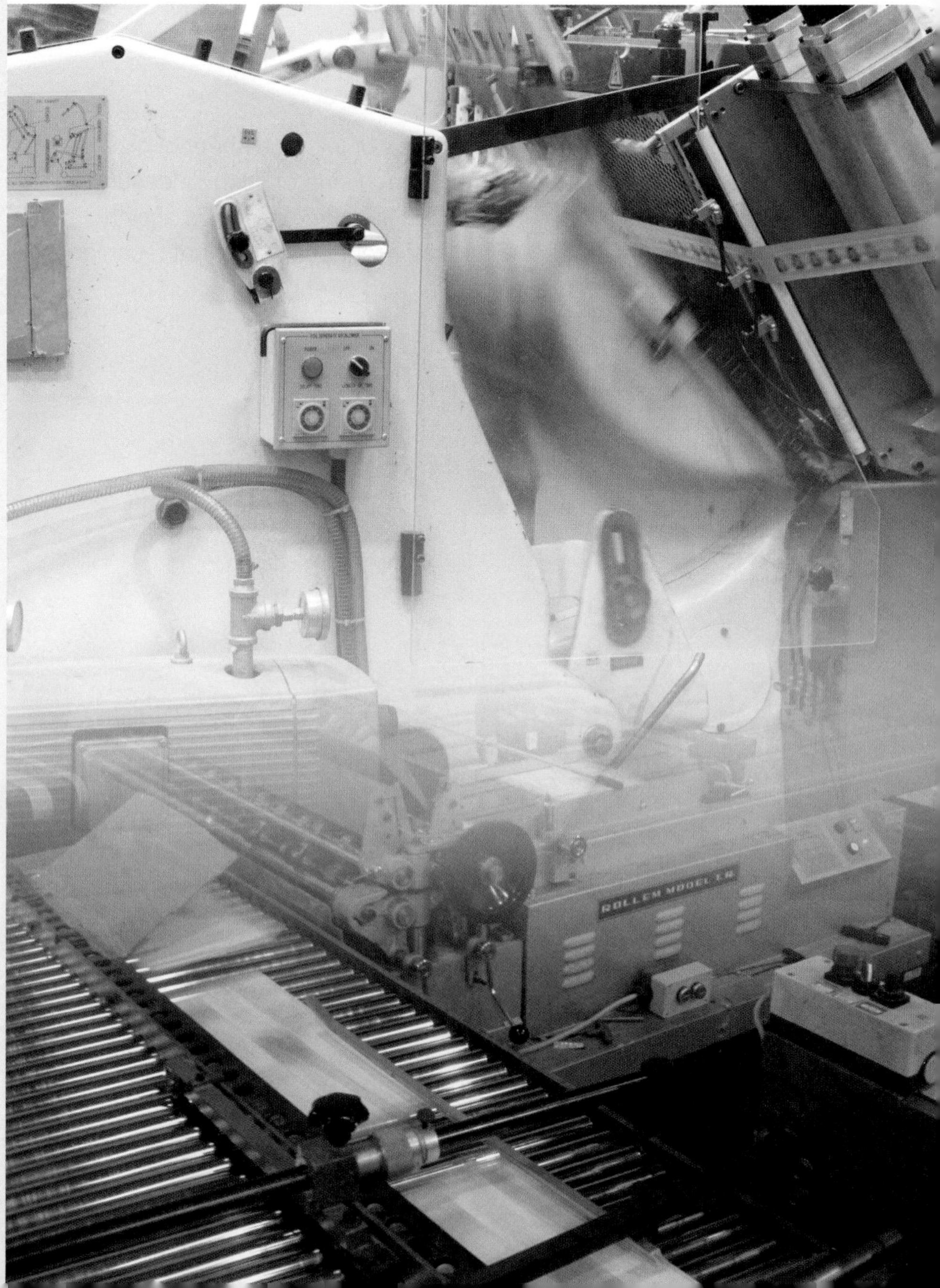

Goodheart-Willcox Publisher

Important Terms

banding machine
binding
blind embossing
coating
collating
converting
creasing
creep
cutting
debossing
die cutting
drilling
edge staining
edition binding
embossing
epoxy
finishing
gathering
indexing
laminating
lift
liquid lamination
mechanical binding
numbering
packaging
perfect binding
perforating
plastic comb binding
punching
scoring
shrink-wrap
slitting
spiral binding
stamping
stitching
taping machine
trimming
varnishing

G-WLEARNING.COM

While studying this chapter, look for the activity icon to:

- **Practice** vocabulary terms with e-flash cards, matching activities, and vocabulary game.
- **Reinforce** what you learn by submitting end-of-chapter questions.

www.g-wlearning.com/visualtechnology/

Finishing is a general term that applies to many types of operations carried out during or following printing, including cutting, folding, slitting, perforating, creasing, scoring, die cutting, embossing, stamping, numbering, drilling, punching, varnishing, and laminating. Exact finishing methods will vary depending on the type of product and its specifications.

Binding is the process of fastening together the sheets of a product with methods including perfect binding, saddle-stitching, case binding, and mechanical binding. It can be considered a finishing operation, but it is usually classified separately since binding is often an operation subcontracted to a specialty house. Like finishing, binding is a general term that can be applied to slightly different tasks depending on the type of product and the process involved. **Figure 17-1** depicts the steps involved in a type of binding operation.

Finishing and binding are as important as the printing itself. If even one finishing process is poorly done, even a very well-printed job will have little or no value. The customer might reject the job and refuse to pay for it, or demand that it be completed again, without additional charge. In either case, the printing company will be faced with a financial loss on the job, instead of the expected profit. This makes it extremely important that all finishing and binding processes are performed correctly. Many printing facilities include packaging and distribution as part of the binding operation. Once the product is printed, it is distributed. A container is necessary to house the printed material. The purpose of packing is to contain, protect, preserve, and transport a product. Packaging is essential to the distribution process.

Cutting

Making a large sheet of paper into several smaller sheets is termed ***cutting***, which should not be confused with trimming. ***Trimming*** is the process of cutting off uneven or unwanted edges of paper, as when trimming the three sides of a book.

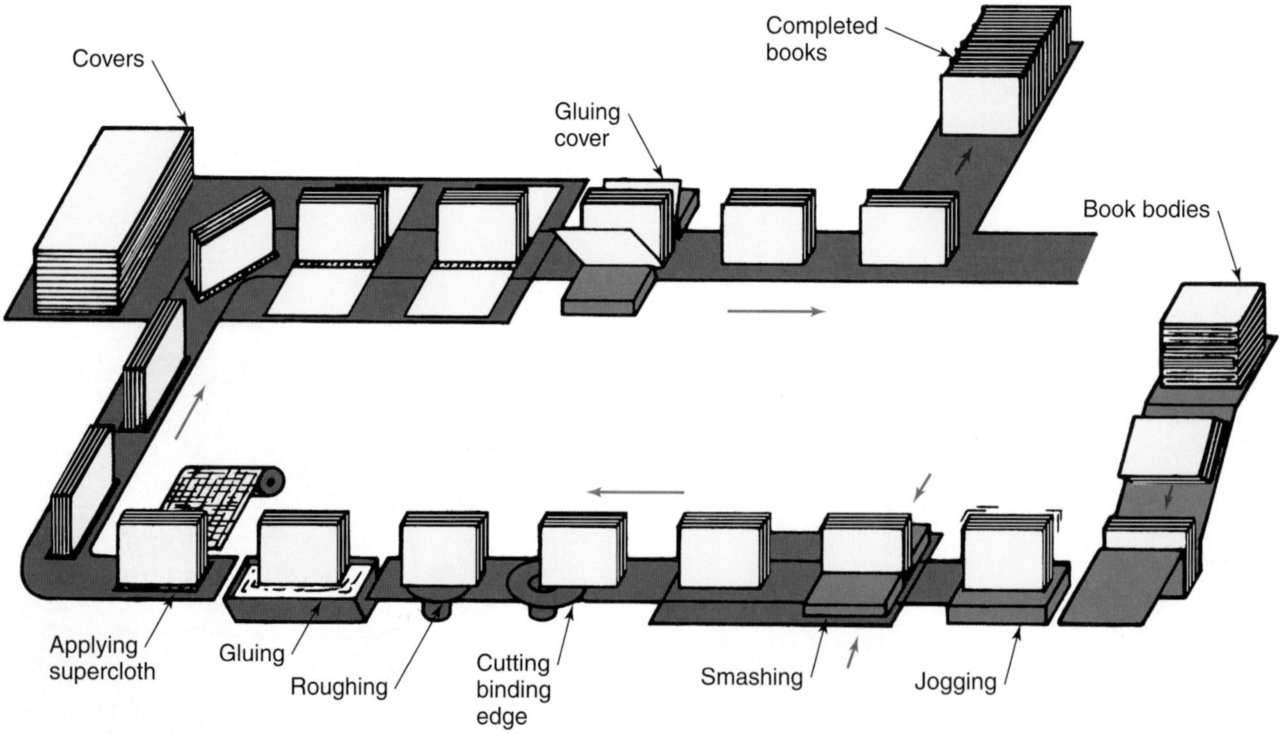

Goodheart-Willcox Publisher

Figure 17-1. The flow of a typical perfect binding operation. Perfect binding is the process of attaching a paper cover to the book body with glue.

Paper Cutter

The most common type of equipment used to cut paper stock is the manual or electronic guillotine cutter, **Figure 17-2**. The knife of a guillotine cutter is forced through the paper at a slight angle to produce an oblique shearing action, **Figure 17-3**.

The blade must be very sharp and free of nicks, since any roughness of the blade will appear as a jagged edge on the cut sheets. Keeping blades in excellent condition is essential for quality trimming or cutting of stock. Most plants send cutter blades out to be sharpened. Extreme care must be taken when removing or installing a cutter blade. Any blade that is out of the cutter should be placed in a sheath to eliminate the possibility of injury from the sharp edge.

Warning

Respect a cutter blade's sharpness. Handle a blade carefully, since it can cause severe cuts.

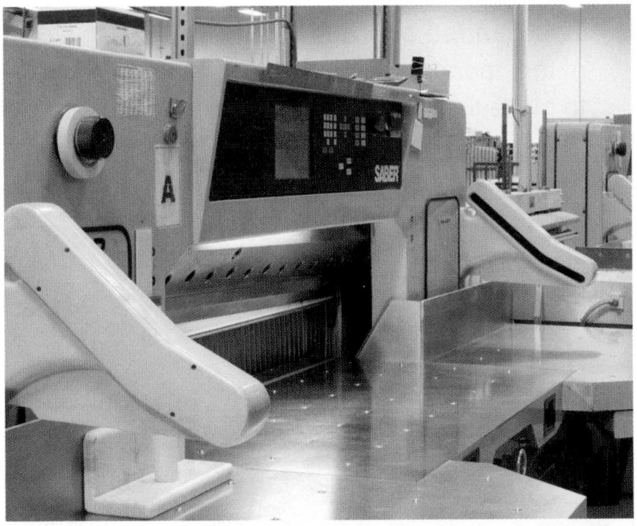

©George Deal

Figure 17-2. This is a powerful computer-controlled guillotine cutter. Cuts can be preprogrammed into computer memory. To help in moving and positioning large stacks of paper, the cutting table is pierced with many tiny holes through which powerful jets of air are blown. The paper stack is slightly raised from the surface by the air, making it easy to move.

Specific equipment instructions should be followed. To correctly position a sharpened blade in the cutter, follow specific directions provided by the equipment manufacturer. Before making any adjustments, place a new wood or plastic shear stick in the table's groove or channel. Refer to **Figure 17-3**.

The shear stick should be rotated or turned periodically to give a new surface under the cutting edge and produce a final sharp, clean cut.

Today's paper cutters come in a wide variety of sizes from tabletop models to huge floor models. Floor models have automatic clamps and are computer-programmed to make planned cuts. The cutter size is designated by the length of cut. A 30″ paper cutter will take a sheet up to 30″ in width, **Figure 17-4**.

A dial gauge or digital readout indicates the distance of the back gauge to the cutting edge of

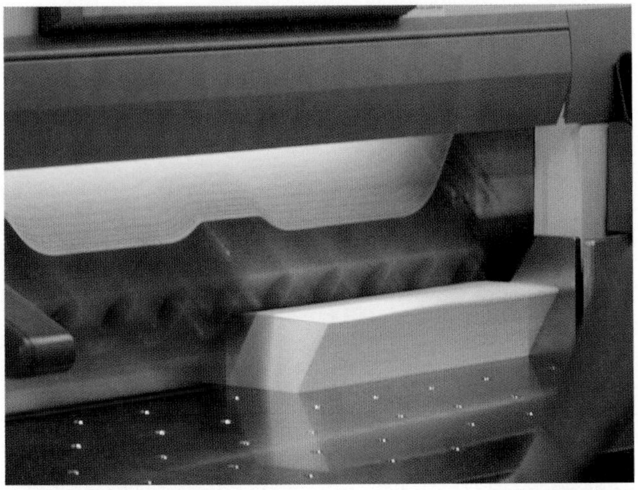

©Kevin Runbeck

Figure 17-3. The guillotine cutter forces a blade through a stack of paper to produce shearing action.

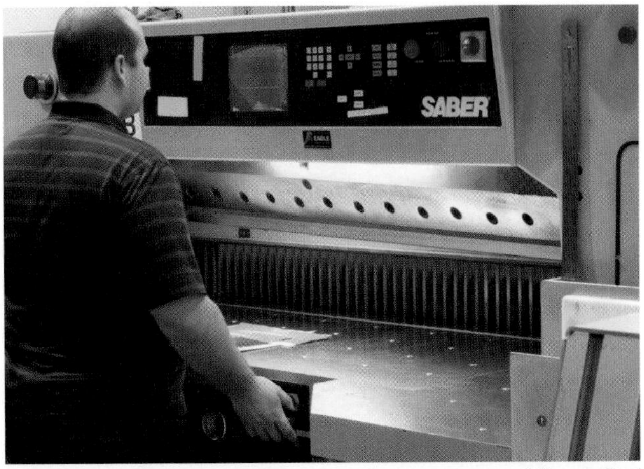

©George Deal

Figure 17-4. The length of cut that can be made by a paper cutter is used to designate its size. Typical sizes are 30″ and 37″, although larger and smaller models are made.

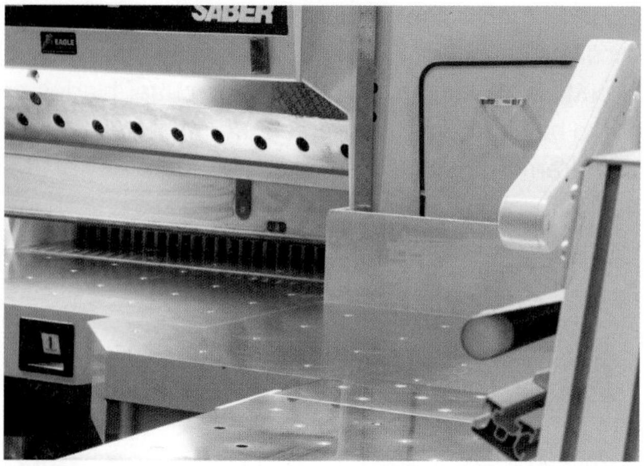

©George Deal

Figure 17-5. Most large cutters use an air jet bed on the table. Air flows up through holes in the table to lift paper for easy movement.

the blade. A properly adjusted cutter will give very accurate cuts.

Most large cutters have a low-pressure air table or bed that allows for easy movement of heavy stacks of sheets. Air is pumped up through the table to form a cushion between the table and the paper. The air lifts the paper so that it floats over the table for easy positioning, **Figure 17-5**.

Many of today's facilities have a vacuum system to remove all of the unwanted paper. The waste stock is sucked to a receiving area, where it is baled for recycling, **Figure 17-6**. Paper dust must be held to a minimum to comply with local, state, and federal health safety regulations.

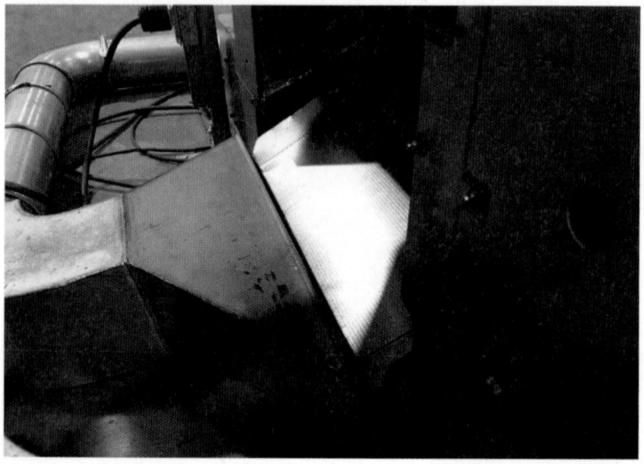

©George Deal

Figure 17-6. Paper waste, such as trimmings from paper cutters, is usually baled for recycling.

The cutting of paper is a very exacting task. A wrong cut can make a job a pile of waste, which can be a very costly mistake. Accuracy is essential when paper is cut down to the size for a given press run. Proper allowances must also be considered when bleeds and trims are specified.

Automatic programmed paper cutters have safety features designed to prevent injuries to fingers or hands. These include:

- **Nonrepeat device.** Cutter blade will only come down once until reset.
- **Two-handed operation.** Buttons on each side of the operator must be pressed simultaneously to make the cutter blade operate. See **Figure 17-7**.
- **Electric eye stop.** A detector that will automatically stop the descent of the cutter blade if a hand, arm, or other object is in its path.

©George Deal

Figure 17-7. On most large paper cutters, the operator must use both hands to press buttons that make the cutter knife operate. This system keeps hands out of the area where the cut is performed.

Warning

Whatever the cutting device, safe operation is essential. If a cutter will slice through a pile of paper like butter, consider what it would do to a hand. Always follow manufacturer's directions and never bypass safety devices when operating a cutter.

Folding Operations

Once images have been printed onto the substrate, they are often folded. Many jobs are printed on one side and backed up with a second printing, commonly called sheetwise imposition. The single sheet might be letter-size and small enough to be folded for insertion into an envelope, or large enough to have 8 or 16 book pages on each side. One common notion is that no matter the size of a piece of paper, a sheet can be folded only seven times.

The most common folding machine for smaller sheets is the buckle type, **Figure 17-8**, which uses roller action to buckle-fold the paper. The stock is placed in a friction- or suction-type feeder. The adjustment on the suction-type feeder is similar to a printing unit feeder, while the friction type requires a very exact setting.

As the sheet leaves the feeder, it travels on belts or rollers that carry the sheet to the fold plate, **Figure 17-9**. As the sheet is forced against the fold plate, the sheet buckles and another combination of rollers folds the sheet and carries it to a delivery station or to another set of folding rollers. The fold will be either parallel with or right-angle to the first fold. **Figure 17-10** shows a parallel fold and a right-angle fold.

Some folders use a folding knife to force the paper between rollers for folding. The operation of a knife-type folder is illustrated in **Figure 17-11**.

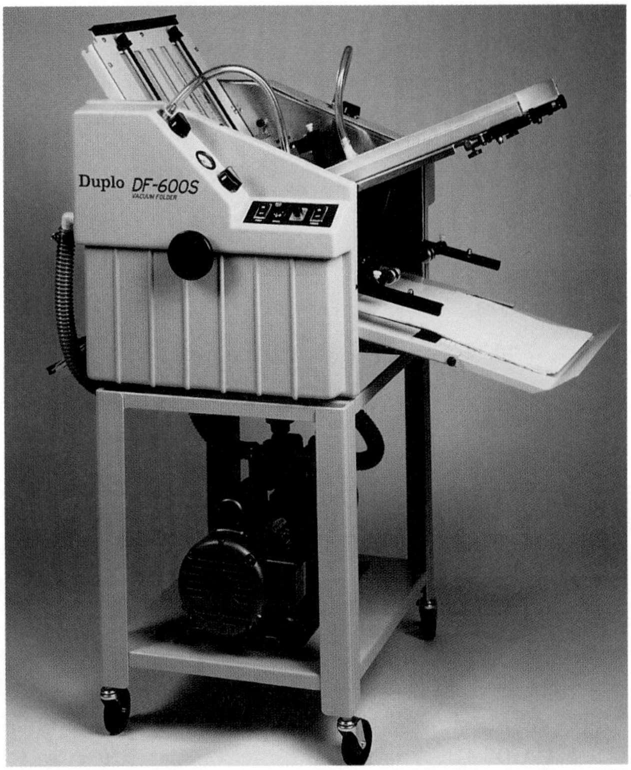

Duplo USA

Figure 17-8. A small folder that uses a suction-type feeder. The suction is provided by a vacuum pump mounted below the folder.

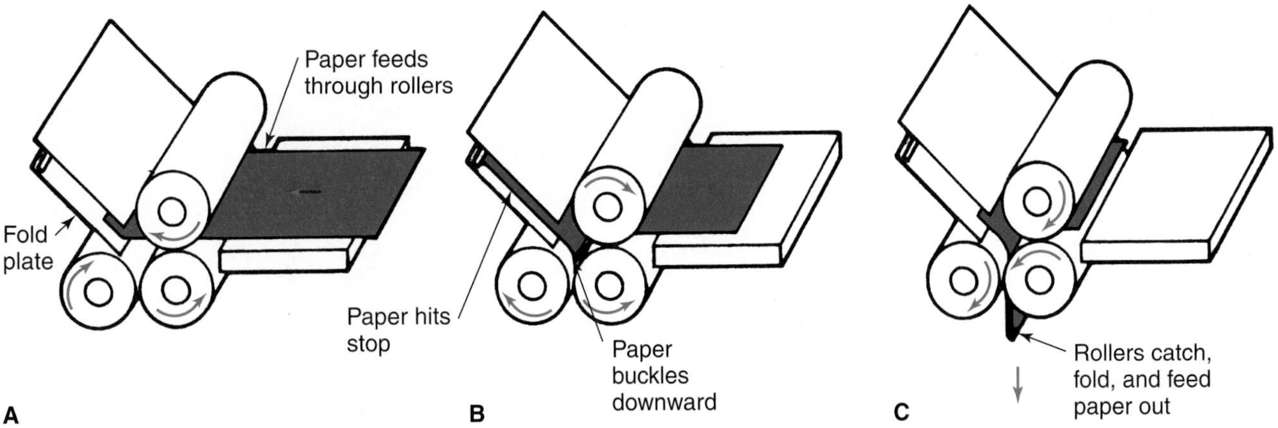

Goodheart-Willcox Publisher

Figure 17-9. The basic operating principle of a buckle folder. A—Paper is fed into the machine by rollers. B—Paper hits the stop on the fold plate and buckles downward. C—Rollers catch the paper and feed it downward to make a fold.

Floor-type folders come in a variety of sizes and are commonly found in graphic communications facilities. Many folders, such as the one shown in **Figure 17-12**, have computerized controls to speed up the process of setting up for different folds and different paper sizes.

The folding requirements of any project should be considered in the planning stage, since it can affect the choice of equipment and the overall production schedule. Most folds are a combination

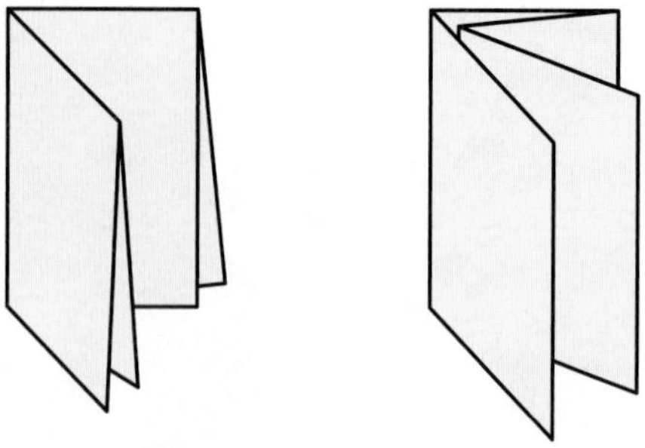

Goodheart-Willcox Publisher

Figure 17-10. Examples of parallel and right-angle folds.

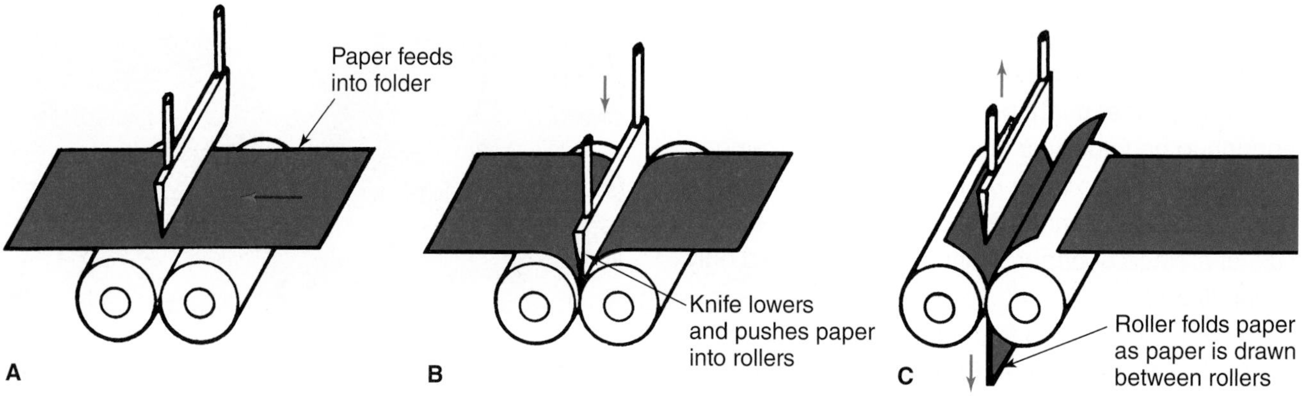
Paper feeds into folder
A
B
Knife lowers and pushes paper into rollers
C
Roller folds paper as paper is drawn between rollers

Goodheart-Willcox Publisher

Figure 17-11. Operation of a knife-type folder. A—Paper is fed into the folder by rollers. B—The folding knife comes down and pushes the paper between two rollers. C—The rollers fold and pull paper through machine.

MBO
M80

©George Deal

Figure 17-12. A computerized control panel on this folder permits quick setup for different paper sizes. Various attachments are available to allow customized setups.

of parallel and right-angle folds, such as those shown in **Figure 17-13**.

Some printing jobs have different folding requirements. Different types of folds include half folds, accordion folds, gatefolds, French folds, and letter folds.

Folding Area Safety

- Tie back long hair and secure any loose sleeves or similar clothing items. The rotating parts of folding machinery could grasp hair or loose clothing and pull it into the machine.
- Keep your fingers clear of pinch points, such as folding rollers.
- Handle paper carefully; the edges of sheets are very sharp and can cause painful cuts.
- Turn off any machine before making adjustments. Follow the manufacturer's prescribed procedures for adjusting machine settings.
- Lock out electrical power when performing maintenance.

Other Finishing Operations

In addition to cutting and folding, there are many other finishing operations that are used as required to produce the final product. In-line operations are additional finishing units performed as part of the continuous process or at the end of the printing

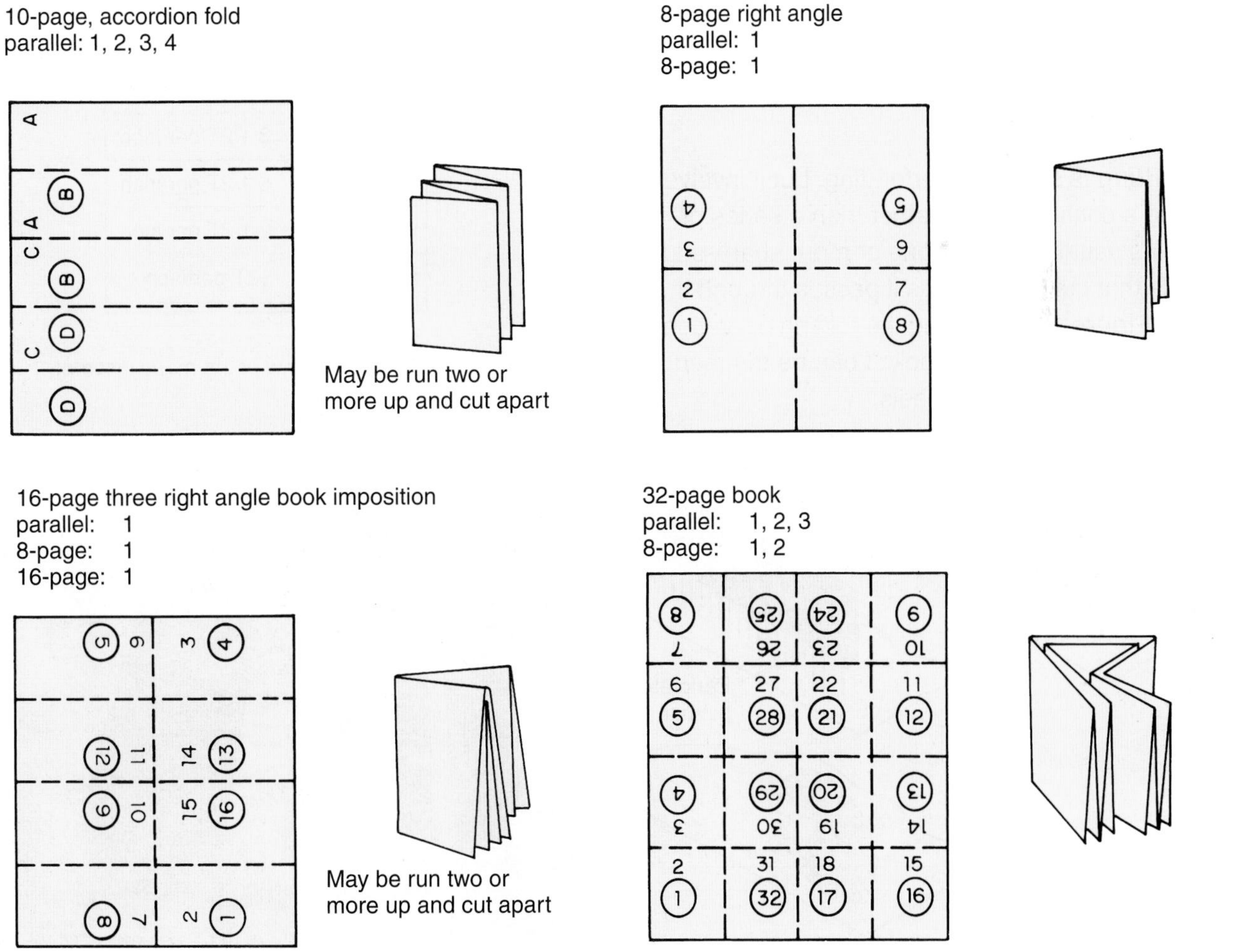

Goodheart-Willcox Publisher

Figure 17-13. These are a few of the common folds used in the industry.

process. Off-line operations are done on stand-alone equipment.

Perforating

Whenever it is necessary to remove a portion of the printed material, stock is perforated, or "perfed." This makes it possible to readily tear off and remove a reply card on an advertising circular or a single page in a workbook. ***Perforating*** places a series of small cuts or slits in the substrate, using various types of blades or wheels, as shown in **Figure 17-14**.

Sometimes, the task can be completed while running the job on the press. In-line finishing processes are common with many of the printing devices. The stock can also be perforated on the folder as an auxiliary process. The type of perforation and the number of teeth per inch to make the slits or holes will depend on the type of substrate used. **Figure 17-15** shows some examples of perforations.

Slitting

Slitting is similar to perforating, but it involves making a continuous cut rather than a series of slits. It is usually done by one or more sharp-edged wheels that cut the stock as it passes through the folder, **Figure 17-16**. During the folding operation, for example, a leaflet or booklet can be trimmed to finished size by slitting wheels.

Creasing and Scoring

Creasing is the process of compressing the substrate so it will fold more easily. This is often accomplished with a rotary creaser attached to the folder, **Figure 17-17A**. Sometimes, creasing is a separate operation using a creasing rule, **Figure 17-17B**, on letterpress equipment or specially designed finishing equipment. A creasing rule is made of a thin piece of metal that is pressed slightly into the stock. It is used to make folding easy. Rule thickness will vary with the stock.

The term *scoring* is used interchangeably with creasing in some operations, but ***scoring*** is actually a slight cut made in heavy stock before it is folded. The correct depth of the cut is important. Scoring

Pinhole	28T per inch
Slot	9T per inch
Slot	8T per inch
Slot	7T per inch
Slot	3 1/2T per inch
Knifecut	6 1/2T per inch
Knifecut	2 1/2T per inch
Knifecut	12T per inch

Rollem

Figure 17-15. These are a few of the many different perforations that are used.

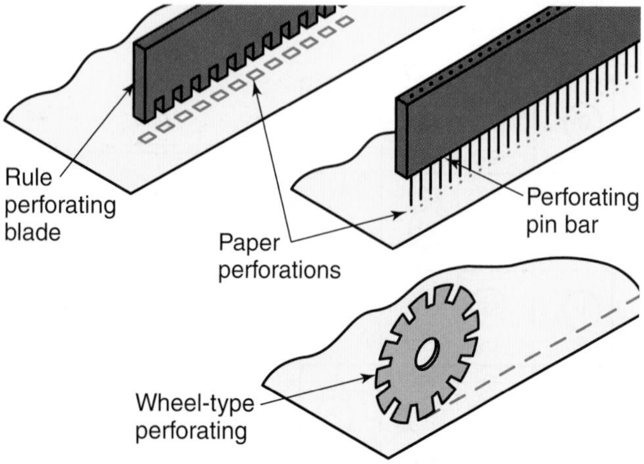

Goodheart-Willcox Publisher

Figure 17-14. Stock can be perforated through the use of various devices on the press or the folder.

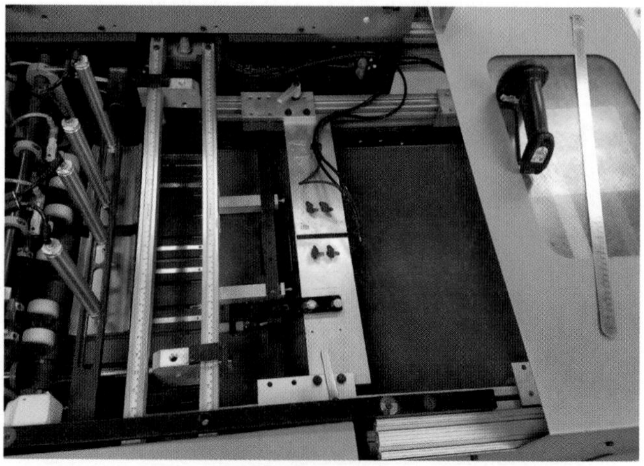

©George Deal

Figure 17-16. Slitting is commonly done by a sharp wheel that cuts paper sheets as it exits the folder.

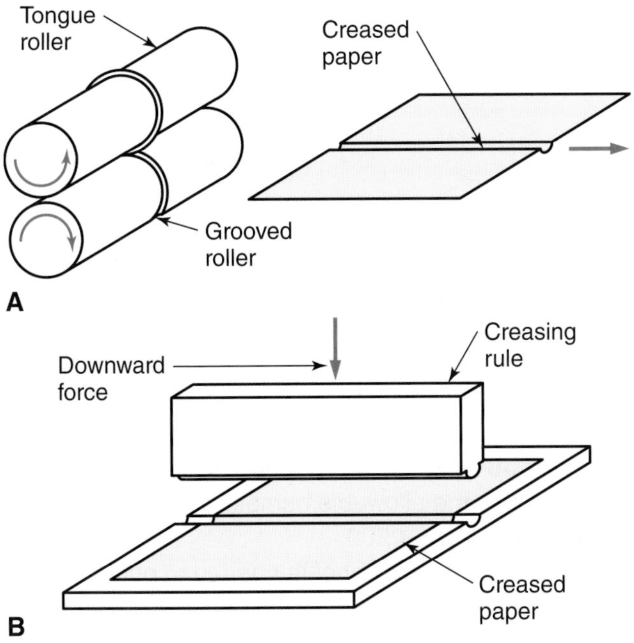

Goodheart-Willcox Publisher

Figure 17-17. Creasing devices. A—The creasing roller method is used on a folder. B—Creasing rules are typically used on letterpress equipment.

©George Deal

Figure 17-18. The exposed strips are for scoring and have rounded edges. The sharp blade edges for the cuts are encased in rubber to release the substrate easily from the blade.

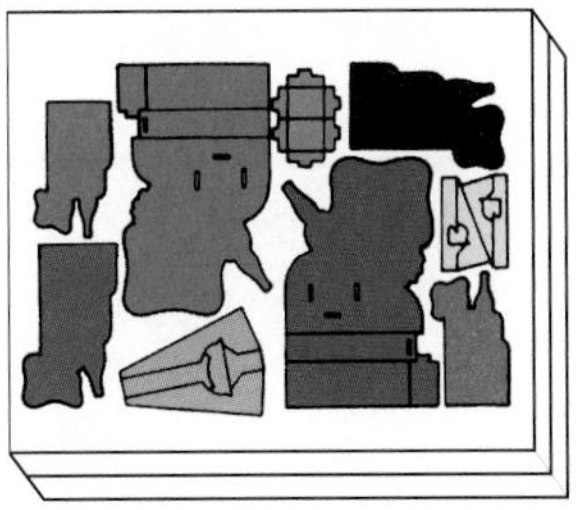

Tag and label dies

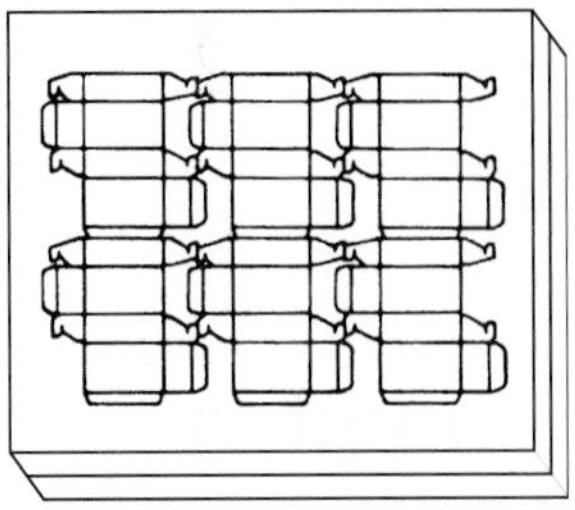

Folding box dies

Accurate Steel Rule Die Mfg., Inc.

Figure 17-19. Irregular shapes can be die cut. These are examples.

is commonly done in the packaging industry, where scores are made at the fold points for cartons.

Die Cutting

Whenever an irregular shape must be cut into a substrate, the method most often used to do the task is ***die cutting***. In the die cutting process, pressure is used to force a sharp metal die through the stock, **Figure 17-18**.

The dies, which look somewhat like kitchen cookie cutters, are used to slice through the substrate to form tags, cards, labels, and boxes, **Figure 17-19**. Dies are also used to cut the irregular shapes after printing labels, decals, and stickers.

Although relief printing is no longer done by most printers, a small relief press is found in many shops because of its usefulness for die cutting and similar tasks requiring pressure. The dies used in the process consist of a base, or dieboard, with steel rules shaped and inserted into a saw kerf. The saw kerf or laser cut is the open area left after sawing or laser cutting the material. Pieces of sponge rubber are glued to the dieboards on either side of the rules to release substrate material after cutting.

Embossing

Embossing is a process that creates a raised image on a substrate by pressing it between two dies, **Figure 17-20**. One die is in relief, while the other is recessed. When the two are brought together with the stock between them, the clamping force creates a raised image on the stock.

High-quality embossing requires expensive dies and must be done to close tolerances, but the results can be very impressive. See **Figure 17-21**. Sometimes, an image is printed, and the stock is then embossed. In other applications, the stock itself creates the image and ink is not used. This technique is called ***blind embossing***. If an image is sunk into the substrate, rather than being raised, the process is called ***debossing***.

Academic Link

Calculating Paper Requirements

Determining the amount of paper needed for a job must be an exact calculation. Ordering too much stock for a job is a waste of money and resources, while not ordering enough stock may delay completion of the job.

Several factors are included in calculating the paper requirements for a job, such as page size, stock size, order quantity, and waste percentage. A waste percentage is typically established when the order is received and should be added to the client's order quantity.

For example, a client orders 8000 copies of a 48-page, perfect-bound booklet to be printed. The page size is 6″ × 9″, the allowable waste is 5%, and the full-size stock is 25″ × 38″. To determine the number of full-size sheets needed:

1. Determine how many 6″ × 9″ pages can be cut from a 25″ × 38″ sheet of stock.
2. Calculate the total number of 6″ × 9″ pages included in the order: 8000 × 48 = 384,000.
3. Divide the total number of finished pages by the number of 6″ × 9″ pages that can be cut from a 25″ × 38″ sheet of stock: 384,000 ÷ 16 = 24,000.
4. Calculate the allowable number of waste sheets: 24,000 × 5% = 1,200.
5. Add the number of sheets needed to print the job with the number of waste sheets allowed to determine the total number of full-size sheets of stock to order for the job.

How many 25″ × 38″ sheets are needed to complete this job?

Stamping

The process of ***stamping***, or foil stamping, is a method of transferring a thin layer of metallic tone or color to a substrate, using heat and pressure. Gold or simulated gold is commonly used as a stamping material, **Figure 17-22**. Silver and other metallics, as well as various color foils, are also available. Some other colors are also available as hot stamping materials.

Stamping is a form of relief printing process. The material to be stamped is set in raised metal type or produced as a cut (an engraving in metal that has a raised printing area), then clamped into a

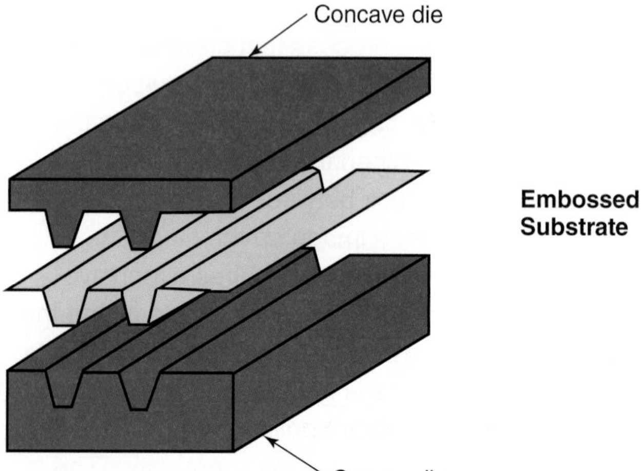

Goodheart-Willcox Publisher

Figure 17-20. A pair of dies is used for embossing an image on a substrate.

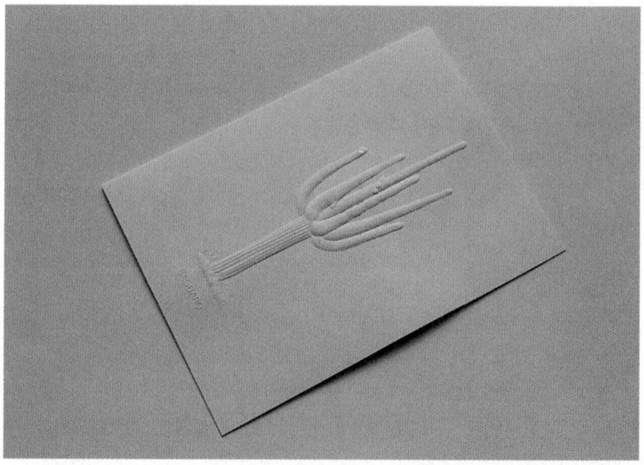

Goodheart-Willcox Publisher

Figure 17-21. Embossed surfaces create a very interesting pattern or design that has depth. This is an example of blind embossing, with no ink used on the raised image.

holding device. The type or other material is heated, then brought into contact with a coated foil laid over the substrate. The heat and pressure transfers the color or metallic film from the foil to the substrate. Proper image transfer depends on the amount of heat and pressure, and the length of time they are applied. In a production situation, the foil stamping unit is automated, but for small jobs, a hand-operated press is typically used.

Numbering

The process of imprinting tickets, certificates, checks, or other items with consecutive figures is called ***numbering***. Using a device called a numbering machine, the figures are transferred from an inked relief image onto the stock. In operation, a plunger is automatically depressed by the press to ratchet the numbering head to a different figure or digit. This permits forward or backward numbering, **Figure 17-23**. Many printing machines have the capability of in-line numbering.

Punching and Drilling

Both punching and drilling produce holes in a substrate but use different means to do so. ***Punching*** is done by forcing a metal rod down through the paper to remove stock. The punch works in a shearing action with a die placed below the paper, **Figure 17-24**. Punching is used for such applications as producing the holes needed to do spiral binding or paper for binders.

Drilling uses a revolving, hollow drill bit with very sharp edges, **Figure 17-25**. After placing stock on the drill table board, the revolving drill is forced through a ***lift*** of paper. The waste stock rises through the hollow center of the drill and is ejected out of the drill top. A guide at the back of the board regulates the distance the holes are drilled from the edge of the sheet, **Figure 17-26**. Most drills have stops to ensure the proper positioning for each lift to be drilled.

Drills are available in various diameters. Many drilling machines have auxiliary devices as attachments. These devices make it possible to slit, fillet, or notch a lift of paper. Also available are multiple spindle drilling machines that make it possible to drill ten or more holes at one time.

©George Deal

Figure 17-22. Foil stamping is used as an accenting or decorative device.

Mega Pixel/Shutterstock.com

Figure 17-23. Tickets are a printed product that commonly must be numbered as a finishing operation.

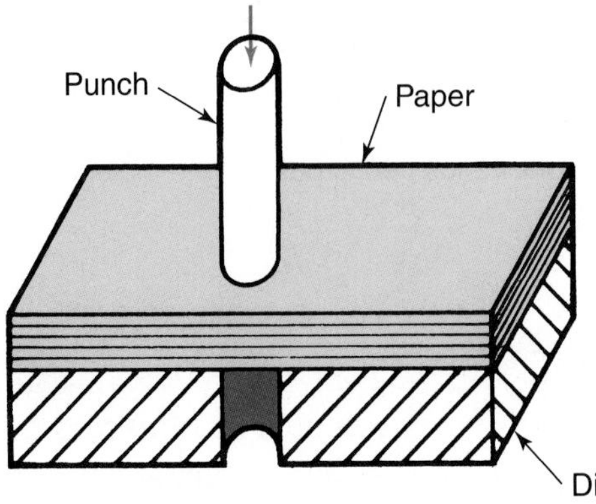

Goodheart-Willcox Publisher

Figure 17-24. A punch forces a metal rod straight down through stock. It does not spin, as does a drill. The die located below the punch shears off stock to form a hole.

Goodheart-Willcox Publisher

Figure 17-25. Paper drills have very sharp edges. Handle drills carefully when mounting or removing them.

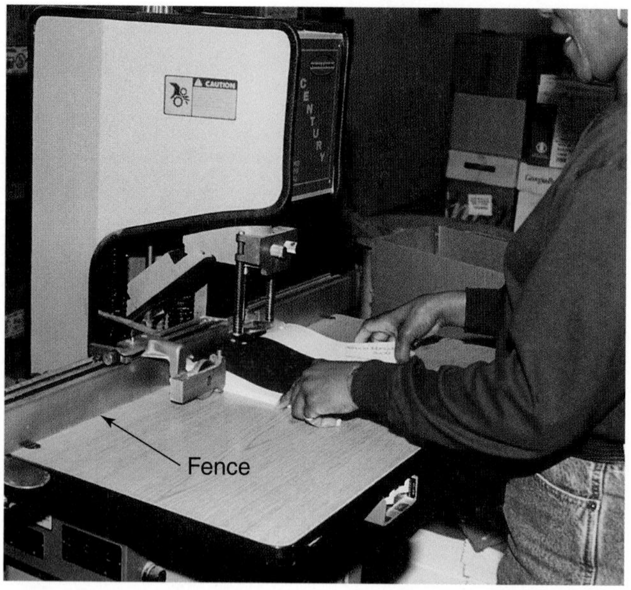

Goodheart-Willcox Publisher

Figure 17-26. A fence at the back of the drilling machine table can be set for proper positioning of the holes being drilled. This machine is operated with a foot switch, leaving the operator's hands free to position the material.

Warning

The drill spindle should be protected by a guard. The high-speed revolving action of the drill tends to draw hair or loose clothing toward it. This is caused by static electricity. Hands and fingers must also be kept away from the revolving drill.

Coating

After an image has been printed onto a substrate, ***coating*** is sometimes used to provide a clear protective surface. Usually, the coating makes the surface resistant to moisture and scuffing. End use and the nature of the substrate determine the type of coating. Some common classified types of coating are protective and decorative.

Glossy brochures, annual report covers, and similar products are typical examples of ***varnishing***. The coating may be full coverage or spot location. The coating materials vary, but some of the coatings are epoxies that give excellent wear qualities. An ***epoxy*** is a resin that forms a very hard surface coating when combined with other chemicals.

Laminating

Laminating is the bonding of two or more materials together to become one common unit. Put another way, it is the sealing of a substrate between two pieces of plastic material. A thin film of plastic with an adhesive coating is bonded to the substrate to provide protection against abrasion and moisture. The laminate material can be applied as an in-line operation on some printing presses, **Figure 17-27**, or as individual sheets of various sizes. Often, restaurant menus are laminated to protect the menu from moisture and constant handling.

The process, called ***liquid lamination***, is actually a coating method. The plastic coating

©George Deal

Figure 17-27. Laminating material being applied. The thin plastic layer protects the printed product.

material is applied in liquid form and then cured into a tough protective layer by exposure to ultraviolet light. For this reason, it is sometimes referred to as a UV-cured coating.

Indexing

Adding plastic index tabs or index thumb cuts to the edge of a substrate is referred to as ***indexing***. The purpose of this is to make it easier to locate specific information.

Edge Staining

Edge staining is when the edges of books or other gathered material is given a different look from the stock. Gilding is an example of applying gold leaf to the edge of a book. Sometimes color is used to identify different sections of a book or catalog.

Converting

Changing a printed piece into another is called ***converting***. The following general operations are also considered converting: bookbinding, laminating, coating, folding, gluing, and die-cutting.

Binding

After printing and such finishing steps as folding, a product may be ready for shipment or it may require *binding* to fasten the sheets or folded signatures together. Many printed press sheets are very large and must be folded, gathered and collated, stitched, and trimmed. See **Figure 17-28**.

Some general or basic types of binding include the following:

- **Adhesive binding.** Also called padding, this is a classification for methods that use glue or

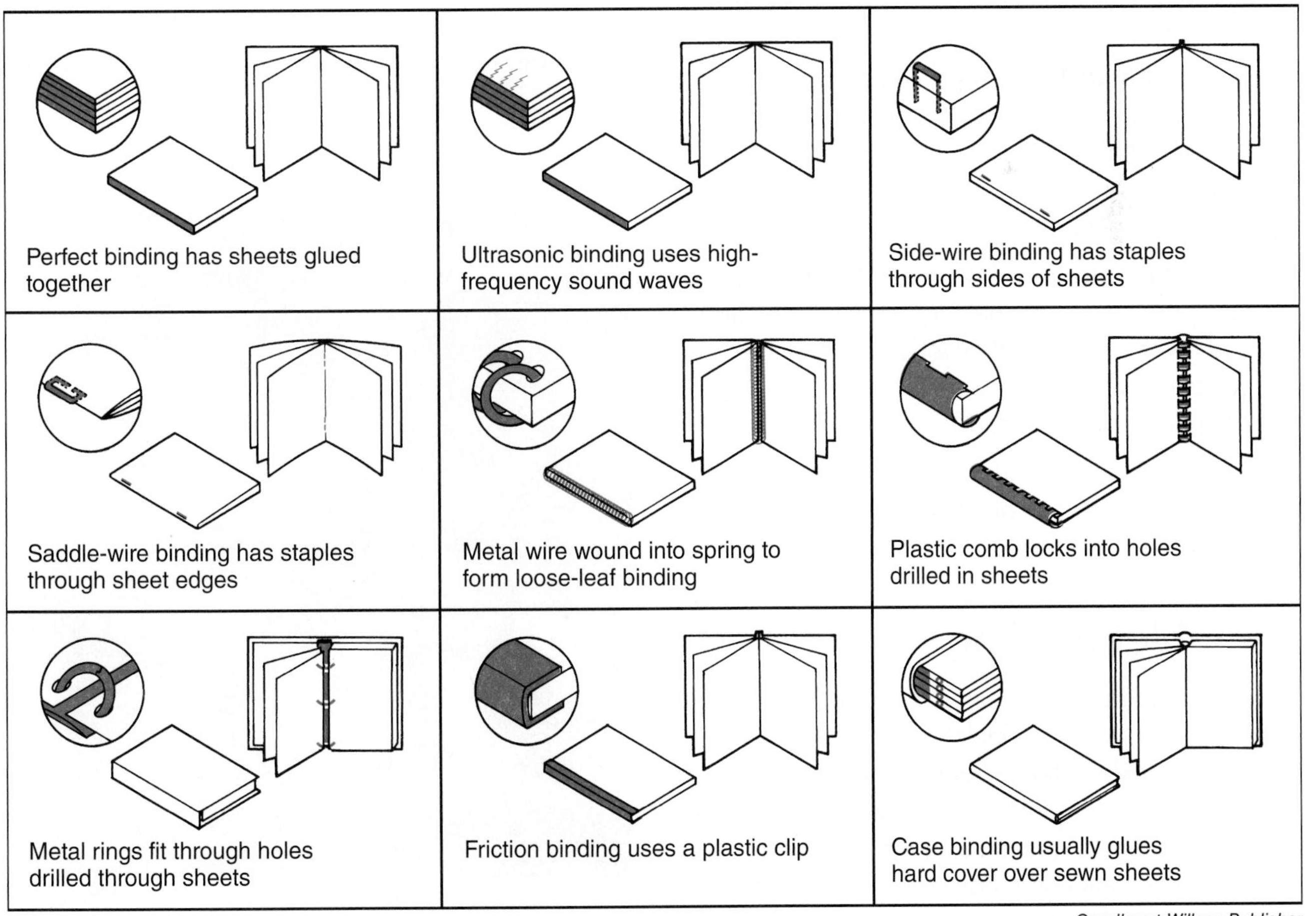

Figure 17-28. Various methods used to bind materials together after printing.

adhesive to hold the sheets together but allow them to be removed, as in the case of notepads.

- **Mechanical binding.** A broad category that includes many different devices used to hold sheets together. Spiral wire, metal posts, metal or plastic rings, plastic combs, and channels that rely on friction to hold are all mechanical methods. Since separate sheets are being fastened together, this is sometimes called loose-leaf binding.
- **Side stitching.** A form of stapling in which metal wire is forced through sides of sheets and formed to hold sheets together. Side sewing is similar, but it uses threads rather than staples to bind sheets together.
- **Saddle stitching.** A method in which metal wire is forced through the folded edge of a signature and formed into staples to hold the pages together. Saddle sewing is like saddle stitching, but it is done with thread instead of wire.
- **Perfect binding.** Also called softcover binding, this method uses an adhesive to hold sheets or signatures together and to fasten the flexible cloth or paper cover onto the body.
- **Edition binding.** The most complex and permanent form of binding, in which a rigid cover is attached to a book body that is held together by sewing. It is also called case binding or hard binding.
- **Self-cover binding.** A term used to describe using the same material for both the cover and body of the book. Self-cover books may be perfect bound, but they are most often saddle-stitched or side-stitched.

Some of the most widely used fastening techniques include pamphlet binding, edition binding, perfect binding, and mechanical binding.

Pamphlet Binding

Most of today's magazines, catalogs, and booklets fall into the pamphlet binding category. One of the simplest techniques is saddle-wire stitching. Sheets are folded, gathered, and stitched through the center, or saddle, of the folded sheets.

Many booklets and magazines are fastened by this method. The folded sheets are placed one over the other and then placed onto the saddle of the stitcher, **Figure 17-29**. The maximum number of pages is regulated by the limit of the stitcher and/or the pamphlet thickness allowing the booklet or magazine to lie flat.

When larger publications are bound, the machine is capable of gathering the signatures and cover. They are then stitched and trimmed, **Figure 17-30**.

Gathering and Collating

Gathering is a general term associated with the assembling of signatures for a book or other multipage product. As discussed previously, a signature is a large sheet that has been folded to form a group of pages, **Figure 17-31**.

The term ***collating*** usually means the assembling of single sheets. However, the term can also mean the checking of signature placement after gathering.

The basic process of gathering is illustrated in **Figure 17-32**. It involves using a gathering machine to stack the signatures on top of each other in the correct order. Note that one type uses a rotating gripper bar and the other uses a gripper arm. Both place the signatures on a moving conveyor. Other variations are also available. **Figure 17-33** shows a gathering machine placing book signatures in the proper sequence.

©George Deal

Figure 17-29. Stitching machine uses rolls of wire to produce staples that are inserted through the saddle of a signature.

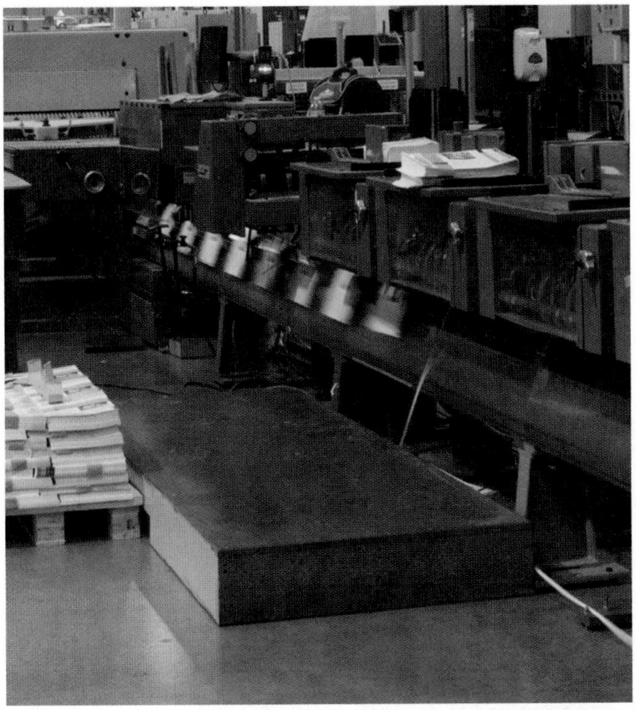

©George Deal

Figure 17-30. This saddle-wire binding machine is used for high-volume production of magazines and booklets.

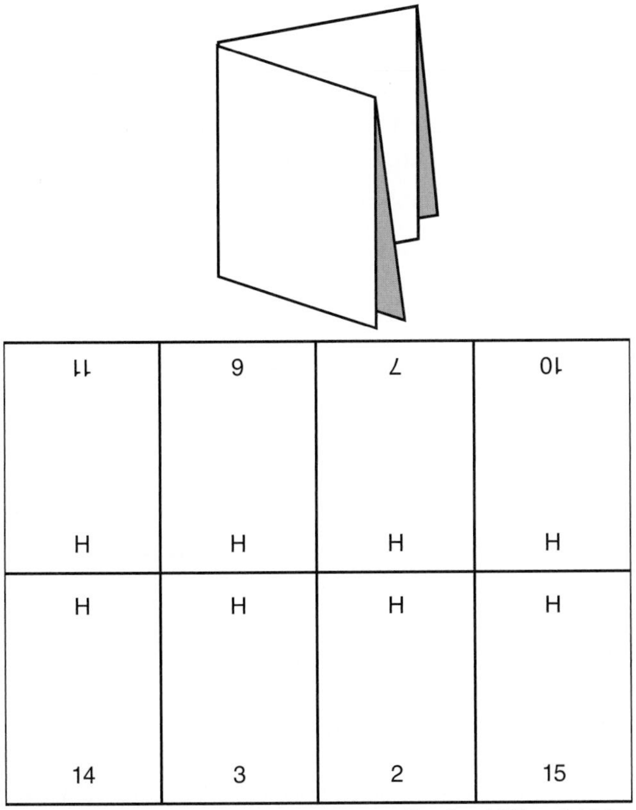

Goodheart-Willcox Publisher

Figure 17-31. A signature is a larger sheet that is folded to produce a series of pages.

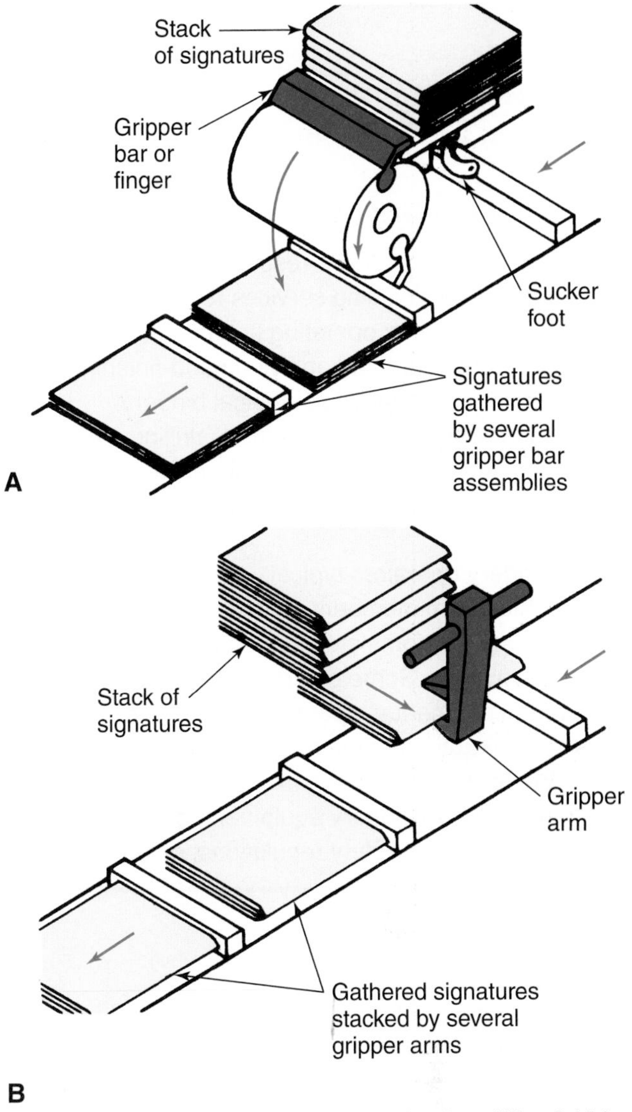

Goodheart-Willcox Publisher

Figure 17-32. Two methods commonly used to gather signatures. A—Rotary gathering. B—Gripper arm gathering.

©George Deal

Figure 17-33. A collator machine like this one places all signatures of a product in proper order for binding.

Career Link

Bindery Operator

A bindery operator is responsible for completing all binding and finishing services required for each job, which includes operating and maintaining all bindery equipment and applying hand-finishing techniques when required. Typical bindery operations include cutting, folding, drilling, stapling, packing, hot stamping, laminating, collating, inserting, padding, wrapping, gathering, and numbering.

Bindery operators typically work very closely with other team members, as many bindery operations are completed in an assembly line of repetitive tasks. Some plants still have equipment that requires manual operation, while many facilities use highly-automated and computerized machines.

Bindery operators are expected to operate and maintain all bindery equipment, enforce all applicable OSHA safety regulations, dispose of all waste material in compliance with EPA regulations, and pay close attention to specifications and details while performing all bindery tasks to ensure quality on every job. Manual dexterity and mechanical abilities are also important qualities. A high school diploma or an associate's degree is needed for entry-level bindery positions, and on-the-job training is often provided by employers. Certification programs are available and may be a requirement for advancement opportunities.

"The more we know, the more we are able to cope in an ever-changing, highly technological society. Various communication systems will be the major link for this rapid dissemination of information."

Jack Simich
Former GATF Educational Director

A suction feed collator with in-line folding, stitching, and trimming for creating finished booklets is shown in **Figure 17-34**. It is shown collating six stacks of pages plus a cover.

Collating marks can be used on signatures to check the accuracy of the signature-gathering sequence. As illustrated in **Figure 17-35**, the collating marks should form a diagonal line when

Duplo USA

Figure 17-34. This is a suction feed collator with in-line fold, stitch, and trim units. It can be equipped with up to 18 bins and handle many different sheet sizes and paper weights.

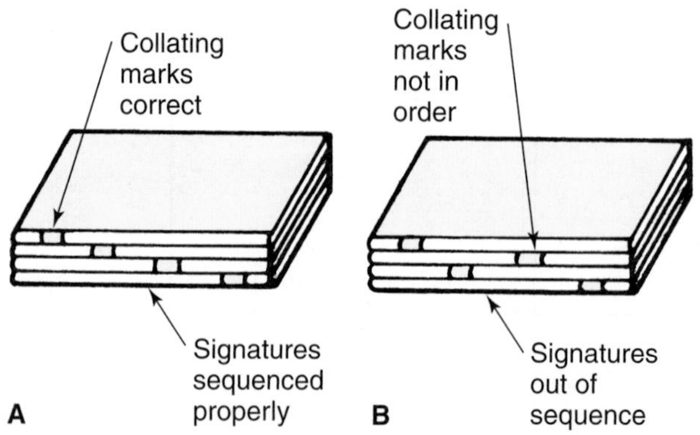

Goodheart-Willcox Publisher

Figure 17-35. Collating marks placed on folded edges of signatures allow a visual check for proper gathering sequence. A—Marks align diagonally, showing correct signature order. As a further check, collating marks often are printed with letters or numbers in proper sequence. B—Marks not aligned diagonally. Signature order is incorrect.

signatures are in the proper order. If the marks do not align, one signature or more is out of sequence.

Stitching

Stitching is a common binding method that holds the sheets together with wire staples. It is typically used on products with fewer than 120 pages. Books with large numbers of pages are bound with other methods, such as sewing or mechanical devices.

Saddle stitching, **Figure 17-36**, is commonly used for booklets or magazines because they tend to lie more flat than side-stitched products when opened. When the thickness of a saddle-stitched product increases, the amount of ***creep***, or shingling, becomes more evident. As shown in **Figure 17-37**, creep is a pushing out, or extension, of pages on the outer edge of the book, caused by the greater thickness at the spine. Although the finished pages will be trimmed evenly, an allowance for creep must be made in the prepress phase, when the pages are being laid out. If allowance is not made, page margins of the finished book will not be even. In extreme cases, type or illustrations along the outer edges could be cut off.

The side-wire stitching technique is another method of fastening several signatures or many sheets, **Figure 17-38**. The cover could be of the same type of stock or a specially printed substrate. One of the drawbacks of this type of binding is that the booklet or magazine does not lie flat when opened.

Side-stitch machines might be of the single-head type, like the one shown in **Figure 17-38**, or a multiple-head configuration that places several staples simultaneously. Multiple-head stitching increases binding speed or volume.

Warning

Never place a finger or hand under a stitcher head. A staple could be driven through your finger or hand if the machine is activated.

Edition Binding

Edition binding, also called case binding, is considered the most durable and permanent method of binding books that will be used extensively over a period of time, such as textbooks and reference volumes. The parts of an edition-bound book are identified in **Figure 17-39**.

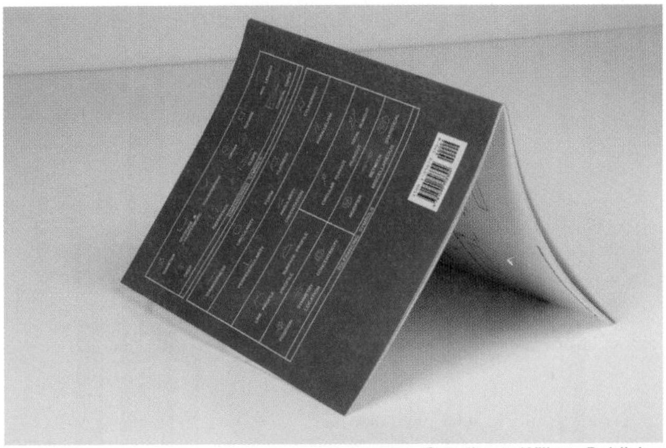

Goodheart-Willcox Publisher

Figure 17-36. Saddle stitching involves stapling through the folded area, or saddle, of the product. It allows a booklet to lie relatively flat when opened.

Goodheart-Willcox Publisher

Figure 17-37. Creep, or shingling, results when saddle-stitched products become thicker. The extended page edges will be trimmed off evenly.

Goodheart-Willcox Publisher

Figure 17-38. Side-wire stitching is used for some booklets and other products. A booklet bound by this method will not lie as flat when opened as will a saddle-stitched product.

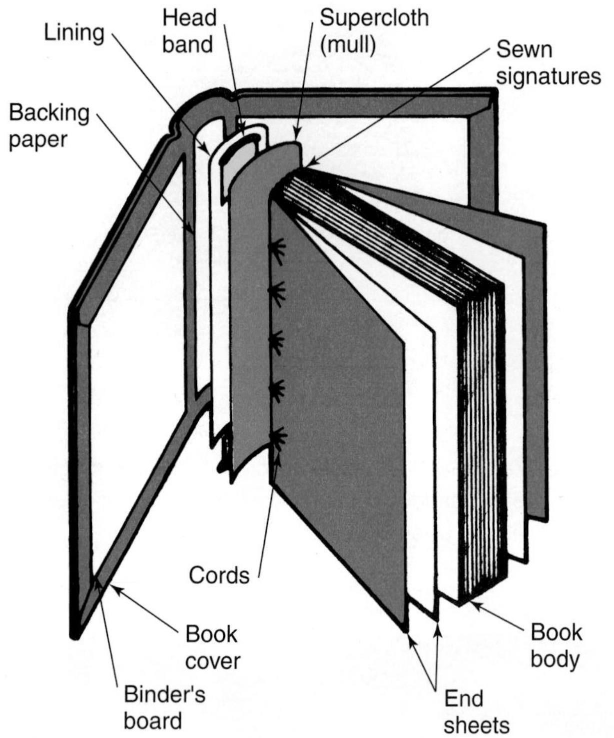

Goodheart-Willcox Publisher

Figure 17-39. The basic parts of a case-bound book.

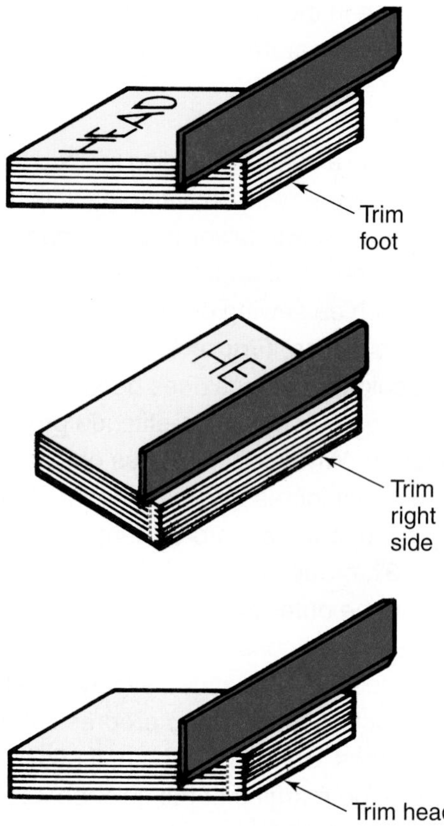

Goodheart-Willcox Publisher

Figure 17-40. A three-knife paper trimmer cuts excess material off the foot, right side, and head of the book body after signatures are sewn together. Although the three trimming steps are shown separately here, they are completed in a single operation.

The binding process involves gathering and sewing the signatures together, then compressing the signatures, and trimming the edges with a three-knife trimmer, **Figure 17-40**. The book body is then glued, the spine rounded, and lining applied. The book cover is manufactured separately by wrapping and gluing a printed cover on binder's board. It is then attached to the body with an adhesive in a process called *casing in*. The bound book is then clamped in a fixture until the adhesive dries. The steps in the binding process are shown in order in **Figure 17-41**.

Although the vast majority of case-bound books produced today are manufactured with machine binding methods, hand-binding is still done for special volumes and other uses. Knowing how to do hand-binding is a useful skill and an aid to understanding the binding process.

Perfect Binding

The ***perfect binding*** process, used for producing books that are usually described as softcover or paperback, is a fast and relatively low-cost method. Since it eliminates the need for sewing and constructing a hard cover, it is more economical than edition binding. Perfect binding is not as long-lasting or rugged as edition binding. For this reason, it is often selected for products that will have a limited life span, such as some children's books. Its low cost has made it popular for mass-market novels and other books where price is a competitive factor. See **Figure 17-42**.

In this process, either signatures or single sheets can be gathered or collated to form the book body. The binding equipment then grinds or saws the binding edge of the book body to roughen the surface, and a flexible glue is applied. The cover is placed on the body and clamped until the glue sets. The book is then trimmed, usually with a three-knife trimmer.

Perfect-bound books intended for greater permanence, such as some textbooks and reference volumes, are often bound with a system called burst binding. This method involves notching the spine of the book body and applying a high-strength adhesive under pressure. Another method that provides greater

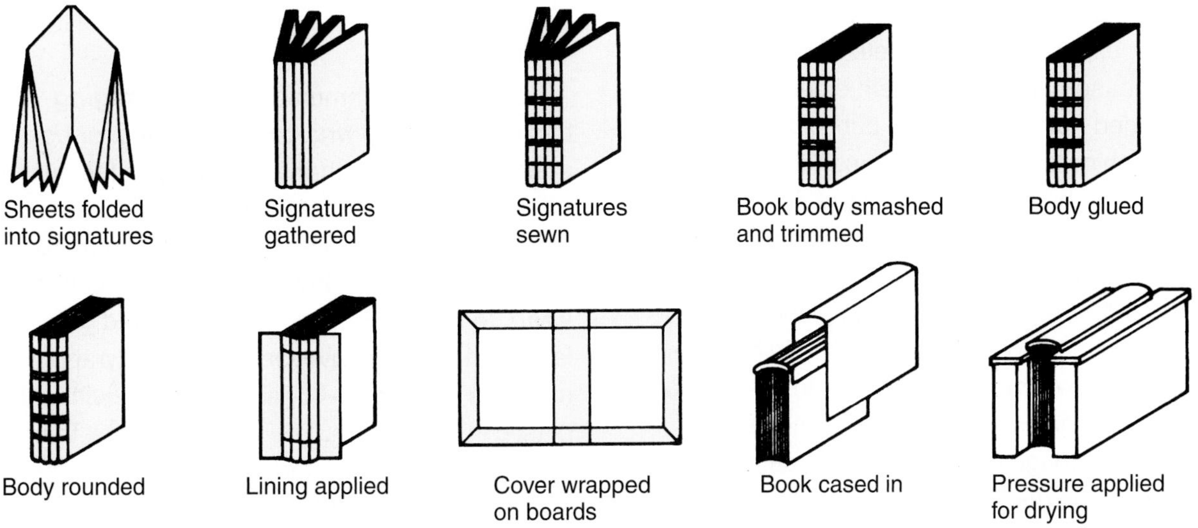

Goodheart-Willcox Publisher

Figure 17-41. These are the major steps that occur during the edition binding of a book.

permanence is sewing the signatures together (like an edition-bound book) before the gluing and covering operations are performed. These methods virtually eliminate pages coming loose and falling out.

Mechanical Binding

The broad category called ***mechanical binding*** consists of a number of methods that employ a mechanical device (metal spring, plastic fastener, etc.) to hold sheets together in loose-leaf form. Two of the methods usually used are plastic comb binding and spiral binding.

Plastic comb binding is commonly used for booklets that might have to be altered by adding or removing pages. Books bound with this method permit the pages to lie perfectly flat when open.

The binding method involves using a special machine, **Figure 17-43**, to punch rectangular holes along one edge of the printed material. After the

Goodheart-Willcox Publisher

Figure 23-42. Perfect binding is a very popular method for use with products as diverse in size as magazines, books, and telephone directories.

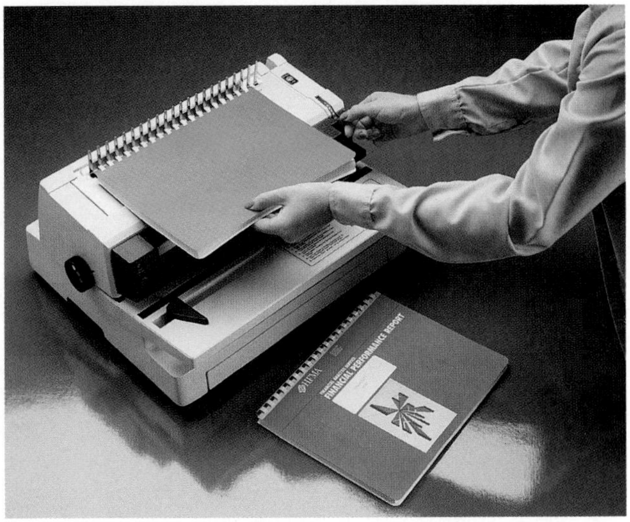

General Binding Corp.

Figure 17-43. A special machine is used to punch the product and insert a plastic binding comb. The finished plastic-bound book can be taken apart to easily add or remove pages.

sheets are punched, they are positioned over the spread or expanded plastic teeth of the fastener. When released, the plastic teeth extend through the punched holes to bind the publication. The same machine can be used to open the comb teeth so pages can be removed or added. Combs are available in various diameters to suit the number of pages being fastened.

Spiral binding is similar to the plastic comb method but does not allow the binding to be opened for the addition or removal of pages. In this method, smaller round holes are punched, then the wire is spiral-fed through the booklet using automatic equipment. The method is used for many types of products from small pocket notebooks to calendars, to books an inch or more in thickness, **Figure 17-44**. Several variations of the spiral method are used, but all follow the same principle. The diameter of each type of binding wire varies with the need.

Like most mechanical bindings, the spiral wire method allows a book to be opened flat and remain that way. The spiral allows for the tearing out of a page but not the insertion of sheets.

Packaging

In graphic communications, ***packaging*** basically involves wrapping, strapping, or boxing the printed pieces together for delivery to the customer. While printed products were once typically wrapped in paper and then packed in boxes, the more common method today is the use of plastic ***shrink-wrap***. In this method, a stack of printed pieces is placed on the conveyor of a shrink-wrapping machine, **Figure 17-45**, and enclosed with a thin plastic in sheet form. The wrapped stack then passes through a heated tunnel where the plastic shrinks to form a tight, sealed package.

The shrink-wrapped products may then be packed in boxes of corrugated board to protect them during shipment. Other printed products, such as books, may be packed in boxes without being wrapped beforehand. Several boxes can be stacked on a pallet and then strapped in place for shipping.

An alternative to shrink-wrapping is to use a ***banding machine***, also called a loop press, to wrap

Goodheart-Willcox Publisher

Figure 17-44. Spiral fastening uses metal or plastic wire wound through holes to bind together loose sheets.

©George Deal

Figure 17-45. A shrink-wrapping machine wraps bundles of product in plastic, then passes the bundles through a heated tunnel to shrink the plastic tightly around the product.

and bond a plastic or metal band around a bundle of booklets, books, boxes, or other products. This holds the products together for shipping.

Larger forms of the banding machine may be used to strap stacks of boxes onto pallets to keep them securely in place during shipping. Plastic wrapping material, similar to shrink-wrap, is often used to bind a stack of boxes on a pallet into a single unit.

A ***taping machine*** is used in shipping departments to automatically apply tape to seal the tops of boxes. As the boxes are fed through the machine, a series of rollers and brushes applies the tape to the top of each box. A cutter also slices off the tape to the correct length. Two belts move the boxes through the taping machine. This helps automate the shipping department of a facility.

Summary

- Finishing is a general term that applies to cutting, folding, slitting, perforating, creasing, scoring, die cutting, embossing, stamping, numbering, drilling, punching, varnishing, laminating, indexing, edge staining, and converting.
- Types of binding include perfect binding, saddle stitching, case binding, and mechanical binding.
- Some general or basic types of binding include adhesive binding, mechanical binding, side stitching, saddle stitching, perfect binding, edition binding, self-cover binding.
- Packaging involves wrapping, strapping, or boxing the printed pieces together for delivery to the customer.

Review Questions

Answer the following questions using the information in this chapter.

1. What does the term *finishing* mean to a printer?
2. Which term refers to eliminating uneven or unwanted edges of paper?
   A. Cutting.
   B. Scoring.
   C. Sheathing.
   D. Trimming.
3. What is the purpose of a shear stick?
4. A(n) _____ lifts heavy stacks of paper off the cutter table for easy movement.
5. How does a buckle folder work?
6. Explain why a folding machine operator should tie back long hair and secure loose clothing.
7. _____ is similar to cutting, but it can be done by a set of wheels as the sheet passes through the folder.
8. Name seven types of binding.
9. _____ is a general term associated with the assembling of signatures.
10. Why are collating marks used?

Suggested Activities

1. Complete an edition-binding project. Visit a writing class in your school and suggest to the teacher that each student write a poem and that your class would print the poems and bind them into a book.
2. Diagram the workflow of a perfect-bound book.
3. Visit a printing plant and identify the binding and finishing tasks that were used to finish three different jobs.

Chapter

18 The Business of Graphic Communications

Learning Objectives

After studying this chapter, you will be able to:

- Summarize practices for planning and growing a successful business.
- Explain the basic fundamentals of business, such as costs, estimates, and productivity.
- Summarize the use and application of various industry standards and specifications.
- Explain how copyright laws apply to printing companies.

Goodheart-Willcox Publisher

Important Terms

business plan
copyright
corporation
counterfeit
fair use
fixed cost
infringement
intellectual property
labor cost
materials cost
partnership
printing estimate
productivity
profit
single proprietorship
trade customs

While studying this chapter, look for the activity icon to:

- **Practice** vocabulary terms with e-flash cards, matching activities, and vocabulary game.
- **Reinforce** what you learn by submitting end-of-chapter questions.

www.g-wlearning.com/visualtechnology/

G-WLEARNING.COM

Graphic communications is a big business that is composed of a few large companies and many small and mid-sized businesses. It is a large industry in terms of the dollar value of products (approximately $90 billion) and the number of establishments (around 35,000). Many commercial printing businesses employ 20 or fewer people. Digital printing is playing a major role in changing the status of the commercial graphic communications market.

Planning for Growth and Success

The growth and success of any operation is dependent on every employee, every process, every supplier, and every piece of equipment. Careful business planning is tremendously important. If a planner or manager makes mistakes, it can cost the firm time, money, and personnel. Mistakes are costly.

The success of a graphics firm is measured by the cost and quality of finished products. The employees, raw materials, and equipment dictate the cost and quality of a printed product. Every phase of production must be well thought out and reviewed periodically. As the old saying goes, "A chain is only as strong as its weakest link." If one phase of production is a weak link in the chain, it can affect the final product and the future of the company.

To help achieve growth and success, effective managers rely on proven business and personnel practices, which include:

- Using efficient, cost-effective equipment to produce better products at a lower cost.
- Developing a "team effort" attitude, where all employees work and communicate as a cohesive unit to outperform competing companies.
- Using worker feedback to analyze and improve production steps. The person performing a task usually has the best idea of how it can be done better.
- Determining pay increases, in part, on company profits. This can generate incentive to improve job performance.
- Making it known that promotions and salary increases are based on job performance. Use worker qualities such as dependability, work quality, efficiency, cooperation, initiative, and innovation to make decisions on promotion.
- Providing workers with the capability of advancement within the company as a performance incentive and means of building employee morale.
- Carefully analyzing and selecting outside sources of supplies and services, weighing cost versus quality factors.
- Applying appropriate quality control and production control methods to all business operations within the company.
- Developing and implementing a continuous training program to help employees keep up to date with advances in technology.

Developing a Business Plan

A ***business plan*** is a document that states the goals of a business and presents a framework for achieving those goals. In any business, planning is essential to success. Once a business plan has been developed, it must be used. The plan is a tool to measure success.

Here are some of the basic reasons to have a business plan:

- It helps the executive officer focus on the factors relating to success and growth.
- It is a management tool.
- It defines many aspects of the business.
- It is a communication tool.
- It helps keep the financial picture in focus.

See **Figure 18-1** for basic factors in business plan development.

Establishing the Organization

Three of the most common organization types for businesses are single proprietorship, partnership, and corporation. Each type has unique characteristics and advantages.

A ***single proprietorship***, also known as a *sole proprietorship*, is a business owned by one person. The business and the owner are a single entity, and the owner has full control of the business operations. The owner's income, minus expenses, is the business' profits. The owner of a single proprietorship also carries 100% of the liability of running a business. For example, if the business incurs bad debt or is sued, the owner is personally liable even if the business closes.

A ***partnership*** is a business owned by two or more people. The owners and the business are considered a single entity and pay income tax on the profits of the business. In this type of business, the ownership responsibilities and legal liability are split between or among all the partners. Unlike a single proprietorship, a partnership shares both the profits and liabilities of a business.

A business that is a ***corporation*** is a separate legal entity from the people who own or manage it. This type of business pays taxes on its own tax return and is liable for its own debt and other legal responsibilities. Typically, a corporation has shareholders who invest in the company and share in the profits of the company.

With a large number of small companies in the printing industry, most businesses are single proprietorships or partnerships. The larger companies (and some smaller ones) are typically corporations. Single owners and most partners are actively involved in operating their businesses, while many of the stockholders in a corporation are not involved in the day-to-day operations of the business.

Factors in Business Plan Development	
Vision statement	Production Staffing Equipment Facilities Projected growth Funding
Product	Range of products Competitive pricing
Market and strategy	Target audience Niche Need for the product Growth potential Advertising Sales Promotion package
Customers	List clients Gain and loss factors
Competitive advantage	Reason for success Why product is better Customer service Distribution Prompt and courteous service
Management team	Qualification of personnel Duties and responsibilities Available resources Accounting system Salaries Benefits
Personnel	Current workforce Future workforce Job descriptions Benefits Salaries

Goodheart-Willcox Publisher

Figure 18-1. Basic factors in developing a business plan.

Business Basics

The success of any type of business involves certain operations tasks that must be performed in order to stay in business.

- **Sales.** Obtaining orders for the company's products or services.
- **Business.** Handling all the financial operations of the company.
- **Production.** All the activities necessary to produce goods or services.
- **Administration.** Coordinating and overseeing all aspects of the company.

In a large business, there may be dozens of people fulfilling each of these responsibilities. In a small company or single proprietorship, however, a few people may fill all the roles. In a small company, for example, the owner may handle both the sales and administrative responsibilities; the office manager may send out invoices, pays bills from suppliers, and keeps business records; and the production manager may operate press equipment and oversee the prepress worker and press helper.

As company size increases, the responsibility for carrying out business operations is divided among a greater number of people. For example, a company that is a two-person partnership may designate one partner as the company president (administrator) and the other as controller (business manager). A variation on this organization might be the addition of a production manager, to whom the plant manager reports. The production manager is responsible to the president, as are the controller and sales manager. When a company becomes large enough to be incorporated, a board of directors is elected by the company's stockholders to oversee the business. Day-to-day operation is conducted by the president or chief executive officer (CEO). Larger organizations are more complex, with a number of different levels of supervision and responsibility.

Business Costs

To remain in business, a company must make a ***profit***. This means that it must receive more income from the sale of products or services than it spends for raw materials, employee salaries, building rent or property mortgage and taxes, utility bills, and other costs of doing business. The difference between income and expenses is the profit of a business.

The key to success is identifying and controlling business costs, and setting prices that cover the costs and provide a desired percentage of profit. A company that does not accurately determine its costs or sets prices too low to make a profit will soon be out of business.

Business costs can be grouped into three categories: materials costs, labor costs, and fixed costs. Accountants have various formulas to assign a portion of the fixed costs to each job that is printed. Materials costs and labor costs are specific to each job: a particular number of worker hours to produce it, along with measurable quantities of paper, ink, and other materials.

- ***Materials costs*** are the prices paid for items that are consumed as a job is printed, primarily paper and ink. Other items, such as packaging for the finished product, are also included in materials costs.
- ***Labor costs*** are the "people costs" involved in operating a business. These include the hourly wages or salaries for workers, the cost of health insurance, paid holidays and vacations, and other employee benefits. Services purchased from outside suppliers and service providers are also considered labor costs.
- ***Fixed costs*** (also known as overhead) are expenses that remain the same, regardless of the volume of business. For example, rent or mortgage payments for the shop premises are the same whether the printing presses are running round-the-clock, or the business is closed for the weekend. Fixed costs also include electricity, gas, telephone, the equipment needed to run the business, office supplies (ranging from copier toner to floor wax), and advertisements.

The computer has become a major tool in almost every aspect of graphic communications, from the creative and prepress areas through all phases of production and business operations. In addition to software for estimating, accounting, billing, and purchasing, programs have been developed to simplify personnel and equipment scheduling, **Figure 18-2**. Some systems use computer terminals at various workstations to gather information that can be used for more accurate cost calculations. Precise information on costs

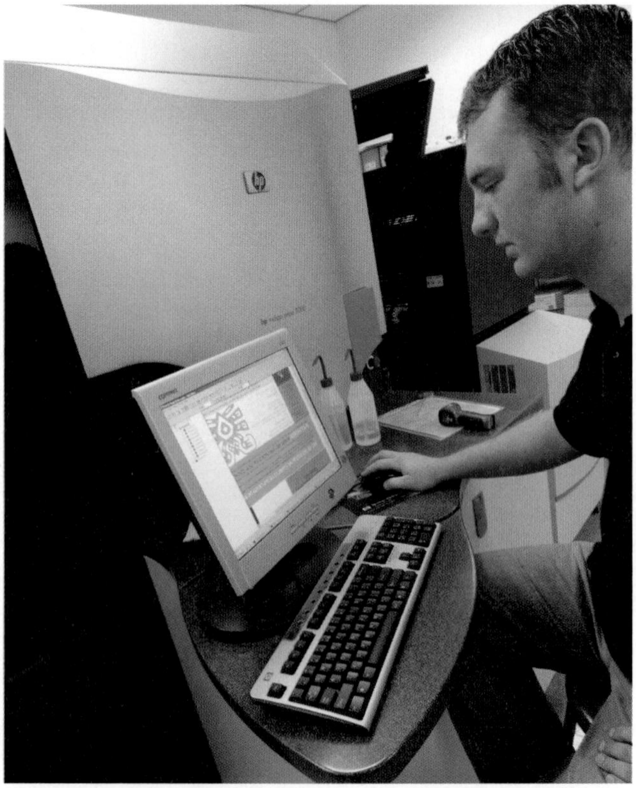

GIT, Arizona State University

Figure 18-2. The computer station on this digital printing system functions as a print server with available image enhancement packages.

allows more closely calculated estimates, which may provide a competitive advantage for a printer. Better cost control can also improve a company's profitability.

Job Estimates

After a job is completed, it is a fairly simple matter to accurately calculate the costs involved in producing it. However, customers want to know in advance what they are going to pay for their order. This is where a printing estimate comes in. A ***printing estimate*** is an offer to print a particular job for a specified price. If the customer accepts the estimate, it becomes a contract that is binding for both the printer and customer.

Developing an estimate can be very simple or extremely complicated, depending on the circumstances. At the simple end are jobs performed day-in and day-out by small shops and quick printers. These jobs are usually handled with a fixed-price schedule rather than an actual estimate and are typically priced in units, such as 100 or 500 sheets. A base price for printing is established and additional charges are applied for variables, such as a different paper stock or color ink. Finishing steps, such as folding or tabbing, are also listed on a price schedule.

More complicated jobs require custom-developed estimates that meet specifications provided by the customer. A custom estimate requires careful calculation of every aspect of the project, from paper cost and availability to operating cost of each piece of equipment, percent of spoilage, and final packaging and delivery.

Preparing an accurate estimate requires a precise knowledge of costs. Many successful firms have developed detailed breakdowns of their operations, which are stored on a database of information for use in developing estimates. Using these breakdowns, a company can determine exactly how much per hour it costs to operate a specific piece of equipment, **Figure 18-3**, or how many worker hours must be allotted to carry out a particular operation. An estimate is generated using hourly cost rates and the specific materials cost for the job. The hourly cost rates developed using this method include a portion of the company's overhead (fixed cost), as well as labor costs. Cost of materials is determined separately because it varies from one job to another.

Many printing firms, especially smaller companies or those performing various types of printing operations, relied on pricing guides that provided average costs for virtually every type of prepress, printing, and finishing operation. Although pricing guides are still in use, they have been replaced in many plants by computers that use specialized estimating software, **Figure 18-4**. There are a number of different estimating programs on the market, but most operate in a similar manner. An estimator enters the specifics of a job, such as size, quantity, paper to be used, and equipment required. The software then calculates an estimate based on cost data and presents it for review.

Some estimating software is designed for use on standalone computers, while other programs are intended for larger operations where a number of different computers and sites are linked, or networked. Some estimating programs allow outside sales personnel with laptop computers

GIT, Arizona State University

Figure 18-3. Accurate printing estimates depend on precise costing information. The hourly cost of operating equipment is a combination of labor costs and overhead.

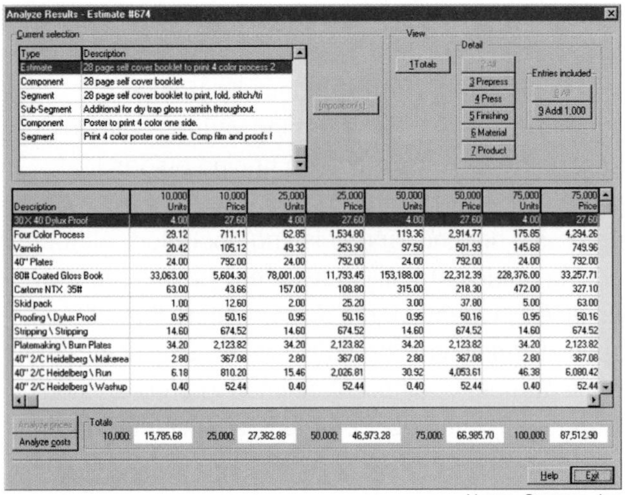

Hagen Systems, Inc.

Figure 18-4. Estimating software can simplify the process of preparing a printing estimate. This summary screen provides the estimator with pricing for various quantities of a job. With software such as this, information can be viewed many different ways before preparing and printing an estimate.

or tablets to prepare an estimate right at the customer's office or plant. A completed estimate is either printed out or e-mailed to the customer, allowing confirmation of prices, scheduling, and material availability.

Organizing Work

Productivity is the amount of quality work completed in a given time span. Efficiency (maximum output with minimum effort) and utilization (maximum use of people and equipment) are two factors that contribute to productivity. To achieve high productivity, good communication among plant workers is essential to prevent costly errors or shipping delays.

To track printing jobs as they move through the plant and provide job-specific information to all departments, some type of job ticket is typically used, **Figure 18-5**. Job tickets are generally designed to meet the specific needs of a company or area within a company. Job tickets vary with nearly every business site.

The information that appears on a job ticket is necessary job specifications for various workers and departments. For example, the stock and ink required for the job is important information for both the purchasing department and press room, and the finishing information applies to the bindery department. In addition to job specs, a job ticket records the customer contact and billing information, proof or approval details, and job

©George Deal

Figure 18-5. A job ticket holds specifications and details about printing jobs that are useful to all departments involved in completing the order.

delivery information. With computer programs, it is possible to trace a job throughout the plant or offsite location any time a client requests job status information.

Matching the Job to the Equipment

To ensure efficient and profitable printing operations, each job should be matched with the most appropriate equipment available. Using a piece of equipment that is not particularly suited for a job can cause delays, increase waste, and cut profit margins. One common choice printers face today is whether to print a job using conventional means or electronic (digital) methods. There is frequently no clear indication of when it is better to use conventional printing or digital printing. Speed, quality, and economics are some determining factors. Run length, page count, and bindery processes are also considerations in determining the optimum equipment.

For each printing process, a point of optimum return can be determined. With experience, users learn to optimize job requirements and printing method.

Digital printing allows variability and customization in the manufacturing process, and can produce fully completed projects if product specifications conform to the options available. A benefit of digital printing is no makeready costs are incurred. However, offset printing makeready costs are decreasing due to technological advancements.High-volume electronic printers have an interrupt feature that requires minimum time and effort to produce another job, even if a different paper is involved.

Plates are an element of traditional printing that introduces variable costs for material, labor, and time. Because digital printers do not require a platemaking step to produce copies, they have a decisive cost advantage. Once running, though, printing ink and chemistry will cost much less than the fuser and toner used in the digital press.

Digital printers have no makeready cost: the first copy produced is the same as the second and the last copies. Thus, the break-even point is when the cost of total copies made on the digital press equals the makeready cost on the printing press plus the lower cost-per-copy volume.

Multiple-page documents require added consideration to be given to the type of binding necessary and the corresponding equipment. Usually, bindery operations for conventionally printed sheets are done off-line. Some electronic printers can saddle stitch work on-line; others require an off-line operation. The key considerations are run length and page count.

Trade Customs

It would be time-consuming and inefficient to write a contract that covers all aspects of each new print job. In the printing industry, trade customs are used rather than formal, individual contracts. ***Trade customs*** are understood rules or implied laws used in the printing industry that have been validated by courts as binding agreements. At times, specific contracts are issued when additional or special terms are desired, however.

The National Association of Printers and Leadership (NAPL) issued guidelines for the use of trade customs. NAPL guidelines state that the printer should:

- Print trade customs on the back of estimates and other order acknowledgments.
- State that all work is subject to trade customs on the order acknowledgment.
- Make sure that customized terms and conditions are enforced in the same manner as trade customs.
- Ensure that salespersons are knowledgeable about trade customs and how they protect the printer.

For years, the industry followed a document called *Trade Customs of the Printing Industries of North America*, **Figure 18-6**. It was considered the guide to transactions, such as Terms and Conditions of Sale. The technology has changed dramatically, making the document obsolete in many areas and not informative in others. The new publication, *Best Business Practices for the Print Industry*, is intended to fill that void.

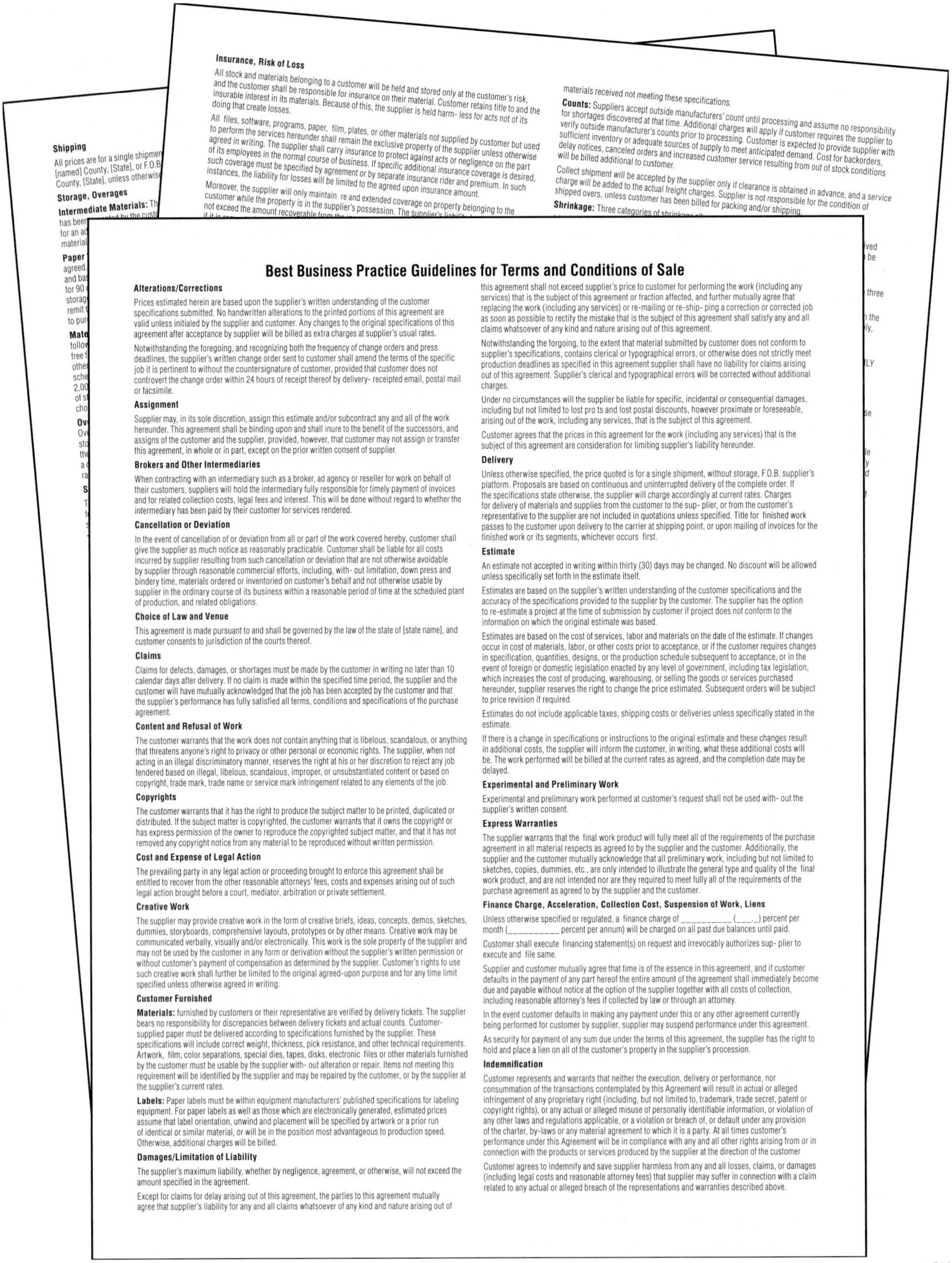

Best Business Practice Guidelines for Terms and Conditions of Sale

Alterations/Corrections

Prices estimated herein are based upon the supplier's written understanding of the customer specifications submitted. No handwritten alterations to the printed portions of this agreement are valid unless initialed by the supplier and customer. Any changes to the original specifications of this agreement after acceptance by supplier will be billed as extra charges at supplier's usual rates.

Notwithstanding the foregoing, and recognizing both the frequency of change orders and press deadlines, the supplier's written change order sent to customer shall amend the terms of the specific job it is pertinent to without the countersignature of customer, provided that customer does not controvert the change order within 24 hours of receipt thereof by delivery- receipted email, postal mail or facsimile.

Assignment

Supplier may, in its sole discretion, assign this estimate and/or subcontract any and all of the work hereunder. This agreement shall be binding upon and shall inure to the benefit of the successors, and assigns of the customer and the supplier, provided, however, that customer may not assign or transfer this agreement, in whole or in part, except on the prior written consent of supplier.

Brokers and Other Intermediaries

When contracting with an intermediary such as a broker, ad agency or reseller for work on behalf of their customers, suppliers will hold the intermediary fully responsible for timely payment of invoices and for related collection costs, legal fees and interest. This will be done without regard to whether the intermediary has been paid by their customer for services rendered.

Cancellation or Deviation

In the event of cancellation of or deviation from all or part of the work covered hereby, customer shall give the supplier as much notice as reasonably practicable. Customer shall be liable for all costs incurred by supplier resulting from such cancellation or deviation that are not otherwise avoidable by supplier through reasonable commercial efforts, including, with- out limitation, down press and bindery time, materials ordered or inventoried on customer's behalf and not otherwise usable by supplier in the ordinary course of its business within a reasonable period of time at the scheduled plant of production, and related obligations.

Choice of Law and Venue

This agreement is made pursuant to and shall be governed by the law of the state of [state name], and customer consents to jurisdiction of the courts thereof.

Claims

Claims for defects, damages, or shortages must be made by the customer in writing no later than 10 calendar days after delivery. If no claim is made within the specified time period, the supplier and the customer will have mutually acknowledged that the job has been accepted by the customer and that the supplier's performance has fully satisfied all terms, conditions and specifications of the purchase agreement.

Content and Refusal of Work

The customer warrants that the work does not contain anything that is libelous, scandalous, or anything that threatens anyone's right to privacy or other personal or economic rights. The supplier, when not acting in an illegal discriminatory manner, reserves the right at his or her discretion to reject any job tendered based on illegal, libelous, scandalous, improper, or unsubstantiated content or based on copyright, trade mark, trade name or service mark infringement related to any elements of the job.

Copyrights

The customer warrants that it has the right to produce the subject matter to be printed, duplicated or distributed. If the subject matter is copyrighted, the customer warrants that it owns the copyright or has express permission of the owner to reproduce the copyrighted subject matter, and that it has not removed any copyright notice from any material to be reproduced without written permission.

Cost and Expense of Legal Action

The prevailing party in any legal action or proceeding brought to enforce this agreement shall be entitled to recover from the other reasonable attorneys' fees, costs and expenses arising out of such legal action brought before a court, mediator, arbitration or private settlement.

Creative Work

The supplier may provide creative work in the form of creative briefs, ideas, concepts, demos, sketches, dummies, storyboards, comprehensive layouts, prototypes or by other means. Creative work may be communicated verbally, visually and/or electronically. This work is the sole property of the supplier and may not be used by the customer in any form or derivation without the supplier's written permission or without customer's payment of compensation as determined by the supplier. Customer's rights to use such creative work shall further be limited to the original agreed-upon purpose and for any time limit specified unless otherwise agreed in writing.

Customer Furnished

Materials: furnished by customers or their representative are verified by delivery tickets. The supplier bears no responsibility for discrepancies between delivery tickets and actual counts. Customer-supplied paper must be delivered according to specifications furnished by the supplier. These specifications will include correct weight, thickness, pick resistance, and other technical requirements. Artwork, film, color separations, special dies, tapes, disks, electronic files or other materials furnished by the customer must be usable by the supplier with- out alteration or repair. Items not meeting this requirement will be identified by the supplier and may be repaired by the customer, or by the supplier at the supplier's current rates.

Labels: Paper labels must be within equipment manufacturers' published specifications for labeling equipment. For paper labels as well as those which are electronically generated, estimated prices assume that label orientation, unwind and placement will be specified by artwork or a prior run of identical or similar material, or will be in the position most advantageous to production speed. Otherwise, additional charges will be billed.

Damages/Limitation of Liability

The supplier's maximum liability, whether by negligence, agreement, or otherwise, will not exceed the amount specified in the agreement.

Except for claims for delay arising out of this agreement, the parties to this agreement mutually agree that supplier's liability for any and all claims whatsoever of any kind and nature arising out of this agreement shall not exceed supplier's price to customer for performing the work (including any services) that is the subject of this agreement or fraction affected, and further mutually agree that replacing the work (including any services) or re-mailing or re-ship- ping a correction or corrected job as soon as possible to rectify the mistake that is the subject of this agreement shall satisfy any and all claims whatsoever of any kind and nature arising out of this agreement.

Notwithstanding the forgoing, to the extent that material submitted by customer does not conform to supplier's specifications, contains clerical or typographical errors, or otherwise does not strictly meet production deadlines as specified in this agreement supplier shall have no liability for claims arising out of this agreement. Supplier's clerical and typographical errors will be corrected without additional charges.

Under no circumstances will the supplier be liable for specific, incidental or consequential damages, including but not limited to lost pro ts and lost postal discounts, however proximate or foreseeable, arising out of the work, including any services, that is the subject of this agreement.

Customer agrees that the prices in this agreement for the work (including any services) that is the subject of this agreement are consideration for limiting supplier's liability hereunder.

Delivery

Unless otherwise specified, the price quoted is for a single shipment, without storage, F.O.B. supplier's platform. Proposals are based on continuous and uninterrupted delivery of the complete order. If the specifications state otherwise, the supplier will charge accordingly at current rates. Charges for delivery of materials and supplies from the customer to the sup- plier, or from the customer's representative to the supplier are not included in quotations unless specified. Title for finished work passes to the customer upon delivery to the carrier at shipping point, or upon mailing of invoices for the finished work or its segments, whichever occurs first.

Estimate

An estimate not accepted in writing within thirty (30) days may be changed. No discount will be allowed unless specifically set forth in the estimate itself.

Estimates are based on the supplier's written understanding of the customer specifications and the accuracy of the specifications provided to the supplier by the customer. The supplier has the option to re-estimate a project at the time of submission by customer if project does not conform to the information on which the original estimate was based.

Estimates are based on the cost of services, labor and materials on the date of the estimate. If changes occur in cost of materials, labor, or other costs prior to acceptance, or if the customer requires changes in specification, quantities, designs, or the production schedule subsequent to acceptance, or in the event of foreign or domestic legislation enacted by any level of government, including tax legislation, which increases the cost of producing, warehousing, or selling the goods or services purchased hereunder, supplier reserves the right to change the price estimated. Subsequent orders will be subject to price revision if required.

Estimates do not include applicable taxes, shipping costs or deliveries unless specifically stated in the estimate.

If there is a change in specifications or instructions to the original estimate and these changes result in additional costs, the supplier will inform the customer, in writing, what these additional costs will be. The work performed will be billed at the current rates as agreed, and the completion date may be delayed.

Experimental and Preliminary Work

Experimental and preliminary work performed at customer's request shall not be used with- out the supplier's written consent.

Express Warranties

The supplier warrants that the final work product will fully meet all of the requirements of the purchase agreement in all material respects as agreed to by the supplier and the customer. Additionally, the supplier and the customer mutually acknowledge that all preliminary work, including but not limited to sketches, copies, dummies, etc., are only intended to illustrate the general type and quality of the final work product, and are not intended nor are they required to meet fully all of the requirements of the purchase agreement as agreed to by the supplier and the customer.

Finance Charge, Acceleration, Collection Cost, Suspension of Work, Liens

Unless otherwise specified or regulated, a finance charge of __________ (___) percent per month (__________ percent per annum) will be charged on all past due balances until paid.

Customer shall execute financing statement(s) on request and irrevocably authorizes sup- plier to execute and file same.

Supplier and customer mutually agree that time is of the essence in this agreement, and if customer defaults in the payment of any part hereof the entire amount of the agreement shall immediately become due and payable without notice at the option of the supplier together with all costs of collection, including reasonable attorney's fees if collected by law or through an attorney.

In the event customer defaults in making any payment under this or any other agreement currently being performed for customer by supplier, supplier may suspend performance under this agreement.

As security for payment of any sum due under the terms of this agreement, the supplier has the right to hold and place a lien on all of the customer's property in the supplier's procession.

Indemnification

Customer represents and warrants that neither the execution, delivery or performance, nor consummation of the transactions contemplated by this Agreement will result in actual or alleged infringement of any proprietary right (including, but not limited to, trademark, trade secret, patent or copyright rights), or any actual or alleged misuse of personally identifiable information, or violation of any other laws and regulations applicable, or a violation or breach of, or default under any provision of the charter, by-laws or any material agreement to which it is a party. At all times customer's performance under this Agreement will be in compliance with any and all other rights arising from or in connection with the products or services produced by the supplier at the direction of the customer

Customer agrees to indemnify and save supplier harmless from any and all losses, claims, or damages (including legal costs and reasonable attorney fees) that supplier may suffer in connection with a claim related to any actual or alleged breach of the representations and warranties described above.

©PIA

Figure 18-6. The Terms and Conditions of Sale section of the Best Business Practices for the Printing Industry address common printing trade business customs.

Career Link

Customer Service Representative

A customer service representative (CSR) in the printing industry is the first, and often only, line of contact customers have with the company. To provide the best customer service possible and build professional relationships with clients, CSRs must have thorough knowledge of the printing plant operations, the computer system for order entry and tracking, and the specifications and needs of each job.

CSRs act as a liaison between the customer and other shop personnel by accurately communicating the customer's requirements, tracking the progress of jobs through the shop, and making the best use of the shop's resources and schedules. In handling orders and customer requests, a CSR may need to calculate figures, such as proportions, discounts, percentages, area, and volume; analyze and interpret technical procedures; and create written and oral reports. In smaller operations, the CSR may also have responsibilities related to sales activities.

The minimum educational requirement for a CSR position is an associate's degree from a two-year college or technical school. However, many CSR positions require a bachelor's degree from a college or university. Depending on the position available, a combination of education and experience may also be given consideration.

"Print has an unequaled history of strength and believability. It has the power to shape ideas and influence action. It is important to note in today's world of sound bites of fleeting impressions, print lasts."

Michael Makin
Printing Industries of America

Standards and Specifications

Under certain circumstances, such as producing work for government agencies, printers may be required to conform to certain standards set by organizations such as ISO or ANSI. In other situations, customers may require the printer to meet specifications set by the company or by specialized organizations. Such specifications as SWOP®, GRACoL®, and G7 are set by IDEAlliance.

International Organization for Standardization (ISO)

The International Organization for Standardization (ISO) is a nongovernmental, worldwide organization of national standards bodies. It covers all fields except electrical and electronic engineering standards, which are covered by another organization. ISO coordinates the exchange of information on international and national standards and publishes its technical work in the form of international standards. The ISO technical committee for graphic technology is TC 130.

American National Standards Institute (ANSI)

The American National Standards Institute (ANSI) is an impartial organization that validates work conducted by organizations accredited as standards development groups. Standards are considered to be voluntary, not mandated. Each standard is identified with the letters ANSI and a number.

Committee for Graphic Arts Technologies Standards (CGATS)

The Committee for Graphic Arts Technologies Standards (CGATS) is accredited by ANSI. The goal of CGATS is to have the entire scope of printing and publishing recognized as the national standards group, and intends to coordinate the efforts of other bodies.

NAICS Code

The North American Industry Classification System (NAICS) provides codes to classify businesses in order to collect and report statistical data, **Figure 18-7**. This information is used to compare data within each industry and among participating regions: United States, Canada, and Mexico. The first two digits in the NAICS code designate industry sectors, the third digit represents the subsector, the fourth represents the industry group level, the fifth digit identifies the international industry level, and the sixth digit designates the national detail.

NAICS Printing Industry Codes	
NAICS Code	**Printing Operation Type**
323	Printing and Related Activities
3231	Printing and Related Activities
32311	Printing
323110	Commercial Lithographic Printing
323111	Commercial Gravure Printing
323112	Commercial Flexographic Printing
323113	Commercial Screen Printing
323114	Quick Printing
323115	Digital Printing
323116	Manifold Business Forms
323117	Book Printing
323118	Blankbooks, Loose-Leaf Binder, and Device Manufacturing
323119	Other Commercial Printing
32312	Support Activities for Printing
323121	Trade Binding and Related Work
323122	Prepress Services

Goodheart-Willcox Publisher

Figure 18-7. NAICS codes and printing industry-related categories.

Think Green

Sustainability Plan

Many business plans in the graphic communications industry now include a sustainability plan. A sustainability plan contains the guidelines and procedures used in order to help organizations use, develop, and protect resources in a way that meets needs without harming the environment. As the demands on our natural resources increase, companies must implement sustainable practices to safeguard the environmental health, economic growth, and quality of life. A company's sustainability plan may rely on individual employee input, but the goals are simple. The sustainable practices a company implements must focus on reducing the use of materials, energy, and water; reducing the pollution put out by the company; reducing the amount of waste produced by the company; and using more nontoxic, recycled, and remanufactured materials. Communication and education within the company are necessary to meet these goals.

Copyright Laws

A ***copyright*** provides legal protection against unauthorized reproduction of literary works (books and other printed materials), musical compositions and recordings, artworks, photographs, film and video works, and dramatic works. These items are considered ***intellectual property***, or creative works of an individual or individuals that can be protected from unauthorized use. Copyright gives authors, artists, and other copyright owners the opportunity to exclusively profit from their creations for a stated period. It protects against financial loss resulting from the sale of their work by someone who has not paid a fee to them. In the United States, a copyright lasts for the life of the author or creator, plus 70 years after his or her death.

In graphic communications or printing, copyrights primarily address printed materials. A textbook, for example, usually has copyright information on the page immediately following the title page. Smaller printed pieces, such as booklets, might have a copyright notice on the first page or inside the front cover. Single page items, such as posters, usually have a copyright notice on the front side. There are a number of forms that the copyright notice can take, but it should include the word "copyright," the abbreviation "copr.," or the symbol ©. A copyright notice should also include the name of the copyright owner and the year first published, **Figure 18-8**.

When a customer brings in materials and asks the printer or copy service to reproduce it, there is a risk of violating copyright law. If the item bears a copyright notice, the customer must produce written evidence of permission from the copyright holder to reproduce the material. It might be wise to have customers sign a release form that protects the printer from liability for copyright or intellectual property ***infringement***. Being convicted of copyright infringement can cost thousands of dollars in fines and damages payable to the copyright holder, in addition to legal fees. Creating counterfeit property is also illegal.

Factors commonly used by the courts to determine and remedy copyright infringement include:

- How the material was used.
- The type of work copied.
- The amount of the material copied.
- The impact on the monetary and market value of the original copyrighted material.

There are exceptions to the law that allow some duplication of copyrighted materials without infringement. These exceptions are known as the ***fair use*** provisions of the law. This does *not* include ***counterfeit*** versions of copyrighted materials. Counterfeiting refers to reproducing an exact copy of a document or something of value without proper permission, with the intent to defraud.

© Jones Publishing 2019

Copyright Jones Publishing 2019

Copr. Jones Publishing

© JP

Copr. JP 2019

Goodheart-Willcox Publisher

Figure 18-8. There are a number of ways that a copyright notice can be presented.

The most common example of fair use is in education. Materials may be copied and used in the classroom for direct teacher-to-student educational purposes only. This means that an instructor may copy a reasonable portion of a copyrighted work (such as a magazine article or book chapter) for classroom use by students. Additionally, students may copy material and use it in a classroom presentation or discussion. If the copyrighted material is to be used outside of the classroom, however, the appropriate permissions *must* be secured.

Industry Challenges

One of the biggest challenges facing the graphic communications industry is the need to lower costs. Because of technological advancements, it is no longer true that nearly all printing is done using a press. Great concentration is taking place in the field of digital printing. Internet publications have given the printing industry another direction. Data distribution through the Internet is now the first step. Digital communications is changing the way that consumers communicate. Analog printing will exist for many years to come, but the business model must change to be successful.

Environmental sustainability is a major concern. It is a huge challenge to develop production models that adhere to sustainability policies. In a highly competitive market, it is no longer essential to merely streamline the production process for survival. Cutting waste is equally important.

Future for the Industry

Some of the forces that are shaping the graphic communications industry are cross media, electronic media, technological innovation, economics, regulations, and mobile and interactive media. Local and national organizations are working to update standards and educate those in the industry regarding these changes. Many of the successful printers are reshaping their businesses to keep up with these changes. Print alone is not going to meet the needs of the customer. Understanding how to utilize all media together, including television, radio, digital, and mobile resources, is the key component to staying vital in this fast-paced, ever-changing industry.

Summary

- Employees, raw materials, and equipment dictate the cost and quality of a printed product.
- The key to success is identifying and controlling business costs, properly calculating business estimates, and maximizing productivity.
- Printers may be required to conform to certain standards set by organizations such as ISO or ANSI.
- A copyright provides legal protection against unauthorized reproduction of literary works (books and other printed materials), musical compositions and recordings, artworks, photographs, film and video works, and dramatic works.
- Having customers sign release forms protects the printer from liability for infringement. Exceptions to infringement laws are known as fair use.

Review Questions

Answer the following questions using the information in this chapter.

1. Identify five business and personnel practices that are effective in growing a successful business.
2. Explain the purpose of a *business plan*.
3. Describe the characteristics of a corporation business type.
4. What are some examples of expenses that are categorized as *materials costs*?
5. Which business expenses are included when calculating hourly cost rates?
6. _____ is the amount of quality work completed in a given time span.
7. How are job tickets used within a printing company?
8. The two primary factors in deciding if a job should be produced using conventional printing or digital printing are _____ and _____.
9. Describe the purpose of The International Organization for Standardization (ISO).
10. Explain the purpose of North American Industry Classification System (NAICS) codes.
11. How long is a copyright in effect in the United States?
12. Describe the *fair use* provisions of the copyright laws.

Suggested Activities

1. Since digital printing has made great strides within the printing industry, identify the products that are commonly printed by the digital process. Before digital printing, what printing process was used to produce these products?
2. What are the benefits of incorporating national specifications in printing operations?
3. Visit the NAICS section of the US Bureau of Labor Statistics website. Research the number of printing establishments in your state and note the number of employees in each category.
4. Compare the role and cost effectiveness of print to other forms of communication, including television, radio, Internet, mobile delivery, and social media.

Appendix A

Several typefaces are presented here, grouped by each of the five classifications. As you study these type designs, refer to the components identified below for features to compare.

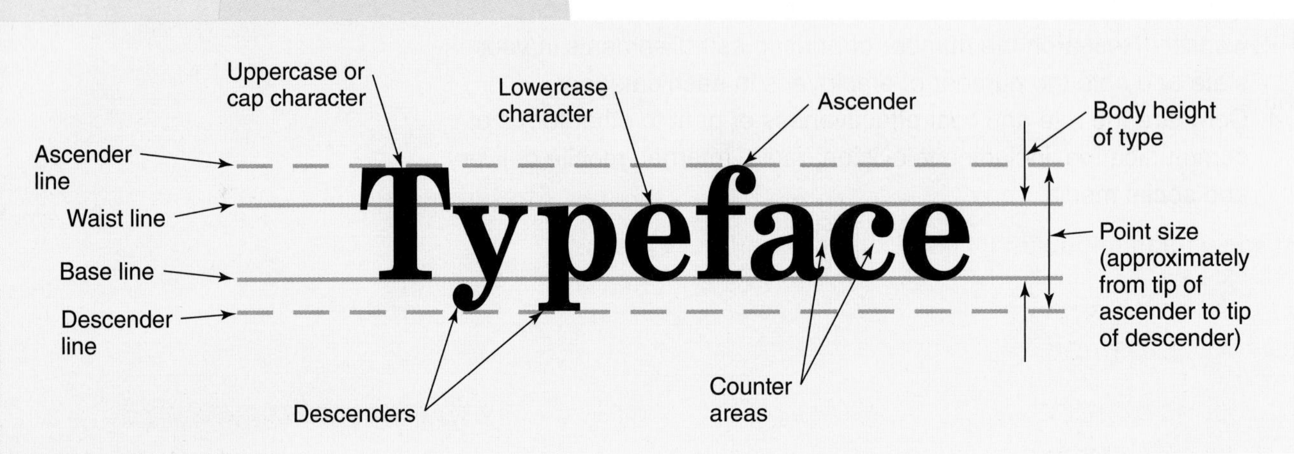

Goodheart-Willcox Publisher

Figure App A-1. When discussing typefaces, using the correct terminology ensures effective communication.

Serif

Palatino
abcdefghijklmnopqrstuvwxyzABCDEFG

Times
abcdefghijklmnopqrstuvwxyzABCDEFGHIJ

Century Old Style Standard
abcdefghijklmnopqrstuvwxyzABCDEFG

Bauer Bodoni
abcdefghijklmnopqrstuvwxyzABCDEFGHIJKL

Cheltenham
abcdefghijklmnopqrstuvwxyzABCDEFGHIJK

ITC New Baskerville
abcdefghijklmnopqrstuvwxyz

Minion Pro
abcdefghijklmnopqrstuvwxyzABCDEFGHI

Italian Garamond
abcdefghijklmnopqrstuvwxyzABCDEFGHI

Caslon 540
abcdefghijklmnopqrstuvwxyzABCDEFGHI

ITC Garamond
abcdefghijklmnopqrstuvwxyzABCDEFGH

Casablanca
abcdefghijklmnopqrstuvwxyzABCDE

Goodheart-Willcox Publisher

Figure App A-2.

Square Serif

Geometric Slabserif 703
abcdefghijklmnopqrstuvwxyzABCDEF

Courier
abcdefghijklmnopqrstuvwxyzABCD

Playbill
abcdefghijklmnopqrstuvwxyzABCDEFGHIJKLMNOPQRSTUVWXYZ12

Sans Serif

Helvetica
abcdefghijklmnopqrstuvwxyzABCDEFG

Futura
abcdefghijklmnopqrstuvwxyzABCDEFGHIJ

Formata
abcdefghijklmnopqrstuvwxyzABCDEF

Ottawa
abcdefghijklmnopqrstuvwxyzABCDEFGHI

Gothic 812
abcdefghijklmnopqrstuvwxyzABCDEFGHIJKLMNOPQR

KabanaBook
abcdefghijklmnopqrstuvwxyzABCD

News Gothic Standard
abcdefghijklmnopqrstuvwxyzABCDEFGHIJK

Myriad
abcdefghijklmnopqrstuvwxyzABCDEFGHIJ

Swiss 721
abcdefghijklmnopqrstuvwxyzABCDEFGHI

Vogue
abcdefghijklmnopqrstuvwxyzABCDEFGHIJK

Goodheart-Willcox Publisher

Figure App A-3.

Cursive and Script

Ex Ponto
abcdefghijklmnopqrstuvwxyzABCDEFGHIJKL

Amazone
abcdefghijklmnopqrstuvwxyzABCDEFGH

Commercial Script
abcdefghijklmnopqrstuvwxyzABCDEFGHIJ

Freehand 591
abcdefghijklmnopqrstuvwxyzABCDEFGHIJKLM

Berthold Script
abcdefghijklmnopqrstuvwxyzABCDEFGHI

Tekton
abcdefghijklmnopqrstuvwxyzABCDEFGHIJKL

Goodheart-Willcox Publisher

Figure App A-4.

Novelty, Decorative, and Miscellaneous

IRONWOOD
ABCDEFGHIJKLMNOPQRSTUVWXYZABCDEFGHIJKLMNOPQRSTUVWXYZ1

Hollow
abcdefghijklmnopqrstuvwxyzABCDEFG

Lincoln
abcdefghijklmnopqrstuvwxyzABCDEFGHIJ

LIBERTY
ABCDEFGHIJKLMNOPQRSTUVWXYZABCDE

Madrone
abcdefghijklmn

Merlin
abcdefghijklmnopqrstuvwxyzABCDE

Kids
abcdefghijklmnopqrstuvwxyzABC

GEOMETRIC SLABSERIF 703
ABCDEFGHIJKLMNOPQRSTUVWXYZABCD

Caslon Openface
abcdefghijklmnopqrstuvwxyzABCDEFGHIJ

Southern
abcdefghijklmnopqrstuvwxyzABCDEFGH

Orbit-B
abcdefghijklmnopqrstuvwxyzABCDEFGH

PALETTE
ABCDEFGHIJKLMNOPQRSTUVWXYZABCDEFG

PENGUIN
abcdefghijklmnopqrstuvwxyzABCDEFGHIJKLMN

ROSEWOOD STANDARD
ABCDEFGHIJKLMNOPQRSTUVWXYZABCD

STENCIL
ABCDEFGHIJKLMNOPQRSTUVWXYZ

UMBRA
ABCDEFGHIJKLMNOPQRSTUVWXYZABCD

Goodheart-Willcox Publisher

Figure App A-5.

Appendix B

Useful Information

Prefix	*Symbol*	*Multiplication Factor*
exa	E	10^{18} = 1,000,000,000,000,000,000
peta	P	10^{15} = 1,000,000,000,000,000
tera	T	10^{12} = 1,000,000,000,000
giga	G	10^{9} = 1,000,000,000
mega	M	10^{6} = 1,000,000
kilo	k	10^{3} = 1,000
hecto	h	10^{2} = 100
deca	da	10^{1} = 10
(unit)		10^{0} = 1
deci	d	10^{-1} = 0.1
centi	c	10^{-2} = 0.01
milli	m	10^{-3} = 0.001
micro	μ	10^{-6} = 0.000001
nano	n	10^{-9} = 0.000000001
pico	p	10^{-12} = 0.000000000001
femto	f	10^{-15} = 0.000000000000001
atto	a	10^{-18} = 0.000000000000000001

Goodheart-Willcox Publisher

Figure App B-1. US Customary and metric conversion factors and prefixes.

When You Know	Multiply By: Very Accurate	Multiply By: Approximate	To Find
	Length		
inches	* 25.4		millimeters
inches	* 2.54		centimeters
feet	* 0.3048		meters
feet	* 30.48		centimeters
yards	* 0.9144	0.9	meters
miles	* 1.609344	1.6	kilometers
	Weight		
grains	15.43236	15.4	grams
ounces	* 28.349523125	28.0	grams
ounces	* 0.028349523125	0.028	kilograms
pounds	* 0.45359237	0.45	kilograms
short tons	* 0.90718474	0.9	tonnes
	Volume		
teaspoons		5.0	milliliters
tablespoons		15.0	milliliters
fluid ounces	29.57353	30.0	milliliters
cups		0.24	liters
pints	* 0.473176473	0.47	liters
quarts	* 0.946352946	0.95	liters
gallons	* 3.785411784	3.8	liters
cubic inches	* 0.016387064	0.02	liters
cubic feet	* 0.028316846592	0.03	cubic meters
cubic yards	* 0.764554857984	0.76	cubic meters
	Area		
square inches	* 6.4516	6.5	square centimeters
square feet	* 0.09290304	0.9	square meters
square yards	* 0.83612736	0.8	square meters
square miles		2.6	square kilometers
acres	* 0.40468564224	0.4	hectares
	Temperature		
Fahrenheit	* 5/9 (after subtracting 32)		Celsius

* = Exact

Goodheart-Willcox Publisher

Figure App B-2. Conversion table—US Customary to SI Metric.

When You Know	Multiply By: Very Accurate	Multiply By: Approximate	To Find
	Length		
millimeters	* 0.03933701	0.04	inches
centimeters	* 0.3937008	0.4	inches
meters	* 3.280840	3.3	feet
meters	* 1.093613	1.1	yards
kilometers	* 0.621371	0.6	miles
	Weight		
grams	* 0.03527396	0.035	ounces
kilograms	* 2.204623	2.2	pounds
tonnes	* 1.1023113	1.1	short tons
	Volume		
milliliters	* 0.20001	0.2	teaspoons
milliliters	* 0.06667	0.067	tablespoons
milliliters	* 0.03381402	0.03	fluid ounces
liters	* 61.02374	61.024	cubic inches
liters	* 2.113376	2.1	pints
liters	* 1.056688	1.06	quarts
liters	* 0.26417205	0.26	gallons
liters	* 0.03531467	0.035	cubic feet
cubic meters	* 61023.74	61023.7	cubic inches
cubic meters	* 35.31467	35.0	cubic feet
cubic meters	* 1.3079506	1.3	cubic yards
cubic meters	* 264.17205	264.0	gallons
	Area		
square centimeters	* 0.1550003	0.16	square inches
square centimeters	* 0.001077639	0.001	square feet
square meters	* 10.76391	10.8	square feet
square meters	* 1.195990	1.2	square yards
square kilometers	* 0.3861019	0.4	square miles
hectares	* 2.471054	2.5	acres
	Temperature		
Celsius	* 9/5 (then add 32)		Fahrenheit

* = Exact

Goodheart-Willcox Publisher

Figure App B-3. Conversion table—SI Metric to US Customary.

Measures of Length	Measures of Weight	Measures of Liquid Volume
10 millimeters = 1 centimeter (cm)	10 milligrams = 1 centigram (cg)	10 milliliters = 1 centiliter (cl)
10 centimeters = 1 decimeter (dm)	10 centigrams = 1 decigram (dg)	10 centiliters = 1 deciliter (dl)
10 decimeters = 1 meter (m)	10 decigrams = 1 hectogram (hg)	10 deciliters = 1 liter (l)
10 meters = 1 decameter (dam)	10 hectograms = 1 kilogram (kg)	10 liters = 1 decaliter (dal)
10 decameters = 1 hectometer (hm)	10 kilograms = 1 myriagram (g)	10 decaliters = 1 hectoliter (hl)
10 hectometers = 1 kilometer (km)	10 myriagrams = 1 quintal (q)	10 hectoliters = 1 kiloliter (kl)
10 kilometers = 1 myriameter (mym)	10 quintals = 1 millier or metric ton (MT or t)	

Goodheart-Willcox Publisher

Figure App B-4. Metric units.

Fraction, Decimal, and Metric Equivalents

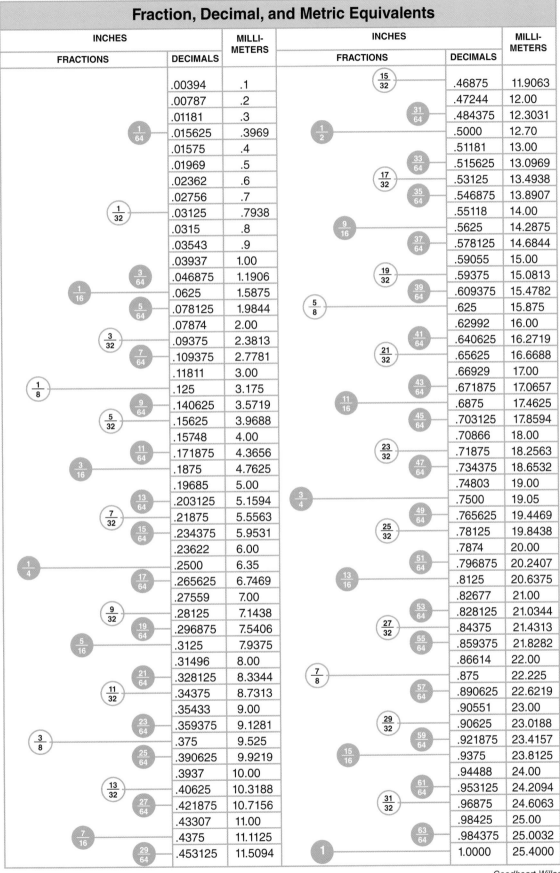

INCHES		MILLI-METERS	INCHES		MILLI-METERS
FRACTIONS	DECIMALS		FRACTIONS	DECIMALS	
	.00394	.1	15/32	.46875	11.9063
	.00787	.2		.47244	12.00
	.01181	.3	31/64	.484375	12.3031
1/64	.015625	.3969	1/2	.5000	12.70
	.01575	.4		.51181	13.00
	.01969	.5	33/64	.515625	13.0969
	.02362	.6	17/32	.53125	13.4938
	.02756	.7	35/64	.546875	13.8907
1/32	.03125	.7938		.55118	14.00
	.0315	.8	9/16	.5625	14.2875
	.03543	.9	37/64	.578125	14.6844
	.03937	1.00		.59055	15.00
3/64	.046875	1.1906	19/32	.59375	15.0813
1/16	.0625	1.5875	39/64	.609375	15.4782
5/64	.078125	1.9844	5/8	.625	15.875
	.07874	2.00		.62992	16.00
3/32	.09375	2.3813	41/64	.640625	16.2719
7/64	.109375	2.7781	21/32	.65625	16.6688
	.11811	3.00		.66929	17.00
1/8	.125	3.175	43/64	.671875	17.0657
9/64	.140625	3.5719	11/16	.6875	17.4625
5/32	.15625	3.9688	45/64	.703125	17.8594
	.15748	4.00		.70866	18.00
11/64	.171875	4.3656	23/32	.71875	18.2563
3/16	.1875	4.7625	47/64	.734375	18.6532
	.19685	5.00		.74803	19.00
13/64	.203125	5.1594	3/4	.7500	19.05
7/32	.21875	5.5563	49/64	.765625	19.4469
15/64	.234375	5.9531	25/32	.78125	19.8438
	.23622	6.00		.7874	20.00
1/4	.2500	6.35	51/64	.796875	20.2407
17/64	.265625	6.7469	13/16	.8125	20.6375
	.27559	7.00		.82677	21.00
9/32	.28125	7.1438	53/64	.828125	21.0344
19/64	.296875	7.5406	27/32	.84375	21.4313
5/16	.3125	7.9375	55/64	.859375	21.8282
	.31496	8.00		.86614	22.00
21/64	.328125	8.3344	7/8	.875	22.225
11/32	.34375	8.7313	57/64	.890625	22.6219
	.35433	9.00		.90551	23.00
23/64	.359375	9.1281	29/32	.90625	23.0188
3/8	.375	9.525	59/64	.921875	23.4157
25/64	.390625	9.9219	15/16	.9375	23.8125
	.3937	10.00		.94488	24.00
13/32	.40625	10.3188	61/64	.953125	24.2094
27/64	.421875	10.7156	31/32	.96875	24.6063
	.43307	11.00		.98425	25.00
7/16	.4375	11.1125	63/64	.984375	25.0032
29/64	.453125	11.5094	1	1.0000	25.4000

Goodheart-Willcox Publisher

Figure App B-5. A decimal conversion chart.

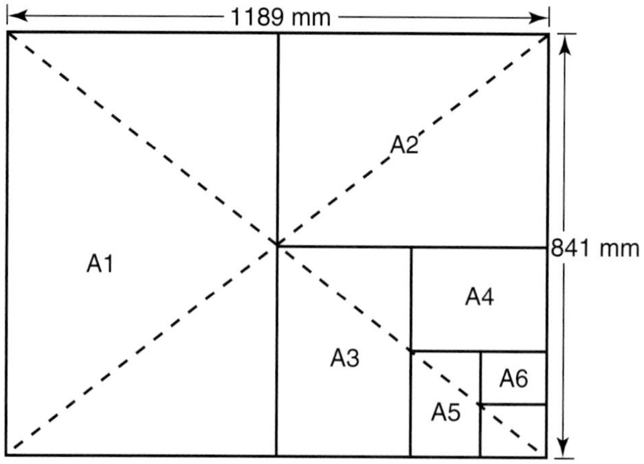

Goodheart-Willcox Publisher

Figure App B-6. ISO A-series paper.

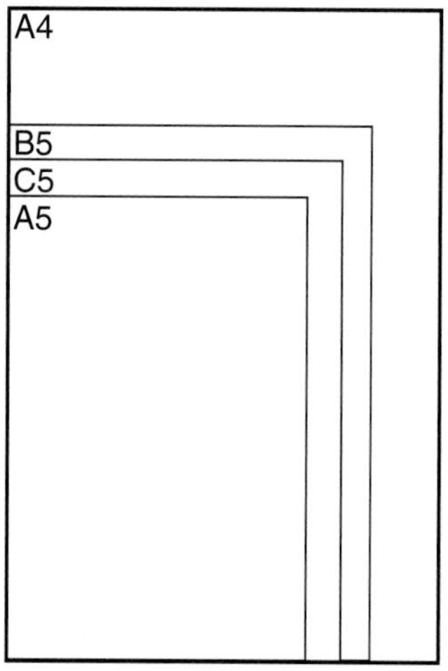

Goodheart-Willcox Publisher

Figure App B-7. The relationships among ISO A-, B-, and C-series papers.

ISO Sizes	Millimeters	Inches
2A	1189 × 1682	46.81 × 66.22
A0	841 × 1189	33.11 × 46.81
A1	594 × 841	23.39 × 33.11
A2	420 × 594	16.54 × 23.39
A3	297 × 420	11.69 × 16.54
A4	210 × 297	8.27 × 11.69
A5	148 × 210	5.83 × 8.27
A6	105 × 148	4.13 × 5.83
A7	74 × 105	2.91 × 4.13
A8	52 × 74	2.05 × 2.91
A9	37 × 52	1.46 × 2.05
A10	26 × 37	1.02 × 1.46

Goodheart-Willcox Publisher

Figure App B-8. ISO A-series paper sizes (metric and US Customary measurements).

ISO Sizes	Millimeters	Inches
B0	1000 × 1414	39.37 × 55.67
B1	707 × 1000	27.83 × 33.11
B2	500 × 707	19.68 × 27.83
B3	353 × 500	13.90 × 19.68
B4	250 × 353	9.84 × 13.90
B5	176 × 250	6.93 × 9.84
B6	125 × 176	4.92 × 6.93
B7	88 × 125	3.46 × 4.92
B8	62 × 88	2.44 × 3.46
B9	44 × 62	1.73 × 2.44
B10	31 × 44	1.22 × 1.73

Goodheart-Willcox Publisher

Figure App B-9. ISO B-series paper sizes (metric and US Customary measurements).

R Series	Bond 17″ × 22″ (432 mm × 559 mm) (g/m²)	Cover 20″ × 26″ (508 mm × 660 mm) (lb/ream)	Index 25 1/2″ × 30 1/2″ (648 mm × 775 mm) (lb/ream)	Bond 24″ × 36″ (610 mm × 914 mm) (lb/ream)	Bond 25″ × 38″ (635 mm × 965 mm) (lb/ream)
20.0	5.32	7.39	11.0	12.29	13.51
22.4	5.95	8.28	12.39	13.77	15.13
25.0	6.65	9.24	13.83	15.36	16.89
28.0	7.44	10.35	15.49	17.21	18.92
31.5	8.37	11.65	17.43	19.36	21.28
45.0	11.97	16.64	24.89	27.66	30.40
50.0	13.30	18.49	27.66	30.73	33.78
56.0	14.89	20.71	30.98	34.42	37.84
63.0	16.75	23.23	34.85	38.72	42.57
71.0	18.88	26.26	39.28	43.63	47.97
85.0	22.61	31.45	46.90	52.27	57.46
100.0	26.60	36.98	55.32	61.46	67.57
112.0	29.79	41.42	61.96	68.83	75.68
140.0	37.24	51.78	77.45	86.04	94.60
180.0	47.88	66.57	99.58	110.62	121.63
200.0	53.20	73.97	110.64	122.91	135.14
250.0	66.50	92.46	138.30	153.64	168.93
400.0	106.41	147.95	221.29	245.83	270.29

Goodheart-Willcox Publisher

Figure App B-10. The R20 series of paper weights and equivalent weights.

Trimmed Page Size (Inches)	Number of Printed Pages	Number from Sheet	Standard Paper Size
4 × 9	4 8 12 16 24	12 12 4 6 2	25 × 30 38 × 50 25 × 38 38 × 50 25 × 38
4 1/4 × 5 3/8	4 8 16 32	32 16 8 4	35 × 45 35 × 45 35 × 45 35 × 45
4 1/2 × 6	4 8 16 32	16 8 4 2	25 × 38 25 × 38 25 × 38 25 × 38
5 1/2 × 8 1/2	4 8 16 32	16 8 4 2	35 × 45 35 × 45 35 × 45 35 × 45
6 × 9	4 8 16 32	8 4 2 2	25 × 38 25 × 38 25 × 38 38 × 50
8 1/2 × 11	4 8 16	4 2 2	25 × 35 25 × 35 25 × 45
9 × 12	4 8 16	4 2 2	25 × 38 25 × 38 25 × 38

Goodheart-Willcox Publisher

Figure App B-11. Cutting charts. Using standard paper sizes can prevent waste, while using odd-size pages can create excess waste and also increase costs, if the correct quantity has not been ordered or there is not enough time to order special-size paper. This chart shows the number of pages to several standard paper sizes. The paper size includes trim top, bottom, and sides. This size does not include bleed.

Grade of Paper	Book 25 × 38	Bond 17 × 22	Cover 20 × 26	Bristol 22 1/2 × 28 1/2	Index 25 1/2 × 30 1/2	Tag 24 × 36	g/m²
Book	**30**	12	16	20	25	27	44
	40	16	22	27	33	36	59
	45	18	25	30	37	41	67
	50	20	27	34	41	45	74
	60	24	33	40	49	55	89
	70	28	38	47	57	64	104
	80	31	44	54	65	73	118
	90	35	49	60	74	82	133
	100	39	55	67	82	91	148
	120	47	66	80	98	109	178
Bond	33	**13**	18	22	27	30	49
	41	**16**	22	27	33	37	61
	51	**20**	28	34	42	46	75
	61	**24**	33	41	50	56	90
	71	**28**	39	48	58	64	105
	81	**32**	45	55	67	74	120
	91	**36**	50	62	75	83	135
	102	**40**	56	69	83	93	158
Cover	91	36	**50**	62	75	82	135
	110	43	**60**	74	90	100	163
	119	47	**65**	80	97	108	176
	146	58	**80**	99	120	134	216
	164	65	**90**	111	135	149	243
	183	72	**100**	124	150	166	271
Bristol	100	39	54	**67**	81	91	148
	120	47	65	**80**	98	109	178
	148	58	81	**110**	121	135	219
	176	70	97	**120**	146	162	261
	207	82	114	**140**	170	189	306
	237	93	130	**160**	194	216	351
Index	110	43	60	74	**90**	100	163
	135	54	74	91	**110**	122	203
	170	67	93	115	**140**	156	252
	208	82	114	140	**170**	189	328
Tag	110	43	60	74	90	**100**	163
	137	54	75	93	113	**125**	203
	165	65	90	111	135	**150**	244
	192	76	105	130	158	**175**	284
	220	97	120	148	180	**200**	326
	275	109	151	186	225	**250**	407

Goodheart-Willcox Publisher

Figure App B-12. Equivalent weights, in reams of 500 sheets. Basis weights are in bold type.

Book (25 × 38)	This grade encompasses the widest range of printing papers. As the name implies, book grade is widely used for books. Other uses include magazines, folders, pamphlets, posters, and other commercial printing. The different grades of book paper are coated (enamel), uncoated, offset, text, and label.
Cover (20 × 26)	Many grades of coated, text, and book papers are made in matching cover weights. There are also many special cover papers with a variety of surface textures, coatings, and finishes.
Bond (17 × 22)	Primarily used for stationery and business forms, this category also includes ledger and writing grades. Available in a wide range of colors and weights. Surfaces accept typewriter and writing inks and erase easily. There are two types: sulphite and cotton fiber (rag content). More costly bonds are made with 25% to 100% cotton fiber.
Index Bristol (25 1/2 × 30 1/2)	Characterized by stiffness and receptivity to printing inks, index is used wherever a stiff, inexpensive paper is required.
Printing (Mill) Bristol (22 1/2 × 28 1/2)	Generally stiffer than index, printing bristols are widely used for menus, greeting cards, covers, and tickets.
Newsprint (24 × 36)	This inexpensive grade is limited primarily to cost-critical uses.

Goodheart-Willcox Publisher

Figure App B-13. Printing papers. All papers have certain properties and characteristics affecting printability and quality. Printability and quality are not always related. The finest quality of paper might not always print well. Weight, bulk, caliper, grain direction, color, opacity, surface texture, coatings, and strength are some of the factors to consider before selecting paper. Papers are generally classified and defined in terms of use, as suggested by the grade names listed in this chart. Basic sizes are shown in parentheses.

Book, Offset, Label (Coated and Uncoated), and Text

Basis 25 × 38	30	35	40	45	50	60	70	80	90	100	120	150
17 1/2 × 22 1/2	25	29	33	37	41	50	58	66	75	83	99	124
19 × 25	30	35	40	45	50	60	70	80	90	100	120	150
20 × 26	33	38	44	49	55	66	77	88	99	109	131	164
22 1/2 × 29	41	48	55	62	69	82	96	110	124	137	165	206
22 1/2 × 35	50	58	66	75	83	99	116	133	249	166	199	249
23 × 29	42	49	56	63	70	84	98	112	126	140	169	211
23 × 35	51	59	68	76	85	102	119	136	153	169	203	254
24 × 36	55	64	73	82	91	109	127	146	164	182	218	273
25 × 38	60	70	80	90	100	120	140	160	180	200	240	300
26 × 40	66	77	88	99	109	131	153	175	197	219	263	328
28 × 42	74	97	99	111	124	149	173	198	223	248	297	371
28 × 44	78	91	104	117	130	156	182	207	237	259	311	389
30 1/2 × 41	79	92	105	118	132	158	184	211	267	263	316	395
32 × 44	89	104	119	133	148	178	207	237	275	296	356	445
33 × 44	92	107	122	138	153	183	214	245	298	306	367	459
35 × 45	99	116	133	149	166	199	232	265	398	332	398	497
35 × 46	102	119	136	153	169	203	237	271	305	339	407	508
36 × 48	109	127	146	164	182	218	255	291	327	364	437	546
38 × 50	120	140	160	180	200	240	280	320	360	400	480	600
38 × 52	125	146	166	187	208	250	291	333	374	416	499	624
41 × 54	140	163	186	210	233	280	326	373	419	466	559	699
41 × 61	158	184	211	237	263	316	369	421	474	527	632	790
42 × 58	154	179	205	231	256	308	359	410	462	513	615	769
44 × 64	178	207	237	267	296	356	415	474	534	593	711	889
44 × 66	183	214	245	275	306	367	428	489	550	611	734	917
46 × 69	200	234	267	301	334	401	468	535	601	668	802	1000
46 1/2 × 67 1/2	198	231	264	297	330	396	463	529	593	661	793	991
52 × 76	250	291	333	374	416	499	582	666	749	832	998	1248

Goodheart-Willcox Publisher

Figure App B-14. Standard paper sizes and weights. It has been traditional practice to price papers based on a ream (500 sheets). 1M pricing is replacing this. These tables give the weight per 1M sheets for common sizes and weights of different paper grades.

Bond, Business, Writing, and Ledger

Basis 17 × 12	13	16	20	24	28	32	36	40
8 1/2 × 11	6.5	8.0	10	12	14	16	18	20
8 1/2 × 14	8.3	10.2	12.7	15.3	17.8	20.4	22.9	25.5
11 × 17	13	16	20	24	28	32	36	40
16 × 21	23	29	36	43	50	57	65	72
16 × 42	47	58	72	86	101	115	130	144
17 × 22	26	32	40	48	56	64	72	80
17 × 26	31	38	47	57	66	76	85	95
17 1/2 × 22 1/2	27	34	42	51	59	67	76	84
17 × 28	33	41	51	61	71	81	92	102
18 × 23	29	36	44	53	62	71	80	89
18 × 46	58	71	89	106	124	142	160	117
19 × 24	32	39	49	59	68	78	88	98
19 × 28	37	46	57	68	80	91	102	114
19 × 48	63	78	98	117	137	156	176	195
20 × 28	39	48	60	72	84	96	108	120
21 × 32	47	58	72	86	101	115	130	144
22 × 25 1/2	39	48	60	72	84	96	108	120
22 × 34	52	64	80	96	101	128	144	160
22 1/2 × 22 1/2	35	43	54	65	76	87	97	108
22 1/2 × 28 1/2	45	55	69	82	96	110	123	137
22 1/2 × 34 1/2	54	66	83	100	116	133	149	166
22 1/2 × 35	55	67	84	101	118	135	152	168
23 × 36	58	71	89	106	124	142	159	177
24 × 38	63	78	98	117	137	156	176	195
24 1/2 × 24 1/2	42	51	64	77	90	103	116	128
24 1/2 × 28 1/2	49	60	75	90	105	120	135	150
24 1/2 × 29	50	61	76	91	106	122	137	152
24 1/2 × 38 1/2	66	81	101	121	141	161	182	202
24 1/2 × 39	66	82	102	122	143	164	184	204
25 1/2 × 44	78	96	120	144	168	192	216	240
26 × 35	61	76	94	113	132	151	170	189
28 × 34	66	82	102	122	143	163	184	204
28 × 38	74	91	114	136	159	182	205	228
34 × 44	104	128	160	192	224	256	288	320
35 × 45	109	135	168	202	236	270	303	337

Goodheart-Willcox Publisher

Figure App B-14. Continued.

Equivalent Weights in Reams of 500 Sheets

Basis Weights in Boldface					
	Bond 17 × 22	Book 25 × 38	Cover 20 × 26	Index 25 1/2 × 30 1/2	Bristol 22 1/2 × 28 1/2
Bond	**13**	33	18	27	22
	16	41	22	34	28
	20	51	28	42	34
	24	61	33	50	42
	28	71	39	58	48
	32	81	45	66	55
	36	91	50	75	62
	40	102	56	83	68
Book	12	**30**	16	25	20
	16	**40**	22	33	27
	18	**45**	25	37	30
	20	**50**	27	41	33
	22	**55**	30	45	37
	24	**60**	33	49	41
	26	**65**	36	53	44
	28	**70**	38	57	47
	30	**75**	41	61	50
	31	**80**	44	65	54
	35	**90**	49	74	61
	39	**100**	55	82	68
	47	**120**	66	98	81
Cover	18	46	**25**	38	31
	25	64	**35**	52	42
	29	73	**40**	60	50
	36	91	**50**	75	62
	40	100	**55**	82	68
	43	110	**60**	90	74
	47	119	**65**	97	80
	58	146	**80**	120	99
	65	164	**90**	135	111
	72	183	**100**	150	123
Index	43	110	60	**90**	74
	53	135	74	**110**	91
	67	171	93	**140**	116
	82	208	114	**170**	140
Bristol	52	133	73	109	**90**
	58	148	81	121	**100**
	70	178	97	146	**120**
	82	207	114	170	**140**
	93	237	130	194	**160**
	105	267	146	218	**180**

Goodheart-Willcox Publisher

Figure App B-14. Continued.

Printing Bristol

Basis Size 22 1/2 × 28 1/2	Weight per 1000 Sheets								
	67	80	90	94	100	110	120	140	160
22 1/2 × 28 1/2	134	160	180	188	200	220	240	280	320
22 1/2 × 35	165	196	221	231	246	270	295	344	393
23 × 35	168	201	226	236	251	276	301	352	402
26 × 40	217	259	292	305	324	357	389	454	519
28 1/2 × 45	268	320	360	376	400	440	480	560	640

Cover

Basis Size 20 × 26	Weight per 1000 Sheets						
	50	60	65	80	90	100	130
20 × 26	100	120	130	160	180	200	260
22 1/2 × 28 1/2	123	148	160	197	222	247	321
23 × 29	128	154	167	205	231	257	333
23 × 5	155	186	201	248	279	310	403
26 × 40	200	240	260	320	360	400	520
35 × 46	310	372	403	495	557	619	805

Index Bristol

Basis Size 25 1/2 × 30 1/2	Weight per 1000 Sheets				
	90	120	140	170	220
20 1/2 × 24 3/4	117	157	183	222	287
22 1/2 × 28 1/2	148	198	231	280	263
22 1/2 × 35	182	243	284	344	446
25 1/2 × 30 1/2	180	240	280	340	440
28 1/2 × 45	297	356	462	561	726

Goodheart-Willcox Publisher

Figure App B-14. Continued.

Formula	Weight of 1000 sheets × the number of sheets ÷ 1000 = total weight
Example	Determine the weight of 1765 sheets of 25 × 38 × 80 (160M) lb stock.
Solution	160 × 1765 = 282,400 ÷ 1000 = 282.4 lb

Goodheart-Willcox Publisher

Figure App B-15. Finding the weight of a number of sheets.

Problem: Determine the weight of a roll of coated (2 sides) book paper that is 30" in diameter and 38" wide.

1. Square the diameter: 30 x 30 = 900
2. Multiply the result by the roll width: 900 x 38 = 34,200
3. Multiply by given factor (.034): 34,200 x .034 = 1162.8

Answer: 1163 lbs.

Factors: (These average factors apply for all weights)

Newsprint	0.016
Antique finish	0.018
Machine finish, English finish, Offset, Bond	0.027
Supercalendered (coated 1 side)	0.030
Coated 2 sides	0.034

Goodheart-Willcox Publisher

Figure App B-16. How to find the weight of a roll of paper.

	Basis Weight	Paper Finish			
		Coated	Smooth	Vellum	Antique
Book	40		.0025	.0031	.0034
	45	.0021	.0028	.0035	.0037
	50	.0023	.0031	.0038	.0041
	60	.0028	.0038	.0046	.0050
	70	.0034	.0044	.0054	.0058
	80	.0040	.0050	.0059	.0065
	90	.0046	.0057	.0065	.0074
	100	.0052	.0063	.0071	.0082
	120	.0060	.0076	.0082	.0100
	150	.0072	.0095	.0106	.0123
Cover	50		.0058	.0070	.0075
	60	.0056			
	65		.0075	.0092	.0097
	80	.0072	.0093	.0113	.0120
	90		.0106	.0130	.0135
	100	.0092	.0116	.0140	.0150
	130		.0150	.0184	.0190
Bond	13		.0021	.0025	.0027
	16		.0026	.0031	.0033
	20		.0032	.0039	.0042
	24		.0038	.0047	.0050
Index	90		.0080	.0084	
	110		.0096	.0104	
	140		.0132	.0140	
	170		.0144	.0160	
Bristol	90	.0055	.0069	.0084	.0090
	100	.0061	.0076	.0093	.0100
	120	.0073	.0092	.0111	.0120
	140	.0085	.0107	.0130	.0140
	160	.0097	.0122	.0148	.0160
	180	.0110	.0137	.0167	.0180
	200	.0122	.0153	.0185	.0200
	220	.0134	.0167	.0204	.0220

Goodheart-Willcox Publisher

Figure App B-17. Caliper equivalents. The numbers provided are averages. Variations occur in mill runs.

Diameter (Inches)	All Bond	Regular Ledger	Posting Ledger	Regular Offset	Regular Tagboard
10	1.86	2.34	1.98	2.10	2.55
12	2.83	3.37	2.94	3.12	3.74
14	3.92	4.58	4.07	4.32	5.07
16	5.13	5.99	5.38	5.71	6.86
18	6.60	7.58	6.86	7.27	8.01
20	8.23	9.35	8.51	9.04	10.21
22	10.00	11.16	10.28	10.90	12.47
24	11.90	13.34	12.30	13.05	14.56
25	13.10	14.62	13.42	14.22	15.96
26	14.10	15.80	14.53	15.41	17.24
27	15.30	17.05	15.68	16.63	18.60
28	16.40	18.33	16.88	17.90	20.00
29	17.70	19.66	18.12	19.22	21.46
30	18.90	21.05	19.40	20.58	22.96
31	20.02	22.45	20.73	21.99	24.62
32	21.60	23.93	22.10	23.45	26.10
33	22.90	26.52	23.52	24.95	27.78
34	24.20	27.89	24.98	26.49	29.49
35	25.70	29.86	26.48	28.06	31.25
36	27.00	31.60	28.03	29.73	33.06
37	28.70	33.39	29.61	31.41	34.93
38	30.20	35.23	31.25	33.15	36.83
39	31.90	37.13	32.93	34.92	38.81
40	33.70	39.06	34.65	36.75	40.82

International Paper Co.

Figure App B-18. Approximate roll weights per inch of width.

No. Out of Sheet	Quantity of Pressrun									
	500	1000	1500	2000	2500	3000	3500	4000	4500	5000
1	500	1000	1500	2000	2500	3000	3500	4000	4500	5000
2	250	500	750	1000	1250	1500	1750	2000	2250	2500
3	167	334	500	667	834	1000	1167	1334	1500	1667
4	125	250	375	500	625	750	875	1000	1125	1250
5	100	200	300	400	500	600	700	800	900	1000
6	84	167	250	334	417	500	584	667	750	834
7	72	143	215	286	358	429	500	572	643	715
8	63	125	188	250	313	375	438	500	563	625
9	56	112	167	223	278	334	389	445	500	556
10	50	100	150	200	250	300	350	400	450	500
11	46	91	137	182	228	273	319	364	410	455
12	42	84	126	168	209	250	292	334	375	417
13	39	77	116	154	193	231	270	308	347	385
14	36	72	108	144	179	215	250	286	322	358
15	34	67	100	134	167	200	234	267	300	334
16	32	63	94	125	157	188	219	250	282	313
17	30	59	89	118	148	177	206	236	265	295
18	28	56	84	112	139	167	195	223	250	279
19	27	53	79	106	132	158	185	211	237	264
20	25	50	75	100	125	150	175	200	225	250
21	24	48	72	96	120	143	167	191	215	239
22	23	46	69	91	114	137	160	182	205	228
23	22	44	66	87	109	131	153	174	196	218
24	21	42	63	84	105	125	146	167	188	209
25	20	40	60	80	100	120	140	160	180	200
26	20	39	58	77	97	116	135	154	174	193
27	19	38	56	75	93	112	130	149	167	186
28	18	36	54	72	90	108	125	143	161	179
29	18	36	54	72	87	103	121	138	156	173
30	17	34	51	67	84	100	117	134	150	167
31	17	33	49	65	81	97	113	130	146	162
32	16	32	47	63	79	94	110	125	141	157
33	16	31	46	61	76	91	107	122	137	152
34	15	30	45	59	74	89	103	118	133	148
35	15	29	43	58	72	86	100	115	129	143
36	14	28	42	56	70	84	98	112	125	139
37	14	28	41	55	68	82	95	109	122	136
38	14	27	40	53	66	79	93	106	119	132
39	13	26	39	52	65	77	90	103	116	131
40	13	25	38	50	63	75	88	100	113	125

Goodheart-Willcox Publisher

Figure App B-19. Paper-stock estimator. Use this chart to determine how many sheets are needed for a particular job. For example, a job calls for 4000 pieces that cut 16 out of 1 sheet. Follow the first column to 16, and then read across that line to the 4000 column. (No spoilage is included.)

To determine the approximate number of linear feet in a roll of paper, use the formula and factors shown below.

Formula: $\frac{\text{Net Weight} \times 12 \times (\text{Factor})}{\text{Basis Weight} \times \text{Width}} = \text{Linear Feet}$

Paper	Factors
Bond	1300
Cover	1805
Book or Offset	3300
Vellum Bristol (22 1/2″ x 28 1/2″)	2230
Index (25 1/2″ x 30 1/2″)	2700
Printing Bristol (22 1/2″ x 35″)	2739
Wrapping, Tissue, Newsprint, Waxing (24″ x 36″)	3070
Tag	3000

Example: Find the number of linear feet in a roll of form bond (20″ width, sub. 16 lbs., net weight 750 lbs.)

$$\frac{750 \times 12 \times 1300}{16 \times 20} = 36{,}562.5 = 36{,}563 \text{ Linear Feet}$$

To obtain a more exact approximation of linear feet, use the formula below:

$$\frac{[(\text{Roll Radius})^2 \times (3.1416)] - [(\text{Core Radius})^2 \times 3.1416)]}{\text{Paper Thickness}} = \text{Linear Inches}$$

$$\frac{\text{Linear Inches}}{12} = \text{Linear Feet}$$

Zellerbach Paper Co.

Figure App B-20. The approximate number of linear feet in rolls.

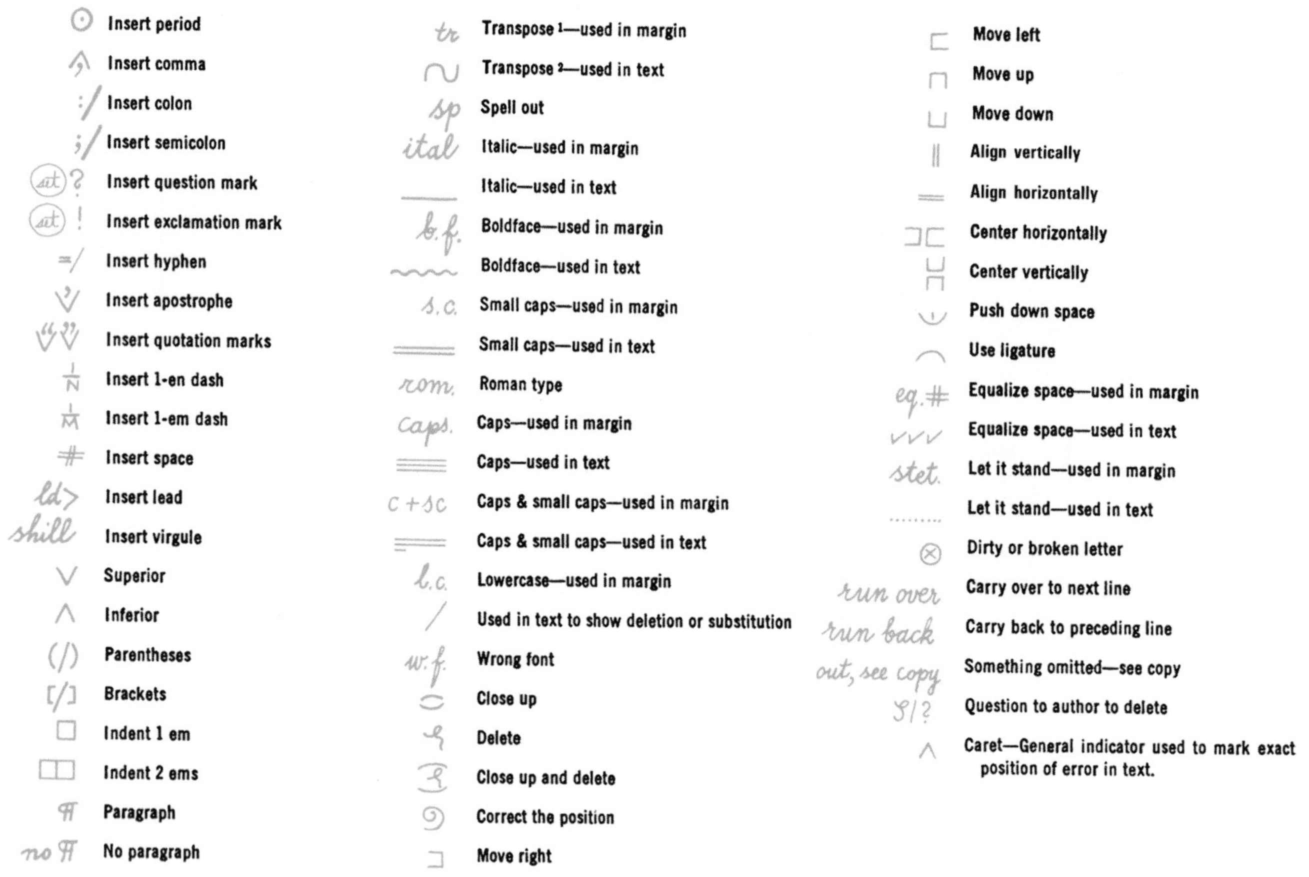

Goodheart-Willcox Publisher

Figure App B-21. Proofreader's marks.

Appendix C

SkillsUSA—Preparing Students for Leadership in the World of Work

Introduction to SkillsUSA

SkillsUSA is a national organization that brings together students, educators, and industry members dedicated to preparing students for excellence in career and technical occupations. The SkillsUSA Framework supports the acquisition of technical skills grounded in academics, personal skills, and workplace skills. Becoming involved in SkillsUSA is a commitment that can provide many lifelong rewards.

History

In 1965, the Vocational Industrial Clubs of America (VICA) formed to fill demand for a national skills organization that could connect industry professionals, educators, and youth in order to train students for future technical careers. While VICA began with just 200 members from 14 states, it grew quickly and expanded its membership to include college students. By 1969, VICA had more than 82,000 members.

VICA held its first competitive events in 1967, giving student competitors the chance to showcase their technical skills for peers, instructors, and professionals. In 1995, VICA changed the name of its national competition, the US Skill Olympics, to SkillsUSA Championships. In 1998, VICA was renamed VICA-SkillsUSA, and in 2004, the name of the organization was shortened to SkillsUSA.

Membership

SkillsUSA represents over 360,000 members in over 18,000 local chapters across the United States, with industry support from more than 600 corporations, trade associations, and labor unions.

Organization Colors and Relationships

The SkillsUSA colors illustrate the importance of the relationship between the national organization and the individual states and chapters. Red, white, blue, and gold represent the national organization itself. Within this color scheme, red and white represent the individual states and chapters, while blue represents their common union. Gold represents the most important part of the organization, the individual member.

Motto, Creed, and Pledge

The SkillsUSA organization lives by its motto, "Preparing for leadership in the world of work," and members follow its creed. In accordance with the creed, SkillsUSA members believe in the dignity of work, the American way of life, fair play, high moral and spiritual standards, and that satisfaction is achieved by good work.

SkillsUSA members also pledge to be productive members of their schools, chapters, and communities:

"Upon my honor, I pledge:

- To prepare myself by diligent study and ardent practice to become a worker whose services will be recognized as honorable by my employer and fellow workers.
- To base my expectations of reward upon the solid foundation of service.
- To honor and respect my vocation in such a way as to bring repute to myself.
- And further, to spare no effort in upholding the ideals of SkillsUSA."

SkillsUSA membership not only helps its members hone their technical skills, it helps them choose their futures. The organization recognizes the importance of diversity in the workforce and gives students from all backgrounds the opportunity to prove their skills and choose their careers. Championship contests are designed to evaluate career readiness, as well as preparedness for applying and interviewing for jobs. In addition to taking assessment tests and career interest inventories, members can try out potential careers in hands-on environments.

SkillsUSA Leadership Opportunities

SkillsUSA promotes good citizenship and expects its members to prepare to become leaders in their fields and their communities. SkillsUSA encourages all its members to contribute to their communities. Chapters can organize community service projects to give back to their communities and submit these projects to championship events.

Mentorship

SkillsUSA members can learn to lead by example through Student2Student mentoring. In these programs, chapters work with middle and elementary schools to help younger students explore future careers. Older students mentor younger students by going on field trips or working on hands-on activities together.

National Officers

Members can learn to lead a community by serving in the House of Delegates and as SkillsUSA National Officers. National officers are elected by vote from the House of Delegates and hold their positions for one year. Potential officers should study the SkillsUSA Leadership Handbook closely and meet the qualifications for candidacy, which include active membership in their chapter and past SkillsUSA leadership experience.

There are strict regulations about where, when, and how candidates may campaign for officership. Campaigning with social media is not allowed, and candidates do the bulk of their campaign work by interacting directly with the delegates. Candidates must give a brief speech, participate in question-and-answer sessions, and attend three Meet the Candidate sessions.

SkillsUSA Competitions

SkillsUSA competitions at the local, state, and national level test for more than a participant's technical skill. The definitive goal of SkillsUSA is preparing members to excel in the workplace. So, participants' preparation, appearance, and behavior are also thoroughly graded as part of a complete work performance. Competitions are held for both technical skills and leadership qualities.

The National SkillsUSA Championship is held annually in Louisville, Kentucky, and more than 6,300 students compete each year in order to earn Skill Point Certificates. Skill Point Certificates are awarded to participants who reach or exceed industry-defined cut scores, regardless of medal standing or contest ranking. The competition holds contests for more than 100 concentrations in the technical, skilled, and service occupations as well as career and leadership skills. SkillsUSA also sponsors competitions on the local, state, regional, and international levels.

Professional Behavior

Each competition requires careful preparation, both before and during the contest event. Participants should study the regulations for their contest and observe all standards for dress, tools, and other preparations. Contest events have multiple parts. Each event typically has the following four components: a professional development program (PDP) test; a technical skills–related written test; an oral professional assessment or interview; and a submission of a hard-copy résumé. Contestants will then complete industry-defined challenges that are specific to their skill set.

The skills required to net the most points are also those required to do good work on the job. Contestants must know their task, tools, and skill set inside and out in order to perform the task proficiently. Often, projects must be prepared within a set time limit, which requires careful time management. Other events may call for teams that require excellent teamwork and communication to ensure all parts of the project are completed correctly.

Professional Ethics

Participants in SkillsUSA competitions are held to high standards of performance and sportsmanship. The SkillsUSA will not tolerate unethical or disruptive behavior. Interrupting other contestants, tampering with other contestants' work, and other unethical behavior can be grounds for immediate disqualification.

Professional Dress

During the SkillsUSA ceremonies, meetings, and similar functions, students should dress professionally and follow SkillsUSA's guidelines for dress. Both genders are expected to wear black SkillsUSA jackets or red SkillsUSA blazers, windbreakers, or sweaters and dress in a business-formal style. For men, this means a white dress shirt, black dress slacks, black socks, black shoes, and black ties. For women, this means a white blouse or turtleneck with a collar that does not extend over the lapels or neck of her blazer or jacket. Women may wear a black dress skirt or slacks with black shoes. Black sheer (not opaque) or skin-tone seamless hose should be worn with skirts.

SkillsUSA is an organization that asks for a commitment from its members, but it provides many rewards. If you are interested in learning more about SkillsUSA, please see their website.

Glossary

A

absolute intent: Rendering intent using exact preservation of colors including the white point, often causing dramatic color shifts. (12)

achromatic vision: Blindness to all colors; ability to see only in shades of white, gray, and black. (11)

active layout: Asymmetrical layout for more energy and excitement. (7)

adaptation: Adjustment that eyes make in different lighting conditions. (11)

A/D converter: A device used to convert an analog charge into digital form. The result of this conversion is stored as pixel data. (10)

additive color formation: Theory based on mixing red, green, and blue light in various combinations to create a color reproduction or image. (9, 11, 12)

additive colors: The primary colors using, red, green, and blue. (7)

additives: Ingredients such as driers, lubricants, waxes, and starches that are added to ink to impart special characteristics, improve desirable properties, or suppress undesirable properties. (16)

adjacency: A property of the eye that changes the perception of a color based on the adjacent or surrounding color. (11)

afterimage: An image that the viewer continues to see after the actual object is no longer in sight. The image is created by the eye's attempt to restore equilibrium. (11)

aliasing: The process in which smooth curves and other lines become jagged because an image is enlarged or the resolution of the graphics device or file is reduced. (9)

analog charge: A series of electrical impulses created with the light received by the charged-coupled device (CCD). (10)

analog format: Film-based format that has image gradations of tone from light to dark. (10)

analogous: Colors that are next to each other on the color wheel. (7)

anchor points: Where two segments of a path meet. (9)

animation: Taking individual still images with slight variations and running them together to create the illusion of motion. (1)

antialiasing: Software technique for diminishing the jagged edges of an image that should be smooth. (9)

apprenticeship: A method of job training in which an employee in a union shop receives classroom training and on-the-job experience as a means of becoming an experienced journeyman. (2)

aqueous inks: Inks that are based on a mixture of water, glycol, and dyes or pigments. (13)

artwork: The graphic elements (line art and photographs) used in producing printed products. (1)

augmented reality: A real world environment with extended 3D, computer generated graphics, sound or GPS data accessed by a computer or mobile device through a marker. (9)

automatic trap: Trap set by building art with common colors. Also called *process bridge*. (12)

B

banding machine: Device that is used to wrap and bond a plastic or metal band around a bundle of booklets, books, boxes, or other products. This holds the products together for shipping. (17)

barrier guards: Machine guards that can be hinged or moved. (4)

baseline grid: Nonprinted set of guidelines on each layout page. (9)

basic size: The standard length and width, in inches, of a grade of paper. (5, 15)

basis weight: The weight, in pounds, of a ream of paper cut to its basic size. (5, 15)

Bezier curve: A vector graphic defined mathematically by two endpoints and two or more other points that control its shape. (9)

binary: System that a computer uses to recognize only two numbers, or digits: 1 (on) and 0 (off). (9)

binder: Substance that holds pigment together and adheres ink to the substrate. (16)

binding: The process of joining together multiple pages of a printed product by various means including sewing, stapling, spiral wire, and adhesives. (1, 17)

bit: Binary digit. The basic unit of digital information. (9)

Note: The number in parentheses following each definition indicates the chapter in which the term can be found.

bit depth: The number of bits of color or grayscale information that can be recorded per pixel. The greater the bit depth, the more colors or grayscales can be represented. (9, 10)

blanket: A resilient material that is attached to a cylinder and used as an image transfer material from the plate cylinder to the substrate. (14)

blanket cylinder: A printing system component that holds the image-receptive blanket on the press and receives the image from the plate cylinder. (14)

bleaching: A chemical treatment to whiten wood pulp. (15)

blind embossing: An embossing process in which the stock itself creates the image and ink is not used. (17)

body type: Type sizes that range from 4-point though 12-point that are used for setting straight matter. (6, 7)

book printing: Graphic communications industry segment that produces physical trade books and textbooks. (1)

brake mechanism: A tension control device designed to produce a slight amount of drag on the web as it travels through a web-fed press. (14)

brayer: A small, handheld roller used to distribute ink on a proof press. (16)

brightness: The lightness or luminosity of a color. An associated value indicates how light or dark a color is. (6, 11, 12)

brush system: A continuous dampening system that uses a brush roller to transfer fountain solution from the fountain roller to the rest of the system. (14)

burned edge: The result of poor cutting or adhering techniques of stencils, which can cause imperfect images. (14)

business plan: A document that states the goals of a business and presents a framework for achieving those goals. (18)

byte: A binary word, or group of eight individual 1s and 0s. (9)

C

cable modem: Broadband connection over cable TV lines using faster coaxial cable. (9)

calendering: The process of flattening and smoothing the paper surface by passing it between a series of rollers. (15)

calibration: A process by which a scanner, monitor, or output device is adjusted to provide a more accurate display and reproduction of images. (12)

career: A position you train for and seek employment for your life's work. (2)

cell distortion: The result of tensioning fabric in one direction without stretching it equally in the other direction. (14)

cell size: The distance across individual open areas between adjacent threads. (14)

cellulose: The raw material used to make paper. (15)

centered text: When lines of text are centered over each other with a common center point. (6)

chain of custody: The process of tracking and recording the possession and transfer of wood and fiber from forests of origin to the end user. (15)

chalking: Condition that occurs when dried ink is easily rubbed off or lost from a printed sheet. (16)

characterization: Describes the color limitations or color profile of a particular device. (12)

characters: The individual visual symbols, such as letters, numerals, and punctuation marks, in a particular typeface. (6)

character styles: A collection of formatting instructions that can be applied to a word or words. (9)

charge-coupled device (CCD): A solid-state, light-sensitive chip receptor that converts light into an analog charge; commonly built into image capturing devices. (10)

chipper: A machine that cuts logs into chips. (15)

choke trap: Trap performed by spreading the background under the foreground object. (12)

chroma: A term used in the Munsell system to indicate the extent to which the color is diluted by white light. (11)

chromatic adaptation: The adjustment our eyes make to color conditions. (11)

chromatic induction: A change in perception where the eye causes a color to look different when surrounded by or adjacent to other colors. (11)

chromaticity: A color quality of an image that includes hue and saturation, but not brightness. (5, 11)

chromaticity coordinates: The *x* and *y* values of the CIE Yxy color space; they represent the hue and saturation of a color. (11)

clipboard: Temporary storage area for information that has been copied. Only one thing at a time can be on the clipboard. (9)

closure: Gestalt principle that says when a space is not completely closed, our eyes fill in the missing information. (7)

cloud-based storage: Offsite storage system maintained by a third party provided remote access to your data. (9)

CMOS: Complementary metal oxide semiconductor active pixel sensor. An active light sensor chip commonly used in low-end digital cameras. (10)

coated paper: Paper with a mineral substance applied to it for a smoother, stronger surface. (15)

coating: Provides a clear protective surface that is resistant to moisture and scuffing. (17)

collating: The gathering of sheets or signatures, usually after they are printed. (17)

color: A visual sensation produced in the brain when the eye views various wavelengths of light. (7)

colorant: Chemical substance that gives color to such materials as ink, paint, crayons, and chalk. (11, 16)

color constancy: The tendency to perceive the color of an object to be constant, even when specific conditions (such as lighting) are changed. (11)

color control bar: A strip of colors printed in the trim area of a press sheet. (12)

color correction: Adjusting images to optimize values for highlight and shadow, neutral tones, skin tones, and sharpness, to compensate for impurities in the printing ink and color separation. (12, 14)

color diagram: A visual representation of color data, used for process ink analysis. (16)

color gamut: The range of colors formed by all possible combinations of the colorants in a color reproduction system that can be shown on a computer display or other output device. (11, 12)

colorimeter: A color measurement device that measures and compares the hue, purity, and brightness of colors in a manner that simulates how people perceive color. (11)

color management module (CMM): Color transformation engine that translates data from one device's color space to another. (12)

color management system (CMS): An electronic prepress tool that provides a way to correlate the color-rendering capabilities of input devices, color monitors, and output devices to produce predictable, consistent color. (9, 12)

color separation: The process of dividing the colors of a multicolored original into the printing primaries (CMY) and black (K). CMYK color separations are used to prepare printing plates. (11)

color space: A three-dimensional area where three color attributes, such as hue, value, and chroma, can be depicted, calculated, and charted. (9, 11)

color strength: The amount of pigment in an ink that determines how well the ink will cover the substrate. (16)

color wheel: A visual tool that illustrates the basics of color. (7)

combination densitometer: A color measurement device that computes both the reflection and transmission densities of an image or surface material. (11)

commercial printing: A segment of the graphic communications industry that produces various products for customers, including forms, newspaper inserts, and catalogs. (1)

comparison proofing: A proofreading method done primarily by one person to find such major problems as copy deletion, incorrect sequence, or copy duplication. (9)

competitive advantage: When a person or company has an attribute or skill that allows it to outperform others. (3)

complementary colors: Any two colors that lie directly opposite each other on the color wheel. (7, 11)

composition: The organization of the elements in the layout. (7)

composition depth: The space measuring from the beginning of a composition until the end of the composition. (6)

comprehensive: A detailed layout showing how the printed piece will look when finished, often completed on the computer. It will usually become the final file. (7)

computer-to-plate (CTP): Imaging systems that expose fully-paginated digital materials to plates in platesetters or imagesetters without creating film intermediates. (1, 14)

concordant: Relationship of typefaces used together, usually from the same family, without a lot of variety. (6)

cones: Light-sensitive nerve cells of the retina that help us perceive light and color (red, green, and blue). Cones detect both intensity and wavelength (color). (11)

conflict: Relationship of typefaces used together that are very similar, but not the same, causing a visual conflict and confusion. (6)

constructive criticism: Analysis that is positively intended, specific and objective, whose objective is to improve or enhance a design. (8)

constructive interference: When two light waves cross a single point at the same time and combine to create brighter light than one wave can emit alone. (11)

content management systems (CMS): Computer applications often used for websites that include the ability to publish, edit content, manage workflow, and organize and maintain data. (1)

continuation: When your eye continues through one element into another. (7)

continuous ink-jet printer: Printer in which a continuously circulating flow of ink through the printhead is maintained while the power is on. (13)

continuous spectrum: Spectrum of colors that is created when sunlight passes through a prism. The spectrum blends smoothly from one color to the next. (11)

continuous tone: An image with an infinite number of tone gradations between the lightest highlights and the darkest shadows. (11)

continuous tone copy: An image with an infinite number of tone gradations between the lightest highlights and the darkest shadows. (1)

contract proof: The proof that acts as an agreement between the customer and the printer as the expected quality and content of the final product. (9)

contrast: The variation of elements in a printed product. (6, 7, 12)

contrast pairing: Opposite combinations that are ways to show contrast in a layout. (7)

conversion: Step of color management systems that performs color correction between imaging devices. (12)

converting: The finishing operations that transform the printed piece into another physical form. (17)

copy: The text elements (words) used in producing printed products. (1)

copyright: A legal protection against unauthorized copying of original, creative works. (3, 18)

cornea: A transparent window at the front of the eye that refracts light to the retina. (11)

corporation: A type of business that is a separate legal entity from the people who own or manage it. A business of this type pays taxes on its own tax return and is liable for its own debt and other legal responsibilities. (18)

counterfeit: The production of an exact copy of a document or something of value without proper permission, with the intent to defraud or mislead someone into thinking that it is the original or official. (3, 18)

craft-centered jobs: Work performed by artisans or others with manual skills. (2)

creasing: The process of compressing the substrate so that it will fold more easily; often done with a rotary creaser attached to the folder. (17)

creative commons: A nonprofit organization that grants licenses to the public allowing free use of a copyrighted material under specific terms. (3)

creep: A pushing out or extension of pages on the outer edge of a saddle-stitched book, caused by the greater thickness at the spine. An allowance for creep must be made in the prepress phase. (17)

critique: A disciplined analysis of work designed to give feedback to enhance or improve a final design. (8)

cross-platform: Describes applications, formats, or devices that work on multiple computer operating system platforms. (9)

cursive: A typeface designed to simulate handwriting, in which the letters are not joined. (6)

cutting: The process of making a large sheet of paper into several smaller sheets. (17)

D

dampening system: A group of rollers designed to apply moisture to the nonimage area of the printing plate. (14)

data centers: Third-party sources that use redundancy to securely store data in a cloud-based environment. (9)

debossing: The reverse of embossing, so that the image is sunk into the substrate, rather than being raised. (17)

decibels (dBA): A unit for expressing the intensity of sound. (4)

decorative typeface: A typeface designed primarily to command special attention, express a mood, or provide a specific appearance for a theme or an occasion. (6)

definition: The sharpness or distinction of the printed image. (6)

definition statement: Opening statement of a résumé that outlines strengths and skills specific to the job opportunity. (3)

de-inking: The process of removing inks, fillers, and coatings from wastepaper. (15)

delivery pile: A uniform stack of paper that accepts sheets from the delivery system of a sheet-fed press. (14)

delivery system: A press system that removes the printed substrate from the printing system and prepares it for finishing operations. (14)

densitometer: An electronic instrument that uses a photocell to accurately measure the amount of light reflected from or through different tone values. (5, 11)

design: The application of proper methods to produce a product that is both artistic and functional. (7)

design forum: An online resource where individuals can post designs for critical analysis. (8)

desktop: Entire screen area of your monitor when the computer starts up. (9)

desktop publishing system: A computerized system commonly used in the graphic communications industry to produce type and images. (5)

destructive interference: When two light waves cross at a single point at the same time and intersect to cause a dimmer light or a dark spot. (11)

dichromatic vision: A form of color blindness where only yellows and blues are visible. (11)

didot point system: The standard system of print measurement used in Europe. (5)

die cutting: A process in which pressure is used to force a sharp metal die through the stock. It is used to make irregular shapes. (17)

diffraction grating: An optical device used to study the colors in light. (11)

digital asset management (DAM): The protocol and resources established to handle all digital files and data. (13)

digital blueline proofs: Two-sided digital position proof for eight-page impositions. (12)

digital camera: A camera that takes digital images or videos and stores them for later reproduction. (9)

digital format: Data stored with measured values and distinct points or positions. A digital image is stored with distinct points of varying brightness and color, which are recorded as pixels. (10)

digital prepress system: A computer-centered process that consists of preparing content, composing pages, and outputting the finished file. (9)

digital printing technology: Any reproduction technology that receives electronic files and uses dots for replication. (13)

digital proofs: Proofs generated by outputting files on a high-resolution, high-quality printer. (12)

digital subscriber line (DSL): Internet connection using 2-wire copper telephone lines. (9)

direct imaging (DI): The process of sending a digital file directly to a press without the use of traditional offset or computer-to-plate processes or chemistry. (13)

direct screen photographic color separation: A method in which a process camera, contact printing frame, or enlarger is used to make color separation exposures through a photographic mask and a halftone screen onto high-contrast panchromatic film. (11)

dispersant: Substance that breaks apart and distributes inks. (16)

display type: Type sizes above 12-point, used to emphasize the importance of a message and capture the reader's attention. (6)

display typeface: A typeface designed primarily to command special attention, express a mood, or provide a specific appearance for a theme or an occasion. (6)

distributed printing: A system of digital printing in which the electronic files for a job can be sent anywhere in the world, through a wide area network (WAN), for output. Commonly used for localized editions of newspapers and magazines. (13)

dot gain: Optical increase in the size of a halftone dot during prepress operations or the mechanical increase in halftone dot size that occurs as the image is transferred from plate-to-blanket-to-paper in lithography. (12)

dot pitch: A measurement of the vertical distance between rows of pixels on a monitor, stated in decimal fractions of a millimeter. (12)

double-sheet detector: A control device that prevents more than one sheet of paper from entering the press. (14)

drawdown test: A method of checking for proper ink mixing by placing a small amount of ink on paper, and then using a blade to spread it and produce a thin ink film. (16)

drilling: Piercing operation that uses a revolving, hollow drill bit with very sharp edges. The waste stock rises through the hollow center of the drill. (17)

Drupa: Held every five years in Düsseldorf, Germany, the largest print trade show in the world. (9)

dry: The point at which the ink is free of volatile substances and has polymerized to a total solid state. (16)

dummy: A small representation of a final document. (7)

dye: A type of colorant that dissolves in liquid. (11)

dye sublimation: A type of thermography that uses heat and pressure to change solid dye particles on a ribbon into a gas to produce an image on a substrate. (13)

dye-sublimation printer: Printer that uses heat to transfer dye onto various substrates, such as plastics, cards, papers, or fabrics. (9)

E

edge staining: Changing stock color on the edges of the sheet. (17)

editing: The final preparation of the author's or writer's manuscript for publication, including checking the text, line art, and photographs. (1)

edition binding: The most complex and permanent form of binding, in which a rigid cover is attached to a book body that is held together by sewing. (17)

effective ppi: The resolution of an image at the scale used in the document. (10)

effective resolution: The "actual" resolution of an image at the size it is placed in a document. (9)

E gauge: A device used to measure point sizes and leading of printed type. (5)

electromagnetic spectrum: The entire range of wavelengths of electromagnetic radiation, extending from gamma rays (very short) to radio waves (very long). (11)

electronic information transfer: Sending digital information instantly via Internet. (2)

electrophotography: Printing process that uses a drum coated with chargeable photoconductors, dry or liquid toners, and a corona assembly to produce an image on a substrate. (13)

electrostatic assist: A process in which a power source feeds electrical charges between the impression roller and the printing cylinder, creating a force that helps release ink from the etched cells. (14)

electrostatic printing: A printing method that uses the forces of electric current and static electricity to fuse toner onto a page. (1, 13)

electrotype: A duplicate relief plate that is produced from a mold through an electrochemical process. (14)

elemental chlorine: Chlorine gas used to bleach paper pulp and to separate the pulp from lignin. (15)

elements of design: Line, shape, texture, space, size, and color. (7)

elements of layout: Text, graphics, and the page itself. (7)

elevator pitch: A 30- to 90-second speech that describes you as a professional. (3)

embossing: A process that creates a raised image on a substrate by pressing it between two dies. (17)

em dash: The longest dash and the most versatile punctuation mark that can take the place of commas, colons, or parentheses. (6)

en dash: Slightly longer than a hyphen, used in place of the word *to* or *through*. (6)

entrepreneur: Someone who starts his or her own business. (2)

entrepreneurship: The process of starting a business. (3)

epoxy: A resin that forms a very hard surface coating when combined with other chemicals. (17)

e-pubs: Electronic publications. (1)

equivalent weight: The weight of one ream of paper of a size that is larger or smaller than the basic size. (15)

ergonomics: The science of fitting the job to the worker. (4)

error-diffusion screening: Screening method that places dots randomly. (12)

exposure latitude: The amount of overexposure or underexposure of an image that is acceptable for final production. (10)

eye span: The width of body type a person can see with one fixation (sweep or adjustment) of the eye muscles. (6)

F

fair use: Exceptions to US Copyright Laws that allow duplication and use of copyrighted materials without infringement. (3, 18)

filament: A single thread. (14)

fillers: Inorganic materials, such as clay or titanium dioxide, added to improve opacity, brightness, smoothness, and ink receptivity. (15)

fillets: The contoured edge or transition from the stem of the letter to the serif. (6)

filter: A feature of image manipulation programs used to apply special effects to images, such as textures and patterns. (10)

financial printing: A segment of the graphic communications industry consisting of plants that primarily print materials such as checks, currency, and legal documents. (1)

finishing: A general term that applies to the many operations carried out during or following printing. (1, 17)

fixed cost: Business expenses that remain consistent, regardless of the volume of work in the shop. (18)

flash drive: Storage device using integrated USB interface. (9)

flash memory card: Small, removable storage device that has high storage capacity with fast access and retrieval speeds. (9)

flatbed scanner: A type of scanner that scans images placed on a glass bed, or scan area. (10)

flexography: A relief printing process that uses flexible printing plates for printing long run jobs. (1, 14)

flooding: In gravure printing, the process of inking the cells of the plate or cylinder. (16)

flush: Term describing the dispersing of a pigment in an undried state (a paste) into a vehicle for ink. (16)

flush left: When text is aligned with an even left margin and ragged right margin. (6)

flush mount: A book where pages are printed on photo paper and then fused onto a heavier and stiffer board. The pages lay flat with minimal gutter. (3)

flush right: When text is aligned with an even right margin and a ragged left margin. (6)

flying splicer: A splicer unit that bonds a new web to the existing web without stopping any operations on a web-fed press. (14)

font: In computer-based or phototypesetting composition methods, it consists of all the characters that make up a specific typeface. (6)

font set: The font list for a document. Font sets can be created for individual jobs and activate only the set needed. (9)

font stack: A list of fonts used as replacements on computers that do not have specified fonts. (6)

formal balance: A design principle that is achieved when the elements of a design are of equal weight and are positioned symmetrically. (7)

former board: A curved or triangular plane that serves as the folding surface on a web-fed press. (14)

forms printing: Industry that designs and prints special paper forms used in many businesses. (1)

foundry type: Individual pieces of metal type that could be aligned with type containing other letters to form words and sentences for printing on paper. (6)

Fourdrinier machine: A paper machine that forms a continuous web of paper on a moving, endless wire belt. (15)

fovea: The most sensitive part of the eye's retina and the area of sharpest vision. It is located at the center of the macula and is packed with cone cells. (11)

furnish: The slurry of fillers, sizing, and colorants in a water suspension from which paper is made. (15)

G

gamma levels: Degrees of contrast of a screen image of a monitor. (12)

gamut: Complete set of colors within a color space. (9)

gamut alarm: Warning used by many imaging or page composition programs to indicate the presence of colors that are out of the printing range. (12)

gamut compression: Technique used to compress colors to fit into a smaller color gamut to give the illusion that all color chroma, saturations, and values are present. (12)

gathering: The assembling of printed signatures. (17)

geometric sans serif: Sans serif typefaces built on geometric shapes that share many components between the various glyphs. (6)

gestalt: Psychology based on the whole being viewed independently from the separate elements. The principles are similarity, proximity, closure, and continuation. (7)

gigabyte: One billion bytes, abbreviated GB. (9)

glyphs: The graphical representation of a specific character. Some typefaces have more than one glyph for a character, called *alternates*. (6)

grade: Category or class of paper. (5, 15)

grain: The direction or structure of paper fibers. (15)

grain long: Grain that runs parallel to the cylinder of the offset press. (15)

grain short: Indicates that the grain runs across the paper. (15)

gram: The standard unit of mass in the metric system. (5)

graphical user interface (GUI): A method of representing computer operations and programs on the screen with icons that can be selected with a mouse to perform activities. (9)

graphic communications: The exchange of information in a visual form, such as words, drawings, photographs, or a combination of these. (1)

graphics: The elements of layout that include the ornamentation, photographs, and illustrations. (7)

graphics tablet: Digitizer that lets user draw images and graphics by hand using a stylus. (9)

gravure: A method of printing from cells or depressions that are engraved below the nonimage area of the printing cylinder. (14)

gray card: A neutral gray card designed to set the middle gray tones to help with the lighting and exposure settings. (10)

gray component replacement (GCR): The removal of equal amounts of cyan, magenta, and yellow areas of a four-color halftone and replacement of these colors with a higher proportion of black. (12)

grayscale: A continuous tone strip used to visually gauge exposure of an image. (5, 12)

GREP: Complex character style defining a character, word, or pattern of characters. (9)

grid: An underlying template for margins and columns that give consistency to multiple pages of a document. (7)

grotesque: Early sans serif typefaces, often with peculiar and awkward weight distribution. (6)

gutter: The measurement of space between columns of text. (7)

H

halftone dot: Printed dot generated by the line screen to simulate a continuous tone image. (9)

hardware: A computer and its associated devices. (9)

harmony: Colors that are visually pleasing together. (7)

hazard: Anything with the potential to cause personal injury or illness. (4)

Hazard Communication Standard (HCS): Designed to give workers a safe workplace and better understanding of workplace hazards. (4)

headline dominant: Layout that has the headline or display text as the main visual element to convey the message. (7)

heavy elements: The darker strokes of a type character that give it identity. (6)

hex color: Color defined in HTML for web design using the hexadecimal system. (9)

hierarchy: The distribution of elements in a design based on level of importance to the message. (7)

hinting: Application that optimizes how type prints at small point sizes on printers with a resolution of 600 dpi or lower. (9, 12)

histogram: A graphic display of highlight, midtone, and shadow values that correspond to the number of pixels affected in each part of the tonal scale. (10)

hue: The color of an object perceived by the eye, and determined by the dominant light wavelengths reflected or transmitted. (7, 11)

humanist sans serif: Sans serif with a strong calligraphic influence and a much higher stroke contrast. (6)

hyphen: A punctuation mark that is used to separate compound words or syllables of a single word that is too long for a given line length. (6)

I

ICC color profiles: Profiles based on the CIELAB color space and used as standards for describing the color characterizations of different devices. (12)

illumination: The brightness of light in an image. (5)

image assembly: The process of electronically assembling line and halftone negatives or positives into pages. (1)

image carrier: A press plate or other intermediate used to transfer identical images onto a substrate. (1)

image resolution: The number and size of pixels in an image, measured in pixels per inch (ppi). (9)

impactless printing: Term for several types of printing that do not require direct contact between an image carrier and the substrate. (1)

impression cylinder: A printing system component that brings the paper to be printed into contact with the blanket cylinder. (14)

incident beam: The beam of light coming toward a surface. (11)

indexing: Tabs or cuts added to the edge of a sheet to locate specific information. (17)

informal balance: A design principle that is achieved by changing the value, size, or location of elements in a design. (7)

infringement: The unauthorized use of copyrighted material. (18)

ink: A colored coating specially formulated to reproduce an image on a substrate. (16)

ink body: Term that describes the consistency of an ink. (16)

ink darkness: A factor that affects the contrast of printed materials. (6)

ink fineness gauge: A device that measures the pigment particle size in an ink. (16)

ink formulation: The amount and type of ingredients used in a particular printing ink. (16)

inking system: A group of rollers designed to carry ink to the image area of the printing plate. (14)

ink-jet printing: A direct-to-paper technology that uses digital data to control streams of very fine droplets of ink or dye to produce images directly on paper or other substrates. (13)

ink-jet proof: A type of job proof that provides four-color proofs generated directly from the digital files. (9)

ink length: The elasticity of ink; referred to as long or short. (16)

ink mileage: The surface area that can be covered by a given quantity of ink. (16)

inkometer: An instrument that measures the tack of a printing ink. (16)

ink sticking: A press problem that occurs when two layers of ink film, on two different sheets, bond together. (16)

ink tack: The stickiness of the ink. A measurement of cohesion between the ink film and the substrate. (16)

ink thickness gauge: A device that measures the thickness of the ink film on the press rollers. (16)

in-plant printing: Term for printing facilities operated by companies whose business is not the production of printed materials. (1)

in port: Beginning of a frame, used to make connections with other frames. (9)

intellectual property: Creative works of an individual or individuals that can be protected from unauthorized use. (18)

interactive PDF: A PDF file that is intended to be viewed on screen, containing actions or buttons that allow the viewer to interact with the data. (3)

International Color Consortium (ICC): Organization established in 1993 by leading manufacturers to create a cross-platform standard for color management. (12)

interpreter: A computer program used with output devices that receive PDL page descriptions. (9)

ionography: Printing process that uses an electron cartridge, a nonconductive surface, and a magnetic toner to produce an image on a substrate. (13)

iris: An opaque diaphragm that contracts and expands to control the amount of light that enters the eye; the colored portion of the eye. (11)

ISO series: The series of standard paper and envelope sizes established by the International Organizations for Standardization (ISO). (5)

IT8 reflective target: Standard color reference tool used to calibrate input and output devices. (12)

italic type: A unique, slanted typeface modeled on a form of handwriting. (6)

J

job boards: A physical or online place where job openings are listed by categories. (3)

job definition format (JDF): A file format based on Extensible Markup Language (XML), which provides a standard format that is compatible with any JDF-enabled equipment. (9)

journeyman: A tradesperson who has completed an apprenticeship or, through experience, is qualified to work without supervision or further instruction. (2)

justify: To adjust letterspacing and wordspacing so lines of type in a block are all equal in length, resulting in even left and right margins. (6)

K

kerning: Adjusting the space between characters to improve appearance or readability. (6)

kerning pairs: Spacing values for letter combinations automatically built into some fonts. (6)

knockout: Clean break between design elements. (12)

L

labor cost: The "people costs" involved in operating a business, including hourly wages, salaries, and benefits for employees. (18)

laminating: Process in which a thin film of plastic with an adhesive coating is bonded to a printed substrate to provide protection against abrasion and moisture. (17)

laser proofs: Digital proofs printed onto paper using electronic files. They are produced by an industrial laser printer and may be in black and white or use process colors. (9)

layers: A feature of image editing programs that creates multiple, editable levels of a single piece of artwork. (10)

lay-flat: A printed book with a flexible binding or hinge that allows the pages side by side to lay flat with minimal gutter. (3)

layout: The plan and roadmap of elements that show the visual hierarchy and provides direction for the viewer. (7)

leading: The vertical distance separating each line of typeset copy, measured in points from one line to the next. (5)

legibility: A measure of how difficult or easy it is to read printed matter. (6)

letter form: The details and specific characteristics of each individual letter shape of a particular typeface. (6)

letterspacing: Changing the spacing between typeset letters, for better appearance or to fit copy in a given space. (6)

lifelong learning: Upgrading and updating one's job skills and knowledge to keep pace with technological changes in a field. (2)

lift: Term describing a pile of paper, usually the amount cut or drilled in a single operation. (17)

ligatures: Joined letter combinations, such as *fi*, *ff*, *fl*, *ffi*, or *ffl*, found in some typefaces. (6)

light elements: The hairlines or other less-dark strokes that tie together the heavy elements of a type character. (6)

lignin: A glue-like substance that bonds wood fibers together. (15)

line: Design element that forms the shape of an image. (7)

line art: An illustrated image drawn by hand or using computer software. (1)

line gauge: A device used to measure type sizes and line lengths in picas or inches. (5)

line length: The distance from the left to right sides of a line or body of copy, usually measured in picas. (6)

linespacing: The space between lines of text vertically, measured from baseline to baseline. (6)

linking: Connecting text boxes so text flows from one box to another. Also called *threading*. (9)

links: Preview graphics in documents that are connected to the original files and their locations. (9)

liquid lamination: A coating method similar to varnishing. The plastic coating material is applied in liquid form and then cured into a tough protective layer by exposure to ultraviolet light. (17)

liter: The standard unit of capacity in the metric system. (5)

livering: A chemical change in the body of an ink that occurs during storage. (16)

lockout device: A key or combination-type lock used to hold an energy isolating device in the safe position to prevent the machine from energizing. (4)

lookup tables: Chart stored in computer memory that lists the dot sizes needed to produce given colors. (12)

lossless compression algorithms: A mathematical formula for image compression that assumes that the likely value of a pixel can be inferred from the values of surrounding pixels. (9)

lossy compression algorithms: A mathematical formula for image compression in which data in an image that is least perceptible to the eye is removed. (9)

loupe: Magnifying device used by printers to see the halftone dots. (9)

luminance: The amount of light in an image. (5)

M

machine guards: Metal or plastic enclosures that cover moving machine parts and protect the operator from being cut, squashed, or hit by flying fragments. (4)

macula: A small hollow in the middle of the eye's retina where the cones are concentrated. (11)

magnetography: Printing process that uses a drum, magnetic toner, and high pressure to produce an image on a substrate. (13)

makeready: The process of preparing a press for printing a job. (13)

manager: A leadership position whose responsibility it is to manage a company, business, or part of a business. (2)

manuscript: A style of hand lettering used by the scribes of Germany, France, Holland, and other countries in the Middle Ages. (6)

margins: The white space defined by a grid at the four edges of a page or around an object. (7)

mask: A feature of image editing programs that protects a specified area of an image from changes, filters, and other effects applied to the rest of the image. (10)

master pages: Pages containing information and elements that will appear on every associated page. (9)

materials cost: The prices paid for items that are consumed as a job is printed, such as paper, ink, and packaging materials. (18)

maximum resolution: Maximum number of pixels that a computer screen can represent in both horizontal and vertical dimensions. (12)

mechanical binding: A broad category that includes many different devices used to hold sheets together. (17)

menu: List of options shown in a dialog box. (9)

mesh count: The number of threads (or strands) per linear inch in a fabric. (14)

meter: The standard unit of length in the metric system. (5)

metric conversion chart: A table of equivalencies used to convert US Conventional and metric values from one system to another. (5)

metric prefix: Word prefix that indicates multiples or divisions of measuring units in the metric system. (5)

modem: A device used with computers to send and receive digital information through telephone lines. (9)

Modern Roman typefaces: Typefaces that have increased contrast between very thin, light elements and heavy elements. (6)

moiré pattern: A visually undesirable dot-exaggerating effect that occurs when two different screen patterns are randomly positioned or superimposed. (5)

monitor: A visual display device that connects to and transmits data from a computer to the viewer. (9)

monochromatic colorimeter: A color measurement device that measures the intensity of a particular color and does not depend on the eye's perception of color. (11)

monospace: A typeface where each character or glyph has exactly the same horizontal space. (6)

mottling: The blotchy or cloudy appearance of an image, instead of a smooth, continuous tone. (10)

N

near-complementary color: A color that harmonizes with colors that lie next to its complement on the color wheel. (11)

neo-grotesque: More refined sans serif typefaces with careful construction and less variation in the line weights. (6)

nested styles: A string of character style formatting that can be set up to work together, so that when one is complete, the next one is applied. (9)

networking: Use of web of friends and relatives to find a job. (3)

newspaper printing: A segment of the graphic communications industry that involves publishing and printing daily or weekly newspapers. (1)

Newton's rings: An undesirable color pattern that results from interference between the exposure light and its reflected beam from the closest adjacent surface. (10)

nip points: The point of contact where two cylinders, gears, or rollers meet or come close to one another. (4)

nondisclosure: A legal contract between parties that protects confidential material or information. (3)

nonpareil: Measuring unit on a line gauge that is equal to one-half pica. (5)

numbering: The process of imprinting tickets, certificates, checks, or other items with consecutive figures, using a device that transfers the figures from an inked relief image. (17)

O

oblique: In electronic composition, the term used to describe a simulated italic character produced by slanting an upright Roman typeface, usually 12°. (6)

off color: When the color of the printed job does not match the intended color. (16)

offset lithographic printing: A printing method in which inked images are offset or transferred from one surface to another. (14)

Old English: A text typeface often used for such applications as diplomas, certificates, and religious materials. (6)

oldstyle: Typefaces based on the handwriting of scribes, with serifs that have thick and thin transitions and a diagonal stress. (6)

Oldstyle Roman typeface: A group of typefaces that have a rugged appearance, with relatively little contrast between heavy and light elements. (6)

opacity: The degree of transparency or ability to see through. (6, 11, 15)

OpenType font: Cross-platform, digital font format offering 65,536 characters, multiple language support, and extensive typographic features. (9)

operating system: The interface between the computer and the user, and the computer and the applications. (9)

optical character recognition (OCR): A system used to translate the bitmap image of scanned text into ASCII characters. (10)

orphan: A very short word, or part of a word, forming the final line of a paragraph. (6)

out port: End of a frame, used to make connections with other frames. (9)

output device: A piece of equipment, such as monitors and printers, used to display, produce, or transfer information processed by a computer. (9)

outsourcing: Sending a product to a service company for specified work needed to complete a product. (2)

overprinting: When image elements are specified to be printed over or on top of other colors. (12)

overset text: A red *x* indicating more text in a frame than will fit. (9)

P

package printing: Industry that uses images printed on many different types of materials, such as plastic, paper, cardboard, corrugated board, and foil. (1)

packaging: The process of wrapping, strapping, or boxing the printed pieces together for delivery to the customer. (17)

page composition: Prepress process of setting type and image layout for a page. (1)

page description language (PDL): A file format that describes a page's layout, contents, and position within the larger document in a manner the output device can understand. (9)

paint effects: A feature of image manipulation programs that contains several tools that allow the user to create and color images. (10)

Pantone®: Proprietary color space most commonly used as spot color. (9)

paper caliper: A device used to measure paper thickness. (5)

paper flatness: How well a sheet of paper remains straight or unwarped for feeding through a sheet-fed press. (15)

paper size: Measurements that describe the length and width dimensions of paper. (5)

paragraph styles: A collection of formatting instructions that can be applied to a paragraph of text. Sizes are expressed in inches or metric units. (9)

partnership: A type of business that is owned by two or more persons. The owners and the business are considered a single entity and pay income tax on the profits of the business. (18)

passive layout: Symmetrical layout for corporate or conservative design. (7)

pasteboard: The area within the application frame that is beyond the document edges. (9)

percent open area: Percentage of area per square inch in a fabric through which ink can pass. (14)

perceptual intent: Rendering intent that changes color data but not the relationship between the colors. (12)

perfect binding: Method that uses an adhesive to hold sheets or signatures together and to fasten the flexible cloth or paper cover onto the body. (17)

perfecting press: Printing system that prints both sides of the substrate at once. (14)

perforating: Operation that places a series of small cuts or slits in the substrate, using various types of blades or wheels on the press or folder. (17)

periodical printing: That segment of the graphic communications industry consisting of plants that are designed primarily to print magazines. (1)

personal protective devices: Clothing or equipment worn for protection from potential bodily injury associated with chemical use or machine operation. (4)

petrochemicals: Petroleum-based chemicals. (15)

pH scale: A measuring scale used to determine the acidity or alkalinity of a solution. The pH scale is numbered from 0–14, with 7 designated as neutral. A pH value below 7 indicates an acidic solution; a value above 7 indicates an alkaline solution. (14)

pH value: A measurement that indicates the acidity or alkalinity of a solution, as measured on the pH scale. (14)

photopigments: Light-sensitive chemicals in the cones of the human eye. Photopigments respond to red, green, or blue light. (11)

photopolymer plates: Plastic relief plates commonly used in flexographic printing. The surface contains a light-sensitive polymer coating that hardens after exposure. (14)

pica: One of the principal units of measure used in the graphic communications industry. (5)

pi characters: In fonts for computer or phototypesetting, such symbols as stars, asterisks, arrows, percent signs, or check marks. (6)

picture dominant: Layout that has the picture or image as the main visual element to convey the message. (7)

piezoelectric ink-jet printer: Printer in which a piezocrystal is charged to cause pressure, which forces droplets of ink from the nozzle. (13)

pigments: Colorants in the form of fine, solid particles that do not dissolve but spread through liquids or other substances. (11, 16)

pixel: Abbreviation for *picture element*, the tiniest image component in a digital imaging or display system. (9)

pixels per inch (ppi): Measuring units for image resolution. (5)

plastic comb binding: A mechanical binding method commonly used for booklets that might have to be altered by adding or removing pages. (17)

plate cylinder: A printing system component that holds the plate on the press. (14)

plate wear: The wearing away of the surface of a plate by coarse particles in the ink. (16)

platen press: A relief press that prints by pressing a type form or plate against a platen, the surface that holds the paper to be printed. (14)

platform: The computer system that is used to operate software. The platform defines the standard around which a system can be developed. (9)

point: One of the principal units of measure used in the graphic communications industry. (5)

point size: A vertical measurement used to identify or specify the size of a typeface. (6)

point system: The system of print measurement used throughout the graphic communications industry in the United States. (5)

portable document format (PDF): File format independent of software and platform that includes all information for viewing, proofing, or printing. (9)

postconsumer paper waste: Used paper products that have served their intended purpose and are separated from solid waste for recycling into new paper. (15)

PostScript: Page description language by Adobe. (9)

PostScript Type 1 font: Consists of all the variations of one style of type; includes the suitcase file and printer typeface file. (9)

power corner: The bottom-right corner of a page; has more visual weight than the rest of the page. (7)

preconsumer paper waste: Scrap material generated by the papermaking process. (15)

preferences: Settings that define how objects and documents behave. (9)

preflighting: Analyzing an electronic document to determine if it meets necessary specifications required for printing. (9)

press proofs: Proof generated with a proof press. One of the best verification proofs; also very slow and expensive. (12)

primary colors: Colors that when combined, create all other colors, and in its purest form, cannot be created by any combination of color. (7, 11)

principles of design: Balance, contrast, unity, rhythm, and hierarchy. (7)

printability: How well fine details are reproduced in a printed image. (15)

print engine: A small computer component inside a laser printer that translates the output of the computer into a bitmapped image for printing. (9)

printer resolution: The number of smaller printer dots per inch (dpi) used to generate the halftone dot. (9)

printing: A process involving the use of a specialized machine to transfer an image from an image carrier to a substrate. (1)

printing estimate: An offer to print a particular job for a specified price. If the customer accepts the estimate, it becomes a contract that is binding for both the printer and customer. (18)

printing press: A specialized machine used to transfer an image from an image carrier to a substrate, usually paper. (1)

printing system: A group of cylinders used to transfer images from the printing plate to the substrate. In a lithographic press, the printing system consists of a plate cylinder, a blanket cylinder, and an impression cylinder. (14)

print strength: How well a paper surface resists lifting of its fiber by high-tack inks. (15)

process color printing: The method of printing full-color materials using the transparent cyan, magenta, yellow, and black inks. (11)

process colors: The four colors of ink used for color printing: cyan, magenta, yellow, and black (CMYK). (1, 7)

productivity: The amount of quality work that is completed in a given time span. (18)

profit: The difference between sales income and business expenses. (18)

project brief: Written research for a project developed through working with the client and answering critical questions for background and foundation. (7, 8)

proof: Any copy or art that is checked before going into print. (9)

proofreader's marks: Widely used symbols that single out and explain when something in typeset copy is to be taken out, added, or changed. (9)

proofreading: The process of checking for typesetting errors and marking them for correction. (9)

proportional scale: A measuring device used to determine the correct reproduction percentage for the enlargement or reduction of images. (5)

proximity: Gestalt principle that says things that are close together will be viewed as a group. (7)

public domain: Works published in the United States before 1923 and works published in the United States before 1964 that have not renewed their terms of copyright. (3)

pulpers: Vats in which coloring or bleaching additives are added to pulp. (15)

punching: Piercing operation done by forcing a metal rod down through the paper to remove stock. The punch works in a shearing action with a *die* placed below the paper. (17)

Q

QR code: An optical label that uses a matrix bar code to embed data that can be read by a smartphone. (9)

quantizing: A filtering process that determines the amount and selection of data to eliminate, which makes it possible to encode data with fewer bits. (10)

quick printing: A subdivision of commercial printing, consisting of shops specializing in rapidly completing short-run printing and photocopying work for business customers. (1)

R

random-access memory (RAM): A temporary computer memory buffer used to transfer data. More RAM will move data faster and allow more applications to be open simultaneously. (3, 9)

raster: A representation of an image on a grid of pixels of predetermined size and depth and is, therefore, resolution dependent. (9)

raster image processor (rip): A device that interprets all of the page layout information for the marking engine of the output device. (9)

ream: Five hundred sheets of paper. (5, 15)

recycled paper: Paper made from old or used paper products. (15)

reflected beam: A beam of light that has bounced off a surface. (11)

reflection densitometer: Instrument used to accurately determine different tone values, such as the highlights and shadows of an original. (5, 11, 16)

register unit: A feeding system mechanism that places paper in register for printing on a press. (14)

relative intent: A more accurate rendering intent that adjusts only the out-of-gamut colors to fit into the print space. (12)

rendering intent: When profiling, a translation that tells how to map color from one space to another. (12)

resolution: An image's sharpness or clarity. (5, 9)

responsive design: The ability of a digital format to conform to different proportions and media displays. (1)

résumé: A document outlining skills and experience used to obtain employment. (3)

retarder: Solvents added to ink to thin the viscosity and slow the drying time. (14)

retina: A layer of light-sensitive cells at the back of the eye. When light reaches the eye, it is focused onto the retina. (11)

retina display: Monitors with higher pixel density for a higher quality display. (9)

retouching tools: Tools used in image manipulation programs to modify images in ways similar to methods used in darkroom photography. (10)

rhythm: The use of elements in an image to create visual movement and direction. (7)

robotics: The use of machines to do repetitive tasks, particularly in manufacturing. (2)

rods: Light-sensitive nerve cells of the retina that help us perceive light and intensity. There are about twelve million rods in the human eye. (11)

Roman typeface: A type style based on the capital letters cut into stone monuments by the ancient Romans. (6)

rough: A redrawn version of a thumbnail to accurate proportions showing more detail. (7)

rubber plates: Flexible relief plates commonly used in flexographic printing. (14)

rule of thirds: Dividing the page into thirds horizontally and vertically. Placing elements at the intersection of the lines adds impact to the layout. (7)

S

Safety Data Sheets (SDS): A document, produced by a chemical manufacturer, that summarizes the physical properties of a particular chemical and the health and safety hazards associated with its use. (4)

sans serif: The classification for typefaces without serifs, or stroke endings. (6)

satellite Internet: Internet connection from a small satellite with a Network Operations Center (NOC) that transmits and receives information with the orbiting geostationary satellite. (9)

saturation: An attribute of color that defines its degree of strength or difference from white. The extent to which one or two of the three RGB primaries is predominant in a color. (7, 11)

saturation intent: Rendering intent that does not maintain color realism and changes hue and brightness. (12)

scan area: The section of a scanning device on which images are placed for scanning. (10)

scanner: An electronic imaging device that measures the color densities of an original, stores the measurements as digital information, manipulates or alters the data, and uses the data to create four color separations. (10)

scoring: A slight cut made in heavy stock before it is folded. (17)

screen: Used to change continuous tone photographs into dotted halftones for printing. (5)

screen angles: Angular relationships of line screens used in making color separations for four-color printing. (5)

screen frequency: Number of lines in a linear inch used to determine the size of a halftone dot. Measured in lines per inch (lpi). (9)

screen printing: A printing process that uses a squeegee to force ink through a porous fabric covered by a stencil that blocks the nonimage areas. The ink pressed through the open image areas produces the image on a substrate. (14)

screen ruling: The number of ruled grid lines per inch (lpi) on a halftone screen. (10)

screen tint: Reproduction screen used to provide a tint percentage of a solid color. (5)

script typeface: A typeface designed to simulate handwriting, in which the letters are joined. (6)

scumming: A condition in lithography when the nonimage areas of the plate begin to accept ink. (16)

secondary colors: Colors created by adding two main colors on the color wheel together. For example, red + yellow = orange. (7)

sentence case: When the first word of a sentence is capitalized and the rest is in lowercase (with the exception of proper names). (6)

serif: The thickened tips or short finishing-off strokes at the top and bottom of a Roman typeface character. (6)

set: The point at which an ink is dry enough to be lightly touched without smudging. (16)

setoff: A condition that results when wet ink on the press sheets transfers to the back of other sheets in a stack. (16)

set size: The width of a typeset character. (6)

shade: A color gradation created by adding black to a color. (11)

shape: Elementary form that defines specific areas of space. (7)

sheet-fed press: A lithographic press that prints paper one sheet at a time as it is fed through the system. (14)

show-through: An undesirable result of poor opacity in which the image on one side of a sheet of paper is seen on the other side. (15)

shrink-wrap: A packaging method in which a stack of printed pieces is enclosed with a thin plastic in sheet form. (17)

SI Metric system: The modern version of the metric system, based on seven internationally recognized units of measure. (5)

similarity: Gestalt principle that says things that are similar will be viewed as a group. (7)

single proprietorship: A type of business owned by one person in which the business and the owner are a single entity; the owner's income is the business' profits. (18)

size: The relationship between elements on a page. (7)

sizing: Material, such as rosin, that is added to pulp slurry to make the paper stronger and more moisture-resistant. (15)

slitting: An operation similar to perforating that makes a continuous cut, rather than a series of slits. It is usually done by sharp-edged wheels that cut the stock as it passes through the folder. (17)

small caps: Capital letters smaller than the normal caps of the font. (6)

smoothness: Freedom from surface irregularities. (6)

soft proofs: Press-ready, electronic files that represent what the final printed page will look like and are most often PDF files that can be viewed on a computer monitor. (9, 12)

software: Computer programs that initiate and accomplish various computer-based tasks. (9)

software-as-a-service (SaaS): A type of data management system in which the data is managed and maintained externally. Clients access the data on demand using system-specific software and an Internet connection. (13)

solid-state drive (SSD): Alternative type of storage device that has no moving parts. (9)

solvent inks: Inks that have a main ingredient of a solvent that evaporates and produces VOCs. (13)

spatial resolution: The ability of a digital imaging device to address data in horizontal and vertical dimensions. (10)

spatial zones: Different ways to utilize a grid to keep it from becoming boring. (7)

specifications: The size requirements, printing specifications, and finishing and binding information. (7)

specking: Tiny dots that appear near an image area, caused by paper fibers or other foreign material in the ink. (16)

spectrodensitometer: A color measuring instrument that serves all the functions of a spectrophotometer, densitometer, and colorimeter in one device. (11)

spectrophotometer: Instrument capable of measuring light of different colors or wavelengths by using a prism or diffraction grating to spread light and isolate narrow wavelengths of light between 1 nm and 10 nm. (5, 11, 16)

spectrum locus: A horseshoe-shaped curve that results when the chromaticity coordinates of visible light are plotted on the CIE chromaticity diagram. (11)

spiral binding: A mechanical binding method in which small round holes are punched through the pages and metal or plastic wire is spiral fed through them. (17)

spontaneous combustion: Ignition by rapid oxidation without an external heat source. (4)

spot screening: Screening method in which dots are laid in a grid pattern based on the color tone. The spacing between the dot centers is held constant, but the dot size is varied to produce different shades or tones. (12)

spread: Two pages side by side, that will be seen together when printed. (7)

spread trap: Trap created by spreading the foreground over the background color. (12)

squeegee: A rubber or plastic blade used to force ink through the open areas of a screen-printing stencil. (14)

stamping: The process of transferring a thin layer of metallic tone or color to a substrate, using heat and pressure. (17)

stitching: A binding method that holds sheets together with staples. Typically used on books with fewer than 120 pages. (17)

stochastic screening: Halftone method that creates the illusion of tones by varying the number of micro-sized dots in a small area. (12)

storage: Space on a hard disk, removable disk, or cloud that allows backup of digital media. (3)

strike-through: An ink-penetration problem that occurs when the ink soaks into the paper too deeply and shows through the opposite side of the sheet. (16)

stroke: The thickness of a line forming a character element. (12)

style sheets: A collection of formatting instructions that can be applied quickly. (9)

Subiaco face: An early version of the Roman typeface, used for several books and named for the town where the printing was done. (6)

substance weight: The actual weight of a ream of paper. (15)

substrate: Any material with a surface that can be printed or coated. (1, 15)

subtractive color formation: The combination of cyan, magenta, yellow, and black inks to produce a printed image. (9, 11, 12)

subtractive colors: Cyan, magenta, and yellow. Colors that reflect when light hits a substrate. (7)

successive contrast: A color-vision effect that causes the viewer to see afterimages. (11)

sucker feet: Devices that provide a vacuum to remove sheets from a stack and position them for access to the press. (14)

supercalendering: Using heated steel rollers and pressure to form a very smooth, high-gloss finish on paper. (15)

T

tablet computer: A mobile computer that has a touchscreen display, hardware, and battery in one unit. (9)

tagout device: A prominent warning device securely fastened to an energy isolating device, to indicate that electrical power is off and must remain off until the tag is removed. (4)

taping machine: Device used in shipping departments to automatically apply tape to seal the tops of boxes. (17)

template: In a page composition program, a reusable form that can be set up to include the page geometry, typography, and other elements of a page that recur in a document. (9)

tensile strength: The amount of stress that will break paper. (15)

tensiometer: An instrument that measures screen fabric tension. (14)

terabyte: One thousand gigabytes, abbreviated TB. (9)

tertiary colors: Colors created by adding two secondary colors together. (7)

text: Words, sentences, or paragraphs. (6)

texture: A projection of emphasized structure or weight. (7)

thermal ink-jet printer: Printer in which the ink is superheated to form a bubble, which expands through the firing chamber, forcing ink out of the nozzle. (13)

thermal transfer: A type of thermography that uses heat and pressure to change solid dye particles on multiple ribbons into a gas to produce an image on a substrate. (13)

thermoformed: Formed by heat and pressure. (15)

thinners: Solvents added to ink to change the viscosity of the ink. They do not affect drying time. (14)

thixotropy: The tendency of ink to flow more freely after being worked. (16)

threading: Connected text boxes that allow text to flow from one to another. Also called *linking*. (9)

thumbnails: Simple, rapidly drawn designs of a layout. (7)

tint: A color gradation created by adding white to a color. (11)

tinting: Problem that occurs when ink pigment particles bleed into the dampening solution, causing a slight tint of ink to appear on the nonimage area of the printed sheet. (16)

title case: Phrase where each word has an initial capital letter. (6)

tonal resolution: The number of bits of color or grayscale information that can be recorded per pixel. The greater the bit depth, the more colors or grayscales can be represented. (10)

toner: Positively charged powder that is attracted to negatively charged image dots to make up the printed image on a page. (9)

tool palette: Menu showing the tools of the application. (9)

totally chlorine free (TCF): Unbleached paper with a slightly brown appearance. (15)

toxic substance: A poisonous substance. (4)

tracking: A feature that allows the control of letter and word spacing together. (6)

trade customs: Understood rules or implied laws used in the printing industry that have been validated by courts as binding agreements. (18)

Transitional Roman typefaces: Typefaces that are a remodeling of oldstyle faces. (6)

transmission densitometer: A color measurement device that measures the fraction of incident light conveyed through a negative or positive transparency without being absorbed or scattered. (5, 11)

trapping: Method used to create a small area of overlap between colors to compensate for potential gaps. (12)

trichromatic colorimeter: A color measurement device that relies on the perception of the eye to match a patch of light by combination of the three primary colors. (11)

trim: The paper that is left over after cutting a sheet into smaller pieces. (15)

trimming: The process of cutting off uneven edges of a product after printing. (17)

tristimulus values (X, Y, Z): Three values that designate the amount of red, green, and blue light in an image. (11)

truetype font: Compact digital font format developed by Apple and Microsoft. (9)

turnaround: The completion time for a product from its inception. (2)

two-person proofing: A proofreading method that requires the reader to work with an assistant, called the *copyholder.* (9)

typeface: Distinctive designs of visual symbols used to compose a printed page. (6)

typeface family: A grouping consisting of all the variations of one style of type. (6)

typeface series: The range of sizes of each typeface in a family. (6)

type metal: A low-melting-point alloy of lead, tin, and antimony used to cast foundry type. (6)

type size: Measurements that describe the size of printed type, commonly expressed in points. (5)

typographer: A print designer who determines how a manuscript should be expressed in type as well as other details of reproduction. (6)

typographers' quotes: A preference set in word processing or page assembly software to specify which quotation marks and apostrophes, or inch marks and foot marks are the result of the key strike on a standard keyboard. (6)

typography: The art of expressing ideas in printed form through the selection of appropriate typefaces. (6)

U

uncoated paper: Paper that does not have a mineral layer applied over the surface, so it has a slightly textured feel. (15)

undercolor addition (UCA): Undercolor addition is used with *gray component replacement* to produce better shadow quality. (12)

undercolor removal (UCR): Technique used to reduce the yellow, magenta, and cyan dot percentages in neutral tones by replacing them with increased amounts of black ink. (12)

undercut: The vertical distance between the surface of the cylinder bearers and the cylinder body. This allows for the thickness of the plate or blanket and packing. (14)

unity: The proper balance of all elements in an image so a pleasing whole results and the image is viewed as one piece. (7)

unsharp masking (USM): A function of some scanners that increases tonal contrast where light and dark tones come together at the edges of the images. (10)

US Conventional system: The standard system of weights and measures used in the United States. (5)

UV inks: Inks that are polymer-made and UV-curable. (13)

V

value: The lightness or brightness of a color, or where it hits on the white-to-black center axis; used in Munsell's color system. (7, 11)

variable data printing: A digital printing process that enables quick and easy content changes at several points within a print run. The "on the fly" imaging resident allows customized and personalized printed materials to be produced. (13)

varnishing: A coating applied after printing to provide a clear protective surface. (17)

vector graphics: Object-oriented, resolution-independent graphics defined by mathematical algorithms. (9)

vehicle: The liquid component in ink that serves as a binding agent. (16)

video card: Board that plugs into a computer to give it display capabilities. (12)

viewing booth: A booth or defined area illuminated with color-balanced lighting (5000 K). Images are viewed at a 90° angle to reduce glare. (11)

viscosity: The internal resistance of an ink to flow; the opposite of fluidity. (16)

visibility: A legibility factor that results from the contrast of a dark typeface against the light reflected by the paper. (6)

visual center: Slightly up and to the right of the actual center. (7)

volatile organic compounds (VOCs): Toxic substances contained in blanket and roller washes, fountain solutions, plate cleaners, glaze removers, degreasers, and film cleaners. (4)

W

warp threads: Threads that run vertically, at a 90° angle to the weft threads. (14)

washup solvent: Solvent used to dissolve ink from a screen. (14)

waste stream: The solid, liquid, or contained gaseous material that is produced and disposed of, incinerated, or recycled by a facility. (4)

watermark: A translucent design impressed in paper. (15)

web-break detector: A device that automatically shuts down the press if the web snaps or tears. (14)

web-fed press: A lithographic press that prints with one long, continuous web of paper that is fed from a roll. (14)

web fonts: Fonts stored on a web server, not on a user's local computer. (6)

web-safe fonts: A small list of fonts that are most likely to appear on a wide range of computers. (6)

web splicer: A device used to bond a new roll to the end of an existing web on a web-fed press. (14)

weft threads: Threads that run horizontally, at a 90° angle to the warp threads. (14)

well sites: Hundreds or thousands of photosensitive elements on a CCD. (10)

white balance: Making the objects that are really white appear white in your image by considering the color temperature of a particular light source. (10)

white point: A movable reference point that defines the lightest area in an image displayed on a cathode ray tube, causing all other areas to be adjusted accordingly. (12)

white space: The areas of the layout that are void of printed images. (7)

wide format printer: Printer that typically produces images from paper rolls larger than 13″ in width and technically limited in length only by the length of the roll of substrate material. (13)

widow: A single line of a paragraph, either at the beginning or end, that is separated from the rest by moving to the next column or page. (6)

wireless Internet: Radio frequency bandwidth with an always-on connection. (9)

word-of-mouth marketing (WOMM): Positive or negative feedback from clients that influences future potential business. (3)

wordspacing: Changing the spacing between typeset words, for better appearance or to fit copy in a given space. (6)

work ethic: Standard to which on-the-job conduct and performance is based. (2)

work for hire: A document that defines ownership of material created for a client at the request of the client. (3)

workspace: Arrangement of panel, bars, windows, and menus on a computer. (9)

wysiwyg: What You See Is What You Get. Allows you to see on the screen what you will get in your final product. (1)

wysiwyp: What You See Is What You Print. A monitor display method used by word processing and page layout programs that uses color management software to produce a CMYK representation of the printed output. (9)

X

x-height: The height of the lowercase *x*. (6)

Z

zero-speed splicer: A splicer unit on a web-fed system that uses a set of festoon rollers to draw out slack from the web and feed the press while a splice is being made. (14)

Index

Q

R

S